Developing Practice Competencies

Developing Practice Competencies

A Foundation for Generalist Practice

D. Mark Ragg

WILEY

JOHN WILEY & SONS, INC.

Library of Congress Cataloging-in-Publication Data:
Ragg, D. Mark.
  Developing practice competencies: a foundation for generalist practice/D. Mark Ragg.
    p. cm.
  Includes bibliographical references and index.
  ISBN 978-0-470-55170-7 (paper/cd-rom); 978-1-118-01855-2 (ebk); 978-1-118-01856-9 (ebk); 978-1-118-01857-6 (ebk)
 1. Social work education. 2. Social service–Practice. 3. Social workers–Training of. I. Title.
  HV11.R312 2011
  361.3′2–dc22

                                                        2010026663

Printed in the United States of America

10 9 8 7 6 5 4 3 2

To Lisa Gebo

Your bright light guided me toward this project.
As I conclude the writing, your light is gone.
This book will keep your energy alive as it guides the paths of new
professionals spreading your influence through their work.

Contents

Chapter 12   **Building Multisystemic Working Alliances 279**

Chapter 13   **Managing Threats to the Working Alliance 303**

Integration of EPAS Core Competencies

Coverage	CSWE Competency and Practice Behaviors	Where Covered
Educational Policy 2.1.1—Identify as a professional social worker and conduct oneself accordingly.		
Well Integrated	1. Advocate for client access to the services of social work.	Chapters 2, 13
	2. Practice personal reflection and self-correction.	Chapters 1, 2, 3, 5
	3. Attend to professional roles and boundaries.	Chapters 1, 2, 4, 5
	4. Demonstrate professional demeanor.	Chapters 2, 3, 5, 6, 7
	5. Engage in career-long learning.	Chapters 1, 2, 3, 6
	6. Use supervision and consultation.	Chapters 2, 3, 4, 12, 13
Educational Policy 2.1.2—Apply social work ethical principles to guide professional practice.		
Well Integrated	1. Recognize/manage personal so guided by professional values.	Chapters 1, 2, 5
	2. Make ethical decisions using NASW and IFSW Ethics.	Chapters 2, 4, 5, 9
	3. Tolerate ambiguity in resolving ethical conflicts.	Chapters 2, 5
	4. Apply strategies of ethical reasoning and principled decisions.	Chapters 2, 3, 4
Educational Policy 2.1.3—Apply critical thinking to inform and communicate judgments.		
Integrated	1. Distinguish, appraise/integrate sources of knowledge, including research-based knowledge and practice wisdom.	Chapters 3, 4, 9, 11
	2. Analyze models of assessment, prevention, intervention, and evaluation.	Chapters 1, 3, 4
	3. Demonstrate effective oral/written communication with individuals, families, groups, organizations, communities, and colleagues.	Chapters 2, 4, 5, 6, 7
Educational Policy 2.1.4—Engage diversity and difference in practice.		
Well Integrated	1. Recognize how cultural structures and values may oppress, marginalize, alienate, or create or enhance privilege/power.	Chapters 1, 2, 4, 5, 6, 7, 8, 9, 10, 11
	2. Gain sufficient self-awareness to eliminate the influence of personal biases and values in working with diverse groups.	Chapters 1, 2, 4, 5, 6, 7, 8, 9
	3. Recognize and communicate their understanding of the importance of difference in shaping life experiences.	Chapters 1, 3, 4, 5
	4. View self as learner and others as informants.	Chapters 2, 4, 5, 6, 11
Educational Policy 2.1.5—Advance human rights and social and economic justice.		
Present and Integrated	1. Understand forms/mechanisms of oppression/discrimination.	Chapters 1, 2, 4, 5, 13
	2. Advocate for human rights and social/economic justice.	Chapters 2, 13
	3. Engage in practices that advance social and economic justice.	Chapters 2, 4
Educational Policy 2.1.6—Engage in research-informed practice and practice-informed research.		
Partially Covered	1. Use practice experience to inform scientific inquiry.	Chapter 3
	2. Use research evidence to inform practice.	Chapters 3, 4, 6, 7, 9, 11

Educational Policy 2.1.7—Apply knowledge of human behavior and the social environment.

Integrated	1. Utilize conceptual frameworks to guide the processes of assessment, intervention, and evaluation.	Chapters 3, 4, 5, 11
	2. Critique and apply knowledge to understand person and environment.	Chapters 3, 4, 5

Educational Policy 2.1.8—Engage in policy practice advancing well-being and effective services.

Referenced More Than Covered	1. Analyze, formulate, and advocate for policies that advance social well-being.	Chapters 13
	2. Collaborate with colleagues and clients for effective policy action.	Chapters 13

Educational Policy 2.1.9—Respond to contexts that shape practice.

Integrated	1. Continuously attend to changing locales, populations, scientific/technological developments, and emerging trends.	Chapters 2, 3, 4, 5, 11,
	2. Promote sustainable changes in service delivery and practice to improve the quality of social services.	Chapters 2, 5, 11,

Educational Policy 2.1.10 (a). Engage individuals, families, groups, organizations, and communities.

Integrated and Sets Foundation	1. Substantively/affectively prepare for action with individuals, families, groups, organizations, and communities.	Chapters 1, 5, 11,
	2. Use empathy and other interpersonal skills.	Chapters 2, 5, 6, 7, 8, 10, 11
	3. Develop a mutually agreed-upon focus and outcomes.	Chapters 2, 4, 5,

Educational Policy 2.1.10 (b). Assess individuals, families, groups, organizations, and communities.

Well Integrated	1. Collect, organize, and interpret client data.	Chapters 4, 6, 8,
	2. Assess client strengths and limitations.	Chapters 2, 4, 11
	3. Develop mutually agreed-upon goals and objectives.	Chapters 2, 4, 11
	4. Select appropriate intervention strategies.	Chapters 3, 4, 9, 11

Educational Policy 2.1.10 (c). Intervene with individuals, families, groups, organizations, and communities.

Sets a Foundation	1. Initiate actions to achieve organizational goals.	Chapters 11, 13
	2. Implement prevention interventions/enhance capacities.	Chapters 11, 13
	3. Help clients resolve problems.	Chapters 5, 6, 7
	4. Negotiate, mediate, and advocate for clients.	Chapters 2, 13
	5. Facilitate transitions and endings.	Chapters 14

Educational Policy 2.1.10 (d). Evaluate progress/outcomes with individuals, families, groups, organizations, and communities.

Sets a Foundation	1. Critically analyze, monitor, and evaluate interventions.	Chapters 3, 4, 14

Levels of Coverage

Well Integrated: Most practice behaviors are explored in multiple chapters and integrated into many discussions, exercises, DVD materials, and provided graded materials.

Integrated: Several chapters contain discussions and references to issues associated with the practice behaviors. Sets a Foundation. Some chapters contain references and discussions associated with the practice behaviors, setting a foundation for future courses to develop more fully.

Partially Covered: Some practice behaviors are covered but others are only referenced or partially discussed. Referenced More than Covered. Issues associated with practice behaviors are identified, but there is very little expansion or further discussion.

Acknowledgments

Thanks to these colleagues, who reviewed this book and provided feedback:

Mary Fran Davis, LCSW, Austin Peay State University, TN
Art Frankel, PhD, MSW, University of North Carolina, Wilmington
Chrys Ramirez Barranti, PhD, MSW, California State University, Sacramento
Michaela Rinkel, MSW, PhD, University of Wisconsin, River Falls
Diana Rowan, PhD, MSW, LCSW, University of North Carolina, Charlotte
Lyn K. Slater, LMSW, PhD, Fordham University, NY
Layne K. Stromwall, MSSW, PhD, Arizona State University

About the Author

Mark Ragg has been a generalist social worker for more than 30 years. After beginning his career in children's services, Dr. Ragg has worked in the fields of developmental disabilities, domestic violence, forensic social work, child welfare, child and family therapy, and mental health. Within this generalist practice career, Dr. Ragg has consistently worked with community groups concurrent with clients and families to provide intervention at multiple contextual levels. This breadth of practice extends to individual, family, group, organizational and communities levels. These 30 years of practice are integrated with research to provide a foundation for this textbook.

For the past 14 years, Dr. Ragg has taught and researched the development of social work practice competencies with BSW and MSW students. As an educator, Dr. Ragg consistently integrates the realities of practice with the rigors of academic teaching. Such integration begins with integrating practice supervision methods with practice education. This hands-on teaching approach enhances student competency acquisition and has become a critical element in all practice courses. In this newest publication, the integration has come full circle. After viewing thousands of student practice tapes, Dr. Ragg has identified concepts and patterns of competency development. These concepts are now integrated with Dr. Ragg's practice background and research evidence to provide methods for developing critical competencies for generalist practice.

Introduction

The social work profession has existed for about one century. While the profession's development was influenced by the social upheaval during industrialization, the profession has survived the social and economic changes over the past century because social workers respond to society's needs by attending to portions of the population that are discarded and ignored by the powerful and elite. Because of this history, the profession has developed at the interface between people and society. This is a unique position for a helping profession because we consistently confront and mediate the impact of powerful social forces.

Given this unique professional position, social work has developed a broad focus. Social work practitioners occupy many roles in society. Professional functions range from distributing resources to those in need, protecting vulnerable populations, advocating for responsive social systems, and helping people to master life's challenges. Consequently, you will find social workers operating in multiple roles. Some roles overlap with other professions, such as psychologists, nurses, and counselors. Other roles do not overlap with professional groups because social work often fills in societal gaps where other professions fear to tread.

The social work niche in society is to help people who are most compromised by social events and forces. As such, we work with many diverse systems. Some social workers provide clinical counseling services with individuals, families, and groups. For that reason, social workers must become competent in roles that require clinical assessment and intervention. However, social work competencies extend far beyond a clinical perspective. Social work practitioners work diligently at the community and societal levels to advocate on behalf of underserved and socially compromised people.

Generalist Practice

The unique domain of social work practice demands a broad range of generalist practice competencies. These competencies prepare you to work in multiple settings and roles. You must be able to work competently with diverse client groups. The discussions and exercises in this textbook are designed to help you achieve these competencies. You will develop a full range of generalist practice competencies that will allow you to work with client systems of all sizes. You will learn how to engage individuals and larger client systems in focused work toward client-specific goals.

Identification With Client-Level Work

Inherent in generalist practice is the need to work with our clients competently. Most social work positions pay us to help specific people. Whether these people are homeless, addicted, traumatized refugees, similar to us or very different, we must competently engage them in service and help them master their situation. Many generalist practice skills help us achieve these job requirements. These skills often are conceptualized as stages of helping, beginning with helping clients entering professional services and then proceeding through assessment, intervention, and ending.

This textbook is organized to help you understand the skills involved with each stage of helping. You will empathically understand the client experience at each stage and learn the skills that can help clients to increase their mastery. Successfully managing the nuances of the helping relationship and the challenges of each stage promotes practice competence. To help with this development, the textbook uses examples and exercises to help you identify the challenges and prepare helpful responses.

Client Context

As we approach direct client work, it is important to identify the cultural and social context of the client situation. This is an important generalist competency because often we must work with the context of client problems as we help the client. This requires skills associated with family-, group-, and community-level intervention concurrent with the skills associated with direct client work.

Throughout this textbook you will develop an appreciation of the contextual elements of client problems. Examples provided in the chapters will begin this sensitization. Discussions will also explore how each skill can be applied in various contexts. As you finish with the foundation skills, the later chapters will build on the earlier discussions to help develop skills associated with working with larger client systems and intervening in the larger contextual realm.

Skill Foundation

Generalist practice competencies are built on a skill foundation. This textbook is designed to help you establish a solid skill foundation for professional practice. It is understood that you already have some very well developed skills. It is unlikely that you would enter a helping profession without already experiencing yourself as a helper. The textbook will focus on establishing a professional level of control over your natural skills to provide a foundation that you can access and use within a professional role.

Skill Development Observations

In the past 15 years I taught multiple sections of introductory and advanced practice classes each and every year. In each class I observed students develop their skills through a series of three to seven videotaped role-plays. This has yielded thousands of observations providing a unique learning experience about sequences of student skill development.

Skill development tends to progress through identifiable sequences because most of us have similar socialization experiences. While our socialization varies across cultures and ethnic groups, every group learns how to interact appropriately with others. Rules of politeness, turn-taking, and expressiveness occur within every culture. Thus, we all have a default set of interactive skills that emerge through socialization. It is our need to expand our socialized skill sets into professional skills that sets up identifiable skill development sequences.

In our fast-paced digital society, new elements of socialization are entering into our interactions. Texting and Facebooking are now part of socialization. Many of us have developed skills of fast communication using digital media. Inherent in these skills, we can now engage in three or four simultaneous discussions. These skills were unknown when most textbooks were written and even now are largely unexplored. While we have not yet learned how to harness these new interactive capacities, we are beginning to understand some of the challenges in the transition into professional-level skills.

Socialized Skill Expansion

The observations of developmental sequences and the nuances of digital communication require a slightly different approach to teaching professional practice skills. This altered approach involves expanding our socialized skill sets to create a set of professional skills that build onto our current interactive habits. To achieve this expansion, we must first understand our current skills so we can consciously adjust and expand. Consequently, the first step in our skill development sequence is to learn about our socialized skills and subsequent expansion challenges.

To assist in this learning, every chapter in this text explores socialization influences including challenges for digital communicators. As each chapter explores skill development, you will begin with an exploration of the socialization influences inherent in our default skills. As we understand these influences, we can begin to identify specific areas of expansion that can build onto our current skills to enhance our professional competence. Early chapters explore the foundation skills. As we approach later chapters we will begin combining skills in application to more challenging client situations.

Cultural Context

We all have a unique cultural context that informed our initial skill development. As we explore our socialized influences, we inherently explore our cultural influences. As we understand our culture and subsequent interaction skills, we learn how culture and environment shapes how we interact and respond to others. We also learn that everyone has similar experiences based on their culture. In effect, everyone establishes normal default settings based on cultural and family experiences.

As we begin working with clients, it is important to understand that our default settings and our client's default settings are inherently different. Consequently, each set of skills in this textbook is provided with cautions and nuances relating to cultural differences. Rather than having a separate chapter discussing the importance of culture, you will find constant reminders of the role that socialization and culture play in the interactive processes that form practice. Try to never speed-read through these discussions; their seeds must take root to help you develop a well grounded professional identity.

Evidence Foundation

As professionals, we are expected to be competent in how we use our knowledge. This competency area requires us to apply research findings in our practice. This competency also requires us to generate new knowledge through evidence emerging from our practice. To generate knowledge, first we must become highly competent in how we use our skills so they are applied with precision in every application. This textbook uses two areas of evidence to help you understand and develop this area of competence.

Practice-Related Evidence

A large body of research helps identify critical practice skills. This research has been amassed over the past 50 years, providing us with clear indications of the skill sets needed for professional practice. This textbook integrates findings from this body of research into skill selection and the discussions of critical practice skills. As you explore the skill sets within each chapter, you will benefit from the conclusions drawn from multiple research studies.

While the chapters draw heavily on research, the presentation of knowledge begins with the practitioner-client interface. As such, there will be no discussions of sampling and statistical analysis; rather you will explore how the research can be applied in your work with clients. As you explore the different skill sets, pay attention to the citations so you can explore the research underlying each skill set.

Evidence-Based Practice

Along with the skill-focused research, the profession has started to amass evidence focused on clusters of skills that can be applied to specific client problems. Evidence-based practice explores research focused on these applications. Frequently, evidence-based practice studies focus on very specific client problems and develop tightly controlled packages of skills that are applied to help clients resolve their problems. Each practice is narrowly focused and narrowly applied.

The evidence-based practices build on specific practice competencies and rely on practitioners to have a skill foundation that can be applied to client situations. This textbook has identified the skills foundations necessary for multiple evidence-based practices. Each chapter will provide you with an understanding of specific skills that when combined can be used in evidence-based models. Many chapters will discuss the models that employ specific skills to help you understand how the skill sets explored throughout the textbook relate to evidence-based practice.

Textbook Organization

This textbook has three sections. The first section focuses on you as a professional. The chapters in this section begin with an exploration of your motivation and values so these can become the foundation for your professional identity. Subsequent chapters integrate professional values and ethics into the foundation so you can begin to identify as a social work professional. The final chapters explore how the knowledge you are gaining in theory and research classes can build onto the foundation to promote professional-level thinking. By the end of the first section, you will be applying your knowledge to understand complex client situations and use professional knowledge to plan change-focused intervention.

The second section expands on your cognitive competencies into the realm of the helping relationship. The early chapters explore the development of an empathic working alliance with clients and larger client systems. You will learn how to apply your knowledge to understand client experiences and system dynamics. You will also learn how to use this knowledge to engage people in goal-directed change efforts. The content from this section integrates with the first section to prepare you for learning interactive skills that can be used with client systems of all sizes.

Throughout this section of the textbook, you begin to learn the core skills of generalist practice. Each skill is explored so you can use it for assessment and change-directed action with client systems of all sizes. There are four core skills in this section. Some skills, such as questioning and reflecting, will be familiar. You will learn how you habitually use these skills and then learn how to use them with increased precision in your professional roles. The concluding chapters develop competencies in using observation skills and providing direction so you can engage in multiple practice roles. These skills become the skill foundation for the final section.

The last section of the textbook explores how to use interactive skills to accomplish client goals. You will begin by learning how to influence people without telling them what to do. This is accomplished by integrating the interactive skills with the empathic working alliance skills developed in the second section. This becomes your foundation for motivating clients and working within a focused alliance. Later chapters explore how to include other professionals and community support people in the working alliance. This leads to understanding collaborative practice with multiple agency and community systems. In conclusion, you will learn how to finish change-focused intervention and help clients to succeed in the future.

The competencies developed throughout the textbook are the foundation of generalist practice. You will learn competencies that can be applied in all social work roles from clinical to advocacy functions. The foundation competencies will prepare you for the full range of professional roles, including many evidence-based practices. The competencies can be expanded in later courses to include unique skills used with specific client groups and types of client system.

Section I
Building the Professional Self

The first section of the book focuses on the core skill sets that help practitioners develop a professional identity. This involves how you identify with our professions, how you maintain self-awareness and control, how you use knowledge, and how you make ethical practice decisions. The section concludes with an exploration of how these elements emerge when you conduct client assessments and establish the goals of intervention.

When reading the chapters of this section, you have the opportunity to use chapter exercises to develop skills in each of these areas. Written material and exercises are provided to maximize your professional development. This book is quite different from texts and materials used in other courses. The difference is associated with the focus on you, the reader. When reading the contents of these chapters, you will be encouraged to reflect on past experiences, feelings, thoughts, and motivations. You will then be assisted in building onto your current skills to develop professional competencies.

By the end of this section, you should be aware of typical patterns of thinking and responding to situations. You should also have a clear sense of the traits that must be monitored and controlled to assure they do not interfere with professional practice. This is critical to the professional use of self. If there are areas that seem particularly challenging, it is important to explore these with faculty advisors because this section provides a foundation for building the skill sets in subsequent sections of the text.

Building the Professional Self

Chapter 1
Professional Self-Awareness

Effective helping professionals tend to be very self-aware and maintain an ability to control how they respond to situations (Jennings & Skovholt, 1999; Jennings et al., 2008). Self-awareness and self-control dovetail with each other to create interpersonal effectiveness. The term "self-awareness" refers to the ability to tune in to yourself, maintaining an ongoing knowledge of your emotional and cognitive responses to external events. "Self-control" refers to the ability to control how you express your feelings and thoughts in interaction with others. Such control keeps your traits, emotional reactions, and personal issues from interfering with ethically grounded professional practice (Brabender, 2007).

Importance of Self-Awareness

The need for practitioner self-awareness is well established in the professional literature (Borrell-Carrio & Epstein, 2004; D. W. Johnson, 1997; Spurling & Dryden, 1989). Because professional practice occurs in an interpersonal context, we must be able to monitor our responses to client situations in order to allow professional skills, rather than reactivity, to govern how we act. Self-awareness serves four critical functions for helping professionals:

1. *A source of personal power.* When people know what they are thinking and feeling, they stay fully informed on how they are influenced by others (Hedges, 1992; Rober, 1999; Tansey & Burke, 1989). When a person is not aware of how others influence feelings and thinking, there is a loss of control and personal power.

Case Example

A practitioner tended to be very protective of misunderstood adolescents. Other than this, she was a very effective practitioner. However, when working with parents and children together, she tended to consistently side with the child, causing angry reactions in the parents. Eventually parental complaints required some focused supervision to help her understand, and gain control of, her side-taking tendencies.

---

2. *Source of insight into differences.* When people are aware of their thoughts and feelings, they are better positioned to understand the differences between themselves and other people (Arthur, 1998; Dettlaff, Moore, & Dietz, 2006). A full awareness allows for differences to be explored without feelings of threat (Dettlaff et al., 2006; Manthei, 1997). This is particularly important when cultural or spiritual differences exist in the client situation (Daniel, Roysircar, Ables, & Boyd, 2004; Suyemoto, Liem, Kuhn, Mongillow, & Yauriac, 2007; Yan, 2005; Wiggins, 2009).

Case Example

A practitioner was meeting with a family from a Native American reservation. When the family came in for the first appointment, the father was not willing to talk with the practitioner. As the practitioner explored the reluctance, the father stated that the practitioner was asking too many questions. Even though there had been few questions in the interview, the practitioner allowed the man to express himself and learned that the questionnaires sent out as part of intake were culturally offensive. The practitioner was able to explore his feelings with him and arrange a different way to gather the information needed for the intake.

---

3. *A source of insight and control* (Hedges, 1992; Rothman, 1999). Everybody reacts to certain situations based on their feelings and beliefs. If practitioners understand their thoughts and feelings, they can separate their reactions from the client's story and proceed in a way that is most helpful to the client. However, when practitioners are not aware, they may superimpose reactive agendas and proceed based on reactivity rather than on a logical understanding of the client's needs. Concurrently, practitioners may avoid client themes, options, feelings, and issues to diminish the intensity of their own emotional reactions.

Case Example

A female practitioner was working with an elderly couple. The husband's constant criticism of the wife was very similar to the dynamics between her mother and father. As they began exploring options for supported living, the practitioner reacted to the criticisms and prompted the woman to confront her husband and state that her needs were not being met in the relationship. The woman followed the directives but was actually content in the relationship. The confrontations, however, began to alienate the husband and cause deterioration of the relationship. Eventually they stopped coming to see the practitioner and did not move into supported living.

4. *A source of emotional connection with clients.* Practitioners' abilities to tune in to their own strengths, vulnerabilities, sensitivities, and feelings provide a set of internal experiential hooks on which they can hang the experiences of others (Rothman, 1999). These experiential hooks are drawn on when others speak of their experiences. The practitioner listens to the other's story and draws on these hooks to imagine the full experience of the client. The hooks, coming from self-awareness, consequently provide for empathic understanding of the client and a focus on improving responses (Manthei, 1997).

Case Example

Several rebellious teens were starting service in a school-based group for high-risk youths. The youths were teacher-referred and knew that they might be expelled if they did not attend. The practitioner knew of the coercion to attend and was concerned about how it might affect the group. The practitioner then reflected on past experiences when others had made him go places and do things that he did not want to do. Issues of resentment, passive defiance, and powerlessness filled his head as he thought about these experiences. In the first meeting, he used these experiences to make sense out of the attitudes presented by the group members. This allowed him to explore their feelings about attendance.

Self-Awareness as an Element of Interactive Practice

The goal of self-awareness is to prevent practitioner attitudes and feelings from interfering with professional interactions (Williams, 2008). It is very important to be able to pay attention and respond to client statements (Bachelor, 1995). When you are in a reactive mode, your focus shifts to acting on your reactive impulses rather than attending to the client's statements. To have a good working relationship, you must understand the content of client statements and also respond to the client's emotional experience (Castonguay, Goldfried, Wiser, Raue, & Hays, 1996; Miville, Carlozzi, Gushue, Schara, & Ueda, 2006). When practitioners are able to accomplish such positive and open working relationships, creative problem-solving and a sense of playfulness can be achieved with clients (Creed & Kendall, 2005; Morgan & Wampler, 2003).

Self-Awareness Based Practice Errors
Two common types of self-awareness errors can interfere with a good working relationship: errors of omission and errors of commission. Errors of omission occur when you interact with another person but fail to pick up on important themes or information during the

interaction. Errors of commission occur when you actively insert your own meaning into the situation or take actions that interfere with the helping relationship. Without an awareness of your beliefs, biases, reaction themes, and feeling patterns, you are at high risk of these types of error.

Errors of omission occur when you do not adequately understand what the other person is attempting to communicate. This can occur if your feelings, beliefs, and attitudes intrude on your listening. In such moments your focus shifts to your thinking rather than fully attending to the client communication. When you miss the details of the client experience, you have huge gaps in understanding. When such gaps develop, there is a tendency to fill them with assumptions and theories of what is occurring rather than relying on information provided by the client. Such errors are hard to identify without first understanding your communication patterns and biases.

Errors of commission occur when you impose your beliefs or feelings onto the client situation. In such situations your thoughts and feelings exert more influence on the interaction than your client's statements. When we start imposing our models onto the client, significant problems often emerge in the helping relationship (Borrell-Carrio & Epstein, 2004; Keenan, Tsang, Bogo, & George, 2005; Price & Jones, 1998; Saunders, 1999). Research on helping relationships concludes that clients relate best to nonjudgmental, positive, and responsive practitioners (Bachelor, 1995; Binder & Strupp, 1997; Hilsenroth, Peters, & Ackerman, 2004).

The solution to errors of omission involves increased awareness of your personal traits, but avoiding of errors of commission requires you to apply this awareness to how you are operating in the here and now. Often when errors of commission occur, you will find yourself talking more than the client as you try to convince him or her to accept your point. If you ever experience an emotional pressure to "sell" your insight or solution to the client, you may be at risk of a commission type of error. The self-awareness task is to notice a shift in the interpersonal dynamics during the session. These dynamics may indicate errors of commission:

- Clients become less active in the conversation as you take over the discussion.
- You start to believe you know more about the client situation than the client does.
- You start explaining the client's reality back to him or her.
- You believe that you know what clients need to do and start imposing your solution.

As self-awareness develops, it will be important to find a balance between observing yourself and observing your client. If you become too self-focused, you can create a new problem as you spend too much time attending to yourself and ignore the client (Williams, 2008). Indicators of errors should operate like red flags, where you notice something in the interaction that provides a clue that you need to alter your approach. To begin this process, the next sections explore the roots of your beliefs and affective reactions.

Socialization, Self-Awareness, and Initial Skill Sets

It is likely that you have already started some self-reflection in your early professional courses. Often reading theories causes us to reflect on our past experiences and current functioning. This is a common experience for people entering professional education programs. It is your personal history that provides a predisposition to care about other people. This same set of experiences develops an initial skill set for exploring situations, understanding problems, and identifying options. If you did not have such experiences and skills, it is unlikely that you would consider a helping profession.

Process of Socialization

As you enter your professional education, it is helpful to understand your predispositions and initial skill sets. These helping foundations are based largely on socialization experiences. As your skills develop, interpersonal habits form. Some habits involve our thinking

Figure 1.1

**Socialization
Influences Cube**

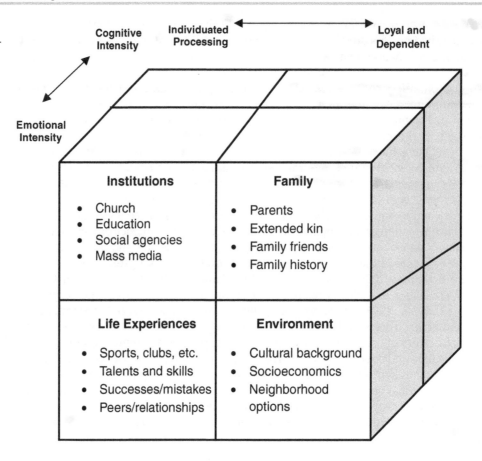

and affective reactions. Other habits involve how you interact with other people. The skill foundation that you bring into a helping profession involves a convergence of your interactive habits and attitudes that promote caring. Although this skill foundation is useful as a starting place, the habitual nature of interpersonal skills leaves you at risk for errors.

To build an awareness of the beliefs and values that control your initial skill sets, it is useful to first understand how socialization forms your thinking and interactive habits. There are several sources of socialization. Figure 1.1 presents four common sources of socialization. Take a moment to consider some of your experiences with these sources and reflect on the values and beliefs that emerged through your socialization experiences.

The nature of our mental socialization is shaped by two continua. The first continuum focuses on how you process events. On one end is reliance on logical processes and thinking. At the other end of the continuum are emotional processes. Although both logical and emotional processes are important, you often tend to favor one type of processing based on your past experiences. The second continuum focuses on the interactive context of socialization. Some people are prone to immediate reactions while others tend to respond slowly through a series of exchanges. Our skill foundation is very heavily influenced by these two continua.

Cognitive-Emotional Elements

The cognitive-emotional continuum ranges from highly cognitive to highly emotional socialization experiences. Emotionally intense experiences tend to stimulate affective reactions. If the experience is positive, you often seek to replicate it in future relationships. If the experience is negative, you tend to avoid similar experiences as you develop. People who have intense emotional experiences during their development may tend to process situations from an emotional position.

At the cognitive end of the continuum, high-intensity experiences promote questioning and critical thinking. This is common in socialization exchanges where experimentation, experiential learning, and negotiation were promoted. Each exchange involves thinking and rethinking situations based on new experiences and outcomes. Lower-intensity experiences may involve socialization experiences where you are told what to think and encouraged to accept rather than question. If negative emotion is linked to certain thinking styles such as feeling rejected for autonomous thinking, a tendency to accept rather than question can be strongly embedded in our socialization experience.

The variations in our socialization form affective and thinking habits as we age. Our patterns of responding to emotion and expressing feelings, beliefs, and values develop and become second nature. Some of us love thinking through complicated problems and will automatically begin analyzing situations as they emerge. Others are more attuned to affect and can easily identify with people's feelings and internal experiences. Still others react to situations with particular emotional or cognitive themes. These automatic tendencies provide the initial skill foundation for how you respond to client situations.

Interactive Elements

The second continuum focuses on relational elements in our socialization. You develop your interpersonal skills within a social context. There is a group of people you lived with, a group of people you learned with, and a group of people you played with. The nature of these groups provides a context for your interactive habits. You have all read about family systems, attachment relationships, and other theories focused on relationship influences. Consequently, you likely have a strong appreciation of the relational context of human development.

Your interactive socialization experiences form habits for conversing. You have learned to wait for your turn to talk. Consequently, many of us listen until we have a thought, then shift our focus to our thinking to remember the thought until our turn emerges. This and other interactive habits shape your initial interpersonal skills. Everyone carries around invisible rules about what is rude and what is acceptable. To promote social success, habits emerge to inhibit rude behavior.

The interactive habits you develop for managing social relationships provide a set of initial communication skills. These skills are the foundation upon which you build your professional practice skills. Your patterns of listening and exploring situations emerge from social situations in your past. Concurrently, your patterns of problem-solving, managing differences, and decision making often are well set before you enter a helping profession. Given that helping professionals all work in a relationship with clients, these habits are very important to understand and control.

Socialization Influences on Response Systems

The habits that emerge from your socialization often form patterns that influence how you respond to situations. Depending on the sources and the intensity of experiences with each continuum, some habits will be tightly held and others will be flexible. Cognitive-emotional habits form beliefs and codes for living; interpersonal habits form patterns of responding. Although these habits have been instrumental in your social successes, as a helping professional you must move beyond habitual responding by building "professional" beliefs and skills.

The discussions and exercises throughout this and the subsequent chapters build on your current beliefs and interactive habits. Through reading, thinking, and applying your knowledge in the exercises, you will start building your professional "self." The professional identity and skill sets you develop should complement, rather than conflict with, the caring habits you have already developed. You will learn to use yourself with greater precision and purpose. This ability to control your responses requires self-awareness.

Understanding Response Systems

As you start building self-awareness, it is useful to first understand your response tendencies. Four areas of experience affect how people react to any given situation. These four areas provide a framework for monitoring reactions. Such frameworks are useful because it is impossible to monitor everything. The four areas of experience can be broken down into two domains: action systems and processing systems. The term "action system" refers to the interactive and behavioral responses that occur in response to a situation. The term "processing system" refers to the internal thoughts and feelings that emerge in the situation. By concentrating on one or the other system on responding, people can scan and monitor how they react in different situations.

Action Systems

The action systems govern what people say or do within a situation. There are two elements in the action system: interaction and behaviors. The interactive response system governs what you say and how you relate to other people. The behavioral response system controls how you act within a situation. Although the two are closely related, it is worth considering each separately so unique contributions can be understood. In helping professionals, interactive people tend to explain, provide advice, or try to discuss situations. More action-oriented people seek to fix things or take over situations until problems are resolved.

To understand how socialization influences your interactive response system, think about some of the rules that govern how you speak to others. You probably have noticed how your interactions change from situation to situation. In some situations you talk more while in others you are content to be passive. Similarly, in some situations you are tentative while in others outspoken. Students learning to be helping professionals have two very common interactive habits (Piers & Ragg, 2008). The first emerges in situations where you talk more. Often talking is preceded by an impulse to say something. In such situations there is often a socialized interactive pattern.

Case example. Two adolescent females are talking. When you observe the pattern of conversation you can notice that as DiAndrea listens to Juanita, she has a thought that triggers an impulse to share the thought. DiAndrea consequently stops listening and focuses on the thought. When Juanita stops talking, DiAndrea shares the thought or story. DiAndrea's story shifts the focus of the discussion. While the thought is triggered by Juanita's story, the thoughts that are expressed shift to a somewhat related story about DiAndrea. This is common when talking among friends; someone tells a story that causes another person to want to share a similar story.

This example highlights a common socialized pattern of interaction. The pattern emerges from our politeness socialization, where authority figures have told us not to interrupt or to wait our turn. Consequently we have developed a pattern of listening and then disengaging to maintain our thoughts until our turn emerges. This pattern, while very helpful in our social relationships, can interfere with the helping relationship because you end up disengaging from the client while focused on your own thoughts. If this pattern is familiar to you, pay close attention to the tuning in and exploratory skills chapters as they will help you develop new habits. At this point, just take note that this is a habit you may want to control.

A second socialized interactive pattern includes advice giving. Most often you learn how to solve problems from parents or guardians. Reflect for a moment on the types of exchanges that occur when you approach your parent/guardian with a problem. Many parents listen for a short period of time and then provide a solution through advice giving. This pattern of problem solving becomes the template you use when friends approach you with a problem. This habit is very useful with friends and is part of being a caring person. Yet the pattern also can interfere with the helping relationship as it involves imposing our vision of the problem on clients.

Similar situations cause people to take action or express themselves behaviorally. At times, you discover this reaction through our bodies. Gestures, feelings of pressure, and muscle tightening tune us into the existence of such reactions. For example, when you hear that someone has been treated unfairly, you often experience a pressure to take some sort of action, such as calling someone or writing a letter. In such situations, it is important to identify the reaction and then assess how the reaction might influence the helping relationship.

Awareness of our reactions can help us prevent mistakes. If you feel impatient to speak or to take action on behalf of the client, this is your reaction, not a request from the client to act on his or her behalf. Awareness of the reaction allows us to identify the pressure as our desire to help. Because this is your impulse, it is up to you to control the response so you can refocus on the client situation to see what the client needs.

Processing Systems

The processing systems involve the thoughts and feelings we have regarding a situation. Awareness of the processing system involves two areas of focus: what we are thinking and what we are feeling. The thinking elements include interpretations, attributions, values, assumptions, and beliefs. The feeling elements include the immediate emotional responses to the client situation (e.g., sadness, helplessness, disgust, hopelessness) and our experience of the client during the session.

Awareness of our thinking and feeling is vital because these become the interpretive frames for understanding the client situation. Often our interpretive guides thread back to socialization messages and thinking habits. As we approach situations, these guides filter and organize our understanding of the situation. This understanding, in turn, dictates how we respond. Several systems of thinking influence the interpretation of situations. Some systems include:

- *Values*. Your socialization provided you with values that set your code for living. Some values are tightly held while others are flexible. Although these are your values for living, they may not be the values that inform your client's decisions. Tightly held values place you at risk of imposing your codes of living on your clients. It is important to understand your values so they do not interfere with your understanding of client situations.

- *Meaning systems*. You have developed systems of assigning meaning to statements, words, events, and situations. These systems often are based on past experiences in similar situations. It is important to be aware of how you attribute meaning and responsibility to events so you can allow your clients to find their own meaning.

- *Expectation systems*. Your socialization experiences provide you with systems for predicting what might and/or should occur within different situations. These systems include expectations based on roles (family roles, social positions, etc.), events (emergencies, disappointments, dates, etc.), and demographics (racial, sexual orientation, religious, economic, gender, age groups, etc.). These socialization-based expectations are based on past information, which often is drawn on for interpreting new situations. It is important to understand your past systems of expectations so they do not control your expectations in client situations.

Without an awareness of how beliefs and models of understanding influence your reactions, you cannot truly understand clients. Consequently your responses to clients will vary in usefulness. For example, if you believe that arguing is "bad" and should be avoided, when members of a client system begin to argue, you might intervene to decrease the arguing. Although this might be consistent with your beliefs about family life, it may not help achieve the family's goals. However, if you are aware of your personal injunctions about arguing, you will be able to control the impulse to stop the arguing and work with the family to bring an argument to fruition.

Concurrent with developing an awareness of patterns of thinking and interpreting situations, practitioners need to be very aware of their feelings. Feelings are automatic responses to situations that can easily communicate your reactions through nonverbal communication. When clients see your reaction, they may interpret it as disapproval. Clients consequently may begin to edit their disclosures to spare your feelings or avoid certain topics because they believe you cannot handle the content area.

The Cultural Context of Socialization

Your socialization experiences occur within a cultural context that sets the norms for your family. Although families within every culture diverge from each other, there is a tendency for families within each culture to have overlapping patterns that influence child guidance, disciplinary practices, family roles, and parental responses to children (Bross, 1982; Ragg, 2006). To help understand your cultural influences, it is helpful first to understand how cultural elements likely influenced your parents. To organize this discussion, cultural influences will be discussed in terms of four parental functions: discipline, guidance, accessibility, and nurturing.

Parents tend to perform specific functions as part of socialization. Notice in Figure 1.2 that accessibility and nurturing functions help children integrate feelings of being lovable. As

Figure 1.2

Cultural Influences on Socialization

a parent attends to their child, the child develops feelings of self-worth and emotional well-being. The parental functions of guidance and discipline promote limiting behavior. These socialization functions help children understand the world and behave in a manner that will promote social success.

Cultural elements that influence parental discipline include abstract mindedness and systems of sanctioning. The term "abstract mindedness" refers to the level of concreteness in the culture. Some cultures are very concrete and operate with very clear rules, expectations, and punishments. Other cultures are very abstract and use stories and myths as part of the socialization. Closely associated with abstract mindedness, cultural norms set standards for the punishment of children. Some cultures use corporal punishment, such as spanking or other physical disciplines; other cultures, such as the dominant North American culture, endorse other methods, such as time out or loss of privileges.

The cultural elements that influence parental guidance include the experience of difference and cultural values. The phrase "experience of difference" refers to the relationship between the cultural group and the dominant culture. Some cultures feel superior to the dominant culture while others feel judged and left out. Regardless of the group's position vis-à-vis the dominant culture, parents must help children understand the differences. In many aspects, these discussions involve helping children understand the cultural values. There is great diversity in cultural values including religious influences, materialism, work ethics, artistic expression, connections to nature, and other domains that make the cultural groups distinct. There are also varying levels of privilege and influence.

Parental accessibility varies greatly across cultures based on the cultural orientation to resources and the collectivist nature of the culture. The orientation to resources again is related partly to the cultural group's position vis-à-vis the dominant group. Some cultural groups have restricted access to higher-paying jobs and monetary resources. Such groups must work in low-status and low-income positions. Often members of such cultures must work more than one job, which restricts parental availability for socializing children. Other cultures may seek to accumulate resources, which can also limit parental availability. In collective cultures, resources are shared more than in individualistic cultures. In these collective cultures, members share in socializing children.

Nurturing children is influenced by the support structures and role expectations inherent in the culture. Some cultures have rigid expectations about nurturing functions. In some cultural groups, these functions are relegated primarily to a specific gender group. It is common for a cultural group to have expectations regarding the amount or quality of nurturing. Within a culture there are also support systems to help develop the nurturing functions. For example, some cultures promote nonfamily day care by funding child care services while other cultures promote kinship approaches to child care. Such systems and expectations influence the structure of socialization.

These cultural elements combine to set a tone for family socialization. The messages and beliefs form our cultural default settings and often are unrecognized until we are confronted by cultural differences. Although racial and ethnic groups may make it easy to identify some cultural differences, not all differences are immediately evident. Cultural groups such as gays, lesbians, and conservative religious groups are often invisible until they self-identify as being different. Consequently, it is useful to build an awareness of our cultural influences prior to working with client groups that may evoke our cultural biases and presuppositions.

Exercise 1.1: Exploring Cultural Influences

This exercise explores your cultural influences using the cultural dimensions just described. All people have cultural influences. If you are a member of the dominant culture, you may be unaware of the influences because they often are embedded in the structure of society. Cultural influences include your status in society, your race, religion, and ancestry. For example, if you are Caucasian and were born in the United States, your culture is probably the dominant culture. However, if you are Asian American and were born in the United States, you will have had very different life experiences. Spend some time thinking about your life experiences, ancestry, and cultural background and identify your cultural group.

Use the next set of questions to reflect on different cultural influences. For each cultural element, think about the questions and then enter some of your observations in the cultural chart (see Figure 1.3).

1. *Abstract mindedness*. In your culture, how much do people rely on principles, symbols, and the like to convey cultural values? Can you tell a person's status by belongings or are other symbols used? How rigid and concrete are the cultural rules? Is your culture very tolerant of gray areas? Are there clear rules that people must follow? How can you tell someone is successful? Do people communicate by telling stories, or is communication more direct?

2. *Experience of difference*. How often do people in your culture talk about cross-cultural differences? Can you identify people from your culture? How do cultural members make sense of racism or cultural oppression? How do parents explain differences to the children? How are economic disparities explained? How are people in your culture different from others? How have people in your life made sense of the differences? Do people talk about the differences, or is this kind of discussion avoided or brushed aside as a topic of conversation? How are the resource differences between different cultures explained? How do differences influence your response to situations?

3. *Values and religion*. What institutions are most influential (e.g., schools, church, government)? What do people do to promote the institutions? How have the important values and institutions influenced your responses to situations?

4. *Individualistic versus collective*. Is your culture more socialist or capitalist? Are common rights or individual rights more protected? Do people have obligations to the larger group (e.g., public service)? Does the tax structure benefit individuals or the public good?

5. *Roles and expectations*. What roles are most important in your culture? What family roles are most respected? What are the expectations for the different family roles? How valued are nonfamily roles that socialize children? What is the ideal family structure in your culture?

Figure 1.3

Cultural Chart

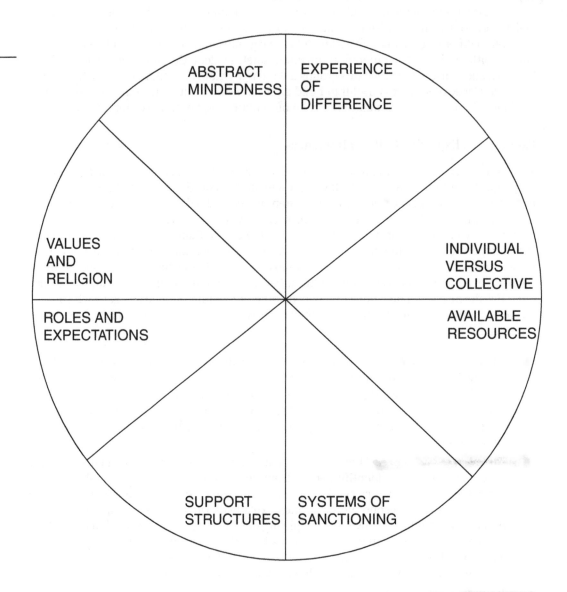

6. *Available resources*. Do most people in your cultural group have enough resources to achieve their goals? How important are possessions in your culture? How much energy do people invest in acquiring resources? Do people share resources freely within the culture or withhold?

7. *Support structures*. Whom do people typically approach for support? What sources of support do people avoid approaching (e.g., social practitioners)? What sources of support bring stigma? Is it okay to need support, or is that a sign of failure?

8. *Systems of sanctioning*. How are children punished in your culture? Is physical punishment okay? How do people hold each other accountable? Do people use lawyers or deal with each other to work out problems? What are the most severe social punishments? How are people rewarded?

After you have reflected on all of these questions, review the cultural chart to identify some of the strongest cultural influences. Try to identify some areas where cross-cultural conflicts may emerge, and develop an initial plan for identifying problems in the helping relationship.

Knowing Your Socialized Background

As you develop your awareness of how you react to different situations, it is useful to explore the influences that underlie your response systems. Most of the events that influence your models of understanding come from socialization experiences and the cognitive constructions you use to make sense out of life. To understand how your family helped to socialize you within the cultural systems, you need to understand family influences. Doing this often involves exploring how you have responded to and made sense of critical events and family history. Such exploration greatly increases your self-awareness.

The next section provides an opportunity to explore your own life so you can begin to identify themes and patterns to monitor in your professional work. The exploration in this book is very brief and serves only as a beginning for your ongoing development. As you proceed with your professional career, it will be important to continue this work as new areas for understanding will emerge frequently in response to new client situations.

In guiding you through the brief self-exploration, exercises are used to help you highlight patterns of thinking, feeling, acting, and interacting. As you use each of the tools, make note of your own experience of exploration. This experience likely will be somewhat similar to your clients' experience during the assessment phase of intervention.

The first exploration begins with family life. In your most formative years, your life experience is dependent on family and neighborhood. As you age, you integrate broader ranges of experience, but much of your response is still inherited from our families. To build self-awareness, you must concurrently develop understanding of how you have adapted to your family-based experiences. Consequently, the self-exploration begins with a genogram.

Family Genograms

A genogram is the first tool that you will use to make sense of your family experiences. The genogram was developed by Murray Bowen and has been broadly used in family-based practice (Marlin, 1989; McGoldrick, Gerson, & Shellenberger, 1999). Many books outline the use of genograms in practice. The next exercise will not provide a full exploration on how to use the genogram but will introduce you to the basics. In performing this exercise, first follow the instructions for constructing the basic genogram. After you have drawn your genogram, read the instructions for the family dynamics and reflect on how they influenced your socialization.

In the family genogram, circles represent females and squares represent males with their current age noted within the circle or square. Generational differences are indicated by vertical position with the parents (or even grandparents) on the top and offspring on lower lines. The lowest line in the genogram is the youngest generation in the family system you are assessing. Typically, the eldest sibling is drawn on the left with younger siblings ordered according to birth order drawn to the right. The current family is always in the middle of the genogram with a dotted line around the family members who live together.

Figure 1.4

Family Genogram

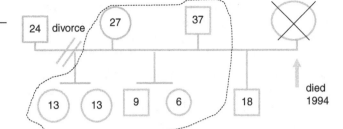

Multiple marriages or relationships are possible to draw. To depict such relationships, draw lines between the adult and first partner. Then break the line and connect the next partner. Although this may sound complicated, the principles of drawing a genogram are fairly simple once you see how it is done. In the genogram depicted in Figure 1.4, you can see that both the current father and mother had prior marriages. One mother died (shown by an X) and the other mother had been divorced (shown by the slash breaking the line between the parent figures). The father in the current family had a son, who is now 18, with the female parent who died. The mother in the current family had, with her first husband, twin girls who are 13. These girls are living in the current family, as shown by their inclusion in the dotted line. Children born from the current relationship (ages 9 and 6) are drawn with a line descending from the union line (the line connecting the two parents).

Figure 1.4 shows a two-generational genogram depicting parents and children. Often practitioners want to assess families using three-generational genograms, such as the one shown in Figure 1.5. Using the same principles, the three-generational genogram places the eldest family members on the top and the youngest on the bottom. The first (eldest) generation is represented by a third-generational line above the parents. This presents a bit of a challenge because the parents forming the current family system are also members of a sibling line. Typically, the children of the first generation who marry to form the next generation are indicated by drawing them lower than the other siblings. A line can then be used to form the parent level of the next generation.

There can be many challenges when working with genograms. For example, if a person is adopted or unsure of his or her parents, or if a person is born from an incestuous relationship, it is hard to map the family. Similarly, some cultural groups have experienced significant traumas, such as the use of boarding schools, lynching, ethnic cleansing, and disasters that will impact the genogram. In such situations, it is possible to place a question mark (**?**) in the genogram and make notes to identify the background information. If clients appear distraught when mapping the family background, it is best to stop the exercise and explore their reactions.

Figure 1.5

Three-Generational Genogram

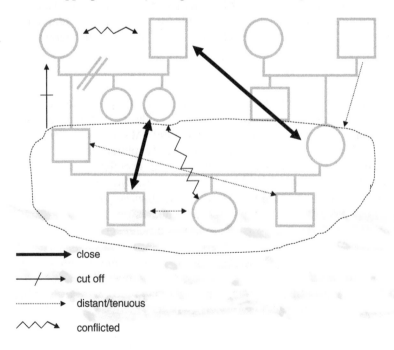

close

cut off

distant/tenuous

conflicted

The relationships among the family members also can be depicted on the genogram using different types of lines, as shown in Figure 1.5. Typical relationship types included on a genogram are conflicted, close, distant or tenuous, and cut-off relationships (no longer talk to each other). Although many more types of relationships exist, these four are enough for the purposes of this example. If you want to include more, add more types of lines to the legend and use them in the genogram.

When using lines to show types of relationships, the direction of energy in the relationship is shown with arrowheads. If the feeling is mutual in the relationship, usually there are arrowheads on both ends of the line. If the feeling flows in only one direction, there is only one arrowhead (which points to the family member who receives the emotion). For example, if Person A was always angry with Person B but the feeling was not reciprocal, the arrowhead would point from Person A to Person B.

In Figure 1.5, the daughter in the current family has conflicts with an aunt on the father's side of the family. This same aunt has a very close relationship with the brother. The brother and sister have a distant or tenuous relationship. The father has a cut-off relationship with his mother in which the emotional energy comes from him. The father's mother is divorced from his father and in a conflicted relationship with him. The mother has a very close relationship with her husband's father, but her father is not close to her. The father seems to have a distant relationship with the youngest brother.

Exercise 1.2: Exploring Your Genogram

It is clear that a genogram contains a wealth of family information. It depicts who is in the family and how they get along with each other. To make sense out of your family, draw a genogram in the space provided below. When drawing the genogram, use the three-generational model (see Figure 1.4).

If you know both of your parents, begin with your father (or previous father figures) way over to the left and mother (or mother figures) way over to the right. Then draw in their parents and siblings if possible. If you are unclear about certain relationships, use question marks where squares and circles would be placed. Make brief notes beside the question marks to document the information gaps. Finally, draw in your brothers and sisters.

After drawing the genogram, read the next lists of questions and reflect on your genogram and family socialization experiences. You may want to make notes on the genogram to capture some of this information or just reflect mentally to ensure privacy. Make sure you address all questions and think about how these aspects of your family influence your action and processing systems.

1. *Tolerance for difference.* As a professional helper, you will be working with diverse groups. Family socialization provides frameworks for understanding and responding to different types of diversity. In your family socialization, some differences will be valued while others may be negatively judged. It is important to understand how your family's approach to differences influenced your responses. Reflect on the next questions to understand how different people in your background influenced your approach to differences.

- *Economic differences.* How did your family make sense of different economic groups? How were rich people valued? What were people's attitudes about poverty? What did family members say caused economic differences? Did your family have friends from different economic groups?

- *Values differences.* What were the major values in your family? How did they deal with people who had different values? Were people able to disagree with each other in the family? What did family members scoff at when the news was on the television? How did you family members feel about politicians? Did they endorse a political party?

- *Religious differences.* How important was religion or spirituality in your family? Did family members subscribe to organized religion? How flexible were family members when it came to religion and spiritual issues? Were family members allowed to question religious teachings? Were family members allowed to believe in religion? Were there other sources of spiritual fulfillment, such as spending time in nature?

- *Racial differences.* How were different racial groups discussed in your family? Were values attached to different racial groups? Did you play with people from different racial groups as a child? What were your experiences like with different racial groups?

- *Cultural differences.* How important was cultural background in your family? What cultural activities were part of your family's traditions? How did your family explain the differences between your culture and other cultural groups? Were there any expectations that you adhere to cultural norms?

- *Privilege differences.* Did you primarily live in one community, or did your family move frequently? If you moved often, was this to improve the family situation? How much choice did your family have about moving? Was your family able to influence community structures and institutions, or were you on the receiving end of other people's influence? What kind of connections did your family have in the community? How active was your family in the community? How was your family viewed by others in the community?

- *Sexual orientation differences.* Who was gay or lesbian in your family? How did family members talk about gay, lesbian, or other sexual populations? How did members of your family distinguish between sexual deviancy and sexual minorities? What meanings were attached to sexual minority groups? How would your family respond if you or one of your siblings told them you were gay/lesbian?

Based on how your family responded to these types of diversity, identify areas of intolerance with the people in your genogram. Jot notes beside these people indicating the types of intolerance. Now consider your relationship with these people, and reflect on how messages of intolerance might affect you when you have to work with diverse clients. Make a mental note of any areas where you will need to focus attention as you develop your openness to diverse client groups.

2. *Support seeking.* You are entering a profession where other people will be approaching you for support. Sometimes the methods clients will use to gain support are disguised and easy to miss if you have a predetermined belief regarding how people should ask for support. At other times, you may find that you have emotional reactions to a client's method of soliciting support from you. Both of these potential reactions come from the historical models of support seeking you have developed through your family experience.

Consequently, it is important to understand how people in your family achieved support. Consider your genogram and reflect on the next sets of questions.

- *Kinds of support.* Was it all right for people to need emotional support in your family? How did others respond to crying or isolating due to unhappiness? When you needed money or rides, how did your family members respond? Were family members good sources of information, or did you need to ask others? Could you trust your family members to give unbiased feedback, or were they judgmental? Did family members listen well, or did they just tell you what you should do?

- *Identified support people.* Do people in your family support each other, or do you need to go outside of the family for support? Does the support tend to come from one or two sources? Are there any features of these people (e.g., gender, age, birth order) that might explain what the support system is based on? What do others do to activate these people to provide support?

- *Identified people receiving support.* Do some people in your family receive more support? What is it about these people (or the people not receiving support) that might explain this pattern? How does receiving support influence status in the family?

- *Rules for whether people are worthy of support.* In your family, do the people providing support place conditions on people such as expectations for how they should think or behave in order to receive support? What are the themes of these conditions that might operate as rules or standards?

- *Patterns of activating support.* How do people in your family activate the support-giving responses in others? Is it okay to ask others directly for help, or do family members need to use indirect methods, such as being visibly helpless or increasing tension in the family (e.g., pouting or tantrums)?

- *Persistent unsolicited support.* Are there any family members who provide support even when others do not appear to want support? Are there patterns that might identify the rewards that the individual gets from this support giving? What is the impact of this support on others?

   Based on the patterns of support giving in the family, identify some themes that might influence how you respond to clients. Perhaps there are experiences or modeling in your family that could cause you to be too abrupt when others seek support. There may be influences in some families that can cause a member to be too free with providing support. Identify possible problems that you will need to prevent when clients approach you expecting support.

   3. *Influencing others.* All people in a family seek to influence others to ensure that their needs are met. The strategies developed by family members to shape the responses of others often form a pattern or trend when a member wishes to influence people. Given that a component of your professional job will involve influencing the behaviors of others, it is important to be aware of the types of influence strategies that might be common to you. Look at the various members in your family genogram and try to determine the methods used by each to influence others. Some of the common influence strategies might include:

- *Logical argument.* Identify people in the family who believe that a person needs to be rational and logical and that these traits should guide behavior. How influential are these members of the family? Is this the primary source of influence?

- *Wearing down resistance.* There may be some people in the family who try to get their way via repeated requests, whining, pouting, or other "wear-down" strategies. Identify these people on your genogram. How influential are they in the family? Are they the ones who get their way? How do you feel about the use of this strategy? Do you ever use this strategy?

- *Escalating tension.* Some people influence others by making them uncomfortable by expressing anger. Often people in a family use this type of strategy to control others. Sometimes people increase the volume of their voice, assume a condescending or angry tone, or become completely silent. Identify people in your family who use tension. Also identify how others respond to them. How have you used tension to get your own way? How do you react when others use tension? Are there certain types of tension that you use more often? Are there certain types of tension that cause you to give in to others?

- *Induction of guilt.* Similar to tension, some family members may use guilt to influence the behavior of other people. Identify those in the family who use guilt as a strategy of influence. Identify the people who are most susceptible to giving in when others use guilt. Think about how you use guilt in your relationships. Think also about how you respond when others use guilt to influence you. Do you give in? Does it make you feel things other than guilt?

- *Loss of approval.* Similar to guilt, some family members may use disappointment or disapproval to influence other people. In some families, loss of approval appears like a loss of love, while in others disapproval is more of a dirty look. How are approval and loss of approval expressed in your family? Identify the people who use this strategy. How do you respond when people express disapproval about what you are doing? How do you use disapproval to influence others?

- *Coercive sanctions.* In some families, coercion is used to gain compliance. At one extreme, this involves becoming violent or threatening harm. Spanking is one form of this strategy, but in more extreme cases, people may punch, kick, choke, throw things, grab, or push. If this has occurred in your family, identify the people who use this type of strategy. When this type of strategy is used, how do you react? How do you feel about the use of coercion? When you see people using this strategy, what do you want to do? In some families, there are more subtle coercive systems, such as being sent to bed, losing privileges, or grounding. How are these strategies used in your family? How have you used different types of coercion in your life? What kinds of issues bring out a desire to use this type of strategy?

In reviewing the strategies of influence used in your life, identify types of client behavior that may evoke a strong response from you. Also identify reactions in yourself associated with the different types of strategies. How will you know when you are reacting to something? Spend some time developing a plan for monitoring and controlling your strategies of influence and reactions to people who may attempt to influence you.

From Socialization to Professional Development

Socialization experiences provide a starting point for your professional career. Somehow in all of those influences you discover that a helping profession is a good direction for your future. For some people, the decision is based on a foundation of caring that emerged from the socialization. Other people may react to experiences and events and choose a helping profession to help vulnerable people either prevent or recover from similar situations. Regardless, most helping professionals have a desire to make the world a better place; this desire threads back to life experiences leading us toward our professional pathway.

Toward a Professional Self

As you begin your professional education, you begin a second identity as a professional. Many of the questions in the last exercise attempt to begin a foundation for the developing professional identity. Although your professional identity builds on your foundation of caring, it is a qualitatively different identity from a personal identity. In your personal life, you are able to maintain values and beliefs that emerge from socialization experiences. This is who you are as a person. As your education progresses, you discover who you are as a helping professional. Although there is some overlap between the two identities, your patterns of responding to people will gain focus and purpose as a professional identity emerges.

Developing a professional identity is sometimes a struggle. As a good son or daughter, you are loyal to your families. As a good citizen, you extend loyalty to institutions such as schools, churches, and other community bodies that influence your development. Now you must add a new loyalty: your professional affiliation. A critical part of self-awareness is ensuring that your loyalty is correctly aligned at any given time. There will be times where clients subscribe to values or activities that seem to violate your family or institutional loyalties. At these times, you must avoid imposing personal or family values. Rather, you must respond from a professional position.

Developing our professional self is a lifelong process. Every day you learn new insights and skills as you gradually increase our mastery as a professional. This developmental process involves applying our skills in practice situations, gathering feedback, and continually adjusting your responses to increase mastery (Ericsson, Krampe, & Tesch-Romer, 1993). As you progress, your professional self develops expertise that is valued by your clients and profession. To begin this process, it is important to take realistic stock of your skills, beliefs, values, and competencies that provide a foundation for the "professional self."

Considerations for Digital Communicators

For those who live large portions of life on the Internet and communicate mostly using Facebook and texting, there may be some unique challenges as you develop self-awareness. These challenges emerge from digitally connected people because you are likely to have an expansive understanding of the world. Inherent in living a connected life, digital communicators have an enormous awareness of events occurring within social networks and the world. You learn about situations in real time, seldom relying on the news media to provide you with information that is already stale. Digital communicators are the ultimate consumers of information.

In your quest for information, you develop skills to access information quickly. As you surf from site to site, you make lateral cognitive moves often stimulated by interest or divergent thoughts that enter your mind. You can immediately explore multiple sources of information with a world of infinite information literally at your fingertips. As a result, your mind becomes quite adept at pursuing facts and fantasies, each existing in a unique universe and linked to multiple parallel worlds. The constant flow of information and entertainment keeps your mind moving at an amazing pace, constantly seeking and exploring.

Concurrent with accessing information, digital communicators maintain large social networks. Social networking, while a critical link to the world, is sometimes an intrusive demand. Twitter, Facebook, and other services that automatically update followers intrude into electronic worlds, each time drawing attention and resulting in a decision to welcome or resist the distraction. Texting promotes similar decisions. Each decision requires you either to respond or to ignore, as the communication enters your awareness.

Distraction Versus Focus
Although digital communicators are excellent at multitasking, developing self-awareness may be frustrating because it is a slow and focused search. This contrasts with the skill sets associated with surfing the Web and managing social networking intrusions. The surfing patterns and social networks develop skills to quickly access information, make decisions, and respond. This skill set may frustrate digital communicators when developing self-awareness.

Self-awareness development is not a fast process because the information is not easy to find. Often the important information seems invisible. Often you must spend inordinate amounts of time reflecting on a situation to learn the subtle influences in your life. This intense, singular focus can seem very slow and tedious for digital communicators. There are very few easily retrievable nuggets of information. To be successful, digital communicators must welcome internally focused exploration as they would a challenging Web search.

Outward Versus Inward
The second challenge for digital communicators is the direction of the search. Digitally connected people are highly skilled at seeking out sources of information on the Internet. Most know different search strategies that can eliminate useless information and increase the likelihood of a successful search. These skills all begin at the keyboard and extend outward into cyberspace. As such, your best-honed skills are outward in focus.

Developing self-awareness is an inward journey. Strategies for an inward search are unique because they require openness rather than active penetration of space. Often self-awareness emerges when you notice patterns in your life and then explore those patterns.

Pattern emergence is a reflective experience that is qualitatively passive and calm. To develop awareness, it may be necessary to relax and reflect inward rather than trying to pursue information actively.

Fragmentation Versus Coherence

A final challenge emerges from the nature of digital information. As you receive digital information through updates or searches, you gather multiple unique elements of information. Many of the information elements remain unique and do not require any integration into a whole. As you multitask, you manage several digital conversations while working on a term paper and watching television. Such management requires skills at keeping each set of tasks distinct from the others.

The tasks used to fragment life into unique manageable packages can interfere with self-awareness. As you explore your experiences and methods of coping, the task is to unify and build a coherent understanding of your values, thinking, and affective processing. The development of self-awareness requires you to explore seemingly unrelated life events and associated responses to find common threads and meaning in the divergent experiences. The skills associated with developing coherence diverge from the habits developed for managing the multiple digital inputs. For this reason, developing self-awareness may feel awkward and frustrating.

Exercise 1.3: Understanding Your Socialized Foundation

In the genogram and cultural exercises, you explored some socialization influences. In this exercise, you will explore your patterns of thinking and responding. This is a summary of the personal you. Take great care in exploring who you are today because this is the foundation that will support your professional self. As you proceed with this exercise, you will respond mentally to several sets of questions. Make sure that you answer every question in your mind. Take time to reflect on each area of questioning. As you respond to the questions, you should have some thoughts and insights; jot down these insights on paper. Use these thoughts to identify areas of your personal self that you want to shape, build on, or control as you start developing your professional self.

1. *Context.* First, let's explore the social context of your life. Read the next sets of questions and mentally answer each as your reflect on how they apply to your life.

- *Neighborhood.* You were raised in a neighborhood and community. This setting provided you with a comfort zone. What features in your neighborhood promoted comfort or fear? What areas of the neighborhood did you learn to avoid? What areas of the neighborhood were sources of comfort? Where did you go to have fun in the neighborhood? How was your neighborhood viewed by others in the community? Compare these features to the types of neighborhood that your clients may come from. Would those neighborhoods be similar to yours? If the neighborhoods are different, how are you going to increase your comfort entering neighborhoods that are different from yours?

- *Culture.* You were raised in a cultural context. Some of you are members of the dominant culture, and others were raised in a minority cultural context. What privileges has your culture provided you? How did your racial or cultural group fare in relation to the privileges provided to other groups? How do those differences influence your perceptions of your culture? How do these differences influence your perceptions of other cultural groups? Think about your culture and race and how these elements of your life fit into the larger society. Are there any other cultural groups that are confusing to you at this time? Are there any groups that seem too entitled? How might these observations present challenges as you start developing your professional self? What values of right and wrong has your culture/background instilled in you? Do these values fit with the larger society values such as work ethic, democracy, competition, and equal opportunity? How might you respond to clients from different cultures, races, or backgrounds?

- *Institutions*. Think about the role that societal institutions had in your life. What influence did school, church, police, neighborhood organizations, social welfare institutions, and economic institutions have in forming your personal identity? Are relationships good with some institutions and not with others? Which are helpful and which are hurtful? How might past experience influence your reactions when you have to interact with these institutions and organizations as a professional? How might these experiences influence how you respond to clients who are having difficulty with social institutions?

2. *Behavior*. This section explores your current codes of behavior. With your genogram and life history in mind, consider the next sets of questions about your action tendencies. As you mentally answer these questions, you will have insights into your patterns of behavior and ways that you manage your actions. Make notes to capture your insights as you proceed.

- *Talents*. What special talents have you developed throughout your life? Do these talents help you see things differently from other people? How do these talents affect how you express yourself with others? How do the talents influence your motivation and drive? How can these talents enhance your abilities as a professional helper?

- *Life experiences*. What experiences have you sought out that helped form your character? What kind of activities did you tend to participate in? How did these activities enlighten you about other people? Did any of the activities expose you to people you might not have met otherwise? How might these experiences help you as a professional helper?

- *Social direction*. What are the things you do that make society a better place? If nobody knew you were doing good deeds, would they be worth doing? What are the expectations you use to organize your educational and work life? What happens if these expectations cannot be achieved? What happens if other people interfere with your plans?

- *Codes for living*. Should people be clean and tidy? What does it mean when people do not take good care of themselves? How important is punctuality? Are the standards for behavior in a family different from how people should act in public? How important is following up on your promises? Should all rules be followed, or is it okay to break some? Under what conditions is it okay to break rules?

- *Public and private behavior*. How is your public behavior different from your private behavior? What are some things you have done you will never tell your parents? What are some things you have done you will never tell another soul? How would your life change if someone found out and went public? How would it feel if a societal institution entered your life and started asking you and your family about these types of behaviors?

- *Injunctions*. How do you keep control of your behavior? Is your self-control something that happens inside you, or do you need others to be watching? Is controlling your behavior important to you? Under what conditions would you become violent? Under what conditions is it okay to take a life? Under what conditions would you consider breaking the law? What sexual behaviors are doable for you? What sexual behaviors are okay for others, but you probably would not do them? How do you distinguish between sexual minorities and sexual deviance?

3. *Interaction*. You developed several interactive habits that control your patterns of relating to other people. Reflect on your systems of interaction that emerged from your early family experiences. As you mentally answer the next sets of questions, take notes when you have insights into your interpersonal patterns.

- *Listening habits*. When you listen to others, do you tend to go into your head when you have a thought, or do you continue listening? Do you find that you lose track of what others are saying when you are listening? When you listen too much, do you get bored? Do you prefer listening or talking? Do you talk more than you listen? Are you a person who gives advice to others?

- *Relating to others*. Do you prefer people who are a lot like you? How do you react when others are different from you? Can you trust others to do what they say, or do you have to check up on them? Can you trust others to respect you, or do you have to analyze what people might mean by what they say (or do not say)? Do you feel others judge you harshly or want to bring you down? Are there differences between groups of people you like and those you do not like?

- *Interpersonal situations.* Are some situations harder to handle than others? When people ignore you, how do you react? How do you respond when you do something embarrassing and people laugh at you? When people confront you publicly, can that cause problems? Sometimes you believe you are right, but others still want to take another direction; is that ever a problem for you?

- *Problem solving.* Given your family experience, how do you approach problem solving? Is there a right and wrong way to raise problems? Are problems between people something that authority figures arbitrate, or do people work things out at their own level? Do you have a tendency to diminish tension when problems are being discussed, or can people battle it out? What is the role of authority figures when other people have problems? Is tension a good thing, or should it be avoided? When others disagree with you, what happens inside you? What feelings are evoked when you prefer one solution to a problem but people select a different solution?

4. *Emotion.* You have had an opportunity to consider many elements in your genogram. Emotional management is something that is heavily influenced by family experiences. Think about your family messages and rules about emotions as you reflect on the next set of questions.

- *Emotional expression.* Are emotions something to be controlled or expressed? What is the right way to express emotion? Should you hold in emotion? Do you tend to ignore or express emotions? Is there such a thing as being too emotional? How would you know if you were too emotional? Is it bad to be emotionally expressive? Is it bad to hold in emotions? Are there right ways to express negative emotions? Should you hide your feelings when upset? How about when you are happy?

- *Emotional value.* Are certain emotions okay and others not? What makes a good emotion good? What emotions should you avoid? What makes these emotions negative? What emotions should you hide from others? Are there occasions when you can share negative emotions?

- *Emotional awareness.* When you experience feelings, do you know exactly what you are experiencing, or do some feelings seem confusing? When you cry during a movie or show, what feeling themes tend to be present? What feelings tend to motivate you to take action? What thoughts tend to go through your head when you are sad, angry, happy, powerless, or ashamed? How do the thoughts amplify or diminish the feelings?

5. *Thinking.* Many of your feelings, actions, and interactions are influenced by your beliefs (Ellis, 1996; Meichenbaum, 1997). You all have different levels of beliefs. Some beliefs are ideological and influence your sense of right and wrong, while other beliefs are of no real consequence in how you live your life. As you answer the next set of questions, reflect on your beliefs that help guide your life. Again, take notes about any insights that emerge during the exercise.

- *Self-conceptions.* Many people feel that they have many flaws. Do these thoughts ever emerge for you? Do you feel that you should be perfect? How pervasive is this belief? What would happen if you are less than perfect? Do you often feel that you must defend yourself or prove something to others? When you judge your own actions, whose eyes or perceptions do you use to observe yourself? Are these people who are friendly or critical? Do you find you need other people to keep saying good things about you? If people criticize you, does it cause you to feel bad or forget your good points? How does your race factor into your identity? What is unique about your ethnic background? How does race and ethnic background influence your self-worth?

- *Family roles.* Are there family roles that are more important than others? Should these roles have special privileges? Do these roles benefit one gender over another? Can two people of the same sex fulfill these roles? Is your answer to the last question based on logic or loyalty? How should children be raised? Whose job is it to raise children properly? What is society's role in helping this to happen? How do these beliefs fit with those from other cultures? How might these beliefs create problems when working with different client groups?

- *Ideologies*. What ideologies tend to influence your codes for living? What is the role of organized religion in your life? Do you follow religious teachings like inflexible rules or more like guidelines? How do feminist beliefs influence your life? What about socialist beliefs? How do these beliefs fit into today's society? How does your ideology help you identify good from bad? Have you noticed that many ideologies are polarized into good/bad categories? Is it good for society to think in polarized terms? How does this style of thinking fit for you?

6. *Motivational orientation.* You are all motivated by different affective orientations. These orientations set patterns in our lives and influence our relationships with others. Reflect on the next sets of questions to identify patterns in your strivings. After mentally answering the questions, consider how your natural motivations might influence how you operate as a helping professional.

- *Some people strive to be the best.* Do you find your values are superior to others? How are your grades compared to those of your classmates? Does it matter if others do better than you? How hard do you work to be attractive? Do you hate it when others see you looking bad? Do you often compare yourself to others? Are you a leader? Do you often assume control when working on group projects?

- *Some people strive to be safe.* Do you worry that others might do things to mess up your plans? Does it bother you if others are angry with you? Do you try to keep everyone happy? How important are rules and procedures? Does it bother you when others do not follow rules? When you need to confront someone, do you bring others with you for support? Do you count on friends to help protect you from others?

- *Some people strive to be close to others.* How much energy do you put into maintaining old friendships? When your friends do not reach out to you, do you continue to put the effort into relationships? Do you tend to do more than your share on group projects? Do you often give in for the good of the group, even if your ideas seem better? When others are not doing their share, do you still do your best?

- *Some people strive to master challenges.* Do you seek out challenges? Are you the kind of person who experiments with new approaches? Do others accuse you of trying to reinvent the wheel? Will you accept failure as long as you learn from your attempts? Do you keep trying even when others tell you that it is not worth it? Are you happy when you start on a new project? Do you keep seeking out new areas to learn?

Now take a few minutes to review the notes you took during the exercise. You should at this point have a sense of the strengths and challenges that emerge from your socialization and life experiences. Treat your socialization as a professional starting point by first circling the insights and thoughts that will help you relate to clients and populations that are different from you. These circled areas will become your foundation for building your professional identity.

The second task is to underline any thoughts or insights that might interfere with serving clients. As you underline, understand that these areas are not bad or negative; these are simply elements of your socialization that you want to keep in your personal rather than your professional life. You will be building new frameworks for thinking and methods of responding that will round out your professional self. At this point, you need to start separating personal traits that can translate into professional competencies from personal traits that might interfere.

When you have finished the underlining, look at your pages and begin planning how you might limit the influence of the underlined areas as you build your professional self. Identify the elements that you might need to control or even eliminate and formulate a plan for each. Develop similar plans for the areas that might be helpful in your profession. Identify the beginning competencies so you can start to shape them into professional skills. Remember that professional development is a lifelong process; these plans will be actualized throughout your career.

Figure 1.6

**Lifelong-Learning
Sequence**

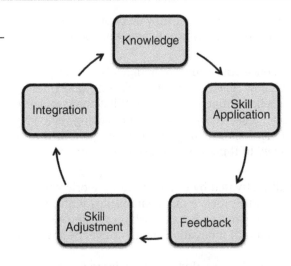

Toward a Lifelong Learning Approach

Based on your current set of competencies, you are now embarking on a career-long journey of professional development. You have now identified values, beliefs, and skills that you can build on to become a competent professional. You have also identified sets of values, beliefs, and skills that you want to retain in the personal rather than the professional realm. This initial separation between your personal and professional selves signifies the beginning of your professional development.

As you continue to develop your professional self, you will discover a pattern of learning and skill development. This pattern is evident in most professions where skills are an element of success. The pattern, depicted in Figure 1.6, involves continual cycles of skill application, feedback, adjustment, and integration with new knowledge. You will continue to learn from this cycle throughout your career.

Although you have some experiences and learning at this point, your professional self will continue to develop as your competencies grow. The first step in this ongoing development is knowledge. You must have knowledge that can be applied in practice (Lane, Mathews, Sallas, Prattini, & Sun, 2008). Knowledge development requires you to understand theories, research findings, and professional principles that inform your practice. You have been acquiring this information through your prerequisite classes and now can integrate your knowledge with your current skill foundation by applying your learning to practice situations.

After applying your knowledge, it is very important to gather feedback and evidence to help you refine your skills (Ericsson et al., 1993). Such evidence includes client outcomes, client feedback, supervisory feedback, and other observation systems that can help you identify effective skill elements. Even in the absence of external data sources, such as supervisors, you will become a skilled observer and will begin to reflect on your interventions to discover skills that are working well and skills that require adjustment.

As you gather information, you will continually adjust and refine your skills, each time learning more about how to use yourself with professional precision. If you practice with self-awareness and openness, the repeated cycles will hone your skills and competencies for working within the helping relationship. Eventually, skills that begin awkwardly develop into competencies and interactive habits that will become second nature.

Critical Chapter Themes

1. It is important for helping professionals to be very aware of themselves. Such awareness provides (a) a source of personal power; (b) awareness of differences; (c) insight into one's reactions; and (d) a source of emotional connection.

2. Self-awareness includes four response systems to be fully aware of how you respond to situations: action, interaction, thinking, and feeling.

3. Our responses are heavily influenced by our family socialization and personal history. Models of understanding, interpreting, avoiding, and behaving evolve as you adapt to early family and community situations. You must understand these adaptations to be fully self-aware.

4. A genogram can help us understand our socialization influences regarding support seeking, tolerance of difference, and influencing others. These are critical areas of awareness for a helping professional. The genogram also provides a tool for assessing client family patterns.

5. Our life experiences and socialization provide a starting point for developing as professionals. You shape this development using self-awareness to control patterns that might interfere with the helping relationship and building on traits that can enhance your work.

6. Competencies continually build on foundation skills by applying skills, gathering feedback, adjusting, and then integrating outcomes with new knowledge. This is the foundation of lifelong professional development.

Online Resources

Psychological games including self-awareness: http://wilderdom.com/games/

Resources with a multicultural focus: www.edchange.org/multicultural/index.html

Recommended Reading

Ericsson, K. A., Krampe, R. T., & Tesch-Romer, C. (1993). The role of deliberate practice in the acquisition of expert performance. *Psychological Review*, *100*(3), 363–406.

Galindo, I., Boomer, E., & Reagan, D. (1989). *A family genogram workbook*. Richmond, VA: Educational Consultants, www.galindoconsultants.com.

Rothman, J. C. (1999). *Self-awareness workbook for social practitioners*. Boston, MA: Allyn & Bacon.

Chapter 2
Conscious Self-Control and Ethical Behavior

As we become aware of how values and models of interpretation can interfere with the helping relationship, it is important to find methods of controlling potential interference (D. W. Johnson, 1997; Murphy & Dillon, 1998). Our ability to exert control over our personal reactions begins with the self-awareness you started to build in Chapter 1. As you develop your professional self, professional groups provide guidelines for self-control through professional values and ethics.

Toward a Professional Code of Behavior

Professional behavior is guided by three related influences working together as a framework: values, ethics, and legal duties. Within every helping profession, these three influences shape the expectations for professional practice. Often discussed separately, the influences tend to reflect different levels of abstraction along a continuum of professional expectation. At the most abstract level, there are values and principles. At the most concrete level, we must all adhere to legal duties that prescribe actions that must be taken in specific circumstances.

Socialization Challenges

Although professional values are not intended to replace personal values, they are a precondition for successful enculturation into the profession. Depending on the profession you choose, professional values may conflict with your personal beliefs. It is important to consider the professional values carefully as you choose a profession. Otherwise you may become upset when your personal beliefs are challenged or you are expected to act on professional beliefs that offend your values. To prevent such conflicts, it is important to understand how professional and personal values become juxtaposed as you enter a helping profession.

To put this challenge in context, try to imagine someone deciding to become a priest while secretly doubting the existence of God. This may not be a very good career choice. If the doubting priest attempts to reconcile these differences by asking the church to drop all references to God, ongoing conflicts can be predicted as long as the priest remains in the profession. Similarly, if a person enters a helping profession without truly subscribing to the professional values, there will be similar conflict.

In Chapter 1 you had an opportunity to identify your personal values. To prevent conflicts in your future, it is wise start with a clear understanding of professional values and their implicit demands on you as a practitioner. You can then seek to reconcile the two sets of values. Understanding professional values is important because different professions stress unique values. It is important to select a profession with values that are not diametrically opposed to your personal values. Many beginning professionals may find some principles in their chosen profession that require them to challenge and adjust personal values. The resolution of potential conflicts is individual. However, the resolution must occur within us because professions, like the church, will not change to accommodate your personal beliefs.

Considerations for Digital Communicators

People who are digitally connected may experience some additional challenges in the professional relationship. Our methods of surfing and managing online relationships can set up habits that interfere with professional expectations. Two areas of potential challenge include issues of consent and issues of appropriate boundaries.

Informed Consent

Many web sites carry material that would not fit easily into an ethical framework. Web sites such as YouTube and other video-sharing web sites often carry material that violates copyright laws. Many of the online videos also involve pranks and material that involves videotaping people without their consent. We are entertained by the content on such sites with little concern or understanding of the ethical issues inherent in the taping and presentation of the material.

Our ongoing entertainment with online material sets habits that will need to change as we enter a profession. We must be concerned with issues of consent and sharing information that might be embarrassing or humiliating. The development of a professional self requires us to become sensitive to the person rather than viewing situations from an entertainment perspective.

Boundaries

In cyberspace we can explore information without boundaries. Abundant information and images are totally accessible. We can find old friends and discover details about people's lives. As we surf the available information, we do not think about the appropriateness of access. Although we have some informal beliefs about "creeping," people routinely invade each other's privacy based on interests and whims.

In professional relationships, we are curtailed in our exploration. As we form a helping relationship, we must limit our discussions to those appropriate to client goals. Although we may be interested in multiple areas of a client's life, we cannot explore these areas unless it is appropriate to the professional role. We also must refrain from using the Internet to access information about our clients without their knowledge and consent.

Professional Values

As we develop our professional selves, we assume a set of values for guidance. Professional values provide the guiding principles for the profession. Some professions are grounded in physical science and others in social sciences. The history and scientific grounding of any profession will influence the value base. The value base, in turn, influences the ethical guidelines that guide professional responses. By understanding and adhering to values, we establish a range of responses we can integrate easily into our professional activities. Values and ethics are discussed in other courses and textbooks, but their link to self-control makes them a critical practice competency. The discussions in this textbook focus on how values and ethics inform practice decisions and activities.

Comparative Values Among the Helping Professions

All helping professions have core values that guide practice and underpin the professional codes of ethics. Each helping profession lays claim to its own practice domain, but the major helping professions have values in common. All professions take a position on human dignity, client determination, professional responsibility, and human conditions. The first three core values are basically the same across professional groups. The last core value, human conditions, contains some differences in focus across the disciplines. To understand how values necessitate professional self-control, explore these values before delving into the ethical principles that follow.

Human Dignity

All of the major helping professions—psychology, counseling, nursing, occupational therapy, and social work—profess values about treating clients with dignity. Inherent in these values is the expectation that professionals will refrain from imposing personal values and accept the client without judgment. If professionals actively discriminate against client populations based on race, gender, age, ability, sexual orientation, or any other trait, they may lose their professional license to practice.

This value of human dignity sometimes has created tension between conservative religious groups and professional bodies. While publicity and court cases may emerge from this tension, professional groups maintain that they have a right to impose professional values just as the American Association of Pastoral Counselors expect their practitioners to adopt religious-based values. At the heart of this debate is the issue of personal versus professional values. Often protagonists argue that professions should change the value base to accommodate individual beliefs.

Inherent in the value of dignity, professional associations insist that practitioners always put the welfare of the client first. Doing this requires us to be able to put our values aside for the good of the client. Practitioners with conservative personal values cannot pick their clients based on sexual values. Concurrently, liberal practitioners cannot refuse to work with clients who profess staunch conservative values. Professional practitioners can never impose their values or political agendas on their clients.

Client Self-Determination
The second core value of the helping professions is client self-determination. Clients are expected to have choices about the way they live. There are two elements to client determination.

1. Clients must be able to make decisions about how they live. Consequently, no professional can tell clients how to live or dictate values-driven outcomes without violating a core professional value.
2. Clients should not be forced to change or enter service without their consent.

Inherent in this value, practitioners are expected to collaborate with clients by forming a helping relationship in an informed and equal manner (Corey & Herlihy, 1996). Practitioners provide clients with options and honor their decisions. Even clients referred due to criminal behavior have a choice, although their options may be limited. Inherent in this decision-making process is an assumption of competence. Even with clients with physical or mental disabilities are assumed to be competent to make independent decisions unless ruled otherwise by a court of law (Hall & Jugovic, 1997).

It is not unusual to experience competency-related conflicts in professional practice. Competency challenges often occur when working with children, adolescents, elderly persons, and disabled persons (Croxton, Churchill, & Fellin, 1988). Consequently, workers must know the competency laws that may impinge on this principle (Croxton et al., 1988; Hall & Jugovic, 1997; Schmidt, 1987). Ethically, practitioners also must challenge structures that interfere with a client's self-determination. Some of the structures that inhibit client autonomy include:

- Managed care determinations (Clark, 1998; Watt & Kallmann, 1998) and empirically driven intervention protocols (Raw, 1998) often limit the options available to clients.
- Paternalistic approaches to service may withhold options or apply pressure to accept favored options (Davitt & Kaye, 1996; Dolgoff & Skolnik, 1996; Stein, 1990).
- The nature of life and death decisions often limits client autonomy, especially when the client wants to take their own life, or the decision may harm others (Clark, 1998; Wesley, 1996).

Professional Responsibility
The third shared value among the helping professionals is professional responsibility. All professions place the interests of the client as the top priority when providing service (Corey & Corey, 1998). This value dictates that workers should keep all of their activities focused on achieving their clients' well-being. Inherent in this injunction is the fact that workers need to avoid putting self-interest, career advancement, other relationships, and politics above the interests of the client.

Professional responsibility to clients can be difficult to achieve due to competing priorities in the practice situation. Agencies often have priorities associated with funding, cost efficiencies, and interagency relationships that can pit administrative agendas against client interests. Sometimes community boards overseeing professional service are fraught with political infighting and agendas that subvert client best interests. Professionals must be prepared to challenge administrative decisions when they interfere with client well-being. All professional disciplines provide guidelines and professional protections to encourage professionals to protect client interests at all times.

Conflicts between employing organizations and client interests can introduce self-interest conflicts for agency-employed professionals. It is difficult to advocate for client interests when you fear that your job or potential for advancement may be in jeopardy. Even in situations of career-related risk, client interests must even take priority over your self-interest. It is useful to know that professional organizations will support workers when they truly are advocating for client interests. Many states also have whistle-blower protections for people who must make these difficult decisions.

Human Conditions

Each helping profession has shared beliefs about the nature of human problems. This core professional value is evident in the theories and approaches endorsed by the professional group. Unlike the core values just explored, the various helping professions view human problems somewhat differently. These core values tend to span from an inner to a societal understanding of human problems.

- *Counseling.* The American Counseling Association views human problems with an emphasis on how individuals adapt within situations. Consequently, counselors often end up in school or occupational settings helping to maximize people's capacity within these spheres of life. Psychology focuses heavily on clinical populations, but counseling traditionally has focused on normal developmental challenges, such as school or work adjustment problems. Today counselors are being used increasingly to diagnose and treat individuals with problems, but they tend to base their approaches on the premises of normal life span development rather than on clinical research and pathology.

- *Nursing.* The American Nursing Association maintains that nursing must promote public health. Like social work, nursing maintains a focus on social justice as it applies to ensuring the optimal well-being of the patient, the family, and society (Halvorsen, Forde, & Nortvedt, 2009; Shaw & Degazon, 2008). Nurses are expected to attend to the needs of society's vulnerable populations by administering to health needs (Fahren-wald et al., 2005). Doing this includes the prevention of mental and physical disease along with treating people with obvious illness. Within the social justice mission, professionals focus on holistic health by treating individuals and groups rather than by attempting to change societal structures.

- *Occupational therapy.* The American Occupational Therapy Association focuses on using activity to promote healthy living. As a profession, occupational therapy promotes the optimal physical, cognitive, sensory, and psychosocial functioning clients. Typically, the profession works with people who have some level of impairment or disability that requires adaptation. As such, the profession focuses on people's strengths and how those strengths can be enlisted to compensate for, and master, limitations. As in the fields of nursing and social work, in occupational therapy, issues of social justice emerge especially in the domain of people's right to live and participate in society without stigma or prejudice.

- *Psychology.* The American Psychological Association, which encompasses branches such as social psychology and industrial psychology, traditionally has focused on the individual and how he or she processes situations. Psychologists attempt to understand behavior through multiple subspecialties ranging from working with brain functions to larger system change. Often the focus of psychology is to help people actualize their internal potential by helping them to understand and change how they respond to situations. Psychologists tend to employ rigorous, scientific assessment strategies to

Table 2.1 **Sample of Professional Activities**

Profession	Common Types of Work	Common Work Settings
Counseling	• Work/school adjustment counseling • Life adjustment counseling • Mental health interventions	• School or workplace assistance offices • Community service agencies • Private practice
Nursing	• Physical care interventions • Administer medications under supervision • Mental health interventions	• Hospitals • Community health settings • Mental health settings
Occupational Therapy	• Disability adjustment counseling • Adaptive skill development • Mental health interventions	• Hospitals • Community health settings • Mental health settings
Psychology	• Psychological assessment (test administration and interpretation) • Mental health interventions • Specialty (industrial, social) consultation	• Hospitals • Schools • Community mental health settings • Criminal justice/prisons • Private practice
Social Work	• Family-centered interventions (child protection, family preservation) • Social benefit interventions • Mental health interventions	• Hospitals • Schools • Community service agencies • Criminal justice/prisons • Mental health settings

understand the inner workings of the mind. Psychology has unique expertise in the area of administering and interpreting psychological tests and measures of human capacities.

• *Social work.* The National Association of Social Work maintains that people cannot be separated from their social context. Consequently, humans must be understood within their life circumstances for change efforts to be realistic and appropriate. If workers miss the context, they might blame their clients for things outside of their control. Inherent in this value is the fact that people and their environments are considered interdependent. Consequently, social workers often see problems located in the environment rather than in the client. Social work practice can focus on changing society and promoting social justice as well as helping clients adapt to their life situation (Watt & Kallman, 1998).

In the preceding discussion, you will have noticed remarkable similarities in the values *of the helping* professions. To help you understand the subtle professional differences, Table 2.1 provides a sample of the different types of work and some common work settings associated with the various professional roles. The table, though far from exhaustive, provides a snapshot of each profession and its scope of expertise.

Importance of Professional Ethics

Professional values provide general principles to guide professional activity. However, professions require a clearer set of behavioral guidelines to ensure uniformity within the profession. Consequently, professional ethics expand on values to provide clear and concrete guidelines for professional behavior (Corey, Corey, & Callanan, 1998; Jackson, 1998; Murphy & Dillon, 1998). Most ethical guidelines focus on the worker's actions by limiting the types of actions and interactions that may occur within the professional relationship. Such guidelines are developed to protect clients from unethical workers. This is a most serious function of ethical guidelines. Professions with licensure may investigate and sanction workers who violate ethical principles.

Every helping profession has a code of ethics that governs the behavior of professionals practicing within that discipline. For the purposes of this chapter, five helping professions are considered—counseling, occupational therapy, nursing, psychology, and social work—because there are the most common professions providing services to clients. Although each profession operates with different domains of expertise, a perusal of each profession's code of ethics yields significant overlaps and similarities. This discussion explores common elements and divergences using professional values as an organizing framework.

This discussion limits the focus on critical ethical principles. The full codes of ethics and other professional materials can be found on the web sites of the professional organization; links to these sites can be found at the end of the chapter. Explore downloadable versions of each organization's code of ethics as you prepare for your professional career.

Relationship Among Values, Ethics, and Legal Expectations

Professional values are abstract principles that shape the core beliefs of practitioners within each profession. However, to guide professional actions, a more concrete set of guidelines is needed. This is the role of professional ethics. Every professional has a code of ethics that translates the values into guidelines for professional behavior. Many professions have ethics committees that monitor ethical behavior and sanction ethical breaches. At the most concrete level, professionals must abide by legal expectations and duties. Legal expectations demand that all professionals respond to situations in a prescribed manner. If legal breaches occur, professionals can suffer legal or civil repercussions.

Role of Professional Bodies
Professional practitioners are accountable through their professional organization's code of ethics. Each organization dictates acceptable public interactions and behaviors. As we enter our chosen profession, we accept these ethical rules as a condition of our professional membership. When a practitioner's behavior violates an ethical principle, the professional association may take corrective action. Corrective actions can involve mandated training, required changes in practice, or suspensions. In states where professions are licensed, corrective action may include a professional losing his or her license to practice.

A professional body's right to control its membership is debated when value conflicts emerge with social groups. Typically such debates focus on an individual's right to live by personal, rather than professional, values and beliefs. As you select your professional membership, remember that membership into a profession is an act of free will. As you become a professional, you enter a contract to accept the values and rules of the profession *as they currently exist*. For this reason, it is important to make an informed decision because the profession will place expectations on you to abide by specific values and ethics. Although values and ethics may change, it is not wise to hope for drastic changes as you enter a profession.

Role of Legal Systems
Professional bodies control their membership's general activities; legal systems set expectations that span across professional groups. These expectations provide a code for all professionals regardless of affiliation. The codes typically assert basic human rights that override professional ethics. Such codes historically emerge to protect both professionals and the public. For example, if helping professionals are aware of child abuse, society insists that they report the abuse. This legal expectation to report makes it possible for society to protect children by providing an out clause that overrides ethical expectations of confidentiality.

Legal rules and duties are often the most concrete expectation governing practice decisions. Typically, these rules focus on situations where a person presents a significant risk to either self or others. Helping professionals, because of their training and relationship with clients, are expected to act to protect people. Consequently most professional settings have policies and procedures outlining exactly what to do in situations that require legally mandated actions. Failure to act on a legal duty can result in civil or criminal action.

Congruity between Beliefs and Actions

As we develop our professional selves, we are challenged to integrate our beliefs, professional values, and actions. It is important that we be able to live by the values and ethics of our chosen profession. It would be agonizing to work daily in a way that is inconsistent with our identity or core beliefs. Consequently, it will be very important to tune in to your feelings and thoughts as you explore the ethical principles discussed in the next section.

If congruity with the values and ethics is a significant challenge, consider that this chapter is focused on five helping professions. Many other helping professions, including pastoral counseling, Christian counseling, medicine, recreational therapy, and legal occupations, may allow for integration of different values. If you feel uncomfortable with the values and ethical principles described in this text, you may want to explore one of the other professional affiliations.

Ethical Principles

The range of ethical principles emanates from the centrality of the client in professional relationships and extends to agency and social situations. Professional groups expect that ethical behavior will be consistent in all situations. Consequently, practitioners are expected to display their values throughout all areas of living. To help understand how ethical principles operate in shaping behavior across the range of professional activity, review the codes of ethics discussed earlier to see how the specific domains yield concrete prescriptions for behavior. For consistency, the ethical principles discussed in the next section are grouped according to the values discussed earlier in the chapter.

Ethical Principles and Human Dignity

All helping professions have ethical principles that ensure that clients are treated in a dignified manner. All professional codes of ethics speak of respect and client rights as important considerations. Although these ethical principles are consistent across professional groups, expectations do vary slightly. For example, all professions promote client rights, yet social workers are expected to actively challenge social structures that interfere with respect and client rights. Other professions take a more limited view of advocacy as a professional obligation. Professions such as nursing include ethical clauses associated with ensuring dignity when performing medical procedures.

Client Primacy

Practitioners spend time with clients for the sole purpose of enhancing the client's ability to master life situations and overcome challenges. All actions and decisions concerning service should be based on this core obligation to clients. This obligation is more important than loyalty to our agencies and even to our profession. Professional helpers must be willing to take significant risks to promote client interests. There are two core elements in this principle: promotion of the client's best interests and ensuring that no harm is done.

1. *Promotion of client's best interests.* All professionals are expected to promote the client's best interests in all professional activities associated with that client's service.
   - *Centrality of client interests.* All professional actions must promote client well-being above all other interests. Practitioners must serve the client and can never reject clients because they disagree with their lifestyle or values.

  - *Conflicts of interest*. Practitioners must avoid dual relationships with their clients (e.g., friend plus counselor, landlord plus service provider, etc.). Practitioners must also avoid economic situations where practitioner interests may conflict with a client's best interests (e.g., prolonging service to maintain a source of income).
  - *Advocacy*. Practitioners must be willing to take a stand when clients' needs are not being met or their rights are being violated. Even when your employer is at fault, it is important to find ways to promote clients' best interests.

2. *Freedom from harm*. When practitioners find that they are unable to help a client, they must ensure that their contact with the client inflicts no harm on the client or members of the client system.
  - *Least intrusive alternative*. Practitioners must begin with the services that will be least disruptive to the client and others within the client system. For example, outpatient services should be ruled out prior to encouraging the client to enter residential or hospital treatment.
  - *No harm*. Practitioners must never take actions that can physically, psychologically, emotionally, or socially inconvenience or otherwise harm a client. Concurrently, a professional cannot withhold beneficial actions that will harm a client through inaction.

Client Respect/Dignity

Professionals must treat their clients with respect. Doing this includes welcoming contact, managing differences, and honoring clients' decisions. Professionals must avoid voicing negative judgments about their clients. Practitioners also must refrain from imposing their standards or value judgments on a client's situation. The only area where practitioners can impose standards is when a legal duty mandates action. Consider these common clauses.

- *Freedom from imposition*. As a professional, you will work with clients with very diverse lifestyles. You must refrain from imposing your standards on the client. Some areas of diversity include:
  - *Hygiene standards*. (e.g., frequency of showering, manner of dress). Even if clients are unkempt or smell unclean, professionals have no right to comment unless hygiene is part of the client's service goals.
  - *Family structures*. (e.g., communal living, common law). Unless people living in the home are placing someone at risk or harm, professionals cannot impose their own standards on the client's choice of family structure.
  - *Personal choices*. (e.g., marital indiscretion, sex clubs, shoplifting). Clients may disclose affairs or other behaviors that violate our personal codes of living. Unless these behaviors are part of the client's goals and expectations of service, you must accept that these are personal choices.
  - *Sexual orientation/identity*. (e.g., gay, transgender). Professional helpers often have clients who are gay, lesbian, bisexual, or transgender and their identity has nothing to do with their reasons for entering service. As a professional, you must accept their true identity and work with them without imposing judgment or seeking to change their identity.
- *Client beliefs*. Although practitioners often challenge client beliefs, you are limited to the beliefs and values associated with the problems and goals that are the focus of the service agreement. Professionals cannot engage in ideological debates or challenge client beliefs that are not pertinent to service.
  - *Religious preferences*. (e.g., fundamentalist, Mormon, etc.). Helping professionals cannot judge others based on their religious affiliations or ideology. It is important to understand and work within the structure of a client's religious or spiritual beliefs.
  - *Values*. (e.g., prefers not to get an education, work, etc.). Clients enter service with a unique set of values and beliefs. Professionals must refrain from challenging values and beliefs unless they are associated with the focus of service.
  - *Political ideologies*. (e.g., conservative, liberal, socialist, etc.). When clients enter service, they often have staunchly held political ideologies. Practitioners must

respect people's ideological positions even if they are inconsistent with personal belief systems.

- *Client language.* Many clients have idiosyncratic methods of expressing themselves. Professionals should avoid correcting client word choices or other elements of client expression.
  - *Language use.* (e.g., trouble finding right word). Sometimes clients cannot find the right words to express themselves. Practitioners should avoid finishing client sentences or correcting word choices. Although you can clarify client statements, you should avoid correcting word choices.
  - *Grammatical errors.* (e.g., using wrong tense, misuse of words). Sometimes clients speak with grammatical errors. It is important to respect their meaning rather than attempting to shape their expressive language skills.
  - *Expressiveness.* (e.g., use of profanity, slang, loud). Sometimes clients swear or speak in loud tones. Although you may react internally to such language use, you have no right to insist that they change based solely on their choice of expressive language.

Client Rights

Helping professions most often provide service in the context of a helping relationship. Within the relational context, clients can be vulnerable, given that they are often in crisis when entering the relationship. Consequently, professional groups identify client rights and protections for clients. Clients entering a helping relationship with counselors, nurses, occupational therapists, psychologists, and social workers are guaranteed these rights:

- *Effective and accessible service.* Clients have a right to expect practitioners to be available and competent in their professional roles. Availability speaks to issues of agency placement in the community, freedom from barriers, and reasonable efforts to accommodate client needs. Competence requires practitioners to be well trained, licensed, and up to date on the best interventions.
  - *Effective services.* Practitioners must be able to provide services with the strongest prognosis for success.
  - *Available services.* Services should be available at the times when clients are most likely to be seeking service and in settings free from barriers to access.
- *Nonintrusion.* Clients have specific complaints that bring them into service. Consequently, professionals are expected to limit their scope of exploration, avoiding areas of the client's life that are not related to the goals of intervention (Smith & Fitzpatrick, 1995). Common intrusion-related concerns include:
  - Exploring or inquiring about the client's life circumstances unrelated to the presenting problems (e.g., finances, leisure activities, friendships).
  - Extending the professional relationship into nonprofessional domains (e.g., dating, social contacts, friendship, sexual intercourse).
  - Entering and searching a client's living space or belongings without a warrant, consent, or legal jurisdiction that permits the intrusion (e.g., looking in backpack, entering living space, reading mail).
- *Confidentiality.* Practitioners must never talk about their clients in an identifiable way without written and informed consent. This includes activities such as:
  - Identifying or affirming to another person that you are providing service to a specific client.
  - Discussing case details with other professionals (other than your supervisor) without prior authorization.
  - Sharing case dynamics or details that could potentially allow a listener to identify the client from situational details.
  - Discussing case material in a public forum or place where other people can overhear your discussion.
- *Human rights.* Although human rights discussions can become long and legalistic, the principles in the Universal Declaration of Human Rights of the United Nations argue that human rights are universal and indivisible. This means that all humans should

have the same set of rights and no group should have exceptional rights. Some rights are evident in the ethical principles; other rights extend beyond common service situations. Professionals must never interfere with a client's human rights. Consider this partial listing of rights and freedoms:

- Right to work
- Right to sustenance
- Right to education
- Right to asylum
- Right to equal treatment under the law
- Right to fair and open hearings
- Right to self-control
- Right to self-expression
- Right to health
- Right to pursue happiness
- Right to government noninterference
- Freedom from arbitrary arrest
- Freedom from torture
- Freedom from slavery and servitude

Ethical Principles and Client Determination

All helping professions promote ethical principles that clients must never be coerced, threatened, cajoled, or otherwise pressured to take an action against their will. Similarly, professional associations maintain that clients should control the goals, direction, and procedures used in the provision of service. These principles are very consistent across the helping professions and are enshrined in the two critical principles: informed consent and the right to challenge.

Informed Consent

Clients must give fully informed consent for many practitioner activities. Informed consent consists of three critical elements:

1. Clients must be capable of giving consent. If a client has an impairment or is a minor child, efforts must be made (e.g., through a guardian, advocate, or parent) to ensure that the client understands or a designated surrogate is providing consent.
2. Clients must be informed about the activities, expectations, and potential outcomes of service and practitioner actions.
3. Given this information, the client must agree to participate. Typically this agreement is put in written form so the client and practitioner can document the decision.

Like other assumptions, informed consent has some challenges. The assumption of confidentiality is often a challenge when working with children and youths because of their minor status (Isaacs & Stone, 1999). Similar challenges exist with dependent populations, such as those who are elderly or have disabilities, because the practitioner may have frequent contact with caregivers. Confidentiality is also at risk in computerized or team environments in which networks allow broader access to client information (Goodyear & Sinnett, 1984).

In certain situations, society gives the practitioner permission to take action without consent. These situations include legal procedures, such as criminal charges, apprehension hearings, and competency hearings. In the absence of legal mandates, the next service elements generally require informed consent:

- *Entering the helping relationship.* Without a legal mandate (e.g., Child Protective Services, guardian consent), treatment or service cannot begin without the client's awareness and permission (Corey & Herlihy, 1996; Prout, DeMartino, & Prout, 1999). Practitioners need to inform clients:
  - That this is a professional helping relationship.
  - Of the nature of the relationship and the practitioner's role.

- *Sharing client information.* (Dickson, 1998; Okun, 1997). Aside from legal reporting requirements, which will be discussed shortly, workers cannot, without written permission, share client information beyond the immediate service team (Isaacs & Stone, 1999; Prout et al., 1999). Common situations requiring informed consent include:
  - Acknowledging to another person that a client is receiving service.
  - Talking about case dynamics outside of the immediate treatment team.
  - Sharing information with other service providers associated with the case.
- *Expectations and procedures.* Clients have a right to know what is likely to happen when they are receiving services (Corey & Herlihy, 1996). This right to information includes expectations, rights, and exceptions. Specific elements include:
  - The likely duration of service and possible events that may extend duration.
  - The efficacy of the approach used at the agency. Ideally this should be based on evidence rather than impressions.
  - The procedures and methods used when providing service.
  - The limitations, expectations, outcomes, and potential risks associated with service.
  - The limits and exceptions to confidentiality and/or other rights.

Challenging Elements of Service

Most professions expect clients to be active participants in shaping service direction and procedures. Consequently, clients have a right to question, challenge, and appeal professional decisions. Even when agencies provide evidence-based practices, clients have a right to request a different type of service. Two critical elements are associated with active client participation: questioning service decisions and requesting changes in the service.

1. *Questioning service decisions.* When a practitioner or agency representative makes a decision that impacts services, clients can question the rationale and contest the decision. Although funding and the voluntariness of the service provided may shape the agency response, clients do have a right to challenge service providers. Doing this includes:
   - *Challenging treatment protocols.* If clients dislike the type of treatment, they have a right to question the importance of treatment elements or the methods being used.
   - *Asking for a second opinion from another source.* If a client disagrees with a practitioner or service provider, he or she has a right to request a second opinion.
   - *Appealing decisions.* If clients disagree with a decision or disposition, they have a right to ask a supervisor or administrator to reconsider the decision.
2. *Requesting a change in services.* If elements of service are deemed unsuitable by a client, he or she can ask for changes. In agencies, there are usually procedures for requesting changes that will activate supervisory or administrative decision makers. Mechanisms of challenging service include:
   - *Asking that the provider identify alternative approaches.* and select a different method that might better suit the client.
   - *Asking for another practitioner.* If a client experiences a poor fit with a given practitioner, he or she has a right to request service from another practitioner in the agency.
   - *Elevating scrutiny.* If a client remains unsatisfied, he or she has a right to continue the challenge to different levels of the agency hierarchy.
   - *Taking civil action.* If a client has challenged professional actions (or inactions) and remains unsatisfied, he or she has a right to go outside of the system by hiring a lawyer and taking civil action against a practitioner and the agency.

Ethical Principles and Professional Responsibility

Helping professions provide expectations of professional responsibility. Often these expectations focus on client exchanges, lifelong learning, public interactions, and responsibilities beyond direct work with clients. There are two common features in the codes of ethics: professional competence and professional comportment.

Professional Competence

When a practitioner is hired to provide professional service, there is a good faith assumption of competence. In other words, clients should be able to assume that a practitioner is able to provide the services as promised by the agency (Reamer, 1998). Clients also should be able to assume that intervention will be delivered in an efficient and effective manner (Corcoran, 1998; Thyer & Myers, 1998). Workers must keep abreast of the literature and upgrade their training (Raw, 1998; Thyer & Myers, 1998). If a practitioner or agency promises to provide a service that staff cannot provide, the agency can be held legally responsible. Elements of competence include skills, standards, and currency.

- *Requisite skills*. Professionals are expected to have the requisite knowledge and skills to perform their professional duties. The expectation of competence extends beyond front-line activities to include supervision and administration. Practitioners must:
  - Engage, assess, and use the helping relationship effectively.
  - Use interpersonal and technical skills effectively to explore, assess, and intervene with client systems.
  - Make informed decisions when selecting interventions to ensure that the selected interventions have the strongest likelihood of achieving client goals.
- *Practice standards*. Professionals are expected to take pride in the professional realms of competence, openly identify themselves as members of the profession, and perform at the highest level in all professional activities. Practitioners must:
  - Maintain professional self-control on the job by refraining from angry outbursts or other acts indicating a lack of emotional control.
  - Maintain sobriety on the job by refraining from ingesting any substance that might impair professional judgment.
  - Avoid dual relationships or other conflicts of interest that may interfere with the primacy of the client's interests or due diligence in performing professional functions.
  - Work collaboratively with other professionals and disciplines to ensure appropriate client services are maintained.
  - Promote professional ethics by reporting ethical violations to the professional association or governing body.
  - Extend professional respect to the clients of other professionals in the service system.
- *Practice currency*. New methods of intervention are developed and tested every day. Consequently, the assumption of a professional identity requires a lifelong learning commitment. Practitioners must work from a current knowledge base. Doing so has two ongoing requirements:
  1. Professional helpers must read the professional literature to understand the latest developments in their profession. Bachelor-level practitioners should read at least one journal article every week. Practitioners with postgraduate training should read three articles every week.
  2. Practitioners must participate in ongoing professional development to integrate new knowledge, skills, and best practices.

Professional Comportment

Professionals must interact appropriately with other professional groups and community members. When you are associated with a professional group, all interactions reflect on the profession as well as on you as a person. Many professional groups will hold practitioners accountable for behavior unbecoming to members of the profession. There are three common areas where comportment is monitored: on the job, in collegial relations, and in the community.

1. *Professional conduct on the job*. Professional groups expect their practitioners to exemplify responsible professional behavior in the workplace. Most work settings

will contain several professional groups. It is important that all professions collaborate and work together to promote client best interests. Doing this includes

- Honoring employment commitments, such as hours of work, session length, documentation, policies, and procedures.
- Providing some services at reduced cost or pro bono to ensure accessibility for economically disadvantaged clients.

2. *Collegial relationships.* Workers are in constant contact with other professionals as part of serving clients. Consequently, there are ethical guidelines to govern the manner in which the practitioner relates to other professionals. These guidelines serve to keep the client interest primary in such interactions and also serve to maintain professional integrity within the service system. Some of the principles focused on inter-professional functioning include:

- Engaging with colleagues to promote the best interests of all clients in the service system.
- Directly clarifying and resolving professional misunderstandings rather than allowing problems to affect collaboration.
- Refusing to comment or cast aspersions about a colleague's practice skills or competence.
- Reporting ethical breaches to the professional body so corrective action can be taken.

3. *Professional conduct in the community.* The public behavior of helping professionals should be consistent with their professional status. Professionals must be contributing community members. Even on weekends and vacations, you should be respectable and consistent with your professional values.

- Professionals are expected to make their services available to the public. Even practitioners in private practice should make allowances so all people can access their services.
- Professionals should strive to make the community a better place for clients and nonclients.
- Professionals should refrain from illegal or disorderly acts that might reflect badly on their professional role.

Ethical Principles and Human Conditions

The final focus of professional codes of ethics is on a professional's obligation to the larger society. This focus extends beyond our responsibility to the community as we expand our influence to the larger society. Two ethical principles enlarge our focus to the societal level: our obligation to contribute to professional knowledge and our obligation to challenge social conditions.

These two obligations are often the most ignored principles of ethical codes. Our tendency to overlook these principles is partly because we do not graduate with enough experience to believe we can contribute to the professional knowledge or influence larger social systems. Nevertheless, it is important that we never lose sight of the larger obligations that we will assume as we join our chosen profession.

Scholarship and Research

As lifelong learners, it is expected that we will continually learn from our experience, integrate new knowledge, and eventually start to share our learning with other professionals. Inherent in this principle is the fact that we must be able to reflect on our professional practice so we continue to strengthen and understand our skills. Over 10 years, we should become very proficient and develop expertise (Ericsson, Krampe, & Tesch-Romer, 1993).

As you progress as a helping professional your contributions to your profession change. Initially you contribute through advancing your ethical practice. Eventually your contribution may involve assuming leadership in your practice setting. Leadership involves modeling competency and best practices through sharing with other workers. It may involve assuming the formal roles, such as team leader or supervisor, as opportunities present themselves. Even if you assume a supervisory position, the ethical obligation to share knowledge extends beyond agency settings.

As the ethical obligation to advance our learning and contribute to the credibility of the profession extends beyond our agency, we begin to share our best practice principles, strategies, and knowledge with other professionals. As we broaden our sphere of sharing our knowledge begins to serve the larger society. Professional groups provide a venue for such sharing when professional associations hold annual conferences. We can also submit articles for professional publication. Regardless of the venue we choose, we should contribute through these activities.

- *Reflective understanding.* As you work with clients and client groups, it is important to understand how their needs emerge and how to respond appropriately to their needs.
- *Integration of knowledge.* When you reflect on our professional practice, you integrate new knowledge and information contained in the professional literature.
- *Unbiased documentation.* As you identify client needs, dynamics, and service outcomes, objectively document and organize your findings.
- *Dissemination of knowledge.* As you gain new insights and knowledge, it is important to share your findings with others, allowing them to review, learn, engage, and use the information.
- *Challenge ungrounded knowledge.* As your expertise grows through lifelong learning, you must start to challenge your chosen profession to incorporate the most up-to-date evidence into theories and practices.

Promote Social Justice and Human Rights

Concurrent with advancing professional knowledge, professional helpers are expected to contribute to the welfare of society. This principle, while evident in most professions, is strongly stated in social work and nursing. Inherent in this ethical principle is the expectation that practitioners must be informed about social conditions and be able to contribute to societal improvement. This contribution involves taking a public position about social conditions that maintain oppression and social-group vulnerabilities. Some of the social issues confronted by professionals include:

- *Social conditions.* Most professionals are aware that the structures of society contribute to inequality and violations of human rights. Some codes of ethics outline a professional role in challenging social patterns of oppression and abuse in society (Murphy & Dillon, 1998).
- *Children's rights.* Professions such as social work and nursing are active in agencies that work with vulnerable children throughout the world (e.g., international adoption). When working with international organizations professionals must be aware of issues such as child labor, child warriors, child abuse, and other infringements on children's rights. When working with international organizations it is important the professionals take a stand about the conditions of children throughout the world (Grover, 2004).
- *Cross-cultural practices.* Some cultural practices violate the rights of other people, especially women and children. Such practices require practitioners to balance human rights with cultural sensitivity (Kakkad, 2005; Ross, 2008).
- *Involuntary treatment.* In mental health and corrections work, people are increasingly being forced to take medications or participate in treatment against their will. Professional groups are ever more challenged by such violations of human rights (Snow & Austin, 2009).
- *Incarcerated clients.* When people are incarcerated, their basic human rights are suspended. Professionals who work with incarcerated clients or consult with prison systems experience a conflict between human rights violations and their professional ethics (Ward, Gannon, & Vess, 2009). This conflict can be difficult to resolve.
- *Coercive interviews.* In recent years governments have violated human rights through surveillance techniques, imprisonment, torture, and other suspensions of human

rights. Increasingly helping professions have had to take hard stands on such violations (Burton & Kagan, 2007). In 2010 the American Psychological Association took a clear position that any member involved in acts of torture will be stripped of their professional membership.

Across professional groups, the ethical principles focused on client treatment have strong similarities. With the social justice principle, there is greater diversity. Most professions have some expectation that members will contribute to society, but the level of expectation varies across professional groups. Historically, social work and nursing have been the most socially conscious professions and expected to challenge social structures that maintain inequality both in practice and in research (Carnegie & Kiger, 2009; Hancock, 2007; Mertens & Ginsberg, 2008; Paterson, Duggett-Leger, & Cruttenden, 2009).

Increasingly psychology is being challenged to increase its focus on human rights and advocating for social change (Kakkad, 2005; Pettifor, 2004). This challenge has been issued about psychology's role in working with incarcerated offenders (Ward et al., 2009), in cross-cultural practice (Kakkad, 2005; Pettifor, 2004), and until recent APA decisions, in the use of torture (Burton & Kagan, 2007). The challenge to include human rights has stimulated professional debates about the role of human rights in a national-based code of ethics (Fisher, 2004; Palmero, 2009).

Exercise 2.1: The Street Kid

A practitioner in a center-city health center working with street kids and homeless young adults was helping a young gay male to find permanent housing. As they explored the young man's finances, the practitioner learned that he earned his money as a prostitute. He looked young and was able to make very good money on the street. In his last conversation he told the practitioner that he makes double money by performing oral sex on the men without a condom. The practitioner told him that he should always use a condom. The youth replied, "It really doesn't matter at all anymore." The practitioner reported the youth to the public health agency, expressing concerns that he might be HIV-positive and presenting a risk to the community.

1. Given the worker's job, list three ethical principles that were violated.

2. If you were the practitioner and had concerns about this young man's safety, how might you proceed without violating professional values?

Legally Mandated Assumptions and Duties

The ethical principles just discussed are enforced by professional bodies. As such, ethical violations result in actions focused on a professional's ability to engage in practice. Beyond the professional realm, there are guidelines that have additional weight and sanctions because they are legally mandated assumptions and duties. Just as violations of the code of ethics can result in professional sanctions, violations of the next assumptions and duties can result in legal sanctions.

Legally Protected Assumptions

Several legal assumptions are inherent in the provision of professional service. The fact that a professional is paid to provide a service in a professional setting should guarantee that the assumptions are met. If a practitioner does not meet these assumptions, clients harmed by the worker's action (or inaction) could claim damages or result in legal sanctions. Most assumptions focus on the service quality and practitioner-client treatment in the professional setting.

All professionals should be aware of these duties and legally binding assumptions. Some assumptions are associated with specific jobs. For example, when your job responsibilities requires expert knowledge, society increases their expectation of competence. It is important to read the legislation, policies, and procedures carefully to see how different assumptions are operationalized within the organization and professional roles. The next set of assumptions can result in civil litigation if violated by a practitioner regardless of professional affiliation.

Assumption of Competence

As discussed earlier, when a practitioner is hired to provide professional service, there is a good faith assumption of competence. This means clients should be able to assume a practitioner is able to provide client services as promised by the agency (Reamer, 1998). Clients also should be able to assume that intervention will be delivered in an ethical, efficient, and effective manner (Corcoran, 1998; Thyer & Myers, 1998). Workers must keep abreast of the literature and upgrade their training (Raw, 1998; Thyer & Myers, 1998). If a practitioner violates this assumption, clients can initiate a lawsuit claiming damages. If it can be demonstrated that the practitioner lacks competence or made decisions that competent practitioners would not make, the suit is likely to be successful.

Assumption of Informed Consent

Clients must give fully informed consent for many practitioner activities. The term "informed consent" means that the expectations, activities, and parameters of service have been described and that written consent has been solicited. Informed consent is needed for entering treatment, sharing information, altering the service contract, and setting expectations. If a practitioner discloses information or engages in professional assessment/intervention activities without informing clients, civil litigation may result. With civil litigation, clients can claim damages if any discomfort or embarrassment arose from the practitioner's actions.

Assumption of the Least Intrusive Intervention

As clients enter service, there is an assumption that they will receive the least intrusive (intensive or drastic) intervention. This means that the practitioner must attempt less intrusive interventions before proceeding with disruptive services (e.g., institutionalization, removal, or medically intrusive interventions). This assumption was the basis for lawsuits that resulted in the closing of residential institutions during the 1960s and 1970s. In these lawsuits, advocates argued that the system of institutionalization had no options that were less intrusive. As a result, institutions were dismantled and community-based services were increased.

Legal Duties of Helping Professionals

Legal duties are more specific and directive than ethical principles and assumptions. The preceding principles are *assumed* conditions of service. If the practitioner or agency does not live up to the assumptions, clients can initiate legal proceedings and claim damages. With duties, clear guidelines specify how the practitioner must respond every time a situation arises. If the practitioner does not respond appropriately, society or a third party may take punitive action. Two types of duties are common to the professional field: the duty to report and the duty to warn.

Duty to Report

A practitioner who is aware of, or suspects, that there is abuse, exploitation, or neglect of someone in a vulnerable position must report the abuse to the proper authorities. Although the details of this duty vary with governmental statutes, it typically applies to child abuse, elder abuse, spouse abuse, and the abuse of persons with disabilities. It is important to know the reporting expectations for your state or province as you enter the field. As explained in the informed consent section, we should advise clients entering service that these duties will override their expectations of confidentiality.

Professionals are required to report several types of abuse. Most commonly, professionals report physical and/or sexual abuse. Agency protocols will dictate steps to follow, but professionals typically report to the authorities how they came to be aware of the potential abuse (relationship, professional role), the indicators of abuse, and contact information for the victim. The decision to report typically is based on these criteria:

- Is there evidence that the person was abused?
- Is there a reason to believe that the person was abused?
- Is there a reason to believe that the person will be abused?

Professionals in some states also must report evidence of neglect or psychological abuse. This is a more difficult duty because neglect and psychological abuse are more difficult to substantiate. If you work in a state that mandates reporting neglect or emotional abuse, it is important to discuss indicators of such problems and documentation strategies with your supervisor.

Duty to Warn

The duty to warn requires professionals to talk directly to potential victims. If we are aware that a client may harm another individual, or if we can reasonably predict (based on past behavior) that a client will seriously harm another person, we must warn the potential victim so safety precautions can be implemented (Sonkin, 1986). There have been several lawsuits in the United States as a result of failure to warn. Mental health professionals also have been found liable for the traumas experienced by family members witnessing a death due to the worker's failure to warn the victim.

The duty to warn requires thoughtful assessment of the situation.. Inherent in this duty is a decision to suspend confidentiality and privacy guarantees to ensure the safety of a third person. For this reason, critical ethical and legal ramifications result. There are three critical elements to consider when assessing a situation to decide whether to warn a person of impending harm: the threat, the victim, and the client's capacity to do harm (Felthous, 2006; Pietrofesa, Pietrofesa, & Pietrofesa, 1990).

1. *Threat*. Practitioners first must assess the presence of a threat. A threat can be expressed in fantasy form (e.g., dreams) or very clearly articulated. Given that as practitioners, we have information about the client and professional training, it is expected that we will be able to identify threats using our knowledge and skills.

2. *Victim*. There needs to be a clearly identifiable victim so the practitioner can identify whom to warn. However, it is not necessary for a client to mention the intended victim by name. If logical deduction or elements in the client situation can be used to identify the intended victim, we are still responsible for identifying and warning.

3. *Risk/Capacity*. The most difficult element in making the decision to warn is assessing the risk or capacity of the client to inflict harm. Typically, risk elevates when the client begins mobilizing and focusing emotions, thinking, and actions that support the threat. If you think the client can access the victim to act on the threat, you must warn him or her.

Legal Duty Enforcement

Failure to perform legal duties to report and warn can result in legal charges, professional sanctions, and civil litigation. Criminal charges are rare, but a pattern of failure to report child abuse could result in other forms of legal action. Practitioners who fail to perform either duty can lose their job, their license to practice, or both. Concurrently, the victim or the victim's family members could initiate a lawsuit for compensatory damages. Annually there are many lawsuits based on this duty. Each suit alters how courts will adjudicate new cases (Walcott, Cerundolo, & Beck, 2001). Typically four criteria are used to judge a practitioner's actions:

1. *Did you consider all information available to you given your professional relationship with the client (history, files, collateral reports, family members, client disclosures, etc.)?* This assessment criterion considers your professional role and your access to information that is inherent in your role.

2. *Did you access and use the same information that other similarly trained professionals would use?* This criterion compares your performance to that of other professionals. If it is determined that you overlooked available information that others would have considered, your decision making will be questioned.

3. *Did you use your professional knowledge and training to interpret the information?* Here the courts consider your assessment of the available information. It is expected that you will use the most current information and research when forming your decisions. It is also expected that you will make logical and well-grounded professional decisions.

4. *Are your conclusions consistent with those of similarly trained professionals?* This final criterion compares your deductions and decision making to that of other professionals. If your actions are consistent with the responses of others, the court likely will decide that the client's actions could not be reasonably predicted.

The potential for legal action can seem unsettling, but remember that underlying all potential action is a code of ethics. If you abide by the values and ethics of your chosen profession, you should be fine. If you act on your intuition, personal values, or beliefs rather than using professional knowledge and skill, you put yourself at risk. Ultimately, you will be compared to others in your profession when your actions are judged.

Ethics, Duties, and Diversity

Our codes of ethics typically are presented within a cultural vacuum, creating the illusion that ethical principles are somehow pristine. Each profession is socially mandated to control the actions of its members, but cultural elements are inherent in all nationally based ethical codes (Pettifor, 2004). In effect, our codes of ethics reflect the dominant culture of a country. Consequently, there are likely to be subtle differences when codes of ethics are compared across nations (Fisher, 2004).

These cultural artifacts in our codes of ethics and legal duties can create conflict when working with diverse client groups because dominant cultural values cannot be separated from legislation or ethics. Culture influences the frame, definition, and legal response to problems and their resolution, and may result in legal responses that are culturally insensitive. Practitioners have little flexibility because we are bound by society's laws and our professional ethics.

Elements of Diversity

Many elements of diversity can create problems. Potential conflict tends to emerge from differences between the dominant culture and minority groups. Table 2.2 contains several dimensions of diversity along with a brief discussion of the influence of dominant culture. As you review this table, consider the experiences of different groups in society.

Diversity-related challenges emerge most strongly with the duties to report and warn. This is because cultural and religious groups often have different models for family living and discipline. When these models diverge from the dominant cultural models, conflict may emerge. As professionals, we must follow the laws of society. Although we attempt to respect diverse points of view, clients may not feel respected when we must take actions that are foreign to their perspectives.

Balancing Ethics and Diversity

Ethically, all helping professionals strive to be culturally competent. Doing this can be a challenge, given the cultural insensitivity inherent in legal duties and service system elements grounded in legislation. When working with diverse clients, it is important to help them understand that inflexible systems such as legal duties are not a criticism of their culture but rather a legal imperative that cannot be changed. Practitioners can work with

Table 2.2 **Dominant Culture and Minority Group Considerations**

Diversity Considerations	Dominant Cultural Influence	Minority Experience
Cultural Influences	Social and family biases reflected in legislation during lobbying and development.	Divergent beliefs and values produce a disconnect between core values and professional ethics and legal duties.
Spiritual Influences	Separation between church and state influences professional functioning and codes of ethics.	Diverse religious groups struggle with the secular nature of ethics and the legalistic nature of professional duties.
Racial Influences	Dominated by white, middle-class, European influences in laws and ethical principles.	Lack of political and social influence concurrent with experience with racism highlights the differential application of laws and ethical principles.
Socioeconomic Influences	Wealthy people influence the development of laws through lobbying and serving on decision-making committees.	Assumptions and values contained in laws are out of touch with people of limited means and those who are socially vulnerable.
Ability-Related Influences	Laws and ethical principles assume that people have the capacity to understand situations and take autonomous action.	People with disabilities often cannot access, understand, and/or navigate the social systems that protect others.

different groups to help them understand the operational definitions of risk and abuse (e.g., when a parent strikes a child to the point where it leaves a welt or bruise). Doing so can help clients understand society's subtleties so they can incorporate the legal injunctions into their cultural framework.

When program values, policies, and procedures interfere greatly with diverse groups, it is incumbent on professionals to challenge the policies that create cultural conflict. At times this may involve helping minority groups to access social resources that can advocate for culturally sensitive policies. Practitioners also can help decision makers identify intergroup differences, hire staff who can operate within the culture, and assist in the development of alternative programs.

Exercise 2.2: The Women's Shelter

You are a practitioner in a shelter for battered women. A young woman in the shelter has described horrendous abuse. In her marriage, ongoing violence often resulted in her needing medical care. She never reported the abuse to the police because her partner threatened to kill her. Just prior to admission, she had been held for three days by her husband at knifepoint and repeatedly raped. She escaped when he fell asleep.

Along with this young woman, you work with several other women at different stages of leaving or reconciling with their partners. You have just become aware of another young woman who left her abusive partner and began dating another man. They are thinking of living together, and she has approached the center requesting donated furniture and supplies for setting up the new apartment.

You discover that the woman setting up the new apartment is planning on moving in with the ex-partner of the first woman. The man has admitted to knowing the staff at the center but has presented himself as a volunteer who helped with fundraising. He even stated that he knows you but, due to ethical guidelines, you said nothing about him. The second young woman keeps informing you that he has told her to say "hi" for him when she comes in for meetings. You want to warn this woman, but you know he would sue or take some action against the agency. You are also concerned that furniture and supplies meant to help battered women are going to be given to a batterer.

1. Consider the next options. Identify the ethical principles breached by each of the options.
   a. Warning the second woman by breaching confidentiality of the first woman.

   b. Saying nothing to the current partner.

   c. Withholding the furniture with no explanation.

2. Does this situation require you to warn the new partner? Explain why or why not.

Resolving Ethical Dilemmas

It is clear from the preceding discussions that professional self-control is much more complex than simply being aware of one's feelings. Legal and ethical considerations in many areas of practice require workers to continually acquire new knowledge about interventions, legislation, and legal outcomes to shape practice responses (Dickson, 1998).

The overlap in values, ethical principles, assumptions, and duties can become confusing. Such confusion often accompanies practitioner attempts to apply professional values and ethics to group settings, management systems, and different types of client populations (Hess & Hess, 1998; Northen, 1998). Workers often must make decisions between two or more courses of action and need some system for deciding which action is most ethical.

Ethical dilemmas and confusion are compounded by competing priorities within the profession. For example, there are differing opinions between empiricists who want workers to use only validated and tested interventions and others who believe that intervention evolves through the interaction between the practitioner and client (Raw, 1998; Thyer & Myers, 1998). Each of these polarized positions can take a value or ethical principle and enshrine the argument within an ethical stance.

Ideological professional debates and multiple choices can confuse incoming professionals. Many professionals currently are proposing that we attempt to balance and unify the values and principles rather than approach them as competing entities (Banks, 1998; Dean, 1998; Herlihy & Remley, 1995; Raw, 1998). Inherent in this debate is the understanding that values and ethics will change and adjust to meet professional and societal demands. We always must be aware of our current ethical principles.

To provide clarity, this section explains a system for resolving dilemmas in situations where two possible actions appear to involve conflicts between ethical principles. Challenges are inevitable when one ethical principle comes into conflict or competition with another. Often the values and principles can provide some guidance. Legal duties will, of course, override the assumptions of informed consent and confidentiality. Although we remain responsible for our decisions, as long as the situation meets the criteria, we have no choice but to perform the legal duties.

Ethical Priorities

There will be times when a practitioner must weigh different ethical principles when trying to decide which action to take with a case. The next weighting or prioritization system helps with this decision making. The system has five levels of priority, beginning with life-and-death issues and ending with subjective judgments of what might yield the best benefit for the client. The five levels are:

1. *Life and death.* When situations have implications for life and death of any person, the practitioner must give this the highest possible priority regardless of other ethical considerations. Although maintaining the service relationship with a client is important, it falls under the maximum benefit (or fifth) category in this system of resolving dilemmas.

2. *Abuse and violation.* Situations of abuse and violation are ranked second because they can compromise safety and well-being even if death is not an imminent risk. If the situation contains evidence of abuse, practitioners should prioritize addressing the abuse risk above other ethical considerations.

3. *Human rights.* The third tier of decision making focuses on violations of client rights. Such situations include many of the assumptions and civil rights previously described. Rights issues can be difficult to resolve because many dilemmas occur among different rights. For example, one practitioner might need to choose to violate a client confidence in order to report another practitioner who violated the client's right to competent service (e.g., refusing to see the client). Given the equal ranking of these rights, a practitioner cannot ethically make such a violation without client permission. If the situation included abuse or a risk of suicide, a violation of confidentiality would be warranted.

4. *Restricted freedom.* The fourth level for decision making focuses on restriction and freedom. Practitioners will be confronted with situations where they want to take action to help clients who are in oppressive situations in their personal relationships, living situations, or other circumstances. In making the decision to act, practitioners must attend to the first three levels of consideration first. For example, if working with an abused woman a practitioner may want to talk to her boyfriend to try to "straighten him out" or engage the couple in service. Doing this however may put her in danger. Given the potential for danger, the practitioner must attend to the first (life/death) and second (abuse) priorities before attempting to challenge the oppression of the woman. These levels would need to be explored and the woman would need to give permission before any contact with the partner would be appropriate.

5. *Maximum benefit.* The fifth category in this system is the principle of maximum benefit. This weighting category asserts that when two alternatives of equal value are considered, practitioners should use a cost-benefit analysis and take the path of maximum gain with the least potential damage. Practitioners should do their job efficiently, with competence and appropriate consultation, and keep the client's best interests primary. This principle often is violated by pressuring clients, speaking badly about clients, inappropriate closures of service, or taking more intrusive types of interventions than are warranted. A practitioner must be able to demonstrate that the chosen course of action will have the best potential for a positive, safe outcome.

In this example, the new graduate paid close attention to the fifth principle of maximum benefit. Notice in the interview that the supervisor placed peer relationships

Case Example

A new graduate applied for a position in a community mental health agency working with consumers with co-occurring substance abuse problems and mental illness. The program was using a storytelling approach to intervention. Consumers would share their life experiences, and the practitioner would explore the stories, helping clients to attribute new meaning to their history. The graduate pointed out to the supervisor conducting the interview that this approach was not well researched and suggested using motivational interviewing or integrated dual-diagnosis treatment, which are evidence-based practices. The supervisor informed the graduate that she had developed the program along with other team members and there would be no changes. The supervisor said, "If you are hired into this program, you will need to get along with the team members. Criticizing their hard work would not be a good start." Upon returning home after the interview, the graduate phoned the supervisor and withdrew her application.

at a higher priority than effective client service. It became clear that the team was organized around principles that were inconsistent with the code of ethics. Based on the ethical decision-making principles, the graduate concluded that the most ethical option was to withdraw.

Weighting Alternatives

To resolve an ethical dilemma, practitioners can use the five categories to consider alternative actions and decide a plan of action. This involves working through a five-step weighting process.

1. Identify the options creating the dilemma.
2. Assess the critical information to determine the weighting category of each option.
3. Proceed with the option to resolve the risks associated with the highest-weighted category.
4. Assess the ethical and service implications of the chosen direction.
5. Work with the client and other individuals impacted by the option to mitigate any potential problems associated with the action.

In reviewing these five steps, it is clear how the different levels of the weighting system work in conjunction with each other. The earlier steps find the appropriate weight to guide the decision, and then the practitioner assesses the ramifications of the decision. The practitioner can then ensure that the principle of least harm guides attention to possible reactions. Attention to multiple perspectives is an important part of resolving ethical dilemmas.

Although the final step in resolving the dilemma can be explored only at the theoretical level at this point, it is helpful to practice resolving practice dilemmas. The next exercise provides an opportunity for you to explore an ethical dilemma from practice. Respond to the exercise associated with the dilemma and practice walking through the steps of resolution.

Exercise 2.3: The Women's Shelter

(This exercise is a continuation of Exercise 2.2.) You are still working in the shelter for battered women and have been in a quandary regarding a woman setting up an apartment with the ex-partner of another woman in the shelter. This man tells his current partner that he knows the staff because he was a volunteer. You want to warn this woman, but you know he would sue or take legal action against the agency. Today the woman comes up to you and says, "Randy [his name] told me to say hi to you."

1. Use the weighting system to identify the level of the ethical issues.

2. Use ethical behavior guidelines to resolve the dilemma without violating any ethical guidelines.

3. The worker in this situation resolved this dilemma in this way: When the new partner told her that the man told her to say hi, she responded, "I am sorry, but due to confidentiality rules I can't talk about him." The woman became curious and pressed for an explanation. Each time the practitioner provided the same response. Eventually the woman went to other women in the shelter, asking if any of them knew her

boyfriend. The first woman involved with this man self-identified, promoting long and involved woman-to-woman discussions. What is the ethical principle that was used?

Critical Chapter Themes

1. Practitioners must be in professional control of their actions and interactions at all times. Values, ethics, and legislated protocols have been developed as guidelines for professional self-control.

2. The core values of helping professions—human dignity, client self-determination, professional responsibility, and concern for human conditions—are common in most health and human service professions.

3. Within the framework of values, there are important ethical principles that emerge to form codes of ethics. Workers can be held professionally accountable for failure to follow ethical guidelines.

4. Some behavioral guidelines have legal implications. These include legal issues that are assumed in the provision of service (e.g., professional competence, use of the least restrictive alternative, informed consent) and legal duties (e.g., the duty to warn and report). Workers can be sued for violations of these guidelines.

5. When different principles are in conflict with each other, workers use a system of weighting different alternatives to identify the best choice for action. The weighting system protects life as a top priority and extends to choosing the least harmful alternatives.

6. Practitioners all have socialized personal values that may conflict with the values of some professions. It is important to ensure that we can abide by our professional values because entry into a profession mandates adherence to professional values and ethics.

Online Resources

American Counseling Association: www.counseling.org/

American Occupational Therapy Association: http://aota.org/

American Nurses Association: http://nursingworld.org/

American Psychological Association: www.apa.org/

Ethics web site with discussions and helpful information: www.ethicsscoreboard.com/rb_5step.html

National Association of Social Workers: www.socialworkers.org/

Recommended Reading

Furman, R. (2009). Ethical considerations of evidence-based practice. *Social Work, 54*, 82–84.

Gushwa, M., & Chance, T. (2008). Ethical dilemmas for mental health practitioners: Navigating mandated child maltreatment reporting decisions. *Families in Society, 89*, 78–83.

Kaplan, D. M., Kocet, M. M., Cottone, R. R., Glosoff, H. L., Miranti, J. G., Moll, E. C., et al. (2009). New mandates and imperatives in the revised ACA Code of Ethics. *Journal of Counseling and Development, 87*, 241–255.

Koocher, G. P. (2009). Ethics and the invisible psychologist. *Psychological Services, 6*, 97–107.

Numminen, O., van der Arend, A., & Leino-Kilpi, H. (2009). Nurses' codes of ethics in practice and education: A review of the literature. *Scandinavian Journal of Caring Sciences, 23*, 380–394.

Chapter 3
Professional Thinking and Knowledge

Chapter 2 explored the need to acquire information as an ethical concern. Practitioners clearly need to keep up on laws and legislation to ensure ethical practice (Dickson, 1998; Prout, DeMartino, & Prout, 1999). Practitioners also must learn effective interventions (Thyer & Myers, 1998). Together, these requirements make it imperative for practitioners to develop and use a strong knowledge base. This chapter explores elements of the professional knowledge base and the thinking skills through which practitioners apply knowledge.

Developing Our Professional Thinking

As we develop our "professional self," education alters how we think so we can better comprehend complex interpersonal and intrapersonal situations (Bromley & Braslow, 2008). Two critical elements are involved in changing our thinking:

1. We must apply our thinking so it can be translated into action.
2. We must integrate new thinking skills into our personality (Sternberg, Grigorenko, & Zhang, 2008). If we can expand our ability to understand complex client situations comfortably, we establish a strong cognitive foundation for practice.

To help integrate our thinking abilities and personalities, this chapter builds on the previous two chapters. We first explore our socialized thinking habits and then start building a foundation for professional thinking. Professional thinking requires us to integrate our experiences with clients with ethical standards and professional knowledge (Pack-Brown, Thomas, & Seymour, 2008; Perry, Stupnisky, Daniels, & Haynes, 2008). Doing this requires the use of logical and creative thinking processes (Groves, Vance, & Paik, 2008).

Socialization and Thinking Styles

Our styles of thinking are largely related to our parents' approach to thinking and problem solving (Zhang, 2003). If we were expected to follow directions with a minimum of questioning, we learned to work from someone else's plan and suspend our own intellectual functions. For many, this same message is replicated through learning experiences in school. As we develop, there is an implicit message that questioning is not valued. Alternatively, people challenged to solve problems without externalized criteria tend to develop a questioning approach to thinking approaching situations from different angles (Zhang, 2003).

Thinking Styles
As we internalize our socialized messages about thinking and problem solving, we develop habitual thinking styles. There are three common thinking styles: creative, conformist, and reactive (Zhang & Sternberg, 2005). When exploring these three styles in Table 3.1, notice an increasing influence of external sources as the table transitions from creative thinking through to reactive thinking. Socialization influences the development of these styles. Creative thinkers are encouraged to explore and experiment, which promotes curiosity and divergent thinking (Suedfeld & Coren, 1992; Zhang, 2006). Conformists are more methodical, following directions and systems that have already been developed. Reactive thinkers require prodding and oversight as they take on tasks.

Table 3.1 Typology of Thinking Styles

Type	Label	Features
Type 1	Creative/ Integrative	• Employs complex thinking at different levels • Integrates multiple concepts into larger picture • Evaluates and questions outcomes and situations • Is hierarchical, able to prioritize and manage multiple tasks and elements • Adopts new approaches to problems
Type 2	Conformist	• Employs fewer, more fundamental concepts • Focuses on the details rather than the whole picture • Follows directions and accepts explanations • Takes thing in order, one task at a time • Favors traditional approaches to problem solving
Type 3	Reactive	• Employs little conceptual organization or planning to the thinking • Reacts to tasks as they emerge rather than anticipating or understanding the larger context • Relies on externally provided criteria and directions to provide order • Attempts to meet basic criteria with little understanding of purpose or function

Socialization Influences

Thinking habits emerge over years of parental and educational influences (Zhang, 2003). As we age, we develop automatic thinking habits that operate unconsciously and independent of our logically controlled thinking processes (Verbrugge & Mol, 2008). Consequently, our thinking styles tend to be habitual rather than a reflection of our intelligence or thinking abilities. Consider the next socialization approaches, and identify how each type of parental response might shape the three thinking styles.

- *Problem solving.* Some parents encourage children to tackle problems and experiment with their own solutions. Such parents are patient and allow children to try their own solutions and learn from their failures. Other parents are very active in their children's problem solving, seeming almost to take over problems and impose solutions. Still others ignore problems, responding only when they must. When responding, they engage only long enough to decrease the tension that required their participation, then they withdraw.

- *Experimentation.* Some parents set up opportunities for children to engage in learning activities. Activities introduce children to new experiences and allow them to explore, experiment, and draw their own conclusions about their experiences. These parents respond to the children's questions and encourage their thinking. Other parents engage with their children during learning activities with a little more direction. They encourage certain learning activities and reinforce those activities they consider to be important. A third group of parents may be passive about learning. They prefer their children to be part of structured activities and do not often take an active role. They respond when they are approached, answering questions with minimal responses or by directing children to someone else.

- *Questioning.* Some parents encourage children to ask questions and spend time helping them understand their situations. They are patient and willing to spend the time to ensure that the questions are answered adequately. Other parents give uneven attention to questions depending on their ability to answer. Such parents do well with procedural questions but may not engage so readily with questions focused on the child's underlying thinking or alternative actions. Some parents struggle with the "why" and "why not" involved in the situation. Answers such as "just do it" or "because I said so" may emerge with such questioning.

- *Relating.* Some parents help children understand interpersonal differences and events by exploring how different people think and react. They help children extrapolate values and beliefs from people's behaviors and statements. Such parents also help children explore methods of understanding and responding in social situations. Other parents maintain a behavioral focus when discussing other people and their reactions. They reinforce certain actions and explain how some behaviors can lead to problems. Another group of parents may adopt a distancing approach, explaining that children should just avoid certain people.

When we reflect on these parental approaches, it is easy to see how different thinking habits can emerge during socialization. Likely some of the parental descriptions reminded you of your parents. We cannot help but be influenced by them, as our parents were our first sources of information and problem solving. Our parents, in turn, were influenced by their parents, creating an intergenerational influence on how we think. However, parental modeling influence only our habits, not our capacity. Regardless of your parental socialization, you can train your mind to adopt other systems of thinking. In your career, at times you will need to be conformist and linear in your thinking and, at other times, circular and creative.

Cultural Influences
In Chapter 1 you engaged in an exercise that explored several cultural influences. In this exercise you discovered some influences on how you think. Culture provides a ring around your family experiences that reinforces values, providing interpretation guidelines for social events and expectations through which success and failure are defined. Given that family and culture are the initial contexts for your thinking, it is also important to understand how your cultural background has influenced your thinking habits.

Much of the cultural influence emerged through your family and kin relationships. You probably can remember the dinner conversations when family members gathered together (e.g., holidays). During these discussions, standards of right and wrong are communicated through family stories and arguments. All of these culturally relevant moments set the stage for your current thinking habits. Cultural messages also provide a loyalty framework that may make it difficult to shed some habits. Revisit your notes from the cultural exercise to understand which thinking habits have ties to your cultural background.

Socialized Habits versus Thinking Ability
The thinking habits we inherit from our parents and cultural institutions, although evident in our approach to situations, are independent of our actual thinking ability. However, these habits do influence how we use our abilities. Five-year-olds have the ability to distinguish their assumptions and thinking from those of others, but this skill tends to be under-developed (Verbrugge & Mol, 2008). As we develop our professional selves, it is important that we begin to separate our past thinking habits from our ability to understand situations. As we begin introducing professional rigor to our thinking, there are challenges to using our thinking ability.

- *Values influences.* People often use their personal values as a template for under-standing situations. Research indicates that the strength of people's values decreases their complex thinking ability when they attempt to understand interpersonal situations (Conway et al., 2008). Values biases actually can elevate problems because an initial biased decision provides the foundation for subsequent decisions leading to sequences of faulty inferences (Wong, Kwong, & Ng, 2008).
- *Externalization.* When people rely on external sources for answers rather than analyzing and evaluating situations, creative and complex thinking is inhibited (Palut, 2008). When the external source or standard is used as an example of the perfect or ultimate solution, people tend to withhold alternative solutions or limit their thinking by dichotomizing potential responses (Egan, Piek, Dyck, & Rees, 2007).

- *Affective responses.* People often experience immediate emotional responses to a situation. However, these emotional responses actually interfere with our ability to comprehend the situation. Interference is particularly strong when the situation is morally challenging (Myyry & Helkama, 2007).

All of these potential sources of cognitive interference underscore the importance of the self-awareness work in Chapter 1. Notice how issues of loyalty and reactions based on past experience are inherent in the sources of thinking distortion just described. As you continue to develop your professional self, you will develop new thinking habits that use professional knowledge rather than family modeling and values.

Professional Knowledge Base

Professional knowledge bases are instrumental in helping us understand and plan intervention. We draw on research and professional observations to help formulate our thinking about current situations. The consistent use of a knowledge base promotes practitioner competence (Staller & Kirk, 1998). As we continue to grow as practitioners, eventually we will contribute new knowledge as part of our ethical duty to advance our profession.

Even though different professions draw on divergent sources of knowledge, effective practitioners are consistently driven to learn and expand their ability to understand client situations (Jennings & Skovholt, 1999; Spurling & Dryden, 1989). Through a comprehensive understanding, intervention direction and client goals emerge. Without direction, practitioners may drift ineffectively from subject to subject with no purpose.

There are two elements in a professional knowledge base:

1. *Theory.* lies at the root of professional knowledge by providing a vision of how different knowledge elements are connected. Theory shapes our thinking as we explore the client situation (McGovern, Newman, & Kopta, 1986).
2. *Research.* tests the propositions contained in theories to ensure that the theories are well grounded rather than conjecture or fantasy.

Role of Theory

Many theories are described in the professional literature. Some are well supported by research while others are primarily conjecture based on practice observations. The vast array of available theories can be confusing for developing professionals as we approach the literature looking for theories that can help us understand client situations. To simplify our thinking, there are three broad theoretical frameworks upon which we base most of our assumptions: biopsychosocial, developmental, and person-in-environment frameworks.

Biopsychosocial Model

A major theoretical framework in the helping professionals is the biopsychosocial model. This theoretical framework integrates multiple theories to explain problems and issues based on development influences. The biopsychosocial model is used to explain how biological, psychological, sexual, cognitive, group, family, neighborhood, and community development issues are involved in client situations (see Figure 3.1).

In the original conceptualization of the model, the focus was on biology, sociology, and psychology (Engel, 1977). The blending of three disciplines was well received in health and human services. In recent years spirituality and culture have been stressed when discussing the model. Consequently, spirituality has been added in Figure 3.1 to allow for the expanded perspective. When using the biopsychosocial model to understand client situations, we often integrate the concepts with a life span understanding of how multiple influences interact in a person's life. The interaction of biology, social factors, psychological development, and spirituality influence how client systems develop and operate.

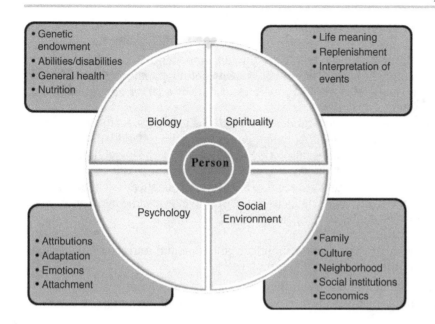

Figure 3.1

Biopsychosocial Model

Developmental/Life Span Models

Many theoretical models emerge using developmental or life span perspectives. The developmental models adopt a longitudinal perspective, making sense of current functioning based on past experiences. When we assess a client, group, family, or other client system, we use a model of development and then compare the functioning of the client system to the developmental stages in the model. If the current function seems appropriate according to the model, we assume there is no problem. Otherwise we use the model to identify where the problems emerged.

Developmental models typically have an optimal direction that helps distinguish normal from abnormal development. When the client system masters one stage of development, it has the foundation for the next stage. Notice in Figure 3.2 how stage 1 builds a foundation for the next stage. The outcomes of stage 2 and stage 1 combined provide the foundation for the third stage. This successive development of the foundation is referred to as the epigenetic principle.

Often the developmental models are combined with biopsychosocial understandings because biological, social, and psychological capacities change at different developmental stages. Developmental theories contain three distinguishing elements:

1. *Optimal direction.* The proper direction is important in developmental theories. To achieve the proper outcome, the client system must develop in the right direction. If the system deviates from the direction, problems are inferred.

2. *Stage-wise development.* Within developmental models, there are several stages leading to the ultimate outcome. Each stage contains at least one task that must be mastered to ensure proper development.

3. *Epigenetic principle.* Each developmental stage builds on the outcomes of the outcomes of the previous stages. If the previous stage is successful, the foundation for the new stage is stable. However, if the previous stage is not properly mastered, problems will occur in the next and all subsequent stages.

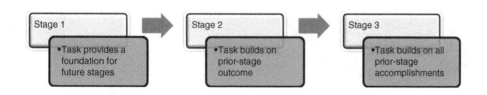

Figure 3.2

**Life Span/
Developmental Models**

Person-in-Environment/Ecosystems Models

The final common framework is referred to as either ecosystems theory or person-in-environment theory. Ecosystemic models focus on subcomponents in mutual influence. Within this model, component parts of the client system continually interact and influence each other. Concurrently, the client system operates as part of a larger environment that influences how the system can function.

Within the person-in-environment model, every entity is viewed as a subcomponent of larger systems in a constant exchange interaction. For example, an individual is part of the family, the family is a system that is also a subcomponent of the neighborhood, the neighborhood is a subcomponent of a town, and so on. In the helping relationship, workers are also nested in larger systems. Observe in Figure 3.3 how each smaller system is nested in a larger unit. Although the figure limits its focus to the next five levels, the number of levels can be expanded from the cellular to the galactic levels.

1. *Social.* Within the social level, there are political, governmental, and economic systems that influence all of the interrelated system levels.
2. *Community.* At the community level, there are supports and other systems, such as associations, school boards, local government, industry, agencies, and service systems.
3. *Neighborhood.* At the local neighborhood level, resources and stressors include schools, gangs, businesses, friends, neighbors, and the like.
4. *Family.* At the family level, there are local relatives, immediate family, kin systems, fictive kin, and other family-focused resources.
5. *Person.* The person is also a system. Biological, psychological, and other systems influence the client's capacity.

When a practitioner and client begin service, multiple systems become involved including families, work teams, agencies, communities, and social systems. These systems all influence each other and in turn are influenced by all of the other systems. Practitioners focus on how the systems interact and track the reciprocal influences. When working from this theoretical model, intervention often seeks to change the relationships among different components of the ecosystem. Ecosystemic models commonly are used to understand individuals, families, organizations, communities, groups, and societies. The ecosystemic model often is integrated with the biopsychosocial approach to achieve a holistic understanding of a client situation.

Figure 3.3

Person-in-Environment Model

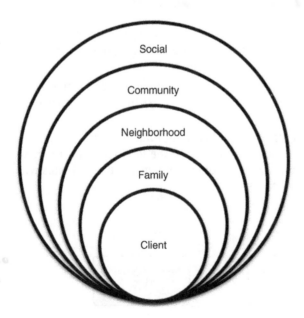

Using Theoretical Frameworks

Theoretical frameworks focus our assessments of the client situation and how we target intervention. The last three frameworks, biopsychosocial, life span, and person-in-environment, all provide models that can help practitioners understand most client situations. The models are sufficiently expansive to include diversity, culture, and oppression as we seek to understand the multiple influences in a client situation.

To illustrate the contributions of theory and knowledge to professional practice, Table 3.2 outlines the knowledge base, elements of knowledge, theories, and commonly known practices associated with each theoretical framework. As you read the table, notice that many individual theories tend to overlap within the theoretical frameworks or models. Also notice that the well-accepted models tend to promote research and evidence-based practice.

Empirical Grounding

It is very easy to generate theories and approaches to serving clients. Some theories are very logical and eloquent while others can border on bizarre and dangerous. Both bizarre and grounded theories can sound good when proponents of a theoretical approach argue

Table 3.2 Elements of the Professional Knowledge Base

Theoretical Framework	Knowledge Elements	Associated Theories	Broadly Known Evidence-Based Practices
Biopsychosocial models	• Trauma and stress • Self-conception • Cognitive functioning • Adaptation • Ability/disability • Psychopathology • Biopsychosocial functioning • Health and illness	• Stress/coping theory • Trauma theory • Addictions theory • Recovery theory • Intergenerational transmission theory	• Integrated dual diagnosis treatment • Assertive community treatment • Health promotion • Public health iIntervention
Developmental and life span models	• Life span development • Stages of grieving • Family development • Group development • Organizational development • Socialization • Attachment and loss	• Freudian/neo-Freudian theory • Psychosocial development theory • Social learning theory • Family development theory • Attachment theory • Loss and grieving theory	• Incredible Years Curriculum • Parent Management Training—Oregon • New Beginnings Program • Nurse-Family Partnership • Headstart
Ecosystemic models	• Relationships • Family systems functioning • Larger system dynamics • Political systems • Cultural systems • Social systems • Power/oppression • Oppression and privilege	• Exchange theory • Systems theory • Field theory • Empowerment theory • Conflict theory • Cultural transmission theory	• Multisystemic therapy • Behavioral couples therapy • Brief strategic family therapy • Wraparound services

the merits of their model. Theoretical discussions can assume almost an ideological position when professionals are dedicated to a specific theoretical approach without critical thinking. Doing this can be dangerous; some extreme approaches have resulted in client death.

Given the potential danger to clients, there is an ethical obligation for practitioners to take great care when selecting their theoretical approach to practice. This is a challenge when anyone can set up a web site for $10 per year and promote an approach to treatment. To protect clients, it is important to select theoretical approaches that have some supporting research evidence. Doing this requires us to select theories from the professional literature rather than trusting our clients to untested approaches.

The constant generation of new theories requires practitioners to remain current by reading the professional literature. The rate of knowledge expansion does not allow practitioners to relax their reading habits. To remain competent reading should include both clinical and empirical works to ensure a broad knowledge base. Along with reading, practitioners should attend professional-development activities to ensure that they are using the best practices available.

Role of Research

Theory and research must work in concert to ensure a viable professional knowledge base. Practitioners apply research findings in their work. Research is the source of grounded knowledge that can replace socialized understandings. Consequently, research provides a solid foundation for our thinking as we form an understanding of client problems (Thyer & Myers, 1998).

Most research builds on theory at some level because theories provide linkages between the different elements in a problem situation. Given that researchers ground their research questions in selected theories, there is a theoretical influence on their selection of variables and interpretation of results. Consequently, we must be aware of the theoretical assumptions as we read research studies.

Two types of research inform the profession: quantitative and qualitative. *Quantitative research* uses statistics to assess relationships, trends, and differences. *Qualitative research* uses themes indicated in spoken, written, or observed data to understand situations. Both types of research are important to glean an understanding of client situations.

Quantitative Research

Most sources of quantitative knowledge are studies exploring or comparing different client groups or intervention methods. These studies are important sources of information and provide empirically tested foci and methods for intervention. Six common types of quantitative research contribute to the professional knowledge base.

1. *Outcome research.* Outcome research assesses the effectiveness of new or different intervention techniques. Subjects in these studies often have similar problems or experience some situation requiring intervention. Such research can be very useful and immediately applied when working with similar client groups.

2. *Program evaluations.* Program evaluations are similar to outcome research when assessing an intervention system. With program evaluations, a broader type of intervention is studied, often a new approach or model (such as Family Preservation programming). Program evaluations often focus on interventions that use a manual to ensure that all practitioners use the same approach. This source of knowledge is important for providing intervention ideas and useful manuals.

3. *Cross-sectional research.* When researchers want to understand the impact of an event or experience, cross-sectional research is used to take a close look at effects. Cross-sectional research provides important information on effects, thinking styles, and other traits that can focus intervention. Cross-sectional research is useful when a practitioner wants to learn about different populations.

4. *Longitudinal research.* Sometimes researchers want to follow the progression of a phenomenon over a period of time. Consequently, they measure a variable several times at regular intervals to identify how the phenomenon develops. For example, a researcher may assess social behavior of many children living in single-parent homes and continue tracking the children until they are adults to identify elements that promote positive or negative relationship functioning in adults. This type of research is excellent for identifying the causes of problems.

5. *Comparative research.* A large body of research that compares two (or more) groups of people or types of interventions is called comparative research. This research allows practitioners to see if the impact on one group is really different or if one intervention is better than another for certain situations.

6. *Epidemiology.* Epidemiological research focuses on the frequency, prevalence, and patterns of different types of problems. Epidemiological findings often become the common knowledge we use to justify intervention programs. For example, most people can report that 1 in 4 women experience unwanted sexual attention by the age of 18 Such epidemiological information anchors our knowledge base about social problems and is used to argue for prevention and intervention funding.

Some forms of quantitative research are difficult to read and apply to practice. The analyses are often complex with many mathematical terms and tables of numbers.. Many practitioners pay close attention to the literature review, the description of the method, and the discussion section when the analysis is beyond their understanding. When taking the research courses in your program, also read professional articles to gain an understanding of how the research can be applied.

Qualitative Research
Although there are some qualitative articles published in journals, the richest sources of qualitative learning are books in which a researcher becomes immersed in situations that can help inform practice. Five common types of qualitative research are used to build professional knowledge.

1. *Ethnographies.* Ethnographies are most often stories of a single person or situation that are developed in great depth and detail. Such stories can provide insight and inspiration to practitioners. Such in-depth documentation helps practitioners at a deeper level than they can get in quantitative research.

2. *Grounded theory.* This approach to qualitative data begins with letting a person or group tell their story without a specific question guiding the research. As the story unfolds, the researcher categorizes and compares themes to come up with the strongest explanatory theory.

3. *Participant observation.* With participant observation, researchers act as if they are one of the subjects. They observe situations and events from the point of view of the people being studied. Often the observations are followed by reflections on their experience and observations.

4. *Narrative interviews.* Narrative interviews involve an unstructured approach to interviewing people about their stories. The researcher then analyzes the content of the answers and uses content themes and presentation styles to make sense out of the situation or story.

5. *Focus groups.* Focus groups involve several people responding to a set of questions—similar to an interview. The researcher tracks the themes and consensus of the group and reports them as findings.

Qualitative research is often easier to read than quantitative research because the report provides a full story. Consequently, the research is very similar to a book. There is very little abstraction, such as statistics, which make it easier for practitioners to digest.

However, often the findings are based on very few subjects, which makes them hard to generalize.

Exercise 3.1: Peter and His Residential Problems

The worker in this case is Glenna, a case manager working in a center for people with developmental disabilities in a rural southern state. The center has educational, prevocational, vocational, and residential programs serving clients of all ages. Glenna is a 29-year-old Caucasian woman living with the supervisor of the residential services (named John).

The client in this case is Peter, a 27-year-old Jewish male of Russian descent who has a rare handicapping condition that causes him to have a small and somewhat frail stature. Intellectual disabilities are minimal with this syndrome, but there is difficulty processing on the abstract level. Peter was diagnosed as a young child and immediately placed by his parents. He has neither seen nor heard from his family since his placement. Peter has lived his life in a series of institutions, group homes, and specialized foster homes.

Peter has consistently done well in the sheltered workshop where he is employed. He is brighter than most of the other clients and produces at a high rate. He has a fairly good relationship with the staff in the workshop and often comes to visit the case managers in their offices. Glenna sees him probably four to five times per day as he drops in to chat and then returns to work. Even with this pattern of chatting, Peter has high productivity at work. Given that he is paid piecework, his high production benefits him with money. Peter is able to take the bus downtown and use his money well. He has bought season tickets to the little theater and loves to read books. He is being considered for competitive employment (part of the general workforce) at a local department store, where he will be stocking shelves and sweeping floors.

The problem area for Peter is maintaining stability in his residential placements. Peter does not do well in group-living situations and will escalate his behavior if placed in a group home. Consequently, he was placed in a specialized foster home. Peter has had several foster home placements since coming to the agency. Although he is bright and participates in community activities, he is demanding of people in caregiving roles. If Peter does not feel his needs are met, he will storm into the room, pound tables or desks, and demand that people do what he wants.

Peter's demandingness is not a constant type of behavior. Often he functions well in all areas of his life. During these times, he is helpful around the home, engages in conversation, and is pleasant company. When Peter is cooperative, he is rewarded with increased freedom and responsibility. One of the rewards during calm periods is a TV for his bedroom. This allows Peter total control over program choice and an opportunity to spend unlimited time in his room watching TV. He is also allowed to go out in the community without restrictions. These periods are positive times for the foster parents, who feel free to leave him at home alone and resume their own lives.

Peter's good periods seldom last longer than four to six weeks, after which he will "blow up" at the foster parents. Typically, there are no warning signs. The foster parents, after being out, are greeted by pounding and swearing when Peter sees them coming into the home. Such behavior jeopardizes his residential placement, given that he is most unkind in the things that he yells. Peter also has smashed items but never attacked a human being.

When Peter gets in his angry state, he generalizes his anger and becomes demanding of everyone in roles of authority. He has gone into the executive director's office ranting and raving about how people in this "f_ _king dump need to pay attention to what I want." During these periods, Glenna builds in extra supports for the residential providers until things stabilize. It takes about two to three weeks to get Peter stabilized and about another month or two before the additional resources can be withdrawn.

Glenna states that Peter's problems are caused by his early institutionalization, which disrupted his ability to trust other people. She argues that his escalation probably developed because he had to cry and escalate to get his needs met. Her rationale for building in the supports is that Peter does not have to be so demanding and can relax knowing that his needs will be met.

1. Given the information provided, what type of theory does Glenna appear to be using: developmental, biopsychosocial, or ecosystemic?

2. What elements in her thinking and behavior support your choice?

3. What elements in Peter's situation can be used to support a developmental understanding?

4. What elements in Peter's situation can support a systemic understanding?

5. What elements in Peter's situation support a biopsychosocial understanding?

Toward Evidence-Based Practice

Over the past 20 years, the role of research in the helping professions has increased dramatically. Helping professionals used to base practice decisions on experience and clinical wisdom. Although these elements of practice still are respected, increasingly practitioners rely on research to understand situations and identify interventions with the strongest prognosis of success.

Using Research to Form Practice Decisions

As you start to replace your socialized understandings of situations, you will discover that the world is very complex. Because very few client situations are simple, your common sense developed through life experience, although helpful in social situations, is insufficient when making practice decisions. Developing evidence-based decisions is difficult because our commonsense understandings are automatic and comfortable. People in our past have made statements that we incorporate into our thinking and habitually use for basing decisions.

As you develop your professional identity, your habitual knowledge used for understanding social and psychological problems must give way to professional knowledge. Doing this requires you to read the professional literature to gain the best knowledge possible. Most practitioners start this process during college as instructors insist that students read certain chapters or articles before attending the lecture. You consequently learn to wade through complex passages to glean new information.

The tedious reading of your college years is really the beginning of your professional learning. To become a competent professional, you must continue reading for the rest of your professional career. Inherently, most practitioners are aware of the value of reading so the transition from being forced to being motivated should be easy. Ultimately, you should be reading chapters and articles every week to keep your knowledge current.

Selecting Research to Read

As you progress in your profession, you will discover two indispensible roles for research: maintaining competence and developing expertise. All professionals have an ethical obligation to remain competent. Doing this requires you to explore research findings associated with the problems and concerns that emerge in your professional practice. Regardless of your professional discipline, new understandings of client problems emerge every day. You must stay current with research findings to ensure that your thinking is consistent with scientific knowledge.

Although ensuring competence sounds simple, doing so requires you to sort through the available research on practice situations. To help select research to read, it is useful to consider the chronological development of researching social and psychological problems. Early research is often basic and seeks to confirm the existence of the problem. Over time, research becomes more complex as it begins to identify nuances and subtleties. For example, in domestic violence research, early studies documented the existence of the problem. Later research provided information about how family members coped with the violence and the impact of violence on different areas of functioning.

As you develop your professional self, it is likely that you will begin to focus on specific client groups or types of problems. As this occurs, you start reading the research with a slightly different purpose as you start to develop expertise in certain areas. With developing expertise, you want to know the body of research in more detail and compare it to your practice experiences. As you read, your minds starts to integrate one study with other findings and your experience. At this point of development, you often start to generate your own thoughts and questions for research.

When selecting studies to read, it is wise to choose the most recent research because each new study tends to build on and expand knowledge gleaned in previous research. It is also useful to sample research from different theoretical orientations. Often clusters of researchers collaborate together, each with a slightly different perspective. By sampling the findings of different researchers, you can discover research that is consistent with your approach to client situations and contrast those findings to other approaches.

Understanding the Promise of Outcomes

As you explore the available research, outcome studies are an important source of information because they contain details about interventions. While reading this type of study, it is important to understand its background. The background will provide the theoretical information and thinking associated with the intervention. These details provide a framework for understanding how the researchers approached the intervention.

The second critical element when reading an outcome study is to understand the interventions. Typically the researcher will describe the intervention used. As you read the described intervention, try to identify the critical elements. If you can visualize the actions of the practitioner during intervention, it is easier to integrate the research into your own practice. If you cannot visualize the intervention, you may need to gather more information on the approach by finding other articles listed in the bibliography or written by the authors.

A third critical element found in many outcome studies is the discussion of alternative interventions. Ideally, the researcher will compare the intervention to another well-accepted intervention. This provides us with information about the improvements the research intervention can make if selected. However, many studies compare their intervention to no intervention at all. This approach provides us with less information to make our decisions.

When you read outcome studies, you want to determine whether the intervention is better than other options. As you read, keep this quest for improvement in mind. If the study identifies only that the intervention is better than no intervention, it can be potentially useful. Stronger studies compare two or more approaches to intervention. This provides a better comparison because most interventions are superior to inaction. Practitioners constantly seek out the most promising interventions or strategies so they can be incorporated into practice.

Understanding Research Limitations

As a practitioner, you must be a critical consumer of the research. Often the studies you read will have features that do not easily fit into your practice. Two elements in research often make it difficult to apply findings in a practice setting: sample limitations and intervention elements.

1. *Sample limitations.* Researchers often limit whom they include in their studies. Sometimes this is to maximize positive outcomes; sometimes it is because the intervention is appropriate only for specific groups of people. It is important to understand these decisions as you seek to apply interventions with your clients. If your clients are not an exact match to the sample in the study, you may need to seek alternative interventions or be very careful with how you apply your new knowledge.

2. *Intervention elements.* Funded research can be quite different from agency-based practice. Often a study has an exceptional level of resources that cannot be replicated in community practice. It is important to understand the differences between the research situation and your practice setting and decide whether the intervention is possible or not. If the differences are minor, you may be able to adapt the new knowledge and employ the intervention successfully. However, if the intervention requires supports or resources unavailable to you or your clients, it is important to proceed cautiously.

Some evidence-based practices are very rigorous and include training, fidelity checks, and ongoing consultation. Although these practices are very consistent, they will require a significant agency investment of time and money to implement in practice. If you are hired into a program that uses this type of practice, you will follow very specific protocols. However, this is not the only use of outcome-based research in practice. Even if agencies are not able to fund additional training or consultation, professionals use the research to adapt their approach to intervention.

When an evidence-based intervention does not easily fit your clientele or practice setting, you must decide if there are elements in the research that can be applied or whether the intervention should be abandoned. Often it is possible to identify elements in the research that can be integrated into our practice even if the intervention is not an exact fit. As you gain knowledge, you will likely find patterns in the research that help identify the most promising elements that can be adapted.

Applying Research in Practice

In professional practice, knowledge is constantly applied to your client situations. Consequently, you need to develop your knowledge base and then find ways of using knowledge to serve clients. The first step in this process is drawing on good information. Doing so requires you to use well-grounded theory and interventions.

Even if an intervention cannot be implemented easily, as you read the research, it is important to identify elements that can be applied to client situations. Often several research articles will have similar elements. For example, cognitive behavioral, narrative, journaling, and eye movement desensitization and reprocessing (EMDR) interventions for posttraumatic stress problems all involve exposure and detailed discussions of traumatic events (Beck, Coffet, Foy, Keane, & Blanchard, 2009; Bugg, Graham, Mason, & Scholes, 2009; Neuner et al., 2008, Tufnell, 2005). Given this consistent element, it makes sense to include exposure and detailed exploration if working with posttrauma clients.

Practice-Based Evidence

As you apply knowledge in professional practice, you begin a cycle of applied learning that will remain with you throughout your career. This cycle involves using your knowledge with clients and in turn learning from the outcomes and evidence that emerges through practice. If you rigorously monitor, collect feedback, and observe for evidence, your outcomes begin to expand your knowledge and inform your practice.

Evidence includes client reactions, changes in client behaviors, verbal feedback, and outcome measures. If you can rigorously identify how intervention is received and used by clients, your practice evidence can help inform your use of the knowledge gleaned from journals, other publications, and training. This sets in action a four-step cycle:

1. *Acquire knowledge.* Theories and research provide a solid foundation for beginning practice. You must read and think continually to keep your knowledge current and ready to use.

2. *Apply knowledge.* As you acquire knowledge, you apply your learning with clients. As you apply the knowledge, your skills develop. You learn to understand clients and adjust your knowledge to meet the unique needs of each client.

3. *Gather evidence.* After applying knowledge, you must observe and gather evidence regarding the impact and effectiveness of your intervention. If the intervention has no impact, reflect on the application to understand the lack of outcome. If the intervention has impact, learn about the impact so you can add the new evidence into your ongoing knowledge base.

4. *Adjust practice.* The final step in the learning sequence is to integrate your new evidence into your approach to practice. Practitioners constantly adjust and change how they work based on the effectiveness of interventions. As you adjust your interventions, reading, observation and client feedback combine to keep your practice optimally informed.

Toward Applied Thinking

We can easily glean new information to replace our socialized understandings, but we also must develop new thinking habits to enhance our old styles of thinking. Ultimately, we must apply our knowledge to client situations (Badger, 1985; Gambrill, 1997). It is the act of applying knowledge that builds our thinking skills as we explore client situations, identify contributing elements and explain problems (McLennan, Culkin, & Courtney, 1994).

Many books, articles, and dissertations have been written about thinking. Some resources focus on principles of thinking, others on brain functions, while others propose novel understandings. Given the plethora of information, it is not possible to explore all of the subtleties and nuances of thinking in a single chapter. Consequently, it is important to understand that the ensuing discussion is but a small scratch on the surface of the debates and controversies in the field. This scratch, however, will provide some stimulation as we start to focus on the thinking involved in making sound practice decisions.

To begin our understanding of our thinking processes, consider two commonly discussed types of thinking: linear and nonlinear thinking. Linear thinking is conventional in nature, building each premise on established facts or principles (DeWall, Baumeister, & Masicampo, 2008). Linear thinking often is referred to as logical or conformist thinking. Nonlinear thinking is more creative and circular in nature (Glassner & Schwarz, 2007). Nonlinear thinking styles often are referred to as creative, critical, or reflective thinking. Nuances and subtypes exist within each broad category of thinking, but these categories are well accepted in the literature and will suffice for our applications to professional thinking.

Concurrent with these thinking styles, two types of mental energy emerge when thinking: expansion and contraction. Expanding energy leads to new conclusions, thoughts, linkages, and options as we think about a situation. Expansive thinking is associated with innovation and holistic considerations. Contraction, however, leads to focusing and clarity as some thoughts are considered irrelevant, leaving only the most important elements of the situation. As we develop our professional thinking habits, both forms of mental energy emerge to service different practice requirements.

Linear Thinking

The term "linear thinking" often is used interchangeably with the term "logical thinking." Logical thinking is conscious and focused in nature (DeWall et al., 2008). It is considered linear because each premise linked to a premise that already is accepted or established

(Vance, Groves, Paik, & Kindler, 2007). Thus, this style of thinking builds in a step-by-step manner; each new thought or premise sits on a foundation of established premises.

Linear thinking is central to understanding the client situation. We use client information and then draw on our knowledge to understand linkages among events (Freeman, 1993). For example, as a child protection service worker, we often work with parents who hit their children. As we explore the situation, we might learn that a parent was abused as a child. Logically, we might infer that the parent's background influences the problem. As linkages emerge, we draw on theories to guide our further exploration (Baron, 1994; Browne & Keeley, 1994; Kassierer & Kopelman, 1991). In this situation, we would likely draw on a developmental theory, such as social learning theory.

In linear thinking, our mental energy influences the decisions we make about connections and premises that emerge. If we are in an expansive mode, we are rapidly establishing new hypotheses and generating thoughts about what might be occurring within a given situation. However, when we are in a contractive period, we carefully assess linkages and thoughts to determine which ideas make the most sense or apply in a given situation.

Linear Expansive Thinking

As we explore client situations, our minds engage to identify possible explanations for the situation. This engagement begins as we listen to our clients tell their stories. As we listen, we mentally draw on our knowledge for possible foundations to explain the problem. Three common linear thinking patterns emerge during this expansive period: identifying linkages and patterns and forming predictions. Notice in the next discussions how these thinking patterns expand our understanding and ability to respond to the client situation.

1. *Identifying linkages.* Often problems are caused by prior events. To help clients understand how problems have evolved, the practitioner explores the history of the problem to identify how one event contributes to the next. Such thinking is linear with clear sequencing of events and outcomes (e.g., A leads to B). In the preceding example, we hypothesized that the parent learned to hit from his or her parents. Cause-and-effect linkages are not always simple. Often people's solutions to past events become today's problems. Similarly, events outside of the situation can contribute to the problem. We must be able to identify connections among different elements of a person's life to fully understand the problem situation. For example, when working with parents who hit their children, workers often explore the situation to find that the parents experienced coercive punishment as children. With further exploration the worker might find that when the child does not listen the parent feels powerless and becomes highly punitive. The childhood experiences logically link to the current behavior as do feelings of powerlessness.

2. *Identifying patterns.* Our professional exploration often involves finding patterns and themes across problem occurrences. Patterns may emerge in interaction, behavior, feeling responses, and thinking. In the previous example, we identified links to feelings of powerlessness and parental history. However, with additional exploration we may find that when the parent drinks they dwell on negative events over which they have no control. This causes the parent to start feeling down on him- or herself for not being able to manage these elements of life. With an increased number of drinks, these feelings become exacerbated, and the parent starts lashing out at others. The situation escalates to violence when the children are defiant. Notice how this type of pattern helps identify possible solutions and services to help control of hitting.

3. *Forming predictions.* We must take action to help clients achieve their goals. In taking such action, we must use our knowledge to select interventions. As we make this selection, we predict how the intervention will affect the client and help to achieve client goals. Such prediction includes identifying positive outcomes and progress as well as anticipating potential negative outcomes. In the case we have been discussing, we could draw on research findings that some multisystemic treatments work well with violent parents who drink while other treatments may not work well with this combination. Consequently, logically we would select a multisystemic type of treatment.

Linear Contractive Thinking

The expansive energy helps us develop an understanding of the client situation, but we also must limit the possible explanations according to the client situation. Contractive energy helps us impose limits on our thinking. This energy brings us out of the theoretical range and back to the client situation as we test our premises by exploring the subcomponents and boundaries of the situation. The next discussions build on contractive thinking. Notice how problem parameters provide limits to the linkages and identify problem elements making the situation easier to comprehend.

- *Identifying problem parameters.* Along with understanding how problems might have evolved, we want to understand where, when, and how the problem emerges. In the previous situation, we likely would explore when and where hitting occurs, who tends to get hit, how hard, and so on. Doing this helps define the problem and the potential interventions for resolving it. In the example we would want to explore the frequency and severity of the hitting, situational factors (such as drinking, stress, etc.), precipitating events, what outcomes emerged after the violence, and other factors to understand the risks involved and the services required to resolve the violence.

- *Partializing situations.* When clients approach helping systems, often their problems seem overwhelming to them. The overwhelming nature of problems often is due to the fact that several smaller problems are combined in the situation. Separating out the smaller problems or problem components makes the situation more manageable. With the previous situation, we would likely consider stress, drinking, and negative self-concept as elements of the problem. By separating the problem elements, we can identify service goals and objectives. This skill also helps us identify necessary changes that can lead to success (Bloom, Fischer, & Orme, 1995).

- *Responding to goals and objectives.* As we select interventions to alter the client situation, we work within a framework of goals and objectives that guide intervention. For this reason, our predictions and selected interventions always must be tempered by our knowledge of the client's desired outcomes (Verbeke, Belschak, Bakker, & Dietz, 2008; Verbrugge & Mol, 2008). We consequently limit and constrict our opinions.

As we develop our professional use of linear thinking, we can build on our personal thinking skills. We have all been in situations where someone was upset with us. As we notice that the other person is angry, our logical thinking reviews past encounters and behaviors to identify our transgression. If we reflect on this process, we draw on our knowledge of the person and relationship to identify potential reasons for the problem. In client situations, we use theories and research about similar client situations, rather than personal information, to guide our exploration. As we discuss the situation with the client, these sources of knowledge help us identify potentially meaningful content, which we then explore in greater detail.

Exercise 3.2: Peter's Escalation

(This exercise is a continuation of Exercise 3.1.) After the last volatile incident, Glenna met with Peter and discussed the problem of his volatility. He had gone into the executive director's office and called her several names. Many of the names and phrases incorporated observations about her obvious weight problem. Peter had suggested that she would do better if she were seated less and did her job taking care of clients like him. Glenna received a call shortly after his visit with the executive director.

Glenna took a firm stand with Peter. She told Peter that he was going to have to redeem himself this time. Peter consequently was prohibited from visiting staff during working hours. He could come to see the staff members only on coffee breaks, and only with workshop staff permission. Peter stated this was not fair to him. Glenna responded that his behavior was not fair to others and stressed that he needed to learn how to work with others.

1. Who is this intervention serving?

2. When Glenna said, "You have to redeem yourself," how does this statement shift the beneficiary of the intervention?

3. Given Glenna's understanding of the case in the last section, how is this intervention inconsistent with her past assertions?

4. What type of theory does Glenna appear to be using now?

When Glenna told Peter he was prohibited from visiting, he became irate. He yelled at her, swore, and called her names. He then escalated and began kicking her bookcase and yelling, "You don't care. Nobody cares about me. You might as well just get rid of me!" He then ran out of the workshop and left for the day. Glenna called John and told him of the escalation in volatility in Peter's final statement before leaving. John phoned the consulting psychiatrist, and they agreed that Peter should be hospitalized for his own safety. It was arranged for him to be picked up by the police when he arrived at the foster home.

5. What was Glenna's apparent interpretation of Peter's statement, "You might as well get rid of me!"?

6. What alternative interpretation could there be for Peter's statement?

7. If Glenna adopted this alternative interpretation, how might it change the intervention?

Nonlinear Thinking

Nonlinear thinking often is referred to as creative or critical thinking (Glassner & Schwarz, 2007). Although linear thinking is very helpful, creative thinking is associated with innovative responses and options that defy a rational approach. Nonlinear thinking helps us to develop a more holistic understanding of complex situations while also identifying a greater range of potential solutions (Payne, Samper, Bettman, & Luce, 2008; Smith, Dijksterhuis, & Wigboldus, 2008; Zhang, 2002). With nonlinear thinking intuition, divergent choices are considered as possibilities in the situation. Creative thinking is an integrative skill using emotional as well as logical processes (Brookfield, 1987). Using creative thinking allows for the development of new perspectives (Browne & Hausmann, 1998).

The use of intuition and hunches in practice requires significant rigor from helping professionals, because intuition and creative options must be validated in the worker-client relationship. The need to tie our assumptions back to the client sets up a circular thinking pattern in which the worker first establishes an assumption or hunch about the client situation, then takes some action based on the hunch to test whether it is operational in the situation. After action, the worker monitors client reactions to determine whether the hypothesis is supported. The support, or lack thereof, is then fed back into the thinking to change or confirm the worker's assumption. In this way, there is a constant interplay between expansive and contractive mental energy.

Nonlinear Expansive Thinking

Creative thinking is known for its expansive nature. Many nonlinear thinkers are exploring situations from multiple perspectives, seeking to find the most promising options. Practitioners using nonlinear thinking approaches are often in an exploratory and expansive mode with their clients. Two common thinking activities are employed during this style of thinking: generative alternatives and challenging assumptions.

1. *Generative alternatives.* Nonlinear thinkers do not readily adopt the most expedient or apparent interpretation or action. Instead, they experiment with alternative interpretations, perspectives, and options. Doing this allows for them to see different aspects of the situation that can be helpful in working with clients (Brookfield, 1987; Gambrill, 1990, 1994). Identifying alternative explanations of events is a necessary skill when using the strengths perspective because the worker must identify positive definitions of situations that might ordinarily promote negative interpretations. With the example used earlier, a creative thinker might seek to redefine the parent's situation as the parent being loyal to his or her parents and showing the loyalty by replicating their system of parenting. Notice how this is a very different understanding from determining that she is a drinker who harms her children when drunk. While either assumption can be true, the strength-based assumption will yield a different emotional response in the client.

2. *Challenging assumptions.* Nonlinear thinkers never take assumptions for granted; instead, they tend to question how an assumption came to be and whether it applies in a particular situation. Each assumption must fit the situation. Workers who use nonlinear thinking always question the status quo and push for a new approach to situations. Critical thinkers do not discount other people's ideas; however, they apply rigorous scrutiny to ensure an idea is the best understanding of the situation. For example, say the parent who has been used as an example throughout this section refers to her children as stubborn or disrespectful. A worker might encourage her to consider other explanations by gently questioning her assumptions and encouraging her to think of other possibilities.

Nonlinear Contractive Thinking

The contractive energy of nonlinear thinkers keeps practitioners seeking feedback and data to confirm or further challenge their assumptions. Contractive energy is important; without testing new assumptions, we may begin to treat our interpretations as the client "reality" and intervene based on conjecture rather than validated information. These two cognitive patterns are typical of creative thinkers:

1. *Maintaining skepticism.* Nonlinear thinkers are never satisfied that they have reached the final conclusion (Brookfield, 1987; Gibbs & Gambrill, 1999). They always review past actions to learn what they can do differently next time. They also review every situation with an element of skepticism that anyone truly knows the right answers. This skepticism keeps them searching and questioning to find better, more effective ways to intervene and also keeps them collecting information and testing their

assumptions. This tendency to look for validating information keeps expansive energy in check because options are only as good as the results they generate. If a nonlinear thinker were to challenge the parent who has hit her children, she would likely use data based on caring exchanges and other acts to help the mother understand that she has the capacity to create a new, positive model of parenting for her family.

2. *Reflective thinking.* Nonlinear thinkers often think in reflexive loops. Doing this involves considering elements in the situation, developing an assumption, testing the assumption, and gathering information on outcomes. Based on the feedback information, assumptions are altered by incorporating the new information and repeating the cycle. Consequently, understanding is always fluid and changing based on the incoming information. In these reflective loops, creative thinkers vary their sources of initial observation and feedback perspectives to incorporate multiple vantage points. When working with a client, a creative practitioner consistently monitors client responses using them as a guide to alter subsequent interventions.

Case Example

A worker was discussing an elderly woman's depression and negative self-feelings. Based on a pattern of extreme negative feelings, the worker suspected there was some sexual abuse in the background. The worker stated, "I have a question in my mind that may seem weird to you at first. I would like to ask it because it may have some influence on what we are discussing." After the client agreed to answer, the worker stated, "When you were talking, I had a feeling that someone did something to you when you were little that made you feel lousy about yourself." The client responded, "No . . . never to me. But my dad used to hit my mother a lot." The worker incorporated the information and then asked, "How were you involved?" The client began to share how most of the mother's beating occurred when she had done something wrong. Apparently, the father would start berating the client, and when the mother attempted to defend her, the father would become violent toward the mother.

In this example, see how initial action yielded information that the hunch was wrong. The worker consequently incorporated the feedback and altered the path of exploration, still believing the client was involved in some type of abuse. The question about how the client was involved yielded confirmation that there was some trauma (witnessing spousal abuse) that impacted her self-concept (the fights were about her).

Exercise 3.3: Peter's Discharge Plan

(This is a continuation of the previous two exercises.) After Peter got out of the hospital, new supports were put in place and he was stabilized again. He did well in both residential and workshop settings. The supports included ongoing counseling, a community/respite support person (to take him out), and an independent living group at the workshop. The period of stability lasted more than 4 months, leading Glenna to put Peter's name forward for a supported independent living apartment and competitive employment. Her plan was to move him into the new services and then pass his case on to a different case manager.

1. What is likely to happen to Peter in this transition?

2. What past events in Peter's life does this plan parallel?

3. What might be done differently to help the plan (apartment and work) succeed?

Building Professional Thinking Skills

As a helping professional, you eventually will integrate your linear and nonlinear thinking skills to bring focus and direction to your exchanges with clients. Although initially you might experience some confusion as you apply knowledge during interaction with your clients, new thinking habits will emerge, requiring you to spend less time sorting out concepts and findings in your head and more time listening and responding to your client.

As you build your thinking skills, you will master multiple elements that contribute to your ability to understand and respond to client situations. Figure 3.4 provides a picture of the multiple elements that influence your thinking and ultimately your actions with clients. Notice how your background and self-awareness remain a consideration even though you add research evidence and theory to your repertoire of considerations. Professional thinking is inherently complex and purposeful.

Interrupting Old Thinking Habits

To help with the integration of new thinking skills, it is useful to begin with a focus on the old thinking habits. Integrating new thinking into an ethical and interactive approach to practice is far from a simple enterprise. Although this chapter is focused solely on thinking and knowledge, all subsequent chapters involve some elements of integrating your professional thoughts into client exchanges.

Given the challenges of building a solid professional skill set, do not feel that you should master new habits right away. Thinking skills first must be integrated with your interpersonal skills for them to become seamlessly habitual. You eventually will have to integrate material from all of your professional courses as you build your practice skill foundation. However, at this point, you will learn how identify the interference of old habits to help with identification and interruption. Consider the next elements as you identify methods of disrupting your old thinking habits.

Thinking and Feeling Clues
It is possible to identify habitual thinking based on your emotional responses when listening to a client. Use the list of internal experiences to gauge whether you are using your complex thinking habits or falling back into personal thinking habits.

Figure 3.4

Thinking Influences

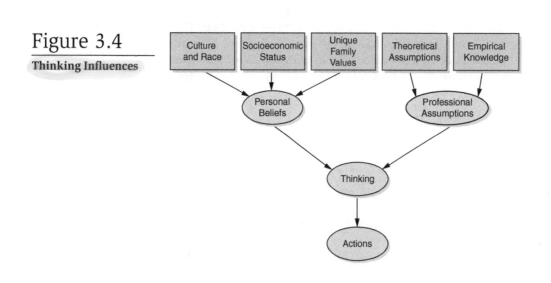

- *Frustration versus patience.* If you find yourself getting frustrated with a client, you may not appreciate the complex pressures inherent in the person's situation. However, if you find yourself calm and open during your exchanges, you are likely open to a more complex understanding.

- *Repulsed versus open.* If you find yourself repulsed or upset about elements in the client situation, you are likely imposing your own values, beliefs, and predetermined understandings. However, if you continue to be open to hearing your client's story, you are likely using complex thinking rather than old models of understanding.

- *Confused versus inquisitive.* If you find yourself confused when listening to your client, it may indicate that you are trying to impose your cognitive frameworks and preexisting understandings onto the situation and they are not fitting. However, if you find yourself inquisitive and mentally trying to piece together elements in the client's story, you are more likely to be open to the complexities of the situation.

- *Certain versus curious.* If you find yourself convinced that you know more about a client's situation than he knows himself, you may be oversimplifying the situation. However, if you find yourself curious about the situation and open to learning more, you are likely to encourage exploration into the complexities and creative options inherent in the situation.

Action Clues

Along with the internal clues, it is possible to identify the emergence of old thinking habits by your impulses to act. Your patterns of action can indicate that you are failing to grasp the complexity of the client situation. Consider the next patterns of activity.

- *Instructing versus exploring.* If you notice that you are spending a lot of time telling clients how they should or should not respond to situations, you probably are working from old thinking habits. However, if you easily construct new questions and your thoughts link well to client statements, you are likely using more complex thinking.

- *Explaining versus listening.* If you find that you are trying to convince clients or explain how your ideas are best for them, you are likely working from your old thinking habits. If your mental energy is invested in listening and understanding clients, you are more likely to be using professional thinking habits.

- *Taking over versus supporting.* If you find that a solution springs to mind and you start implementing your solution rather than helping clients find a resolution, you may be working from old thinking habits. When you find yourself asking clients questions to help them discover their own solutions, you are developing new habits.

As you read these approaches to responding, you will discover that some of the professional values and ethics are inherent in the professional thinking models. Notice a focus on client primacy, self-determination, and allowing clients to direct their service. You will also notice that self-awareness skills are associated with professional thinking. Professional thinking styles must reflect an ethical approach to serving clients.

Developing New Thinking Habits

As we relinquish our socialized thinking habits, we must replace them with new habits. This may be a struggle because you are just beginning to develop your professional thinking skills. Complex cognitive skills require repetition. Initially we are unaware of our thinking processes; however, with practice, our thinking becomes integrated with our consciously controlled mental processes (Verbrugge & Mol, 2008). With practice, you will continually develop new insights and abilities to identify elements in the client situation. These moments occur as your thinking skills become more honed.

As we transition from socialized to professional thinking, our old habits diminish and give way to three professional habits. Professional thinking habits tend to be integrative because we must view situations from multiple angles before we respond. These professional thinking habits involve integrating knowledge, contextual information, and other perspectives during our interaction with clients. You will use three core professional habits in remaining chapters of this book:

1. *Extending perspectives*. The first professional habit is extending your thinking so you can understand situations from other people's perspectives. This habit builds on your ability to be aware and in control of your old thinking habits. To achieve this skill, first you must identify the thinking and perspectives of the other person. Doing this requires you to suspend your beliefs about the situation so you can apply the client's frameworks of understanding. After you identify another person's thinking, the challenge is to apply his or her thinking to the situation. Finally, you must be able to incorporate the person's thinking into your approach to helping so that you do not impose your knowledge and beliefs (Verbeke et al., 2008; Verbrugge & Mol, 2008). This thinking ability provides a foundation for empathy.

2. *Developing situational understandings*. Practitioners integrate multiple elements as they approach client situations. First you must understand the client's perspective, as discussed. As you listen to clients, however, you also use professional knowledge to understand how the elements of the situation link together to explain the problem. This integrated information also provides a direction for change. Developing situational understandings requires you to objectively collect information rather than inserting assumptions. You then assess situations using professional knowledge. Good situational understandings underlie client assessments, treatment contracts, and the selection of intervention strategies.

3. *Maintaining goal directedness*. Practitioners tend to retain goals and situational understandings in the back of their mind as they select strategies and responses. The goals form a filter through which options are assessed; they are not the core focus of mental energy. Your knowledge and theories merge into the filter, allowing you to focus on the client situation while still using your professional knowledge (Waldman, 2007). This ability allows you to stay actively engaged with clients while still responding in a manner that promotes goal achievement.

Exercise 3.4: Helping Peter

(This exercise is a continuation of the previous three exercises.) You are Peter's new case manager. He is now living in an apartment complex downtown where the agency has supported independent living. As you get to know Peter, you begin to appreciate his complexities. You shared your thoughts with Glenna, who stated that he was simple to understand and was just a manipulative man. You are not so sure.

1. What are some of the environmental challenges Peter has had to overcome?

2. Given these challenges, what behaviors may indicate creative adaptations to the environment?

3. How have professionals made these adaptive responses worse rather than better?

4. What limitations does Peter have that might make it harder for him to manage these challenges?

5. How has Peter creatively dealt with his limitations?

6. From what sources does Peter appear to be drawing his meaning in life?

7. How do these sources influence his challenges?

8. What theoretical model did you use to draw these conclusions?

Role of Supervision and Consultation

As we develop our professional thinking, we are lucky to have support. Just as family, friends, teachers, and others helped form our socialized thinking, supervisors and consultants help us refine our professional thinking. In the early stages of our careers, supervisors are critical in our professional development. As we share information about our client work, supervisors ask questions and challenge us to develop strong professional thinking skills.

Supervisors are often busy so it is critical to have access to your supervisor on a regular basis. Most often, new practitioners meet with their supervisor weekly. During these meetings practitioners share information about their clients and solicit input when there are areas of confusion. It is very important to be able to approach supervisors with questions and concerns. A good supervisor will help you develop professional thinking and interactive skills.

Beyond supervision, you will ask others to consult on case situations. Sometimes consultation is informal, such as asking a colleague how she might proceed with a case situation. Formal consultation often involves a trainer or paid consultant. When engaging in consultation, ensure that you maintain your ethical obligations to client rights. You may have to disguise information so your colleagues cannot identify your client. At the same time, it is important to maintain your ethical obligation to your employer. Remember that your supervisor is your formal source of input so you should approach him or her first.

Critical Chapter Themes

1. Practitioners use knowledge gleaned from theory, research, and past practice to develop interventions.
2. The application of knowledge is guided by theory. There are three common theoretical frameworks: biopsychosocial, developmental/life span, and person in environment. These frameworks guide the assessment and the practitioner's understanding of situations.

3. Research is critical in helping to understand and respond to client problems. There are two types of research: quantitative and qualitative.

4. We all have thinking habits that set our cognitive style of understanding situations. Some habits are creative; others, traditional, and others, reactive. We must control our past thinking habits.

5. As professionals, we need to develop new cognitive habits that allow for complex thinking during exchanges with our clients.

Online Resources

Brainteasers Organization—contains thinking development games: www.brainteasers.org/

e-how Thinking Activities: www.ehow.com/thinking-skills-activities/

Foundation for Critical Thinking: www.criticalthinking.org/index.cfm

Social work podcasts and blogs: http://socialworkpodcast.blogspot.com/

Recommended Reading

Balen, R., & White, S. (2007). Making critical minds: Nurturing "not-knowing" in students of health and social care. *Social Work Education*, *26*, 200–206.

Gambrill, E. (2006). *Critical thinking in clinical practice: Improving the quality of judgments and decisions* (2nd ed.). Hoboken, NJ: John Wiley & Sons.

McCracken, S. G., & Marsh, J. C. (2008). Practitioner expertise in evidence-based practice decision making. *Research on Social Work Practice*, *18*, 301–310.

Sternberg, R. J., Roediger, H. L. III, & Halpern, D. F. (2007). *Critical thinking in psychology*. New York, NY: Cambridge University Press.

Taleff, M. J. (2006). *Critical thinking for addiction professionals*. New York, NY: Springer.

Weston, A. (2007). *Creativity for critical thinkers*. New York, NY: Oxford University Press.

Chapter 4
Assessment and Service Contracting

This chapter builds on the first three chapters as we pull together awareness, ethics, thinking, and knowledge to focus the client intervention. This chapter is also dependent on the next few chapters because part of the assessment process involves interviewing and exploring client situations. For this reason, this chapter is precariously placed at the juncture where mental skills and interpersonal skills meet. The placement of this chapter in the book builds on the mental skills. As you read this chapter, bear in mind that assessment ideally occurs within an empathic relationship and employs several interactive skills. In later chapters you will learn to use these skills to explore client situations. These skills are critical elements of any assessment.

Throughout this chapter we explore the thinking and cognitive skills associated with conducting an assessment. Chronologically, these skills are applied after clients have entered service and have committed to engaging with a practitioner. At the point of assessment and contracting, we help clients orient to service by mapping out what service will look like for them. Doing this involves two separate but related procedures:

1. We must develop an understanding of the client situation. Doing so involves an assessment of the problem that underlie the client's entry into service.

2. Based on the assessment, we work with the client to extend this understanding to identify a direction for change. This direction becomes the foundation for developing goals and objectives that can rectify the problem situation.

Professional Affiliation and the Assessment Focus

Assessment, although often considered a static point of service, actually is a dynamic exchange through which practitioners begin to understand what must change in client situations to help them achieve their goals. In its pure form, assessment involves exploring multiple dimensions of the client situation to develop a unified sense of direction. The emergent sense of direction provides an understanding of how best to respond to the client situation. We often identify assessment with the beginning of service; however, our understanding and subsequent direction continues to change as we discover new information during service.

Understanding the Professional Role

Assessment strategies and activities traditionally have varied depending on the practitioner's professional affiliation and role. In Chapter 2 we explored the values and ethics of various professional groups. Our professional affiliation directs how we focus our exploration during assessment. Remember that psychology tends to focus on clients and their internal processes that relate to the situation. Counseling professionals often consider internal processes yet also consider the life span context of clients' adaptations. Nursing and occupational therapy often include some exploration of physical health. Social work is likely to focus on environmental dynamics as part of the assessment. Although these focus shifts are over-simplified, it is important to remember that the values and history of the professional role influence our focus throughout the assessment process.

Limits and Possibilities
In human service organizations, professional affiliation influences the types of assessment we are expected to perform. All professionals help clients manage aspects of their

life; our training provides different professional domains for understanding the dynamic processes within the situations. Consider these dynamic processes that occur in client situations. Each process provides a partial understanding of the client and their challenges. Consequently, restricting our exploration to a single domain limits our potential understanding.

- *Client-level biological processes.* All people are influenced by their biology. Some of us have special abilities and some have disabilities. Concurrently, our diet, exposure to elements, level of activity, metabolism, neurological systems, and physical constitution influence our options within any situation.
- *Client-level cognitive-emotional processes.* Within any given situation, clients have emotional and spirited responses and attribute meaning to events in their life. The interplay of emotion and thinking influences how clients experience this situation. This internal experience in turn influences how clients interact with and behave in the situation.
- *Systemic processes.* Clients do not live in a vacuum. Rather, they are part of multiple systems and networks including families, groups, organizations, and communities. As a member of these systems, clients engage in reciprocal interactions. These dynamic interactions and relationships form patterns and follow predictable paths that influence the client situation.
- *Life span processes.* Clients change in response to the demands and supports that accompany their life stage and current age. As their abilities, demands, resources, and environments change, clients must respond and adapt. If situational elements or past adaptations interfere with their response, problems may evolve.
- *Social processes.* The social environment can exert very powerful influences on the client situation. Some social elements can be supportive (e.g., culture-specific traditions); others can limit clients' ability to respond to their situation (e.g., poverty and structural racism).

As you read the listed process categories, you probably gained a sense of the enormity of a client's potential experience. You also may have gained some appreciation that professionals ideally should understand all of these dynamic forces when assessing the client situation. However, we cannot possibly remain current and competent in all domains. Consequently, professional groups tend to focus on limited domains; interdisciplinary assessments enable us to glean a comprehensive, competent assessment. For this reason, many agencies employ members of several professions.

Influence of Professional Identity and Ethics

As each professional group approaches assessment, discipline-specific competencies, values, and ethics guide the focus and methods employed. It is very important that practitioners in each profession be well versed in the research and knowledge associated with their field. Our command of our professional knowledge base is what allows us to generate an appropriate understanding of the client situation.

Ethically, all professionals must achieve competence in the content areas required for assessing clients. Given the slightly different domains of expertise, each professional group will have specific areas of competence. For example, psychologists and counselors regularly are required to conduct cognitive evaluations on clients. Social work practitioners seldom conduct such assessments but may need to conduct an environmental assessment. Occupational therapists often are engaged to assess the impact of disabilities. Nurses assess physical care needs and capacities. These lists are tremendously incomplete, but it is clear that each professional group must master its basic content competencies.

Beyond professionally specific basic competencies, professionals are also ethically required to master issue-specialized competencies. Some content competencies are job specific. For example, if your position involves working with substance abuse, content areas such as detoxification risk assessment, and substance abuse intervention models are associated with your job.

Toward Interdisciplinary Collaboration

While each professional group has domains of expertise, in agency practice there are high levels of overlap among the professional groups. All groups engage in helping relationships to assist clients master their life situations. When working in interdisciplinary settings, we learn about other professional groups to understand how their domains of competency dovetail with our own. Every group contributes toward client success. Problems arise when professional groups vie for superiority and influence rather than supporting and collaborating across disciplines.

Because there are overlaps and unique domains of competence, collaborating with other professional groups requires us to engage and form interdisciplinary relationships. This outreach is important because each group uses similar language yet the words may have unique meanings for each professional group. As we forge interdisciplinary relationships, we learn the subtleties of each profession. Such exposure and knowledge provides a foundation for collaboration. The next four principles guide the development of interdisciplinary collaboration.

1. *Relationship*. Spend time with other professionals, learning how they approach clients.
2. *Currency*. Remain current on the disciplinary-specific and cross-disciplinary research.
3. *Respect*. Seek input from other professionals when their perspective can help.
4. *Humility*. Sidestep power struggles and competitiveness with other disciplines.

Ethics and Hidden Assessment Functions

Within an agency environment, some assessment functions may extend beyond simply understanding the client situation. These hidden assessment functions can create ethical dilemmas for practitioners when agency or programmatic concerns begin to influence assessment decisions. Consider these three areas where practitioners may experience pressure when making an assessment:

1. *Funding concerns*. Sometimes funding levels are associated with diagnostic categories. For example, some insurance companies limit the number of sessions according to the *Diagnostic and Statistical Manual of Mental Disorders* (*DSM*) system diagnoses (e.g., depression). Similarly, in foster care, the cost per day of service often changes based on behavioral problem assessment results. Practitioners may be pressured to assign different labels to clients to maximize income or minimize expenses.

2. *Programming concerns*. Sometimes agency programs are designed for specific types of clients (e.g., domestic violence). When there are long waiting lists for other services or when a program needs clients, practitioners may be pressured to shape the assessment so clients will be directed into the program.

3. *Litigation concerns*. When an assessment involves identifying potential harm to others, agency administrators may become concerned about the possibility of lawsuits. Practitioners may be pressured to be conservative in assessment recommendations to protect the agency.

Notice in these areas of assessment that the hidden functions result in indirect beneficiaries. When assessing clients, we need to be aware of the hidden beneficiaries and ethical considerations that stem from them. Remember that an assessment or diagnosis remains in a client's files and becomes part of their permanent record. When the primacy of the client's well-being is compromised to serve a secondary beneficiary, the ethical decision-making system in Chapter 2 can be useful in deciding whether to raise concerns with your supervisor or professional association.

Working With Multifactorial Causality

Professional affiliation notwithstanding, all practitioners must be able to understand the client situation. Ultimately, we must be able to explain the nature of the problem and identify what must change to help clients achieve their goals. Doing this requires achieving a balanced understanding of contextual and individual factors as we explore client situations. To achieve this balance, it is important to understand that problems are multidimensional. Although research may indicate that a life event (e.g., exposure to violence) is associated with a problem (e.g., delinquency), many factors shape the development of a problem (e.g., parenting, peers, learning ability, aptitude).

As we proceed toward intervention with clients, it is very important that we understand the factors that contribute to the problem situation. Ultimately, such understandings cover multiple areas of assessment. We need to understand the complex interplay between events and forces inherent in the client situation when we assess and plan intervention. For example, environmental factors such as economic downturns may trigger problems that occur on the individual level. We have all heard of individuals who have been laid off and elect to kill themselves as a solution to their problem situation. Ultimately, a decision to cut production costs was the starting point of the current situation. However, past decisions to drop out of school and to purchase a home may have equal weight in the client's feelings of powerlessness.

Locus of the Problem and Professional Domains

Even though practitioners must have an appreciation of the complex situations that contribute to client problems, there will be different areas of emphasis across professional affiliations. As a result, professional groups tend to locate the problem differentially in the client situation. Counseling and psychology often use psychometric assessment tools and adaptation knowledge bases leading to problem definitions that focus on the individual client. Nursing and occupational therapy identify physical adaptation issues. Social work tends to include many environmental variables in the assessment.

The differences across professional domains should never result in competitive comparisons. Rather, there are slightly different domains of professional expertise. Each professional adopts different priorities when developing the content competencies in Table 4.1. However, all professions develop some understanding of each content area. This results in similarities in the professional domains. When it comes to assessment, it is useful to have multiple perspectives to capture the complexity of client situations. This is why most agencies adopt multidisciplinary approaches to service.

Table 4.1   **Basic Content Competencies and Problem-Focused Variations**

Assessment Area	Basic Content Competencies	Problem-Focused Variations
Biopsychosocial processes	1. Biological processes	1. Substance abuse/addiction
	2. Emotional processes	2. Trauma responses
	3. Cognitive processes	3. Disabilities and handicaps
	4. Psychological adaptation	4. Mental illness (*DSM*-IV)
	5. Human attachment and relationships	5. Physical illnesses
		6. Medications
	6. Trauma effects	7. Interpersonal violence
		8. Sexual perpetration
Person in environment processes	1. Individual adaptation processes	1. Family violence
	2. Culture and ethnicity influences	2. Family system variations
		3. Criminal justice systems
	3. Interactive dynamics	4. Employee supervision
	4. Family dynamics	5. Workplace management
	5. Neighborhood influences	6. Funding systems
	6. Larger system dynamics	7. Community systems/ networks
	7. Community dynamics	

Life span processes	1. Normal developmental sequences	1. Gay/lesbian identity development
	2. Life stage dynamics	2. Gender differences
	3. Identity development	3. Racial group differences
	4. Cultural contexts	
Social processes	1. Political and legislative systems	1. Social oppression
	2. Economic systems and influences	2. Structural racism
		3. Social justice
	3. Social service systems	4. Torture/crimes against humanity
	4. Human rights	

Intervention Options

As a practitioner, your professional position dictates your role in the service setting. For example, in the example of client suicide, the practitioner is well aware of the influence of past trauma. However, if her job is to help the person develop skills for alternative employment, integrating past traumatic events into the professional focus would be difficult and often inappropriate. Frequently, we will identify needs that are not related to our role. Sometimes other professionals will respond to those needs, but often clients must face the unmet needs without professional assistance.

When limitations associated with professional roles interfere with resolving a client problem, it is important to work closely with a supervisor to ensure an adequate response is possible.

Case Example

A child welfare practitioner was working with an African American father who had been laid off from his job in an auto-parts manufacturing plant. He had dropped out of school during grade 7 to take the position and had worked in the plant for 18 years. His decision to work was based on being the oldest child in a sib line of six born to a single-parent, addicted mother. The father had worked hard all his life and married a woman who also worked in the plant. She quit work after having children. The family recently moved to a larger, single-family home in the suburbs. Shortly after the move, the father was laid off. He became frustrated, started drinking, and recently hit his son who was very defiant when his father withheld the car. Although the practitioner identified that the father was a victim of circumstance, her professional role dictated that she help him change how he dealt with his frustration. She also worked closely with her supervisor to find a job retraining program and helped the man enroll.

Assessment Process

Four phases are inherent in the assessment process. These phases involve activities that transition from general statements of need to a dynamic understanding of what must change to improve the client situation. The early phases of assessment involve the interactive skills discussed in subsequent chapters (questioning, reflecting, observing, and directing). Later assessment phases apply our knowledge, theories, and thinking skills to identify contextual issues and individual patterns (behavior, interaction, thinking, and feeling) that contribute to the client problem.

During the assessment process, information is gathered and honed to provide direction for intervention. In Figure 4.1, observe that assessment is like an upside-down triangle. At the top is all of the client information. As the assessment progresses, that information is honed down to the most important information for explaining the problem. That explanation is then honed further to identify intervention direction.

To help understand the dynamics of each assessment phase, they are discussed separately. However, in agency practice, often the steps are blended as we continually gather information, form hypotheses (or hunches), check out our hunches by gathering more

Figure 4.1

**Assessment
Progression**

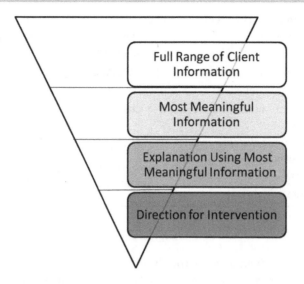

information, and formulate new directions based on the information already gathered. Assessment and intervention is a circular process where our understanding is constantly expanded. However, many agencies insist on a formal assessment as clients enter service. The four phases will help you understand the formal assessment process.

Phase 1: Data Collection

When we first meet clients, we have very little information about their situations. Although there may be some information in agency files from past contacts or other organizations, we must build a relationship with our clients based on their current concerns. Doing this always involves meeting them and exploring the situation. Some theoretical approaches use unique methods of data collection; all require an initial meeting to collect some data on the client situation.

There are four common sources of data when conducting an assessment: (1) interviewing, (2) observing, (3) third-party reports, and (4) psychometric data. Depending on the agency and types of service provided, it is not unusual to include all of these data sources in an assessment. Consequently, it is important to understand how to use all four types of data when conducting your assessments.

Interviewing

Most professional assessments involve some form of interview where a practitioner and client meet to explore the situation. Successful interviews typically require an initial level of client engagement so people are comfortable sharing their story. The interactive skills of data collection are discussed in subsequent chapters; here it is important to understand the critical nature of interactive skills during the assessment process. During assessment, we select very specific and focused questions to explore the situation and build an understanding. Concurrently, we often observe client actions/interactions and use interpersonal skills to clarify and deepen our understanding of the situation.

Depending on the client request and/or size of the client system, practitioners use different skills when conducting the interview. For example, if we are meeting with an individual, we tend to rely on asking questions about the situation and tracking the client's verbal description of the story. With families or couples, we are able to use observation to identify elements of the family system. Similarly, with organizations and communities, we rely more on observation and are selective about who we interview directly.

Interviews are helpful because we have face-to-face contact with the client. This begins the engagement process concurrent with data collection. It also allows us to use observation of nonverbal communication during the data collection. The limitation of interview data collection is the reliance on client verbal self-reporting. If a client is uncomfortable about content areas, he or she may misrepresent information or avoid topics. This can limit the utility of the data that we receive.

During a client interview, we tend to focus on three general areas of inquiry: historical factors, contextual factors, and client responses. These broad categories of inquiry provide a contextualized understanding of the client situation. Reflect on how these elements tend to influence all elements of your life and how important they might be if you were seeking help.

1. *Historical factors.* Historical elements provide a sense of continuity across time and allow us to identify how the problems developed. The client history also provides information about other agencies and supports that have been involved with the client system.
   - *Biological history.* We often want to explore for biological contributors, such as disability, injury, and intergenerational health patterns. These historical elements can be very important to understanding client situations.
   - *Personal history.* We often want to solicit information on clients' personal and relational background, institutional involvements, and developmental highlights leading to the present time.
   - *Cultural history.* All clients have a cultural and ethnic background, even if they are members of the dominant culture. It is important to explore culture to understand reference groups and support systems.
   - *Oppression/trauma history.* Many clients have a background of social injustice, human rights violations, and trauma. Histories may include witnessing death, experiencing torture, refugee experiences, and other events. Such experiences are critical when seeking to understand current situations.
   - *Problem history.* Problems tend to emerge over time. We often want to gather information on the onset, history, duration, and severity of the problem. Doing this allows us to position the emergence of the problem in historical context and track changes in the problem.
   - *History of problem-solving attempts.* Often we want to understand how clients have responded to the problem. Entering service is typically just the latest attempt to resolve a problematic situation. By knowing about past attempts, we can avoid duplicating problem-solving strategies and identify the most promising interventions.
   - *History with the helping system.* Practitioners frequently want to explore other services used in the past. Doing this provides additional sources of assessment information and helps identify patterns of help seeking.

2. *Contextual factors.* Concurrent with the historical context, it is important to understand social contextual factors. Often problems are in response to events in the social environment. Some important contextual elements include:
   - *Social situations and events.* Often it is important to understand client situations within a broader social framework. Issues concerning the economy, community factors, and social oppression influence client options and help explain client responses. Social factors such as culture help identify potential support systems and cautions for selecting interventions.
   - *Systemic functioning.* When working with a larger client system such as work groups and families, it is important to understand how the system and subsystems are functioning.
   - *Support systems.* All clients need a blend of formal, informal, cultural, and kinship supports to function well. From these support systems clients derive emotional, instrumental, informational, and feedback support. Practitioners often want to understand the array of supports and how clients meet their needs for support.
   - *Risk factors.* Practitioners often seek information about what stressors and risk factors have emerged in relation to the problem situation and the sequencing of stresses vis-à-vis the problems. If events such as job loss are involved in the problem situation, there may be some need for environment-focused intervention, such as job training or other options.

3. *Client response patterns*. At the client level, it is useful to consider how the individual responds to the problem situation. There are four response systems: Two influence how the client processes events (affect and thinking), and two dictate the client's actions (interaction and behavior). Understanding all four systems of responding is important during assessment because it helps us focus our intervention.

   a. *Affective responses*. The affective response system focuses on people's feelings. Feelings generate instant responses to situations and events. Everyone can recall times when an action was taken or something was said based on feelings, even though logic cautioned against such action. Some feelings, such as powerlessness, hopelessness, inadequacy, euphoria, and joy, can exert powerful effects on behavioral responses.

   b. *Cognitive responses*. As we explore a situation, it is important to understand how a client interprets its elements and attributes meaning to different events. Client reasons, excuses, and thoughts before and after problematic situations provide important information about how problems emerge.

   c. *Interactive responses*. It is important to understand how clients relate to other people in the situation. Sometimes the nature of the relationships and interactions can provide very important information about the problem situation.

   d. *Behavioral responses*. The behavioral response system focuses on client behavior, or lack thereof, in response to the situation. Behavior typically is observable and measurable, allowing us to judge the frequency and intensity of responses. We also learn about the timing and sequencing of different people's actions.

Observing

Practitioners often observe clients to glean information about interaction or skill performance. Observation is very important when identifying problems associated with injury or disability. It is also useful with larger systems, such as families, groups, organizations, and communities, because we can observe the dynamics among people and units. Observation is useful because we are not relying solely on client descriptions of an event; we witness the actual event. Doing so provides information that includes a fuller range of data (interactions, context, and behaviors).

Depending on the exchanges or skills we want to assess, we sometimes structure the observation. For example, when assessing some skill performances, we may limit the time for performing a task. We may also use systems of interpreting actions or interactions (e.g., types of words used, frequency of themes/behaviors). At times we may want to be invisible (e.g., observing from a distance or through a one-way mirror). There are three common methods of observing client situations:

1. *Naturalistic observation*. We sometimes want to go into the client's environment to observe the context and dynamics of the situation. Doing this can involve interaction through activities such as home visits. Sometimes we want to remain passive when observing (e.g., school observation) so our interactions do not interfere with the dynamics.

2. *In-session observation*. When working with families and groups, we constantly are observing interactive dynamics during the session. Often this observation involves intervention and is part of the ongoing assessment-intervention cycle.

3. *Constructed observation*. Sometimes we construct opportunities to observe clients by assigning a task or event. For example, a practitioner might ask a family to solve a problem, then observe them through a one-way mirror. This method is less natural than the other forms of observation but allows for more structure.

The core limitation to the utility of observational data is our frameworks of interpretation. Observation allows for data collection that is unedited by the client, but we edit the information as we interpret the meaning of client behavior. Consequently, we must monitor our thinking to ensure that we are not inserting our own meanings into the observed data. The risk of misinterpretation increases during cross-cultural observations because we may not have access to the appropriate interpretation systems. When working cross-culturally, it is useful to explore observations with clients to get an indication of the client's interpretation and meaning systems.

Third-Party Reports

Practitioners sometimes want to use information provided by people other than the client. Typically these are people associated with the client situation either currently or in the past. Information may be written, or we may want to conduct live interviews depending on the situation. Such data gathering tends to supplement and support information gathered from the client.

Two cautions are associated with third-party information: First, it is important to understand that the information will be filtered through the client's relationship with the other person. For this reason, there may be assumptions or beliefs that taint the information we receive (e.g., the past practitioner may have had difficulty with the client). The second caution is to ensure that we act within our code of ethics. Ethically, we must always gather such information with the informed consent of the client and in a way that will not disrupt or otherwise harm the third-party reporter or his or her relationship with the client. The three common forms of third-party information include:

1. *Third-party interviews.* Sometimes we want to interview people associated with the client situation (e.g., teachers, estranged parents, relatives). At times such people have a perspective we cannot otherwise access. In such situations, we must protect client rights as we proceed with the assessment. Typically we must ask client permission and secure written permission before approaching the third party.

2. *Third-party reports.* When clients have been involved with other agencies or received service from the agency in the past, we often want access to closing summaries or assessment reports to help understand the client situation. Such third-party reports sometimes are contained in the client file allowing us to read reports prior to the first meeting. If they are not in the file, we must secure for informed consent before soliciting information from other professionals.

3. *Third-party consultation.* We often rely on supervisors or consultants to help us to understand client situations. Sometimes we ask the third party to meet with the client and share their findings (e.g., a psychiatric consult) with us. In other situations we may share case information and solicit input. When we work with supervisors, they are considered part of the intervention team; however, some consultants may require informed consent before you solicit their input.

Psychometric Data

Structured questionnaires, indexes, and other forms of measurement are increasingly common during client assessment. Such measures can be used with client systems of all sizes, so they are very useful whenever engaging in assessment activities. Many psychometric formats are used in assessments, ranging from projective techniques, structured interviews, observations, to scaled questionnaires. For a format to be considered a psychometric assessment tool, typically it has a very structured and standardized method for scoring and interpreting the information. Almost all professional groups use standardized measures; however psychologists and counselors receive specific training and have expertise in using these assessment methods.

Psychometric assessment tools tend to use a list of questions, statements, or activities that will yield a score. Frequently all of the items have an underlying theme (e.g., alcohol use, anxiety, etc.). Some questionnaires will have several scales with a common theme (e.g., behavior checklists). Most often clients are asked to provide a very specific response to each item on the questionnaire. Later scoring yields a numeric value used in interpretation. When practitioners use standardized systems (such as scales or psychometric instruments) to gather data, there are three critical considerations: reliability, validity, and test type. This textbook does not provide an in-depth exploration of psychometrics, but it is important to understand some of these concepts as they pertain to assessing clients.

1. *Reliability*. Reliability is a measure of a tool's consistency. It is important that a tool measure consistently every time it is used. For example, if we want to assess aggressiveness, comparably aggressive children should score about the same. Reliability is scored on a scale from 0 to 1.0 with scores close to 0 indicating a very weak scale and scores near 1.0 reflecting a highly reliable measure. For making clinical judgments about a client, you will want to ensure that the reliability of the scale is .80 or higher. There are multiple types of reliability. You will learn more about reliability in your research classes. For the purposes of this discussion, consider reliability coefficients like someone shooting at a target. If they hit the bull's-eye 90% of the time, they are a good shot. The reliability in this situation would be .90.

2. *Validity*. "Validity" refers to whether the scale is measuring what it is supposed to measure. Even if a measure consistently measures the same way (reliability), you need to be concerned that it is measuring what it is supposed to assess. Like reliability, there are many forms of validity that you will learn in your research classes. For the purposes of this discussion, remember that validity is important. Hitting a target 90% of the time is not useful if the person is shooting at the wrong target. Validity helps us ensure that the target is appropriate.

3. *Test type*. A final consideration when selecting a standardized instrument for assessing clients is the type of test. Three types of tests commonly are used when assessing clients: descriptive, normed, and cutting-score tests.
   a. *Descriptive tests* typically provide information about a client or systemic dynamic. These tests don't indicate problems; they simply identify the presence of some trait such as contentment or rigidity. These scales are not sufficiently developed to provide norms or cutting scores; they simply indicate the level of the attribute that the scale measures. They are best used for assessing the client before service and then again after service to determine the level of change.
   b. *Normed tests* compare the client's responses to a pool of other people to indicate how the client is functioning compared to others. Typically a client's results can be graphed to see how the client differs from people considered "normal." Scoring higher than the normal group often indicates a problem or an area of strength. Scoring in the normal range indicates that the client functions similar to others in this area.
   c. *Cutting-score tests* have critical scores that indicate whether the client is in a problem range or not. If a client scores above this critical score, problems are indicated. Typically cutting scores are developed by comparing groups who have a problem with groups who are considered free from the problem. The cutting score is established where one group's scores drop off and the other groups begin.

Selecting measures for assessment requires careful consideration of the psychometrics and the purpose of the assessment. Many measures allow us to get very specific information about the client situation. However, it takes time to complete measures so we want to be judicious about the number of structured measures we include in our assessments. Spending more than 30 minutes completing measures may become a burden for clients. We typically want to use a few well-selected measures rather than including multiple instruments.

It is also important to understand that the use of some measures requires specific training or credentials. Psychology and counseling professions tend to include more training on using these types of measures; it is not unusual for instrument publishers to limit the availability of complex measures to certain types of professionals or people with specific training.

Although measurement tools are helpful in achieving a numeric score of client attributes, it is important to remember that often the measure has a very narrow focus. For example, a measure of child abuse risk may provide a good assessment of parental hostility toward a child. However, the measure may ignore parental stress, past trauma, and other important considerations. Measures are like trying to guess a picture by looking at a small section. They provide a good view of that small section, but the rest of the picture may be unclear. Also, many measures are developed on specific groups and may not be appropriate for specific clients or cultural groups.

Data Collection with Larger Client Systems

The nature of data collection changes depending on the size of the client system. Table 4.2 contains content variations for client systems of different sizes. When reading this table, pay attention to the progressive shift to systemic subcomponents and dynamics as the size of the client system becomes more complex. Increased complexity makes it harder to collect information through interviewing and necessitates some data collection through observation.

Table 4.2   Common Content Areas of Data Collection for Different Client Systems

Individuals	Family	Groups	Organizations	Communities
Historical Elements				
• Personal history • Relational history • Meaning attributions re: historical events • Problem development • Moves and relocations • Problem-solving attempts • Help seeking history • Past/current history of oppression or violation	• Personal history of adults up to couple stage • Development of couple relationship • Addition of children and adaptations • Problem development • Past solution attempts • Past/current oppression or violation	• Personal history • Problem development • Problem-solving attempts • Member social relationships • Member past group experience • Member past/current oppression or violation experience • Group formation • Group developmental milestones	• Organizational inception • Developmental milestones • Organizational changes • Subcomponent histories • Current situation development • Relational histories • Subgroup development and functioning • Past/current oppression or violation	• Community inception • Developmental milestones • Boundary change history • Impactful events • Problem development • Past adaptations or problem solving • Subcomponent development and functioning • Critical community elements • Past/current oppression or violation
Contextual Elements				
• Cultural background • Demographic influences (age, race, gender) • Socioeconomic status • Community and neighborhood dynamics • Support systems	• Parental cultural backgrounds • Community participation and emersion • Parental demographics (age, race) • Economic activity and resources • Relationship to dominant culture • Kinship systems • Support systems	• Cultural background • Demographic influences (age, race, gender) • Cross-cultural relationships and past experiences • Context of problem occurrence • Social networks and groups	• Cultural groups and dynamics • Demographic influences (age groups, racial groups, gender distribution) • Relationship to funding sources • Task and mission accomplishment • Boundary maintenance • Community integration and networks	• Cultural groups and interactions • Cultural group support systems • Community demographics (average age, racial groups, etc.) • Economic activity and opportunities • Community resources • Viability of community systems
Systemic Response Elements				
• Affective processing patterns • Belief systems and values	• Emotional climate and processing • Tension management	• Group atmosphere • Group cohesion • Tension management • Shared beliefs	• Organizational climate • Organizational mission and subsystem adherence • Subsystem functioning and contributions	• Community efficacy • Management of difference • Intergroup relations and interactions

(continued)

Table 4.2 (*Continued*)

Individuals	Family	Groups	Organizations	Communities
• Attribution and interpretation patterns • Interaction patterns • Relationships with others • Behavior patterns • Frequency, severity, and duration of problem behaviors	• Subsystem functioning (parent, spouse, sibling) • Family task accomplishment • Boundary maintenance • Involvement of fictive kin and supports • Member and difference management • Power and control systems	• Norms and member expectations • Interaction patterns • Role distributions and flexibility • Decision making • Managing difference • Member control and power dynamics • Leadership dynamics • Authority dynamics	• Systemic organization • Decision-making and input systems • Information management and sharing • Accountability systems	• Community management • Member development options • Boundary management and social integration • Access to decision makers • Safety and control • Community responsiveness • Support and recreation

Cultural and Social Implications

As we collect data, it is very important to understand cultural and social contexts that can influence data collection (Shmelvov & Naumenko, 2009). Many assessment protocols are developed with a dominant cultural bias. As we approach clients, we often assume that our assessment strategies are culturally unbiased. This is not an accurate assumption. Although many cultural and social groups will adapt to our methods, some cultural groups and people with diverse backgrounds may find assessment protocols rude or oppressive. It is very important to be open to diverse perspectives so we can adjust our approach to data collection. Consider the next elements of diversity.

- *Cultural groups.* Some cultures find too many questions rude and intrusive. They often prefer less direct methods of data collection. For example, a children's mental health agency with two Native American reservations in its catchment area found that very few Native American families completed their referrals for service because the agency sent every family a package of standardized measures to complete prior to scheduling an interview. The families experienced the measures as impersonal and rude. The agency eventually had to develop a different intake protocol for its Native American referrals.

- *Oppression and human rights violations.* Some client populations, especially immigrant populations, have had experiences of past abuses by governments or social agents. As these populations approach agencies for service, they will experience higher levels of mistrust than families within the dominant culture. Measures, assessment results, and the contents of the client file will be areas of concern. It is important to screen for a possible history of violations or oppression and adjust the data collection procedures so that clients can disclose information as they become comfortable.

- *Relationship with dominant culture.* Many racial, economic, and cultural groups have a strained relationship with the dominant culture. As members of these groups enter an assessment, they may be very suspicious about how their information will be used. It is important to remember that an assessment results in a permanent record; groups that experience tension with the dominant society may be hesitant about disclosing some information. It may be important to explore the types of information that such groups want to exclude from the record so you can understand the situation while still responding to client concerns.

Phase 2: Data Weighting

After data collection, we end up with a lot of information about the client situation. Consequently, the second phase in the assessment process is to separate important information from information that does not deepen our understanding of the situation. In this phase we identify information elements in the client story that warrant further reflection and consideration. This process involves applying our theories and professional knowledge to the client story.

The first step in this phase is to identify information in the client situation that seems important for deepening our understanding. Identification begins as the client shares his or her story and our thinking is activated by elements of the story. These activation triggers can come from diverse aspects of professional practice. Some aspects hinge on the client's presentation of information, some on professional knowledge, and others from past practice experiences. Five common triggers for identifying information worthy of further consideration include:

1. *Repeated themes or patterns*. Repeated elements, patterns, processes, or themes in the client story often suggest importance.

2. *Nonverbal indications of importance*. Nonverbal indicators of client meaning, such as tonal changes, watering of the eyes, and clenched fists while talking, often indicate that the information being shared has some importance to the client.

3. *Convergence with evidence*. We often find that the client story reminds us of articles that we have read, which helps us to identify potentially important elements.

4. *Theoretical consistency*. When client information fits our preferred theories or frameworks of understanding, we draw on theoretical assumptions to determine meaningful from meaningless information.

5. *Past practice*. Many practitioners have developed habits of working and select information for further consideration based on what they traditionally consider during the assessment phase.

In reading this list, you can see that some activation triggers can easily lead you to assessment frameworks. An assessment framework uses linear thinking skills to apply knowledge to the client story. We apply our professional knowledge by identifying the most important elements of the client situation. Then we use the knowledge to create linkages among story elements to help explain the nature of the client problem. Ultimately, we are seeking to use knowledge to create a dynamic understanding of how the elements of the situation interact to create and maintain the problems. Four common frameworks are applied: (1) existing evidence, (2) existing theories, (3) the *DSM* system, and (4) practice wisdom.

Using Evidence

In Chapter 3 we discussed the different types of evidence in the professional literature. It is important that we use these sources of knowledge when assessing the client situation so we can select the most promising interventions (McNeese & Thyer, 2004). As we use evidence, we identify elements in the client situation that indicate that the problems are consistent with those of known client populations. Three aspects of the client story can help us apply empirical knowledge: causal events, adaptive responses, and symptomatic clusters.

1. *Causal events*. Often client problems occur in response to events or situations. These events can lead us to identify sources of knowledge that promote understanding and to determine possible interventions. When we review the client situation, it is useful to explore the causal events to identify whether they can help explain the problem (e.g., past trauma). If the causal events converge with available knowledge, intervention options become apparent.

2. *Adaptive responses*. As we review the actions and thinking that clients use to adapt to their situations, we can identify specific problem-solving strategies in the client

information. When obvious patterns emerge, we are able to identify elements in the adaptive response associated with the current distress. When we understand how clients have adapted, we can use our knowledge base to explain how the adaptations are related to the problems and identify potential interventions.

3. *Symptomatic clusters*. When we identify groups of symptoms we can turn to the literature to understand the underlying problem. Often clusters of symptoms are identified in the research of client problems. We consider the research leading us to potential explanations and problem definitions. For example, a child may be defiant, withdrawn, and moody. As we read the literature, we discover that this can be caused by past abuse, physical disorders such as learning disabilities, and parenting problems. When we consider these symptom-related findings, we are guided to explore other elements of the situation to clarify the possible problems.

As we use evidence to help understand the client story, our knowledge base brings focus to the wealth of information already provided. The application of knowledge helps us to select potentially related information as we reflect on the client situation. When we base decisions on valid research, it is easier to communicate across professional groups because most research is broadly accepted. Evidence-based knowledge often has an added benefit of providing possible directions for intervention.

Although evidence-based decisions provide a valid foundation for our judgments, it is important to understand that many of our clients do not fit the research. Some client problems have yet to be researched. Likewise, many clients have multiple problems that make their situations a difficult fit with the available research. We often have to draw some ideas from the research and adapt them to our practice experience to guide our selection of important material.

Using Theory

This discussion of theory is presented as distinct from the evidence-based discussion, but the two domains of knowledge overlap. Many research studies are based on theoretical assumptions. As such, most evidence is linked to a theory that guides the study. By understanding the theories underlying the research, we can identify empirically supported theories from those that have no evidentiary support. Ideally, we will draw on well-supported theories and shy away from ungrounded ones.

Theories are very useful during the assessment phase because they contain concepts that are logically linked together. As we reflect on elements of the client situation, we can use theory to attach elements of information. For example, social learning theory suggests that childhood exposure to violent parents results in children abandoning assertive responding in favor of demanding aggressiveness (Kalmuss, 1984; McCord, 1988). Given this link between the past and the present, when we assess an aggressive child whose mother left the father due to past abuse, we can comfortably consider the aggression and the violence exposure to both be important factors in the problem. When using theory to identify important informational elements, consider these aspects of the theory:

- *Concepts/Constructs*. Theories contain concepts or constructs working together to explain phenomena. Typically there will be several concepts that are important to understanding the theory. For example, systems theories tend to focus on boundaries, subsystems, energy exchanges, and other concepts. As we review client information, we often use the theoretical concepts to organize our thinking. There are three types of concepts in theories: main, moderating, and mediating. Each is important when understanding and assessing clients.
  - *Main concepts* include events or elements that are central to understanding the theory. For example, in social learning theory, it is often assumed that exposure to violence (first concept) in the family leads to violent behavior in children (second concept).
  - *Moderating concepts* include elements that influence the direction and strength of another concept. For example, research finds that if a child receives social support, the relationship between violence exposure and the development of violence decreases in strength.

○ *Mediating concepts* account for the influence between one concept and another. For example, it is assumed that children learn that they can get their own way by using violence. Consequently, learning how to achieve outcomes might be included as a mediating concept because it reinforces the use of violence.

• *Linkages*. In most theories, the concepts are linked together in an order that explains the phenomenon. The links depict the relationship that one concept has with the others. There are four very common types of relationships or links between concepts:

a. *Chronological links*. If we were sketching the concepts, chronological links would be the arrows that link concepts in order from left to right. Typically, the concepts on the left occur at an earlier time. The earlier concepts most often influence the later concepts, eventually explaining the end-result problem. These links often are used to depict linear phenomenon.

b. *Hierarchical links* tend to show how one concept or construct provides a foundation for additional constructs. With organizations and families, the highest levels of a hierarchy often are presented at the top of a page with other levels depicted in succession below.

c. *Circular links* tend to be used to show how one concept influences subsequent concepts or events, which in turn will influence the original concept (often at a later time). These links depict cyclical phenomena and are drawn in a circular form.

d. *Reciprocal links* depict bidirectional relationships where one concept influences another, which in turn influences the first concept. For example, a supportive relationship promotes prosocial behavior in a child. Prosocial behavior in turn increases positive supportive exchanges with others.

The array of concepts and links leads to theoretical explanations about how phenomena occur. As we review client information, the theoretical assumptions immediately cause us to identify specific information elements as potentially important. As we identify a possible link between a client event and a theoretical construct, we note the possibility and then monitor for other evidence that the link is meaningful. We do this with multiple links, bearing in mind that the explanation can be biological, psychological, environmental, or social in cause.

Case Example

Consider working with a young man with developmental disabilities referred due to outbursts in the sheltered workshop. During the assessment we learn that he was exposed to domestic violence in the past. We are likely to identify this exposure as important, given that it may help explain the outbursts. We also consider the effects of the disability and how they interact. We then monitor for other elements that help us confirm the disability and violence exposure effects. As we identify other important elements, we continue the identification and monitoring functions with each one.

Theoretical sorting of information is common among practitioners. This method often is selected because it is easy and consistent. The ease and consistency should also bring cautions, however. Many theories are not well grounded in research. Consequently, the theories may be constructs of people's imagination rather than well-established systems of understanding client situations. Ethically, we must make our practice judgments on the most rigorous sources of information.

Using the DSM System

Increasingly professionals are expected to use the *Diagnostic and Statistical Manual* as part of the assessment process. The *DSM* system was developed by the American Psychiatric Association as a tool for diagnosing mental illnesses based on symptom clusters. Practitioners using the *DSM* system explore the client symptoms and compare them to the manual to diagnose the client's problems. This method of assessment has strong links to medical practice and is very influential in most agencies that take third-party reimbursement through Medicaid or health insurance companies.

The *DSM* system is organized around four primary axes, each identifying a specific range of problems. The axes were developed through an analysis of how psychiatric symptoms tended to cluster together. This analysis allowed the developers to identify specific clusters of symptoms that tended to emerge together. The *DSM* committee then explored the clusters of symptoms and sorted them into different categories or axes. The four axes include:

Axis 1. Clinical and major disorders such as psychosis (schizophrenia, bipolar disorder), depression, and developmental disorders

Axis 2. Pervasive personality conditions such as personality disorders (borderline, narcissistic, antisocial, etc.) and mental retardation

Axis 3. Medical conditions and physical diseases

Axis 4. Psychosocial factors and environmental conditions that contribute to the problems

When we use the *DSM* system to assess clients, our primary focus is on the presenting symptoms. The exploration is very focused as we attempt to rule various diagnostic options either in or out. We commonly explore four features of client symptoms, which help us rule out some disorders while giving clues toward providing the most accurate diagnosis:

1. *Symptoms*. We want to get a full descriptions of all symptoms associated with the problem. Examples of symptoms include manifestations such as behaviors, interactions, perceived interactions, feelings, visual images, or thoughts.

2. *Symptom onset*. We attempt to understand the age of symptom emergence and the life events that appeared to accompany the development of symptoms. The timing of symptoms is very important for diagnosing some disorders.

3. *Symptom severity*. We typically want to understand how the symptoms disrupt the client's life. Consequently, we explore the impact and severity of the symptoms and any changes in severity across situations.

4. *Symptom duration*. Often the symptoms must be in evidence for a period of time before they are considered a feature of a disorder. Consequently, we want to explore how long the symptoms have been evident and any fluctuations in the symptoms since their emergence.

As we gather information during our client interview, we must constantly check the symptom information against the criteria in the *DSM* manual. We strive to find the cluster of symptoms and symptom dynamics that best correspond with a specific diagnosis. With experience, we often have some indication of the nature of the problem (e.g., someone reporting that she hears voices is likely schizophrenic) so we do not constantly have to search through the manual. We do, however, use the manual to finalize and confirm our diagnosis.

The *DSM* system is well accepted in the field and often linked to funding sources, making it a preferred method of weighting information in many settings. The difficulty in using the *DSM* emerges in the permanence associated with a psychiatric diagnosis. When clients are diagnosed, it remains a label in their file for life. This can be problematic, especially if the diagnosis is in error. Errors are common in some *DSM* categories because the weighting of data is symptom based. The same symptom can be present in many diagnoses, which elevates the risk of errors.

Developing Practice Wisdom

Experience is important in developing our instincts about which elements of information are most important. Early in our careers we have very little experience so we must rely on our supervisor or consult with more experienced practitioners to help sort through the array of information provided by our clients. As we approach others with questions, we can integrate their responses into our skill sets to help sharpen our data collection and weighting skills.

As we gain practice experience, we can begin to match our past experiences with our knowledge base. We begin to use information and techniques that worked well with past clients to inform our judgments with future clients. The integration of knowledge, new information, and experience is the foundation of our lifelong learning. As our experience expands, we are better able to identify important information.

Using practice wisdom often becomes second nature. Practice wisdom is consequently a double-edged sword. On one hand, it helps us quickly identify important information when exploring the client situation. On the other hand, we run the risk of assessing clients based on our past experience rather than on our knowledge base. To avoid this issue, we must continue to merge our experience with the professional knowledge base.

To keep our assessment skills sharp, it is important to expand our knowledge base by continually reading and integrating new information into our practice wisdom. As we develop our practice wisdom, the nature of supervision changes. We no longer seek wisdom from our supervisor; rather, we begin to seek stimulation. Supervision can become a time when we explore new findings and discuss the best methods for using our information during assessment and treatment planning.

Cultural and Social Implications

As we develop our skills of weighting client information, it is important to remain aware of cultural and social dynamics. There is a risk of inserting our cultural bias as we attribute meaning to specific informational elements. Most of our knowledge and practice wisdom will be developed within our cultural cocoon. Cultural assumptions, priorities, and experiences silently influence our thinking, creating many unacknowledged biases in how we respond to client information. Even the *DSM* system has some cultural bias as many professionals involved in developing the manual practice in North America.

When we work with people from other cultures, we must mistrust our linear thinking as we apply knowledge to the client situation. Linear thinking tends to lead us to simple connections where we match elements in the client situation to our knowledge. However, this simple match may not be accurate in some situations. The risk of a mismatch is highest when we are working with clients whose culture, racial background, social, or economic situation diverges significantly from dominant models. In such situations we must reflect carefully on alternative interpretations for client responses.

For example: You are working in a homeless shelter. An elderly African American man with an apparent walking disability has just moved into the shelter and has had an altercation with two Caucasian men in the lounge. As you enter the room, the man looks at you and says, "They [the men] are evil. They are trying to get me. I listen to the 'larger world' and I know evil when I see it." The man's enunciation was difficult to follow, and his use of language seemed somewhat primitive. You were close enough to notice no obvious signs of alcohol impairment.

In this example, you have very little information. In such volatile situations, practitioners often screen first for substance abuse and then immediately draw on the *DSM* knowledge base, suspecting a possible mental illness. Although there are many addicted and mentally ill people living in homeless shelters consider, some of the possible explanations for this man's responses include:

- *Past racism.* The client may have had multiple experiences of oppression and racism. Although he has difficulty expressing himself, his statements may be a result of these racist experiences. It is possible that the other men said something to trigger a reaction.

- *Low income.* The client may have grown up in a low-income neighborhood. His schools may have been underfunded, and he may have needed to drop out to earn money. This can influence his expressiveness, especially when he is angry.

- *Culture.* Some cultures are more emphatic in how they express themselves. His agitation may be a result of cultural expressiveness rather than anger or paranoia.

- *Spirituality.* Some cultures are very spiritual and have different levels of connectedness to the spiritual world. It may be that the listening to the "larger world" is due to a different spiritual connection.

Notice that there are multiple possible explanations for most behaviors and responses. We cannot always trust that our knowledge is appropriate, given the cultural and racial diversity among our clients. It is important to use nonlinear thinking to consistently question our conclusions in light of social, economic, racial, and cultural differences.

Phase 3: Formulating the Dynamic Assessment

As we identify and organize the most meaningful information, it is important to reflect and think about how the different data elements fit together with the problem situation. As we reflect on the possible linkages between the findings and the problem, we consider possible interpretations and configurations as we attempt to find a plausible explanation of the problem situation. Through this reflection, we link the meaningful information to the presenting problem in a way that explains the nature of the problem.

This assessment phase is referred to as dynamic because the goal is to identify elements of the situation that are connected and changeable. We want to understand the connections among events and experiences to determine how the pieces fit together and influence each other. Through this understanding, we can begin to identify elements in the client situation that can and should change. There are three aspects to the dynamic assessment: the situational explanation, the client needs, and the service direction.

Situational Explanation

The first element in a dynamic assessment is the explanation. If we cannot explain how the situation exists and is maintained, it is difficult to identify a direction for intervention. Our explanation should identify behaviors, thoughts, and environmental factors that can resolve the problems with change. If we identify biological elements, we also identify the need for interdisciplinary collaboration to help the client.

As we move into explanation, we employ our thinking skills to integrate the meaningful information into a coherent explanation. As a clear understanding of the problem emerges, we tie the various elements of the situation together. These ties involve linking events and behaviors in a way that explains how the problem exists and what needs to change to help the client master the situation. Often we integrate several influences to achieve a satisfactory explanation.

- *Biological influences.* In a biopsychosocial assessment, it is important to consider possible biological contributions. Many problems have a biological element that must be considered lest we waste time and money on ineffective interventions.

- *Chronological influences.* Sometimes problems have emerged over a long period of time. For example, a traumatic event can shape emotions and thinking. Likewise, dropping out of school often influences a client's economic options. As we integrate the client's history, we try to identify pivotal events that might shape the current situation.

- *Adaptive influences.* Past solutions to problems often emerge as subsequent problems as situations change (Watzlawick, Weakland, & Fisch, 1974). As we integrate the client's history, it is useful to consider past solutions to problems and reflect on how those solutions might inhibit responses in the current situation.

- *Reactive influences.* Sometimes client responses involve emotional reactivity to elements in the situation (Docherty, St-Hilairen, Aakre, & Seghers, 2009). As we integrate these influences, it is useful to understand past events that promote the reactivity concurrent with elements in the recent situation that trigger the response (Skowron, Stanley, & Shapiro, 2009).

- *Attributional influences.* Frequently the meaning attributed to past events and experiences sets a framework of interpretation that can lead to problems or, alternatively, prevent problematic reactions (McNulty, O'Mara, & Karney, 2008). As we explore the client's history, we want to integrate how the person has interpreted past events and how these interpretations influence the current situation.

- *Reciprocal influences.* Sometimes problems are caused by relationships where one person or element in the situation conflicts with another person or element. These situations often contain reciprocal influences, where each element escalates the problematic responses in the other. As we integrate the multiple people and elements in the situation, it is important to consider possible reciprocity among the people and elements involved.

- *Environmental influences.* Sometimes problems are maintained or moderated by elements in the client's environment. One of the most critical environmental elements is support. If support is not forthcoming, stress tends to mount and problems may emerge in the client's relationships (Sachs-Ericsson, Cromer, Hernandez, & Kendall-Tackett, 2009). If a lack of support is accompanied by harsh negative judgments, stress and difficult reactions increase (Willemen, Schuengel, & Koot, 2009).

Identifying Needs

Concurrent with the situational influences, we often find that unmet client needs are a central element of their difficulties. Needs are different from event-based influences; an unmet need indicates a gap where a resource is required. Resources can be internal (e.g., emotional regulation, frameworks of understanding) or external (e.g., an income, education, safety). When we assess a client situation, it is important to consider the unmet needs as part of the dynamic understanding because many situations will require resolving the unmet need. These types of needs often emerge in client situations:

- *Collaboration needs.* Many client situations are complex and require collaborators. Clients may require referrals to medical practitioners, other professionals, and/or spiritual or cultural supports to effectively resolve the situation. As we develop an understanding of the situation, we consider the formal and informal support systems that can be used to resolve it.

- *Cultural needs.* Clients who are members of a minority culture such as sexual orientation, religious, or racial group often become alienated or isolated. Sometimes it is important to work in partnership with cultural resources or help clients connect to them. At other times, we need to consider the cultural needs as we begin planning an intervention strategy.

- *Basic needs.* Every client has basic needs that must be met for survival. Food, shelter, health, and safety are excellent examples of these types of need. If these needs are not met, we have no foundation to build on. In that case, changes in other areas likely will not be successful because clients' attention will shift back to the foundational needs (Raikes & Thompson, 2005). After we identify unmet foundational needs, we must focus on meeting them before we attempt to deal with more esoteric goals.

- *Promotional needs.* All clients require resources that can be mobilized to help them meet their goals (Barnett, 2008; Kasper, Hill, & Kivlighan, 2008). Resources may include support, money, education, or other elements that will help them take action toward achieving their goals. These needs involve resources beyond foundational need level. For example, we all need money to survive (pay rent, buy food, cover utilities, etc.). However, to meet our promotional goal of becoming a helping professional, we also need money for tuition.

- *Affirmation needs.* Clients must feel valued and affirmed as they grapple with life's problems (Creswell et al., 2005). If clients' situations contain no validation or affirmation, often they cannot identify their strengths and skills. Without strengths and skills, their lives are filled with nothing but shame and problems. It is very difficult for clients to focus energy on mastering challenges when they cannot identify strengths to build on. As we integrate information about client situations, we must be aware of how the environment affirms, or fails to affirm, their strengths (Reibeiro & Cook, 1999). Often we must search for potential sources of affirmation in client situations.

- *Motivational needs.* A final category of need is motivation. Even if all of the other needs are met, if clients cannot muster enough motivation to focus their energy toward a goal, they may fail to achieve the goal (Niemiec, Ryan, & Deci, 2009; Poynor & Haws, 2009). Somewhere in client situations, it is critical to find motivating emotions or relationships.

Exercise 4.1: Working With Information to Infer Influence

Think about your upbringing and family life when you were a child. Begin with writing down any biologically based challenges or genetically derived challenges that emerged during your childhood.

In the next worksheet, write down significant events during your childhood. Include such events as losses, traumas, exciting, or fun times. After listing events, jot down patterns that existed in your family. Include patterns of problem solving, supporting each other, expressing emotion, and other patterns that come to mind. Do not list great detail; simply jot down a few words to remind you of the events and patterns.

Events		Patterns	

After completing your lists, think about how you developed and your current patterns of living and responding in relationships. Use a biopsychosocial or person-in-environment theory (whichever fits best) to identify the events and patterns in your life that influenced your development. Circle the events that had the greatest impact on your motivation to succeed. Next consider how you function in your romantic relationships. Take a moment to underline the events and patterns that influenced those relationships.

Now look at the events and patterns that you have circled, and reflect on how they helped to shape your current patterns of relating to others. In the next space, briefly assess the influence of these events on your life.

Finally, identify one element that you might want to change to make your romantic relationships better. Do not write it down; just reflect on how the patterns and events lead to habits that influence your life and how they can be the focus of change.

Phase 4: Identifying Service Direction

The final step in the assessment process is to identify a direction for intervention. In some assessments, we are expected to make service recommendations; in others, we must identify specific changes to be made in the client situation. Regardless, the assessment should build on Phase 3, linking necessary changes to important elements in the situation. When providing the treatment direction, we highlight the important elements identified in the dynamic assessment, then identify what must change to correct the problem.

As we reflect on the client information, we begin to identify the elements that require change. The direction emerges as we apply our knowledge of interventions that might best help the client. Often this involves considering the evidence-based interventions used in situations similar to those the client is facing. This process works best when we can clearly categorize the problem type. Most often evidence-based practices are designed for specific client populations, such as traumatized adults, people with schizophrenia, and acting-out juvenile delinquents. Notice how these examples refer to a problem and a population. We can find evidence-based practices by searching in the literature or online intervention sites to identify practices that work with specific types of problems. Some online sites include:

- CWLA's Research to Practice
     www.cwla.org/programs/r2p/default.htm
- National Registry of Evidence-Based Programs and Practices
     www.nrepp.samhsa.gov
- The Campbell Collaboration
     www.campbellcollaboration.org/
- The Cochrane Collaboration
     www.cochrane.org
- Bandolier Database
     www.jr2.ox.ac.uk/bandolier/index.html
- Center for Reviews & Dissemination
     www.york.ac.uk/inst/crd/welcome.htm
- What Works Clearinghouse
     http://w-w-c.org/

When we work with populations for which there is little guiding evidence, we must rely on our logical thinking capacities to identify elements in the situation that should change (e.g., family, support systems, thinking, etc.). As such, we rely on thinking skills as we identify elements that sustain the problem (e.g., interpretive frameworks, relationships, weak muscle groups, neurological processing, etc.). These problem-sustaining elements provide indications of the necessary changes to correct the situation. These changes are associated with interventions and services that can facilitate the changes.

The service direction often concludes the assessment in the form of recommendations. Some assessments recommend specific types of service or methods of intervention; others suggest specific changes in the client situation. The way you present the recommendations will vary according to your professional role. If you are a case manager, you may focus more on the types of service. However, if you are working in a clinical role, often you will identify changes that clients can make in how they respond to their situations.

Documenting the Assessment

After we complete the mental work inherent in the assessment, often we must write an assessment report. When documenting the assessment, we structure the report so people can easily read and understand the client situation. Typically, practitioners use section titles to help organize the assessment. Although the structure tends to change according to the type of setting and agency procedures, the next list presents headings that are common to assessment reports. Because reports are shared among professionals, it is important to proofread and revise an assessment report to ensure professional-level writing.

Headings Common in Assessment Reports

- Background or Presenting Request
  - In general terms, document the purpose of the assessment. Make sure you include a description of the events leading up to the assessment and the intended recipient of the assessment.
- Assessment Procedures
  - Describe the assessment procedures used (e.g., what scales, how often and where you met with the family, did you do any observations [when and where with whom], what third-party information was used [e.g., files, informants [make sure releases are in order]).
  - You may also include a paragraph on how the client responded to the assessment procedures (e.g., Was the person hesitant or easy to engage? Did he or she complain or try to verbally influence you to believe certain things? If you use a lie scale or social desirability measure, what were your findings? How do all of these considerations impact the validity of the statement?).
- Client (Family, Couple) History
  - Often this section is difficult to write because there is a lot of information to organize. It is useful to use frameworks for organizing this information, both during the interview and in the report.
  - One framework for organizing historical information is the beginning, middle, and end framework. Divide the history into three sections: (1) the early period before any problems existed, (2) the period when problems were developing or becoming evident, and (3) the current state of the problem. These sections will change from client to client, but by thinking in three time slots, you can keep from getting lost in the details.
- Findings
  - Introduce the important findings from the assessment procedures and make sense of each in light of the client's history. Keep sentences simple and direct to allow for easy comprehension. For example, with a couple that is having difficulty resolving problems, you might say, "Both Bob and Velma had elevated problem-solving scores on the Couple's Interactional Style Inventory. These elevated scores indicate that both Bob and Velma tend to avoid problems rather than directly addressing their concerns as a couple. This finding is consistent with their backgrounds. Because both Bob and Velma's families are very volatile, we can expect that this may be a weakness in their relationship."
  - When the findings are associated with interviews and observations, it is useful to use frameworks for organizing the information. The response system framework (action, interaction, beliefs, feelings) is useful, especially when working with individual clients. With families, practitioners often use family subsystems such as the marital dyad, the sibling system, and the parents to organize the information.
  - With groups and organizations, structural frameworks (roles, hierarchy, decision making, authority, procedures/norms, etc.) and interpersonal dynamics frameworks (atmosphere, tension management, interpersonal communication patterns, etc.) are useful.
- Assessment
  - Here we build on the findings to tease out what is actually occurring for the client. At this point we can write our conclusions, as long as they fit with the documented findings. For example: "Bob and Velma seem to be having problems with problem solving. When they attempt to resolve differences, such as whether they wanted to buy a dog, it was noted that each tended to select a different problem and argue the

case (Bob did not want to be saddled with the responsibility and Velma wanted to relieve the children's grief about losing the last dog). This pattern makes it difficult for the couple to define a single problem and generate options. Both Bob and Velma expressed a commitment to the relationship but at times of significant opinion differences, arguments escalate through increasing volume and beginning their statements with words like "You" and "Always." Arguments consequently become hurtful exchanges. These problem-solving challenges appear to be based in both families of origin."

- Often the documentation challenge in this section is avoiding jumble and jargon. It is useful to make short, clear statements and then ground them in the data that lead you to your conclusion. Grounding statements in findings is important if other professionals (e.g., lawyers) are going to challenge the assessment. Notice in the Bob and Velma example how conclusions were illustrated by descriptions. This level of description clarifies the conclusion and allows the reader to understand through illustration.

- Recommendations
  - Recommendations document the changes in the client system that will need to occur to resolve the situation. It is important to outline the actual changes that must occur before discussing any type of service. For example: "The couple needs to develop a system for solving problems and settling differences. Currently, no system is in place other than yelling and blaming each other. The cycle of arguing can be interrupted through acquiring skills such as tabling, exploring, and selecting/implementing solutions. Couple counseling is recommended to help them to improve their problem solving."

Cultural and Social Considerations

Many health and human services are funded through federal and state legislation. For this reason, the nature of service is heavily influenced by values of the dominant culture. For example, child abuse laws were promoted largely by middle-class advocates in the early 1900s, and domestic violence legislation was influenced by the women's movement through the 1960s and 1970s. Likewise, mental health and disability legislation was expanded in the 1960s and 1970s when large public institutions were sued and dismantled for being oppressive and restrictive.

When working with nondominant cultural groups, it is important to understand that their approaches to mental health, disabilities, child rearing, problem solving, and family life may vary from those of the dominant society. When minority cultures and racial groups are assessed, often subtle conflicts exist between the values that underlie the services and the client's values. Some areas of conflict include:

- *Systems of sanctioning* (Ragg, 2006). Different cultures and social groups have unique methods of enforcing rules and expectations (e.g., use of spanking or corporal punishment). When assessing risk, it is important to understand cultural norms. Although the laws may require professional action, it is important to respect and acknowledge the cultural norms.

- *Systems of support* (Ragg, 2006). Some cultures are tightly bound to the nuclear family while others rely heavily on kin networks. This diversity may make it difficult to identify caregivers and supports when assessing family systems for risk. It is important to understand that parental functions and risk elements may reside in people who are not the biological parents.

- *Roles and expectations* (Ragg, 2006). Cultural and social groups often vary in the expectations placed on family members. Some groups may expect children to fulfill roles that diverge greatly from those of the dominant culture. This is very common when economic scarcity coincides with minority group membership. It is important to understand how the culture and economic forces influence family roles and expectations.

Developing the Service Contract

The intervention direction that emerges from an assessment typically provides a foundation for a treatment or service contract between the practitioner and client. The contract identifies the services that the client will receive, including the goals and objectives that will govern change efforts. For this reason, contracting operationalizes the assessment's direction into goals, objectives, and services. The assessment operates like an upside-down triangle, gradually taking a wealth of information and distilling it down to a focused direction. The contract is like an upright triangle transitioning from a semiabstract goal statement to very concrete methods of intervention. This triangle is depicted in Figure 4.2.

Establishing Service Goals

In Figure 4.2, the top of the triangle is a goal statement. This is the most abstract element in the contract because it is a general statement that emerges from the treatment direction. Even though this is the most abstract element, there are limits to the level of abstraction used. The goal statement must abstract enough to capture direction but sufficiently clear to provide a foundation for subsequent steps in developing a service plan, such as developing objectives and identifying methods. These elements of the contract form the broader, more expansive layers of the triangle.

When establishing goals, it is useful to limit the number you are trying to achieve with clients. Ideally, one or two goals can provide a focus for intervention. If you attempt to focus on more goals, the work can become unfocused and confusing, similar to what occurs when you have papers due for multiple classes at the same time. To minimize the number of goals, it is useful to select goal statements that are sufficiently abstract to capture the treatment direction. At the base of the triangle, several objectives and methods are provided. There should be enough objectives to ensure that the goal can be achieved.

Abstraction Challenges in Goal Statements

The greatest challenge to developing a goal statement is to ensure the optimal level of abstraction. Statements can err in two directions. At the most concrete level, practitioners often state a service (e.g., medication, anger management group) rather than describing what the client needs to accomplish (e.g., decreasing anger outbursts). This is a problem because simply attending a service is not truly a client accomplishment. After the client has taken a pill or attended the service, the goal is accomplished. The client may, however, still be very violent.

At the other extreme, practitioners sometimes make vague goal statements. A statement that is too vague lacks an adequate sense of direction. For example, a practitioner working with a volatile client might say, "The client needs to control himself" rather than "The client will decrease his anger outbursts." Notice how the first statement fails to identify

Figure 4.2

Goal Setting and Plans of Care

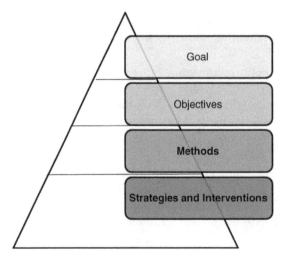

the behavior and fails to indicate a direction for change. A client who uses highly controlled violence will meet the first goal. Highly abstract statements cannot help guide treatment because there is no implicit continuum to help gauge the direction of treatment.

The goal statement is very important because it focuses the work. It is also a tool that communicates what a practitioner is seeking to accomplish with a client. The client, the practitioner, the agency, and the funders should all be able to listen to a goal statement and have a sense of the intervention being provided. A goal statement that is either too concrete or too abstract cannot enable others to understand the work. Read the next case example and observe how a misguided goal can have severe consequences.

Case Example

A three-agency domestic violence partnership was finishing the pilot period and seeking ongoing funding. The program provided separate groups for all family members, individual counseling, and coordinated intervention. Every family had a case manager and two additional practitioners so the father, mother, and children all had separate practitioners. Every case was discussed in weekly team meetings to ensure communication and safety. When planning the meeting to advocate for ongoing funding, the program staff elected to share a case presentation to illustrate the comprehensive services. However, the practitioner whose case was being presented had a single concrete goal. She began presenting a complex case where a battered woman who had been undermined by her husband was trying to regain parental authority with three very challenging children. As the practitioner presented the case, she stated that the goal was to "Have the 2-year-old stay in his car seat when the mother was driving." The funder asked about the goals several times during the meeting, and each time learned that there was only one goal. Ongoing funding was denied.

Balancing the Goal Statement

By now the astute reader will have noticed how extremely abstract and extremely concrete goal statements interfere with functional goal statements. Both tend to be vague, incomplete, and fail to reflect the client situation. There are three important features to consider when developing an optimally concrete statement: client accomplishment, direction for change, and capacity for measurement. Consider this goal statement, and then apply the three criteria to it: "The parent will increase daily use of positive discipline strategies."

1. *Client accomplishment*. A good goal statement will ensure that the change is a client accomplishment that alters how he or she functions in the situation. In the goal statement just listed, using positive disciplinary strategies is an accomplishment.

2. *Direction for change*. A good goal statement will ensure that there is a direction for change that allows for observation (e.g., increase/decrease the frequency, severity, duration). In the goal statement, the word "increase" provides direction.

3. *Capacity for measurement*. A good goal statement offers the potential for measuring/verifying that the goal has been accomplished. In the statement provided, the focus on daily use will allow us to identify specific practices and have the parent track how often he or she uses the strategies.

Notice that the goal statement includes an optimal level of abstraction. The term "positive disciplinary strategies" is an abstract term that borders on categorical. However, the term "increase" grounds the statement in the client's reality. It is possible to identify positive strategies and develop a baseline of how often the parent is using them. The term "increase" also injects concreteness, given that it assumes that there will be some sort of observation or count to assess progress.

Measuring Goal Achievement

As we develop intervention goals, it is important to ensure that they are measurable. To be measurable, the goal's outcomes must be observable. In the goal statement used in earlier, there was a focus on decreasing outbursts. If we have a clear definition of an outburst (e.g., voice volume increases accompanied by aggressive gesturing and swearing), we can observe how often the outbursts occur. Doing this allows us to assess the frequency of outbursts, rendering the goal measurable.

Measurable goals are important for assessing outcomes and to start building evidence of intervention effectiveness. This is particularly important when evidence-based practices are not available for the client situation. Frequently, practitioners use single-case designs to ensure that their interventions are effective. Over a period of time, this clinically focused evaluation can start to build knowledge. Consequently, the importance of measurability begins with ensuring effective intervention but extends to promoting the professional knowledge base. There are several methods for making the goal measureable. The next three are used very commonly in agency practice.

1. *Standardized measures.* Earlier in the chapter we discussed psychometric measures used for assessing clients. When appropriate, these same measures can be used to assess change in symptoms due to intervention. This type of measurement is very strong for building evidence; however, using standardized measures may be awkward if multiple instruments or administrations are used. Multiple measures will take a lot of client time and energy. As professionals, we must balance the burden on the client when selecting this method for measuring goal outcomes.

2. *Behavioral counts/goal attainment scaling.* Helping clients to assess how often a symptom or behavior occurs is an easy method of forming measurable goals. For example, we may ask how often the teams in the agency fight during an average week. We may also observe or have team members observe the conflicts to gather information on the frequency, severity, or duration of problems. We can then follow the same procedure during and after intervention to assess how often the problem occurs. In a goal statement, we may even dictate the level of change (e.g., the teams will decrease conflict exchanges from five times per week to once per month).

3. *Scaled questions.* A very useful but less rigorous approach to evaluating goals is the use of scaled questions. A scaled question involves asking a client to use a scale to assess the goal. For example: "On a scale of 1 to 10 with 1 being totally content and 10 being very conflicted, rate the level of current conflict between your team and the intake team." Notice how this system is less standardized and scientific but very easy to use.

Capacity Elements of a Good Goal Statement

The second critical element of a goal statement is the developmental capacity of the client. It is important that the client be able to achieve the goal. Capacity requires us to integrate the client's values, resources, and motivation when considering intervention outcomes. If we select goals that clients cannot (or will not) achieve, we inadvertently set the client up for failure.

Case Example

A 15-year-old female was placed in a hospital psychiatric ward because she was "out of control." She had been partying with friends, staying out until about 3 a.m., and was very defiant of authority. In a meeting to plan her discharge, a practitioner laid out a plan with these three goals:

1. She would live with her aunt rather than with her parents.
2. She would attend school.
3. She would come in at 10 p.m. on school nights and 11 p.m. on weekends.

The girl agreed to the goals because she had to sign the contract to be discharged. She did move in with her aunt but never followed up on any of the other goals.

In the case example, the goals were not negotiated with the girl, nor were they reasonable, given her past behavior. In effect, they exceeded her capacity to succeed. Additionally, the plan provided no additional supports to help her succeed. It is important to consider supports and methods that can maximize the client's success and to incorporate those supports into the contract so that intervention is well integrated. Perhaps the practitioner could have included a multisystemic service that would work cooperatively with the school, the girl, the family, and other support systems as necessary.

As we reflect on a client's capacity to succeed, we must consider several elements of the situation to help shape the goal. These elements include the challenges, supports, resources, values, and motivations of the client and involved others. Given these elements, we must consider four dimensions of the goal:

1. *Realism.* The change goals must be realistic for clients, given their circumstances. We need to carefully consider clients and their situations as we ask ourselves what is realistic to expect. When we negotiate intervention goals, we use the sense of realism to ensure that the goals can be achieved.

2. *Adequacy.* Intervention goals should be adequate for solving the presenting problem. As we consider the goals, we need to make sure that they are sufficient given the client situation. If a single goal is not sufficient, a second goal should be discussed to ensure that the intervention is sufficient to help the client resolve the situation.

3. *Integration.* During the assessment and intervention considerations, we have a good sense of the client situation. As we start to formulate goals, we consider all of the elements of the situation and attempt to tailor the goals to fit.

4. *Partialization.* Partialization refers to breaking the goal down into smaller units that when combined, will achieve the desired outcomes. The goals should lead easily to establishing clear objectives and methods that can achieve the goals. We should be able to read the goals and have a sense of different outcomes, interventions, services, and supports that can maximize the client's success.

Exercise 4.2: Assessing Goal Statements

The next goal statements all have problems. Read each statement and identify the problems that will interfere with developing a good service contract.

1. The couple needs to learn to get along better.

2. The couple needs help with their communication skills.

3. The couple will decrease their arguing from three times daily to once per week.

4. The couple needs an anger control group.

5. The couple will decrease their fighting from 10 times per week to zero.

Forming Objectives From Goals

Just as goals operationalize the direction of the assessment, objectives operationalize the goal into smaller components that, when accomplished, will achieve the goal. After a goal is established, we break it down into objectives. We do this for each goal in the service plan. In setting objectives, we must be true to the assessment and goal statements by focusing on specific changes in the situation associated with each goal. If we capture all of the critical elements in the situation, the changes should promote goal achievement.

Transitioning From Observations to Objectives
As we work with a goal structure to identify possible objectives, we typically revisit the weighted or most meaningful information that supported the assessment. As we reflect on this information, we start identifying situational elements associated with each goal. We use these elements to develop subcomponents that require change. As we break the problems down into potential objectives, we consider the capacity of the client system to ensure that the objectives we select can change. For example, if the couple fights because they cannot pay their bills and the practitioner cannot influence finances, increasing money is not a realistic objective. However, you can develop objectives around how the couple deals with situations out of their control or teach them money management skills.

Objectives often focus on skill or capacity development (e.g., learn problem-solving skills, learn how to interrupt escalation, identify problems before they begin, identify our buttons, take control of our own buttons, etc.). Often many objectives arise as we identify elements that seem to contribute to the problem. For example, a practitioner was helping an agency where there was a lot of interunit conflict. She observed interactions in the agency and met with several practitioners, noticing how the conflict tended to emerge. The interunit conflict was a definite problem, and the goal was set as decreasing interunit conflict. As the practitioner was transitioning from the goal toward identifying objectives, she used the observations taken during assessment to identify elements for change. Table 4.3 contains the observed elements, logical links, and eventual objectives.

Notice in Table 4.3 that multiple elements easily transform into objectives. As we explore the table, we can see that three objectives emerged from the list of observations. Although there are likely to be additional objectives (e.g., dealing with individual power needs), the practitioner did well to keep the assessment and objectives focused on the organization rather than on the individuals involved. This is important when working with larger client systems where we often tend to focus on individuals.

In writing up objectives, it is important to do three things:

1. Break the goal into component units that can accomplish the goal outcome if achieved.
2. Create tasks that are specific achievements, each related to the others. (In the last example, you can see that each objective represents a piece that can contribute to the success of the goal by dovetailing with the other objectives).
3. Establish objectives that logically lead to techniques or methods that can help accomplish the objective.

Building on Evidence-Based Knowledge
As you identify goals and objectives, you will start to integrate the professional knowledge base as you consider methods for achieving the goals. This is the point of the assessment process where intervention decisions are made. When you reflect on the goal and subsequent objectives, you use your knowledge base to identify intervention strategies that have the best prognosis of success. As intervention options emerge, discuss them with

Table 4.3   Transitioning from Observed Elements to Objectives

Observed Element	Logical Link	Objective
Teams stay together and do not intermingle.	There are tight boundaries around teams that limit sharing and communication.	The agency needs a mechanism for safe interteam sharing.
Communication is channeled through the executive director by supervisors behind closed doors.	There may be triangulation as each team vies for the director's support.	The director needs to develop ways for the supervisors and teams to collaborate.
People take things personally when feedback is provided.	People are reactive and seem to feel vulnerable when problems are addressed.	The agency needs a mechanism for safe interteam sharing.
Front-line workers avoid dealing with problems and are told not to raise issues by the supervisors.	Supervisors and administrators are invested in controlling the communication and problem solving.	Front-line workers need to be able to share and resolve issues at their own level.
The director takes charge and tells people what to do without discussion.	The director is stuck in the middle of problems rather than allowing people to resolve issues.	The director needs to develop a way for the supervisors and teams to collaborate.
People talk about each other behind their backs.	An atmosphere of mistrust has developed that interferes with direct communication.	The agency needs a mechanism for interteam sharing.
Teams formulate their own procedures, which do not fit together effectively.	The lack of communication and problem solving is impacting the structure.	Front-line workers need to be able to share and resolve issues at their own level.
The supervisors dislike each other and share their opinions with the front-line staff.	The supervisors are allowing their feelings to interfere with agency functioning.	The director needs to develop a way for the supervisors and teams to collaborate.

the client so the methods of goal achievement can become part of the service contract. Three considerations can ensure that you offer clients intervention options with a strong probability of success:

1. *Consider available evidence-based interventions*. If evidence-based practices fit the needs of the client, explore them with him or her so the client can consider the most efficient approach to meeting goals. If a client is not comfortable with the methods you describe, provide other options so the client can pursue a course of intervention that best meets his or her needs.

2. *Consider available applicable evidence*. When there is no evidence-based practice to incorporate into the contract, it is useful to consider research and knowledge that can inform the intervention. Explore the possibilities with the client so he or she can make informed decisions about the intervention approaches that will be used.

3. *Consider available promising practices*. If no research applies to the client situation, you may have to involve your supervisor to help identify promising practices. You will find that often this is an important step because many client situations are unique, and some guidance on intervention options is often warranted.

Additional Contracted Elements
Along with the goals and objectives, some agency settings include other elements in their plan of care/service contract. These elements may be included in service contracts:

- *Methods*. Some service contracts spell out the methods that will be used to accomplish the client goals. In direct service, this might include explaining out the configuration of meetings (e.g., individual sessions, couple sessions, group sessions, home visits, medication, exercises, etc.) that will be used to accomplish the different objectives and goals.

- *Services*. In a case management situation, this is where the services are included. It is implicit that the service will help the client toward a specified accomplishment. Often practitioners must follow up and support the referral with the client after the service has begun to monitor objective and goal achievements.

- *Time frame.* Some contracts limit the number of sessions or weeks. These time frames should be logically associated with the goals and objectives described. Limiting the sessions can be useful to keeping people focused, but some practitioners also find that such limits are very rigid and limiting. If you work in a setting that enforces session limits, having clear, achievable goals is even more important.

- *Review schedule.* A final contracted element is the review schedule. Goals and objectives are useful only if they are monitored. You should review progress toward goals to ensure accountable service. When goals are measurable, you can measure progress periodically (e.g., "Over the past two weeks, how often have you had volatile outbursts?"). Such monitoring should occur at regular intervals so that the pace of change can be observed and treatment can be altered accordingly. This monitoring also can be used for documenting outcomes.

Critical Chapter Themes

1. Assessment is an area of practice where our thinking is directly applied to the client situation.

2. We collect information through interviews, observation, psychometric measures, and third-party reports to ensure that our impressions are based on factual information rather than conjecture.

3. We sort and organize information using logical and linear thinking to identify important elements.

4. We use our knowledge and theories to help organize the situational information into a coherent form that can adequately explain the client's concerns.

5. We develop direction from the assessment, and use this to formulate goals to guide our intervention.

6. We must craft goals carefully to ensure that they capture the client situation, are measurable, and can help resolve the situation through creating objectives.

7. The goals, objectives, and methods usually are negotiated with the client to form a treatment contract (also known as plan of care or service contract).

Online Resources

Child Welfare Information Gateway, Family Assessment Model: www.childwelfare.gov/famcentered/casework/assessment.cfm

Pain and disability assessment tools: http://pain-topics.org/clinical_concepts/assess.php

Review and links to culturally appropriate assessment tools: www.transculturalcare.net/assessment-tools.htm

Scottish government Web site covering risk assessment: www.scotland.gov.uk/Publications/2007/08/07090727/0

Recommended Reading

Dziegieleski, S. F. (2008). Problem identification, contracting, and case planning. In W. Rowe & L. A. Rapp-Paglicci (Eds.), *Comprehensive Handbook of Social Work and Social Welfare, Vol. 3* (pp. 78–97). Hoboken, NJ: John Wiley & Sons.

Farmer, R. F., & Chapman, A. L. (2006). Principles, goals, and structure of initial assessment sessions. In R. F. Farmer & A. L. Chapman (Eds.), *Behavioral Interventions in Cognitive Behavior Therapy:*

Practical Guidance for Putting Theory into Action (pp. 21–51). Washington, DC: American Psychological Association.

Nugent, W. R. (2008). Assessment and data collection. In W. Rowe & L. A. Rapp-Paglicci (Eds.), *Comprehensive Handbook of Social Work and Social Welfare, Vol. 3* (pp. 46–77). Hoboken, NJ: John Wiley & Sons.

Schwalbe, C. S. (2008). Strengthening the integration of actuarial risk assessment with clinical judgment in an evidence-based practice framework. *Children and Youth Services Review, 30,* 1458–1464.

Section II

Developing the Helping Relationship

This part of the book shifts focus from the practitioner to the helping relationship. Previous chapters explored skills that function primarily inside the practitioner. Self-awareness, self-control, and thinking skills are important; they must be applied in an interpersonal context to help other people. The next series of chapters explores the interpersonal skills required for effective practice.

This section of the book begins with forming the helping relationship. Chapter 5 helps you apply your thinking skills to understand the client experience. You then learn how to respond to clients in an empathic but focused manner as you engage them in service. In later chapters you develop questioning and reflecting skills. The five chapters in this section provide core interpersonal skills that you can use for many purposes in the helping relationship.

Chapter 5 begins building the interpersonal competencies by extending the internal practitioner capacities into forming an empathic working relationship. Chapter 6 then develops questioning skills that can be used to explore client situations and subtly challenge clients. This chapter is followed by developing reflecting skills. Perhaps the most difficult skill set is developed in Chapter 8 where we learn how to observe and share our observations. The final competency, developing direction is the focus of Chapter 9.

After learning the core interpersonal skills, you will learn slightly more complex ones, including how to use your observations and provide direction when helping clients. Although these skills can fulfill the same functions as questioning and reflecting, they require more conscious thought and often are used more strategically.

These chapters all use a response system framework to help you learn how to focus your responses. Reading the chapters will help you develop abilities to identify and influence the client's processing (thinking and feeling) and action (behavior and interaction) systems. These chapters integrate the interactive skills with the internal skills covered in Section 1. Written material and exercises help establish a firm skill base for empathically responding to clients and helping them change.

Chapter 5
Tuning In and Empathic Engagement

In Chapter 4 we used knowledge to understand the nature of the client's problem. Assessment thinking is important for identifying a service direction and establishing goals. We also use knowledge to understand clients' experience through establishing an empathic link. This style of thinking is nonlinear as we seek to understand situations from clients' experiential perspective. If we can achieve this perspective, we can achieve an empathic position in the helping relationship.

Tuning In and the Empathic Connection

Empathy is a critical precondition for effective service (Angus & Kagan, 2007; Block-Lerner, Adair, Plumb, Rhatigan, & Orsillo, 2007). Research consistently identifies the practitioner-client relationship as one of the most influential factors in client satisfaction and treatment outcomes (Lutz, Leon, Martinovich, Lyons, & Stiles, 2007; Dong-Min, Wampold, & Bolt, 2006). In its simplest form, empathy is the ability to accurately understand the client's experience. Ideally, we can understand all elements in how the client responds to their situation (feeling, thinking, actions, and interactions). Empathy requires us to mentally construct the client's experience through the careful use of awareness and thinking skills. High levels of empathy are one of the critical practitioner traits, separating effective from less effective practitioners practitioner(Lafferty, Beutler, & Crago, 1989; Ridgway & Sharpley, 1990).

Empathy and the Working Alliance

Inherent in working from an empathic position is forming a helping relationship or working alliance (Hilsenroth & Cromer, 2007). The working alliance involves two important skills: empathic tuning in and engaging clients. Tuning in involves our thinking skills as we open up our mental processes to consider situations from the client's perspective (Shulman, 1999). Others refer to this process as empathy, or empathic attunement (Egan, 2010; Rowe & MacIsaac, 1989). Empathy, consequently, is the end product of the internal process of tuning in. As the means to such an end product, tuning in to the client situation serves to sensitize us practitioners before meeting the client and when responding to client disclosures.

Tuning In: The Foundation for Empathy

As we work with clients we seek to tune in to their internal experience of the situation. This tuning in to clients is a critical element for establishing the empathic connection with them (Shulman, 1999). Research finds that in effective practitioners tend to approach clients in a more intellectual fashion and lack empathy for the client experience (Bozarth, 1997; Lafferty et al., 1989). The intellectual approach to clients involves a heavy reliance on logic with very little circular thinking. It is important that we tune in to the client experience concurrent with developing an understanding of the situation.

When we are empathically attuned to a client, we understand his or her experience and situational needs by viewing situations from the person's perspective (Angus & Kagan, 2007). This requires us to be able to accurately tune in to the client's emotional experience (Block-Lerner et al., 2007; Miville, Carlozzi, Gushue, Schara, & Ueda, 2006; Vivino, Thompson, Jill, & Ladany, 2009) and motivations (Huppert, Barlow, Gorman, Shear, & Woods, 2006; Moyers & Martin, 2006). Three personality characteristics are consistently related to achieving an empathic working relationship:

1. *Openness*. Research finds that practitioners who form the strongest working relationship with clients are positive, accepting, and understanding (Beck, Friedlander, & Escudero, 2006; Beutler, Castonguay, & Follette, 2006; Hersoug, Høglend, Monsen, & Havik, 2001).

2. *Concern*. Research indicates that practitioners who form the strongest working relationship respond in a concerned and inquisitive manner rather than being challenging or judgmental (Ackerman & Hilsenroth, 2003; Block-Lerner et al., 2007; Shechtman, 2004).

3. *Purpose*. Practitioners with strong working relationships are able to find common ground and a sense of purpose with the client (Beck et al., 2006; Beutler et al., 2006; Creed & Kendall, 2005; Littauer, Sexton, & Wynn, 2005).

Given these requirements, our ability to build an empathic working relationship with clients begins with our personality (Ackerman & Hilsenroth, 2003).

When we cannot relate from this position, problems emerge in the relationship (Schröder & Davis, 2004). The development of an empathic relationship can be a challenge when our personality characteristics, culture, and life experiences are different from those of the client (Fiorentine & Hillhouse, 1999; Keenan, Tsang, Bogo, & George, 2005; Spinhoven, Giesen-Bloo, van Dyck, Kooiman, & Arntz, 2007). We build our capacity for empathy by building on our self-awareness and adjusting our socialized patterns of thinking and responding.

Fighting Socialization-Based Preconceptions

In Chapter 3 we explored our socialized preferences for logical and linear thinking. This type of thinking occurs easily and often results in an intellectual understanding of a situation. Given that most of this activity occurs in our mind, we have little difficulty believing that we know what is occurring in a situation because we only use one perspective. This very quick and simple approach to understanding situations can interfere with developing empathy because empathy requires us to use the perspectives of other people.

As we develop our capacity for empathy, we must shift from tuning in to our thinking to tuning in to another person's perspective. As we begin this shift, many of us will struggle with socialized thinking habits that maintain our self-focused thinking. Three socialized habits that emerge for many people are described next. These habits develop through our social interactions; they serve as our cognitive default settings as we seek to understand situations.

1. *Focus on factual understandings*. As we listen to people talk about their situations, often we focus our listening on the observable facts in the situation. We want to know who said what and who did what. We have learned through the years that these elements of situations lend themselves to forming quick opinions. When we explore other people's interpretations and experiences of a situation, we often end up debating the facts (e.g., sequencing of events, meaning of statements) rather than understanding the other person's perspectives on the situation. Consequently, many of us tend to prefer the clean observable elements in a situation. To develop empathy, we must move beyond facts and focus on affective responses and interpretations of the situation. Doing this requires us to become open to multiple perspectives and experiences of the same phenomenon.

2. *Focus on internal experience*. When we seek to understand situations, our attention often turns inward as we dwell on our mental processes. As we shift to an internal focus, we tend to tune out other people and external events. This internalized focus is automatic as we reflect on situations. Consequently it is unusual for us to consider other perspectives and experiences. This thinking habit makes it difficult to extend our thinking to clients. As we start to tune in to other people, we must consciously force our focus outward to break the natural tendency to shift our focus inward.

3. *Tendency toward simplicity*. Throughout our lives we have been told not to dwell on situations. We hear messages about moving on and not complicating situations by overthinking. Consequently we tend to accept simple understandings to keep harmonious relationships. However, as we simplify understandings, we abandon using

multiple perspectives to understand situations. For simplicity's sake, we insert assumptions based on our life experiences rather than considering other people's understandings. This tendency to simplify interferes with our ability to understand how other people experience a situation.

When we start to tune in to other people's perspectives, these old habits may cause us to experience some interference. Often we first struggle with the assumption that everyone thinks and feels as we do. This assumption occurs as we struggle to apply other people's life experiences to the situation. First we must consider the other person's life and then extend that consideration to the current situation. If we can extend our perspective in this way, we may discover that the individual's experience is very different.

Case Example

Members of the dominant culture who watch the news and see a picture of a wanted African American criminal experience the message as one of caution and information provision. Consider how different the different experience is for African Americans. Although the basic information does not change, the experience of receiving the information does change. Experiences of identification, racism, and past profiling may be evoked while watching the newscast, yielding a very qualitatively different experience. Very consistently, diverse cultural groups will experience the same broadcast very differently depending on their position of dominance and their identification with the group identified in the broadcast.

Achieving an Affective Connection

In the previous discussion, astute readers will have noticed that there is a shift away from a cognitive understanding toward understanding emotional experiences. Our connection to clients must resonate at the emotional level. When clients sense caring, concern, and understanding in the practitioner, they are able to relax in the helping relationship (Miville et al., 2006; Vivino et al., 2009). This sense can occur only if we tune in to the emotional experience of our clients.

In the last case example, a cognitive knowledge that African American citizens have experienced racism and profiling is insufficient. When we apply this knowledge toward understanding a situational response, we must understand the affective impact of these experiences. If you are African American you will have experiences that facilitate this understanding. If you are of any other cultural group, you must extend your perspective to tune into the experience. Only then can we approach a cross cultural understanding of the client response. It is this ability to tune in to the emotional elements of the client's experience that promotes the empathic connection (Miville et al., 2006). Specific elements of the affective connection include:

- *Positive acceptance* (Beck et al., 2006; Dilallo & Weiss, 2009; Fluckiger & Holtforth, 2008). Clients must feel that the practitioner will accept, without judgment, their feelings, beliefs, and behaviors.
- *Integration of client life experiences* (French, Reardon, & Smith, 2003). Practitioners need to understand the impact of past experiences and subsequent adaptive responses.
- *Accurate emotional attunement* (Miville et al., 2006; Vivino et al., 2009). Practitioners must accurately understand the emotions and motivations of the client.
- *Building on client motivation* (Moyers & Martin, 2006). Clients have feelings that motivate them to make changes in their lives. Practitioners must work effectively with these feelings to promote change.

As we master our socialized influences, we become open to understanding clients' internal experiences of situations—both of past life situations as well as of entering the helping relationship. As we tune in to these experiences, the helping relationship becomes a safe place for clients to explore and master problematic situations.

Tuning In: The Relational Foundation

Tuning in begins long before the client enters treatment. This level of attunement involves taking time to understand the client experience of entering service. The empathy resulting from this level of tuning in allows us practitioner to more fully understand and respond to the client as we first meet (R. Miller, 1999; Shulman, 1999). Consequently, this preliminary empathy sets the tone for the working relationship by helping the client feel welcome, understood, and comfortable (Satterfield & Lyddon, 1998).

Preliminary Tuning In

Preliminary tuning in occurs before the client officially meets with the practitioner. In preparation for meeting the client, we often gather as much information as possible to understand his or her reasons for entering service. As we reflect on these reasons and other elements of client information, we can also tune in to the client experience of entering service by asking ourselves: What must it be like for someone with *this background* and *these concerns* to be coming *here* to meet *me*? This act of tuning in begins the practitioner-client relationship (R. Miller, 1999; Shulman, 1999).

Elements of Preliminary Tuning In

In the above tuning in questions, four critical elements emerge. These areas of concern can cause clients to be very ambivalent about engaging in service. It is important to tune in to these four areas so we can respond appropriately. All four areas of consideration tend to occur simultaneously, yet we will discuss them separately to provide the fullest possible exploration. The four elements include:

1. *Client background.* Given what we know about the client and his or her history, what must it be like asking an agency for assistance? Some clients have abuse or neglect in their background. Such histories can engender anxiety or mistrust with authority figures. Background events are not limited to historical mishaps. Culture, race, religion, sexual preference, and socioeconomic background can all influence a client's experience of approaching an agency for assistance. We must try to tune in to every client's background and how that might predispose him or her to certain reactions or hesitancy. Doing this requires that we reflect on the general impact of background events and how they might apply to entering service at this agency.

2. *Presenting problem.* The nature of the client problem can promote emotional distress about entering service. This is particularly true when the client has engaged in behaviors that are not strongly endorsed by society. For example, child abuse, some sexual behaviors, and violence often prompt negative judgments in other people. When clients believe that the practitioner might judge them harshly, they are likely to withhhold the details of their problem until a supportive relationship is formed.

3. *Agency.* Agencies often have reputations in the community. Some are viewed as helpful and supportive while others are considered negative and intrusive. Similarly, the types of service provided by an agency may be stigmatizing. Clients may experience some services as a sign of failure and others as an indication that they are bad people. It is important to understand how incoming clients might experience your agency. Concerns about the agency may be elevated if a client has received service in the past.

4. *Practitioner.* A fourth area of concern for clients will be you. Clients enter service initially screening for similarities and differences. If they find similarities, they may experience some comfort; however, differences are likely to evoke caution until they build a relationship with you. Racial, cultural, gender, age, and other demographic differences may raise some initial concerns. Although these can be overcome as the relationship develops, clients may be watchful until they believe you can understand and relate to them.

Preliminary Tuning In With Larger Systems

When working with larger client systems such as families, organizations, and communities, there is no single client; rather we must understand the unique perspectives of multiple people. To do so, we must be able to tune in to the experience of several people all involved in the problem situation. As we start tuning in to the larger systems, it is important first to be able to identify individual perspectives. These perspectives are influenced by an individual's position in the system. Consider how the next dynamics can change the experience of any situation.

- *Systemic roles.* Some individuals have positions of responsibility and are privy to information and power that is not available to all members. Other individuals are expected to perform in a dutiful manner and follow directives. These positions will greatly influence how each person experiences a problem situation and the preferred solutions.

- *Attribution systems.* People develop patterns of attributing responsibility for situations. Sometimes there is individual diversity in attribution patterns. However, systems often develop patterns of attribution. For example, some families will put the blame on one person rather than sharing responsibility. Other families will blame forces outside of the family. Organizations and groups often develop similar patterns. How system members attribute responsibility for problems will influence how they define the problem that brings them into service.

- *Problem definitions.* Every person in a larger system will have a unique definition of the problem. This fact presents challenges because often one person's feelings will compel group entry into service. This person often presents the problem definition when referring for service. If we accept this one person's definition, we run the risk of alienating other members of the client system. To preempt adopting the perspective of the most emotionally involved person, it is useful to consider two types of perspective among the system members.
  - *Primary felt perspective.* The person whose feelings drive the referral tends to provide the primary definition of the problem because he or she has the most emotional investment in resolving the situation. This person may be a member of the system, such as a parent or marital partner. For example, a husband may ask for marriage counseling because his wife is having an affair. Notice how his perceptions and definitions of the situation will be different from his wife's. The primary perspective may be external to the system, such as a teacher who insists that parents refer their child for treatment because he is disruptive in class.
  - *Secondary felt perspectives.* All other people in the system have a different definition of the problem so it is very important to avoid accepting the first person's definition. Children will define problems differently from parents. Similarly, practitioners often define situations differently from administrators. It is important to tune in to each members' experience and potential definition of the situation as we begin to engage larger client systems into service.

- *Relationship systems.* With larger systems, people may have preexisting relationships that will influence how they respond to interventions. For example, it is common for triangulation (Bowen, 1978) to occur in families where one parent sides with a child against the second parent. In organizations, we also find team loyalties and friendships. Alliances and other patterns of relating that occur in a larger system influence how people respond when entering service. It is useful to tune in to these dynamics when engaging larger systems:
  - *Loyalties.* When people live or work together, obligations and loyalties tend to emerge. For example, children often side with each other against parents, and vice versa. Similarly, team members tend to support each other because they are familiar with each other's work and styles.
  - *Affiliation patterns.* It is not unusual for people to prefer some system members to others. We all have friends at work and often can identify other people whom we do

not care for. As we engage larger systems, we note patterns of responding and contributions that indicate how people like each other and work together.

● *Coalitions*. Sometimes people collude with each other to disempower others in the system. It is important to identify these coalitions and alliances when tuning in to each member's experience. To identify coalitions we look for triangles and patterns where members take sides or one member is consistently left out.

Given these systemic dynamics, every person in the client system—whether it is a family, group, organization, or community—will have a slightly different experience and definition of the problem. Consequently it is critical that we avoid accepting a single person's definition; otherwise we will alienate others in the system. We must tune in to how each person experiences the situation and how each might define the problem.

Tuning In to Client Concerns About Service

As clients enter service, they have many unspoken concerns about you, the agency, and the helping process. Some concerns involve a lack of knowledge while others are associated with vulnerability. Knowledge-based concerns can be addressed directly. However, vulnerability concerns will require the client to use their experience of the helping relationship to resolve the concern.

A client's knowledge-based concerns are easy to tune in to because they are fairly consistent across clients. Most people approaching an agency for help have questions about what will occur. Some questions focus on the agency's services and expectations; others more directly focus on the service provider. Three types of concern are common for most clients: service, confidentiality, and you.

Concerns About Service

Clients inevitably wonder about what will happen to them as they begin services at the agency. Most will have some experience answering screening questions and filling out forms before they meet you. These experiences often are very impersonal, promoting healthy cautiousness as clients attend their first appointment. If your agency serves involuntary clients, concerns will be elevated because other practitioners or social agents will have coerced the clients into attending. Given these experiences, you can expect these types of questions.

● *What is the structure of service?* This includes the types of service, general program information, and hours/locations of service.
● *What are the demands of service?* This includes service expectations about who must attend, how often, and what they will be made to do.
● *How does the client fit?* This includes identifying how much control clients have over the service focus, timing, and expectations.

Concerns About Confidentiality

Most clients will have some concern about what will happen to their information. You can reasonably expect some concerns about who you might talk to about them and who might find out about their problems. If the client is involuntary or referred by a coercive agency, concerns will be elevated as the person also will wonder about the information exchanges between your agency and others.

Concerns About You

Most clients will be concerned about who you are. At the simplest level, diversity concerns will emerge about your age, gender, race, and cultural background. However, clients also want to be sure that you will treat them with respect and respond appropriately to their needs. There are two components to the knowledge-based concerns:

1. *Diversity-based concerns.* Most clients look for similarities when they first enter a new situation. If you are visibly dissimilar to the client, they may seem a little reserved (e.g.,

old vs. young, male vs. female). Being different is not necessarily a problem. If you can relate effectively and understand the client, his or her experience of you will diminish these concerns (Fiorentine & Hillhouse, 1999). However, if past traumas or events compound the difference (e.g., past sexual abuse), problems may emerge.

2. *Approachability concerns.* The second practitioner-focused area of concern involves your openness and approachability. All clients hope that practitioners will be respectful and understanding. As you attend to their needs and respond to them, these concerns diminish. Your introduction and explanation of services will set the tone for resolving these concerns.

Vulnerability Concerns

Vulnerability concerns are more personal to clients than knowledge-based concerns and are less amenable to content-focused resolution. Many clients feel powerless as they come in for assistance (Greene, Lee, Mentzer, Pinnell, & Niles, 1998). Agency reputation, procedures, or past experiences may elevate feelings of vulnerability and powerlessness. Similarly, the nature of the client problem or background can cause feelings of vulnerability to increase. It is important to tune in to possible vulnerabilities in order to address them as clients enter the helping relationship.

Types of Vulnerability Concerns

Four common categories of vulnerability arise as clients enter service. Minor vulnerabilities can be resolved during introductions if you respond to the client in a respectful and empowering manner. However, many vulnerabilities take time to resolve. It is important to resist the temptation to avoid or dismiss client concerns about entering service. It will be very difficult to develop a positive helping relationship if you start by dismissing client concerns. Consider these types of vulnerability that clients may experience when entering service:

1. *Client history.* Many clients have life experiences that make it difficult for them to trust others. Many also have difficulties with authority figures and people who should have been caring. Given that you are an authority figure and are expected to care, anxieties associated with past experiences may cause clients to be cautious when they first meet you.

2. *Presenting problems.* Similar to the client history, a client's presenting problems can evoke emotional responses to entering the helping relationship. This is most evident with behaviors that often result in negative judgments by others. Clients may experience shame about things they have done. Because of this fact, they can be cautious and ambivalent when entering the helping relationship.

3. *Agency concerns.* If a client has had a negative agency experience, agency or system concerns can interfere with engagement because clients will be watching for you to replicate the negative events. This behavior is most pronounced with clients who have long histories with helping services, such as youths who are in foster care and hard-to-serve client populations.

4. *Practitioner differences.* Clients tend to prefer practitioners who are similar to themselves (Fiorentine & Hillhouse, 1999). When clients see that you are different in some way, they may become cautious, believing that you will not be able to understand them or may judge them. They will monitor you closely to confirm or disconfirm these concerns.

Responding to Client Service Concerns

As clients enter the helping relationship, it is important to respond to their service-related vulnerabilities and their experience of meeting you for the first time (Ackerman & Hilsenroth, 2003). Doing this is especially important when clients have had previous experiences with the helping system that might influence their current experience (Keenan et al., 2005). As practitioners, we must respect these vulnerabilities as we open up discussions about how clients experience their entry into service.

Discussions about the service system and client experiences of it can be uncomfortable because you are part of the system and may feel partially responsible for it. If clients criticize the system, you may feel pressure to respond on behalf of the system. It is very important to remain client focused during these discussions because it is the client's experience that is important. If a client is critical, affirm the experience without taking a position about the system. Doing this allows you to maintain your ethical obligations to your employing agency while concurrently supporting your clients.

Most knowledge-based concerns can be addressed by providing information. Agencies often provide handouts and forms to inform clients about services and service requirements, but these are impersonal. When clients enter your office, they want you to respond to their informational needs. Much of this occurs as you introduce yourself to clients. Many diversity-based concerns are of course immediately answered as you enter the waiting room to greet your client.

Using Introductions

Your introduction of yourself and your services begins the resolution of knowledge-based concerns. Although the content of the introductions is fairly superficial, how you handle them and engage clients in conversation sets the tone for the relationship. Often an introductory sequence consists of four elements. The order of the first two elements is often interchangeable, as you and clients learn how to address each other. Later clients learn about the service they will receive and what will occur during their first meeting.

These four elements are often somewhat perfunctory and will not vary much after you develop your pattern of meeting and greeting new clients. As you develop your pattern, try to include these elements.

1. *Introducing self.* Often as you reach to shake a client's hand, you start telling them your name. Your decisions about formality (e.g., "Hi, I am Mrs. Jamison") will start responding to the client concerns. If you are too formal, some clients may react; however, informality also may evoke negativity. Often you observe clients as you approach and make your decision. If they look formal, you want to start formal (e.g., "Hello, I am Mrs. Jamison, but you can call me Janet if you feel comfortable using first names.").

2. *Reciprocal introduction.* Typically after you introduce yourself, you request clients to share their names. It is important to allow them the opportunity to control how you will refer to them. Even if you want to use first names, some cultural groups prefer formality in professional exchanges. Because you will not automatically understand your clients' preferences, it is usually best to ask them how they would like to be addressed (e.g., "You must be Mrs. Williams; do you prefer Mrs. Williams, or is there another way you would like me to address you?").

3. *Introducing services.* Frequently, clients benefit from a brief description of your services. This may include some information about the agency, program, or specific service that you represent. You do not want to bore them with trivial details, but they should understand the parameters of service. Usually this is the point at which you bring up the rules about confidentiality, expectations, and limitations. If clients already have signed consents to share information and receive treatment, often you can make this introduction brief. However, if reception staff simply hand out forms to sign, make sure you take some time to explore the service parameters (e.g., "We are a program that specializes in helping families experiencing financial crisis. Many clients with financial pressures worry that we might share their information with creditors or other people. I know you signed a form about your information rights, but I want to make sure that I answer any questions you might have. Are you clear about your rights as you come into this program?").

4. *Orienting the session.* As you finish the introductions, you will want to bring the focus of discussion to the present meeting. Many practitioners advise clients about how the

introduction session will proceed to help them make the transition from program content to discussing client concerns (e.g., "Today we are mostly going to get to know each other. I will have some questions about your situation, but before we start, do you have any concerns about coming here today?").

The four elements of the introduction respond to common knowledge-related concerns, helping clients to relax at the beginning of the meeting. Although protocols vary across agencies, many service settings have specific elements of information that they expect practitioners to cover during the first session. When agencies have mandated content to cover, it is important to balance that content with opportunities for clients to relax and get to know you so the relationship can progress concurrently with the formal tasks.

Responding to Vulnerability Concerns

Vulnerability concerns are far from perfunctory. You probably will never develop a set pattern of responding because vulnerability concerns are unique to each client. As a result, you must start with tuning in to the client concern. After you have identified a given client's type of concern, you must identify how to best respond to it.

There are two common considerations when responding to vulnerability concerns. First, you must decide on whether to be direct or indirect in your approach. This decision depends on the nature of the client's concerns. If directness will elevate feelings of vulnerability, it is wise to soften your approach by making the concern seem more general and normal rather than something specific to the client.

The second consideration is the method of responding to the concern. There are two methods for responding to vulnerability concerns: opening statements and interactive responding. Opening statements require practitioners to focus directly on the concerns so we can help clients express and resolve them. Interactive responding requires us to monitor themes in client interaction so we can identify and respond to the concerns. As you address client concerns, you decide whether to respond directly or indirectly to the concern.

Table 5.1 lists the approaches and methods of responding to vulnerability concerns. Notice that some concerns warrant a direct response while other concerns require a softer response. Similarly, practitioners choose their interactive and opening statement strategies based on the various types of concern presented.

Table 5.1 Strategy Decisions for Responding to Vulnerability Concerns

Type of Vulnerability	Directness Concerns	Strategy Considerations
Client History Concerns		
Past abuse Authority figure issues Low trust History of negative judgments	A direct focus identifying potential issues may seem intrusive and judgmental.	Use an opening statement that responds to their fears about entering service. Avoid focusing directly on the client or their history. Rather focus on the impact of the historical that emerge in the concerns (e.g., confidentiality, negative judgments). Use generalized statements, such as "Many clients are concerned about . . . " Normalize concerns: "It is normal for people to be concerned about how information is shared." End the opening statement with a question about their experience entering service rather than on their presenting problems. After exploring their entry concerns, move on to the presenting problems.

(continued)

Table 5.1 (*Continued*)

Type of Vulnerability	Directness Concerns	Strategy Considerations
Presenting Problem Concerns		
Behaviors that draw negative judgments Embarrassing problems	An early direct focus may increase client feelings of vulnerability.	Use an opening statement. First explore the challenges inherent in coming into service and how many people resent professionals meddling in their lives. Avoid discussing the difficult behaviors until comfort is achieved. Rather, focus on the context of the problem, moving into thinking and feeling. After the client has set a context and discussed how he or she feels in the problem situation, move on to discussing problem behaviors.
Agency Concerns		
Negative agency experiences Negative helping experiences	Require a direct and early focus because they can disrupt the alliance.	Use an opening statement. Identify the past experiences in the statement. Affirm the difficulties in coming in. Invite the client to share concerns and anxieties about entering service.
Worker Concerns		
Age differences Gender differences Racial differences Cultural differences	Avoid a direct focus. Wait for the client to identify issues of concern.	Do not include in an opening statement unless the client has raised concerns during introductions. Watch for client statements that indicate a potential concern. Explore the client concern as statements are made.

Indirect Responding to Vulnerability Concerns

The decision to be direct or indirect usually is based on the potential impact of addressing concerns with the client. For example, if the client is worried about being crazy, many practitioners indirectly address the unspoken question by using a response that normalizes people entering service.

Case Example

A practitioner in a family service agency was conducting her first interview with a new client. The client presented initial concerns about relationship problems with her husband. There appeared to be some anxiety in the client, who began asking about the type of people usually coming in for service at this agency. She seemed most interested in the types of problems that people came into service to address. The practitioner felt the questions either reflected anxiety about the seriousness of her problems or anxiety about whether the client was okay. Given two possibilities, the practitioner chose this indirect response: "This agency serves many people with many different types of concerns. Often these concerns are very normal concerns about situations that are outside of people's control, such as normal relationship frustrations. Usually exploring what is controllable in life is very helpful for people."

Direct Responding to Vulnerability Concerns

There are other times when you will want to be more direct in responding to the client concern. Directness becomes necessary when the client concern is likely to interfere with the development or maintenance of a positive working relationship. When you believe that the client concern is critical to the relationship, pick up on it and open it up for discussion.

Case Example

A young practitioner was providing supportive services to men and women in a nursing home setting. She noticed that many of her clients made comments about her age and compared her to their children. She felt these comments might indicate concern about her ability to understand elderly people. She thought about how to address the concern and selected this response: "I notice you refer to me as a 'nice young lady' and once you even called me a 'child.' This stayed with me and I began to wonder if you might be concerned that I may not understand what you are going through because of my young age. Do you find that this is a concern for you?"

In reviewing both types of responses, it is clear that the indirect response attempts to address the concern without any exploration with the client. Such responses are most useful to address a concern where a direct response might shift the focus away from the work by changing the focus of discussion, when the concern is not clear and the practitioner wants to address more than one possibility, or when the concern is not critical to the relationship. The direct response is useful when the practitioner feels the concern needs to be addressed in order for the work to proceed.

Table 5.1 outlines directness concerns and strategy options associated with different types of client vulnerability. Notice how the different types of vulnerability yield different concerns. Also notice how you can phrase statements to respond to concerns without elevating client vulnerability. You can use this table to plan both interactive and opening statement responses to vulnerability.

Exercise 5.1: Identification of Client Concerns

Read the next client statements, and identify and respond to the client concerns.

1. A client booking the first appointment says, "I have been to practitioners before and it was never too helpful."
   a. What type of concern is the client is probably experiencing?

   b. Write a response that can speak to the client's concern.

2. An older client with a younger practitioner asks, "How many kids do you have?"
   a. What type of concern is the client probably experiencing?

   b. Write a response that can speak to the unspoken concern.

3. A client coming into service for the first time says, "I have never been to a place like this before. What kind of things do you do here? I bet you hear some pretty crazy things."
   a. What type of concern is the client probably experiencing?

b. Write a response that can speak to the unspoken question.

Using Opening Statements

An opening statement is a method for directly responding to client vulnerability concerns. Typically, an opening statement is used to open up discussion about the concern right at the beginning of service (Shulman, 1999). After sharing names and describing the service, practitioners begin to orient clients to the session. If clients have no vulnerability concerns, you can ask what problems or concerns led up to their decision to come to the agency. Because the concerns that brought them in are more pressing than their concerns about entering service, they will respond.

When clients have vulnerability concerns, they may not feel safe enough to openly discuss their problems. In such cases, a more complex opening statement is necessary to bring focus to their concerns before addressing their presenting problems. Timing is important because the concerns must be addressed early. The easiest time to do this is after the introductions as you begin orienting clients to the session. There is an awkward moment as you finish superficial discussions and focus on more personal issues. The opening statement fits into this moment to help the transition.

To help understand how opening statements work, a table provides a useful metaphor. Picture an empty table between you and the client. This is an apt metaphor for the early relationship. Because the table is empty, there is nothing to discuss. However, if the client feels vulnerable, we need to get those feelings on the table to explore them with your client (see Figure 5.1). In figure 5.1 the opening statement places a communication package on the table that can highlight the feelings.

The opening statement is your tool for getting the most critical concerns on the table for exploration and resolution. The opening statement involves a five-step process.

1. *Identify the vulnerability.* Through tuning in, you first identify the client vulnerability.
2. *Decide on directness.* Very quickly, you decide whether to be direct or indirect in your statement.
3. *Affirm the client concern.* The first part of the opening statement should affirm the client concern. This part can be indirect (e.g., "Many people are concerned about . . . ") or direct (e.g., "I understand you had a bad experience last time you were here."). Notice how both affirm the experience while getting the concern on the table.
4. *Make a brief statement.* After the affirmation, often you want to follow up with a statement that can begin resolution. The statement should promote feelings of being understood. Two common types of statement include:

Figure 5.1

**Communication
Package**

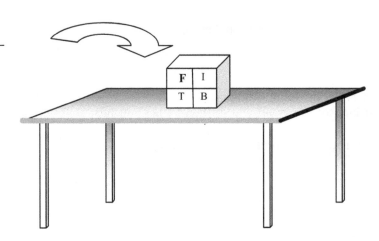

a. *Providing information.* If you believe that helping the client know what to expect can start resolution, you can insert important information into the opening statement (e.g., "In our agency, we want clients to have a lot of say about what happens.").

b. *Providing validation.* If the client is experiencing difficult emotions about entering service, a validating statement can provide an empathic link (e.g., "Coming into a place like this often feels like people are poised to start meddling with your life.").

5. *Invite a response.* An effective opening statement will have captured the most pressing client concern. After making the opening statement, it is important to engage the client. Doing this often involves some sort of question to encourage client discussion.

Case Example

This example is taken from a family-based program associated with Child Protective Services. The practitioner, meeting the clients at an office, completed the introductions and told them about the home-based approach to service. The family is sitting quietly, and there is an awkward moment of silence. The practitioner starts his opening statement. "I am glad that both of you came in today. On the phone you mentioned that the two of you do not agree on disciplining Johnny. It is sometimes hard to openly discuss such hot topics with a third person, especially when Child Protective Services has forced you to come here. Many people feel pressured and judged and want to hold back until they get to know me. That is pretty normal. Before we start talking about your parenting differences, are there any concerns you have about coming here today?"

In the example, the practitioner tuned in to a potential concern about the agency's connection to Child Protective Services. In response, he ensured that this concern was put on the table for the clients. He also validated and normalized the vulnerability concerns; the practitioner then opened the discussion up for the parents to talk about their concerns before proceeding to explore the situation.

Using Interactive Responding

Interactive responding occurs as the practitioner tunes in to the client concerns as they emerge during conversation. Practitioners continually seek to understand how clients are experiencing the service and to respond to clients' feelings (Najavits & Strupp, 1994). Clients consequently begin to feel understood and thus are more willing to engage in the service being provided. As clients feel understood, engagement deepens through frequent exchanges between clients and practitioners.

Picking Up on Concerns

Practitioners often encourage disclosure by picking up on elements in a client's statement that indicate that concerns exist (Baenninger-Huber & Widmer, 1999). Indicators may be verbal or nonverbal signs that are embedded in the statement, causing practitioners to think there is more to the story than meets the eye.

When you hear a client concern, respond in a way that allows clients to feel included and understood. Consequently, it is important to involve clients in exploring and shaping the meaning of the concern (Broome, 1991). This means that the goal of your response is to encourage discussion rather than to try to dismiss or resolve the concern by offering reassurances or explanations. This type of responding involves five basic steps:

1. *Listening to the client statement.* The practitioner listens and observes the client as he or she makes a statement. For example, the client says, "I came here before and really wasn't sure that I wanted to come back."

2. *Identification of processing elements.* While listening and observing, the practitioner reflects on the client statement and mentally labels the important thinking and feeling themes in it. If concerns are evident in these themes, they are identified. For example, in the above statement the client indicated ambivalence about the agency based on past experience.

3. *Tabling the core concern.* From the thinking and feeling elements of the client statement, the practitioner identifies which elements appear to be most important to the client. These become the focus of the response. For example, the practitioner responds, "It sounds like your last experience here wasn't all that you had hoped for."

4. *Validating the concern.* As the practitioner responds to the concerns, the response affirms and validates the client's affective response. This validation may be generalized or normalized to avoid increasing anxiety; however, the client must feel that the concern is valid. For example, "If your experience was not very good last time you came here and you still came in, this must be very important."

5. *Exploration.* When a practitioner has tuned in to the concerns and questions that might be evident for the client, the challenge is to get the concern out in the open and address it. For example, "Tell me about your concerns as you came in here today."

Case Example

As a male client entered treatment in a family service agency, he stated, "I don't know why I am here. People told me I should come and talk to you to see if it will help. I don't even know what to do. Everyone tells me something different. What's the use? You can't help me either. I shouldn't even be bothering you." The practitioner identified a vulnerability concern so she picked up on the feelings that the man was confused and anxious about entering service. She responded, "It sounds like things are getting confusing with many people telling you what to do. This can make you feel like giving up on doing anything about a problem. Do you feel a little like that today?"

In this statement, the practitioner used an indirect response normalizing the concern. She then validated the internal experience and invited the client to open up and explore any concerns he might have. This response picks up on the concern while helping to focus vulnerability so it can be discussed.

Professional Ethics and Negotiating the Helping Relationship

The critical outcome of engagement is the development of a collaborative helping relationship (Gelso & Hayes, 1998; Ridgway & Sharpley, 1990; Walborn, 1996). As a collaborative and open relationship develops, the client is more receptive to intervention (Mallinckrodt, 1993; Reandeau & Wampold, 1991). The ability to engage clients in the helping relationship distinguishes effective from less effective practitioners (Gaston, 1990; Jennings & Skovholt, 1999; Najavits & Strupp, 1994; Pritchard, Cotton, Bowen, & Williams, 1998).

Facilitating Autonomy

Engagement must not be confused with confronting or telling clients what to do. Such behaviors interfere with engagement (Bischoff & Tracey, 1995; W. R. Miller, Benefield, & Tonigan, 1993; Patterson & Forgatch, 1985). In Chapter 2 we discussed the ethical priorities of client self-determination and informed consent. These priorities emerged again when discussing contracting in Chapter 4. As we conclude our discussion on preliminary tuning in and engagement, the priorities reemerge in an interactive form. It is very important that we allow clients to have input into how the service will develop and be delivered. This is a critical element in resolving both knowledge-based concerns and vulnerability-based concerns.

As we respond to client concerns about service, we need to ask their preferences so they can provide input. This input helps shape the goals and methods during contracting and planning. We also allow clients to have input into how we conduct ourselves during service. There will be times when we must point things out that might be uncomfortable, or when we must challenge or encourage clients. We also must support them without taking over their problems. These elements warrant some discussion as we finish preliminary engagement.

The negotiation will use all of the skills (questioning, reflecting, sharing observations, and directing) to be outlined in subsequent chapters. At this point in your learning, you must clearly commit yourself to embodying the ethical principles of informed consent and self-determination as you begin the helping relationship. These principles dovetail with the ethical principle of competence as you use your knowledge to offer clients best practices and evidence-supported options. Adhering to ethical principles ensures that the helping relationship is well grounded and focused from the onset.

Exercise 5.2: Preliminary Tuning In and Engagement

You are a new graduate hired to work with families receiving welfare. You were hired on a grant funding a pilot project. Although you do not know all the details of the grant, you know the basic premise is that children living in poor, single-parent families are at a higher risk for child abuse and child adjustment problems. The project is run through the local Department of Social Services. The agency is located on the edge of town where the buses do not run in the evenings. Consequently, you had many phone contacts with the parents who will be attending the program to arrange rides. Most of the parents are African American and live fairly close to the agency. You are teamed up with a child protection practitioner who is also a member of your graduating class. The program, which includes presentations and lectures, involves a 10-week psychoeducational program focusing on helping the mothers to better understand and attend to their children's emotional needs. You are preparing to meet your first group of parents. You watched them enter the building and noticed many looked older and appeared to have had difficult lives. As you prepare to meet with this group, tune in to the clients.

1. In this situation, whose feelings are driving the development of the group?

2. How might the parents experience the assumptions guiding the program?

3. How might the parents experience your partner?

4. How might the way the program is structured interfere with the parents' experiences?

5. What are the most pressing vulnerability concerns likely to be?

6. Write an opening statement that can begin to get some of these concerns on the table.

Interactive Engagement

Preliminary engagement is achieved when the client resolves their early concerns and makes an emotional decision to continue coming in for service (Warwar et al., 2008). If preliminary engagement does not occur, clients are not likely to continue or actively participate in service (McKay, Nudelman, McCadam, & Bonzales, 1996; Samstag, Batchelder, Muran, Safran, & Winston, 1998). When clients continue, they must then achieve interactive engagement.

Interactive engagement influences the levels of honesty, cooperation, and openness in the helping relationship. Consequently, interaction is a critical element in the empathic relationship (Wynn & Wynn, 2006). As clients begin sharing, we can identify their concerns, priorities, and conflicts. We then respond back in a way that captures their core concerns, and motivation engagement deepens (Huppert et al., 2006; Moyers & Martin, 2006). This back-and-forth pattern of listening and responding is the foundation of the helping relationship.

Socialization Challenges to Interactive Engagement

Several major socialization challenges are associated with interactive engagement. Almost all of our interactive habits are an outcome of socialization experiences. The difficulty with socialized interactive habits is that we often are unaware that they exist. Consequently, we must first discover the habit, then take control. Doing this can be frustrating because discovering our habits is not always a welcome quest. We tend to assume that our interaction is effective because it has supported our social successes. When we discover that our habits are insufficient for professional communication we are often surprised and do not want to invest the conscious energy required to alter our habits.

When we confront our socialized habits, it is useful to remember that most socialization is designed to promote social success. Parents and teachers invest time and energy to ensure that we are polite so we do not alienate other people when we speak. They teach us to take turns, avoid offensive comments, and be helpful. Although these interactive habits promote social success, they can interfere with the optimal use of our skills in the helping relationship. Three major habits can interfere with engagement:

1. *Turn-taking.* As part of our politeness socialization, we learn to wait our turn to speak. Over the years we develop a habit of listening until we have a thought. The thought is triggered by something the other person said, which leads to our impulse to express the thought. We then shift our focus to our mind, waiting for our turn to speak. When our turn comes, we download our thought, putting a "new package" on the table. This habit results in disengagement as we focus on our thought and cease listening to the other person.

2. *Advice-giving.* Our problem-solving socialization has a heavy emphasis on providing advice. Parents, teachers, and authority figures consistently help us identify problems and then provide helpful suggestions about what we should do. The consistency of this pattern in our socialization promotes advice giving as our default setting when we help other people with their problems. Rather than engaging people in solving their own problems, we tend to construct our own solutions and impart those solutions onto their situation.

3. *Arbitration.* When there is conflict involving more than one person, the advice-giving patterns seem to evolve into arbitration. This variation involves the authority figure briefly listening to each person's position in the conflict before imposing a solution on the situation. We have experienced this pattern with parents, teachers, and even supervisors whenever there is conflict in a larger system.

These interactive patterns are socialized into us through repeated experiences during our formative years. Now, as well-socialized beings, we repeat the patterns in our own relationships. It is only natural that the patterns will seep into our helping relationships unless we consciously alter how we interact. Doing this requires us to understand and interrupt our habits as we develop new patterns of interaction. The next discussions can help develop new patterns of interaction for professional helping relationships.

Tuning In to Interaction

Interactive engagement builds on our ability to tune in to a client's communication. As we begin to understand interactive engagement, it is useful to consider the response system framework. In earlier discussions we have used the response systems to identify the elements of how people respond to situations. There are two major response systems: action systems (behavior and interaction) and processing systems (thinking and feeling). As clients respond to their situations, all elements of these systems are in operation. Consequently, as people talk about their situation, all elements will be embedded in their discussions.

As we listen to our clients talk, we can hear all four elements—feeling, thinking, interaction, and behavior—if we carefully tune in to their communication. As the client speaks, all four response systems are placed on the table (see Table 5.2). As we observe the communicated package, some elements tend to be more visible while others are implicit. We are comfortable finding action themes because they tend to carry the content (e.g., who did and said what to whom). The thinking and the feeling may be embedded in assumptions and expectations and harder to find.

As we tune in to the response elements embedded in the client's statements, we can focus on the most important ones. For example, the mother says, "I have tried everything and I don't know what to do." This statement action suggests that she has tried multiple solutions with no outcomes. Processing themes suggest that she is currently feeling helpless and has run out of options. As we tune in to this statement, the emotional themes of helplessness emerge as most important. Consequently, we are most likely to pick up on these themes to build our response.

Table 5.2 Identifying Response Systems

Mother	14-Year-Old Son
Statement:	
"I don't know what to do. I have tried everything and I don't know what to do. He just keeps ignoring me and acting like I don't exist. I set the rules and he should follow them."	"It's no big deal. I just want to be with my friends. You expect me to stay a baby forever. It doesn't happen that way. . . . I am growing up, treat me that way. Every time I go out you want me in early and start phoning around if I am late."
Content:	
This mother feels she is trying to do her best but it is not working. Her son is moving away from her influence and defying her.	This son is stating that he is a normal teenage kid and wants to be treated like his friends.
Processing Elements:	
Thinking: The mother wants to be a good parent and believes doing this requires being central and in charge.	*Thinking:* The son believes that the mother is treating him like a baby and this is unrealistic.
Feeling: The mother feels powerless and inadequate in her role.	*Feeling:* The son is embarrassed and also powerless because he cannot influence his mother.
Action Elements:	
Interaction: The mother engages in cycles of arguing to convince the son to obey her rules.	*Interaction:* The son continually argues for more autonomy but does not feel heard.
Behavior: The mother continually attempts to gain control of the son by interfering when he goes out with friends.	*Behavior:* The son goes to his friends and often stays late.

Critical Elements in Interactive Engagement

As you build your interactive tuning in skills, two elements are involved: effective listening and an atuned response.

First, you must listen to clients effectively. Important information is embedded in client statements, both in the content and in the delivery. As you listen, focus on the statement to identify the most meaningful and important elements. This focus involves three basic skills:

1. *Attending behaviors.* Attending behaviors include verbal and nonverbal behaviors that communicate that you are listening and the client should continue talking. Some nonverbal behaviors include nodding, eye contact, gestures, and body position used to indicate a full interest in the client's disclosures. Verbal behaviors include "uh-huhs" and other short verbalizations that show listening.

2. *Perception checking.* It is helpful to check your understanding of what clients are saying (Wubbolding, 1996). Doing this involves asking for clarification or restating the understanding so clients can correct or validate it. You can start perception checking with statements such as "So, are you saying . . . "

3. *Identifying critical response elements.* Every client statement contains elements of feeling, thinking, relationships, and actions (Ragg, 2001). As you listen to your clients, monitor all elements, so you can identify which areas of responding are most important. It is important to consider all response elements because many client concerns are expressed in their thinking and feeling rather than in the words.

The second critical element is your atuned response. Clients must feel that you understand and care about what they are saying. If your responses promote this experience, clients will begin to trust you with the details of their life story (Goldin & Doyle, 1991). If you fail to understand or respond appropriately to client statements, engagement can be compromised.

Interactive engagement involves a back-and-forth rhythm between you and the client. After you set the table using the opening statement, the client responds, beginning an interactive cycle (see Figure 5.2). The client response puts a package on the table, which becomes the foundation for your next response. You then use the skills described earlier to understand the statement and identify its important elements. As you respond back (based on careful listening) you place your own communication package (containing important client elements) on the table. The interactive sequence contained in Figure 5.2 contains five important steps.

Figure 5.2

Interactive Flow

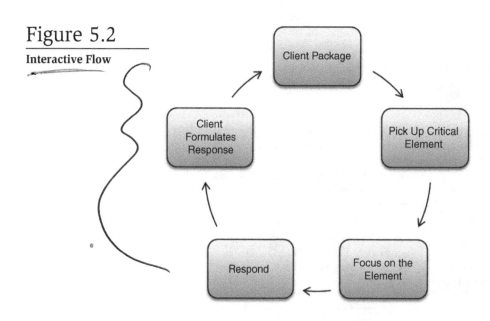

1. Client package. The client makes a statement that puts a communicated package on the table.
2. Critical elements. You identify the critical element embedded in the client's communication.
3. Focusing. As you prepare your response you focus on the critical element.
4. Response. When you respond you place your own communication package on the table that includes the critical element.
5. Client response. The client hears your response and responds to your treatment of the critical element.

Continuing with the table metaphor, you are constantly working with the communication packages that arrive on the table. Consequently, you must keep your focus on client communication to pick out the most important elements from the table. Only then can you respond in ways that deepen your understanding and promote movement toward client goals. The interactive flow builds on this back-and-forth pattern where you respond to the client communication and the client in turn responds back to you based on what you put on the table. This back-and-forth pattern is called interactive engagement.

Exercise 5.3: Interactive Engagement

1. An adolescent girl talking with a counselor says, "It is so hard in this family. People are down on you when you mess up but nobody cares when you are doing well. I worked hard at school to bring my grades up and was so happy when I got six As. I brought my report card home excited. When Dad read it, he didn't even look up at me. He just grunted and said, 'They must have given you the wrong report card.' I couldn't believe it. After hard work, all I got was a grunt and crap like that. But if I got six Ds, you know darn well he would spend time on it. I don't know why I even try to do well. I don't even know why I try at all."

   a. What are the action elements (behavior and interaction)?

   b. What are the processing elements (feeling and thinking)?

   c. What are the most important elements to pick up on?

   d. Write a response that can get these elements on the table.

2. You are a practitioner in the Department of Social Services talking with a single mother. She says, "Sometimes I just don't know if I can manage. It is the beginning of the month and the mailman just brings me pressure and pain. Bills, bills, and more bills. On top of that, I have to take care of my kids. They always want more things. Snacks, sneakers, school trips . . . it just gets impossible. Now you are telling me I have to work 20 hours every week just to get my benefits. The store wants me to work in the evening. That is when I need to be home with my kids. I feel like I can't win."

a. What are the action elements (behavior and interaction)?

b. What are the processing elements (feeling and thinking)?

c. What are the most important elements to pick up on?

d. Write a response that can get these elements on the table.

Socialization, Culture, and Interactive Responding

When we enter the helping professions we have no preexisting method for responding to vulnerability concerns. Most of us have been socialized to retreat from conversations when people are expressing concerns. We often avoid entry into such discussions, especially when we have other things we want to talk about. Consider these socialization influences:

- *Scripted responses.* We all have social scripts that keep vulnerabilities out of our daily conversations. When people ask "How are you doing?" we immediately answer "Fine." There is no consideration; these responses are automatically scripted. If people started providing honest answers to this type of question, many people would stop asking.
- *Problem avoidance.* We are heavily socialized to shift focus quickly away from problems. In our social relationships, when people express a problem, we often listen for a moment, provide a brief response, then we change the subject. We have all expressed problems to others only to get responses like "That's okay, it will get better," "You'll get over it," or "That sucks . . . sorry you are going through that." Then the subject gets changed. When the problem involves us, our response usually is to apologize, then change the subject.
- *Advice giving.* When we cannot avoid discussions of vulnerability, we often move into an advice-giving mode. This involves a slightly longer discussion where we listen to the problem, ask some questions, and then provide advice. If the person persists in discussing the problem, we often stick with our advice and try to end the discussion.
- *Past experiences with vulnerable people.* As we age, many of us have had experiences where we asked a simple question and were hooked into long discussions about a person's problem. We discover that after a person gets to a certain point in a problem-focused discussion, there is no easy way to end the conversation. Consequently, we find ways to detect vulnerability early in a discussion so we can exit before we get too deeply involved.

These socialization influences vary from person to person, yet we can easily identify with some of the exchanges. Consider these socialization influences your default settings for responding to people's concerns. Given this, you must be careful not to dismiss client concerns about service. A common dismissive attitude emerges as we quickly attempt to explore client problems rather than service-related concerns. Beware of attempts to dismiss concerns with brief comments, apologies, and advice. As professionals, we must develop methods for focusing on the concerns so they can be resolved.

Challenges for Digital Communicators

Digital communication is largely a one-dimensional medium providing content through text. Emotional content emerges through word selection or through the insertion of deliberate symbols or letters intended to convey an emotional response. When we rely on digital media for our main source of interaction, we lose practice at tuning in to the subtle communication elements that provide information about emotion and interpretation.

Digital communications may face tuning in challenges. First, as you begin building empathic responding skills, you are faced with many nonverbal communications that require attention. This can challenge people who prefer communicating through text-based digital media. Often the content is but a minor element in a verbal message.

A second challenge emerges in the pace of communication. Digital communication, while interactive, allows people the liberty to reflect on a situation prior to scripting a response. There is no expectation to respond immediately. Interactive tuning in, however, requires us to grasp a person's full meaning and respond immediately. There is little opportunity to hesitate and plan a response. This immediacy can be a challenge for people who are used to a digital-based communication system.

Interactive Engagement With Larger Client Systems

When we engage individual clients, we focus on one person and align our responses accordingly. Larger client systems are more complex as we must attend to several people all putting packages on the table. In the discussion of preliminary tuning in and engagement, you learned that each person within the larger system has his or her own unique perspective.

The multiple perspectives can make interactive engagement seem confusing; each person often asserts his or her own perspective, hoping to influence the practitioner (Buttny, 1996; Ivey & Ivey, 1998; Patalano, 1997). Successful engagement requires that we help system members to find common ground and a sense of shared purpose (Beck et al., 2006; Beutler et al., 2006; Creed & Kendall, 2005). To develop this shared vision, we must be able to manage the divisive systemic energy and develop a new understanding of the problem that can achieve common purpose among the members.

Managing Divisive Energy

When larger systems enter service, we often find that people's unique perspectives on the problem are in competition (Cunningham & Henggeler, 1999). Consequently, practitioners initially must neutralize divisive energy so common ground and shared purpose can be established.

- *Deescalate arguments.* To deescalate conflicts, it is useful to affirm each person's emotional experience without taking sides or affirming an individual's definition of the problem. The goal is to allow each person to identify and share emotions so commonalities in their emotional experience can emerge.
- *Neutralize negative attributions.* People within larger client systems often harbor negative attributions and beliefs about other people and events. These attributions maintain problems in the system. It is important to help system members accept neutral or positive attributions to decrease the negative energy in the system.
- *Build common ground.* Common desires, values, and goals are often ignored when system members are in conflict. As the negative energy subsides, highlighting the commonalities allows people to identify more strongly with each other.

Reworking the Problem Definition

As negative energy is neutralized and common ground highlighted, it is possible to develop a new definition of problems. To help redefine or reframe the client problem, first it is important to tune in to the clients' initial understanding and attributions. Inherent in the initial definition are client vulnerabilities, as clients often set up problem definitions to feel safe. However, these initial frames inadvertently keep problems intact. Most often the initial definitions attribute responsibility in a way that makes it hard to coordinate action (e.g., with another person or past events). To build a common purpose, we need to shift the definition so all members of the system are committed to the change. To set a more hopeful frame (or definition of the problem), use this four-step process.

1. *Listen to and understand each client's definition of the problem.* In such listening, track the themes in the situation. For example, an aging woman who appears depressed says, "I don't know what to do. I get so tired. Tom had a stroke last year and doesn't remember things. I send him up to put on his pajamas and he comes down in a suit. I can't go out anymore because he gets so confused. I sometimes find I don't even like him anymore. This is my retirement and all I seem to do is work." Tom shares, "I know it is hard . . . my mind just isn't working. I see her so upset and I know it is about me. I just don't know how to fix things."

2. *Identify problematic elements.* Identify the elements of the current understanding that interfere with solving the problem. For example, the couple places the responsibility for the problem on Tom as a result of his physical ailments. The health of the partner cannot change, so the definition of the problem is quite hopeless. This makes the problem hard to resolve because the couple cannot influence the disease.

3. *Find potential flexibility.* Discover elements in the situation that can be identified differently. Review the themes, constructs, and language in the situation, and consider how the definition can be shifted. For example, the problem can be redefined so it is not attached to the disease but rather to the woman's exhaustion.

4. *Create an alternative definition.* Use the important themes and constructs to formulate a different definition of the problem that is close enough to the original definition but different enough to be hopeful. For example, say: "It sounds like you are very tired of having to always put out energy for your partner, and you don't get a chance to refill your energy. It seems that we need to explore ways you can start replenishing yourself. That may give you more energy and allow Tom to feel less of a burden. What do you think?"

When thinking about how to set the problem definition, make sure clients can experience some hopefulness about the solution. Also present the problem definition in a manner that is safe for the clients. Consider alternative definitions of the problem that fit the problem behavior patterns but avoid the traps inherent in the current definitions. In making the new definition, it is useful to maintain a positive or a strengths focus.

Exercise 5.4: Problem Identification and Reframing

The family of a young woman who was recently diagnosed with schizophrenia was referred for service after she attempted suicide. The family consists of the girl, a father, and a stepmother. At the beginning of the session, the girl reports, "It is so hard in this family. I don't know what to do. People look at me like I am weird. They talk about me all the time and are just waiting for me to mess up. I can't stand it. They are just so negative." In response to this statement, the stepmother states: "I don't know why you always blame us. We just can't keep you happy. We are busy and have to rest after work. We can't give you all of our attention; we need some for ourselves." The father then touched the stepmother's arm and said: "I don't know why you always have to fight with her. Just relax and it will get better."

1. How does the daughter frame the problem? (Write her definition.)

2. How does the stepmother frame the problem? (Write her definition.)

3. How does the father frame the problem? (Write his definition.)

4. Write a new problem definition that can make it easier to engage the family in problem solving.

Maintaining Interactive Engagement

As the helping relationship deepens, be vigilant to ensure that you maintain active engagement with the client. It is important to continue listening and responding rather than falling into socialized interactive habits. As you first develop your skills, there will be frequent moments of disengagement. This is common. The first milestone of the skill development is to notice the disengagement. After you can identify disengagement, it becomes possible to reengage and eventually to avoid disengagement.

Signs of Disengagement

One of the risks in the helping relationship is losing focus on the client concerns (Allen, Gabbard, Newsom, & Coyne, 1990; Elkind, 1992; Patalano, 1997). Your mind can drift in many directions, and you may not even notice that you have broken active engagement because you are thinking about something the client said rather than listening. When you disengage from clients, you will find that your mental energy has shifted focus. Often you will either be thinking about something or planning to take action. Self-awareness is important in identifying disengagement in order to reconnect with clients. Use the list of disengagement indicators to help you tune in to your patterns of disengagement.

1. *Downloading agendas.* You may find yourself downloading an agenda in response to your thoughts stimulated by the client situation. As you listen to the client, if you get caught up in your thinking, believe you have a solution, and begin to propose your solution you have likely disengaged. Consider these variations on downloaded agendas.
   - *Pitching solutions.* When you find yourself really wanting to help, you will experience an internalized pressure to provide a solution. With more difficult situations, the pressure increases. Your focus on the solution creates disengagement because the solution is based on your conjectures about the client situation. Solutions also disempower clients by having them depend on you for solutions.
   - *Imposing a need to change.* Sometimes you may find yourself correcting or stressing a need to change something in the situation. Statements such as "You need to understand," "Let's look at this logically," or simple corrections move the focus of the relationship from client disclosures to your thoughts of what the client should be doing. This form of disengagement provokes counterargument and highlights differences rather than collaboration.
   - *Counterpositioning.* At times you will disengage from a client's story by taking the position of other people trying to force their perspective on the client (e.g., "What do you think they felt when this happened?" or "How would you feel if someone did that to you?"). Such disengagement may cause clients to feel that you are taking sides by supporting other people.

2. *Downloading personal reactions.* Agendas are prompted by your thinking, but reactions often emerge from a sense of caring for the client. When you react, typically you want the best for the client so you download an impulse to make things better. This behavior may be noble, but it still creates disengagement and can disrupt the working relationship. Consider these three variations on downloaded reactions:

○ *Consoling.* Sometimes you will feel that you want to make clients feel better. For example, you may have an impulse to assure your client that he or she is a good person or otherwise help them feel better by imposing a positive judgment (For example, "You are a good parent; you just need to learn more problem-solving skills"). Such dynamics disengage you from empowering the client or using client strengths because you adopt a position of judging, which elevates your power.

○ *Rescuing.* Sometimes you may react by immediately starting some action, such as planning to go with the client to perform a task. For example, a client was talking about difficulties with his lawyer. The practitioner responded, "Well! We will see about that," and asked for the lawyer's phone number to book an appointment for both of them. Although attending appointments with clients can be an appropriate intervention, clients need to request that you take such action.

○ *Doomsday predictions.* These predictions involve warning clients about what might happen. This response may emerge when you hear a client story that contains an element of risk. If you find yourself warning the client what might happen, you have disengaged and are basing the warning on your conjecture. You and the client are no longer partners in the story.

3. *Downloading personal needs.* There are times when your responses download material onto the table that has nothing to do with the client. Rather, the response is controlled personal needs. Some needs are noble. We all have a need to be helpful; otherwise we would not be entering a helping profession. However, when your needs dictate your response, you are at risk of being self-serving rather than serving your client. Notice the self-serving elements in the next types of responses.

○ *Exerting knowledge.* If you begin informing the client about what is wrong with him or her (e.g., "See, because of your history you just can't help yourself. This is called learned helplessness") you inadvertently elevate your power in the relationship. When you adopt an expert position you retreat into thinking. Clients may feel threatened by such judgments or believe that you can see right through them. With feelings of threat, clients may disengage to protect themselves.

○ *Unfocused self-disclosure.* A subtle form of disengagement is to share your story with the client. Doing this can be helpful when sharing has a very specific purpose that cannot be met through other methods, but unfocused sharing can diminish the goal focus of the relationship, causing it to appear more like a friendship than a professional relationship.

○ *Imposing standards.* One of the most difficult forms of disengagement is when you disapprove of client's decisions and actions. This may result in some form of chastisement or negative reaction. For example, when a client tells you of a mistake, you might say: "What were you thinking when you made that decision?" Such statements make clients feel judged and disempowered.

Methods of Reengagement

The solution to disengagement is rapid identification and reengagement. First be aware when you stop listening and start downloading. Often the first sign is that you will talk more and the client begins to talk less. After you are aware, it is important to reengage as quickly as possible. There are four common methods of reengaging.

1. *Using recall.* The simplest form of reengaging is to mentally reconstruct the conversation to bring yourself back to the client situation. This method works best if the disengagement is brief and has not yet resulted in a loss of focus in the discussion. For example, if you find you are offering suggestions say, "Oh, sorry . . . I am getting ahead of myself here. You were mentioning your partner is sometimes challenging."

2. *Reorienting to the client story.* Another simple system for reengaging is first to notice the disengagement and then to begin listening intently. If you can immediately recall the central themes of the story and little time has elapsed, you can reengage without saying anything. However, this can be dangerous as you may have missed content that the client feels is important. Consequently, you should use this strategy with care.

3. *Reengaging through feelings.* Sometimes you can reengage by using your feelings to reconnect. This begins when you notice that an emotional response has triggered disengagement. You can then use the feeling response to reconnect. For example, if you find you want to change the subject to get away from emotionally heavy material, you can say, "When you were talking, I found myself wanting to change the subject to avoid facing the pain in your life. Do you find things overwhelming at times?"

4. *Creating a bridge.* If you have moved too far away from the client's story, you often have to create a bridge back to the earlier discussion. Doing this involves self-awareness about where you were attempting to take the process. Then you can make a clear statement of where you are trying to go and ultimately make a connection to the point of departure from the client's story.

Case Example

A practitioner was listening to a mother complain about her son's behavior. The practitioner offered suggestions for solutions that are rejected by the mother. He became aware that he was moving in a nonfruitful direction (had disengaged). The response is, "Awhile back you were talking about your frustration and I seem to have jumped into trying to solve things, but I am not sure I truly understand what you were trying to tell me. You were talking about how you get so angry. Can you tell me more about the things that get you most angry?"

Maintaining Engagement

Frequent disengagement is not good for the helping relationship; consequently, an important skill is learning to maintain our engagement with clients. The first step is awareness of our disconnections. The second skill element is to direct your focus. As you become aware of your interactive habits, shift our focus back to the table. It is quite easy to practice this skill element because you are often in conversations. Every conversation is an opportunity to listen better.

With practice you can maintain focus and eventually resist reactions or impulses to download. Typically, the third element of skill development is to keep engagement at those moments when you want to take care of the client or provide advice. For this skill element, you need to develop skill options to past habits. The skills in subsequent chapters will help develop new habits. Consequently, engagement skills will continue to develop and solidify as you add interpersonal skills to your repertoire.

Critical Chapter Themes

1. Effective practitioners establish an empathic relationship with their clients by tuning in to the client and responding to the client's internal experience.

2. Preliminary tuning in occurs before the client enters service, when we use information to understand the client experience of beginning service. Doing this helps identify fears, concerns, and vulnerabilities. We respond to these concerns either directly by getting them on the table or indirectly through monitoring.

3. Knowledge-based concerns can be resolved by introducing and explaining the elements of service. Vulnerabilities require a more sensitive approach to responding.

4. Interactional tuning in involves identifying the underlying content, interactions, affect, and beliefs in client statements. After these elements are identified, the practitioner can respond with empathy to the client.

5. We must establish a system of picking up on the most important elements in the client communication so we can respond directly to client needs.

6. It is important to remain focused on the client communication instead of on our own thinking and beliefs.

Online Resources

Child Welfare Information Gateway: httpwww.childwelfare.gov/index.cfm

PractitionerFamily Engagement: A Web-Based Practice Toolkit: www.hunter.cuny.edu/socwork/nrcfcpp/fewpt/index.htm

The New Social Practitioner Online: www.socialworker.com/home/index.php

Recommended Readings

Decety, J., & Meyer, M. (2008). From emotion resonance to empathic understanding: A social developmental neuroscience account. *Development and Psychopathology, 20,* 1053–1080.

Escudero, V., Friedlander, M. L., Nuria, V., & Abascal, A. (2008). Observing the therapeutic alliance in family therapy: Associations with participants' perceptions and therapeutic outcomes. *Journal of Family Therapy, 30,* 194–214.

Kirmayer, L. J. (2008). Empathy and alterity in cultural psychiatry. *Ethos, 36,* 457–474.

Watson, J. C. (2007). Reassessing Rogers' necessary and sufficient conditions of change. *Psychotherapy: Theory, Research, Practice, Training, 44,* 268–273.

Chapter 6
Questioning Skills

Questioning is a critical skill for any helping professional (Shechtman, 2004; Sween, 2003). Without the skillful use of questions, client exchanges would lack direction and depth because the practitioner would be unable to access information. Questions solicit information about the client, the client situation, and the problems influencing the client. Effective practitioners select questions based on their understanding of the client situation and the goals of service. Consequently, questioning builds on the thinking and tuning in skills discussed in earlier chapters.

As we explore the use of questioning in the helping relationship, we quickly learn that questions help focus, expand, challenge, or confirm our understanding of the client situation. We will also discover that questions can be very brief or quite complex. Brief questions (e.g., "And then?") are not even complete sentences. Often they are referred to as probes or prompts. Other questions can be so complex that they last two or three sentences. Regardless of the length, questioning skills pick up on client statements and respond in a way that encourages the client to expand on the statement. This chapter explores the full range of questions in professional practice.

Power of Questions: Socialization and Culture

Questions are powerful professional tools. When people hear a question, they respond in a unique manner (Buttner, 2007). This is because every question contains an implicit obligation to answer (Wang, 2006). As a student, you are aware that whenever the instructor asks a question, tension rises in the classroom until someone provides an answer. If an answer is not forthcoming, the tension continues to build until some brave soul rescues the class by attempting an answer. The tension emerges from the implicit obligation to respond. Questions are powerful because people feel obligated to respond.

Concurrent with the obligation to respond, people who answer questions expect that the person listening will receive and understand what they have said (Pingree, 2007). When the practitioner responds in a way that conveys that the answer has been heard and understood, empathy and understanding emerge (Hammond & Nichols, 2008; Pachankis & Goldfried, 2007; Wynn & Wynn, 2006). Research finds that active, explorative approaches, typified by questioning, are associated with a stronger helping alliance (Huber, Henrich, & Brandl, 2005; Moyers & Martin, 2006; Sexton, Littauer, Sexton, Tømmerås, 2005). Concurrently, a lack of understanding or distraction is associated with problems in the helping relationship (Keenan, Tsang, Bogo, & George, 2005; Shechtman, 2004).

Socialization and Questioning

The inherent power of questioning emerges from our socialization experiences. We have all had a parent or authority figure issue commands, such as "Look at me" and "Answer me," during questioning. Over the years we internalize these commands so when we make eye contact after a question, we feel compelled to answer. This is why most people's eyes drop to the paper on their desk whenever the instructor asks a question in class. As students, we believe that the obligation to answer can be ducked if we do not make a social connection to the instructor through eye contact.

Other socialization experiences shape our use of questions. As very young children we learn that if we want to know something, we have to ask. During our inquisitive years, we inundate parents with questions about every experience we have. This establishes a long history of using questions to learn. By the time we enter college, we have asked billions of questions. Questions are one of our preferred methods of interaction. As a result, we are usually very comfortable asking questions as they spring from our lips with very little conscious effort or thought.

Questioning and Culture

Our experience with questioning occurs within a cultural context. Members of the dominant North American culture tend to value questions. Most people within the dominant culture have heard the statement "If you want something, all you need to do is ask." Many of us have also been raised with the mantra "Question authority." Inherently, there are cultural beliefs that asking a question is a good thing. In college settings, instructors reward asking and answering questions with participation grades. Such educational reward systems further reinforce the value of questions. Consequently, most students from the dominant culture feel comfortable and competent when it comes to asking questions.

Although the dominant culture values questioning, other cultures vary in their reaction to questioning. For example, some Native American people feel that questions are intrusive. Listening and observing are more highly valued so too many questions can feel rude. For this reason, it is critical to consider potential cultural differences when using the skill of questioning.

A second cultural consideration emerges due to the implicit obligation to respond. Members of the dominant society expect people to respond when they ask a question. Not all cultures experience this same pressure to respond. Concurrently, the power differences between dominant and minority cultures may cause resentment when members of the dominant culture ask too many questions.

Socialization Challenges

Even though we have a long history of asking questions, our precision in using questions is often lacking. We often rely on the implicit content rather than paying attention to the actual question (Hurvitz & Schlesinger, 2009). For example, we may ask, "Are you sure you want to do that?" when what we mean to say is "I don't think that is wise." Similarly, we often ask how people feel when we want to know what they think.

Based on this socialized use of questions, our interactive habits have caused us to be quite sloppy in how we formulate questions. At the same time, implicit content has caused us to respond based on our thoughts rather than the actual content of the question. This habit of responding from our thinking involves a disengagement from the other person. Although this may be commonplace in social relationships, it can create difficulties in a professional relationship.

Questioning Formats to Avoid

With socialization as our primary influence in developing our approach to questioning, it is important to understand that some of our interactive habits can interfere with professional practice. Observe how questioning habits in our social relationships are often off target, showing very little listening. Friends and family members are invested in the relationship, so our questioning styles are often understood or forgiven. Questions directed at strangers are often impersonal and safe. Consequently, there is no depth. Both social experiences do not provide a solid foundation for using questions in a professional relationship.

Several types of questions are counterproductive in a helping relationship. Although these types of questions are common in social relationships, they are not helpful with clients. Consequently, many of the question types listed next will represent habits that you will need to break. In the list of problematic questioning formats, the first three ("why," leading, and closed-ended questions) represent questions where practitioner power may be elevated, resulting in client disempowerment. The last two types of questions (multiple and vague questions) involve the practitioner disengaging from the client.

Problematic Questioning Formats
1. "Why" questions
2. Closed-ended questions

3. Leading questions
4. Multiple questions
5. Vague questions

"Why" Questions

In social relationships, we often ask each other "why" questions when we want to understand something. In the helping relationship, although we often want to know why a client is engaging in a certain behavior, it is important to resist the impulse to use the automatic "why." "Why" questions are a problem for three reasons.

1. There often are complex reasons underlying people's actions. People may be influenced by a combination of childhood experiences, current motivations, impulses, anticipated rewards, and perceived injunctions. When you ask a "why" question, you assume that the client has thought through all of these influences and made an informed decision. When this presumption is not true, the client feels pressured to guess at the real reason to construct an answer to the question (Patton, 1980).

2. A "why" question limits potential causes for clients' actions. Clients feel that they must come up with a single cause for their decision or action. Consequently, answering the "why" question leaves all other reasons undisclosed. When clients respond with a single reason, they are bound by the simple response even though they are aware that the real reasons for their choices are much more complex (Heineman, 2008; Patton, 1980).

3. "Why" questions present respondents with a challenge (Monzoni, 2008). When you ask "why," clients are put in a position where they must explain or defend their actions to you (Patton, 1980). Clients can become defensive and eventually resent you. If this is an ongoing pattern in the helping relationship, the resentment and constant disempowerment can cause clients to withhold information or withdraw from the relationship.

Case Example

A practitioner in a youth drop-in center was talking with an adolescent boy who had run away from home. The teen used to be in a relationship with a girl who frequented the program. The boy was sharing the problem that led to the breakup of this relationship.

> **Teen:** *I was really messed up. She was talking with John and I got jealous. I asked her nicely to stay away from him but she kept saying they were just friends. I started to get pissed . . . she wouldn't do one simple thing for me . . . you'd think she would if she really loved me. I loved her and I didn't flirt around with other girls, but she wouldn't do that one thing. I thought if John is more important than me, then have him . . . so I told her to go f#%k herself.*
>
> **Practitioner:** *If they were just friends, why would you break off with her and tell her to f#%k herself?* (Note that this is both a multiple and a "why" question.)
>
> **Teen:** *When a man and a woman are together they should be together.*
>
> **Practitioner:** *But he was just a friend, why dump her?* (Another "why" question.)
>
> **Teen:** *'Cause she was my woman . . . not his.*
>
> **Practitioner:** *I still don't understand. . . .*
>
> **Teen:** *That's just it, man . . . nobody understands. . . .*

In this example, observe how the youth was very open and talking freely before the "why" question was asked. After the question, he became defensive and limited his responses. As the practitioner persisted with the "why" questions, the youth began to shut down, and the relationship with the practitioner started to disintegrate. Eventually the youth included the practitioner in with everyone else who failed to understand him.

Closed-Ended Questions

Closed-ended questions are somewhat useful when you want to confirm or rule out information (Monzoni, 2008). However, they are useful only when there are two possible answers (e.g., "Did you phone your doctor?"). When there are more than two possible responses, the question style is problematic because it closes off additional information (Evans, Hearn, Uhlemann, & Ivey, 1998; Murphy & Dillon, 1998). When closed questions are used in a situation of multiple possibilities, you must use follow-up questions to glean a full understanding. Consequently, you have to use a series of questions, which the client may experience as an inquisition (Walton, 2006).

Case Example

A female client was talking about her fiancée. She was very ambivalent about remaining in the relationship. The practitioner picked up on this, and the following sequence of questions occurred rather than an open-ended question.

PRACTITIONER: *Do you want to leave him?* (Closed.)
WOMAN: *(pause) Well yes, but . . .*
PRACTITIONER: *Do you want to stay?* (Closed.)
WOMAN: *Well . . . no, but you know he is sometimes so sweet and I am not sure that I will ever find someone who loves me as much as he does.*
PRACTITIONER: *Does he make you feel loved?* (Closed.)
WOMAN: *I guess so.*
PRACTITIONER: *Do you love him?* (Closed.)
WOMAN: *I don't know.*
PRACTITIONER: *What do you mean?* (Open.)
WOMAN: *Well, we have been together since high school. I loved him so much then and was so happy when he asked me out. But that was five years ago, and I am not sure I have been able to really get to know who I am. . . .*

In the example, notice how closed-ended questions box the woman into choosing between two possible answers, both of which fail to capture her situation. The practitioner then used additional questions to elicit more information. Also notice how the open-ended question allowed the woman to open up about her feelings. Had the practitioner started with an open-ended question such as "How are things going on the relationship front?" the client could have provided information based on her priorities and experiences.

Leading Questions

Leading questions are a specific form of closed-ended question where the person asking the question first establishes knowledge or a premise and then asks a closed-ended question formatted so the responder has little alternative except to affirm the information (Heinemann, 2008; Steensig & Larsen, 2008). We often use leading questions when we believe that we know what is happening with our friends. In our conversations, we first state what we believe and then expect the friend to affirm our thinking. This habit is useful with people who know and love us, but it can be problematic in professional relationships.

When practitioners assume they know what is happening with a client, they are at risk of asking a leading question. With leading questions, practitioners superimpose their mental image of what has happened when setting up the question. There is no option to generate information so clients feel that all they can do is confirm the assumption in question (Steensig & Larsen, 2008). Such questions limit clients' ability to disclose their own information.

Case Example

A child protection practitioner suspects that a child has been sexually abused because of something observed in her drawing. The practitioner has been told that others in the family have been molested and is convinced that the child is a victim as well. The practitioner wants to have the child admit to the abuse.

PRACTITIONER: *I was looking at your picture, and it tells me that there is something going on in your family, right?* (Leading question and so vague that one must say "right.")

> **CHILD:** *Yeah.*
> **PRACTITIONER:** *This kind of thing has happened before, hasn't it?* (Again, vague and leading.)
> **CHILD:** *What kind of thing?*
> **PRACTITIONER:** *Well, I know that your sisters were taken away for good reasons, right?* (Vague and leading.)
> **CHILD:** *Well, yeah.*
> **PRACTITIONER:** *And now the same thing is happening to you, isn't that true?* (Leading.)
> **CHILD:** *No . . . .*
> **PRACTITIONER:** *It's okay. Tell me how are you being abused.* (Leading.)

In this example, notice the pressure being placed on the child because there are already predetermined answers to the questions. The child is being boxed into responding in certain ways. With the pressure and limited options, the child may affirm the question to make the practitioner stop. It is most unfortunate when faulty questioning results in disruptive actions with clients and their families.

Multiple Questions

Multiple questions emerge when practitioners shift focus to their thinking while in the act of questioning. Often as a question is being delivered, practitioners sense that it is not clear or focused the way they would like. In an attempt to clarify the question, they deliver a series of questions (Kasper & Ross, 2007). The intent is to clarify the question, but often the delivery becomes more confusing. With multiple questions to select from, the client does not know how to respond (Murphy & Dillon, 1998; Patton, 1980). The direction of the exploration may diverge because the client selects an easy question rather than a question that contains a helpful direction.

Case Example

In this excerpt, the practitioner is checking in with a client at the beginning of a meeting. The client is a homeless man who in the previous meeting decided to approach a church to see if it could give him relief money. He hoped to use the money to put down on a room above a hotel. As it turned out, the church needed a custodian, and the man was able to get some temporary work. However, at the beginning of the meeting, as a result of multiple questioning, the practitioner makes it hard for the man to share this information.

> **PRACTITIONER:** *So how did it go? Did they give you money, or were you turned down again? Have you checked into the hotel?* (Multiple closed questions.)
> **MAN:** *(selecting the most recent question) No, I didn't check into the hotel yet.*
> **PRACTITIONER:** *That's too bad . . . I really thought that they would come through for you. Do you want me to phone them?* (Closed.)
> **MAN:** *No, don't phone them.*
> **PRACTITIONER:** *Well, I really want to make sure you are okay. I want to do something for you.*
> **MAN:** *You don't need to do anything. I am fine.*
> **PRACTITIONER:** *How can you be fine if they turned you down?* (Open.)
> **MAN:** *Well, when I went to the church some guy had gone home sick and they really needed someone to clean up the hall. There was going to be a supper that night and the reverend asked me if I wanted to earn some money. . . .*

Notice how the multiple questions forced the client to choose one of several questions to answer. It is not unusual for clients to choose the last question because it is the easiest to remember. If the practitioner stopped with the first question "How did it go?" she would provided an open-ended question (albeit somewhat vague). Quite likely, the open-ended question would solicit the information the practitioner wanted rather than having to go through a long questioning process.

Vague Questions

A second type of disengaged question is a vague question. Often, when practitioners shift their focus to their thinking while a client is talking, they are not attuned to the statement on the table when the client finishes. As the practitioners form their responses, the connection to the client's last statement is weak. This can be a problem in a professional relationship because there is an expectation that you are listening and able to form an educated response. When professionals respond with vague questions, clients become confused and do not know how to answer (Patton, 1980).

Case Example

A practitioner in a battered women's shelter was talking with a woman about an argument with her partner. The practitioner wanted to help the woman understand how verbal abuse was undermining her feelings of competence. However, the way she formed the question was so vague that the focus was lost.

WOMAN: *I couldn't believe it. All I said was, "How was your day?" and he was off on me. He said all I did was sit on my ass all day and think of ways to make him feel bad when he came home. I had his supper cooked for him and was trying to be good to him. He said I was the worst wife in the world and that I needed to learn to greet a man when he comes home.*

PRACTITIONER: (Reflecting on how the partner was able to make the client second-guess herself.) *When you were talking it seemed that . . . well, I was wondering what did you think about when he said that?*

WOMAN: *I thought . . . hey, I have been working my ass off all day long here. I don't sit on it . . . I work it bone thin. How can he say that crap to me?* (She took the question concretely.)

PRACTITIONER: *He just doesn't know what goes on when he's not home. How do you respond when he says those things?* (Since the client ended with a question, the practitioner must follow.)

WOMAN: *I can't respond . . . he will beat me.*

In the example, observe how the opportunity to explore the woman's thinking was lost because of the vague question. The woman picked up on part of the question and answered. This took the discussion in a different direction. If the practitioner had been more specific, the direction might have gone as planned. For example: "When he said that you needed to learn to greet a man, what did that cause you to believe about yourself?"

Toward a Professional Use of Questions

All questioning occurs within a relational context (Borge, 2007; Enfield, 2009). In a helping relationship, it is very important to become skilled in how you use questions because you have a mandate to ask ones that would be unacceptable in other relationships (Borge, 2007). However, our socialization experiences provide default settings and interactive habits that lack precision. In the professional relationship, more thought and precision is needed. Questioning must occur systematically with clear purpose and focus. To help develop a greater sense of purpose and clarity, the next sections explore specific elements of questioning.

To begin, questioning builds on the engagement skills explored in Chapter 5. The table metaphor used to explain interactive engagement is a critical element in forming questions. If you consider that the client statement puts a package on the table, your questions must respond to that package. Every package also contains implicit and explicit elements that can be selected (Hurvitz & Schlesinger, 2009). Multiple elements in the package—thinking, feeling, relating, or behavior—can help focus your questions. Selecting an element can be challenging because socialized listening habits promote tuning in to our own thinking rather than attending to other people's disclosures.

Purpose of Questions

When forming a question, practitioners must have a clear sense of purpose. The sense of purpose relates to the client's goals and reasons for entering service. For example, if a parent with developmental disabilities is working toward getting his children back because of past neglect, the practitioner should be picking up on elements in the client statement that are linked to issues of parenting. If a practitioner asks about the cost of groceries, there should be some reason or connection to the neglect (such as the parent having to spend too much time out of the home earning an income).

In purposeful questioning, the question focuses on one of four possible functions. The first two functions—clarifying and exploring—focus on understanding the client situation. The second two functions—positioning and promoting change—focus on helping clients increase their ability to master the situation. Early in service, practitioners spend most of their time attempting to understand and assess the situation so most questions clarify and explore. Later, questions that position and promote change are used during intervention.

Exploration

Exploration helps us understand the client situation. Exploratory questions are critical early in service to facilitate the assessment; they also are used throughout when clients describe new situations or events. With exploration, the practitioner picks up on specific elements of the client statement that appear important to client goals. The practitioner selects the important elements from the table and adds a question in response to the client's communicated package. With exploratory questioning, we constantly seek to uncover new elements in the situation that develop understanding and service direction.

To understand the situation accurately, exploration must be focused. The response system framework described in Chapter 4 and 5 can be a useful framework for focusing exploratory questions. The response system framework focuses on how the client responds to their situation. Client system responses include how the situation is processed (beliefs and affective responses) and how it actively responds to the situation (behavior and transactions).

The practitioner explores the situation by picking up on the elements that appear most important in the client statement. As the client speaks, we tune in to the client statement to identify these important elements. Figure 6.1 (see page 145) shows the response system framework in a three-dimensional form. The third dimension in the figure is time. Time is a useful addition because client system responses change over time. By understanding changes (and anticipated changes), practitioners can explore the situation from multiple dimensions and perspectives.

Case Example

Continuing the example of the abused woman, she begins to talk about her future plans. Notice how the practitioner focuses on different responses systems and times while exploring the woman's decision to leave her partner. As you observe the shifts in focus, read the woman's statement carefully to see how different time and response system elements appear to elevate in importance and how the practitioner picked up on the elements that seem most pressing in the client statement.

WOMAN: *I have been thinking about leaving him for a long time now.*
PRACTITIONER: *What kept you in the relationship?* (Past focus exploring relationship —moving to present.)
WOMAN: *I kept hoping he would change.*
PRACTITIONER: *When did your feelings of hope stop?* (Past focus on affect.)
WOMAN: *Last winter. He kept promising to change but never did.*
PRACTITIONER: *Did anything else happen last winter?* (Focus on partner's past behavior.)
WOMAN: *Yes. . . .*
PRACTITIONER: *Sounds like he did something that hurt you badly.* (Shifting focus to past feelings.)
WOMAN: *. . . he had an affair.*
PRACTITIONER: *How did that get resolved?* (Focus on past relationship.)
WOMAN: *He promised to leave her.*
PRACTITIONER: *He makes many promises. How did he do with this one?* (Highlighting an interactive theme transcending time; shifted focus to present behavior.)
WOMAN: *I think okay. But I don't trust him anymore.*
PRACTITIONER: *How does the lack of trust affect you right now?* (Focus on present feelings.)
WOMAN: *I just don't think I want to spend my life with someone I can't trust.*
PRACTITIONER: *So as you look forward, you don't want to live with someone who is not trustworthy?* (Focus on future feeling.)
WOMAN: *Absolutely not.*
PRACTITIONER: *What is so important about being trustworthy?*

Clarification

In a professional helping relationship, an accurate understanding of the client situation is critical. Confusion about the situation can result in interventions that at best are not helpful and at worst can be harmful. Think about a time when you were talking with friends and assumed details or events that were not accurate. If you can recall the conversation, you will likely remember tension emerging as your mind moved in a direction divergent from your friend. In such social situations, friends simply correct each other, and there is no harm done. However, in the professional relationship, clients may not feel comfortable correcting a worker's assumptions.

It is important to listen very closely to the client's responses to ensure an accurate understanding. When we are unsure, we use clarification questions. Doing this requires self-awareness because often we do not recognize when we insert our own assumptions. Assumptions tend to emerge when a client statement is vague. We also form assumptions when we react to themes in the client statement. Themes such as danger, overwhelming emotion, or taboo subjects often cause us to assume rather than asking follow-up questions that might be uncomfortable or feel inappropriate.

Case Example

The abused woman from the previous example continued talking with the practitioner about how she was feeling about the relationship. As she spoke, the practitioner became concerned that there might be a risk of suicidal thinking.

WOMAN: *I can't stand it anymore. No matter what I do, he just gets on me, making me feel like garbage.*

PRACTITIONER: *It sounds stressful. How do you cope with it?* (Wanting to explore her reactions to the situation.)

WOMAN: *I don't anymore. I just want to give up.*

PRACTITIONER: *Are you nearing the end of your rope?* (Seeking to clarify what "give up" means.)

WOMAN: *Oh yeah, I am beyond ready to give up.*

PRACTITIONER: *What does giving up mean to you?* (Still unsure about the meaning.)

WOMAN: *It means it is time to get out.*

PRACTITIONER: *Do you mean divorce, or is there some other plan you have in mind?* (Knowing that there are multiple meanings for getting out and wanting to clarify further.)

WOMAN: *Yes . . . I have already spoken with a lawyer and am looking into jobs in another town.*

In the example, notice how many of the woman's statements could indicate a plan to leave the relationship or a plan to end her life. When the practitioner was not convinced that she truly understood the situation, she continued to clarify the woman's statements until she felt that the woman was safe from self-harm. The practitioner could then work with the woman to ensure that her plan was also going to keep her safe from harm at the hands of her partner.

Positioning

To achieve client goals, we often need to introduce direction into the client exchange. During conversations with clients, we notice parallel situations, themes, or other situational elements that can help enhance movement toward their goals. We also may notice that the client situation coincides with research we have read. Frequently, when such insights emerge, we want to give advice or tell clients something about their situation (McAuliffe & Lovell, 2006). Such impulses emerge because of our socialized history of problem solving. We have a long history of parents, teachers, supervisors, friends, and other people who have given us advice or shared their insights about our situation.

Even though we may tell friends and family how to act, think, and respond, in professional relationships, automatic advice giving is not helpful (Ackerman & Hilsenroth, 2003; Bischoff & Tracey, 1995). Most clients have already received advice from multiple people. To repeat advice that has already failed is really not a service to our clients. Rather, professionals want to highlight and explore aspects of a situation that promote new ways of responding (Sween, 2003). Consequently, we use questions to shift the focus of exploration to topics that can enhance goal achievement. These questions are called positioning questions because they move the client into a better position to develop mastery.

Positioning questions link to elements in client statements that allow the practitioner to shift the focus toward important topic areas. Although this skill may sound new, most people have used positioning questions in their social life. For example, when you wanted to date someone as an adolescent, you would somehow shift the focus of the discussion to the weekend in order to identify whether dating was an option. Most often, our personal use of positioning questions focus on self-oriented outcomes. These same skills can be used altruistically to promote client goal achievement.

The critical skill in positioning questions is first to identify an element in the client statement that has potential for the focus shift. The most useful elements may be subtle, but the response system framework can help identify potential links. As you get used to seeing all four responses systems in client statements, you will see elements of thinking, relationship, and feeling along with the content of the statement. Often the best links are in the thinking and affective elements of the client response. After you identify a possible link, the skill becomes easier as you simply need to add the new focus to your question.

Case Example

As the practitioner in the previous examples continued working with the abused woman, she wanted to ensure the client's ongoing safety. However, the focus was on issues of trust. Observe how the practitioner begins to shift the focus using questions rather than launching into advice.

> PRACTITIONER: *You mentioned that you gave up on your partner because of trust issues, but he was also violent to you. It seems that he is very impulsive. Do his violent impulses bother you as much as his sexual impulses?* (Linking violence to sexual impulsiveness.)
>
> WOMAN: *I don't like either set of impulses.*
>
> PRACTITIONER: *What things tend to bring out his violent impulses?* (Adding issues of violence and safety to the discussion.)
>
> WOMAN: *If he doesn't get his own way, he goes off on me.*
>
> PRACTITIONER: *So if he can't control you, he becomes violent?* (Clarification and possible reinforcement of risk theme.)
>
> WOMAN: *Absolutely. He treats me like I am his personal property.*
>
> PRACTITIONER: *As you reclaim your life and let him know that you won't be his property, what is the likelihood that he will want to hurt you?* (Exploring the risk.)
>
> WOMAN: *Oh . . . pretty high, I would say.*
>
> PRACTITIONER: *So do you have a plan to keep yourself safe when he figures out that you are leaving?* (Shift focus toward safety planning.)
>
> WOMAN: *Not really. I guess I just figured my life would be better as soon as I left.*
>
> PRACTITIONER: *Do you want to explore things to see if we can make sure you are safe when you leave?* (Introduce safety planning.)
>
> WOMAN: *I think that might be wise.*

Notice how the practitioner had a sense that safety planning might be needed but maintained an exploratory feel to the discussion. She consistently linked her questions to the content of the woman's last statement but added direction to each question. The insertion of direction moved the conversation toward issues of risk. She could have started by telling the woman that she was at risk and advising her on safety issues. However, the questions allowed the woman to come to her own realization that there might be some risk and need for safety planning.

Change Promotion

When trying to help clients change, new practitioners often face the strongest impulse to tell clients what to do. Our training and experience allows us to identify options and solutions that seem invisible to our clients. However, we do not want simply to tell our clients what to do. Doing so is not part of an effective helping relationship (Ackerman & Hilsenroth, 2003;

Marshall, 2003). Advice giving also imposes our solutions onto our clients. Questions can present challenges effectively without promoting disagreement or escalating the situation (Halonen & Sorjonen, 2008).

Change promotion questions allow us to influence our clients without necessarily telling them what to do. By embedding direction, consideration, or demand into a question, the change-producing questions provide an exploratory alternative to advice giving. The act of answering a change-producing question provides a subtle nudge that can move the client toward considering an alternative to the current approach to the situation. This type of question has become very popular in recent theories of intervention, such as cognitive, cognitive-behavioral, solution-focused, and narrative treatment. All of these approaches use specific types of questions that require clients to reflect on something prior to answering.

Case Example

Notice how the practitioner from the previous examples uses questions to challenge the woman's thinking and embed suggestions that promote a safety plan.

PRACTITIONER: *Have you ever asked a neighbor to be watchful for signs of violence?*
WOMAN: *I thought about it but never have.*
PRACTITIONER: *What causes you to hold back from asking others to help keep you safe?*
WOMAN: *I really don't want to impose on other people. I don't want to trouble them.*
PRACTITIONER: *Do you think they would be troubled if something bad happened to you and they did nothing to help?*
WOMAN: *Yeah . . . probably. My neighbor on the south side is a pretty good friend.*
PRACTITIONER: *Has she ever seemed concerned about your welfare when things have gotten violent in the past?*
WOMAN: *Oh, yeah.*
PRACTITIONER: *How do you think she might respond if you asked her to keep an eye on things when your partner is getting out of hand?*
WOMAN: *She would jump on it. She has been telling me to dump him for about a year.*

Notice in the example how questions were used to provide suggestions and challenges to the woman's thinking. Initially, the woman believed that neighbors would not welcome her asking them to help her stay safe. However, questions about her beliefs and relationships quickly identified some options. At no point did the practitioner tell the woman what to do yet the movement toward a safety plan was evident.

Building Professional Questioning Skills

To help you hone your questioning skills, questions are broken down into two subcomponents. The first subcomponent, the setup, brings focus to the question. This part of the skill highlights the elements that you want the client to consider when answering the question. The second subcomponent, the delivery, is when you actually ask the question. The delivery shifts the interactive focus to the client much like the ball in a tennis game being lobbed across the net. Once the question is delivered, you must wait for your client to respond before resuming your interactive activity.

Question Setups

The setup brings focus to the question. Setups should link to the last client statement to provide continuity (Steensig & Larsen, 2008). Even simple probes such as "Then what?" link the practitioner question to the last client statement, encouraging the client to elaborate on the action themes. Other setups can be more elaborate first linking to the client statement and then providing up to two or three sentences to focus the question. Simple setups are based on elements in the client's statement that are clearly on the table. More elaborate setups involve the practitioner highlighting, elaborating, or shaping elements of the client's statement to focus the question.

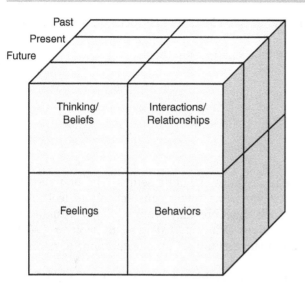

Figure 6.1

Response Systems as
an Exploratory
Framework

Linking the Question

As practitioners listen to the client statement, they tune in to response system elements that seem most important or have the best potential promote the client goals (Adams, 1997; Brown 1997b). Like the cube depicted in Figure 6.1, thinking, feeling, relating, or behavior will be present in the statement. If emotional themes are amplified, you will want to pick up on the emotional elements. For example, "You sounded hurt as you shared that story with me . . . "). However, if relationship seems appear particularly salient, you focus on the transactional themes For example, "It seems that you wanted a different response when you . . . ").

When we focus on elements in the client statement, we can alter time dimensions as we link our questions. Often, especially during the assessment phase, we want to explore the client's past and present. However, there will be times when we want to extend our focus into the future (see Figure 6.1). As we link our questions, we can extend the focus to any of these dimensions in the client situation.

Exercise 6.1: Linking to Client Statements

You are on a student placement in a nursing home. One of your jobs is to meet with people entering the home for the first time. You are sitting down with an elderly woman who is not totally happy to be entering a nursing home. She says, "I have always taken care of myself. I still remember the Great Depression and have always felt it was important to do things for myself. Now they tell me I can't. My son says I have to come in here and let you take care of me. He just out and tells me I have to go. I don't know what to do."

1. Circle two of the client's statements that contain emotional elements.

   Now write a question setup that brings a focus to one of the emotional elements.

2. Underline one element that indicates a strongly held belief.

   Write a question setup that focuses on the woman's belief.

3. Put brackets at the beginning and end of two elements that focus on a relationship.

Write a question setup that picks up on a relationship theme.

Elaborate Setups

Two client-practitioner situations frequently require elaborate setups. The first situation emerges when we want to ask about behaviors that might cause clients to feel judged negatively or elevate their vulnerability. Such situations may prompt lying so respondents can save face or otherwise protect themselves (Vincent, LaForest, & Bergeron, 2009). Consequently, in sensitive situations, we must carefully set up our questions to minimize perceived threats.

The second practice situation that requires elaborate setups is when we want to challenge clients. In these situations, we want to focus the question carefully so we do not offend clients. With such setups we often provide a context, parameters, or requirements to shape client thinking before we ask the question. As clients prepare their response, they focus the answer according to the setup requirements. In either situation, setups allow us to insert direction into the discussion without advice giving or otherwise taking over the discussion.

For example, if the question solicits information that might make clients feel disloyal to their family, a setup can adjust for these feelings. Consider this statement: "Many families express anger by becoming silent, maybe even for weeks at a time. Other families yell, scream, and throw things." Notice how this statement covers a full range of family expressiveness, making it easier for clients to respond. Also notice how this setup elaborately focuses client thinking before you even ask the question.

Common Setup Strategies

Potentially hundreds of setups can be used with clients, but practitioners often choose from six common setups. Each setup introduces an experience or perspective that focuses the question. Setups can be used for all questioning purposes: clarification, exploration, positioning, and change promotion. As you read the list of setup strategies, try to envision using them for the different purposes. Also pay attention to how they help gently focus the client response.

1. *Presumptive*. Presumptive setups presume the behaviors or actions exist (Patton, 1980). By using the presumption, the practitioner sidesteps having to ask initial questions that might heighten resistance. For example, "When you and your partner fight [setup], how violent do things get [delivery]?"

2. *Examples*. Example-based setups provide clients with an example on which to base their response. Examples can normalize feelings or reactions that clients may experience (Patton, 1980). For example: "Many people would feel hurt when their partner treats them like that [setup]. How do you feel about this treatment [delivery]?"

3. *Balanced*. When the focus of the question may create resistance or uncomfortable feelings, providing both positive and negative examples in a balanced manner can give permission for a full range of reactions (Patton, 1980). For example: "When some people feel hurt, they want to give up and crawl into a hole; other people tend to want to get back at the people who hurt them [setup]. How do you respond when people hurt you [delivery]?"

4. *Experiential*. Often practitioners want clients to focus on a past experience so they can benefit from the worker's acquired skills. Practitioners either base the setup on

information they know about the client or experiences that probably will have occurred in the clients' past. For example: "Think of a time when you could have yelled at your child but you stopped yourself [setup]. What are some of the ways you kept yourself calm [delivery]?"

5. *Simulation*. Sometimes you want clients to pretend that something has happened and use the imagined event as a foundation for answering the question (Patton, 1980). This setup requires clients to respond from a different perspective. For example: "If I had a magic wand and solved your problem just by waving my wand [setup], what would you see different when you returned home after the session [delivery]?"

6. *Scaling*. When practitioners want to understand the magnitude of a client experience, they often use a scaling setup where the smallest possible number indicates an absence of something and the largest number means full saturation. As the client responds with a number, the practitioner can better understand the situation. For example: "On a scale of 1 to 10 with 1 indicating that you have no fear of your husband and 10 indicating that you fear your husband may kill you [setup], how much fear do you experience when your husband becomes angry [delivery]?"

As you read the list of setup strategies, the discussion may have seemed technical and confusing. We are not socialized to focus our questions carefully. Rather, we operate from our default setting and spontaneously generate questions almost on a whim. When we start to discover that we can be more focused, the transition to greater precision can feel awkward and uncomfortable. As you practice the different setups, try to get comfortable with a limited set rather than trying to integrate all six into your repertoire right away. Doing this will allow you to insert focus in a natural manner. Ultimately, you will be refining your skills constantly throughout your career. Do not feel you have to master these skills by the end of the chapter.

Exercise 6.2: Setting Up the Question

You are a student doing your placement at a Child Protective Service agency. You are meeting with a family already assessed and receiving services. The family has had problems with both spousal and child abuse in the past. Today the father came in to meet with you. He looked dejected so you asked him how his week had been. He responded that it had been a rough week. You think that there may have been violence so you want to explore the situation.

1. Use a balanced setup and ask this client to explain what a "rough week" means.

The father indicated that there was a lot of fighting so you want to make sure that people are okay.

2. Use a presumptive setup as you check in to see if there was any violence.

The father indicated that there was a "little violence" so you want to determine how violent he became.

3. Use a scaling setup to determine the level of violence during the week.

Question Delivery

Question delivery is when you add the final query to your response. The query is the actual question that prompts the other person to begin formulating their response. Timing the delivery is important. The instant that you deliver your question, you become the listener and must wait for the client to respond. If you ask your question too soon, you will run the risk of becoming distracted as you shift focus to your thinking, trying to compose your next response to get the discussion back on track (Pingree, 2007). This can lead to problems maintaining the communication flow. Consequently, it is best to make sure you are ready for the client response before delivering the question.

Although not all questions require a setup, they all must be delivered to prompt a client response. It is the question delivery that prompts the obligation to respond. Typically, the delivery is directed to one person. However, the focus of the question may be elsewhere in the family system (Penn, 1982). For example, a practitioner might ask a child which parent usually wins when the parents disagree. Notice that the information elicited is focused on the parental relationship even though the child is directed to answer.

Several authors have developed questioning typologies with very minute differences. The typologies are interesting, but they can be confusing in practice, causing us to spend too much time trying to determine which question to use. Within this ocean of potential questions, five common delivery strategies can be used with a client system of any size: (1) descriptive, (2) perspective-taking, (3) comparative, (4) embedded, and (5) sequenced questions.

Descriptive Questions

We constantly explore client situations to understand their problems, strengths, concerns, and options. Consequently, we frequently ask clients to describe some element of their situation. When exploring their responses, we tend to focus on the response systems. As we ask clients to describe aspects of their situation, we can focus on the past, present, or future to glean a full range of information.

- *Thinking*. "What went through your mind when she said that?" or "What do you think you might do?"
- *Feeling*. "When she said that [setup], what was your immediate feeling?" [delivery] or "Did you feel that way last time she said this type of thing?"
- *Interaction*. "How did you respond?" or "How will you respond differently next time?"
- *Behavior*. "What did you do?" or "How will you make this situation better?"

As we explore the client situation, we intuitively identify a need to understand the problem context. Consequently, our focus of descriptive questions constantly switches from exploring the external context and then the client response. Some of the more common elements include:

- *Situational cast*. "Who do you live with?"
- *Situational patterns*. "How do others on your team respond to the supervisor?"

- *Situational setting.* "Where were you when you asked her to set the table?"
- *Situational barriers.* "What seems to be interfering with your ability to finish school?"
- *Situational requirements.* "What do you need from your supervisor to be successful?"

Perspective-Taking Questions
Practitioners often deliver questions with an instruction to adopt someone else's perspective when answering (Tomm, 1988). This type of question requires the client to respond using the thinking and feeling of other people involved in the situation. For example:

"How would your wife describe your shortcomings?"

"When it comes to chores [setup], what would your parents like you to do more [delivery]?"

"If you were your supervisor [setup], what would you say about this [delivery]?"

Notice how this question requires clients to move beyond their own experience when formulating their answer. As the client answers they anticipate the other person's perspective and place it on the table. We can then use the material to explore the situation or challenge the client.

Comparative Questions
Practitioners frequently want to understand issues of difference in the client situation (White, 1986). Comparative questions are effective in getting differences on the table for further exploration. When we use a comparative question, we must establish a focus on two situational elements and then ask the client to contrast them. Sometimes we use a setup to establish one element and then embed the second in the delivery. At other times we can deliver both elements simultaneously. Comparative questions are very useful for positioning and change promotion.

When we use comparisons to advance change, the comparative elements emerge from the client's goals and situation. When selecting these elements, we monitor the situation for opportunities to highlight differences that might enhance motivation and capacity for change. Read the next differences and notice how this questioning strategy can stimulate client thinking concurrent with exploration.

- *Differences between past and present.* "Are you happier now than you were before you left your husband?" or "You said you were madly in love with her [setup]. What has happened to those feelings [delivery]?"
- *Differences between desired outcomes and acquired outcomes.* "So you were hoping this would get you a raise [descriptive setup]. Did it work [delivery]?" or "When you yell at John [simulation setup], does it make him go to bed right away, or does it seem to make things worse [delivery]?"
- *Differences between people.* "When you brought home your report card [setup], who was more upset, your mother or your father [delivery]?" or "Which of your parents lets you get away with coming in late?"
- *Differences between situation and norms.* "So would you say this is how most people would react?"or "You swore at your boss [descriptive setup]. Is this something you often do [delivery]?"
- *Differences between present and future.* "If you keep on yelling at your child [setup], how do you think this might effect your future relationship [delivery]?" "As you grow older and wiser [setup], what do you think you are going to need to change [delivery]?"

Embedded Questions
In previous chapters we learned that telling clients what to do is both unethical and ineffective. However, we also want to help clients consider options and gently insert

suggestions into our responses (Sween, 2003). Embedded questions provide a method of getting options and challenges on the table without overpowering clients or interfering with their autonomy. Embedded questions prevent direct advising by keeping suggestions or direction tentative. Tentativeness is maintained by making suggestions an inquiry rather than a statement.

When we embed direction into a question, we must work hard to maintain a curious position. A curious position requires us to genuinely seek new information from the client rather than asking redundant or perfunctory questions. With embedded questions, it is important to avoid power shifts that occur when a client must explain actions or inactions. Rather, we want to ask a question that gently places potential direction on the table. Consider the next embedded questions.

- *Options.* "You mentioned going back to school [setup]. Have you considered the local community college as a place to start [delivery]?"
- *Suggestions.* "You seem to have some real skill in this area [setup]. Have you ever thought about getting a degree [delivery]?"
- *Hypotheses.* "You seem uneasy about applying to school [setup]. Did you have other educational experiences that contribute to your uneasiness [delivery]?"
- *Challenges.* "What are the thoughts that go through your head [setup] that convince you that going back to school will be a waste of time [delivery]?"
- *Quandaries.* "You seem unhappy with your job but also are not sure you want to go back to school to upgrade [setup]. How do you think you can resolve this dilemma [delivery]?"

Sequenced Questions

A sequenced question delivery involves a series of linked questions to explore a pattern (Patton, 1980; Penn, 1982). The pattern can focus on behaviors, interactions, feelings, or thinking. With sequenced questioning, the practitioner requests step-by-step information with each new question building on the last answer. The goal is to develop a vivid understanding of the entire sequence. For example, a practitioner wanting to understand a father's beliefs about bedtime might engage in the next exchange.

> PRACTITIONER: *What is the problem if John does not go to bed on time?*
> FATHER: *Kids need to get a good night's sleep.*
> PRACTITIONER: *How is it a problem for you if he does not get a good night's sleep?*
> FATHER: *If he doesn't get a good night's sleep then I am not doing my job.*
> PRACTITIONER: *What is so bad about not doing your job?*
> FATHER: *Then you are not a good father.*
> PRACTITIONER: *And if you are not a good father, what is so bad about that for you?*
> FATHER: *Then I am no good.*

In this example, notice how each successive question leads the father deeper into his beliefs, trying to uncover the personalized beliefs. You also can focus on interactive sequences. Notice how the next example follows a progression similar to that in the last example. However, in the next example, the focus is on interaction rather than thinking.

> PRACTITIONER: *When you asked John to go to bed, what was he doing?*
> FATHER: *He was watching TV.*
> PRACTITIONER: *Was the show on or did you catch him during a commercial?*
> FATHER: *It was during a commercial.*
> PRACTITIONER: *Were you in the same room?*
> FATHER: *No, I was in the kitchen, but it is attached to the family room.*
> PRACTITIONER: *What exactly did you say to him to get him started to bed?*
> FATHER: *I said "John . . . bedtime."*
> PRACTITIONER: *What was his immediate response when you said this?*
> FATHER: *He ignored me.*

PRACTITIONER: *When he responded this way, what did you say next?*
FATHER: *I said, "John . . . I said bedtime."*
PRACTITIONER: *You sound calm right now; were you that calm at the time?*
FATHER: *No, I was getting angry.*
PRACTITIONER: *Say it again as you said it that night.*
FATHER: *(Loudly) John . . . I said bedtime!*
PRACTITIONER: *What was his response?*
FATHER: *He threw down the remote and stomped off to bed.*
PRACTITIONER: *When this happened, what did you do . . .*

This same style of questioning can be used with multiple people involved in the situation. For example, the practitioner may include the father, John, and possibly other family members, asking each to contribute their actions and thinking at each step of the sequence. When involving multiple people, it is important to control their responses to avoid arguments.

This type of questioning is tedious but can be effective in exploring interactive and cognitive patterns in a step-by-step manner. The detailed mapping of interpersonal or cognitive processes can be very useful in promoting a fuller understanding of the client situation. If we map the steps of the sequence while questioning (see Figure 6.2), we also develop a powerful tool for identifying moments of escalation and possible points where the cycle can be interrupted. Notice in Figure 6.2 how the situation elevates after the father raises his voice. When working with clients, this point can be explored to identify the potential for changing responses.

Questions for Larger Client Systems

The preceding questioning strategies can be used with client systems of any size. However, the questions typically are directed to a single person in the system with the expectation that

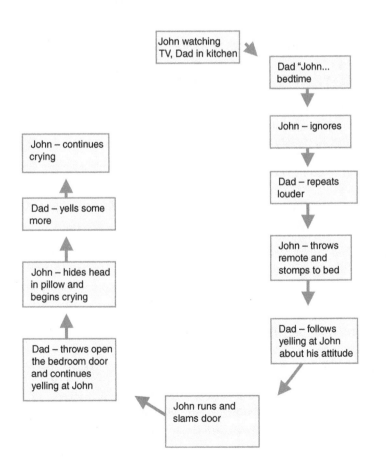

Figure 6.2

Tracking the Interaction Sequence

there will be a single dyadic answer. The next questions are specific to larger systems and operate with the multiple members in mind. The first strategy, circular questioning, is a system that builds on each member's contribution and perspective. The second strategy, triadic questions, engages one member commenting on the process between other members of the system.

Circular Questions

Circular questions are used with larger client systems, such as families and groups (Penn, 1982). The goal of this type of question is to explore the situation from the unique perspectives of the people in the system. The practitioner begins by asking one member of the system a question. After the person responds, the practitioner briefly explores and affirms the contribution, then uses that information as a foundation for exploring the situation from other perspectives. Consider the next example.

> PRACTITIONER: *Dad, you seem to feel it is important for John to go to bed on time. What are your concerns for John if he stays up late?*
> FATHER: *He won't get enough sleep.*
> PRACTITIONER: *And if he doesn't get enough sleep, how is that a problem?*
> FATHER: *He won't be able to succeed in school.*
> PRACTITIONER: *So you want to make sure he is successful?*
> FATHER: *Yeah.*
> PRACTITIONER: *Mom, Dad is worried that John will not be successful if he is not well rested. What are your concerns for John?*
> MOTHER: *I want John to be happy and well adjusted.*
> PRACTITIONER: *So your concerns for John are slightly different than his father's?*
> MOTHER: *Well . . . I want him to be successful, but I also want him to be happy.*
> PRACTITIONER: *Are you concerned that he is not happy the way things are now?*
> MOTHER: *Yes . . . I don't think all the arguing is good for John.*
> PRACTITIONER: *So you agree that John needs to be successful in school but want him to be happy at the same time?*
> MOTHER: *Yes . . . I want both things for John.*
> PRACTITIONER: *John, were you aware that your parents have these concerns about you?*
> JOHN: *Sort of.*
> PRACTITIONER: *What concerns did you sort of know about?*
> JOHN: *I knew my mom wants me to be happy.*
> PRACTITIONER: *How did you know about that concern?*
> JOHN: *I hear Mom arguing with Dad after I go upstairs.*
> PRACTITIONER: *So do you feel that she kind of takes your side on this issue?*
> JOHN: *Yeah.*
> PRACTITIONER: *Do you kind of talk to her about things once in a while to keep her on your side?*
> JOHN: *Well . . . sort of . . . I can talk to her about how I feel and she listens to me.*
> PRACTITIONER: *So would you call her an ally?*
> JOHN: *Yeah.*
> PRACTITIONER: *Does your dad have any allies in his concerns about you doing well at school?*
> JOHN: *Not really.*
> PRACTITIONER: *So it is kind of like you and Mom against Dad?*
> JOHN: *Sort of.*
> PRACTITIONER: *Dad, is that how you feel when things erupt?*

Notice how the practitioner in this example develops part of the story with one family member then moves to another member to tease out his or her perspective. When reading the excerpt, you can see how the practitioner senses triangulation between the parents and John, using the multiple perspectives to explore the relationships. Circular questioning is very useful for identifying alliances, coalitions, and other types of troubled relationships.

Triadic Questions

Triadic questions enable the practitioner to gather relational or interactive information by asking one member to report on the transactions among other members (Palazzoli-Selvini, Boscolo, Cecchin, & Prata, 1980). In a triadic question, the practitioner first identifies a relationship or transaction that appears important. The practitioner then engages a third member of the system to report on the relationship. As the practitioner sets up the question, he or she ensures that the transaction or relationship is clearly the focus of the question.

For example, a practitioner in a multisystemic intervention program is meeting with a family where the son has engaged in delinquent behavior. The practitioner wants to explore the parental responses to the behavior.

> PRACTITIONER: *Robert, when the police bring you home, what conversations tend to occur between your parents?"*
> ROBERT: *Well, Dad is always angry and Mom tries to calm him down.*
> PRACTITIONER: *What does your father say when he is angry?*
> ROBERT: *He usually yells at me and sends me to my room.*
> PRACTITIONER: *When he yells at you, how does your mother calm him down?*
> ROBERT: *She tells him to be quiet or the neighbors will hear.*
> PRACTITIONER: *What happens next?*
> ROBERT: *He starts yelling at her and telling her not to interfere.*
> PRACTITIONER: *After they start arguing with each other, do they ever get back to talking about the problems you have with the police?*
> ROBERT: *I don't think so . . . they just get mad at each other.*

In the last example, notice how the initial triadic question gets the parents' relationship on the table for exploration. This allows the practitioner to explore parental interactions and reactions to Robert's problems. The brief exploration identifies tensions that interfere with effective responses to Robert's problems.

In groups and organizations, triadic questions sometimes are referred to as process illumination questions (Yalom, 1985). An example of such a question is: "Samantha, when the manager of the casework team wants to change the program but the manager of the assessment team does not, how do they resolve their disagreement?"

Exercise 6.3: Delivering the Question

You are a practitioner in an adult mental health program. You are meeting with a family comprised of a mother, father, and two children (Anthony, age 11, and Felicia, age 9). Mother has been diagnosed with a bipolar disorder. She has been in a manic phase, which interfered with the family's ability to function. You think Mother may be experiencing some new stresses that interfere with her stability. You want to explore who in the family might create these stresses and who might mediate the stresses. You are meeting with the family. You are going to use a triadic delivery to find out who supports the mother when she is upset.

First, whom would you select to answer the question?

1. Write exactly what you would say to this person. (Remember the triadic delivery of the question.)

The family member answers that Anthony tends to be the mother's strongest supporter. You want to explore his rationale for being the primary source of support.

2. Use the circular questioning approach (affirming the last statement then moving to Anthony), ask Anthony about his thinking about Mother's needs.

You have just started working in a family service agency where two teams have been arguing about case management procedures. The intake team states that the other team does not care about clients on the waiting list because they are keeping clients in service too long. This makes it hard to move clients from the waiting list into service. The counseling team argues that the intake team does not understand the complexities of long-term service. You notice that neither team really listens to the other. Rather, they just make an unrelated statement supporting their own position. You believe that part of the misunderstanding between the two teams is due to the fact that their jobs are so different. You are talking to some of your colleagues on the intake team.

3. Use an embedded hypothesis question to get the possibility that the problem is due to unique approaches to service on the table for discussion.

4. Your colleagues respond to your question in a way that makes you think that the problem really is due to each team having a very different job. Use a perspective-taking question to help the intake practitioners understand how the other team might describe them.

Bringing It All Together

As we start learning interactive skills, the mental energy involved in breaking our communication habits can feel overwhelming. It is important that you do not let the lists of setups and delivery strategies clutter your brain when you are interacting with clients. Feeling pressured to remember lists can cause you to disengage, which would be counterproductive. Try to become comfortable with the questioning process and then expand strategies. The biggest challenge for beginning practitioners is to avoid socialized questioning habits.

As you gain control of past habits, try to integrate some of the more common setup and delivery strategies. Select three setups that are easy to integrate (such as experiential, simulation, and examples) and three delivery strategies (such as descriptive, embedded, and triadic), and use them whenever interactive situations allow. When talking with friends, pay attention to how you set up questions rather than running on automatic. Doing this will help you become more comfortable with your new skills. Over time, those new skills will become automatic for you based on what you are trying to achieve. After you achieve some level of comfort, start integrating new strategies.

Critical Chapter Themes

1. Questioning is one of the critical skills for clarifying, exploring, positioning, and promoting change with clients. Skilled questioning can deepen and focus the working alliance with your clients.

2. There are five types of questions practitioners should avoid using: closed-ended questions, multiple questions, "why" questions, vague questions, and leading

questions. These questions can interfere with information gathering and the working relationship.

3. Questions respond to the client's last statement by picking up one of the important elements in that statement. In linking your question, you can pick up on situational elements or response system elements.

4. To focus questions, practitioners can structure questions using common setup strategies. These strategies provide a framework that focuses the client response.

5. Question delivery strategies prompt different types of responses from the client. Some strategies require clients to reflect on situational elements before answering while others require clients to provide very specific types of information.

6. Some questioning strategies involve a series of questions that are linked together to achieve the desired result.

7. Specialized questions can be used with larger systems. These questioning strategies capitalize on the multiple relationships in the larger systems, such as families, groups, organizations, or communities.

Online Resources

Basic Counseling Skills Web site: www.basic-counseling-skills.com/asking-questions.html

Focus for Change, business-oriented development Web site: httpwww.coachingforchange.com/pub10.html

1000 Ventures, business-oriented professional development Web site: www.1000ventures.com/business_guide/crosscuttings/communication_questions.html

Recommended Readings

Adams, J. F. (1997). Questions as interventions in therapeutic conversation. *Journal of Family Psychotherapy, 8*, 17–35.

Dickson, D., & Hargie, O. (2006). Questioning. In O. Hargie (Ed.), *The handbook of communication skills* (3rd ed.), pp. 121–145. New York, NY: Routledge.

Marquardt, M. (2005). *Leading with questions: How leaders find the right solutions by knowing what to ask.* San Francisco, CA: Jossey-Bass.

Petress, K. (2006). Questions and answers: The substance of knowledge and relationships. *College Student Journal, 40*(2), 374–376.

Sween, E. (2003). Accessing the rest-of-the-story in couples therapy. *Family Journal, 11*(1), 61–67.

Tomm, K. (1988). Interventive interviewing: III. Intending to ask lineal, circular, strategic, or reflexive questions? *Family Process, 27*, 1–15.

Chapter 7
Reflective Responding Skills

"Reflective responding" refers to the ability to identify and communicate back to clients an accurate understanding of the most important elements in their communication. Along with questioning, reflecting is one of the most commonly used practice skills. In professional communication, reflecting back an accurate understanding helps the client feel understood (Evans, Hearn, Uhlemann, & Ivey, 1998; Murphy & Dillon, 1998). This outcome helps deepen the helping relationship by putting the client experience into words.

Use of Reflection in Professional Practice

Reflection is a skill that can greatly enhance service delivery for the client. The reflection of empathic understanding is associated with effective workers (Lafferty, Beutler, & Crago, 1989). Reflection is associated with client responsiveness to worker intervention (Uhlemann, Lee, & Martin, 1994). Reflection also is associated with a more positive helping relationship (Chang, 1994).

Power of a Reflective Response

The power of questioning lies in the implicit obligation for another person to respond; the power of a reflective statement lies in its ability to promote client thinking. This power resides in the lack of interactive demands placed on the client. There is no implicit obligation for clients to respond back; consequently, they can take their time and consider what was said before forming their next statement. This freedom provides an opportunity for cognitive processes to take hold. Consequently, we often use a reflective response when we want to help clients think about something.

In previous chapters we have used the response system framework (action themes = behavior and interaction, processing themes = feeling and thinking) to focus skills. Like other interactive skills, reflective responding can be used differentially with action and processing systems to generate specific influences. Typically an intervention focus on action themes provides a platform for work while a focus on processing themes promotes consideration and reflective thinking in the client.

Reflective Platform for Client Consideration
When we use reflection in response to a client statement, we organize the client's information so it can be restated in a manner that promotes client thinking. Reflection often is used at the end of meetings to set the stage for future planning. Similarly, we often summarize a discussion before proceeding with the next steps of action or planning.

When using reflection to prompt client consideration, we often identify a potential direction in the content of the discussion. This can occur with an individual client as we identify themes in his or her conversation that logically link to the client goals. Similarly, in discussions with several people, we may notice similar concerns even though the participants may not recognize the commonalities. We can use reflection to highlight the commonalities to draw attention to a common direction. For example: "Today we talked a lot about needing to let the department of mental health know about our need for sustainable fidelity assessment systems. This has been a consistent theme."

Concurrent with identifying direction to take action, we also use reflection to help clients change their internal responses. When we summarize feeling or thinking themes, we often organize information that is ignored or only partially considered by clients. When we place this information on the table for clients to consider, the reflection often provides a platform for them to integrate new information about their internal processes.

Regardless of the content we highlight in our reflections, the impact is very similar. We select and organize elements in the client statement and present them back to the client. Because the reflective response is a statement, the material we present back to clients carries no implicit command for them to respond. Rather, the statement allows clients time to consider and reflect.

Using Reflective Responses

Reflection, like all interactive responses, is used purposefully by practitioners. When we elect to use a reflective response, we listen carefully, select an important element that can promote goal achievement, and place this back on the table to stimulate client consideration. In doing so, we seek to achieve one of four possible outcomes:

1. *Exploration*. We want to learn more about the client situation because we do not have enough information.
2. *Clarification*. We want to ensure that our understanding of the situation is accurate.
3. *Positioning*. We want to identify and explore specific content that will be useful for goal achievement.
4. *Change promotion*. We want to put information on the table that will help the client consider or integrate into his or her approach to the situation.

Exploration

We constantly explore client situations. During assessment, we explore the details of the client situation and later, during the intervention phase, we explore current situations so we can tailor our interventions for the client. For this reason, we must continually draw out information from the client so we can understand and respond appropriately.

In the last chapter you learned about questioning as a common exploratory skill. However, if we used only questions to explore, the interaction would feel like an inquisition because the client would constantly feel obligated to respond. Reflection is very useful to break up the constant pressure of questioning when exploring the client situation. Reflection does not present any pressure to respond and has an affirming tone because we restate part of the client's information. There are three common uses of exploratory reflection.

1. *Promoting further disclosure* (Murphy & Dillon, 1998). Sometimes we want the client to continue telling his or her story. Reflective responses are used to summarize and focus what the client has said. In response, the client can continue disclosing and elaborating on what was said. This is most useful when a client is unfocused. For example: "You mentioned that you were trying to be more positive with the children."
2. *Focusing the discussion* (Evans et al., 1998). When we wish to encourage specific areas of examination, we can use reflection to highlight issues for further exploration. For example: "I have heard a lot about what John has been up to but very little about how you respond to him when he is so unreasonable."
3. *Building platforms of understanding*. As we summarize the contents, thoughts, or feelings that emerge during a discussion, we organize the information so it becomes useful. The organization of information helps establish a shared understanding or platform on which to base ensuing discussions. For example: "You mentioned several times that you feel all alone having a disabled child and that you would love to talk with other parents."

Clarification

When clients share their stories, they are well acquainted with the details. Consequently, they often provide a short version of events. As they edit out details, their description can become cryptic and incomplete. When faced with vague or incomplete information, we risk filling in our own details or assumptions rather than truly understanding what the client is communicating.

If we intervene based on our assumptions about the client's story rather than on an accurate understanding, our intervention is misguided. At best this is a waste of time; at worst we can intervene inappropriately. To ensure an accurate understanding, we must clarify our perception with the client to ensure that we base our actions on real, rather than imagined, information. There are two common uses of reflections associated with clarifying client statements.

1. *Clarifying vague statements.* Sometimes client statements contain vague references or mysterious themes that we do not quite understand. When we hear these themes in the statement, we often have a sense that there is something important but we are unclear about the meaning. In such situations, we reflect back the part of the client statement that seems important so the client can elaborate. For example: "So when John talks back, you 'lose it.'"

2. *Affirming understandings* (Murphy & Dillon, 1998). To avoid misunderstandings, practitioners often wish to ensure that their perception of a client's situation is accurate. Reflective responses are used to check the understanding. This is vital early in the helping relationship when the worker is exploring the situation for assessment and goal setting. For example: "It seems that you are most upset because you want a better relationship with your children."

Positioning

As we interact with clients, there are times when we need to highlight specific content areas so we can proceed with our intervention. If we work with people who have substance abuse problems, for example, somehow we must get drinking and drug use on the table or we cannot do our jobs. Positioning is the skill used to elicit and develop specific types of information during our interaction with clients.

Reflection is a useful tool to use with positioning because we select the important information embedded in the client statement and restate it in a way that highlights these elements. When we put the information back on the table, it is then focused so that the client must integrate these elements into his or her response. Reflection is particularly useful for positioning because it requires the client to consider the elements before responding. There are two important uses of reflection when positioning.

1. *Transition into work.* Often larger client systems, such as groups, families, and organizations, will talk about different aspects of the problem from multiple perspectives. All of the individual discussions provide no direction. When we summarize the discussion so that common concerns are evident, it is easier for members of the system to take action. For example: "Mom, it seems that you have been pulling back a bit so Dad can support John with his homework and Dad has been trying to be less critical about John. It is like you are both working independently on the problem."

2. *Focusing on goals.* When clients first enter the meeting room, they often engage in discussions about the past week. Reflections can be used to highlight themes in conversation that are consistent with the goals of service. This is particularly useful at the beginning of the meeting or session. As we pick up on content that is pertinent to the goals, we can reflect back that content to transition into goal-relevant discussions. For example, a practitioner is working with a substance-abusing client. After a moderately long discussion about the trials and tribulations of the week, the practitioner reflects, "You talked about several methods you used to stay busy during the week with no mention of drinking at all."

Change Promotion

The final use of reflective skills is to promote change. In the earlier chapters you have been cautioned about too much advice giving or telling clients what to do so you do not damage the helping relationship. As a result, you probably are eager to learn subtle methods of promoting change. Reflection is one of the skills that can be very helpful in nudging people toward new ways of thinking and behaving.

When we reflect, we build on client statements by picking up specific elements that they have just shared with us. We are very judicious about the elements we select so we can place the most important material back on the table. The client then hears the material and has the opportunity to reflect and integrate the information. In the reflective exchange, clients retain control of how they respond to our reflection. There are three common uses of reflection for promoting change.

1. *Promoting insight* (Murphy & Dillon, 1998). Sometimes we want to stimulate client critical thinking about their situation. We can accomplish this by reflecting back elements in the situation that clients have been ignoring. For example: "It sounds like you really disagree with Hank even though you say nothing."

2. *Inserting challenges* (Evans et al., 1998). When we want to challenge a style of thinking, we select elements in the statement that allow us to insert alternative interpretations, discrepancies, or strengths that can promote reconsideration. For example: "You tell me how much Anthony loves you and you also tell me that he beat you up so badly that you had to go to the hospital."

3. *Reframing meaning.* Sometime a client's negative interpretations of situational elements maintain the problem. In such situations, we want to introduce alternative attributions by picking up on elements that can support a new definition of the problem. For example: "When you talk about Marcella you describe her as defiant, yet she also seems a little lazy."

The different uses of reflection will be expanded on in the upcoming chapters. At this point it is important to understand its different uses so you can start to be more purposeful in how you use reflection. You may have opportunities to practice exploration, clarification, and positioning in your social relationships. As you enter professional relationships, you will increasingly use the full range of reflections. As you branch into using reflection for promoting change, you may want to explore the skill with your supervisor so you can ensure that you remain reflective.

Reflection and Evidence-Based Practice

Concurrent with research identifying reflection as a critical practice skill, reflection emerges as a critical foundation skill when using evidence-based interventions. Reflective exploration and clarification is an important element in most evidence-based practices. Many practices also employ reflection to affirm clients and help with the engagement process. Some, such as family psychoeducation, integrated dual diagnosis therapy, and multisystemic therapy, use reflection to explore situations without directly challenging clients.

Some of the evidence-based practices, such as motivational interviewing, multisystemic therapy, and dialectical behavior therapy, use a reflection because they all attempt to use subtle challenges to stimulate client thinking and internal problem solving. As you become acquainted with the different evidence-based models, you will start to understand how each uses reflection skills to explore, clarify, position, and challenge clients.

Components of Reflection

Reflection builds on many of the skills outlined in the previous chapters. Most important, we use thinking, tuning in, engagement, and goal directedness to provide a helping context and focus to our reflections. These skills are integrated into three basic steps: (1) identifying critical elements, (2) setting up the reflection, and (3) delivering the reflection. These steps are consistently used in varying degrees whenever we reflect. Although we discuss them as separate steps, as we get comfortable with reflection, the steps blend and become second nature.

As you become more familiar with reflective responding, you will notice a cycle forming (see Figure 7.1). The cycle always begins with the client's communication package on the table. We pick up a critical element of the package, set the focus, and deliver the

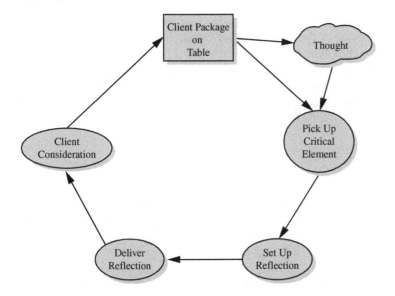

Figure 7.1

Reflection Cycle

reflective response. The client can then consider the response and, in turn, place a new communication package on the table. As the cycle repeats in our practice, the steps in the reflection process will become seamless, requiring very little conscious effort.

Step 1: Selecting the Elements for Reflection

Reflection begins with the client placing a communication package on the table. We listen to the communication and monitor for the most important material. As we listen to the clients communication, we consistently use three cognitive skills.

1. We tune in to the client statement to identify the elements that are most important to him or her.
2. We use our thinking skills to apply research and theory toward understanding the client situation.
3. We maintain the client goals and intervention direction so we can integrate our understanding with client priorities.

Critical Considerations

Through these cognitive skills, we identify the important elements for reflection (Rober, 1999). Doing this requires balancing client emphasis and goals as we listen to the client statement. By tuning in and thinking, we identify the most critical content themes, feelings, meanings, or strengths in the client statement. As we consider the elements of the client communication, we briefly reflect on four questions.

1. *Emergent needs*. Is there something that is preventing the client from moving forward?
2. *Client goals*. What elements can help the client achieve his or her goals?
3. *Client mastery*. What elements can help the client master the current situation?
4. *Client enhancement*. What elements can help the client increase his or her capacities associated with the reasons for entering service?

The consideration of these questions is very brief as we mentally scan the communicated material and then shift our focus away from thinking and back to the interaction. This quick consideration allows us to remain engaged with our client while still maintaining direction in our responses. Initially this will feel slightly awkward as you try to select the most important elements. It is important to struggle through the awkward phase by forcing your mind to select a single element for reflection without disengaging from the client conversation.

The selection process will become more natural as you gain experience in keeping goals, mastery, and enhancement in the back of your mind. Ultimately, these selection criteria are based on promoting the client's best interests, which is consistent with the ethical priorities discussed throughout the text. Eventually, selection will become second nature as you almost intuitively identify an element that can promote client interests. Three common elements in client communication promote reflection: emphasized response system elements, client strengths, and discrepancies.

Response System Themes

As we listen to clients, their inflection and emphasis often identifies critical response system elements. Sometimes the important elements are obvious; at other times they form themes that we can identify through repetition. For example, a common theme for adolescents is to resist parental (and authority figure) control. This relationship theme might become present in discussions about parents, teachers, and even the worker. Recurring themes are important to select. Consider the next patterns that can prioritize specific response system themes.

- *Behavior.* Sometimes client statements indicate that he or she is ready or eager to take some form of action.
- *Interaction/Relating.* Sometimes the relationship elements appear to be a priority as the client continues to cycle back to relationship themes.
- *Thinking.* Often the client expresses confusion or emphasizes thinking themes, such as beliefs and values indicating thinking priorities.
- *Affect.* Often the client's communication has affective overtones or hidden feelings that are not addressed.

Client Strengths

When there are no obvious response system themes to provide direction, often it is useful to select elements that demonstrate that the client has exhibited mastery and ability within the problem situation (Saleebey, 1997). For example, the teen mentioned previously might discuss a school situation in which he felt controlled but, rather than lashing out (as done previously), took another form of action. Even if the other form of action was not highly successful, strength is indicated through the attempts to gain mastery.

- *Motivation.* Even when outcomes are negative, a client may have noble motivation.
- *Determination.* Sometimes in situations with negative outcomes, we can clearly see a client's willingness to risk or persevere.
- *Mastery.* Clients often share moments of mastery, partial mastery, and incremental changes that can be identified in their statements.

Discrepancies

Often in the client's discussion themes of discrepancy emerge that may be associated with his or her problems (Evans et al., 1998). It is important to highlight differences and discrepancies so clients can consider the potential meaning and attempt to resolve them. Consider three common discrepancies.

1. *Goals versus outcomes.* Often what we want to achieve is not the outcome in a given situation. Reflecting on such moments allows us to consider how our goals and behaviors are inconsistent.
2. *Feelings versus actions.* Sometimes our affect is inconsistent with our current behaviors or nonverbal communication. By identifying the inconsistency, often we can discover elements in the situation that are currently unacknowledged.
3. *Past versus present.* We often make changes in incremental steps and are unaware of progress. When our past is compared to our current performance, many times we can identify changes we have made.

Exercise 7.1: Identifying Critical Elements

You are a practitioner in a women's health center. You are meeting with a young mother of a 5-year-old son and a 3-year-old daughter. The woman came in due to severe domestic violence. In the most recent violent incident, the son tried to protect his mother by getting into the middle of the fighting. He was knocked to the ground, bruising his head and causing brief unconsciousness. Even after injuring the child, the husband continued hitting and yelling at the woman for making him hurt the son. The woman is talking with you and says, "I just couldn't believe it. It is bad enough he hits me all the time, but he didn't even stop when John got hurt. I kept trying to get to John hoping he would stop, but he kept hitting me and yelling that I was a bad mother. He feels it was my fault because I didn't mind him. That just doesn't seem right. I was trying to get to my son like a good mother. I can't put up with this crap anymore. I just gotta do something."

1. What are the critical content elements in the woman's statement for the action and interaction systems?

    a. Action:

    b. Interaction:

2. Identify the feelings conveyed in the woman's statement.

3. Identify the thinking conveyed in the woman's statement.

4. What elements seem most important to reflect back to the woman to help her feel understood?

5. What elements seem most important to reflect back if you want to explore the details of the violence?

6. What elements seem most important to reflect back if you want to explore how the son is coping with the violence?

Step 2: Setting Up the Reflection

After we select the elements to put back on the table for client consideration, we need to set up a response that will promote client reflection. In Chapter 6 we learned that questions evoke an obligation to respond; with reflection, we want to evoke a contemplative response. Our setup begins this contemplative process. There are four common types of setups:

1. Direct setups
2. Sensory setups
3. Directive setups
4. Comparative setups

Direct Setups

The simplest setup is to use material left on the table by the client's most recent statement. This material is already in focus because the client just finished saying it. For this reason, it is easy to use this material to set up a reflection. We simply select some of the client's content, bringing focus to the element we want considered. When we tune in to the client's statement, we link our response to the content that can move the conversation forward.

As we reach for content to link our reflection, we typically must choose between the obvious and less obvious elements on the table. The obvious, or overt, elements are evident in the content of the client's statement. The less obvious elements are implicit in the statement. Sometimes we want to link to the implicit material rather than obvious elements because the reflection will have a different impact.

For example, a team member might say: "I am tired of this. Some of us work hard and do our best while others do whatever they want." Notice the overt elements in this statement will set a focus on who is working. However, the less overt elements in the "I am tired of this" will set the focus on the fact that something has happened for the team member causing her to think that the balance of work has tipped. We can start this focus by simply setting up a reflection by repeating "You are tired of this."

Sensory Setups

In our habitual reflective responses we often use sensory setups when we reflect. Although these are not as simple as directly setting up a reflection from the table, the habitual nature of sensory setups makes them feel natural. We frequently use auditory setups like "It sounds like . . ." or tactile setups like "It seems like . . ." without thinking. Typically we do not select the sense that we are using with careful consideration; rather, we just launch into our reflection, habitually selecting the sensory focus. As we build on our socialized use of setups, the challenge is to select the sensory focus purposefully.

We can increase the power of our reflections by carefully selecting the sense that we use. In the 1970s, Neuro-Linguistic Programming (NLP) therapists began observing how skilled therapists conversed with their clients. Through these observations, they discovered that people have sensory preferences. Some people organize their experience using visual cues while others use auditory or tactile cues (Bandler & Grinder, 1975). They also found that skilled therapists tended to match their use of language to the preferences of their clients. Although NLP has waned in popularity, setting up our reflections using the client's preferred senses can increase our impact. Consider these sensory options for setting up your reflections.

- *Thinking.* Thinking setups require caution because we often end up sharing our conclusions. This can be a problem if the client simply accepts our interpretation of events rather than reflecting on the situation. Remember that we want to stimulate client consideration. Common setups include: "I am wondering if . . ." and "I can't help but wonder if . . ."

- *Hearing.* Hearing setups share what we have heard rather than sharing a direct conclusion based on our private thoughts. For this reason, clients are more likely to consider your reflection as tentative rather than that you are telling them what to think. Common setups include: "It sounds like . . ."; "What I hear you saying is . . ."; and "I heard several themes . . ."

- *Seeing.* Visual setups are similar in style and impact to auditory setups because they involve sharing our observations. Common setups include: "It looks like . . ."; "It looks to me that . . ."; and "From what I can see . . ."

- *Feeling.* Tactile setups are based on our gut feelings and bodily sensations. These are particularly useful when focusing on a client's affective responses because the language is very body-based. Some of the common setups include: "I get the sense that . . ."; "It seems like . . ."; and "I get the feeling that . . ."

Directive Setups

Sometimes we want to prompt a very specific client response with our reflection. When we operate with specificity, we need to use a more complex setup to focus on specific elements prior to delivering the reflection. Often this type of setup requires us to make an initial statement to establish our focus prior to proceeding with the reflection.

When we use a focused setup, we begin by identifying something in the client's statement or interactions. We then direct the client to approach the element in a specific manner. Only after providing the directions do we finish delivering the reflective response. As the reflection is delivered, the client carries out the direction. Consider the next directive setups commonly used in practice.

- *Process focusing.* Sometimes in larger client systems we observe exchanges and interactive sequences that seem important. In groups this type of reflection is referred to as process illumination (Leszcz & Yalom, 2005). When we want the system to consider these interactions, we must first focus their thinking on the processes occurring in the group. Consequently we focus the group through a setup line, such as: "I have noticed a pattern whenever we talk about problems. I am wondering if anyone else has noticed that . . ."

- *Instructive focusing.* We sometimes want to direct the client to use certain cognitive processes as they consider the reflection. Consequently we must provide instructions as we set up the reflection. Consider how the next instructions sets a tone for client thinking: "I noticed some themes in our discussion today. Listen to these themes and tell me how they fit together . . ."

Comparative Setups

A final type of setup injects a comparison into the reflection. This type of setup begins the reflection by focusing on one dimension (e.g., group membership, time). After the reflection is delivered, a second dimension is introduced so the two dimensions can be compared. The comparison can be set for normalization (e.g., "Most people become upset when they lose their job . . ."), allowing us to contrast the client situation with others.

Comparative setups are very useful when working with discrepancies because we use two dimensions to allow for contrast. This might include such things as words and actions, past and present, male and female, or any other dimension. The critical element in the setup is ensuring that one pole of the comparison is clearly present on the table so we can use it for contrast. Consider these common setups.

- *Past/Present setups.* When we want to highlight progress, we often compare current functioning to the past. As long as either the current or past functioning is on the table, we can set up a comparison by focusing on either time period.
   ◦ *Highlighting the present.* Sometimes when we want to compare the past and present, we allow the past to remain implicit by highlighting the present. For example: "I noticed a difference in how we managed conflict today."
   ◦ *Highlighting the past.* We can also implicitly highlight an element in the present by focusing on how the client might have behaved in the past. For example: "Last year you would have relapsed in this situation . . ."

- *In-group/Out-group setups.* We can use reference groups (group membership, gender, race, professions) to set up comparisons. Similar to working with time comparisons, group comparisons only require us to pick up on some dimension we wish to compare or implicitly contrast to other groups.
  - ○ *Highlighting an element in the current group.* If we want to reinforce an element in group functioning, we highlight that element to promote an implicit comparison. For example: "I noticed a lot of caring in your arguments . . ."
  - ○ *Highlighting an external group.* We can also introduce a comparison by focusing on another group. For example: "Last year I sat on a committee that really struggled with making decisions. . . ."

Step 3: Delivery of the Reflection

After the focus is set for the reflection, we provide a statement that will cause the client to consider, or reconsider, elements of the situation. This statement triggers client contemplation. The reflection builds on, and completes, the setup. After the reflection is delivered, we remain silent, allowing the client to consider the statement prior to responding. There are five common types of reflection delivery.

1. Restating reflections
2. Paraphrased reflections
3. Focusing reflections
4. Challenging reflections
5. Indirect reflections

Restating Reflections

The simplest reflective response is to restate part of what the client has said (Murphy & Dillon, 1998). Commonly, a single word or a phrase can communicate the important components back to the client by picking up directly from the client's statement rather than using a setup sentence. Such responses are a punctuation type of reflection, briefly supporting the client's initial disclosure while shifting focus back to the client for elaboration. Be careful about overusing this type of reflection because it may sound parrotlike or mimicking. Two of the most common restatement reflections include:

1. *Word restatement.* Practitioners can select a specific word used by the client, drawing attention to the word by repeating it. Implicitly the client is encouraged to elaborate on the choice of word. For example, a parent of a child with autism might say: "This has been a week from hell." In response, we might simply say "Hell . . ." and wait for the client to elaborate on why the word was selected.
2. *Phrase restatement.* Practitioners often select an important phrase from the client's statement and repeat it to solicit elaboration. For example, when a client states his or her week has been a "week from hell," the worker might respond: "An entire week from hell . . ." This short response affirms the client's meaning while concurrently implying a need for more information about the week.

Paraphrased Reflections

Paraphrasing is slightly more elaborate than restating. With paraphrasing, practitioners use their own words to pull together the critical content or themes in the client statement (Murphy & Dillon, 1998). Often paraphrasing uses a brief setup, such as "sounds like" or "seems like," to soften the focus and wording choices. Notice how these setups alert the client that we are synthesizing their information. As we synthesize the information, paraphrasing organizes the content themes. This helps focus and organize the client's thinking. Two common methods of paraphrasing include:

1. *Thematic highlights.* Practitioners often summarize the critical themes in a client statement or series of statements. For example, a practitioner talking to a teen with

a learning disability might say: "It seems that at school teachers are telling you what to do and at home you say your parents are telling you what to do. Now you are here and I am telling you what to do. It seems everywhere you go people are trying to tell you what to do."

2. *Summarizing.* Practitioners sometimes want to summarize the content of client statements to organize the information prior to action. Summarizing is like paraphrasing yet tends to focus on all of the themes in a client's discussion. For example: "You mentioned that people tell you what to do and that you often fight back. These moments of fighting back often get you into trouble. Sometimes you prefer trouble but not all the time." Summarizing often is used prior to changing the focus, ending a session, and assigning homework.

Focusing Reflections

Often we want to focus client thinking about their situations. There may be elements of the situation that they are ignoring or that they have not integrated into their current thinking. In such situations, a focused reflection allows us to highlight one element. By using reflection we can put the element on the table so they must consider it in relation to the current conversation.

The most common use for a focused reflection is when clients fail to consider something in the situation. For example, a mother of a child diagnosed with attention deficit/hyperactivity disorder may angrily punish her child for putting himself in danger by playing on thin ice by the river. As the punishment unfolds, the mother believes she is punishing the child because she cares. However, the child experiences the mother as a very angry person. Such situations are common when people are not attuned to their emotions. To help we may want to focus on the emotions so they can be integrated into the situation. Consequently, we highlight the affect by saying: "I hear you talk a lot about caring. As you talk I also hear a lot of fear and anger in your voice."

Notice how the focusing reflection simply highlights the ignored element in the discussion by putting it back on the table for consideration. A client can then reflect on the element and either integrate it into the discussion or reject it. Many focused reflections are used in practice because this type of reflection allows us to inject influence into clients' thinking and feeling. Some very common types of focused reflection include:

- *Highlighting a response system.* Frequently we notice that clients are unaware of an important element in how they are responding to their situation. As we respond to the clients, we focus on the ignored response system element so that clients can include it in their thinking. In the last example, the worker included emotion in the reflection.
- *Highlighting personal positions.* When people focus on generalized or external others, it is difficult to help them because the focus of discussion is not present. Consequently, we want to shift the focus back to the person by focusing on his or her investment. For example, a youth states: "Teachers and workers really don't care about kids." A practitioner might respond: "You said that teachers and workers don't really care. Sounds like you have had some experiences that made you feel this way."
- *Highlighting strengths.* We highlight strengths and positive elements in clients to help them integrate areas of strength into their self-concepts. We often use strength-focused reflections to help clients integrate positive attributes and strengths that they may be overlooking. For example: "You have shared a lot about workers and teachers who didn't care about kids. I hear a well-developed sense of fairness as you talk."
- *Highlighting normalcy.* Often clients make statements that contain a harsh judgment or focus on themselves. In our response, we frequently want to soften the harsh focus by generalizing the judgment or reinforcing that their reactions to the situation are normal. For example, a practitioner working with an elderly patient having to move into a nursing home might reflect: "When you talked about having to go into the nursing home, you sounded sad. I guess there is not much else to feel when facing such a difficult move."

Challenging Reflections

We often want to nudge our clients toward another approach to their situations. Reflections help with promoting change by inserting alternatives into the client discussion. A challenging reflection tends to maximize the difference between two alternative client responses. One response is the status quo response that the client currently uses in the situation. The second alternative then is presented so the client must consider both prior to responding. For example: "You are probably the only person I have talked to that didn't care when his girlfriend broke up with him. Most people are flooded with different feelings."

We must be careful using this type of reflection because it can seem argumentative. As we highlight alternative responses, clients may feel a little defensive. It is important to use the actual client information when presenting a challenge rather than inserting our judgments or assumptions. Such reflection also requires a solid helping relationship that provides a context and history of support. Common examples of challenging reflections are listed next.

- *Reflecting discrepancies*. When client discrepancies emerge, we often want to highlight these so the client can explore and integrate these aspects of the situation. For example: "It is striking how you desperately want your kids to tell you about their lives, but your reactions sometimes make them want to keep their private lives private."

- *Reflecting alternatives*. Often client interpret situations in a manner that maintains problems. Many times we want to reflect alternative interpretations that fit the details of the situation but have a less problematic meaning. For example: "Your kids aren't sharing much about their friends. Sometimes kids keep information from parents so they won't worry. However, you don't seem comfortable believing this."

- *Reflecting cognitive patterns*. Similar to reflecting alternatives, sometimes we also want simply to challenge a belief when it appears there might be a pattern of cognitive distortion. For example: "It seems that when your health starts to fail, you talk more about being an athlete when you were in college."

Case Example

A family service worker was working with a husband, helping him to decrease his angry outbursts with his wife. The man came in for a meeting looking somewhat distraught. As the worker explored the situation, the man said that his wife had been totally unreasonable during the past week. As he spoke about the situation, he stated that she was unreasonable because she wanted to go out with her friends two nights in a row. Knowing that the wife stayed in the house all day, the worker wanted to challenge the thinking and reflected: "Oh . . . when you stay at home all day, wanting to get out a couple nights is a sign of being unreasonable." This reflective challenge caused the man to pause and backtrack slightly, saying "Well, wanting to go out is not unreasonable, but I wanted her to spend time with me."

Indirect Reflections

The final type of reflection is less confrontational than the challenging reflections. Indirect reflections share an understanding of the situation without directly responding to details. Workers often use indirect reflections during conversations to help clients feel understood without interrupting the flow of their disclosure. Workers use nonverbal expressions and brief metaphors to help clients feel that the practitioners understand the situation. There are two common types of indirect reflection.

1. *Nonverbal reflection*. Nonverbal reflection of affective meaning is achieved through using facial expressions or sounds to communicate an understanding without using words. For example, a practitioner may groan or grimace when the client shares a story of disappointment. Many positive client responses are related to the nonverbal expressions by the worker (Wiseman & Rice, 1989).

2. *Metaphoric reflection*. Sometimes metaphors or analogies can be used to reflect client feelings or meaning through an image (Kopp, 1995). This allows the client to experience the reflective communication without a lot of practitioner talk. For example, when a client says she is overwhelmed with all of her family obligations, the practitioner says: "It is kind of like you have a short leash and people keep pulling you back when you really want to explore."

Case Example

A 14-year-old girl diagnosed with oppositional-defiant disorder is in residential care because she refuses to obey family rules. She and her mother frequently fight, and some fights have become physical. The mother is a recovering alcoholic and the girl raised herself. The mother sobered up one year ago and decided to implement rules. The daughter resisted the rules, leading to ongoing power struggles in the home. After six months in residential treatment, the daughter is about to return home. As the worker informs her of the return, the following exchange occurs.

WORKER: *So, you are going home soon. How does that feel?*
YOUTH: *Not bad.*
WORKER: *Not bad!* (Restatement/)
YOUTH: *Yeah . . . I don't care one way or the other.*
WORKER: *You know, I have worked with thousands of kids in care, and you are the only one that has said that to me.* (Reflective challenge.)
YOUTH: *Well . . . I just don't know. For years things were okay, then she comes on like some tyrant with rules for this and that. She doesn't have a right to tell me what to do. Not after what I've been through.*
WORKER: *Sounds like things were rough for a while.* (Reflection of meaning.)
YOUTH: *Yeah . . . She would be passed out and I would have to do everything for myself. She wasn't the mother, I was. I took care of her. Now she stops drinking and thinks she can pick up as if nothing happened.*
WORKER: *After raising yourself and giving up on her it almost seems too little, too late. That would make any kid mad.* (Focused reflection.)
YOUTH: *Well, it sure made me mad.*
WORKER: *(Sneers) Uh-huh . . .* (Nonverbal reflection of feeling.)
YOUTH: *. . . and when she tries to lay down rules it all comes out.*
WORKER: *So things have been bottled up for so long that when she tries to open it up, it goes off on her.* (Metaphoric reflection.)
YOUTH: *Yeah.*
WORKER: *Have you talked to her about how you feel?*
YOUTH: *Yeah, whenever she pisses me off, I tell her.*
WORKER: *You only express your feelings when you are angry.* (Focused reflection.)
YOUTH: *No. I can express myself other times, but it seems to come out that way.*
WORKER: *Would it help if I sat down with you and your mom before you went home to get some of this out on the table?*
YOUTH: *Maybe . . .*

Notice the multiple types of reflection used in the last exchange and how each tends to elicit a different type of client response. As you develop your reflecting skills, your use of the reflective strategies will become second nature. As you tune in to client statements and maintain client goals in the back of your mind, you will intuitively know what elements to pick up on when you want to stimulate thinking in a client.

After the reflection, it is important that we gain some indication that the reflection is accurate (Broome, 1991; Omer, 1997). Consequently, after reflecting back to the client, we need to be highly attentive to make sure the understanding or expression is consistent with the client's experience. Doing this uses observational skills to detect looks and other indications of affirmation. If the client appears puzzled, we need to question whether the reflection fits his or her experience. Exploring this allows the client to correct our misunderstandings of the situation.

Exercise 7.2: Setting Up and Delivering a Reflective Response

You are working in a vocational program for people with developmental disabilities. Your client is a young woman with Down syndrome. This woman is 19 years old and operates at a moderate to mild level of disability. You have been working with her to increase her assertive social skills in preparation for a work placement. She has been unassertive in many social situations, and the team wants her to increase her skills. She is talking to you about her boyfriend. This is the first you have heard about her boyfriend, and you want to understand the nature of her relationship, but you know she will stop talking if you ask too many questions. Consequently, you need to be reflective to encourage her to talk. She begins the conversation by saying, "I have a boyfriend named Tom. He goes to my school with me. He is not in my classroom. He goes down the hall where the big machines are [machine shop]. He doesn't come by my class much because he doesn't like people seeing us together. I think we might be getting married after school ends. I like him a lot and we go to his car and kiss during our lunch hour. (She giggles and looks down.) I like him, that is important. He is almost 20, you know. I am getting to be pretty grown up. Mom doesn't know that, but I am."

1. You want her to expand on her intimate behavior with the boyfriend. Write a reflective response that will promote further exploration.

2. You want to clarify how the boyfriend will not allow them to be seen together. Write a reflective response that can clarify this part of the relationship.

3. You want to affirm her joy about feeling loved. Write a reflective statement that can affirm these feelings.

4. You want to plant a seed of doubt about this relationship because you fear that the boyfriend might be exploiting her. Write a reflective response that might stimulate some doubt.

Using Reflection With Larger Client Systems

So far, most of the chapter discussion has focused on work with an individual client. This is because the mechanics of a reflective response are the same with client systems of all sizes. We select, set up, and then deliver the reflective response. Concurrently, some types of reflection are almost identical across client systems of different sizes. For example, content-focused reflections such as restating and paraphrasing still capture and focus on discussion regardless of the number of people in the group. Likewise, indirect reflections can be used with a system of any size.

When using reflection with a larger client system such as groups, families, and organizations, we can also focus interpersonal processes. As such, larger system reflections tend to capture dynamic patterns in the system and/or common features among the people in the system. Other courses will focus on families, groups, organizations, and communities; here it is important to learn how reflecting skills translate into systems of any size.

Pattern Reflection

Larger systems have dynamic patterns. Some patterns are good for the system while others are related to systemic problems. Often we want to reflect on these patterns to reinforce some and highlight others for change. Reflecting patterns begins with pattern identification. As we observe and interact with members of the larger system, we notice sequences and patterns. If these appear important to the problems and goals, we take note of the patterns and begin to formulate a reflective response that can help the system rectify the problems. We then set up and deliver the reflection. Practitioners focus on two common systemic dynamics using reflection:

1. *Sequences*. In larger systems, there are sequences of interaction and events. When the sequences may help to explain a problem, we want to highlight the pattern so the people in the system can explore and rectify it. To accomplish this type of reflection, practitioners set up the reflection and then describe the sequence to bring reflective attention to the sequence.

Case Example

Two teams in an agency were competing for resources. One of the teams was attempting to have the waiting list declared the agency's top priority so promised program expansion money would be directed to its team. The other team provided evidence-based practice and argued that interventions that were effective and helped clients achieve independence should be the priority. In a staff meeting, intervention was identified as the critical priority because graduating consumers would also open up possibilities for clients on the waiting list. However, every subsequent staff meeting had an agenda item retabling the waiting list priority. These discussions were time consuming and interfered with agency business. After three meetings a worker stated: "I notice that three months in a row we discuss the waiting list, each time only to affirm the need for efficient treatment. However, the next meeting, we end up rehashing the same discussion." This stimulated a discussion about the need to honor decisions and accept outcomes.

---

2. *Systemic inclusion/exclusion*. A second type of pattern in larger systems includes inclusion and exclusion. Frequently, some members of the system have more influence than others, which effectively excludes some system members from positions of influence. Because such patterns can become permanent fixtures in a system, often we want to identify the imbalance so people in the system can consider the impact.

Case Example

A mental health agency was planning new programming for families in which one parent was suffering with severe and persistent mental illnesses. Several research-supported models of intervention were considered. Some of the professional staff had preferences, and eventually the discussion about programming became bogged down in lobbying for preferred models of intervention. After several unfruitful meetings, a practitioner stated: "We have met several times arguing for different models of treatment, but I have not heard anything from our consumers and their families about what might work best for them. This feels like a missing piece for me."

Highlighting Commonalities

People in larger systems often are focused on divisive issues, causing them to lose sight of their commonalities. This is very common with families, organizations, and community groups that have a shared history. When there is divisiveness in a larger system, people often focus on each other's behaviors and interactions because they are observable. When another person's behavior is different from what we might do, we often believe we are working toward divergent outcomes.

When divisiveness occurs in larger systems, we frequently want to shift the systemic focus from divisive dynamics to common ground among the members. This shift of focus requires us to tune in to the larger system. As people share their stories and concerns, we listen for shared themes that reflect commonalities. Even when two people are arguing with each other, they may have a very similar concern. When we search for commonalities, it is useful to tune in to internal elements, such as concerns and feelings, because they are abstract making it easy to find common ground.

If we can identify the similarities, we can use our reflective responses to put shared elements and common ground on the table. We then can use these shared elements to promote collaboration. Four common internal elements can be used for reflect commonalities.

1. *Goals*. Often people are attempting to achieve very similar outcomes but using different means. If they remain focused on the different means, collaboration is difficult. Highlighting the common goals helps to facilitate combined effort. For example, "Don, you want Anthony (son) to come home on time so he doesn't get into trouble. Yvette, you have been arguing that Anthony needs to be responsible for himself. It seems that under it all, both of you want Anthony to be successful."

2. *Concerns*. People's behavior often is motivated by issues of concern. The behavior is observable so many people in the system are aware of their actions. However, concerns are hidden so few people understand the underlying motivation. By highlighting underlying concerns, we can help people find shared concerns and commonalities that can motivate collaborative action. For example, "As you were talking it seems that everyone is upset about having to retire because we don't know what to do with our time."

3. *Values*. In previous chapters we learned that our values often support our behaviors. We also tend to collaborate best with people who have values similar to ourselves. As we help people in larger systems we try to help them identify shared values to provide a common base for working together. For example, "Throughout the staff meeting people repeatedly expressed concerns about clients accessing service without long delays."

4. *Feelings*. Feelings tend to underlie people's reactions. When we approach larger systems where people are operating in a reactive mode, it is helpful to identify underlying feelings and the affective overlaps among the people in the system. Doing this promotes understanding and can lead to increased collaboration. For example, "Tom, when you were talking about feeling unworthy in your relationships, others in the group were nodding and a couple of peoples' eyes started to water slightly."

Case Example

The two teams discussed earlier tended to accuse each other of being insensitive to client needs. The assessment team claimed that the treatment teams kept clients in service too long, causing the waiting list to grow. The treatment teams argued that they needed to work with families until their goals were met so they could retain the gains made in treatment. Eventually a new staff member stated: "We all seem to be very concerned about the clients that we see on a regular basis. We want to make sure that families function at their best, and we are putting a lot of effort into making sure that they are okay."

Exercise 7.3: Reflecting With Larger Client Systems

You are attending a community mental health committee meeting representing your agency, a street-level mobile response program for homeless people who have mental illness and co-occurring substance abuse problems. There have been funding cuts for the past two years so most community programs are operating on very meager budgets. At the meeting a funding proposal is being discussed. The representatives from two university-based hospitals continually takes over the discussion. After anyone from a small community-based program speaks, the hospital representatives speak right after and change the subject back to their plans for the money. As you listen, you notice that the smaller programs are focused on providing services for poor families that have no insurance but the hospitals tends to focus more on middle-class families.

1. Write a reflective statement that can capture the commonality among the various members of the committee.

2. Use your observations about the populations that different programs serve and formulate a reflection that can stimulate thinking about who can be best served.

3. Use your observations about the patterns of interaction and write a reflective statement that can identify the pattern for the group.

Culture, Socialization, and Reflection

Reflection is a powerful skill because it puts selected information on the table in a way that will stimulate client thinking. As professionals, we have control of what we select and how we highlight critical information for clients to consider. Thus, we have a lot of influence when we use this skill. Because we have the potential to influence clients, it is very important to be cautious in how we use this skill. There are two points to be aware of:

1. It is important to understand how cultural and social differences might influence the exchange.
2. We must once again consider our socialized habits so we can be purposeful in how we use the skill of reflection.

Culture and Social Power

Most of this chapter has focused on the mechanics and uses of reflection. As we apply the skill, it is important to understand the cultural and social context of intervention. When we work with clients, we are in a professional role, which creates a power difference between us and our clients. Depending on the race and cultural background of us and our clients, the power differential and dynamics can change. Issues of social privilege and cultural communication styles can converge with the professional role to elevate power and compound power differences in the helping relationship.

Culture and Social Privilege
As members of helping professions, we recognize that members of the dominant culture have social privileges not afforded to all groups. Concurrently, some of the nondominant cultural groups have some privileges and social power that other groups do not have. Within this social pecking order, clients approach us for help. Our professional role has power which can accentuate social differences.

Given the array of power differences, we must be careful when selecting and placing content back on the table. If we have more social power than our client, we must be careful that the social power does not amplify our influence when reflecting. If you find that clients accept what you say without question, or acquiesce to your suggestions, power differences may be amplifying your reflections. When amplification occurs, we need to explore the client reactions to ensure that the client responses are genuine.

Cultural Communication Patterns
When we select and place elements of the client's statement back on the table, there is directness to our communication. Some cultural groups welcome directness while others

may experience our communication as interference. For example, many African American people living in the United States are comfortable with expressive and direct communication. However, people from some Native American communities may experience direct and expressive communication to be rude. Given the difference among different cultural groups, it is important that we tailor our presentation of the reflective response to the cultural patterns of our clients. Tailoring our presentation of the reflection requires us first to observe how the members of the client group communicate. As we observe the cultural communication, we should also be aware of communication-relevant values, such as respect, hierarchy, and formality, so we can highlight information without offending members of the client system.

Power Differences and Professional Ethics

In Chapter 2 we learned that the helping professions value client autonomy and self-determination. This value can be violated easily because of the power inherent in our roles. Our professional position can cause clients to view us as authority figures and give our opinions more credence than might otherwise be warranted. It is important to be aware of our perceived power lest we inadvertently impinge on client autonomy.

When using reflection, our power can emerge in a manner that undermines autonomy if we assume an "expert position" rather than remaining tentative. We assume an "expert position" when we respond as if we know more about clients than the clients themselves. Consider the statement: "You are really angry about this." Notice how this reflection elevates our power rather than allowing clients to remain the experts on their own experiences.

When we use our reflective skills, it is important to remain tentative. Doing this means carefully avoiding phrases that might assume an expert position. To start this process, first try to avoid beginning a reflection with the word "you." When we start a response with the word "you," it is easy to assume an expert position because our response becomes a proclamation about the other person. It is also helpful to use tentative verbs, such as "It seems," "It appears," and "It sounds like."

Socialization and the Use of Reflection

Concurrent with influences associated with cultural backgrounds, our socialization can influence how we use reflection. Some workers may find that reflection is a skill that is difficult to integrate into their professional response repertoires. Others may find reflection very easy to use. Our relationship to reflective responding is linked to socialization through response biases, parental modeling, and our anxieties about silence.

Response Biases

Some of us are very comfortable using reflection while others tend to prefer questions. These preferences tend to be habitual and part of our common systems of interacting with others. Although social habits are sufficient in friend, collegial, and family relationships, in professional interaction, we want to use a full range of skills so we can use the power of each type of response.

If you are a habitual questioner, it will feel awkward to make a statement without ending with a question. Be aware that a question requires a response rather than stimulating thinking. Consequently, it will be important for you to become comfortable using reflective statements without turning them into questions. With practice you can gain control over how you use your responses.

Parental Modeling

One of the greatest challenges to using reflection is our tendency to give advice and assume expertise on the client situation. We have years of experience with parents and authority figures responding to us, and we tend to replicate this response style when we are helping others with their problems. Given our years of advice receiving, imparting advice is an easy habit to fall into when we work with clients. Consequently, we must be vigilant as we develop our reflecting skills.

An inherent threat in the "expert position" is our selectivity in the elements we choose for our reflections. It is important to avoid advancing our opinions and judgments. Rather, we must respond to the client's priorities and goals. If we select material from the table that advances negative judgments, we may stimulate resentment.

Practitioner Anxieties

A final element of socialization is our comfort with silence. When we use a reflective response we make a statement and leave the client to consider our response, silence will emerge in the conversation. This is inevitable as the client thinks about what we have said. Sometimes the silence is short, but at times silences can be prolonged. A silence that lasts longer than a couple of seconds can create anxiety for both the practitioner and the client.

Our reactions to silence have a socialization link. If we were raised in family settings where silence was used to increase tension or to punish people, we may become very anxious when clients are silent. We then may find ourselves filling the silence by explaining the reflection or adding a question to ensure that the client will end the silence. Because it is important to allow clients sufficient time to consider the content of our reflections, we must manage our anxiety about silence.

Bringing It All Together

When you become comfortable using reflections, you will find that you can advance client goals by selecting important elements and placing them back on the table for client consideration. This process is pictured in Figure 7.2. Notice in this diagram how the practitioner begins by selecting one element from the table (T, for a thought). As the practitioner places the element back on the table, he or she makes some addition to the thought. The client then considers the thought and alters the next communication package

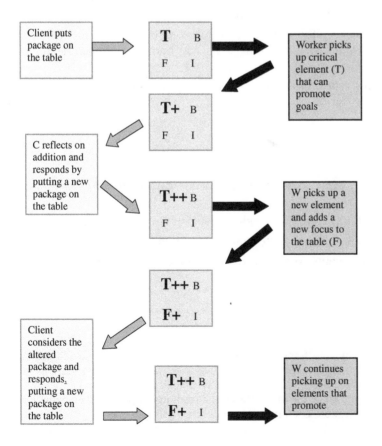

Figure 7.2

Ongoing Reflective Cycles

placed on the table. This process of selection, reflection, and consideration continues throughout the process.

It is likely that reflections will feel a little awkward as you begin focusing on this skill. Initially, it is useful to pay attention to your socialized habits so you can block any potential interference. Doing this often requires blocking the impulse to turn reflections into questions or to interrupt silence. It may also require you to work hard to remain tentative rather than assuming the expert position. Whatever the challenge, start with identifying and interrupting your socialized habits.

As you master your habits, you can begin paying attention to how you focus your reflections. Initially, we are lucky just to include some of the words or content from the client package. As time passes, we begin to notice the range of material on the table. As you start to notice different feelings, beliefs, relational contexts, and other content on the table, you can begin to become selective in the material that you highlight.

As you notice your options on the table, you will also become more skilled at including different elements in your reflections. At this point, setups and delivery will become more natural and require less thinking. Eventually, the goals will remain in the back of your mind, and you will respond directly to the material on the table. Although this takes some time and practice, your reflecting skills will become a new interactive habit that will continue to grow with your practice experience.

Critical Chapter Themes

1. Reflective responding involves communicating important aspects of the client's disclosure back to him or her. This skill is instrumental in deepening the relationship, promoting insight, assuring an accurate understanding, and continuing the exploration.

2. Practitioners use reflection to explore, clarify, position, or promote change with clients.

3. In the reflective response, the worker (1) identifies the critical component in the client disclosure, (2) communicates the critical component back to the client, and (3) monitors feedback about the accuracy of the reflection.

4. There are several methods of communicating the critical components back to the client. These include verbal (paraphrasing, restating, etc.) and nonverbal (touch, sounds) reflections.

5. Receiving feedback on the reflection is important to ensure that the worker is aligned with the client.

Online Resources

Communications skills page: http://spot.pcc.edu/~rjacobs/career/effective_communication_skills.htm

Listening skills: www.mindtools.com/CommSkll/ActiveListening.htm

Observation Skills Test: www.calculatorslive.com/Observation-Skills-Test.aspx

Observational exercises: www.ehow.com/how_4519784_hone-observation-skills-writing.html

Recommended Readings

Bozarth, J. D. (1997). Empathy from the framework of client-centered theory and the Rogerian hypothesis. In A. C. Bohart & L. S. Greenberg (Eds.), *Empathy reconsidered: New directions in psychotherapy* (pp. 81–102). Washington, DC: American Psychological Association.

Broome, B. J. (1991). Building shared meaning: Implications of a relational approach to empathy for teaching intercultural communication. *Communication Education, 40,* 235–249.

Chang, P. (1994). Effects of interviewer questions and response type on compliance: An analogue study. *Journal of Counseling Psychology, 41*, 74–82.

Rober, P. (1999). The therapist's inner conversation in family therapy practice: Some ideas about the self of the therapist, therapeutic impasse, and the process of reflection. *Family Process, 38*, 209–228.

Uhlemann, M. R., Lee, D. Y., & Martin, J. (1994). Client cognitive responses as a function of quality of counselor verbal responses. *Journal of Counseling & Development, 73*, 198–203.

Chapter 8
Observing and Describing Skills

As we work with clients, we notice that some of the most important communication emerges from how they present themselves and their stories. This information is hard to put on the table because it emerges from facial expressions, tonal qualities, and how clients act when describing situations. This information usually is referred to as nonverbal communication. Although we often want to explore client nonverbal communication, it is difficult to begin the exploration because the important information is not explicit.

This chapter explores the nonverbal elements in client communications so we can highlight and explore their nonverbal messages. There are two important elements in this skill set: observing and describing. Observing is an internal skill that helps us identify the important communicated elements. This skill builds on the tuning-in discussions of Chapter 5. Describing is a complex skill that allows us to place nonverbal information on the table for exploration.

Challenges to Nonverbal Communication

We all observe nonverbal information when we communicate with others, but typically our ability to use nonverbal information is unformed. Many types of challenge inhibit our ability to work skillfully with nonverbal information. Some challenges evolve from our socialized communication habits, some from our brain structures, and others from our professional education.

Socialization Challenges

In North America, our communication is often very pragmatic. We are taught to get our message across as succinctly as possible. The adage that time is money tends to underlie how we approach our communication with others. More involved communication is saved for special relationships. This pragmatic approach to communication inhibits our ability to identify and explore nonverbal information skillfully.

The greatest socialization challenge is a tendency to interpret nonverbal communication automatically. In such cases, the nonverbal information becomes a conclusion about the person or the story rather than remaining an observation. For example, we might notice a man's clenched jaw and unblinking stare and conclude that he is angry. From the moment of conclusion we operate based on our assumptions rather than working from observed information.

Interactive Impact
The tendency to form assumptions creates interactive problems because the assumption is seamlessly inserted into a response without being checked or tested. Notice in Figure 8.1 how each person interprets and incorporates assumptions into their next response. As interpretation and incorporation occur, we cease working with observed information because we have altered its form. It is very difficult to remove a conclusion after it has been included in the interactive sequence.

We all have experience with conclusions tainting our interactions. Consider a sequence where we believed our romantic partner might be angry. Initially we observe a tight jaw, pursed lips, and an unblinking stare. We interpret this information as anger, and immediately our anxiety increases as we mentally scan the situation to identify possible infractions that might explain the person's mood. As we respond with "What's wrong?" we insert our anxiety and interpretations into the response. This becomes the communication package upon which the other person must respond.

Figure 8.1

Interpretation Cycles in Communication

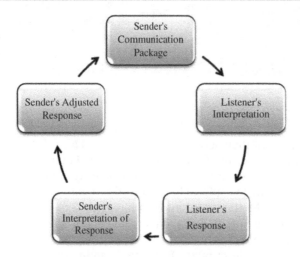

Let us consider that the other person might be tired rather than angry. However, after being asked "What's wrong?" he or she will of course respond "Nothing," which builds on the interpretation that we have placed on the table. We must then defend our interpretation by saying something like "Well, you look upset," which continues the distortion caused by our initial interpretation. As the conversation continues, it is very difficult to remove the interpretation after the communication sequence has been launched.

Challenges for Digital Communicators

People who prefer to communicate through texting and computer-mediated networking orient toward communication systems with very little nonverbal information. Although it is possible to use capital letters, symbols, and bold type to emphasize aspects of the communication, these embellishments are consciously chosen and obvious in text-based communication. Most communication is brief and to the point, leaving little room for nonverbal elements to emerge.

Nonverbal elements tend to emerge in word choices. Most communication is accepted at face value, but readers tend to interpret words based on their relationship with senders of messages. For example, "Fine" may indicate a problem or possibly be taken at face value, based on relationship history. This inclination to use the relationship to insert nonverbal meaning compounds the natural tendency to inject conclusions rather than working with observed information.

Observation and Brain Functioning

A second challenge to our ability to explore nonverbal communication evolves from the structure and specialized functioning of our brain. Observation requires us to use parts of our brain that many times are ignored. Most often, we pay attention to the content and story lines, which is a linear thinking process. Nonverbal information tends to be processed in a different area of the brain, which makes it difficult to use this information during interaction.

Hemispheric Brain Functions

To understand the neurological challenge to using nonverbal information, it helps to understand the structure of the brain. The human brain operates through two hemispheres (see Figure 8.2). The two hemispheres of the brain serve distinct functions so the division of mental labor is unique with no overlapping specializations (Hugdahl & Westerhausen, 2009). The corpus callosum tends to transmit stimulation across the hemispheres. When one hemisphere cannot manage the stimuli, they are transmitted across to the other hemisphere (Bloom & Hynd, 2005).

The hemispheric brain functions develop early in childhood and become increasingly prominent with age (Everts et al., 2009). Even memories tend to be stored according to the hemispheric functions (Evans & Federmeier, 2009). Typically the left hemisphere is considered dominant for right-handed people; the right hemisphere is considered dominant for

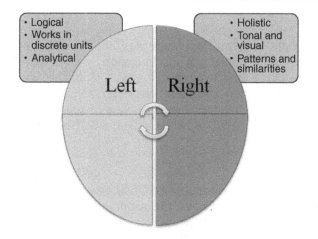

Figure 8.2

Brain Hemispheric Functions

people who are left-handed. Language, written words, and logical functions tend to be processed on the dominant side of the brain (Evans & Federmeier, 2009; Hornickel, Skoe, & Kraus, 2009; Klann, Kastrau, Semeny, & Huber, 2002).

The nondominant hemisphere typically processes visual, spatial, and tonal inputs (Vogel, Bowers, & Vogel, 2003). This hemisphere processes holistic and symbolic information (Schmidt & Seger, 2009) and monitors for patterns, relationships, similarities, and divergences (Evans & Ferdermeier, 2009; Gainotti, 2007; Lutcke & Frahm, 2008; Mohr, Landis, & Brugger, 2006). As the brain scans for these patterns and similarities, memories are retrieved and compared to the current situation as the brain seeks to find appropriate matches (Marchewka et al., 2008; Shin, Fabiani, & Gratton, 2006).

Brain Engagement during Interaction

When we interact with others, both brain hemispheres are active. Our dominant hemisphere decodes the content of the other person's statement, helping us understand the story (Hornickel et al., 2009; Hugdahl & Westerhausen, 2009). Concurrently, our nondominant hemisphere tracks the other person's inflections, tonal qualities, patterns of presentation, gestures, and facial expressions (Gainotti, 2007; Obleser, Eisner, & Kotz, 2008; Wildgruber et al., 2004). The combined brain functions help us understand the communication at multiple levels.

The ability to use both sides of the brain is an important skill in maintaining an emotional bond. As someone shares emotional content, we simultaneously track the story line content and the nonverbal expressions that convey emotional content. This requires our nondominant hemisphere to track tonal qualities, gestures, and facial expressions that convey emotional meaning (Bach et al., 2009; Demaree, Everhart, Youngstrom, & Harrison, 2005; Hornickel et al., 2009; Obleser et al., 2008; Wildgruber et al., 2004).

Professional Education Complications

Professional education can complicate our tendency to inject judgments by causing us to become more elaborate in our interpretations. As we learn theories and professional knowledge, we use them to form interpretations of people's nonverbal behavior. In this way, our developing thinking skills interact with our socialized habits. We can now use theories and research to identify possible "issues" in other people. This can become problematic because people may feel judged if we transparently insert our new knowledge into judgments when we observe behavior.

If we persist in using interpretations rather than working from our observations, problems may emerge in our exchanges with clients. When there is something in a client's nonverbal communication that appears important, we must find ways of using this information. Doing this is particularly important when there are mismatches between the levels of communication (verbal versus nonverbal content) or when the nonverbal communication indicates that there is something important to discuss.

Social and Cultural Considerations

When we explored the biology of nonverbal communication, there was little discussion of the social and cultural influences. It is important to understand that biological trends occur in a broader context that shapes how individuals use their observation skills. Some broader contexts promote seeing and integrating phenomena while others deter observation. For this reason, some contexts influence the value and meanings attributed to observed information. As we develop our observational skills, it is important to be aware of these influences so we can understand them in practice.

Cultural Approaches to Observation

Some cultures promote observing phenomena. When this occurs, cultural values often help members focus their observations and incorporate observed information into community life. For example, in the dominant society, high value is placed on observing economic trends. Many decisions, ranging from the health of the country, to vacation planning, are made based on whether the stock market is up or down. In contrast, some Native American cultures promote observing and understanding nature. Similarly, members of the culture use nature cues to help form decisions about how to live.

Although both of these cultures promote observation, the culturally endorsed focus is different. In the dominant culture, there is a focus on wealth accumulation. This is promoted through political discussions, newscasts, and other systems of promoting the observation. Concurrently, there are methods dissuading observation of people who are living in poverty. Ghetto crimes tend to be broadcast, dissuading people from venturing into areas of poverty, while white-collar crimes receive relatively little attention. In some Native American communities, endorsed observations focus on nature and the meaning of natural events for the community. Community members celebrate their connection to nature in dances and cultural rituals.

Spirituality and Ideology

Religious and spiritually focused groups also promote specific observations. Spirituality promotes observing events and phenomena and attributing broader meaning. When spiritual people observe events, they tend to identify order, higher powers, and additional meaning that others may not identify. Thus, religious and spiritual people have attribution systems that emerge when they observe specific events. Patterns within the attributions are consistent with the ideology that guides their beliefs.

Some groups restrict believers' observations based on ideological principles. We are all aware of the religious beliefs inherent in terrorist acts. Similar belief systems have been used to persecute social groups. In such situations, the group restricts the use of attributions. Often the in group draws positive interpretations, while other groups become the focus of negative beliefs. Value-based attributions are applied to the differences validating ideological beliefs.

When ideology results in differential attributions, observations become distorted because all interpretation is channeled through a rigid set of beliefs. For example, radical groups observe the wealth of the United States and condemn the values of the country. Observations of wealth among members of the in group are viewed qualitatively different. When ideologies reach these levels of polarization, they are often referred to as radical or extreme. Extremes can emerge among any ideological or religious group when polarization and differential attributions are used.

In-Group versus Out-Group Observation

Social group membership provides a perspective that can influence observations. People within any group become aware of the subtleties and nuances of phenomena within the group. Consequently, observations are more distinct because the group context is included in the interpretation. The depth of the in-group perspective allows for increased definition of events. When people observe across groups, observations are often more generalized because group-specific information is lacking. This lack of knowledge sometimes makes it more difficult to understand observed phenomena across groups.

When group membership differences include privilege disparities, it becomes increasingly difficult to understand observations. Identical behaviors may have divergent meanings depending on group membership. For example, people within a group can refer to each other using epithets with no offense. However, if someone from outside the group uses the same language, it is offensive. When we observe people, we must consider that their in-group behavior may differ from cross-group interactions. If we observe only one set of actions (in or out group), we must remind ourselves that we never have the full picture.

Interpretive Dangers

Given the tendency for cultures and contextual groups to influence how behaviors and phenomena are interpreted, we must be very careful when observing. If we are observing within our own group, we may interpret situations through our own lens. This can cause us to overlook important information. Similarly, when observing people from other groups, our interpretations can skew our understanding through a lack of good information.

Regardless of perspective, it is important to keep our focus on the nonverbal phenomenon rather than immediately jumping into interpretation. Doing this requires self-awareness to interrupt the automatic interpretative impulse. To accomplish this, we must maintain focus with our nondominant hemisphere rather than allowing our dominant brains to dominate our experience. In order to do this, we must consciously track and retain the details of what we observe.

Using Observation in Professional Practice

Previous chapters have underscored the importance of observing. In Chapter 3 we developed a cognitive foundation for these skills as we explored nonlinear thinking. This style of thinking is consistent with using the nondominant hemisphere of the brain. When we explored interactive tuning-in skills in Chapter 5, we began honing our observational skills. As we combine observation and listening, we become fully involved in our interactive sequences with clients. The next sections outline nonverbal communication elements that can help us focus when listening to others.

In the last two chapters we discovered that every practitioner response evokes interpersonal power: questions obligate answers, and reflections promote client thinking. Observation draws power from our ability to identify critical information that has not been expressed through verbal content. As we observe, we identify critical yet unexpressed elements of the client situation. When we place these elements on the table for exploration and consideration, we can help clients better master their situations.

Often nonverbal behavior occurs below a client's conscious consideration as internal responses to events cause muscles to tighten, inflections to change, and other manifestations. Physical changes are most common with powerful negative emotions, which are processed in the nondominant hemisphere, where they are less accessible to cognitive mediation and expression (Balconi, Falbo, & Brambilla, 2009; Demaree et al., 2005; van Stegeren, 2009). In contrast, positive and neutral emotions are processed in the dominant hemisphere, where they can be expressed through language (Ruge & Naumann, 2006; Wolynski, Schott, Kanowski, & Hoffmann, 2009). If we are attuned to these nonverbal changes in clients, we can respond to their emotional concerns when they emerge.

As we use observation with clients, our non-dominant hemisphere scans the client, the content and the interactions for patterns and similarities. We quickly consider these elements of client communication for importance. In doing so, we first identify and then flag patterns for exploration. We then transfer the information to the dominant hemisphere so we can help clients to overcome obstacles and master their situations. There are three types of patterns that we look for: nonverbal patterns, content patterns, and interactive patterns.

Observing Nonverbal Patterns

Very often, while telling their stories clients produce actions and expressions that provide us with clues about their emotions and meaning. These patterns emerge below the actual content and are expressed nonverbally as clients present their story. When a pattern of presentation emerges, we identify that there is something important in the communication. Two elements in a client's presentation are easily observed: vocal and physical communication patterns.

Patterns of Vocal Communication

Vocal patterns emerge from the noncontent elements of client communication. The patterns emerge as clients tell their story; the meaning and importance of the communication lies in the quality of the vocal delivery rather than in the words themselves. The noncontent elements of client communication provide information about the attributions and emotion behind their words. These elements often are used to identify affect and meaning.

- *Communication pace.* The speed at which people talk can provide clues about their affective experience. For example, someone talking very slowly might have something on his or her mind that is drawing attention away from the current topic (de Luynes, 1995; Murphy & Dillon, 1998). People who talk quickly and do not allow others to enter into the conversation may feel driven to get their point across.
- *Communication flow.* In addition to the speed of discussion, take note of the rhythm or flow of what is being said by the client (Angell, 1996). If sentences tend to drift off or there is hesitancy in client responses, there may be some indication that emotions are underlying the discussion. Similarly, if the flow is forced or seems pressured, the client might be trying to convince the practitioner of something.
- *Communication tone.* The vocal tone of client statements can provide a clue about the client's affective state. Low-pitched sound quality can indicate sadness or preoccupation. Higher pitches often are associated with nervousness and anxiety. Cutoff words may indicate anger or frustration.
- *Communication volume.* The volume of client statements is an important indicator of affective responses. Quiet statements often can be interpreted as indicating sadness or shyness on the part of the speaker. Higher volume can indicate anger, frustration, or an attempt to increase tension.

Patterns of Physical Communication

Concurrent with vocal communication patterns, clients behaviorally express emotion and meaning through physical communication. As we observe the actions associated with client communication, we can identify clues to the client's internal state. Although we discuss the physical and vocal elements separately, they often occur simultaneously. The physical communication elements include:

- *Posture.* When clients experience emotion, it can influence how they hold their body. When clients are slumped over, rigid, or relaxed, their emotional state is immediately communicated.
- *Position.* How clients position or angle their bodies (e.g., seating choices, who people look at, aversion of eye contact, leaning, etc.) communicates information about their relationships and feelings in the situation.
- *Gestures.* Many clients move their hands while speaking (e.g., punching movements, pointing, arms crossed on chest, open palms, etc.). Gestures are strong indicators of a client's emotional state.
- *Movement.* Frequently clients shuffle or fidget while talking or listening (e.g., picking, rubbing, doodling, etc.). These behaviors provide information about how the client experiences the situation.
- *Eye contact.* How clients make, maintain, or avoid eye contact with others may indicate an emotional response (e.g., timing of eye shifts, avoidance of eye contact, etc.).
- *Eye movement.* Often clients shift their gaze while talking or responding. These shifts can provide clues about their thinking (House, 1994). Eyes cast down often indicates an affective experience; eyes shifting to the side may indicate recalling spoken words or

Looking up is a sign of visual processing.

Looking down is a sign of tactile processing.

Looking to the left side is a sign of auditory recall processing.

Looking to the right is a sign of auditory construction processing

Figure 8.3

Eye Directional Cues and Processing Preferences

Source: Bandler & Grinder, 1975.

thinking what to say; and eyes looking up may indicate visual recall (Bandler & Grinder, 1975). (See Figure 8.3.)

- *Facial expressions.* Movement of the face and different facial expressions can indicate mood or affect (e.g., eyebrows up may indicate surprise, clenched teeth may indicate anger).

- *Behavior-verbal mismatches.* Sometimes the physical communication negates or conflicts with a verbal expression. When the two levels of communication are incongruent, often ambivalence or conflicts are occurring for the client.

- *Physical manifestations.* Clients sometimes communicate important information through their bodies. When we notice physical manifestations, such as labored breathing, flushing, tearing, and bruises, we quickly identify potential problems.

Observing Content Patterns

Concurrent with the noncontent communication, we can observe emotion and thinking in multiple content-related patterns. Clients often select words and phrases that contain additional meaning or emotion. As such, their choice of words contains an emotional load. When we notice a pattern of loaded words and phrases emerging in discussion, we identify that there is meaning or emotion to uncover. There are three types of content patterns: word choice, themes, and mystery patterns.

Word Choice Patterns

The wording chosen by clients provides clues to the affective or cognitive components in the statement. People sometimes choose words to create emphasis. At other times, they select words with no conscious thought, even though they reflect emotional responses. Either way, word choices can identify underlying information as patterns emerge. Word choice patterns often seem polarized (e.g., good versus bad, happy versus sad) with an emphasis on one extreme. When we notice such patterns, we are in a position to pick up on important thoughts and feelings. Five of the most common patterns include:

1. *Negative versus positive interpretations.* Some clients will tend to tune into the negative elements or interpretations of a situation even when there are positive alternatives.

2. *Negative versus positive affective loading.* Sometimes clients focus on a single pole of their affective experience. For example, they may feel inadequate and fail to identify past accomplishments.

3. *Absolute versus tentative wording.* Some clients will use words suggesting that there is never an exception to the problem situation. For example, words like never or always are used when describing a situation.

4. *Internal versus external wording.* Often clients who feel out of control of their own situations choose words that indicate the control is outside of themselves.

5. *I versus you statements.* When clients begin statements with "You," they talk as if they are the expert on the other person's experience and actions. With "I" statements, people talk about their own experience.

Thematic Patterns

More subtle than word choices, clients will often cycle themes into their interactions (Murphy & Dillon, 1998). Initially we may miss themes because they do not emerge until there have been repetitions. When we notice repeated themes, we often can identify critical beliefs, values, and feelings.

Processing themes are common in client communication. They include feelings and thoughts associated with the client's story. In these themes, we often find the power that the situation holds over the client. Frequent powerful themes include:

- *Loss.* Individual clients and even larger client systems often have themes of loss in their stories. At the individual level, this might include such events as divorce, abandonment, death, and geographic moves. At the organizational or community levels, events such as multiple deaths, changes in leadership, business or community leader relocations, high turnover, and layoffs can indicate themes of loss.

- *Disempowerment.* Client stories often include themes in which people and systems have negatively interfered in their lives. At the individual level, this might include intrusions by others, controlling authority figures, exploitation, and backgrounds of being controlled. At the larger system levels, events such as oppressive management systems, takeovers, coups, business ultimatums/power plays, and oppression can indicate disempowerment.

- *Power.* Often events described by the client depict situations in which they have little to no power and other people or systems have much higher levels of power. Alternatively, client may also share stories highlighting their own power or importance. When several such situations are described, a theme of powerlessness might be inferred.

- *Rejection.* Sometimes clients describe situations in which they are emotionally rejected. Events that can cluster into themes of rejection include exclusions of the client system, secrets that do not include the client, denial of requests/overtures, ignoring of the client system, and neglect of obvious needs.

- *Victimization.* At times, client stories will include descriptions of events in which the client system has experienced itself as a victim in the themes inherent in the story. In such situations, we identify a clear oppressor in each described event concurrent with a clear identification of the client system as a victim.

Mystery Patterns

There are times when themes in the client communication indicate unspoken issues that are important for understanding the situation. This is the most difficult type of theme for monitoring and responding. Mystery themes are inferred from observations of missing and incongruous elements. Some of the indicators of mystery themes include:

- *Gaps in congruity.* We often scan client content for consistency across time and situations. If client statements are internally consistent, we can infer a stable pattern of responding across time and place. However, when there is a lack of congruity, there may be some indication of additional meaning in how the client interprets the situation (Watzlawick, Beavin, & Jackson, 1967).

- *Door openers.* Often statements contain unclear meaning during client interaction. Many times these statements are "trial balloons" sent out by the client to see how we will respond, or they may indicate that a subject that has emotional energy for the client (Baenninger-Huber & Widmer, 1999). Statements such as "I am not sure it is even worth it" indicate that clients have feelings that are difficult to express and they need help.

- *Disguised content.* Often clients will avoid open disclosures of powerful themes by expressing themselves through metaphors or analogies. This is similar to someone saying "I feel like I was hit by a truck." When we hear such statements, it is clear that the client has a story to tell.

- *Content shifts.* When the other person changes the subject as we are discussing a situation, it often indicates that we are venturing into a content area that has triggered an emotional reaction. When we experience content shifts, it is important to note the content associated with the shift.

Exercise 8.1: Observing Client Wording and Presentation

You are a practitioner placed in a senior citizen drop-in/support service for people living in the community. Your job is to help clients resolve any problems that might interfere with community living. A woman entered the center and approached you. As you look at her, you notice she has dark skin but her ethnic origin is not immediately clear. She is wearing older-style clothes that are clean but worn and faded. As she walks toward you, she glances up, but then her eyes appear to focus on your mouth as she begins to talk. It is hard to really tell much about her eye contact as she is wearing dark glasses, but the angle of her head suggests she is looking down. You notice there are some dark marks around her neck; the rest of her skin is very smooth and clear. She is soft-spoken, appearing monotonic when speaking.

The woman begins, "I really don't know what to do with Mike. I try to do what's right with my son, but he doesn't want to listen to me. He moved in with me two months ago and he just does what he wants. I try to get him to get a job and plan for his life, he is now 47, but he just tells me that I'm an unfit mother. Then he watches TV or goes out drinking with his friends. I am left there, like a servant discarded after people get what they want. (Sighs quietly and stops for a pause.) I try to get him to pay attention to my needs but he doesn't care."

1. In this exchange, focus on and record the spoken aspects of the meeting and identify content and nonverbal indicators that help you interpret what the client is saying.

2. Read the case situation again and record indicators that help you identify (a) the emotion felt by the client and (b) the meaning that the story appears to have for the client.

   a. Indicators of emotion:

   b. Indicators of meaning:

3. What in the presentation, content, and nonverbal aspects of the client story lead you to hypothesize that there might be more going on in this family?

Observing Interactive Patterns

When working with clients, we have many opportunities to observe them in interaction. With larger client systems, there are multiple people interacting with each other, which allows us to scan the interaction without feeling a need to respond. When observing system members talking, we have an opportunity to identify multiple perspectives and dynamics.

Interactive Function Patterns

Multiple types of interaction emerge in a larger system. Table 8.1 contains five common interactive functions, each with a set of indicators. Notice how each function has multiple

Table 8.1 Larger-System Interactive Patterns

Interactive Category	Interactive Patterns
Decision making	Deference patterns (e.g., acquiesce to another person) Dominance patterns (e.g., people taking over the discussion) Collusion patterns (e.g., consistent siding with one another) Participation patterns (e.g., obstructing or facilitating decisions) Loyalty patterns (e.g., self-interest versus group interest)
Affiliation	Friendship patterns (e.g., people talking with and supporting each other) Antagonism patterns (e.g., people attacking or disrespecting others) Alienation patterns (e.g., people not invested in the group) Approval-seeking patterns (e.g., seeking attention or approval from others) Alliance patterns (e.g., side taking or teaming up together)
Influence	Coercive patterns (e.g., threats and sanctions used to force compliance) Manipulation patterns (e.g., sequences used to get favorable outcomes) Consensus patterns (e.g., taking leadership framing issues and concerns) Reward patterns (e.g., systems of providing benefits or rewards) Persuasion patterns (e.g., systems of convincing others to comply)
Atmosphere	Agitation patterns (e.g., restlessness among people) Distraction patterns (e.g., giggling/joking or sidebar discussions) Work patterns (e.g., people redirecting and focusing others) Avoidance patterns (e.g., silences and aversion of eye contact) Respect patterns (e.g., listening to others versus talking over, eye contact)
Cohesion	Identification patterns (e.g., frequently referencing ''we'' or ''us'') Disclosure patterns (e.g., open sharing among people) Continuity patterns (e.g., following up on past discussions) Celebratory patterns (e.g., noticing accomplishments and special events) Relinquishment patterns (e.g., trusting others to fulfill commitments)

patterns that can indicate the presence or absence of problems. Although the table does not present all larger system functions, it provides an initial set of functions that frequently emerge when working with client groups.

Sensory Preference Patterns

When people store their memories and make sense of their life experiences, they tend to organize those experiences through a sensory hierarchy (Bandler & Grinder, 1975; Young, 2004). Some people attend more closely to visual stimuli; others, to auditory stimuli; and still others focus on tactile experience. As people recall their experiences and tell their stories, this hierarchy is revealed through their interaction (Linder-Pelz & Hall, 2007). We can observe people's sensory preferences in their communicative patterns (Hoenderdos & van Romunde, 1995).

When observing people interacting, we can study their sensory preferences, because each sensory preference has a distinctive vocabulary. Table 8.2 provides comparable alternatives in visual, auditory, and sensory language. When responding it is possible to match

Table 8.2 Language Alternatives for Different Expressions

Visual Language	Auditory Language	Sensory Language
I see . . .	I hear . . .	I feel . . . , I sense . . .
It looks like . . .	It sounds like . . .	It seems like . . .
You look . . .	You sound . . .	My gut tells me . . .
I noticed . . .	I heard . . .	I sensed . . .
Let's look at this . . .	Let's talk about this . . .	Let's explore this . . .
Let's see what is going on . . .	Let's talk about what's going on . . .	Let's find out what is going on . . .

people's language preferences. Findings suggest that interviewers who match language are viewed as more empathic (Türan & Stemberger, 2000).

When we interact with others, it is helpful to consider their processing patterns. People tend to respond better when feedback is delivered in a language consistent with processing preferences (Gacitua, Sawyer, & Rayson, 2008; Linder-Pelz & Hall, 2008).The typical types of processing are:

- *Cognitive.* Clients tend to use words that reflect cognitive functions and process information through rational capacities (e.g., "Things just don't *make sense.*").
- *Visual.* Clients tend to use their visual observations to interpret situations and express their understandings through visual language (e.g., "I don't *see* what the problem is.").
- *Auditory.* Clients tend to use their hearing and talking capacities to sort out situations. When talking, they will often frame things in verbal terms (e.g., "It's like *talking* to a brick wall.").
- *Kinesthetic.* Clients tend to be somewhat intuitive in making sense of situations and will use sensory or action-focused language (e.g., "Something just doesn't *seem* right, but I can't *put my finger on it.*").
- *Gustatory.* Clients tends to use smelling and tasting metaphors in their use of language (e.g., "This really *stinks.*").

Exercise 8.2: Client Disclosure

A client is meeting with you for the first time. In the first meeting, this woman makes this following statement.

> *(Sigh.) I am not sure what is happening to me. (Looks down and avoids eye contact.) I feel like things are slipping through my fingers. I have worked at the brake plant for 20 years, and I just heard they are closing down. It is just rumors right now, but it is eating away at me. I feel frozen and unable to do anything. I come home and my husband is on me to do things for him, and all I can do is keep this sick feeling from bursting out all over the place. Then I go back to work and the rumors greet me at the door, and we go round and round again. It is getting so I can't sleep at night and I don't want to have anything to do with my family. (Looks straight at you.) I just want to crawl in a hole and pull the world in on top of me.*

1. What is the woman's processing (visual, auditory, etc.) preference?

2. What themes are evident in her choice of words that might lead you to think she is in a distraught emotional state?

3. Identify a mystery theme about her emotional state that would need to be checked to assess her emotional situation.

4. Write a brief (10-word) summary statement of what she was saying to you.

Describing Observations

Observing clients is a specific skill set used in all phases of practice. At times—for example, during assessment—we use it to identify unspoken elements of the situation. Throughout intervention, we observe during every client interaction. We never rely solely on the content of a client statement. We always validate our understanding by checking the nonverbal communication. When the nonverbal communication indicates that there is something important, we follow up our observations. This exploration begins with describing our observations.

Power of Describing Observations

Like questioning and reflecting, describing observations yields a unique influence during interaction with clients. The power of describing observations emerges as we place previously unacknowledged information on the table for exploration. Inherent in this skill, we tap into the power of the nondominant side of the client's brain. This power is activated when we use descriptive language and effectively provide a picture rather than relying on questions and reflections, which stimulate the dominant side of the brain.

The shift across hemispheres is powerful because activating processes in one hemisphere amplifies the influence of that hemisphee while concurrently deemphasizing functions of the opposite hemisphere (Perez et al., 2009; Spironelli, Tagliabue, & Umilta, 2009). In effect, if we are sufficiently descriptive to activate the nondominant brain, we tune out the influence of the dominant hemisphere. When we consider that rationalization, justification, and defensive arguments originate in the dominant hemisphere (Demaree et al., 2005), speaking directly to the nondominant hemisphere may be helpful when working with difficult or well-defended emotions.

Describing can also sidestep scripted responding. The dominant hemisphere often anticipates and automates interactional sequences. For example, when someone asks "How are you doing?" we automatically respond "Fine." This response is common even when life is falling apart; we simply respond without thinking. These expectable sequences are automated and stored in our dominant brain like an interactive formula (Gladwin, Hart, & de Jong, 2008). Descriptive language stimulates the nondominant hemisphere which helps sidestep peoples' automated responses which emanate from the dominant hemisphere.

Uses of Describing an Observation

Like other interactive skills, describing observations can be used to fulfill four possible functions. However, describing observations sometimes are followed closely by a second type of response, such as questioning or reflecting. Practitioners tend to combine describing with a second skill because description effectively places material on the table but contains no command. If we want the client to respond to the material, we often provide a second element in our response to encourage action. When reading the next examples provided with each function, notice how the impact changes when description is accompanied by another type of response.

1. *Clarification*. When clients present nonverbal information that conflicts with their content or verbal assertions we can describe the nonverbal communication to clarify the mismatch and achieve an accurate understanding. For example: "You stated that you love your mother, but as you made the statement you pounded your leg with your fist. What is your fist trying to communicate about your mother?"

2. *Exploration*. When we describe nonverbally expressed information, it puts it on the table so we can explore the thinking and feeling inherent in the client situation. For example: "When you were speaking, I noticed your voice became louder and you clenched your fist."

3. *Positioning*. Sometimes the nonverbally expressed information is critical for focusing interaction toward goal achievement. In such situations, we want to get the information on the table. For example: "When you talked about your daughter's plans, your eyes

flipped back into your head and you smiled. Tell what you were thinking about as you reflected on your daughter's plans."

4. *Change promotion.* Describing observations is a critical element in confrontation and challenging clients because it gets information on the table without judgment. For example: "When you said you were going to stay on your medication this time, you laughed. Are you saying you will stay on your meds so I will stay off your back?"

Deciding to Share an Observation

Given that we are always observing clients, a shift to highlighting nonverbally communicated information requires a decision to move beyond the normal functions of listening. Guiding this decision, we want to pick up on nonverbal communication that is pertinent to the client's well-being. We can measure importance by the perceived impact of the emotion on the client. We should also consider client goals. Whenever we elect to place material on the table, it should promote goal achievement and client mastery of the situation.

Assessing the Need

There are two steps in the decision to describe an observation. First, we consider the observed phenomenon and its importance to the client goals. When the nonverbal information has no relevance, we consider the helping relationship. If the observed phenomenon may impact our ability to help the client, we may elect to describe our observations to strengthen the working alliance. After assessing the importance of the information, the second step is to highlight the nonverbal communication so it can be used to help the client.

Making the decision to include information or not requires discipline. Some information may be interesting but not critical to the work. For example, a client may appear angry when talking about her supervisor. We may be intrigued by this relationship, but unless it is associated with client goals, we let the observation pass. We may want to share the observation if the client goals are associated with anger management or work. However, goals about depression or family life may not warrant a focus on the nonverbal communication.

Assessing Accessibility

A second consideration when deciding to share observed information is the client's access to their underlying thoughts and feelings. If clients are angry and know they are angry, they have full access to the information. There is no need to highlight it; any attempt to do so would be redundant. However, if clients do not seem aware of their nonverbally communicated emotion or thinking, we may want to identify it so they can use the information to master the situation.

When clients appear to have no insight or access to their emotional experience, we must be careful about describing our observations because this may be the clients' first introduction to the information. If clients feel judged or that we are being intrusive, defensive reactions may occur because introducing new information is a form of confrontation. This is why we seek to be totally descriptive by purging conclusions and judgments from our communications. Doing this allows clients to process the information in the nondominant hemisphere.

The Challenge of Describing

Describing observed nonverbal information is a complex skill. Most of us have used questioning and reflecting in our social life, but we very seldom describe our observations. Most of the complexity emerges through our lack of practice with the skill. Inherent in our lack of practice is the fact that we have preferential habits for questioning or reflecting. We also have preferential thinking habits. We discussed the automatic concluding and integrating habits earlier in the chapter. These habits contribute to complexity because we seldom pay attention to nonverbal details. Consequently, we must direct our focus to observed, rather than assumed, information.

Along with the challenges inherent in our communication preferences, the mental processes involved in describing are more complex than in questioning and reflecting. Most often, our interpersonal responses involve the dominant hemisphere as we assess and focus. However, describing requires us to engage both hemispheres. The complexity of our brain functions makes this skill mentally challenging. To understand this complexity, it is helpful to quickly recap how our brain works during description.

Brain Processing and Descriptive Language

The neurobiology of language challenges our use of description because our observations occur in the nondominant hemisphere (Obleser et al., 2008; Vogel et al., 2003) while language is formed in the dominant hemisphere (Hugdahl & Westerhausen, 2009). The brain functions involved in descriptive language are more complex because both hemispheres are involved. Questioning and reflecting require less brain processing, which makes them neurologically simpler processes.

Our tendency to formulate conclusions rather than remaining focused on observed elements, may be associated with our interpersonal habits. Conclusions, like questions and reflections, are generated in the dominant hemisphere. As such, there seems to be a habitual reliance on the dominant brain functions. A descriptive response involves both sides of the brain. Typically, the dominant hemisphere concludes that something is important. This is followed by a shift to the nondominant hemisphere to identify the nonverbal components. Finally, we must shift back to the dominant hemisphere to formulate the description.

Because of the complexity involved in formulating descriptions, it is easy to understand why we are not naturally drawn to describing our observations. Consequently, we must consciously develop this skill; it is unlikely to emerge if left to natural development. When we draw a conclusion, we must consciously shift focus back to what we observed that led us to that conclusion. After we identify the observed elements, we can formulate a description of our observation.

Socialization Challenges

Compounding the challenges associated with mental gymnastics across hemisphere, many of us are socialized to withhold observations. As children, we might recall saying "Mommy, that man has a big belly," only to have our mother actively dissuade us from sharing such observations. These parent-child exchanges provide an ambivalent foundation for developing our descriptive skills.

As we age, our descriptive skills typically emerge as justification skills. When our conclusions are challenged, we find we must defend them by dredging up the details upon which those conclusions are based. In social situations, these exchanges often are filled with tension because we often use the skill after we have been accused of something egregious.

Concurrent with these socialization experiences, many of us live in a world where logic and conclusions are valued. In school we are asked to formulate decisions based on data and rational thought. Emotions often are viewed as distracting rather than informative. Consequently, we learn to come to conclusions and base our decisions on those conclusions. The combined socialization experiences promote a focus on the dominant hemisphere, predisposing us to integrate our conclusions rather than attending to the nonverbal communication and observations.

Cultural and Social Considerations

The preceding discussion of socialization influences is based on dominant cultural experiences. It is very important to understand that these experiences will not necessarily extend to other cultures. Each culture develops its own systems of nonverbal communication. These systems become embedded in the culture and are used to socialize members into the cultural systems (Weisbuch & Ambady, 2008). As we work across cultures, we must be aware that every culture has its own systems of using and interpreting nonverbal communications (Dietrich, Hertrich, Alter, Ischebeck, & Ackermann, 2007; Kita, 2009).

Similar to systems of interpreting nonverbal communication, cultural groups differentially value observation. Although the dominant culture values questioning and verbal exchanges, many cultures value observing and imitation as a primary vehicle for learning (Paradise & Rogoff, 2009). When working with cultures that value observation, attempts to promote verbal exploration may be resisted and nonverbal exchanges may be more highly valued (Iwakabe, 2008). Consequently, we must be patient and observe silently prior to asking too many questions.

As we observe and attempt to use nonverbal information in our practice, it is critical that we avoid integrating our conclusions; integrating our own conclusions injects our cultural biases into the exchanges. We must allow clients to form their own interpretations within their cultural frameworks. We must also be aware that our nonverbal communication may be experienced differently by other cultural groups. This is most important as we attempt to influence other people (Kong, 2003; Ruzickova, 2007; Yu, 2003).

Using Description to Promote Client Work

Observations are useful to the degree that they can help clients achieve their goals. Consequently, a critical skill is being able to place our observations on the table for a client response. Doing this requires us to describe objectively what we observe and then invite the client to respond. This skill is easier said than done because describing our observations, like reflections, often end in a moment of silence as the client considers the material that we describe. These moments of silence can create more anxiety because we are placing unacknowledged material on the table. We must consequently be careful of our tendency to continue talking. It is important to allow the silence so the client can consider the new information.

Accessing the Observation

Getting started is often a challenge especially for people from the dominant North American culture. People from storytelling cultures and those with a background in the arts or play therapy may have some experience being descriptive, but very few readers can quickly access the details of an observation. Most of us begin by working back from conclusions. If we can successfully ladder back to the details that support the conclusion, we can access the details of our observations. From these details we set up and describe the observation.

Working Back from Conclusions
Many of us initially find that we continue to draw conclusions when we observe nonverbal communication. For example, we immediately assume that someone is angry, sad, or otherwise affected. Noticing our conclusion is the first step in developing our descriptive skills. This probably will be the case for most students because the dominant cultures in North America promote drawing conclusions.

If you find yourself working from conclusions, the first step is to refocus your mind on the observation. Doing this will require conscious attention because it will require you to access the nondominant hemisphere. There will be a transition in focus that requires conscious mental work. As you refocus, ask yourself what you noticed that led to the conclusion. Briefly scan again what you saw and heard as the client was speaking to identify the observations that triggered the conclusion.

Finding the Observation
As you identify the observed elements that supported your conclusion, you access the details of your observation. At first you may find too few or too many details. This can be frustrating. Identifying too many elements in the client's statement is a sign that you are heightening your observation to the point where everything appears meaningful. If you have a large list, ask yourself which elements stood out as different in the client's communication. Perhaps certain words were stressed, or a look emerged at a certain point. Identifying the moments when the communication varied from "normal" will help you identify important elements in your observation.

If you find that there are too few elements in your list of observations, it is most likely due to your socialized training to use the dominant side of your brain. If this is the case, you may have to relax and become comfortable observing different aspects of the world. You can practice observing in all aspects of life including classroom discussions, sitting in a coffee shop, walking in a mall, watching movies, and any setting in which people interact. As you become comfortable identifying elements in people's interaction that cause you to assume specific emotional or cognitive states, you will become more skilled.

Forming a Descriptive Response

After you have accessed the observed details, you have a foundation for forming a descriptive response. You now shift focus to the dominant side of your brain to frame your statement. Doing this sometimes is awkward because we are not used to fitting observed phenomena into sentences. Our habit of sharing the conclusion will also contribute to the awkwardness because describing the observation will not feel natural.

Setting Up the Description

It is important to focus the discussion prior to describing the observation because nonverbal information initially is unacknowledged. For example, when the client walks in with a slumped posture and sighing, we may notice the behavior, but the client may be unaware. Consequently, the behavior is in the room but not officially on the table for exploration. Our initial challenge is to shift focus to the observed actions.

Unlike the other interactive skills, describing an observation is very simple. We introduce the fact that we have observed something. There are limited ways to accomplish this focus. The simplest setup is to state that you noticed something. The most complex is to focus briefly on a context and then share that you noticed something.

- *Simple.* "I notice that . . . "
- *Focused.* "When you walked in, I noticed that . . . "

Both of these setup lines include the words "I notice(d)." This phrase is useful because it logically leads into a description. If you use setup words associated with reflection (e.g., "it seems"), it is likely to lead to a conclusion. As you build your descriptive skills, try to use the words "I notice" because it will lead you to describe what you noticed. As you become comfortable with the skill, you can start to add "I heard . . . " or "I saw . . . " Regardless, it will be easier to build the skill if you can keep your setup line simple.

Delivering a Descriptive Response

Although the distinction between conclusions and observations may seem insignificant when talking about something minor, such as "looking flushed," the distinction becomes very important when describing indicators of emotional processing. We have all had experiences in which someone has said, "You look angry" and been either wrong or unwelcome. However, if the person had said, "I notice that your fists are clenched and your voice seems louder than normal. Is something going on?" a change might occur in how we respond.

The usefulness of describing observations to get someone to open up seems to come from two elements.

1. We are only describing an observation. We are making no conclusion, assumption, or judgment that may make a client defensive.
2. The technique is descriptive, which tends to provide a picture for the client to reflect on. Visual images tend to be experienced holistically in the nondominant hemisphere and are less prone to logic-based defenses.

When describing observations, first we must practice sharing observations rather than conclusions. "I notice your face is flushed today" is qualitatively different from "You look flushed." In the first statement, we share an observation with the client so the latter can respond. Notice how we use an "I" because it is our observation. In the second example, the practitioner shared a conclusion. Notice the statement starts with "you" because the conclusion is focused on the client. Consequently, try to keep an "I" focus as you start your description. This beginning will help direct you toward a description.

Inviting a Client Response

When describing an observation, we want to get the observed information on the table so it can be explored with the client. Given that the statement made to the client is descriptive, he or she often needs to be invited to comment. Many times a simple probe or question, such as "What feelings are you experiencing under that red face today?" can prompt the client to open up.

When we invite a client response, it is useful to build on the description. Notice above that the "red face" remains on the table. This keeps the focus. If we ask, "Is something happening that we need to talk about?" we end up soliciting an opinion on whether the client believes the situation warrants exploration. Such questions shift our focus away from the observation. Make sure that the focus does not shift so that the client responds to the description.

Exercise 8.3: Sharing Observations

You are working in a drop-in center for at-risk families. Your program is in the center of a medium-size city. You are watching a mother and her 8-year-old daughter interacting when you notice the mother constantly correcting the child's behavior. In less than three minutes, she identified seven things the child should do differently. Whenever the mother made a correction, the child would stiffen and ignore her mother. The mother kept talking at the child until the child threw down a game and swore at the mother. You moved closer to make sure things did not escalate. The mother turned to you and said, "She is impossible. I try to help her, but she has such a temper. What would you do?"

1. Identify the elements you observed that indicate the thinking or feeling under the mother's interactions with her daughter.

2. You want to explore the thinking or feelings that underlie the mother's correcting of the daughter. Write what you would say to the mother to set up your description. Use a focused setup and then describe your observations.

3. Now write a question or probe you could use to help the mother begin to explore the situation.

Sharing Observations and Larger Client Systems

Observing and describing skills are used in all forms of practice, but these skills are critical when working with larger client systems. This is true in part because there are more interpersonal processes in larger systems. With the increased interpersonal processes, there is a parallel increase in nonverbal communication. Practitioners consequently must spend more time observing the client system. We also must become very skilled at describing these observations in order to influence the system dynamics. There are two important applications of observing and describing skills: scanning dynamics and highlighting processes.

Scanning Dynamics

In a larger client system, we often shift our focus from the content being discussed to the dynamics occurring within the system. In these systems, very important information emerges from the nature of interaction. This information includes how people relate and work together. These are the elements in a system that can interfere with success. Consequently, we must observe these dynamics so we can intervene at the system and at the individual levels.

To achieve this level of observation, we often mentally withdraw from the content of discussions to observe how the system members are interacting and relating with each other. This skill is referred to as scanning. When working with larger systems, we move in and out of scanning mode depending on the observed dynamics. This is a core skill involved in group work and community work.

Highlighting Processes

When we identify a potential problem at the system level, we move out of scanning mode and use our description skills to help the system members identify and change how they work together. This use of description is often referred to as highlighting processes because we effectively identify a dynamic and highlight it for discussion among the members.

Highlighting processes follow the stages of description identified in this chapter. We first identify the dynamic, then assess the importance, and describe our observations. Although it may take longer to observe the dynamic in larger systems, the basics of working are very similar to using description with a single client. The core difference is that after describing our observation, there will be several people responding. Some may affirm the observation and others may argue or change it. This diversity underscores the need to be highly descriptive because there are more people to take offense when we place material on the table.

Case Example

A practitioner was serving on a community committee setting priorities for the county health resources. There were physicians and representatives from health and mental health agencies and from health insurance organizations. The committee was bogged down in repeated debates about managing uninsured patients. Some members wanted to prioritize attracting new physicians to the community while others argued that there needed to be funds to manage people who were uninsured. Although the committee would vote and affirm the need to manage uninsured patients, the next meeting inevitably would focus on attracting physicians. These discussions tended to be ideological in nature, stressing that without doctors, there would be no systems for anybody. After several meetings, a practitioner said, "I have noticed a pattern where we have a vote, but the next meeting we engage in the same discussion as if the vote was never taken. Have others noticed this pattern?" This response initiated a discussion about the need to honor votes and proceed with decisions that the committee had made. In the ensuing week, one of the members who was heavily invested in giving more money to physicians resigned from the committee.

Bringing It All Together

As you proceed into your professional role, you will find many opportunities for practicing your observation skills. Your observations will grow in complexity as knowledge and experience refine your skills. With ongoing practice you will be able to identify people's thinking and feeling with very little effort. You will also become sensitive and attuned to others as you deepen your understanding.

Although there are ample opportunities to practice observation, it is hard to find opportunities for describing observations. In your interactions, describing is often not a welcome response because people may feel scrutinized. To get practice developing descriptions, you may need to comment on scenes of beauty and music. If you can become comfortable identifying and describing pleasing elements, you can interrupt your conclusion impulse and gain some comfort in being descriptive.

As you build comfort in describing observations, you will find that it is a powerful interactive skill for getting information on the table. With experience, you will discover that the judicious use of describing can enhance your ability to master many client situations. In later chapters you will learn how describing is a critical element in expressing concern, confronting, and dealing with threats to the helping relationship.

Critical Chapter Themes

1. Practitioners explore the client situation through attending to the client's verbal and nonverbal communication. Doing this requires active listening and observation skills.

2. Verbal communication with clients is easy to misconstrue and requires active listening skills to make sure the practitioner understands the client story.

3. Workers observe the clients' presentations and interactions to identify underlying feelings and thoughts that are important for understanding the situation.

4. In the communication, the practitioner monitors the content themes in client disclosures (wording choices, content themes, and mystery themes).

5. When observing the client, the practitioner scans the nonverbal communication (pace, tone, volume, etc.), the actions (behaviors, presentations, and physical manifestations), and client interactions with others (interactions and interpersonal processes).

6. Workers share observations in descriptive form to get nonverbal material on the table to be explored with the client.

Online Resources

Communications Skills page: http://spot.pcc.edu/~rjacobs/career/effective_communi cation_skills.htm

Listening skills: www.mindtools.com/CommSkll/ActiveListening.htm

Observational exercises: www.ehow.com/how_4519784_hone-observation-skills-writing .html

Observation Skills Test: www.calculatorslive.com/Observation-Skills-Test.aspx

Recommended Reading

Angell, G. B. (1996). Neurolinguistic programming theory and social work treatment. In F. J. Turner (Ed.), *Social work treatment: Interlocking theoretical approaches* (4th ed., pp. 480–502). New York, NY: Free Press.

Emmerling, R. J., Shanwalt, V. K., & Mandal, M. K. (2008). *Emotional intelligence: Theoretical and cultural perspectives*. New York, NY: Nova Publishers.

Hoenderdos, H. T. W., & van Romunde, L. K. J. (1995). Information exchange between client and the outside world from the NLP perspective. *Communication and Cognition, 28,* 343–350.

Ting-Toomey, S. (2005). *Understanding intercultural communication.* Los Angeles, CA: Roxbury Publishing.

Watzlawick, P., Beavin, J. H., & Jackson, D. D. (1967). *Pragmatics of human communication: A study of interactional patterns, pathologies, and paradoxes.* New York, NY: Norton.

Chapter 9
Providing Direction

In previous chapters we explored nondirective methods for helping clients to master their situations. The skills that you learned are focused on helping clients to discover their own solutions. Such skills are consistent with the ethical principles of client autonomy and self-determination. Nondirective skills are also consistent with research findings that suggest an empathic practitioner promotes positive outcomes. The content of this chapter diverges from this pattern of nondirective skill developments because intervention also must have a sense of direction. This chapter explores directive skills designed to promote goal achievement.

Need for Direction

There is ample evidence that a strong working alliance is a critical precondition to effective service (Block-Lerner, Adair, Plumb, Rhatigan, & Orsillo, 2007; Hilsenroth & Cromer, 2007; Lutz, Leon, Martinovich, Lyons, & Stiles, 2007). Previous chapters developed skills associated with developing a client-focused working alliance. Along with the working alliance research, there is evidence that interventions with a strong focus and direction are effective (Berliner, 2005; Cohen, Mannarino, & Knudsen, 2005). Consequently, many argue in favor of a directive approach to intervention.

Evidence-Based and Directive Practice

The debate between directive and nondirective approaches is not new in the human service professions. In the mid-1900s, behaviorist approaches emerged as an alternative to the nondirective Freudian treatments. Later, Carl Rogers developed a new nondirective model. This was followed by directive cognitive-behavioral approaches, which were in turn countered by postmodern alternatives. As we view the history of treatment models, there is a constant tension between directive and nondirective approaches.

In the current debate, people often contrast working alliance research to evidence-based practice outcome research. Working alliance research tends to focus on elements in the practitioner-client relationship and interaction. Outcome research focuses on treatment outcomes. In outcome research, it is normal to use treatment manuals outlining the activities and principles of the intervention. Such manualized intervention approaches are easy to evaluate because several practitioners can use the model and their results can be compared. This provides evidence of success. Increasingly, interventions based on this type of research are referred to as evidence-based or evidence-informed practices.

Directive Intervention
The development of evidence-based practices (EBPs) has converged with the debate between directive and nondirective approaches to intervention. Proponents of empirically based interventions criticize many of the nondirective models. Increasingly, proponents of EBP argue that there is an ethical obligation to use well-researched, directive practice models (Kennedy, Mercer, Mohr, & Huffine, 2002; Thyer, 2007). It is further postulated that a worker-client relationship is secondary to using well-supported interventions (Thyer, 2007).

The EBPs have advanced professional knowledge in the helping professions rapidly. Manualized (standardized interventions that are guided by a step-by-step manual) treatments are endorsed by federal agencies that fund mental health research; for this reason, evidence-based models have proliferated. These same funding agencies have promoted the adoption of these models by community agencies. Increasingly, funding bodies such as United Way agencies and state governments insist that service providers use EBPs.

Levels of Evidence-Based Practice

EBPs have emerged from medical and empirical approaches to intervention, where practitioners are expected to apply the most efficacious intervention. As EBPs have transitioned into the nonmedical helping professions, we have tried to apply the best research practices to assess interventions with specific populations. Practices have emerged that are very effective with specific populations (Leis, Mendelson, Tandon, & Perry, 2009). At the current time several types of EBP are emerging. All are commonly referred to as evidence-based practices, but there are differences in cost and effectiveness. These practices include:

1. *Manualized programs with fidelity assessment protocols.* Many EBPs are resource intensive. Such programs require significant levels of initial training, ongoing consultation requirements, monitoring protocols, and follow-up training agreements. These EBPs are clearly the most expensive practices, requiring an ongoing monetary commitment. These practices use fidelity measures to ensure that people using the program remain consistent with the program used in the research. While the fidelity measures retain adherence to the researched model, they may inhibit agency responsiveness to client population dynamics and unique needs. It is critical to evaluate how such programs are effective with specific community-level client populations.

2. *Manualized programs.* Some EBPs provide clearly manualized programs with examples and guidelines for program implementation. These programs do not promote independent fidelity measures and ongoing consultation but do expect some agency personnel to understand the program and internally monitor program fidelity. Although the monetary commitment is less, agencies must be diligent to ensure the program is implemented as intended. Evaluation of such programs will need to monitor the program implementation concurrent with costs and outcomes.

3. *Public domain EBPs.* Many EBPs are published in the literature. Often no published manuals or training programs are associated with these programs because the research funding did not provide a large budget. Agencies can access these programs and arrange for training through the researchers. Like the programs mentioned above, agencies must assume responsibility for program fidelity.

4. *Adapted EBPs.* Many agencies have taken EBPs found effective with certain populations and adapted the practices to meet the unique needs of client populations. Most often such adaptations are implemented when client populations were excluded from the original research samples so effectiveness with the current population is unsupported. Such adaptations effectively negate the past supporting evidence and require agencies to collect their own evidence to ensure that the adaptations do not disrupt program effectiveness.

5. *Promising practices.* The least rigorous category of EBPs are programs based on informal research, clinical findings, or distilling practice principles from multiple EBPs. Although such programs are based on evidence, testing is required to determine their effectiveness and efficiency. These types of programs require thorough evaluation on outcomes, preferably with scientific rigor in the evaluation design.

In recent years there has been a proliferation of evidence-based practices. As funding sources insist on using EBPs, there has been a parallel proliferation of proprietary practices. Many manualized practices with fidelity protocols now charge agencies training and consulting fees as part of their systems. In extreme cases, consultants make critical practice decisions yet never work directly with the client. Proponents of such models focus primarily on the principles and techniques of the manualized intervention with little consideration of practitioner skills and working relationships.

Toward a Balanced Direction

EBPs are clearly a feature of current professional practice and have advanced the argument in favor of directive practice. Some proponents argue from a polarized position when discussing EBPs. Similarly, some proponents of nondirective practice latch onto the working alliance research and use it to dismiss evidence-based findings. When viewed from the polarized positions, the debate can appear confusing and irreconcilable. However, if viewed from a position of balance, the politicized and dismissive positions of each extreme can be moderated. Clearly there is evidence supporting a working alliance and evidence showing the effectiveness of many directive techniques.

Although it is conceptually easy to promote a balance between working relationship and a directive approach, achieving this balance requires a delicate three-way balance among practitioner knowledge, practitioner skill, and client motivation. In this three-directional balance, each element—empirical knowledge, practitioner skill, and client motivation—must be equally weighted. If our approach is too directive, client motivation may decrease (Bischoff & Tracey, 1995). If we ignore the relationship and rigidly follow protocols, the working alliance also can suffer (Ackerman & Hilsenroth, 2001; Johansson & Eklund, 2006).

To achieve an effective balance, it is important that we enter the helping relationship with a strong skill set and a genuine concern for our clients (Barber et al., 2006; Jennings et al., 2008; Keijsers, Schaap, & Hoogduin, 2000; Littauer, Sexton, & Wynn, 2005). Concurrently, we must base our intervention plans and direction on good evidence (Littauer et al., 2005). Consequently, some direction is necessary. This is especially true in practice settings employing short-term intervention (Scheyett et al., 2009).

Need for Core Skills

Some research has found that the differences across models of intervention tend to be minimal (Leis, Mendelson, Tandon, & Perry, 2009). Research also indicates that variance in the outcomes within a model is attributable to practitioner rather than client effects (Shechtman, 2004; Trepka, Rees, Shapiro, Hardy, & Barkham, 2004). Even when EBP fidelity is adequate, practitioner skill deficits can undermine program effectiveness (Macpherson, Hovey, Ranganath, Uppal, & Thompson, 2007). These findings underscore the need for practitioners to have a strong interpersonal skills foundation. Practitioners must employ these skills with well-informed focus and purpose (Creed & Kendall, 2005; Watson & McMullen, 2005).

Given the effectiveness of EBPs and the concurrent need for practitioner skill, we cannot simply rely on a manual to do our work for us. In previous chapters, we learned several skills that remain important in EBP. First we must be able to tune in and respond to client communications. We also need to question, reflect, and share observations in response to client communications. When we do not use these types of skills effectively, even EBPs will lose effectiveness (Marshall et al., 2005).

Activity-Based Intervention

Many EBPs use structured activities as an element of intervention. Some activities emerge from practitioner-client interaction while others are constructed and implemented as part of a program. Regardless, we often use activities to bring focus to client interventions. The ability to facilitate activities has become a critical practice competency. The nature and content of activities vary depending on the practice model and focus of the approach (Diamond, Diamond, & Hogue, 2007), activities have two elements in common: focus and demand.

1. *Focus*. Activities are focused on specific areas of the client situation. Consequently, we must be purposeful as we select client information on which to focus our activity.
2. *Demand*. When conducting activities, we place demands on clients to explore and respond in ways that are different from normal patterns. Consequently, we must ensure that we have an alliance strong enough to survive the demands.

In manualized EBPs, activities are organized into a sequence with instructions outlining the focus and implementation of each activity. An alternative to such highly structured interventions is to explore multiple EBPs to identify the types of activity we want to use with specific clients. Five common types of activity are used in practice. These include activities that:

1. Provide information.
2. Challenge thinking patterns.
3. Influence affective processing.
4. Influence skills and behavior.
5. Alter problem contexts.

Activities that Provide Information

Often EBPs include psychoeducational sequences providing clients with critical concepts. This is true in many parenting, violence abatement, substance cessation, and mental health programs (Karp & Dugas, 2003; Lane, Mathews, Sallas, Prattini, & Sun, 2008). Practitioners must understand the core concepts of these programs so they can help clients develop a deeper understanding of their situations. Some programs then expand into other types of activity to develop skills and thinking strategies. Two core skills are involved information provision: sharing and applying concepts.

1. *Sharing concepts.* Intervention programs sometimes rely on specific concepts that can be used throughout the intervention. In such situations it is important that all people involved have the same understanding of the concepts. Without a shared understanding among members, there is a risk of misunderstanding. Consequently, practitioners must share or help the members develop a unified method of conceptualizing events and elements in their situation. There are two common forms of directive activity:
   a. *Developing concepts.* Sometimes it is useful to explore an experience and help the client or a group of clients conceptualize events. As clients label and conceptualize their experiences, they provide a framework for future work.
   b. *Teaching concepts.* When well-developed concepts apply to client situations, practitioners often teach clients the concepts so they can be used during the intervention.

2. *Applying concepts.* Concepts are most useful when they can be applied to client situations in a way that enhances client mastery (Bornhofen & McDonald, 2008; Fox, 2009). Consequently, intervention programs tend to apply concepts after a shared understanding is achieved. It is the application of concepts that enables clients to generalize learning to their life situations. If clients cannot generalize experiences from the intervention setting to home, long-term effectiveness will be compromised. Three types of activity help apply concepts:
   a. *In vivo intervention.* Sometimes intervention programs are implemented in the client life space. These interventions use real situations and coach client responses as events emerge.
   b. *Life situation applications.* Often intervention programs meet in agency settings but ask clients to apply concepts to their life situation. As they apply the concepts, the practitioner provides feedback and assistance so clients can use the concepts to better manage their life situations.
   c. *Constructed applications.* Some programs provide case examples or videos, and ask the clients to apply concepts to a standardized situation. This method uses the same content and activities with all participants providing more programmatic control for the practitioners but less generalization to the client situation.

Contextual Cautions

Psychoeducation and concept-based programming has mixed results with some client populations. Ample evidence indicates that it is of limited use as a sole intervention with clients living in poverty with multiple problems (Dumas, Nissley-Tsiopinis, & Moreland, 2006; Goodson, Layzer, St. Pierre, Bernstein, & Lopez, 2000; Jones, Sellwood, & McGovern, 2005; Mueser et al., 2009). Outcomes are also moderated by race and educational levels (Mishel et al., 2003).

Some of the difficulty with education-based programming emerges from the implicit requirement that participants can understand and generalize concepts beyond the treatment condition (Jones et al., 2005; Springer & Reddy, 2004). This requirement assumes a style of cognitive processing and application ability that contains cultural and economic biases. Consequently, many concept-based programs include multiple types of activities that build on the initial conceptual focus.

Activities That Challenge Thinking Patterns

In many EBPs, practitioners use activities designed to challenge and alter people's patterns of thinking. Depending on the EBP, interventions to alter thinking patterns often help clients identify and challenge irrational thinking so feelings and behavior can be altered (Floyd, Whelan, & Meyers, 2006; Sarkisian, Prohaska, David, & Weiner, 2007). Most research focuses on individual outcomes, but similar findings exist for challenging attributions to achieve organizational change and employee retention (Proudfoot, Corr, Guest, & Dunn, 2009).

Pattern of Cognitive Intervention

When we work with clients to alter their thinking, we follow a predictable pattern of activity:

1. We help clients identify irrational beliefs carefully matching the thoughts to identified client problems.
2. We challenge the irrational beliefs so clients can identify how they contribute to problems.
3. We help clients replace their problem thinking with new thoughts that can help them master the situation.

The specifics of this three-step intervention pattern will change depending on the type of problem (e.g., anxiety, depression, anger, marital infidelity). Each of the three steps can involve many activities that incorporate the skills described in previous chapters. Some of common activities used in this three-step process include:

- *Identifying irrational beliefs*. The first step in cognitive intervention activities involves identifying irrational thoughts that contribute to the problem (Floyd, et al., 2006; Sarkisian, et al., 2007). Doing this involves careful exploration of the client's problem situations with a focus on the underlying thinking that underlies them. This exploration sometimes occurs interactively in the session but often is supplemented with assignments and homework exercises for the client to complete outside of the session. Specific interventions to identify problematic thinking include:
  - *Situational exploration*. When identifying irrational thinking, we begin by exploring problem situations associated with client goals. Throughout this exploration we focus on how the client's thinking (expectations, beliefs, etc.) contribute to the problem.
  - *Homework assignments*. Often we use homework assignments, asking clients to monitor their thinking for a period of time or in specific situations. Part of the homework is to return with a list of the thoughts regarding those situations.
  - *List negotiation*. Prior to intervention, it is important to develop a list of the thoughts that promote problems. Doing this involves discussing already identified thoughts so each can be linked to specific problems and identified as something the client wants to change.
  - *Contexualizing*. As a list of irrational thoughts emerges, the thinking needs to be linked to the problems (feelings and behaviors) that brought the client into service. As we finalize the list, all thoughts need to be understood in terms of how they interfere with the client's ability to master the situation. Doing this involves a situational exploration so clients can make their own linkages.
- *Challenging current thinking*. After a list of irrational thoughts is identified we explore the list carefully identifying how they maintain client problems. As the link to current problems is established, the focus of intervention shifts to challenging the irrational thinking (Floyd et al., 2006; Sarkisian et al., 2007). In many cases, irrational thoughts

involve adaptations to events in the client's past. The goal of challenging is to help clients discover how their thinking does not apply to their current situations. Some activities focus on the future to adjust expectations and prepare for events (Venning, Kettler, Eliott, & Wilson, 2009); others focus on the past to adjust historical patterns of interpretation and adaptation (Gregory & Embrey, 2009).To challenge client thinking we engage in the these types of activity:

- *Experiments*. Practitioners have clients experiment with their thinking (Newman & Stiles, 2006). The experiments help clients identify situations where the thinking is clearly faulty.
- *Feedback*. Practitioners provide feedback that help clients to challenge irrational thinking and support rational thought processes (Le Foll, Rascle, & Higgins, 2008).
- *Using evidence*. Often practitioners provide direct challenges to the client's interpretations by exploring the evidence and helping the client see how the thinking does not fit the evidence.
- *Expectation assessment*. Practitioners explore the client's expectations of self and others within situations to help clients identify how expectations cannot be achieved realistically (Kearns, Forbes, & Gardiner, 2007; Voth & Sirois, 2009).

- *Developing alternative thoughts*. The final step begins as clients begin to understand the impact and irrationality of their beliefs. At this time, it is important to provide new frameworks for interpreting events so the client can replace the irrational thinking. New interpretations, if properly matched to events and practiced, can reduce the emergence of problems (Tafrate & Kassinove, 1998). Specific practitioner actions include:
  - *Option identification*. After clients understand that their thinking habits do not accurately fit situations, practitioners engage them to identify new options for understanding situations. This activity is highly exploratory so clients can present their attribution options without feeling pressured by the practitioner (For example, "So if your son is not attempting to drive you crazy, what might he be trying to achieve?").
  - *Reframing*. Frequently practitioners share alternative interpretations for events. When reframing, we help clients develop new interpretations that fit the details of the situation. Because the new interpretations are less locked into problem emotions and behaviors, clients can increase their mastery over their situations (For example, "It seems like your son will do almost anything to get your attention. You are a very important person in his life."). Reframing often is difficult because beginning practitioners attempt to impose their meaning on the client situation. It is important to ensure that the new interpretation fits the details of the client situation so that it will be accepted.
  - *Shifting the locus of control*. Some practitioners shift the locus of control to change client thinking. This shift typically moves responsibility for the problem outside of clients (White, 1984). The shift moves the sense of ownership of the symptom that allows clients to experience the symptomatic behavior as some external enemy rather than a loathed part of their personality (For example, "When you make a mistake and those thoughts start going through your mind, identify the people who first said those things to you. Can you picture them in your mind?"). When clients successfully externalize elements of the problem, it makes it easier for us to collaborate with them to overcome the external problem. Similarly, when clients habitually blame others through excessive externalization, we often want to help them shift the locus of control to internal so that they can identify elements over which they do have control.

Activities That Influence Affective Processing

A third type of activity focuses on helping clients identify and express feelings. Many behaviors and irrational thoughts emerge when difficult feelings are evoked (Greenberg, 2004; Heard, 1996; Whelton, 2004). The cognitive-focused activities discussed earlier, although effective in changing thinking, have less impact on emotions and behavior (Hobbs & Yan, 2008; Kearns et al., 2007; Szentagotai, David, Lupu, & Cosman, 2008). This is particularly true when powerful emotions underlie the problem situation. Emotionally expressive activities build on the idea that exploring the details of difficult events diminishes the emotional impact of the event, making painful feelings more manageable (Frueh et al., 2009).

Understanding Emotional Processing

Before describing feeling-focused activities, it is useful first to understand the nature of emotional experience. Emotional experience is initially processed in the nondominant hemisphere of the brain as the brain triggers bodily changes in response to a situation (Russell, 2003). The bodily changes promote visceral experiences, as the brain sends signals to parts of the body in preparation to react (Greenberg, 2004; Nabi, 2002). The visceral sensations are then acknowledged by the dominant hemisphere which interprets the event and formulates a plan to respond (Goldsmith & Davidson, 2004; Hoeksma, Oosterlaan, & Schipper, 2004).

Many researchers and theoreticians refer to the visceral level of feelings as primary feelings (Russell, 2003; Zurbriggen & Sturman, 2002). When a person notices the visceral changes, the brain immediately attempts to interpret and understand the situation (Olson, Plotzker, & Ezzyat, 2007). This activity includes scanning the situation to prepare a response (Banks, Kamryn, Angstadt, Pradeep, & Phan, 2007; L. A. Miller, Taber, Gabbard, & Hurley, 2008; Sanchez-Navarro, Martinez-Selva, & Román, 2006). If a threat is perceived, the brain alters the emotional experience to prepare a behavioral response (Umberson, Williams & Anderson, 2002; Winstok, Eisikovits, & Gelles, 2002).

The altered experience often is referred to as secondary emotion. Secondary emotions have a sense of controllability and focus that does not exist with primary feelings. With a secondary emotion, we have identified a source of our emotional response, which allows us to attribute responsibility. For example, when you are driving down the road and late for class, you may drive fast trying to save time. However, this is not possible if there are slow drivers on the road ahead of you. In response, you may feel powerless or helpless. However, these feelings provide no sense of control so you may shift the feeling into anger. As you become angry, you can identify slow drivers and hold them responsible for your lateness. Table 9.1 contains a list of primary feelings and related secondary emotions. In the table, the primary feelings are polarized containing a positive and negative pole. The secondary emotions respond to these polarities.

Table 9.1 Selected Primary Feelings and Associated Secondary Emotions

Primary Feeling Poles	Possible Secondary Emotions
Powerless ↔ Masterful	− Anger, frustration, depression, impotence + Competence, superiority, boastful
Discounted ↔ Valued	− Victimization, anger, humiliation, dismissed, invalidated + Elevated, important, favored, special, acknowledged
Helpless ↔ In Control	− Anger, frustration, fear, sadness, victimized, needy + Independent, unencumbered, fearless
Despair ↔ Elation/Joy	− Depression, insignificance, desperate, unlucky, unfair + Lucky, blessed, on a roll, omnipotent, worthy
Inadequate ↔ Competent	− Anger, impotent, incapable, jealous, criticized + Boastful, expert, impervious
Shame ↔ Pride	− Embarrassment, humiliation, anger, persecuted, guilty + Superior, self-righteousness, right
Anxious ↔ Comfortable	− Fear, depression, threatened, judged, persecuted, at risk + Impervious, omnipotent, familiar, supported
Discounted ↔ Validated	− Objectified, anger, betrayed, humiliated, victimized + Present, important, noticed, right, valued
Insular ↔ Intimate	− Lonely, victimized, unlucky, vulnerable + Lucky, horny, dependent, close, attractive
Alienation ↔ Connection	− Alone, insignificant, disconnected, rejected + Engaged, loyal, connected, important, wanted
Hopeless ↔ Hopeful	− Victimized, disadvantaged, futility, anger, frustration + Optimistic, lucky, blessed, happy
Attraction ↔ Repulsion	− horny, friendly, connected, interested, fascinated + disgusted, grossed out, disinterested, bored

Given the interpretive processes, there is an ongoing interplay between feelings and thinking when people respond to situations. This cognitive-emotional interplay can lead to problems. Figure 9.1 outlines the interplay between cognitive and emotional processes in the development of problem behavior. When reviewing the figure, notice first that emotions tend to emerge in response to a situation. We learned in Chapter 8 how feelings are processed on the nondominant side of the brain. However, the dominant side of the brain is used to understand the feeling. Notice in the figure how on the dominant side cognitive processes progressively amplify the emotional experience. As the power in the emotional experience focuses and expands, logical abilities diminish, making it harder to manage the feeling and subsequent behavior.

In our emotional interpretation of a situation, our brain immediately retrieves memories of similar situations. If the memories are emotionally laden, they can amplify the feeling (Daselaar et al., 2008; Phelps, 2004). As amplification occurs, cognitive distortions can emerge in our interpretation and processing of the feeling (Dougal, Phelps, & Davachi, 2007; Kensinger, 2007; Phelps & Sharot, 2008). These distortions are most prevalent with negative emotional memories (Kensinger, 2007). As these memories emerge, a sense of emotional threat permeates our experience of the situation.

If the level of amplification does not interfere with logical processes, we can respond effectively to the situation (DeWall, Baumeister, & Masicampo, 2008; Lewis & Todd, 2007). However, if our attributions are irrational, they can amplify the situation and erode our capacity to manage it cognitively (Dougal et al., 2007; Kensinger, 2007; Phelps & Sharot, 2008). In Figure 9.1, notice how negative emotional amplification can lead to rationalizations and distortions in how the situation is understood.

Some secondary emotions activate deeper regions of the brain to prepare a behavioral response (Nabi, 2002; Ramirez, Santisteban, Fujihara, & Van Goozen, 2002). In these cases, the brain's focus shifts from the prefrontal logical functions to the limbic functions that prepare for action. This activation increases an external focus as we start to scan the environment for the source of the emotional response. Given that the scanning occurs simultaneous with retrieving association memories irrational thoughts can emerge at this point amplifying the emotional experience (Hogan & Linden, 2004; Martin & Dahlen, 2004). As the experience of the emotion amplifies and the body prepares for action, it is difficult to distract attention from the emotion (Hogan & Linden, 2004). As rumination emerges, the likelihood of transgressions and self-defeating behaviors rises (Bandura, Caprara, Barbaranelli, Pastorelli, & Regalia, 2001; Tice, Bratslavsky, & Baumeister, 2001).

Emotional Processing Activities

Given the progression outlined in Figure 9.1, we can see that practitioners must be able to work with both thinking and feeling. The cognitive activities described earlier in the chapter often are combined with emotion-focused activities so that both thinking and feeling can be resolved together. Doing this requires very clear focus as we shift back and forth from attending to emotions, then uncovering and challenging the thinking that modulates the emotional experience. There are four common types of emotion work: emotional identification, emotional expression, emotional exposure, and symbolic expression.

1. *Emotional identification.* Often clients are unaware of their affective responses. This is most prevalent with clients who shift quickly to secondary emotions. During emotional identification activities, practitioners help clients identify emotions by tracing back thoughts and exploring experiences. They then facilitate expressiveness. Four steps are involved in this type of activity:
   a. *Tracking thoughts.* When people do not understand their feelings often we must help them explore their thinking in a situation and then identify the affective elements underlying the thoughts.
   b. *Laddering back to primary feelings.* When clients are focused on secondary feelings and beginning to amplify emotions, practitioners direct their focus on thinking so they can begin to track the cognitive sequence back to the primary feeling and situation.

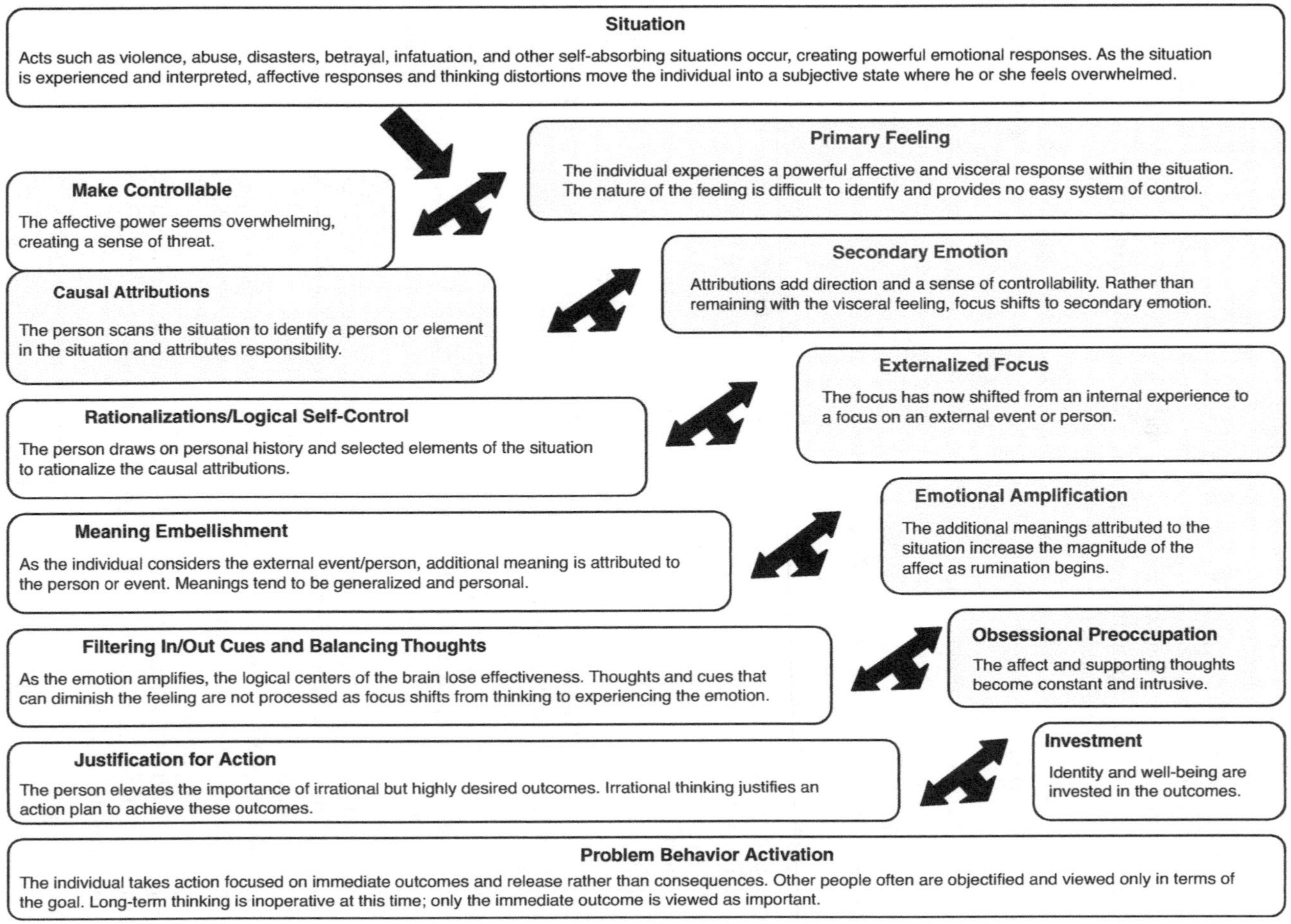

Figure 9.1

Situation

Acts such as violence, abuse, disasters, betrayal, infatuation, and other self-absorbing situations occur, creating powerful emotional responses. As the situation is experienced and interpreted, affective responses and thinking distortions move the individual into a subjective state where he or she feels overwhelmed.

Primary Feeling

The individual experiences a powerful affective and visceral response within the situation. The nature of the feeling is difficult to identify and provides no easy system of control.

Secondary Emotion

Attributions add direction and a sense of controllability. Rather than remaining with the visceral feeling, focus shifts to secondary emotion.

Externalized Focus

The focus has now shifted from an internal experience to a focus on an external event or person.

Emotional Amplification

The additional meanings attributed to the situation increase the magnitude of the affect as rumination begins.

Obsessional Preoccupation

The affect and supporting thoughts become constant and intrusive.

Investment

Identity and well-being are invested in the outcomes.

Make Controllable

The affective power seems overwhelming, creating a sense of threat.

Causal Attributions

The person scans the situation to identify a person or element in the situation and attributes responsibility.

Rationalizations/Logical Self-Control

The person draws on personal history and selected elements of the situation to rationalize the causal attributions.

Meaning Embellishment

As the individual considers the external event/person, additional meaning is attributed to the person or event. Meanings tend to be generalized and personal.

Filtering In/Out Cues and Balancing Thoughts

As the emotion amplifies, the logical centers of the brain lose effectiveness. Thoughts and cues that can diminish the feeling are not processed as focus shifts from thinking to experiencing the emotion.

Justification for Action

The person elevates the importance of irrational but highly desired outcomes. Irrational thinking justifies an action plan to achieve these outcomes.

Problem Behavior Activation

The individual takes action focused on immediate outcomes and release rather than consequences. Other people often are objectified and viewed only in terms of the goal. Long-term thinking is inoperative at this time; only the immediate outcome is viewed as important.

c. *Labeling feelings*. After thinking has been explored, the practitioner directs the client to label and acknowledge feelings.

d. *Contextualizing feelings*. Practitioners direct the client's focus back to the situation that evoked the emotional response. The practitioner encourages the client to disentangle memories that do not apply and to reappraise the situation using logical, rather than irrational, beliefs and interpretations.

2. *Emotional expression activities*. Findings suggest that activities that promote expressiveness and interconnectedness among the members of larger systems encourage feelings of being supported and positive experiences (Berg, Sandahl, & Clinton, 2008; S. Kim et al., 2006). Such activities also can be conducted with individuals (Fosha, 2004). According to Pingree (2007), expressive activities achieve four levels of impact:

a. Clients must mentally prepare to share the affective material. The practitioner supports this process by ensuring a safe environment for sharing emotional material. The practitioner then directs this process by helping clients focus on the situation.

b. Clients must access memories associated with the feeling. The practitioner directs this process by guiding clients to recall the details in the situation.

c. Clients must condense and conceptualize the emotional experience so they can formulate it into words. The practitioner explores client reactions and thinking in the situation to help clients put their feelings into words.

d. Clients experience emotional release as they share feelings and receive validation. The practitioner uses empathic tuning in and reflective responding to help clients feel understood. The practitioner also adopts a strengths perspective to help clients identify their competencies in the situation.

3. *Exposure activities*. Often activities intentionally focus a client's attention on emotionally powerful experiences and situations. This type of activity is a component in many evidence-based interventions such as Imaginal Desensitization and Eye Movement Desensitization and Reprogramming (EMDR). When a practitioner directs clients to describe the details of emotionally upsetting events, it helps clients stop avoiding thoughts and situations (Newman & Stiles, 2006). During such activities, we use our questioning and reflecting skills to help clients explore past situations. Throughout our guiding of the exploration, we must be very directive but supportive. Frequently, exposure activities are repeated and detailed, which evokes very difficult feelings. Our directedness promotes a thorough exploration of details while our supportiveness reminds clients that they are not alone. The next six components help maintain a supportive balance:

a. *Ensuring safety*. Initially practitioners must ensure that the relationship is safe and comfortable for clients to share very vulnerable material.

b. *Establishing a check-in and cuing system*. Practitioners develop a cuing system so they can check in with clients about their emotional experience during the activity.

c. *Focusing on a situation*. To begin the exploration, practitioners help clients explore the background, timing, and setting of emotionally arousing events to situate clients and begin memory retrieval.

d. *Deepening the exploration*. As the exploration proceeds, practitioners explore the details of the event, including observations (sight, smell, tactile experience, sounds, etc.), actions, thoughts, and feelings in an attempt to exhaust the details of client experiences.

e. *Monitoring arousal*. Practitioners use the cuing and check-in system to continually monitor client emotional responses as the situation is explored. If a client's emotional arousal is too high, we attend to the emotions and then assess whether continued exploration would be counterproductive. If arousal is too high, we end the exploration with a shared understanding that we may need to return to the memories in the future.

f. *Repetition*. Practitioners repeat the exploration several times, monitoring client reactions each time. Repetition is continued until the emotional power in the memories is diminished.

4. *Symbolic expressive activities*. Symbolic activities, such as play therapy and music therapy, have long been used by nondirective practitioners. Increasingly, directive

practitioners have adopted some expressive interventions to access emotional material in the nondominant hemisphere of the brain. The next three directive activities have emerged in directive practice.

a. *Art-based activities*. Expressive activities, such as drawings, can be implemented to facilitate exploring emotionally laden events. It is assumed that exploring the events through symbolic means allows the nondominant hemisphere to process the emotions and decrease the affective amplification similar to exposure activities (Adúriz, Bluthgen, & Knopfler, 2009). In such activities, the practitioner provides drawing or other art materials and asks the client to draw specific scenes. These activities are often sequenced, with each successive activity building on the previous expression.

b. *Guided imagery*. Many practitioners are demonstrating success with combined relaxation and guided imagery with clients (Lahmann et al., 2009; Weigensberg et al., 2009). When vivid images are a component of a client's emotional reactions, some practitioners have had success rescripting images. This activity involves having clients describe images in great detail. Then, over a series of sessions, practitioners guide clients through the situation, each time modifying the images (Brewin et al., 2009).

c. *Communicative activities*. Many practitioners have clients express feelings and unresolved conflicts to an imagined protagonist. Variations of these activities include journaling, empty chair work, and letter writing. Clients are coached in confrontation and emotional expression; sometimes they switch positions to process the situation from multiple perspectives. These types of activity have demonstrated positive outcomes with people who have difficult emotional memories (Greenberg, Warwar, & Malcolm, 2008).

Activities That Influence Skills and Behavior

A very common type of directive activity focuses on client behaviors and interactions. While helping clients manage their thinking and affect, it is important to provide them with new skills for responding (Venning, Kettler, Eliott, & Wilson, 2009). As clients engage in behavior-focused activities, participants receive feedback on their performance so they can adjust and refine their actions (Bailey & Butcher, 1983; A. Johnson, 2003; Timler, Olswang, & Coggins, 2005). When we provide feedback to clients, it must be clear and specific to each client's skill performance so subsequent skill attempts can be altered. Consequently, we must observe clients during activities and then provide feedback.

Some forms of feedback promote repeating specific actions while others are designed to decrease client motivation to reenact skills (Gunner, 2006). As we provide feedback to clients, we often insert the perspective of others so clients can understand the impact of their actions (Seedall & Butler, 2006). The provision of alternative perspectives during activities can challenge misconceptions and irrational beliefs while also focusing on skill performance. Two common skill-related activities are enactments and focused skill building.

Skill-Building Activities

Skill-building activities provide clients an opportunity to practice skills that can be applied to life situations (Hakman, Chaffin, Funderburk, & Silovsky, 2009). Skill-building activities work on specific skill sets that can be modeled, explained, and practiced (Brooks, 2007; Lane, Mathews, Sallas, Prattini, & Sun, 2008). When such activities occur in EBP, early activities often provide a foundation for later, more complex skill applications (Greene, 2003; Mueser & Bellack, 2007; Shebilske, Goettl, Corrington, & Day, 1999). Two common forms of skill-building activity are enactments and constructed skill-building activities.

1. *Enactments*. Practitioners often ask clients to enact situations. Enactments originated in psychoanalytic interventions when clients acted out unresolved relationship issues in the helping relationship (Bennett, Parry, & Ryle, 2006). Enactments are a central element in many models of activity-based intervention (Diamond et al., 2007; Haen, 2005; Haen & Brannon, 2002). Often enactment activities occur in response to current

client situations as the practitioner pick ups on client concerns and engages the client in activity. Common types of enactment activity include:

   a. *Naturalistic enactments*. When working with families, groups, or other larger systems (e.g., organizations), it is possible to allow the members to interact naturally. The practitioner then scans the interaction, observing how the system members respond to each other. If a conflict begins, practitioners can direct members to resolve the conflict and then observe and intervene with the members from a coaching type of role. These interventions can help shape client responses to a real conflict or event. Due to the realism of enactments, they are very powerful activities (Seedall & Butler, 2006).

   b. *Role-Plays*. During sessions, clients often identify situations that threaten their capacity to respond. Practitioners often introduce role-playing as an activity that can help clients expand their ability to respond effectively. The suggestion to begin a role-play is an immediate response to a client statement; the practitioner must propose the activity and convince the client that it will be worthwhile. In individual interventions, the practitioner adopts one role and encourages the client to take his or her traditional role. In larger systems, the practitioner often engages others to fulfill the supporting roles. Sometimes roles can be reversed, depending on the desired outcomes of the role-play.

2. *Constructed skill-building*. Often practitioners use activities designed to help clients develop and practice specific skills. Many of these activities involve a blend of teaching, practice, and feedback over time. Constructed activities contain less realism than enactments because they are standardized based on the practitioner's knowledge or intervention plan rather than in response to a specific client situation. Often we must work hard to adapt constructed activities to the client situation in order to improve the realism. Two very common types of constructed skill-building activities include:

   a. *Problem solving*. Several activities focus on the client circumstances and attempt to organize client efforts so they can master their situations. Many activities focus on the stages of problem solving: assessment, exploring options, selecting options, evaluating outcomes. Other activities present clients with a challenge and encourage them to plan solutions and actions that can resolve the situation (Lucey & Staton, 2003). In both types of activity, the practitioner presents a constructed challenge that parallels the client situation, then engages clients in an activity to apply skills to the challenge.

   b. *Homework*. Frequently, intervention programs ask clients to perform activities in their life situations to aid in generalizing skills. These activities are often referred to as homework (Hay & Kinnier, 1998; Scheel, Hanson, & Razzhavaikina, 2004). Homework activities emerge from the work of the session as practitioners ask clients to engage in such activities as attempting the skill, reading a book, playing a game, or monitoring elements of the situation (Hobbs & Yan, 2008; Lupu & Iftene, 2009).

Activities That Alter Problem Contexts

The final type of activity focuses on specific contextual elements in the client situation. Contextual intervention activities become necessary when there is a mismatch between the client's capacity to respond and the environmental elements in the situation. If the demands of the situation exceed the client's capacity, we intervene with the people and agents within the client environment. There are four common reasons for extending intervention into the environmental context:

1. *Capacity to respond*. When clients have a condition (e.g., illness, disability, age) that limits their capacity to respond, often we must work simultaneously with the client and the context.

2. *Acute crisis*. When events occur that suddenly increase demands on the client (e.g., loss of a loved one, psychotic break, traumatic event), his or her internal resources may become overwhelmed temporarily, requiring us to work with the environment to increase supports.

3. *Low motivation.* There are times when clients do not want to change their situation but others are insisting on compliance. This is common with court-ordered clients and those who derive pleasure or addictive sensations from the problem. In such situations, often it is necessary to work with external agents concurrent with the client.

4. *Environmental challenges.* When a client's living conditions or environment contributes to the problem (e.g., poverty, restricted options, oppression, rights violations), at least part of the intervention plan adopts an external focus to help resolve environmental impingements.

Typically, environmental interventions seek to increase support in the client in their natural environment. Research indicates that many client populations lack adequate supports (Grizenko & Pawliuk, 1994; Lacharite, Ethier, & Couture, 1995; Spoth, Redmond, Hockaday, & Chung, 1996). Given this, we must be able to help clients identify and activate supports that fit for their situation. When we determine that clients require some additional resources, we begin by helping them assess available options, ranging from informal to formal supports. Four types of support tend to be available for clients. As we explore client environments and situations, we seek to identify possible sources of support across these categories.

1. *Kinship supports.* Often family members or extended kin are a good source of additional support.

2. *Friendship supports.* Depending on the situation, friends and neighbors sometimes can provide critical support.

3. *Informal supports.* Clubs, sports teams, and informal groups such as Al-Anon can provide important supplements to intervention.

4. *Formal supports.* At times other professional services or programs may be necessary to help clients achieve their goals.

Activating Supports

As we work with clients to access supplemental resources, our role changes, depending on how clients relate to the identified support options. If there is tension in the relationship, we must provide motivation and mediate the relationship between the client and the support people (Walitzer, Dermen, & Barrick, 2009). Even when engaging formal supports, often we must reach out to help clients and the new support person achieve a mutual understanding of roles and activities. The following activities are commonly used to help clients engage additional supports.

- *Support system activation.* Sometimes we must engage support from people who are part of the client's situation, such as family members, friends, teachers, probation officers, coaches, and other professionals. This is common in evidence-based interventions such as multisystemic treatment (Henggeler & Borduin, 1990) and wraparound interventions (Burchard, Burchard, Sewell, & VanDenBerg, 1993). When we engage people who currently are involved with the client situation, we seek to change their roles and activate them in specific support functions.

- *Referrals.* Often situations arise where we must help clients access additional formal services. When we do so, we help them identify and connect with services. As clients approach the new service, we help them complete the referral. Sometimes doing this requires us to contact the other professional, accompany clients to initial meetings, and follow up. Such activities help you, the new provider, and the client to develop a mutual understanding of roles and functions. As we add formal services, our job assumes case management functions because we must now support the client while promoting collaboration among the service providers.

Toward Developing Directive Skills

Our directive skills can be very simple or complex. Simple directives pick up on client communications and direct them to engage in some activity in response to the material on the table. These directives are often referred to as prompts or simple directives. Complex directives include activities such as homework or enactments where there is prolonged activity. Our use of directives seeks to achieve one of four purposes: clarification, exploration, positioning, and change promotion.

1. *Clarification*. During client interactions, comments often are made that are vague, disguised, or unacknowledged. When we are confused or feel that the communication is incomplete, we often use prompts or simple directives to make the comment clear for all involved. Often clarification directives include very brief responses, such as "Tell me more about that" or "Tell her exactly what you mean when you say that."

2. *Exploration*. Exploratory directives can range from quick responses to very involved activities. Quick responses often attempt to prompt clients to expand on a specific aspect of their story (For example, "And so you did . . . "). Complex exploratory directives include activities such as role-plays or tasks designed to observe interaction.

3. *Positioning*. As with other interactive skills, positioning ensures that specific information is placed on the table so we can build on it for change-focused intervention. Positioning can involve brief responses when the material is already on the table. In other situations, practitioners must direct activities that can help the important information emerge. When we assign homework and other tasks, often we are attempting to highlight new information that can be used to promote change.

4. *Change promotion*. As clients learn new skills and knowledge, we often want them to apply their knowledge. Consequently, we use directives to change client actions within their life context. Practitioners often must occupy a coaching role to help clients apply and practice intervention elements.

Although providing directives is presented as a distinct skill, it builds on all of the skills covered in earlier chapters. Thinking, tuning in, engagement, and all of the interpersonal skills are necessary to set the stage and support client activity. When we provide directives, the goal is to prompt clients to act or think differently from the status quo. By providing directives, we skillfully dovetail our knowledge of options with clients' situations by instructing them to take some action. As they follow our directive, they have new experiences that can help them master their situations. The core power of this skill lies in client-level outcomes as they follow directives.

The success of a directive lies in the client's willingness to follow our instructions. As we ask clients to pursue new directions, actions, or patterns of thinking, we trust that they will comply. This is the most complex element in giving directives, as compliance is not guaranteed. Research indicates that many clients respond with initial resistance when practitioners provide a directive (Watson & McMullen, 2005). Consequently, the skill of providing a directive is complex; we must develop presentation styles that enhance compliance.

Working From a Socialization and Cultural Perspective

Socialization challenges are frequent when engaging in directive practice because our authority is elevated. Unlike questioning, where most people feel an obligation to respond, a directive involves us, powerful professionals, instructing a client to do something. Given that we are operating with professional power, client reactions to our directives will be influenced by their history with authority figures. Past experiences with parents, teachers, and other authorities can influence how people respond to our instructions. In addition, our experiences with power and authority influence how we present our directives. Thus the socialization challenges to this skill emerge from both practitioner and client levels.

We all can remember parents, teachers, coaches, and employers telling us what to do. Sometimes these were supportive instructions, and at other times these experiences undermined our sense of competence. Regardless, we learned how to give advice and take over other people's problems. As we provide direction and instructions to others, these models of helping emerge as our default settings. Although we changed our simplistic thinking in Chapter 3, when we start to become directive, we still may fall prey to a tendency to follow these old models.

Table 9.2   **Differences between Stimulation and Taking-Over Approaches to Directives**

Stimulation	Taking Over
Explores the client situation to tailor experience	Applies the exercise with little or no adaptation
Negotiates engagement into an activity	Dictates participation in an activity
Creates experiences then explores incorporation	Creates experiences then expects compliance
Explores how to apply the experience in the client's life situation	Tries to convince clients to use the new skill
Explores concerns and solicits client solutions	Attempts to diminish or dismiss client concerns
Encourages clients to make their own decisions about incorporation	Continually pressures clients to adopt the new skill or position

It is important to understand that providing directives does not entail simply telling clients what to do and what to think. We direct clients to engage in activities that can help them master situations; however, these activities must stimulate clients to change rather than insist on change. There are subtle differences between stimulating a client through a directive experience and taking over the client situation. Notice in Table 9.2 how stimulation responds to the relationships and life context of the client while taking over tends to provide a suggestion and insist on client compliance.

Clients also have experiences with people advising and telling them what to do. Similar to our own experiences, some client experiences are positive and some are negative. Unlike us, clients are on the receiving end of the directives in the helping relationship. Consequently, their reactions to our directives may approximate their responses to other authority figures. If clients had difficult experiences with authority figures, they may react with resistance. Similarly, clients who always sought to please authority figures may be very quick to comply.

Given that clients may respond based on their past experience, it is important for us to understand that their initial reactions may be habitual rather than an element of the working relationship. Consequently, we may need to explore their experience of engaging in directive activities to orient their experience to the working alliance and intervention goals. Notice in Table 9.2 how the stimulation column provides this level of exploration that will allow clients to understand the directive in the context of their current life situation.

Cultural and Social Considerations
As we seek to balance directive and nondirective approaches, it is important to consider our clients' cultural and social context. Many populations receive more directives than they give. Clients from such social positions may react based on their social experiences. Again, it will be important to ensure that their response is genuine rather than habitual before proceeding with our instructions. It is always important to consider the level of social power afforded to clients when planning intervention.

When providing direction, often we must adjust activities and programming to account for cultural differences (Morsette et al., 2009). Some cultures tend to prefer a structured and directive approach rather than emotionally expressive forms of intervention (Türküm, 2007; Wong, Chau, Kwok, & Kwan, 2007). Consequently, clients from such cultures may interpret nondirective methods negatively, and they may withhold full engagement (Raz & Atar, 2003). It may be important to work closely with people from minority cultural groups to help adapt methods.

Another cultural consideration emerges with evidence-based intervention. Research studies have inclusion and exclusion criteria for the study. For example, studies on parent training often insist that two parents attend the groups. When applying this model in poor, predominantly minority communities, the initial criterion may exclude the most vulnerable clients. For this reason, the agency may have to either abandon or adapt the program. When choosing an EBP, the cultural and social requirements of the practice are important considerations.

Professional Facilitation Skills

There are so many intervention activities to alter client processing and actions that it can appear overwhelming. However, we initiate activities in response to client needs, which simplifies our work. We begin with the client situation and goals and select activities that fit. Doing this may involve selecting a specific evidence-based intervention program, or it may require us to implement spontaneous activities in response to the client situation. As we proceed we use several intervention skills as we implement activities with clients. In particular, we use activity facilitation, prompting, and coaching.

Facilitating Activities

When facilitating activities, engagement is critical because the effectiveness of most activities is contingent on client compliance with our instructions. Consequently we must become very skilled at helping clients understand and engage in activities. This venture can be somewhat awkward because introducing an activity involves interrupting the flow of a conversation and changing the focus of discussion to the activity or program.

A critical element of engagement is to assess the fit for clients. If the activity does not fit clients' perception of their situation, the prognosis for success diminishes. An assessment of fit considers the next five factors.

1. *Effectiveness.* As we consider activities or interventions, we attempt to match the client's needs with the most effective intervention possible (Thyer, 2007). Doing this requires us to know the available options and the evidence in support of each one.

2. *Motivation.* The severity of the problem and client motivation to resolve their situations will influence their eagerness to engage in a proposed activity (Scheel et al., 2004). If clients are not motivated, compliance can suffer.

3. *Capacity.* Clients must have the capacity to fulfill the activity requirements (Butler & Gardner, 2003). This includes the requisite skills, cognitive ability, and self-control. Capacity also considers client personality, values, and other life demands (Scheel, Seaman, Roach, Mulling, & Mahoney, 1999; Tokar, Hardin, Adams, & Brandel, 1997).

4. *Fit.* The activity must have some association with clients' perceptions of their problem. If the activity is only peripherally associated with what clients consider important, compliance may suffer (Butler & Gardner, 2003; Scheel et al., 2004).

5. *Alliance.* The activity needs to occur within the context of the working alliance. This requires a clear connection to the agreed goals of service (Hay & Kinnier, 1998; Scheel et al., 1999). If there is no connection, compliance may be compromised because it does not make sense according to the goals.

Setting Up Activities

Shifting the interactive focus from a back-and-forth exchange with clients to implementing the activity is awkward because you must break the interactive flow. Often doing this requires picking up on some element of the interaction as a pivot point during the transition. The pivot is used to link the current discussion to the activity. Ultimately, we must help clients discover a rationale for the activity so they are more likely to engage. After linking the activity to client material, we must begin by outlining the purpose and requirements of the activity (McKelley & Rochlen, 2007). Three steps are common when introducing an activity.

1. *Develop a link.* It is helpful to integrate the activity with the focus of ongoing interaction. Doing this requires careful timing based on the nature of the material on the table. Avoid moments when the material has a heavy emotional component because initiating the activity requires cognitive engagement. When the material on the table appears conducive, develop a potential link. Possible linkages include:

○ *Relating to material on the table*. For example, if the client is talking about relationship problems and you want to implement an activity about irrational thinking, pick up on how the client interprets the actions of the other. Then move toward introducing the activity.

○ *Relating to past material from the table*. If there was recent material on the table that can help establish a rationale for the activity, refer back to that specific material and mention that it stimulated some ideas that might help. When interest shifts, introduce the activity.

○ *Relating to goals and direction*. If the material on the table is not conducive for developing a link, refer to the appropriate intervention goal and inform the client that you have an idea that can help. When interest shifts, introduce the activity.

2. *Initiate the activity*. As we propose engaging in an activity, we need to outline general information about the roles and expected actions (Davis & Butler, 2004; Somov, 2008). Clients need to understand what will be asked of them if they elect to participate in the activity. The discussion does not need to be extensive at the initiation stage, but clients have a right to make an informed decision. Consider outlining these types of information:

○ *Roles*. Often it is helpful to outline the roles that will be assumed by the practitioner and the client(s) during the activity (Davis & Butler, 2004; Somov, 2008).

○ *Nature of the activity*. Clients require some information about what they will be asked to do, the level of risk/vulnerability, and the investment required.

3. *Solicit agreement*. Clients need to determine whether they will engage in the activity (Tokar, Hardin, Adams, & Brandel, 1996). Such a choice should be negotiated as the intervention develops. As the work of the session is concluding, the worker might say, "You know, we could strengthen this skill if you did some practice at home. Are you interested in a couple of practice exercises?" Without being offered a choice, clients are not fully involved in the decision to engage in the task and may feel that they must answer to, or perform for, the therapist.

Delivering Instructions

After clients agree to participate in the proposed activity, it is important to provide very clear guidelines about how to perform the activity. Although clients do require clear direction, we should avoid being too explicit or providing so much information that is interferes with client ability to perform and generalize their skills (Takimoto, 2007). There are three main practitioner actions when delivering instructions: setting the stage, providing instruction, and activating the client.

1. *Setting the stage*. Some activities require advance work to make them possible. Often this involves practitioner work, such as arranging chairs or providing materials. At other times clients must take action, such as gathering information to bring it into the next session. There are two important elements to setting the stage: providing focus and structuring the activity.

   a. *Focusing the activity*. Identify the focus of action, specifics about skills or behaviors, and how clients are expected to respond (Davis & Butler, 2004; Somov, 2008). For example: "In this role-play I want you to play the part of the teacher, and I will be you. We are discussing John's report card. When you play the teacher, make sure you are realistic and say things the way she would. Can you do that?"

   b. *Structuring the activity*. We often need to position people, furniture, provide materials, or lay out the rules prior to beginning an activity (Davis & Butler, 2004; Somov, 2008). For example: "Okay. You sit there facing me and I will sit right here. We will pretend that we are in the classroom."

2. *Providing the instruction*. After the arrangements for the activity are complete, it is important to provide very clear instructions so clients know what to do. Instructions can be verbal or written, depending on the complexity of the activity. Consider these four systems of providing instructions:

a. *Three-step instructions.* If you are providing verbal instructions, it is easiest to lay out instructions in three steps. For example: "First I want you to identify when you are angry. When you notice your anger, pay attention to what is happening in your mind. Later, write down the thoughts that were going through your mind."

b. *Step-wise instructions.* If the instructions are more complex, you may want to break them down into specific steps or phases. For example, in a productive argument activity, the practitioner might explain there are four phases to a good argument: identifying a disagreement, clarifying the disagreement, exploration, and resolution. The instructor can then include instructions for each phase in a serial fashion.

c. *Complex instructions.* When several steps are involved in the instructions, it can be difficult for clients to remember and respond. When engaging clients in complex activities, it is very important to break the instructions into clear and logical steps. The steps should be clear and presented without a lot of explanation that can distract clients (Takimoto, 2007). Having written instructions can be helpful if the activity requires clients to engage in autonomous activity (e.g., homework).

d. *Serial instruction.* Serial directives lay out one part of the instructions at a time. We begin with asking the client to engage in some action. When they begin the action, we add a new instruction. As the new instruction is followed, a new caveat is included. These additions continue until the full range of activities is complete. When using serial instructions, it is important to structure input so each step is logically connected to the next (Takimoto, 2007).

3. *Activating the clients.* The final step in providing instructions is to activate the clients to perform. Doing this involves disengaging from the highly active role of providing instructions so we can begin to monitor client performance. These strategies are helpful when activating the clients.

a. *Direct the client's first action.* Sometimes we need to instruct one client to start. For example: "Tell Tom what you felt as he shared his story" or "Think about what you just said and tell me how your past is haunting you decision." Notice how the practitioner statement triggers client actions, allowing the practitioner to adopt a monitoring role.

b. *Negotiate an activation plan.* With homework, referrals, and support activation, the practitioner needs to work with clients to develop an activation plan. Doing this involves discussing the situation and negotiating roles for clients, practitioner, and possibly others. After negotiation, it is important to secure a commitment to act.

Exercise 9.1: Placing Mother

You are a practitioner working in a home for the elderly. You are meeting with a 57-year-old woman who is at a point where she can no longer provide in-home care for her aging mother. She is aware that she must place her mother to ensure adequate medical care but feels very guilty and does not want to engage her mother in a discussion about moving to the home. You want to help her prepare for this discussion. She has just said, "I don't even know how to bring it up. She has been so good to me. She paid for my education and was there for me when my marriage ended. How can I just abandon her?" As you read this statement, identify an element that can begin focused work (thinking, feeling, relationship, or action themes). Identify the element that can promote work in the next space.

1. You elect to pick up on the thinking element that placing the mother is abandonment. Formulate a response that can begin to explore these irrational beliefs. Remember, you must negotiate the change from exploration to focused activity. Start by picking up on the element, then propose the activity.

2. At the end of the meeting you want to provide a homework assignment to help the woman identify the irrational beliefs that keep her feeling guilty and prevent her from engaging in the discussion with the mother. Propose a homework assignment to the woman by linking to her thinking. Ensure the homework assignment will develop a list of irrational beliefs.

3. During the next meeting, this woman provided you with a list of beliefs that convince her that placing her mother would be abandonment. The beliefs tended to focus on the care the mother provided when she was a child and how she owed the mother equal care as she ages. You know that the mother requires a lot of personal care (she is incontinent so requires frequent bathing and bed changes) and medical care (she requires shots and monitoring). Engage the woman in an activity that will help her challenge these beliefs.

4. As the meeting progressed, it appeared that the woman may be ready to approach a discussion about placement. As she spoke she said, "I know it would be best but I wouldn't know what to say. She's my mother. How do you tell her that she can't stay in my home?" You want to engage the woman in a role-play. Link to her statement and respond with a proposal to engage in a role-play. Use a three-step instruction to keep the activity simple.

Prompting Skills

During directive exchanges, we often want to encourage clients to expand what they are saying or engage in some action but do not want to interrupt the flow of interaction. Prompting allows us to direct clients without stopping the activity. Prompting involves the delivery of very brief directives or instructions while the client is engaged in an activity. Prompting is a critical skill when using focused activities with clients because we constantly insert directions and feedback to influence the activity. For this reason, prompting is a foundation skill for many EBPs and focused interventions.

When prompting, we want to avoid interrupting clients' activity or interaction with extended explanations or instructions. Rather we briefly focus or direct clients, then stop talking so the activity can continue. This is similar to the comments made by coaches when an athlete is in competition. We observe clients in action, making brief comments during the activity that helps them adjust their focus or actions to better master their skills.

Prompting should be minimally intrusive. When clients are sharing their story or interacting with each other, we provide intermittent or periodic directives (For example, "Make sure he understands you"). We keep our insertions simple so clients can respond without having to interpret or reflect on our statements. There is a constant cycle between observing and prompting. We observe to ensure that clients' direction is consistent with goals, then prompt to help strengthen the potential for goal achievement.

When we prompt clients, we are always monitoring the communicated material on the table. The material on the table can involve affect, thinking, relationship themes, or behavior. When we want clients to expand or adjust the communicated material, we use prompts to stimulate them. There is no question in a prompt; rather we provide a focused instruction to expand on or alter what they are doing.

Table 9.3 Prompting in Response to a Client Statement

Client Statement I can't stand it (sigh). I wake up in the middle of the night and can't get to sleep. I just keep thinking about it. Nobody really understands (sigh). I don't even know what to tell them.

Elements	Material on the Table	Prompt Response
Affective	Helplessness/ powerlessness	"You sound powerless. Describe what that's like for you."
Thinking	I am all alone in this	"Help me understand how others have abandoned you."
Relational	People should be able to help	"You say others don't understand. Tell me what you need from people."
Behavioral	Waking up during the night	"You wake up at night. Describe a good night for me."
Nonverbal	The sighs	"You sighed twice. Tell me what they're saying."

Setting Up Prompts

Prompts are brief and focused so our response to the client statement cannot involve a long discourse. We focus immediately on the element we want expanded and provide our instruction. In Table 9.3, notice how the client statement contains multiple elements and how a prompt can be used to expand on each one. There are two types of setup when prompting. The first simply picks up material from the table. The second uses a very brief sentence to focus on a specific element in the client communication.

1. *Direct setups*. A direct setup immediately identifies an element in the clients' last statement and instructs them to expand on that element.
2. *Focused setups*. When there is a lot of material on the table, we sometimes have to focus on one element prior to the prompt delivery. A focused setup uses a brief observation or reflection to focus on that element.

Delivering Prompts

Delivering a prompt is equally simple. When we make our statement we provide very brief and specific instructions so the client understands how to respond. Typically we ask the client to expand content, change focus, or adjust their actions. When we focus on content we are often attempting to understand or explore the material. However, when we emphasize action elements we often seek to influence the client toward change. Notice in Table 9.3 how some prompts expanded content but others bring an emphasis that can promote change-focused work.

When prompting, we first identify an element that requires emphasis, instruction, or focus. We then pick up on the element and quickly direct clients to engage in some action. Five delivery methods are commonly used when prompting.

1. *Elaboration prompt*. Some prompts seek to expand our understanding of the statement. In our instruction to clients, we tell them to expand on an area that will deepen our understanding (for example, "You say you are sad. Tell me how you are different when you are angry.").
2. *Emphasis prompt*. When we want to bring an increased focus on one element, we can instruct clients to revisit that element in the statement but rework the material to strengthen it (for example, "You said you were angry, but your voice sounded sad. Tell me again with an angry voice.").
3. *Repetition prompt*. With repetition prompts, we ask clients to repeat something that we believe is important (for example, "What you did with your hand; do that again."). The repetition brings focus to that element in the interaction so it can be used.

4. *Directive prompt.* During interaction clients, sometimes withdraw or fail to pick up on some element in the situation (for example, an emotional reaction, someone's rudeness). We can highlight the situation and direct clients to use that element as they respond. For example: "You looked hurt when he said that. Tell him how that comment made you feel."

5. *Redirection prompt.* When clients drift off focus during a discussion or focused activity, often we need to redirect their attention back to the discussion or task. When we notice that the focus has drifted, we pick up on the new focus and direct them back to the task at hand (for example, "You started off explaining your anger, but now you are talking about the past. Tell him what is upsetting you today.").

Coaching Skills

Coaching is a focused activity that involves a series of prompts as the practitioner monitors a client, or group of clients, in action. Coaching allows us to detach from the activity, enabling us to observe and intervene directly in the clients' skill performance. As the term "coaching" implies, our role is to help clients develop and refine their application of concepts or skills. There are two common forms of coaching:

1. *Ongoing coaching.* When we help clients develop complex skills we observe their skill performances constantly shifting from observing to prompting them to adjust their actions. We provide prompts as necessary to help clients shape their skills (Hakman et al., 2009).

2. *Interactive coaching.* When intervening with larger systems, we often mediate interaction among the members. In such situations, we direct the exchanges between members to help shape relationship dynamics and interactive skills (For example, "Tony, you seemed upset when Kwame said that. Were you upset? . . . , *Yes.* Tell Kwame how you feel.").

Coaching interventions are easily embraced by clients because most people have a nonstigmatized view of coaches (Fabiano et al., 2009; McKelley & Rochlen, 2007). Businesses often use coaching interventions to develop effective administrators (Abbott & Rosinski, 2007; Libri & Kemp, 2006). In addition, coaching has long been used to increase positive health behavior (Newnham-Kanas, Irwin, & Morrow, 2008; Sacco, Malone, Morrison, Friedman, & Wells, 2009) and decrease difficult behaviors (Chen, Matthews, Charese, Kuo, & Linehan, 2008; Kerr, Muehlenkamp, & Larsen, 2009).

Coaching types of interventions are a central element in many EBPs. The skills can be applied in client systems of all sizes, from individual work to organizational and community work. Popular EBPs such as Critical Time Intervention (Draine & Herman, 2007), Dialectical Behavior Therapy (Chen et al., 2008), and Parent-Child Interaction Therapy (Hakman, et al., 2009) all use coaching interventions to help clients develop skills.

Coaching is one of the core skills associated with using activities. As clients engage in activities, we monitor the activity and provide input to help maximize success. We provide feedback, suggestions, and encouragement during the activity through coaching skills. Although coaching is related to prompting, some unique skill elements are associated with the ongoing interactive nature of coaching.

When we operate from a coaching role, we occupy a unique position vis-à-vis clients. Coaching, as the name implies, occurs from a role outside of the action. We observe the action and then provide feedback and input to the clients. Five critical skill sets are involved in working from this position:

1. *Scanning.* We begin by observing and monitoring clients in action.

2. *Timing input.* As we monitor, we identify moments when we must intervene with clients.

3. *Setting up feedback.* As we begin to intervene, we must set the focus for input.

4. *Delivering feedback.* We provide clients with suggestions and instructions to improve their performance.

5. *Disengaging.* After intervention, we return to scanning mode so we do not interfere with the client activity.

Scanning Activity

Because we coach from a position external to the ongoing action, first we must ensure that we are positioned as an observer rather than an active participant. Doing this requires us to withdraw from active participation in content of discussions or activities. As we shift to a less active role, we focus on the action without feeling that we must contribute content. Rather, we monitor the dynamics and flow of the action, comparing it to intervention goals (Davis & Butler, 2004; Somov, 2008). We remain in the scan mode as long as client performance is proceeding toward the goals. Two core skills are associated with scanning:

1. *Participant observation.* To be able to observe the interaction or skill performance of clients or client systems, first we must disengage from the content of ongoing discussion. However, we remain involved and invested as we monitor the interactions and skill performances of others. To remain as an observer, we direct clients toward active roles using these three strategies.
   a. *Redirecting client focus.* When clients shift their focus to us, we respond by directing the focus back to the interaction or task at hand.
   b. *Encouraging activity.* When clients appear unsure or appear to need reassurance, it is important to support their efforts as we encourage them to continue in the activity.
   c. *Prompting activity.* When the flow of the client activity breaks, it is important to prompt them to reengage in the activity.

2. *Mental focus.* After we disengage from the ongoing activity, we shift our mental focus to the dynamics and processes occurring with the clients. Inherent in this focus, we monitor progress using knowledge and/or performance criteria associated with the activity. For example, with groups, we consider the stage of development, purpose, and membership as we monitor their performance. Often there are three areas of scanning:
   a. *Comparative assessment.* We monitor client performance and compare it to what might be expected given the clients, problems, goals, point in treatment, and so on. In EBP, the treatment manual often provide criteria to guide our scanning.
   b. *Focus monitoring.* As we monitor the ongoing activity, we track client focus to ensure that they remain on task. If they diverge, we may continue to observe, allowing them an opportunity for self-correction, or we may redirect them, depending on the purpose of the activity.
   c. *Safety monitoring.* It is important to consider issues of client harm and safety when scanning client activities. If interactions escalate or clients may engage in activity that will have negative repercussions, we prepare to intervene.

Timing Input

As we monitor client activity, we balance the need for them to find their own way with the goals and objectives (Davis & Butler, 2004; Somov, 2008). If we are too quick to intervene, we interfere with autonomy and client learning through experience. Alternatively, if we fail to intervene, clients may have strayed too far, making intervention futile. Sometimes the balance is difficult, requiring high levels of self-awareness so that we respond based on client needs rather than our anxiety. Four skills are important as we attempt to master this balance.

1. *Identifying redirection points.* When our scanning indicates that the activity appears to be off track, we move from scanning mode to intervention mode and prepare to provide instructions. If clients cannot refocus the activity on their own, we may need to redirect the process to bring them back on track.

2. *Identifying stuck points.* There will be times when client feelings, thinking distortions, or other events disrupt the activity. When the process seems stuck, we help clients

clarify the immediate situation to reorient them to the activity. If the situation escalates or safety is a concern, it is important to intervene immediately.

3. *Identifying growth points.* As clients perform their tasks, there are moments where they need additional instruction to continue their development. As we monitor the action, we watch for these points so we can reinforce client development.

4. *Identifying strength points.* Often there are moments in the action when clients display strengths and admirable qualities. At those times, often we want to reinforce clients.

Setting Up the Coaching Moment

As we prepare to intervene, we shift our focus from scanning to identifying opportunities to reinsert ourselves into the action. It can be difficult to reinsert ourselves into the action because the clients are engaged in activity and we are not in an active role. Consequently, we must find openings for reinserting ourselves into the action to deliver input. To set up the coaching moment, we must first interrupt the action, then focus our prompts.

- *Interrupting the action.* As we move from scanning into intervention mode, we interrupt the action. Doing this requires redirecting client attention away from the activity toward our input. Common interruption strategies include:
  - *Gesturing.* Sometimes hand gestures reaching toward the source of interaction can distract clients and draw attention to you.
  - *Verbal interruption.* Frequently we must verbally inject ourselves into the action by announcing our presence (For example, "I need to interrupt for a moment here").
  - *Moving.* There may be times when you must stand up or move your chair to garner attention. If you must stand up in a situation with several clients in interaction, move calmly toward the person whom you want to engage with so his or her attention is immediately secured.

- *Focusing the input.* Although most of the setups and prompts outlined in previous sections are useful, sometime it is necessary to focus the prompt on the identified concern. Consequently, we often focus on dynamics or interpersonal processes prior to input. These two strategies are useful for setting focus prior to providing a directive.
  - *Process illumination* (Yalom, 1995). In interactive client systems, we often focus client attention on patterns of interaction among the members. This is a descriptive moment where we describe what we observe occurring among people (For example, "Tell me about the tensions you notice between the intake team and the group work team?")
  - *Focused setup.* In larger client systems, many dynamics and interactions are occurring. Consequently, when we want to set up a coaching moment, often we must focus the attention of the multiple members. Doing this usually requires us to describe the element on the table that we want to use (For example, "Tom said something important when he pointed out how the board might react badly to our suggestion.").

Delivering Feedback

After we have the clients focused, we briefly provide input to guide their activity. Whether we are exploring thinking patterns with an individual, running a group, or conducting a meeting, we use brief prompts, instructions, and comments to move the activity toward our goals. Our comments activate clients to assume a new direction. To promote activation we provide brief, clear, and simple comments. Common delivery strategies include:

- *Process commentary* (Yalom, 1995). During interaction between members of a family or other client groups, often interpersonal processes go unnoticed by clients. Although these processes are not conscious, many times they contribute to the problems. Practitioners often want to raise the processes to a conscious level so clients can explore and change them. Doing this often begins with describing the process, then encouraging the clients to work with the new information. For example: "Notice how whenever Tom speaks, Jamie says something that is the opposite of what Tom said. What do you think is going on between Tom and Jamie?"

- *Providing encouragement.* When individuals are engaged in an activity or interaction with others, they often hit a point of hesitation. During these moments, clients often are experiencing a thought or feeling that causes them to partially withdraw from the activity. At these moments, practitioners often want to encourage them to continue in the activity rather than run the risk of losing the potential benefit. At these times, practitioners often use encouraging prompts, such as "Stay with it, Tom. Find the thoughts going through your head."
- *Guiding interaction.* Often we must help clients to focus their interactions by prompting continued discussion (For example, "Tom said something important when he pointed out how the board might react badly to our suggestion. Develop a plan for handling their reactions.").
- *Reinforcing learning.* As clients interact, they use skills and concepts learned earlier in service. Coaching often monitors for concepts to emerge and intervenes to reinforce and strengthen how clients are using skills and concepts. Doing this allows clients to adjust or integrate the skill (For example, "I know you have resolved this kind of issue before. Use those skills from Janice's argument with Fiona.").

After providing prompts to the clients, it is important to disengage so the input does not interfere with client activity. If the input is brief, disengagement is easily accomplished; however, when we talk too much, we must reorient clients to the activity. If we note any awkwardness at the end of our input, it is helpful to instruct clients to resume the activity so we can avoid occupying a central focus.

Integrating Direction

After completing an activity or directive intervention, it is important to integrate client experiences during the focused activity with the service goals (Davis & Butler, 2004; Somov, 2008). The integrative discussion has two parts:

1. We debrief any observed moments that might interfere with generalizing the experience to clients' life situations. If we see rationalization or hesitation during the activity, we can explore and discuss it in light of how such feelings and thoughts might interfere with achieving goals.
2. We explore how clients might use their experiences to increase their mastery. Three methods commonly are used to promote integration:
   a. *Client linking.* Often it is helpful to invite clients to create their own links between their experiences and their service goals. If clients can identify how they can apply their experiences to their life situations, generalization may strengthen because they are identifying areas for potential application.
   b. *Extending experiences.* As we explore experiences, sometimes it is useful to have clients identify other settings where their skills or new thinking patterns might be valuable. If we are aware of situations that might challenge their learning, it is helpful to identify these situations and discuss how new learning can be applied.
   c. *Follow up.* Often it is helpful to use follow-up contacts to help with integrating experiences. By phoning clients between meetings, we can reinforce their learning and enhance integration. This is a common strategy in EBPs such as Dialectical Behavior Therapy (Chen et al., 2008; Kerr et al., 2009).

Exercise 9.2: Preparing Mother

The woman from the first exercise continues to work with you. Your role is to help her to settle her mother into the home for elderly citizens. The mother requires a high level of care that the daughter cannot provide. The woman continues to struggle with engaging her mother in a conversation about entering the home. She has engaged in several role-plays with you but is still tentative. You scheduled a session in her home so you can help her with the conversation. The woman begins the conversation.

WOMAN: *Mom, I need to talk to you about something.*
MOTHER: *Okay, anything you want.*
WOMAN: *This is a difficult thing to discuss.*
MOTHER: *That's okay, dear. You can tell me anything. Is everything all right?*
WOMAN: *Well, sort of . . . but not really.*
MOTHER: *If there is something you need, I can try to help.*
WOMAN: *No . . . I don't need your help . . . . It is just . . .*

You want to help the woman get her concerns on the table. Provide a prompt to help the woman focus on her concerns about the mother's health.

WOMAN: *Mom, I am concerned that staying in my home may not be the best thing for you.*
MOTHER: *Is there a problem?*
WOMAN: *Not a problem, I just don't think I can give you the help that you need.*
MOTHER: *You have been a great daughter. Nobody could be better than you.*
WOMAN: *It's not whether I have been a good daughter or not.*
MOTHER: *Well, you have been and I am proud of you. Most daughters would not do what you have done.*

You notice that the focus has shifted from the woman's concerns about the mother's care to whether she has been a good daughter. You want to refocus the discussion on the mother's health needs. Provide a prompt to help the woman refocus.

WOMAN: *Mom, it is not about me. I am concerned about your health care. I can't do it.*
MOTHER: *You can't do what?*
WOMAN: *I work full time and can't be here for you as much as I would like.*
MOTHER: *It's okay, dear . . . I know you have to work. I am fine.*
WOMAN: *It's just . . .*
MOTHER: *I know you care.*

You want to help the woman get the issue of the home on the table. Pick up on the term "care" and help her raise the issue of the mother's medical needs.

Cultural Considerations

As we integrate focused activities into our intervention repertoires, there are areas of promise and areas of caution. Promise emerges from the apparent effectiveness of many directive interventions. The evidence-based interventions are particularly important when the working alliance between a practitioner and client is not strong (Barber et al., 2006). However, when the working alliance is strong, multiple methods and choices can promote similar outcomes. Consequently, as we consider the use of directive methods, we also must consider our working relationship with our clients.

Inherent in understanding our working alliance is consideration of the social and cultural backgrounds of our clients. As clients approach practitioners for assistance, they carry with them their cultural norms and social experiences. Their experience of the practitioner is filtered through these experiences. For this reason, we must consider cultural influences and social conditions as they pertain to the helping relationship. Like our clients, we enter the relationship with socialization experiences that may, or may not, match theirs. We also carry our professional role and obligations.

A critical consideration is our orientation to collectives. In the dominant North American culture, we often speak of individualism. Human rights are understood and discussed as individual rather than collective rights. These social messages cause us to be more comfortable focusing on individual processes rather than collective ones. For example, consider the last group project you worked on and the problems that emerged as it progressed. As the problems emerged, it is likely that the group members attributed the cause to an individual in the group rather than something at the group level (e.g., decision making, cohesion, group roles).

Our tendency to think at the individual level predisposes us to ignore group level and collective processes. Given that many activities and EBPs are employed in larger systems, this socialization can place us at a disadvantage. We need to tune in to the larger system processes and use collective knowledge to intervene with those larger systems. Often these skills are not part of our socialization, which requires us to become comfortable observing interactive processes so we can intervene easily without attempting to set up individual conversations.

Critical Chapter Concepts

1. Clients require both a strong helping alliance with their worker and a strong sense of direction. We must provide both to ensure adequate service.

2. Directive intervention tends to use focused activity with clients. This is very different from telling clients what to do.

3. Cultural groups have different reactions to directive interventions. It is important to understand how cultural and social contexts influence client responses to directive intervention.

4. As we provide direction, we shift from back-and-forth interaction into focused activity with clients. This transition must be negotiated to ensure we honor client autonomy.

5. There are four common types of focused activity: providing information, challenging thinking, identifying/expressing feelings, and learning skills.

6. We must engage clients in the activity to ensure that they are willing and active participants. We cannot impose our will or force clients to participate.

7. As we use focused activities, we employ prompts and coaching to guide clients and help them apply their learning.

Online Resources

Dramatic enactment resources: www.rehearsalsforgrowth.com/index.html

Facilitation skills tips: www.executivebrief.com/blogs/10-tips-to-boost-your-facilitation-skills/

Group facilitation skills information: http://managementhelp.org/grp_skll/grp_skll.htm

Psychotherapy Brown Bag (CBT discussions): www.psychotherapybrownbag.com/psychotherapy_brown_bag_a/

Recovery Today Online (substance abuse intervention focus): www.recoverytoday.net/

Recommended Reading

Creed, T. A., & Kendall, P. C. (2005). Therapist alliance-building behavior within a cognitive-behavioral treatment for anxiety in youth. *Journal of Consulting and Clinical Psychology, 73*, 498–505.

Davis, S. D., & Butler, M. H. (2004). Enacting relationships in marriage and family therapy: A conceptual and operational definition of an enactment. *Journal of Marital and Family Therapy, 30*, 319–333.

McKelley, R. A., & Rochlen, A. B. (2007). The practice of coaching: Exploring alternative to therapy for counseling-resistant men. *Psychology of Men & Masculinity, 8*, 53–65.

Watson, J. C., & McMullen, E. J. (2005). An examination of therapist and client behavior in high- and low-alliance sessions in cognitive-behavioral therapy and process experiential therapy. *Psychotherapy: Theory, Research, Practice, Training, 42*, 297–310.

Section III
Using the Working Alliance to Promote Change

The last section provided a foundation of interactive skills that practitioners use to explore, clarify, position, and promote change when working with clients. Although the four skill sets were described as discrete competencies, they are all used within the context of a helping relationship. This section of the book explores how practitioners enact the skills within that relational context.

As we explore the upcoming chapters, we will learn how to employ the interactive skills while respecting and nurturing the helping relationship. To accomplish this task, many of the skills in Section 1, such as thinking and tuning in to clients, are integrated with the interactive skills described in Section 2. It is important to integrate skills so they can become second nature as we interact with clients rather than feeling forced.

This section begins with a chapter focused on integrating our interactive skills as we work within the helping relationship. Chapter 10 integrates tuning in, applying knowledge, providing direction, and interaction. Subsequent chapters explore how the relationship can provide a foundation to motivate, manage the working alliance and focus change efforts. Chapter 14 provides a strategy for ending the helping relationship and sustaining changes.

Chapter 10
Integrating Direction Through Transitional Responding

The past four chapters provided the core interactive competencies needed for generalist practice. All of these skills—questioning, reflecting, sharing observations, and providing direction—are used seamlessly to help clients achieve their service goals. In Chapter 9 we learned that direction is important; we also learned that the helping relationship is equally important. Even in highly directive interventions, a collaborative working relationship is associated with effective treatment (Hall, 2008; Hammond & Nichols, 2008). For that reason, a collaborative working alliance and a goal-focused direction are equal priorities in professional intervention.

Given these two priorities, this chapter begins an exploration of how practitioners provide direction within the context of a working relationship. As you explore the transitional responding competency, you will learn how your interpersonal skills can maintain a goal direction as you simultaneously attend to client communication, engagement, and relationship. This skill provides a foundation for achieving balanced direction during intervention. As we use our interactive skills to influence change, we begin to use power and influence in the helping relationship.

Power and Influence in the Helping Relationship

As we work with clients, part of our job is to use our professional influence to help clients achieve their goals (Guilfoyle, 2003). This expectation of influence can be daunting because it requires us to balance three professional responsibilities:

1. We are responsible to use our professional competencies to influence clients toward achieving their goals (Berliner, 2005; Cohen, Mannarino, & Knudsen, 2005).
2. We are responsible for ensuring a positive and productive helping relationship (Allen et al., 1996; Johansson & Eklund, 2006).
3. We are responsible to abide by our professional ethics, allowing clients self-determination and respecting their rights within the helping relationship.

As we balance these three responsibilities, we use our self-awareness, knowledge, and ethics to shape how we use our skills to influence clients. We must be careful to balance our use of power, especially with clients who possess very low levels of personal and social power (Jahoda et al., 2009). Concurrently, we must ensure that we attend to our ethical principles because there are many sources of power that do not fit well into ethical codes. In Chapter 2 we learned that all codes of ethics promote client autonomy and informed consent. These ethical prerequisites must be met as we begin to use our power and influence.

Types of Power and Professional Ethics

There are many forms of power in interpersonal relationships. Sociologists, politicians, and psychologists have long explored and categorized power. For the purposes of understanding how we use influence in the helping relationship, it is useful to first provide a quick understanding of interpersonal power. Table 10.1 contains five power categories and outlines how each emerges in a helping relationship. These types of power include:

1. *Power through manipulation and power elevation.* The types of power contained in this section of the table tend to be unethical when they are used with clients. We should avoid using these types of power as our source for influencing clients.

2. *Power through persuasion and social pressure.* These types of power involve pressuring or trying to convince clients. These border on unethical because they interfere slightly with client self-determination. Consequently, these are not the best forms of influence because we pressure the client rather than allowing them to identify their own solutions.

3. *Power through the practitioner position.* The power sources in this section of the table outline sources of influence that accompany the professional role. While these are ethical forms of influence, they are also fairly weak forms of power because they emerge from our job rather than from us.

4. *Power through client needs and projections.* The sources of power in this section of the table are similar to practitioner position sources of influence because the source of the power is not in us. Rather, these sources of power come from how the client perceives or needs us. These sources of power cannot be relied upon from client-to-client.

5. *Power through how the practitioner relates.* This is the power associated with the helping relationship. When you review these types of power notice how they reflect the concepts you have learned in previous chapters. These sources of influence emerge from how we approach and respond to situations.

Table 10.1 Types of Power and Influence

Type of Power	Power Definition	Power Requirement	Power Source	Practitioner Actions
Types of Power Based in Manipulation and Power Elevation				
Coercive Power	Power is the actions that can be used to influence another's actions.	Ability to punish or otherwise harm.	Harm potential.	Threats, punishment, telling what to do.
Pity Power	Power is causing others to relinquish expectations and compensate for perceived afflictions.	Client sees vulnerability and assumes a caregiving role.	Client feeling pity.	Sharing stories, concerns, and struggles that create pity response.
Scapegoating Power	Power is facilitating group projections of responsibility for negative events, shortcomings, or failures onto another group or person.	People believe worker assertions that a person (client, other person, or group) is responsible for shortcomings and problems occurring in the treatment situation.	Others believing the projected blame.	Find an identifiable person or group that others will believe is responsible for the negative events, then convince others that responsibility attributions are warranted.
Diminishment Power	Power is when others relinquish their autonomous position because they are convinced by assertions that their personal power is illusionary.	Clients believe that they are weak, inadequate, and dependent on the worker for advice and help.	Clients believing that they are inadequate.	Focus on client weakness and problems to the exclusion of strengths. Take over situations on behalf of clients.
Disruptive Power	Power is interfering with another's ability to maintain routine patterns of operation.	Sufficient access that one can interfere with client situations.	Disrupted patterns.	Tracking, interrupting, meddling in client behavior pattern.
Types of Power Based in Persuasion and Argument				
Legitimate Position Power	Power is the endorsement of your position or actions by an external, well-accepted, and legitimate body.	Clients accept the position of the legitimate body and acquiesces to its position.	Client acceptance of the external body and acquiescence of power.	Sharing findings of the external body and convincing clients that compliance is warranted.
Majority Power	Power is accumulation of people taking a specific position vis-à-vis a smaller group.	Clients give in to the position held by the majority in the situation.	Convincing the larger group to assume the desired position and clients to give in.	Manipulate the majority of group members to take your position, cajole clients to acquiesce.

Persuasive Power	Power is the ability to convince other people that your position is correct for them in their situation.	Client engagement in a discussion and a willingness to accept your argument.	Acceptance of an alternative position.	Argue and advise to convince client that your position is superior to theirs.
Types of Power Based in Client Needs and Projections				
Charismatic Power	Power is the attractiveness and popularity that one emits from others.	Other people to like the worker and seek out contact, attention, and input.	Adulation from others.	Try to impress others so they will like you and do as you suggest.
Projected Power	Power is the focused externalization of another person's autonomous function.	Client sees things in you that are really in themselves.	Illusions and externalization.	Maintain the illusion that you are what the client perceives.
Referent Power	Power is the synergy between one's traits and another person's future-focused strivings.	Traits that the client wants to emulate.	Client strivings.	Just being who you are.
Types of Power Based in Practitioner Position				
Bureaucratic Power	Power is the decisions and latitudes made possible by occupying a role.	Position of authority over the client.	Client need.	Granting requests, negotiating systems, providing access
Expert Power	Power is the superior knowledge and experience in a specific area.	Information or skills needed by the client.	Client vested interest.	Teaching, instructing, doing things for the client.
Information Power	Power is the possession of information or the delivery of information critical for others to adequately perform their roles or make decisions.	Client needing information to function and accept your presentation of the information.	Control over information delivery.	Crafting and sharing information in a way that results in desired outcomes.
Reward Power	Power is the possession and contingent willingness to share objects and behaviors valued by the client.	Access to resources that the client values.	Valued resources or acts.	Giving or withholding rewards based on client performance.
Types of Power Based on Relating to Others				
Personal Power	Power is the integrated and purposeful control of one's feelings, thinking, interactions, and behaviors.	To be able to understand and respond to situations with no interference from personal needs or agendas.	Openness to situations and ability to explore.	Developing an accurate understanding and responding with appropriate knowledge.
Transformative Power	Power is the implied direction contained in altering the meaning attributions of another person.	Client to reflect on their current situation using an alternative meaning system.	Client openness to alternative frames.	Explore situations and respond in a manner that challenges clients to consider things differently.
Relational Power	Power is mutual valuing, respecting, and consideration between two (or more) people resulting in self-monitoring and accommodation.	Mutual respect and concern causes client to consider positions.	Shared experience and common ground.	Partnering with clients in a way that they feel supported in their struggles.

(Adapted from French & Raven, 1959)

Given the types of power available and the ethical concerns associated with some forms of power, we are challenged as we help clients change. Some forms of power are clearly inappropriate and should be avoided. Other forms of power fluctuate based on how we are perceived or what the client needs. These sources of influence are fickle. Although they may be useful with some clients, they are not under our control. The only sources of influence that are ethical and controllable are contained in the relational power section. Given that our main ethical source of power and influence emerges from the relationship, we must learn to insert influence into the relationship rather than rely on other forms of power.

Toward a Professional Use of Influence

As we develop our skills for imparting direction into the helping relationship, it is important to consider our professional roles. As professionals, our job is to help clients understand their situation from different perspectives. We also influence clients to respond differently within their situation. The way we interact with clients is intended to influence how they understand, experience, and respond to situations.

A professional use of influence is qualitatively different from its use in other relationships. We influence clients to analyze situations at deeper levels. We also influence client responses. Most important, our use of influence allows clients to remain autonomous and in control; we do not take over, rescue, or chastise clients. We sidestep the temptation to tell them what to do and allow clients to remain the "experts" in their own life situations.

Practitioners who manage to maintain a strong helping relationship are able to resist the desire to provide clients with long speeches and advice giving. Such practitioners adopt what is often referred to as a collaborative approach (Sutherland, 2007). This type of approach involves practitioners listening intently and responding to client communications and priorities without taking over the situation (Osborn, West, Kindsvatter, & Paez, 2008). The level of collaboration in the relationship is associated with a stronger working alliance and client perceptions of being helped (Boardman, Delwyn, Grobe, Little, & Ahluwalia, 2006; Lafave, Desportes, & McBride, 2009).

Influencing Depth

When working with clients, we seek to deepen their understanding of the situation. The focused movement toward depth allows us to help clients achieve a different perspective. Anyone can listen to shallow descriptions of a problem situation. Many friends, bartenders, and hairdressers operate at this level of problem exploration. Professionals must achieve deeper levels of exploration to help clients move from simple descriptions of the situation to an exploration of the action and processing themes within the situation. Figure 10.1 shows how transitional responding can take both practitioner and client deeper into the client's understandings of the situation.

In Figure 10.1, situational concerns are listed down the left side of the diagram. This list illustrates the elements that may be in the problem situation. They begin with contextual and biological elements and extend to interpretations or feelings that may contribute to the

Figure 10.1

Exploring Client Situations

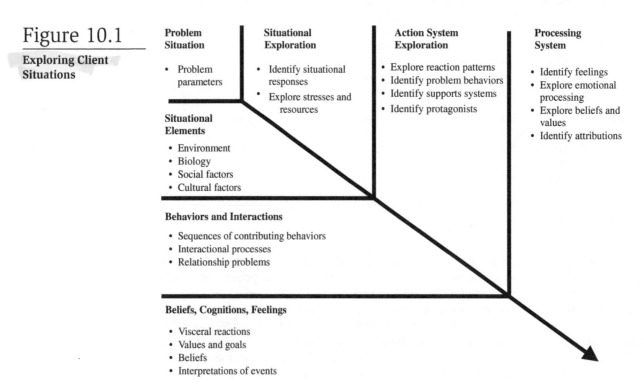

Problem Situation	Situational Exploration	Action System Exploration	Processing System
• Problem parameters	• Identify situational responses • Explore stresses and resources	• Explore reaction patterns • Identify problem behaviors • Identify supports systems • Identify protagonists	• Identify feelings • Explore emotional processing • Explore beliefs and values • Identify attributions

Situational Elements

• Environment
• Biology
• Social factors
• Cultural factors

Behaviors and Interactions

• Sequences of contributing behaviors
• Interactional processes
• Relationship problems

Beliefs, Cognitions, Feelings

• Visceral reactions
• Values and goals
• Beliefs
• Interpretations of events

problem. Across the top of the diagram, practitioner responses are listed. The large arrow sloping down depicts the path of transitional exploration. Transitional responses bring the exploration to the deepest possible levels one step at a time.

Influencing Client Actions

As we promote change, we are often challenged. As a thought or impulse to help the client change enters our mind, we must fight the impulse to launch into advice giving or otherwise telling the client what to do. These approaches to promoting change are well modeled in our lives but telling people what to do provides little opportunity for clients to develop mastery (Bachelor, Laverdière, Gamache, & Bordeleau, 2007). When we promote change, we must find ways of including clients so that they can approach their situation differently rather than simply following our well-meant advice (Osborn et al., 2008). Doing this involves two common practitioner responses: positioning and change promotion.

1. *Positioning for change.* Often the material placed on the table by clients provides a poor foundation for helping them change. Positioning responses solicit material that can better provide a foundation for change promotion. We carefully listen to identify possible material that can extend toward client goals. As we respond, we build on the client material to draw out issues and content that can be used to develop change. For example, a father referred because of hitting his child may state that his parents used spanking, and it was good enough for him. The practitioner may pick up on the statement and begin to explore the man's childhood experiences, anticipating that some of the experiences will help promote change.

2. *Change promotion.* As we explore situations with clients, the back-and-forth exchanges provide opportunities for us to embed small challenges, suggestions, and other considerations into our responses. Each exchange of information involves picking up on material that can advance client goal achievement and then using the material in a response that will promote client changes.

Toward Transitional Responding

The underlying skill of inserting influence is referred to in this text as transitional responding. The term implies that each response helps clients transition into movement rather than remaining stationary. The process of helping clients achieve their goals involves ongoing back-and-forth exchanges between practitioner and client (Flaskas, 2004).

Inherent in the practitioner-client exchanges is the fact that clients must feel that they are being heard as practitioner responses expand on, rather than dismiss, their disclosures (Clarke, Rees, & Hardy, 2004; Giampaolo et al., 2006). Change-focused intervention must be responsive to client statements by building on what clients have shared and adding elements that can help them (Levitt, 2001). Notice how the following dialog begins with exploration then transitions toward helping the client resolve feelings of guilt.

> **CLIENT:** *I feel so overwhelmed by all the pressure in my family. I feel like I am carrying the load for everyone and nobody seems to care. I just don't think I can take it anymore.*
> **PRACTITIONER:** *It sounds like things are stressful. Tell me more about this stress.*
> **CLIENT:** *I just feel like I am always having to work. Even when I am home it is work, work, work . . .*
> **PRACTITIONER:** *Who in the family seems to put the most pressure on you?*
> **CLIENT:** *Everyone . . . I work, I cook, I clean up, and nobody lifts a finger to help me.*
> **PRACTITIONER:** *If someone would lift a finger, who would you want it to be?*
> **CLIENT:** *John, my husband . . . but he can't. He goes off to work and with overtime he can't help with the kids because I have already put them to bed when he gets home. That leaves it all to me, and with my mother living with us, there is so much to do.*
> **PRACTITIONER:** *Your mother sounds like a new addition. When did she move in?*
> **CLIENT:** *She just had surgery and moved in with us to recuperate.*

PRACTITIONER: *Are you providing all of her care as well?*

CLIENT: *Yes. She does not have good insurance and I have to do it all. I don't mean to complain, but it is just so much work.*

PRACTITIONER: *The addition of the health care pressures seems like it is putting you over the top, but you also feel guilty about your stress.*

CLIENT: *I'll say . . . I mean, I shouldn't resent having Mom in the home after all she has done for me.*

PRACTITIONER: *So it's not okay to resent your mother. How about exhaustion . . . are you allowed to feel exhausted without betraying your mother?*

In this example, the worker linked each response to the material placed on the table by the client. The worker picked up some material from the table then used the client material as a platform for responding. The practitioner then uses reflection, questioning, or prompting to encourage further exploration.

Transitional Responding and Interactive Skills

Transitional responding builds on the interactive skills covered in the previous four chapters. As you learned each skill, functions and outcomes were described. These outcomes (see Table 10.2) are the implicit direction that can be achieved in any interactive response. Two of the outcomes, clarification and exploration, are used to deepen our understanding of the client situation. The other outcomes are used in change-focused interactions with the client.

In transitional responding, we insert direction and influence emerge through our use of our interactive skills. Interaction begins with the client's package of communication. It is the themes in the communicated package that provide the foundation for building influence. We use the response systems in the client's communication (feeling, thinking, relating, and actions) to identify themes that can help us develop this direction (see Figure 10.2). When the client communicates, often one response system appears most important. In Figure 10.2, this is the feeling "F" quadrant in the communicated package. The communicated themes provide a foundation for preparing our response.

Benefits of Transitional Responding

Transitional responding contains two elements; (1) tracking material placed on the table by the client, and (2) inserting direction. By using material stated by the client, we affirm the client as we begin the transition. Affirmation is important during transitional responding because the second element in the response includes a demand. The demand is for increased detail, clarity, new content, or new ways of approaching the situation.

The use of a two-part response combining affirmation and demand promotes the working alliance while concurrently providing direction. The alliance is preserved by consistently

Table 10.2 Desired Outcomes and Implicit Direction

Desired Outcome	Implicit Direction
Exploration	To continue exploration, we insert a query in our response. A query encourages the client to expand on the communication package, adding new information.
Clarification	To clarify, we implicitly ask the client to expand on a statement. Rather than pursuing additional depth, clarification requires the client to remain focused on elements already on the table.
Positioning	When we use a response to position the client, we attempt to get the client to put new information on the table that will provide a better platform for building direction.
Change Promotion	When we insert change promotion into our response, we use a response that causes the client to reconsider the current situation or the response to the current situation.

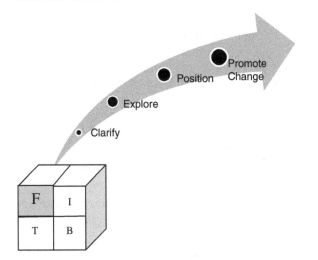

Figure 10.2

**Linking the Response
Themes**

building onto client statements, often repeating elements of the statement as part of the response. The alliance receives focus as we insert direction into the response. This pattern of affirmation then insertion of direction illustrates the transitional responding process.

Transitional Responding Process

Transitional responding is a method that allows us to embed direction as we respond to our clients. Rather than parceling out instructions or advice, transitional responding inserts small directives that shape the focus of the client's next response. It is the size of our insertions that provides the power of transitional responding. There are never long practitioner soliloquies or lectures. We simply respond in a back-and-forth manner; over a series of responses, movement occurs.

To understand transitional responding, it is important to understand how we insert direction into simple responses. We all have the rudiments of this skill, but very few of us can use it with purpose and precision. Typically our insertions in our social relationships are self-serving. Consider how we mention items we like into our conversations before our birthday or work in content about the weekend when conversing with someone we like. These social moments provide us with the rudiments for using transitional responding. To use these skills in a professional context, we follow four skill elements.

1. *Maintain a goal focus.* Transitional responding maintains the client goals and purpose of the relationship as the practitioner listens and responds to the client communication.
2. *Transitional tracking.* Transitional responding picks up on important elements in the client communication, building the practitioner response onto the communicated elements.
3. *Insert direction.* Transitional responding provides direction embedded in the practitioner's response.
4. *Activate a client response.* After the practitioner finishes responding to the client, he or she waits for a client response rather than continuing to talk.

Maintaining a Goal Focus

When we are in conversation with clients, they share so much information it is often difficult to retain our focus. We want to avoid cutting off clients and simply proceeding with intervention (Creed & Kendall, 2005). However, we also must maintain a sense of purpose. As we listen to clients, we pay close attention to the themes in their communication. Some themes are unrelated to the purpose, and some themes provide material that can advance goal-directed work. While we listen to the entire communication, we mentally track themes that are pertinent to our professional role.

Identifying Goal-Related Themes

As professionals, we retain the client goals and purpose of the helping relationship in our minds during client discussions. As the client speaks, we use the goals to filter the important information. We use critical thinking skills as we listen to content and compare the communicated material to our knowledge. Four types of knowledge are used to flag client communication for further attention.

1. *Client emphasis.* Sometimes important themes come with client emphasis as nonverbal behavior highlights the importance of communicated material.
2. *Client background.* Often our relationship with and knowledge of our client helps us to identify the themes associated with problem situations.
3. *Empirical knowledge.* Our knowledge of research and well-grounded theory helps us identify critical content themes if the client's concerns are well researched.
4. *Practice wisdom.* As we gain experience, we develop practitioner intuition that helps us identify patterns and situations that require our attention.

As goal-related themes emerge, we make a mental note that the communicated material needs attention. Some material is ripe for promoting positive outcomes. Other material may indicate movement away from client goals. Regardless, our professional thinking allows us to retain our purpose so we can flag communicated messages as important.

Transitional Tracking

Transitional responding merges our tuning-in skills with interactive skills. As we filter content themes for goal relatedness, we first tune into themes identifying the most important elements in the client communication. As we tune in to the goal-related elements in client communication, we select content that will easily transition into goal-focused work.

Scanning Client Content

A core skill in transitional tracking is scanning the communicated material in the client statement. We find critical content embedded in the response systems themes. Sometimes the most useful material on the table is not immediately obvious, so we also must use our observation skills. Many communicated elements are implicitly on the table rather than firmly embedded in the content of the client's statement. For example, when an elderly client says, "It was a tough week. Friends keep dying and I stay all day in my room," the content is largely about behavior (friends dying and staying in the room). However, there may be very important emotional information that is implicitly communicated.

In this example, the implicit emotional content appears to be more important than the behavioral content. For some practitioners, concern about possible depression may emerge in such statements. These concerns are important indicators of the critical content. In our professional role, we learn to pick up the critical elements associated with the purpose of our work. In the last situation, doing this would include the emotions as we would begin formulating a response that can explore the woman's emotional experience.

The material we select for linking a response is critical for providing direction. If we pick up on the woman staying in her room, we may end up in a discussion about reading novels or how she used to play bridge. However, if we pick up on the implicit emotional themes, we can form a response such as "Things sound pretty lonely." Notice how this response begins to form direction.

Scanning With Larger Client Systems

Scanning can be challenging when working with larger client systems because there are several people placing their communication packages on the table. When there are multiple people involved in the discussion, we must scan for pressing material for each of the individuals and consider how that material fits into the larger system. Often we scan for common themes and overlapping concerns to identify the important themes in the larger system.

A second level of large-system scanning involves the relationships between individuals and the collective. Some communicated material pertains only to the individual while other material is important to the collective. With larger systems, most often we want to select material that is germane to the system when building a response. Consistently selecting individual-focused material can diminish the importance of the collective while elevating individual agendas.

Exercise 10.1: Identifying Elements That Promote Goals

You are working in a parent support program helping high-risk parents respond nonviolently with their adolescent children. A parent comes in and tells you, "I got so mad at her last week . . . she wouldn't do anything she was told. I just wanted to shake her."

1. What are the response system elements in the statement?

   a. Feeling.

   b. Thinking.

   c. Relating.

   d. Behavior.

2. Which element can provide movement toward developing nonviolent parenting skills?

3. How would you use this element in your response?

You work in a day program for people who have a mental illness. The program is designed to help clients prepare for competitive employment. You are meeting with a client who is very upset about another person in the program. You begin by asking the client about what is occurring and the client responds, "Well, you know, she just blew me off. No matter what I said to her, she just would not respond. So I pounded the table and started yelling."

1. What are the response system elements in the statement?

   a. Feeling.

   b. Thinking.

      c. Relating.

      d. Behavior.

2. Which element can provide movement toward developing competitive employment skills?

3. How would you use this element in your response?

Inserting Direction

When we respond to the client's statement, we can insert direction into our response. Ideally, our direction influences movement toward client goals. There are two critical conditions for successful insertion. First, the insertion must logically link to and build on the client statement. Establishing this link requires us to think clearly. If our links fail to pick up on the spirit of the client statement, our insertion will lose credibility. The second condition is selecting appropriate direction. The insertion should increase the depth of exploration or direct the conversation toward goal achievement.

Forging a Link to the Client Communication
There are many ways to link to the client statement. All of the interactive skills use links to the material on the table, so this is not a new concept. However, in transitional responding, we attempt to link in a way that promotes direction for the client. Until this point you have worked to identify the material on the table and simply pick up some element to build your response. Now we add thinking and tuning-in skills so you can pick up material that can promote client goal achievement.

      As we listen to the client statement, we identify direction based on how the content on the table can help us proceed toward goals. We constantly assess our understanding of the situation and the capacity of material to promote goal achievement. If we do not have a clear picture, we often link to material that simply explores. If we believe that we understand the situation, we seek content that will allow us to proceed toward change promotion.

      In establishing a link to the material on the table, we can use response systems (feeling, thinking, relating, and actions) to help identify useful information. At times we select feelings; at other times, one of the other response systems, depending on how the content can move things forward. Table 10.3 illustrates possible goal-related links. Notice how each response system provides unique themes that can be used in our response. All of the responses on the table build on this client statement by the wife of a resident: "I am so sick of being old. Retirement started out well, but then Donald had his stroke and things were never the same." In this situation, consider yourself a practitioner helping residents and families adjust to life in the residence.

      When reviewing Table 10.3, notice how some links promote useful exploration. Also notice how questions, reflections, observations, and directive responses each create a unique demand for the client response. We carefully select our link and our delivery to subtly influence the client response. Imagine being the client responding to each of the links. Notice

Table 10.3 Using Goal-Related Themes

Response System Elements	Content Themes	Response Type	Possible Link
Feeling	Powerlessness Loss	Question	How are these changes affecting you?
		Reflection	Sounds like life is running out of control for you.
		Observation	You told me that things were never the same after the stroke.
		Focused activity	Give me a list of the things that changed after the stroke.
Thinking	Life has changed for the worse	Question	What changed in your life after the stroke?
		Reflection	It seems that you believe life is on a downward decline.
		Observation	You stated that you are sick of being old.
		Focused activity	Tell me all the ways that your life changed as a result of getting old.
Relating/Interaction	Relationship with Donald was disrupted by the stroke	Question	Is Donald totally incapacitated?
		Reflection	So the Donald that you retired with is not the Donald you have today.
		Observation	You stated that life was good until Donald had his stroke.
		Focused activity	Tell me more about the changes after Donald's stroke.
Behavior	As I age, life is changing	Question	How has Donald's stroke curtailed your life?
		Reflection	So life is changing and you feel caged in a bit.
		Observation	You mentioned that things have never been the same.
		Focused activity	Walk me through your day and how it has changed since the stroke.

how each of the links takes a slightly different direction. Some responses will promote the goals of helping adjust to the home while other responses seem superfluous.

Directional Insertions
As we respond to clients, our insertions provide subtle demands and conditions that shape their responses. These demands focus client attention while providing conditions for their responses. Conditions usually include requiring consideration prior to responding. Although practitioners insert many elements in their responses, the three insertions provided in Table 10.3 are important tools for influencing the client response. Each insertion communicates a specific demand to the client.

- *Query*. A query communicates that we require more information. As we discuss the situation with clients, we must be aware of our level of accurate understanding. If we are unclear about elements in the situation or find that we are tempted to fill in the gaps based on theory or conjecture, we need to insert queries so we can prompt the client to expand their story.
- *Positioning solicitation*. In Table 10.3, positioning solicitations emerge when we identify that the material on the table will not support change-focused interventions. A client may be venting or may not be ready for action. Positioning solicitations direct the exploration into new content areas that have a better prognosis for supporting goal-directed work.
- *Change promotion*. The term "nudging" is used with change promotion because it implies small insertions designed to help clients take some steps toward change. A nudge provides a quick challenge. We then observe the client response. If we detect movement toward the goals, the nudge is effective; if not, we may need to shift into queries or positioning solicitations until another nudge-able moment emerges.

Figure 10.3

**Directional
Considerations**

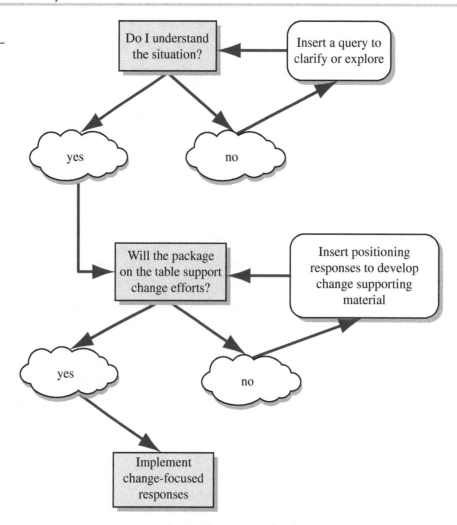

Inherent in transitional responding, we listen very strategically to understand the client situation and select directions that can help clients progress toward their goals. This strategic thinking is depicted in Figure 10.3. Notice that a series of considerations occurs as we listen and prepare our response. We mentally check our understanding and then immediately select a direction to insert into our response.

For example, when working with parents who have been violent with their child, a practitioner may want to solicit material that can promote empathy with the child. If a parent has just said, "That kid drives me nuts. Sometimes I just lose it," there is not much to promote empathy because the thinking is externalized. A positioning response might be "When you drove your parents nuts, did they lose it too?" Notice how getting childhood experiences might provide a better platform for building direction.

Integrating Direction

The schematic in Figure 10.3 may appear complex, but the mental activity of scanning client material occurs very quickly. As we become accustomed to goal-directed thinking, our decisions become second nature. We begin to discover that we can direct conversations comfortably in multiple directions. With careful linking, we direct the conversation in a direction that responds directly to client needs.

To understand how direction builds, review Table 10.3. Notice in this table that our response can build on any of the four response systems: feeling, thinking, relating, and action. We also create differential impact, depending on the interactive skill we select for our response. When you review the different types of responses, observe how each one inserts a unique direction.

Table 10.4 builds on a client situation in a nursing home. In this situation, consider yourself as a practitioner helping residents and families adjust to life in the residence. The

Table 10.4 Directional Insertions and Linkages to Response Systems

Response System Elements	Element Themes	Response Type	Query	Positioning Solicitation	Nudge toward Change
Feeling (Explicit)	Powerlessness, Loss	Question	How are these changes affecting you?	What areas of your life still provide you some control?	Insufficient material for a nudging question.
		Reflection	Sounds like you have gone through many changes.	It seems like you had some good days for a little while.	So Donald's stroke totally destroyed everything that was good.
		Observation	You stated that things were never the same after the stroke.	You noted that things started out well when you first retired.	You stated you were sick of being old but tied your problems to the stroke.
		Focused activity	Give me a list of the things that changed after the stroke.	Describe for me the things that were so good when you first retired.	For the next two days, please list all of the good feelings you experience.
Thinking (Implicit)	Life has changed for the worse	Question	What changed in your life after the stroke?	Did anything change for the better?	Did anything get better as you aged?
		Reflection	It seems that you believe life is on a downward decline.	It seems that other than the stroke, things were going well.	So the stroke totally destroyed your life.
		Observation	You stated that nothing has been the same.	You mentioned that things were good for a while.	Everything you just said had a negative focus.
		Focused activity	Tell me more about the ways your life has changed for the worse.	Tell about some of the changes that seem all right for you.	Tell me about the thoughts that convinced you that life is so bad.
Relating/ Interaction (Explicit)	Relationship with Donald was disrupted by the stroke	Question	How has Donald's stroke changed your relationship with him?	What strengths do you use to manage Donald's illness?	Who are the people you enjoy being with?
		Reflection	It seems that Donald has changed since the stroke.	It sounds like retirement began very well for you and Donald.	It seems like the stroke snuck into your life and robbed you of everything good.
		Observation	I heard you say that Donald's stroke was the moment of change.	When you were talking you spoke of good times with Donald.	When you described the changes, you said Donald's health was responsible.
		Focused activity	Talk about the life you had with Donald before his stroke.	The stroke was pretty devastating. Talk about how Donald has rebounded.	The stroke seems like an evil force. Tell how it rises up to mess with your life.
Behavior (Implicit)	As I age, life is changing	Question	How has Donald's stroke curtailed your life?	What things are you still able to do?	If you could get out, what would you do?
		Reflection	Your options in life seem to be getting smaller.	It seems like old options have diminished, leaving fewer choices for you.	It seems that some options were taken from you and others were given up.
		Observation	You stated that getting old is difficult at this time for you.	As you spoke you indicated that there have been changes after a period of good times.	When you spoke you stated that nothing is the same as before.
		Focused activity	Tell me more about the way your life has changed.	You say life has changed. Tell what you do with your free time.	Talk to me about how you are taking care of yourself in the midst of turmoil.

239

wife of a resident says, "I am so sick of being old. Retirement started out well, but then Donald had his stroke and things were never the same." Earlier we explored possible links to the statement. In Table 10.4, queries, positioning solicitations, and nudges have also been included. Notice how many possible directions emerge when direction insertions and combined with interactive skills and links to the four response systems.

As you read the responses associated with each response system, you will notice several patterns. First, notice how each response system will take the discussion in a different direction. This is most noticeable in the query column because it is still very exploratory. Some of the directions will take you away from helpful responses and the goals of intervention. Also notice how this client statement does not provide well for inserting a nudge toward change. Most of the nudging responses are unlikely to be successful, and some may appear argumentative to the client. This is because the material on the table does not provide a foundation for change. See how the positioning solicitations can help develop a stronger foundation.

Building Insertion Skills

When viewed in a table, the possibilities associated with a simple statement can appear overwhelming. Fortunately, you will never be handed a table and asked to think through every possible direction. The direction comes from the goals that reside in the back of your mind. As you listen, you will develop a sense of the most important material on the table. In the simple statement "I am so sick of being old. Retirement started out well, but then Donald had his stroke and things were never the same," there is clear distress. Given that your job is to help families adjust, you are likely to reach for the emotional material and either explore (add queries) or attempt to position (solicit material that can help).

It is important to understand that there are never right answers. There are only directions that take you closer to, or further away, from client goals. Over time you will become comfortable identifying the material on the table that will maximize direction toward the goals. This process will become faster as your skills improve. It is important continually to practice identifying the material placed on the table when people make statements. As this identification process develops, you will concurrently identify more options.

Case Example

This example involves a worker from a battered woman's shelter interacting with one of the residents. The client is angry and starting to escalate. The worker is attempting to get her to calm down. As you read this excerpt, notice the thinking and selective use of directional inserts.

CLIENT: *I have had enough of this. All my life I put up with people dumping on me, and if anyone thinks I am going to keep putting up with this crap, they have another think coming.*

PRACTITIONER: *(Wonders if the client has a history of victimization that might need to be overcome.) So your husband is not the first one to treat you this way?* (Positioning solicitation.)

CLIENT: *No, almost everyone in my life has dumped on me.*

PRACTITIONER: *(Wanting to explore supports and move toward strengths.) You say almost everyone . . . was there someone in your life you felt was supportive to you?* (Positioning solicitation.)

CLIENT: *Yes. I had an aunt I used to go to.*

PRACTITIONER: *What kinds of things would you go to her for?* (Query.)

CLIENT: *Oh . . . when things were not good at home she would always be there for me.*

PRACTITIONER: *It sounds like she was an important refuge for you. What kinds of things would happen at home to make you want to see your aunt?* (Query.)

CLIENT: *We used to fight a lot.*

PRACTITIONER: *(Wanting to identify role of aunt.) When the fighting happened at home, how were you involved?* (Positioning solicitation.)

CLIENT: *I would do something or get fresh and then Dad would go off on me.*

PRACTITIONER: *(Wanting to get at emotional responses to start a focus on inner strengths) When he went off on you, what thoughts and feelings did you experience.* (Positioning solicitation.)

CLIENT: *I kind of felt guilty but then I would just think he was a jerk.*

PRACTITIONER: *(Wanting to clarify the nature of feelings) So you felt that you caused some of the fighting . . . ?* (Query.)

> CLIENT: *(Pause) Yes . . . I caused a lot of trouble for my parents.*
> PRACTITIONER: *(Wanting to contrast parental relations and the aunt) But you were never any trouble for your aunt.* (Positioning solicitation.)
> CLIENT: *Never.*
> PRACTITIONER: *(Wanting to establish the difference) So even though you are the same person, you never caused problems when with your aunt.* (Positioning solicitation.)
> CLIENT: *I said never . . .*
> PRACTITIONER: *(Wanting to highlight the calm side of the client) So which one is the real you, the person who blows up and causes trouble or the person who stays calm and never causes trouble?* (Nudge.)

In the example, notice how the practitioner continually shifted from exploratory queries and positioning solicitations, trying to get material on the table that could support a nudge. In the final statement, notice how the practitioner nudged that client to become calm and rational. This is a common pattern with several queries and positioning attempts with very few nudges.

Activating a Client Response

As soon as we respond to clients, the onus shifts to them. They must consider our statement and construct a response. As clients respond, we monitor how our statement is understood and integrated into the client position. Just as we pick up on elements of their communication, they select part of our statement to integrate and use in their next statement. The material that clients use provides important information about how work is progressing. If clients integrate the direction, their response will reflect a change.

Often clients will demonstrate partial integration or will assume an unanticipated direction. When the ensuing client direction is counterintuitive, this often indicates that their integration of our input included unanticipated factors. As we observe and listen to client responses, we assess the new direction to determine its fit with client goals. If the direction will promote goal achievement, we can follow the clients' leads. If the new direction is problematic, we must find an opportunity to insert new direction into the material on the table.

Monitoring for Client Reactions

As clients assume the speaker position, it is important to observe their reactions to our statement. If they disagree or are uncomfortable with our response, most often their reaction will emerge in their nonverbal behavior. Although verbal reactions may accompany the nonverbal behavior, we cannot always count on clients feeling comfortable confronting our misinterpretations or mistakes (Dalenberg, 2004; Estrada & Holmes, 1999). Regardless of clients' open communication, practitioner mistakes *do* negatively impact the working alliance (Dalenberg, 2004; Hollands, 2004).

Given the potential harm to the working alliance, it is important that we remain watchful for misunderstandings and reactions when we insert direction. When we notice a reaction it is we need to explore the client response to resolve any possible problems (Muran et al., 2009). In this exploration, it is important to affirm and validate the client experience while taking responsibility for adjusting understandings and perspectives to reflect more accurately the client perspective (Binder, Holgersen, & Nielsen, 2008).

Adjusting the Practitioner Position

As we work with clients, it is very important to adjust our approach proactively to reflect their priorities and perspectives (Sutherland & Couture, 2007). As we monitor client responses, we continually reflect on the alliance and alter our approach to maintain a collaborative relationship. If our insertions of direction are consistent with client perspectives, progressive insertions continue to pursue a trajectory toward accomplishing client goals. Our adjustments build on observations of client progress and the material on the table as new steps are continually made through listening, assessing, inserting, and responding to client communications.

Transitional responding allows for fast adjustment because each directional insertion is minute. For this reason, we can easily change direction when client responses indicate a potential problem with the last insertion. Resolution occurs as the reaction is put back on the table with a query that can begin an exploration of the client response. Consider the next excerpt where a practitioner provided a change-focused nudge that was not well received by the client.

Case Example

This excerpt is taken from an exchange between a rehab counselor and client in a day program for developmentally disabled clients. The client is a male diagnosed in the mild range of developmental disabilities. He is scheduled for competitive employment and is anxious about the expectations that might be placed on him.

CLIENT: *I am not sure that I want to go to Kmart to work.*
PRACTITIONER: *What's the matter, don't you like making money?*
CLIENT: *(Pause): You know I like money.*
PRACTITIONER: *I do know you like money. I also noticed that you were quiet after I asked you about liking money, so I think maybe there is something else that makes you not want to go to Kmart.*
CLIENT: *Uhhm*
PRACTITIONER: *Tell me more about why you don't want to work at Kmart.*
CLIENT: *Well, it's not about money.*
PRACTITIONER: *You are right. I shouldn't have made that comment about liking money. I know you like money . . . so what's up that makes you want to stop the work placement?*
CLIENT: *I don't know.*
PRACTITIONER: *What is it that you don't know?*
CLIENT: *I don't know what to do.*
PRACTITIONER: *So you are not sure what will happen when you go to the work placement.*
CLIENT: *Yeah . . . I don't know where to go when I get there . . . I'll be lost.*
PRACTITIONER: *Would you like to take a trip to Kmart and look around as you are making up your mind?*
CLIENT: *Yeah.*
PRACTITIONER: *When we are there, would you also like to meet the supervisor and other people who are placed there?*
CLIENT: *Can we do that?*

Notice in the excerpt how the practitioner initially provided a flippant response to the client's communication. This response disrupted the collaborative relationship and threatened the alliance. The practitioner picked up on the potential problem and immediately put it back on the table to be explored. As the impact from the flippant response was discussed, the potential damage was resolved and the discussion resumed a helpful direction.

Establishing an Interactive Rhythm

As we use transitional responding, a back-and-forth rhythm is established. In the rhythm, we listen to the client communication, identify goal-related content, embed direction, and present new communication to the client. The client then picks up elements of our communication, integrates the new material, and responds back to us. This communication cycle continually repeats itself. The rhythmic quality of these exchanges establishes a relaxed atmosphere during the information exchange with each person taking turns putting material on the table and responding to the other.

Movement emerges in the back-and-forth communication as we pick up communicated material from the client and inject small parcels of direction in our response. With each successive client communication, the conversation moves in a goal-oriented direction. Because the inserted directive is small, each step in the rhythmic dance is subtle. If our understanding is off base or our direction does not fit for a client, he or she can correct us, allowing the direction to be shifted immediately.

The back-and-forth rhythm initially requires attention and effort because it is not always a natural method of communication. In regular social conversation, people tend to "download" their thinking. This occurs as a result of mental activity during conversation. When we listen to others share their experiences, our brain continually retrieves connections and memories (Buchanan, 2007; Daselaar et al., 2008). When we respond, we often begin to download this material, placing it on the table in a stream of memories and thoughts.

Constant downloading can dilute the direction in our conversations. Consequently, we must be focused during the back-and-forth exchanges. As clients respond to our statements, we must be prepared to pick up material quickly so we can respond rhythmically. If we wait too long, downloading is likely and a rhythm will be harder to establish.

Establishing the rhythm requires a balance. If we pick up on client content too quickly, we run the risk of cutting them off. However, if we wait too long, downloading patterns may set in, making it harder to establish a direction in the discussion. Achieving the balance requires us to observe clients. After they finish their responses, the client often pauses slightly. This is the moment when we start to move into our response.

To avoid seeming rude, it is helpful to signal that we are about to respond. Subtle signals can interrupt automatic downloading, helping to establish a rhythm. Two common methods signal that a response is upcoming:

1. *Leaning into the conversation.* As we lean toward clients, our body language indicates that we are about to respond. Clients often will wait for us to talk after we lean toward them.
2. *Gesturing into the conversation.* Often a slight raising of the hand or reaching slightly toward clients indicates that we are about to engage in the conversation.

After several exchanges, a rhythm will develop with minimal downloading and embellishments. We can then relax as a natural turn-taking pattern develops.

Managing Client Breaks in the Rhythm

There are times when clients will hesitate after we have made a response. Such moments of silence break the rhythm. As we learned earlier, sometimes a break may indicate that clients do not understand or agree with our last statement. However, breaks are also common after reflections or descriptions because clients must consider our statement prior to responding. Regardless, these moments often promote internal tension as we wait for a client response. If there is indication of a problem, we deal with the situation as described earlier. If the break involves a prolonged silence, we must approach clients gently.

Many new practitioners struggle with moments of silence and begin explaining their statement or downloading a rationale. This is not helpful for clients. It is important to allow clients to consider our statement as they formulate a response. Doing this requires us to avoid filling the silence to quell our internal tensions. When client silences break the rhythm, consider these actions:

- *Maintain focus on clients.* Rather than shifting focus to your internal anxiety, keep your focus on the clients and watch how they process your last statement.
- *Observe and wait.* Observe the clients' nonverbal communication to gain a sense of their experience of your response. Allow 5 to 10 seconds for clients to begin their statement.
- *Describe and prompt.* If a client appears not prepared to respond, describe your observations during the silence and invite him or her to clarify the silence.

Exercise 10.2: Proposing a Group Program

You are meeting with your supervisor about developing a group program for aggressive adolescent girls. You have identified the need and have a plan to take about 10 teen girls from the waiting list and start them in group work. Your supervisor is unsure and responds to your proposal saying, "This agency is a clinical agency. We provide therapy to people in need and do not engage in simple support. We are an important resource in this community."

1. Identify:
   a. Affective components:

   b. Thinking components:

   c. Relational components:

2. Construct a positioning solicitation question that will build on the agency's relationship in the community. Make sure the question solicits information about the agency's relationship that might be used for developing an argument in favor of your group proposal.

3. How might you use the affective and thinking themes to reinforce the relationship theme?

4. Your supervisor continues the discussion and eventually says, "I will not support any treatment approaches that are not clinically grounded. Many groups are more recreation or support rather than treatment." Identify how you can use the phrase "clinically grounded" to nudge the supervisor toward considering a group program.

5. Construct a question that uses your strategy to nudge the supervisor.

6. Your supervisor finally states, "The problem is that group work has always been in addition to case work in the agency. If we ran groups, who would do the paperwork and case management functions? It doesn't seem feasible." What thinking themes provide the most promise for movement toward accepting the group program?

7. Construct a response that can nudge the supervisor toward agreeing to consider the group program.

Socialization Challenges

Very few people naturally use transitional responding in their social relationships. We may use some elements of the skill when hinting about something we want, but it is not a natural way of responding. When listening to other people's problems, our brains often make multiple connections, retrieving thoughts and memories associated with similar situations.

We then construct solutions and download the solution for our friends. As we explain our thoughts about how our friends may solve the problem, we talk rather than engage in a back-and-forth exchange.

Helping exchanges easily can become convoluted if we begin sharing a solution. Be watchful of the following two indications that solution downloading is a risk.

1. We find ourselves monopolizing the conversation. As we begin to talk at length, the back-and-forth rhythm stops and often clients silently gaze in our direction.

2. Another clue to downloading is the frequent use of the word "and" to indicate that we have more to say. The word "and" signals that it is still our turn to talk. Consequently, clients will remain silent rather than engaging in the conversation.

Our friends manage to survive downloading, but the behavior is less useful in a helping relationship. If we download solutions and attempt to convince clients to comply, the solution is the product of our mental processes rather than an autonomous client decision. The lack of autonomy can interfere with client competency development. Furthermore, there is no assurance that our solutions will fit a client's situation. When we feel a pressure to act or solve a problem for our clients, our sense of urgency becomes a warning beacon of impending downloads. We then can shift our focus from our thinking to the client's communication so we can reengage and use transitional responding.

Integrating Transitional Responding

As our professional skills develop, transitional responding becomes second nature and part of our personal style. To enhance adaptation, it is important to practice monitoring themes when listening to a conversation. Initially, doing this involves simply identifying the themes in people's statements. As we become more efficient at identifying themes, our ability to respond develops as we link our questions, probes, reflections, and prompts to the material on the table.

As we develop transitional responding skills, it is important to practice using the full range of interactive skills: questions, reflections, descriptions, and prompts. These skills allow us to differentially pick up on other peoples' response system themes. The ability to quickly pick up will become a critical feature in influencing clients.

Case Example

The following excerpt is taken from a session in a community mental health center. The worker is meeting with a woman upset that, during her daughter's Christmas concert, her partner informed her that he was leaving. The woman is recovering from a depressive episode. She has one son and her partner has two daughters, all residing in the home. During times of tension, the man threatens to leave and sometimes becomes violent. The woman came into this meeting after attending the Christmas concert. Notice how the worker uses all of the interactive skills while shifting focus among the response systems and transitioning from exploration, positioning, and change promotion.

> CLIENT: *I was so angry, he has always treated me bad, but to tell me he was leaving at Colleen's [his daughter] Christmas concert was the worst thing he could do.*
>
> PRACTITIONER: *You told me about many of the things he has done. This must have been horrible to be considered the worst. What was it about telling you at the concert that made this worse than all of the other things you have suffered?*
>
> CLIENT: *It was just so humiliating.*
>
> PRACTITIONER: *Humiliating, was there someone watching?*
>
> CLIENT: *Yeah, Colleen's teacher. She is always taking Colleen's side against me. Tom talks to her about Colleen's needs and the two of them are forever ganging up on me.*
>
> PRACTITIONER: *So it often feels as though they are against you. When this happens, do you feel under attack as a mother?*
>
> CLIENT: *Damn right . . . I am attacked. They have no right to judge me.*
>
> PRACTITIONER: *What do those judgments say about you as a mother?*
>
> CLIENT: *They say I am no f#!ing good, that is what it says . . . but they just don't know what it is like. They always take her side.*

(continued)

(Continued)

PRACTITIONER: *You said they think you are not a good mother, but somehow there seems to be more to it . . . something to do with Colleen. How does she seem to benefit when they make these kinds of judgments about you?*

CLIENT: *She wins. She always wins by making me look bad. No matter how much I try to get her to tow the line, she connives and gets her dad on her side and then I lose every time.*

PRACTITIONER: *So it sounds like you are always the one who loses. Can you think of a time in your life when you felt like you were the winner?*

CLIENT: *Never, first it was my sister setting me up and now it's Colleen.*

PRACTITIONER: *Someone has always beaten you out, first your sister and now Colleen. When they beat you out and you lose, what do they win?*

CLIENT: *Love, respect . . . nobody ever treats me right. They always set me up so I don't get the love.*

PRACTITIONER: *So when you get set up by your sister or Colleen, it robs you of the love and respect you feel you deserve. How were you robbed today at the concert?*

CLIENT: *He told Colleen before the concert, and I know they told the teacher. Now I can't ever get her respect. No matter what I do, I just can't seem to win.*

PRACTITIONER: *It seems that all your life you have wanted love and respect but have felt powerless. It seems that somehow people are robbing you of your power over yourself and your feelings. Tell me about a time when you kept your power.*

Transitional Responding With Larger Client Systems

In larger systems, transitional responding must be concerned with system retention and achieving shared goals. Larger client systems must work collaboratively toward identified outcomes. This can be challenging because collaboration must occur between the practitioner and the system as well as among the system members. The addition of cross-member collaboration and relationships provide additional dimensions when using transitional responding. These dimensions can be challenging because we often approach interaction from a dyadic rather than a group understanding (Dunbar, 2009).

When we observe communication in larger systems, multiple members are putting material on the table. As we observe and consider the material, we must now determine whether the material is unique to the individual or shared among the membership. If the material is individual in nature, we deal with it as such. Doing this employs all of the transitional responding skills described throughout this section. However, often material on the table is common for multiple members. This shared material requires some additional consideration.

Larger Systems and Self-Regulation

In larger systems, communication patterns form early. These emergent patterns reflect the dynamics of the larger system (Pincus, Fox, Perez, Turner, & McGeehan, 2008). When practitioners work with larger systems, they must influence the systemic dynamics at the same time they work to influence individual members of the system. The way we respond to the system and its members is our core source of influence (Yamaguchi & Maehr, 2004). Consequently, we observe and work with the exchanges among the members to identify and influence important dynamics in the system. As we engage with larger systems, we must set a tone that allows members to share openly even if they disagree with us (Sani, 2005). Doing this helps establish a collaborative and open relationship between us and the system.

As we continue working with larger systems, our goal is to activate the collaborative forces in the systems so members can work together in meeting shared goals. To help the system members achieve their goals, we monitor system forces so we can intervene at the collective level. We also must intervene with individuals in the group. Two important forces require attention in larger client systems: cohesion and division. Cohesive forces help the group work together toward shared goals. Inherent in cohesiveness is a shared identity and sense of belonging together (Bauman, 2009). Divisive forces promote the disintegration of the system. Such forces are typified by individual rather than shared interests (Finn, 2008).

Divisiveness versus Cohesion

When monitoring the dynamics among system members, we constantly scan for indications of how the members collaborate. If members cannot commit to a shared vision or goal, personal aspirations and goals will interfere with achieving shared outcomes. As we work with larger systems, we monitor for dynamics that can enhance or diminish the collective ability to the system to accomplish its goals. Transitional responding with larger systems often requires us to pick up on dynamics associated with cohesion. As in other client systems, the forces can be understood in terms of the response systems.

The divisive and cohesion-building dynamics in the group can be understood using the same response system framework used earlier. Larger systems contain affective, cognitive, relational, and behavioral dynamics similar to individuals.

- *Affect.* It is important that larger systems maintain positive affect and identification among the members (Pollack, 1998). One of the important elements in larger systems is a social trust and openness among members (Bond & Ng, 2004; Phan, 2008). If members trust each other to perform their roles and prioritize collective goals, the system remains strong and viable. As trust erodes, the system begins to disintegrate, making it harder to achieve goals (Welch et al., 2005).

- *Beliefs.* When strong beliefs are held by one faction in the system, divisiveness can emerge as the beliefs tend to forge a separate identity within the group (Bauman & Skitka, 2009). It is important that members of the larger system are able to maintain different beliefs and values and have them respected by others (Smokowski, Rose, & Bacallao, 2001).

- *Relationships.* When there is competition among factions in a larger system, problems can emerge achieving shared goals (Saunders, 2008). This is most pronounced when the competing factions each has a unique shared identity that is attempting to assert influence on the larger system (Finn, 2008).

- *Behaviors.* To be successful, members of the larger system need to forgo individual strivings and invest in the goals of the larger unit (Beech & Hamilton-Giachritsis, 2005). The goals must be clear and accepted by members (van Andel, Erdman, Karsdorp, Appels, & Trijsburg, 2003). If individual strivings supersede the collective goals of the system, divisiveness may emerge (Finn, 2008).

Working with Divisive Energy

The greatest impediment to larger system success is divisiveness. When a larger system fragments into subgroups and cliques, it is very difficult to influence the system toward achieving shared goals. One of the most important elements to consider is the diversity within the system. Diversity can become divisive if it is not addressed and explored (Nishii & Mayer, 2009). Consequently, it is important to promote each member sharing experiences and perspectives. As these emerge in the system, we attempt to minimize the power of differences so common ground can be highlighted.

As we monitor larger system communications, it is important to scan for possible dynamics that might interfere with collaboration among members. If people appear hesitant to take risks or share, we need to identify these dynamics so they can be addressed (Beech & Hamilton-Giachritsis, 2005). It is important to identify and address dismissive and attacking communication (e.g., eye-rolling, whispering) in relation to other members (Bayazit & Mannix, 2003; Martin, Milne, & Scantlebury, 2006). When using transitional tracking to diminish divisive dynamics, we begin by describing the dynamic and then contrasting it to the shared goals. For example: "I noticed that whenever Tom shares his thoughts, Tammy and Linda roll their eyes back into their heads. Is this how we want the group to support each other?"

Working with Commonalities

The common ground and shared vision among the system members promote cohesion in the system (Burke et al., 2005). Consequently, as we listen to members communicate, it is important to monitor for commonalities among members. When we notice commonalities, we can use transitional responding to solidify shared concerns and engage the group in discussing how these common elements can be used toward communal goals (LeBaron & Carstarphen, 1997). For example: "I noticed that Roberto, Chalmers, and Anthony all mentioned that being diagnosed with a mental illness is something they want to hide from other people. This group is designed to start planning how we can change the system. What about the system makes us want to hide who we are?"

Sharing commonalities among members builds cohesion. Applying the commonalities toward shared goals helps focus the system on its goals. Notice how the transitional response used in the last example is very similar to the transitional responses used throughout the chapter. The only difference here is how the observation focuses on multiple people rather than on an individual. This type of response requires a higher level of observation as we must track the material each person places on the table and then identify similarities in the content themes.

Cultural and Social Considerations

It is important to consider the cultural and social contexts of clients as we implement any professional skill. Transitional responding, is heavily reliant on active listening. The process of listening varies from culture to culture, with each culture extracting unique elements from another person's statements (Flaskerud, 2007). Some cultural groups identify spiritual, affective, and beliefs as they listen; others limit comprehension to the communicator's content (Carbaugh, 1999; Cueva, 2006). Consequently, it is very important to ensure that communicated messages and priorities are consistent between practitioners and clients (Flaskerud, 2007; Stephens, Porter, Nettleton, & Willis, 2006).

Cultural patterns of listening are well entrenched. Some cultures can adjust to listening styles across cultures, but others remain consistent (White, 1989). When working with clients from diverse cultural backgrounds, the onus is on the practitioner to listen carefully and capture the subtle meaning of clients' communications. Transitional responding can help with this process by maintaining a focus on the client response systems and interrupting our predisposed patterns of downloading. The ability to alter the focus quickly is useful when cultural differences interfere with understanding or direction.

Monitoring Influence

As we listen to people from other cultures, it is important to understand that they think and identify as a member of a cultural community (Harrell & Bond, 2006). As such, they will have identifications and traits that overlap with others while still maintaining individuality. The uniqueness of ethnic group members will emerge as clients respond to our statements. If our meaning or direction fits well, clients will respond with ease. However, if we miss cultural nuances, hesitation or nonverbal reactions are likely. When these occur, transitional responding can be used to place the reaction on the table for exploration and correction.

Transitional responding can be useful for tracking the perspectives of ethnic groups because it allows us constantly to monitor the impact of our responses. Many argue that the best approach to interacting with ethnic minority groups is through active listening, observation, and participation (Paradise & Rogoff, 2009; Skultans, 2006). Participation is important because many ethnic groups learn more through partnering and engaging in a learning experience than through verbal instruction. These findings underscore the importance of pacing carefully in a step-by-step manner so potential misunderstandings can be corrected.

Critical Chapter Themes

1. Workers must be able to respond to client disclosures in a way that both validates the disclosure and helps move exploration to increased depth.

2. Based on perceived importance of the different themes, the practitioner selects one aspect of the package on the table to provide a foundation for direction.

3. Transitional responding links worker responses to the package that the client has placed on the table. Workers link their responses to the action, interaction, thinking, or affective themes in the client's last statement.

4. In moving toward increased depth and goal achievement, practitioners build on the client communication by inserting queries, solicitations for additional content, and nudges toward change.

5. Questions, reflections, observations, and prompts all can be used as transitional responses in moving the discussion in a direction without disengagement.

Online Resources

Communication and Conflict—self-improvement Web site: www.communicationand conflict.com/index.html

Livestrong.com—self-improvement Web site: www.livestrong.com/article/14657-improving-listening-skills/

Mindtools—a career development Web site with an emphasis on communication skills: www.mindtools.com/index.html

Recommended Readings

Jahoda, A., Selkirk, M., Trower, P., Pert, C., Kroese, B. S., Dagnan, D., & Burford, B. (2009). The balance of power in therapeutic interactions with individuals who have intellectual disabilities. *British Journal of Clinical Psychology, 48,* 63–77.

Nardone, G., & Salvini, A. (2007). The strategic dialogue: Rendering the diagnostic interview a real therapeutic intervention. London, UK: Karnac Books.

Parr, P., Boyle, R. A., & Tejada, L. (2008). I said, you said: A communication exercise for couples. *Contemporary Family Therapy, 30,* 167–173.

Schnitman, D.F. (2008). Generative inquiry in therapy: From problems to creativity. In T. Sugiman, K. J. Gergen, W. Wagner, & Y. Yamada (Eds.), *Meaning in Action: Constructions, Narratives, and Representations* (pp. 73–95). New York, NY: Springer.

Sutherland, O. (2007). Therapist positioning and power in discursive therapies: A comparative analysis. *Contemporary Family Therapy, 29,* 193–209.

Chapter 11
Motivating Change Within an Empathic Working Alliance

In the last chapter, we learned how to insert direction using interactive skills. Transitional responding allows us to pick up on the client communication, validate the client, and respond in a manner that can provide influence. This influence will be effective only when a client is motivated to act on our input. We cannot assume that a client enters the relationship highly motivated to change; nor can we assume that the client will remain consistently motivated as services progress. Consequently, this chapter explores methods of helping the client identify and capitalize on their inherent motivations for change.

Toward a Change Focus

As the practitioner and client focus on achieving goals, the helping relationship becomes a working alliance. In the working alliance, the practitioner and client collaborate with each other in an intense but goal-focused set of exchanges. The working alliance is critical for successful service. Success is based on three outcomes of the alliance:

1. Without the establishment of a working alliance, many clients withdraw from service (Samstag, Batchelder, Muran, Safran, & Winston, 1998).
2. A working relationship is associated with intervention receptivity and a commitment to work (Gaston, Marmar, Thompson, & Gallagher, 1988; Reandeau & Wampold, 1991).
3. The working alliance predicts positive service outcomes and goal achievement (Gaston, 1990; Mallinckrodt, 1993).

The engagement skills explored in Chapter 5 provide a foundation for the working alliance. Practitioners build on this foundation as service progresses by focusing the interaction and decisions on client goals. Inherent in this focus, the relationship must change from an authority relationship to an egalitarian partnership (Crits-Christoph, Demorest, & Connolly, 1990). The change in authority underscores the need to attend closely to the relationship while still focusing on the work. We cannot rely on practitioner authority; changes occur through the strength of the working alliance (Gelso & Hayes, 1998).

Socialization Challenges to Motivating Others

One of our critical roles throughout service is motivating clients to change. However, very few people have natural motivation-related skills. We lack motivating skills because there are very few developmental experiences where we learn to motivate other people. Although parents, teachers, friends, and coaches all provide encouragement, these people pay little attention to teaching us how to motivate others. There are two challenges inherent in our socialization experiences: our ambivalence about ambivalence and our tendency to cheerlead rather than motivate.

Ambivalence About Ambivalence
Most people are highly ambivalent about change. We all have payoffs in our current situations even if we are unhappy. We also may fear the unknown elements associated with change. At best, we experience the mild discomfort of newness. At worst, we undermine our change efforts because we become anxious. We seldom acknowledge and share ambivalence. When we do share any misgivings, others tend to point out the positive outcomes to help us tip the balance toward change.

If we assess our lifetime of decision making, we will likely find very few models for helping a person explore his or her ambivalence about change. Caregivers tend to provide emotional support, stress the positive, and tout the positive value of success rather than exploring emotional conflicts (Brown & Dunn, 1996; Cunningham, Kliewer, & Garner, 2009). Many support people deny the costs of change, keeping a focus on positive outcomes. The just-try-it approach is repeatedly modeled throughout our lives causing it to become our mantra as we attempt to motivate others to try something new. This mantra is a significant challenge when we are confronted by client hesitation and ambivalence about change.

Even in the helping professions client ambivalence is often misunderstood. Such hesitation traditionally has been called resistance in the helping professions and discussed as something to be overcome rather than explored (McKelley, 2007; Mitrany, 2009). The assumption typically is that there is a problem in the client that must be overcome before progress is possible. Newer conceptualizations suggest that ambivalence is a normal reaction to change, indicating client needs for understanding and exploration (Frankel & Levitt, 2009; Miller & Rollnick, 2004).

Given the newer understandings of people's change reactions, we cannot rely on our socialized skill sets to help people overcome ambivalence. Socialized skill sets are likely to stimulate an impulse to convince clients that they should attempt the change rather than exploring the full range of costs and benefits associated with change. We must avoid being argumentative, which elevates our power while simultaneously diminishing clients' autonomy.

Cheerleading Versus Motivation

Along with struggling with ambivalence, socialization agents tend to have a limited view of motivation. Authority figures most often promote action from a behavioral perspective rather than attending to people's feelings and visions for their lives (Nebbitt, Lombe, & Lindsey, 2007; Reynolds & Burge, 2008). The promotion of action often occurs through messages of "Go on . . . I know you can do it." The expression of faith in our ability denies our internal reality and hesitation. Notice how these approaches also keep the motivating source external rather than helping people use their internal motivations.

The tendency to promote action is more like cheerleading than motivation. The external force makes a lot of noise about our capacity and encourages us to act. There is no alliance; rather there is an external source expressing faith in us. If we rise to their expectations, they affirm us by saying things such as "I knew you could do it." Notice how even the accolades keep the focus external rather than acknowledging our internal realities.

The tendency to provide cheerleading, rather than exploring our motivating feelings and visions, sets a dangerous precedent. As we start to encourage and motivate clients, we will find ourselves wanting to express faith and cheer them on. Remember that doing this will shift the power away from clients and erode their autonomy. When we find this occurring, we interrupt the process and redirect our focus back to clients' motivating feelings and visions of change.

Motivation in the Working Alliance

Motivation is a fickle force in the alliance. Often clients' motivation fluctuates based on their pathway into service, practitioner responses, and current life situations. As client motivation ebbs and flows, it is our job to help them maintain the focus on their goals. As motivation declines, we explore the situation to rekindle commitment; when motivation is high, we support clients' inherent efforts. To fulfill such roles, first we must learn how motivation operates.

Service Entry, Autonomy, and Client Motivation

As clients enter service, the locus of motivation is an immediate concern. Some clients are motivated by internal forces while others really do not want services. The client's level of autonomy in the service decision sets the tone for initial motivation. Three common levels of autonomy are associated with a client's entry into the helping relationship.

1. *Voluntary clients.* Most voluntary clients enter service because they are in a situation that exceeds their capacity to respond. They want help mastering their situation and are seeking professional input and support to build their capacity. As they enter service, most voluntary clients are motivated to master their situation to make changes in their lives.

2. *Semivoluntary clients.* Many clients enter service because they are under some sort of stress that is limiting their options. Possibly they have exhausted their normal responses, and problems persist, or the problems may be slightly different, rendering past solutions ineffective. Most often these clients are motivated to bring the situation under their control to diminish stress, and many are open to making permanent changes.

3. *Involuntary clients.* Many clients would not enter service except for an authority figure insisting that they attend. This is true of many parents involved with child protective services, substance-using clients, violent clients, children and youth, and others whose behaviors negatively impact others. Involuntary clients are told by courts, romantic partners, parents, administrators, or others that they need to enter service and demonstrate changes. Many of these clients are not highly motivated because they feel that they have no choice.

When reviewing the pathways into service, it is easy to understand how different autonomy experiences are associated with various levels of motivation. Regardless of clients' entry paths, practitioners must work to help them identify reasons to be in service and access the inherent motivation in these reasons. This is a difficult task because some clients have yet to admit that they have a problem that would warrant involvement with a helping professional. It is very difficult to achieve a working alliance when clients cannot envision a reason for being in service.

Motivation and the Stages of Change

In the mid- to late 1970s, practitioners noticed that clients with lower levels of autonomy were unmotivated in the helping relationship. This pattern was particularly evident in situations where clients were engaged in problem behaviors that were disturbing to others yet often resulted in benefits to themselves. Professionals began experimenting with different approaches to help clients identify reasons to change. This movement gave rise to the transtheoretical model of change motivation (Prochaska, DiClemente, & Norcross, 1992). The stages of change model involves five phases:

1. *Pre-contemplative.* Clients have not yet considered that there may be a problem that warrants intervention and are not yet motivated to make changes in their situation.

2. *Contemplative.* Clients begin to consider that changes may be necessary but while acknowledging the possibility of changing, they are not yet ready to take action.

3. *Preparation.* Clients begin gathering information and identifying areas where change might improve their situation.

4. *Action.* Clients begins taking focused action to alter their situation and/or responses to their situation.

5. *Maintenance.* Clients have made changes that improve their situation and now must find ways to ensure that their environment can sustain the changes.

Within the stages of change, practitioners work with clients to help them discover their inherent motivation. As clients tap into their motivation we support them by helping them focus on mastering their problem situations (Ryan & Deci, 2008). Inherent in the stages of change, it is important to understand that motivation is not a linear constant force; rather, it is cyclical, ebbing and waning throughout the change process (Bados, Balaguer, & Saldaña, 2007; Prochaska et al., 1992).

Motivational fluctuations influence client investment in the working alliance. We must monitor our clients' level of motivation and be prepared to rekindle client motivation when they begin to second-guess or abandon their efforts to change. This is a sensitive balance because clients may legitimately change their goals outside of our awareness. This potential for change requires us constantly to allow clients to define their own direction while simultaneously supporting their change efforts (Ryan & Deci, 2008). To achieve this sensitivity, it is important to understand how people develop and maintain their motivation.

Toward Understanding Motivation

Motivation is multidimensional drawing on aspects of people's past experiences and their beliefs about the current situation. The aspects of past experiences that motivate individuals are based on life experiences, socialization, and personality traits. These converge with the individual's interpretations and beliefs about the situation, providing a motivational foundation. We must listen carefully to clients to understand how they understand and experience their situations. From this understanding we help clients master the situations (Ryan & Deci, 2008).

As we tune in to client motivation, we must understand two general dimensions: internal versus external motivation and affective orientation. These dimensions influence how people organize their approach to life. On the internal versus external dimension some people feel as if they are controlled by external forces and events while others believe that they influence their life situations. Affective orientation influences the feelings that motivate people. Every person is motivated by slightly different emotions. If we can understand a person's cognitive and affective orientation to the situation, we are better able to help the person maintain motivation to master the situation.

Internal Versus External Motivation

Some people are motivated primarily by internal forces while others focus on people and events in their environment. As people make changes in their lives, these motivational sources influence how they sustain energy in their attempts to change. People who are internally motivated measure success based on their internal strivings and possibilities (Ryan & Deci, 2006). However, many clients enter service with other sources of motivation. Many enter service anticipating rewards or responses from other people; others, to avoid negative consequences. Thus, there are diverse motivations for accessing professional services.

Internal versus external motivation is often called locus of control. The working alliance is influenced by the locus of control because a client's source of motivation may locate the desired outcomes outside of the working relationship. If the client's perceptions of success rely on another person's response, outcomes become harder to achieve when the other person is not an active participant in the working alliance (Ryan & Deci, 2006). Alternatively, when a client is motivated by internal strivings and a desire to change, the working alliance is easier to achieve because mastery in the situation becomes the desired outcome.

Internal versus external motivation provides a continuum of motivation. Ryan and Deci (2000) developed a theory known as self-determination theory that outlines five points along the continuum between external motivation and internal motivation. In reading these five points, notice how it is easier to maintain motivation over a period of time as the motivation becomes increasingly internalized.

1. *External motivation.* A person is motivated to change because external forces insist on the direction of change and outcomes.
2. *Partially internalized motivation.* The person agrees in principle with some of the outcomes and needs for change but is motivated primarily because others think he or she should change.
3. *Identified motivation.* The person agrees with the necessary outcomes and takes action to change. Commitment may diminish if the costs of changing increase.

4. *Value-consistent motivation*. The person wants to achieve the outcomes and has no meaningful ambivalence about the changes. Motivation may change from time to time, but the changes are not resisted.

5. *Intrinsic motivation*. The person has an inherent sense of direction and appropriateness in the situation. He or she wants to maximize potential and mastery in the situation.

Challenge of Externalization

When people enter service because of external forces, they often present arguments that indicate that they are somehow victimized in the situation and are not responsible for the events that preceded entry into service. The focus of most discussions remains on others, situations, and events outside of the people entering service, making it very difficult to achieve common ground or an alliance. We must be careful during these moments lest we collude with clients and focus an alliance on people who are not involved in service.

If we attempt to build a working alliance when clients are heavily externalized, we run the risk of triangulating ourselves into clients' situations. Once we fall into the triangle, we will spend our time trying to change the responses of people who are not engaged in service. Difficulties arise because the source of motivation is not accessible, causing energy to be directed outside of the service situation. We have two alternatives when such situations emerge: We can work with the client to include the other person in the working alliance, or we can help the client identify internal motivations that can support a working alliance.

Case Example

The chief executive officer from a women's shelter and a children's mental health agency began meeting because they felt that a third agency, the substance abuse agency, was not responsive to family needs. They met several times, then began asking for meetings with the governmental director who funded substance abuse services in the county. As they met with the governmental director, they argued that substance abuse services should have a systemic approach and service all family members. The director suggested that they arrange a meeting with the executives from the substance abuse agency to discuss programming ideas for the community. The community executives argued that the governmental director should be the one to plan the meeting so the substance abuse agency could see the importance of a family approach. The director stated that he might become involved later but community meetings should occur first.

In this example, the two community executives were attempting to achieve a working alliance with the governmental director to pressure a third agency executive to alter programming. The governmental director identified the externalized motivation and avoided setting up an alliance unless the third community agency was involved. If the three agencies approached him, then an internal motivation would be possible and an alliance could be achieved.

Indentifying Internalized Motivation

When clients are externally motivated, our work is to help them discover possible benefits associated with the change. Although we acknowledge that change will have some negative outcomes, such as having to assume responsibility or having to give up payoffs associated with old behaviors, we also help clients visualize reasons why change would enhance their lives. As clients begin to identify areas where change would be welcomed, they can begin to develop some internal motivation.

Even as we help clients achieve some internal motivation, it is important to understand that a lifetime of externalized interpretations will not change quickly. It is important to respect externalized beliefs and allow clients to share their perspectives. As we explore situations, however, we work with clients to find elements in the situation where they can achieve some control or internal motivation. Doing this balances in some internalized perceptions that we can focus on from time to time to help clients identify their capacity for autonomous control.

Case Example

A program working with men who assault their female partners continually struggled with the men presenting themselves as victims in their situation. They often deflected responsibility to their wives and the court system that insisted that they attend the program. The program director restructured the yearlong program into five phases with the first phase focused on achieving internal motivation. The men could not move out of the first phase until each had discovered 10 reasons why he belonged in the group. As the men worked together on this task, many of the externalized beliefs were challenged and internalized motivations were discovered.

In this example, notice how the restructuring of the program directly focused on the men's externalization and used the group members to help each other dismantle externalized beliefs. This process allowed the members to start identifying possible reasons for engaging in change efforts. After achieving and arguing the 10 reasons, they could move forward in the program. However, if they were not able to identify 10 reasons, they would be challenged within the program, and their probation officers would be advised that progress was not possible. Probation officers provided a focus for continued externalization, but the group and program worked to enhance internal motivation.

Affective Orientation

It is common for feelings to motivate people's behaviors. We all have certain feelings that motivate our approach to life. Even if we are not highly emotional people, we find that affective patterns emerge in our decisions and responses. Inside these patterns we find feelings that motivate. These are the feelings that cause us to tear up during movies or create distress when situations interfere with our patterns of living. These are also the feelings that motivate us to speak up, take action, or seek out specific types of people.

In this section we are interested in the underlying feelings that guide people's approach to living. These are the feelings that provide ongoing motivation. When we understand the feelings that motivate our clients, we can ally with these emotions when forming the working alliance. Forming an alliance with the natural motivating forces provides a foundation for the change efforts that are consistent with clients' normal systems of activation. We then draw on motivating emotions when clients are ambivalent about change.

Feeling Clusters

Feelings have been an enigma to social sciences for centuries because they tend to operate automatically while yielding powerful influences over human behavior. Feelings have been a topic of concern for philosophy, religion, and more recently psychology. Scientists historically have believed that feelings are vestiges of our primitive past where we instinctually responded to our environment (James, 1895). Thus, feelings have a long history of helping humans survive individually and as a species.

Four survival functions are associated with feelings: self-advancement, self-preservation, social connectedness, and mastery. Within each function there are clusters of feelings. To understand how feelings contribute to motivation, it is useful to consider the four clusters as a rough gauge to underlying feelings.

1. *Self-advancement.* Feelings associated with this function often are identified with procreation functions (Insel & Fernald, 2004). Such feelings are often competitive, seeking to elevate the person in the social group (Annesi, 2006; Arndt et al., 2009).

2. *Self-preservation.* Humans could not survive without an ability to identify and respond to dangerous situations (Eippert et al., 2007). Fear stimuli deemphasize critical thinking while amplifying the scanning functions to identify potential sources of danger (Etkin & Wager, 2007; Thielscher & Pessoa, 2007). Concurrent with scanning, our limbic systems are primed so we can either fight or run (L. A. Miller, Taber, Gabbard & Hurley, 2008). Self-preservation feelings are concerned with preserving a person's safety and security (Woody et al., 2005).

3. *Social connectedness.* Humans cannot survive without a connection to other humans (Tomasello, 1999). Our children are dependent for a very long time. Likewise, we must collaborate with others to meet our goals (e.g., securing food, shelter, etc.). Our brains respond immediately to facial expressions and nonverbal communication associated with our connection to other humans (Ashwin, Baron-Cohen, Wheelwright, O'Riordan, & Bullmore, 2007; de Vignemont & Singer, 2006).

4. *Mastery.* Mastery feelings promote autonomous functioning, allowing us to respond to environmental challenges. Doing this requires the focusing of the prefrontal cortex (Dehaene & Naccache, 2001), which allows us to formulate goals and plan our actions (Eisenberger & Lieberman, 2004; Spence & Frith, 1999). People motivated by this feeling cluster respond to challenges and tend to push limits to discover their capacities.

Identifying the motivating feeling can be difficult because behaviors and decisions can look identical but be motivated by different feelings. For example, a student motivated by self-advancement feelings studies hard and engages in multiple activities to ensure that she gets a good grade. She is motivated to stand out in the class and be noticed as an excellent student. Another student engages in similar study habits and learning activities but is motivated by mastery feelings. In contrast to the first student, this student loves learning and solving problems. She seeks the stimulation of mastering new concepts rather than standing out. A third student may engage in the same behaviors out of fear of disappointing a parent if she gets low grades.

Although all of these students engage in similar behaviors, they are motivated by very different feelings. We cannot identify the motivating feeling based on their behaviors. We must explore their thinking and rationales for their actions to begin to understand how they are motivated. As we learn about the reasons for their actions, we can begin to identify the feeling cluster that captures their motivation. As we learn which feeling motivates clients to take action, we can begin to work with their naturally motivating feelings to help them sustain their change efforts.

We identify motivating feelings by monitoring client themes. As clients describe their situation, affective, cognitive, interpersonal, and activity themes emerge. Embedded in these themes are the feelings that are most influential. We track patterns to themes to identify the most influential motivating feelings. Table 11.1 contains interpersonal and

Table 11.1 Identifying Feeling Cluster Themes

	Interpersonal Themes	Cognitive-Affective Themes
Self-preservation	Seeks support prior to taking a stand. Associates with powerful others. Has a consistent friend-group that are willing to support. Avoids confrontation when upset. Placates others when they are upset.	Wants people to act predictably. Nervous about upsetting others. Distrustful of others' intentions. Constant scanning for possible threats. Unwilling to take actions that might increase risk of failure.
Self-advancement	Compares self to others (attractiveness, intelligence, morals). Controls decisions in social groups. Surrounds self with weaker friends. Corrects and challenges others. Attacks or undermines competitors. Mentors weaker and less adequate.	Frequent need to assert superiority. Believes self is superior to others. Interprets others' successes as a threat to superiority. Disagreement experienced as a personal challenge. Needs a group of followers.
Social Connectedness	Maintains meaningful friendships for long periods. Engages readily with others. Accepts diversity and difference. Puts effort into maintaining connections with others.	Lives up to commitments. Commits fully to shared goals. Secure in relationship to others. Attends to other people's needs. Unsettled when apart from friends and family.
Mastery	Tests limits in an experimental way. Tends to pursue new directions. Approaches situations as challenges. Frequently engaged in goal-focused projects.	Inquisitive about how things work. Adopts a playful approach to challenges. Enjoys multiple types of challenge. Enthusiastic about new projects.

cognitive-affective themes that can help identify the feeling clusters. As we identify clients' feeling orientations, we have a better sense of what they hope to achieve.

Primary Feelings and Secondary Emotions

As we monitor activity, interaction, and cognitive themes, sometimes it is a challenge to identify the underlying feeling. This is because feelings often are covered by layers of thinking. The concepts of primary feelings and secondary emotions help distinguish between actual feelings and the combination of feelings and thinking. Primary feelings tend to occur outside of cognitive awareness. These feelings are visceral sensations evoked as neuro-transmitters begin to trigger bodily responses (Russell, 2003). As we notice the sensations, we try to understand our situation. Secondary emotions involve the subsequent blend of feelings and thinking (Flemke & Allen, 2008; Russell, 2003).

When feelings come to conscious awareness, our thinking shapes the emotional experience, creating secondary emotions. For example, anger is a secondary emotion that may have vulnerability, powerlessness, shame, or other primary feelings underneath. Anger allows us to focus on a person or situation as a target for actions (Carver & Harmon-Jones, 2009; Zurbriggen & Sturman, 2002). As thinking begins to change the emotional experience, the intensity of emotion can be amplified or attenuated by the thoughts evoked in response to the emotion.

Table 11.2 shows three common primary feelings associated with the feeling clusters. Notice how very similar primary feelings and secondary emotions exist within the various feeling clusters. To identify the primary feelings that are motivating clients, we explore the situation, client thoughts, and secondary emotions to gather hints about the underlying primary feeling. Through the exploration, we can begin to understand client motivations.

Emotional Investment

Feelings are often illogical because the emergence of feelings often results in tuning down critical thinking functions. Many people know that their activities are harmful, yet they

Table 11.2   Selected Primary Feelings and Associated Secondary Emotions

Feeling Cluster	Primary Feeling Poles	Secondary Emotions
Connectedness	Discounted → Validated	− Objectified, invisible, betrayed, humiliated, victimized + Important, right, valued, acknowledged, respected
	Insular → Intimate	− Lonely, unlucky, vulnerable, insignificant, indifferent + Lucky, horny, dependent, close, happy, important
	Alienation → Connected	− Alone, insignificant, ambivalent, unrooted, unwanted + Engaged, included, secure, wanted, valued
Mastery	Powerless → Masterful	− Angry, frustrated, overwhelmed, impotent, dependent + Competent, skilled, unencumbered, independent
	Inadequate → Competent	− Angry, impotent, incapable, envious, criticized, judged + Expert, impervious, confident, able, respectable
	Manipulated → Autonomous	− Duped, dependent, led, contingent, out of the loop + Free, in control, spontaneous, unfettered, carefree
Self-Preservation	Anxious → Secure	− Fearful, worried, threatened, persecuted, at risk + Impervious, safe, familiar, supported, carefree
	Hopeless → Hopeful	− Victimized, disadvantaged, futile, frustrated + Optimistic, lucky, blessed, happy, carefree
	Despair → Elation/Joy	− Depressed, insignificant, desperate, unlucky, cheated + Lucky, blessed, on a roll, omnipotent, worthy
Self-Advancement	Repulsive → Attractive	− Ugly, unattractive, marred, unwanted, disgusting + Beautiful, handsome, noticed, envied, coveted
	Shame → Superiority	− Embarrassed, humiliated, judged, guilty, worthless + Superior, attractive, confident, omnipotent, infallible
	Flawed → Ideal	− Insignificant, wrong, humiliated, undesirable, worthless + Self-righteous, superior, omnipotent, significant

continue to engage in high-risk health behaviors such as smoking, substance abuse, tanning, overeating, and gambling (Arndt et al., 2009). This is because feeling-level processes are governing the behaviors. In its most extreme form, emotionally governed people perpetually react to their emotions with little concern about logic or rationale (Bueno, Weinberg, Fernández-Castro, & Capdevila, 2008; Wood, Heimpel, Manwell, & Whittington, 2009). Concurrent with problem behaviors, unregulated feelings are associated with mental health problems (Trosper, Buzzella, Bennett, & Ehrenrich, 2009). Many argue that good mental health is contingent on understanding, regulating, and harnessing feelings (Izard, Stark, Trentacosta, & Schultz, 2008).

Most often, motivating emotions operate as a subtle influence. They underlie daily decisions and patterns of responding with little conscious awareness. This influence is different from overwhelming moments of emotional agitation. Strong emotional reactions often occur in response to an event. Our motivating feelings tend to operate without triggering events: They simply form patterns of action and interaction. We have belief systems and values consistent with our feelings, providing a seamless system of response. When feelings are triggered, our thinking activates, allowing us to integrate and respond to situations.

Tendencies of Balance

Within the systems of responding, some people are more emotional while others regulate the emotional influences through their thinking. Most people strike a balance between thinking and feeling; very few people are totally emotional or totally logical. The balance between affective and logical processes mediates the power of emotional experience, allowing emotions to be focused and used (Thompson, Lewis, & Calkins, 2008; Trosper et al., 2009). It is our higher-order thinking and associational processes that moderate our emotional experiences, allowing for reflection, insight, and applying the emotion (Haga, Kraft, & Corby, 2009; Izard et al., 2008; Thompson et al., 2008).

As we apply our mental processes to regulate feelings, our locus of control (internal versus external) influences our actions. People who are heavily externalized constantly react to situations in their environment. They seldom establish personal goals or plans; rather, they favor a reactive manner of living. Similarly, people who are heavily internalized often ignore relationships. They are driven by internal processes, which are often an enigma to others. Extreme orientations toward locus of control and thinking-feeling tend to create problems. Mental health tends to require balance in affective processing and locus of control.

As we create balance, a pattern of motivation emerges. Figure 11.1 shows a circumplex model of motivation depicting the blending of the four polar extremes of motivation sources. When reviewing the figure, notice how movement between the four extreme points provides a blending of influences. Points of blending are indicated to illustrate possible trends that occur with different levels of balance. Personal patterns at each point will vary depending on feeling cluster (self-preservation, self-advancement, mastery, or connectedness) and personal experiences.

Accessing Motivating Emotion

We have already learned that clients are motivated by their feelings when entering service (Stein, 1995). The initial motivating affect is an important consideration because it is central to engaging clients and establishing focus. To help clients, we must understand and enhance their motivation to improve their situations (Nordbø et al., 2008). The level of client motivation predicts their successful completion of intervention (Huppert, et al., 2006; Velicer, Norman, Fava, & Prochaska, 1999).

Integrating Motivating Feelings Into the Alliance

As we meet with clients, we tune in to their unique blend of thinking and feeling that forms the motivational system. With voluntary clients, their motivational system is instrumental in

Figure 11.1

Circumplex Model of Motivation

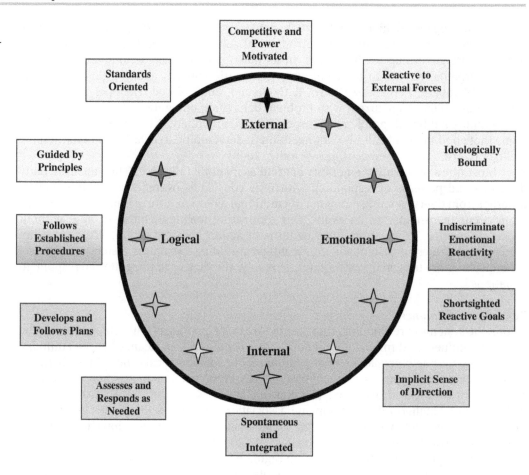

their decisions to enter service. With many other clients, patterns of motivation tend to emerge from the patterns of action and interaction surrounding the entry into service. Regardless of the entry decision, we detect motivation as clients describe their situations and how they respond to life events.

Motivation in the Early Alliance

As we glean information about clients, we form a working alliance by using their desires and motivation to form intervention goals and service plans (Ridgway & Sharpley, 1991). We quickly partner with clients' inherent motivation to promote this working alliance (Harris, 1996; Sommers-Flanagan & Sommers-Flanagan, 1997). When formulating goals, we use the motivating feelings to help frame the goals, suggest appropriate interventions, and negotiate roles that can maximize clients' inherent motivations.

Accessing motivating affect can be challenging with clients who did not independently elect to enter service. When working with nonvoluntary clients, we initially help them identify a reason to be in service. Even court-referred clients have motivations that can be identified. For example, they may want to avoid prison. If we begin with the reality that their motivation is to avoid punishment, we can explore the actions guaranteed to bring on the punishment (Slonim-Nevo, 1996) and build an alliance to help gain control of those behaviors. Such exploration must occur early in service. If it is delayed, there is a risk of colluding with clients.

To begin working with client motivations, we need to understand and enhance their motivating feelings. Two common elements emerge as we help clients change their situation. These affective elements shape how clients' innate motivations emerge and energize their change efforts throughout service. By understanding these elements of motivation, we can respond appropriately as client motivations ebb and flow during their time in service. The affective elements include:

Case Example

A man was referred to a substance abuse program due to persistent public drunkenness and driving under the influence. He came into the program to avoid doing time but initially did not want to attend. The practitioner resisted the temptation to use the legal mandate and instead began exploring why he had chosen the program over jail time. The man outlined a solid rationale, explaining that he had a job, a wife, and his own apartment. The practitioner explored these elements of his life and asked what might happen if he were to go back to court. The man explained he would lose everything and would have to do time. The practitioner shifted exploration to the man's connections and motivation to keep his marriage and possessions that drinking was putting at risk. From this motivation, the man was able to commit to working on his drinking behavior.

- *Allying with motivating feelings.* The first affective element focuses on the feeling sets that traditionally motivate clients. Each client will have different feelings that motivate him or her to take action. Knowing the influential feelings helps us tap into a client's motivation.
- *Developing affective tension.* The second affective element involves emotional tension that is generated when clients reflect on themselves in their situations (Dijkstra & Dijker, 2005). The tension emerges from the difference between the current situation and their desired outcomes. This tension between "what is" and "what is desired" helps motivate action.

Allying With Motivating Feelings

As we seek to motivate clients toward change, we help them access their own motivating feelings. Doing this requires us first to tune in to their descriptions of their experiences so we can identify the feeling clusters that are operational in client situations. When we identify the client motivations, we use their affective patterns to help us forge the change alliance. It is this affective unity that keeps our efforts attuned to client desires.

Finding the Motivation Link

When exploring situations for motivating feelings, it is sometimes useful to identify whether the motivating affect lends itself best to personal or social situations. Connectedness and mastery feelings tend to provide the most fertile ground for promoting change in interpersonal situations (Conroy, Elliot, & Pincus, 2009; Okada, 2007). In contrast, self-preservation and self-promotion strivings have a personal orientation that extend better to self-oriented goals (Anessi, 2006; Aron et al., 2005; Conroy et al., 2009). Given these tendencies, it may be useful to scan for general orientation themes first.

As we reflect on the thinking and interpersonal themes in client descriptions, we begin to identify the affective themes that motivate clients. These themes are embedded in client stories as they share information about current and past situations. We scan the stories as clients share their thoughts and feelings. We also listen to their interpersonal and behavioral responses to situations. Through this scanning, we monitor for themes, identify secondary emotions through the thinking themes, and eventually begin to appreciate the primary feelings that motivate the client. To help with identification, Table 11.2, presented earlier, provides a sample of secondary emotions and primary feelings associated with the feeling clusters.

Working With Affective Polarities

You will notice in Table 11.2 that the emotions and feelings are presented in a polarized manner. This is because affective experience can either be positive or negative. Whether clients speak of negative or positive affective experiences, we can begin to identify their most powerful feelings by the feeling frequency. The primary feelings that cycle through multiple stories are likely to be the feelings that can help motivate clients.

The feelings that are frequently referenced by clients suggest emotional investment in that feeling cluster. We can then assume that these feelings have higher likelihood of motivating clients toward change. When we attempt to motivate clients, we often want to use the positive primary feeling because it helps to highlight desirable outcomes rather than negative memories. To ensure that our observations are accurate, we describe our observations so clients can affirm their investment in specific feelings. As clients consider the influence of certain feelings in their lives, we increase their awareness of their feeling processes, allowing these feelings to become an ally in our change efforts.

We must be careful when clients continually revert to negative affective poles. When clients elect a negative focus, it may indicate an attempt to divest rather than continuing to invest in the situation. Many of us have decided to end a romantic relationship at some point in our lives and began by focusing on the negative elements. When clients continue to adopt a negative focus, it may have implications for the goals and direction of service.

Motivation and Strength-Based Practice

When we ally with clients' motivating affect, it is important to avoid pressuring clients. Feeling autonomous and in control promotes positive motivation (Downie, Mageau, & Koestner, 2008; Thøgersen-Ntoumani & Fox, 2007). People tend to perform better, and retain motivation, when they feel that their activity is of their free will rather than compelled by others (Adie, Duda, & Ntoumanis, 2008; Gagné, 2007). Autonomy and confidence are associated with learning and mastery motivation (Hänze & Berger, 2007; Lopez, 2008).

Concurrent with feelings of autonomy, motivation is enhanced when people feel competent in the situation (Mouratidis, Vanseenkiste, Lens, & Vanden Auweele, 2009). As people develop a sense of competence, they begin to believe that they can accomplish their goals, which results in an increased motivate to take action (Adie et al., 2008; Nordbø et al., 2008; Thomas & Barron, 2006).

When working with clients, we try to maintain a focus that promotes a maximum level of client autonomy. This is consistent with the ethical principles outlined in Chapter 2 and also enhances client motivation. It is important to avoid arguing or pressuring clients because that will erode their natural motivation (Miller & Rollnick, 2002; Ryan & Deci, 2008). The skills covered in the last five chapters can be used in lieu of pressuring to ensure that clients are permitted opportunities to develop their own directions.

Motivation and the Social Context

Along with autonomy strivings, interpersonal connectedness produces positive affect and motivation (Downie et al., 2008). Humans have social needs that motivate them to form and maintain relationships with other humans (Patrick, Knee, Canevello, & Lonsbary, 2007). This sense of connection is associated with motivation for success (Moller, Elliot, & Friedman, 2008) and for recovery (Engström & Söerberg, 2007).

When working with clients, it is important to understand their relationships in order to identify connections that can help motivate change. It is possible to work with the web of relationships that surround people to alter the relationships and generate increased motivation (Garrett & Landau, 2007). This is a core principle in many evidence-based practices such as multisystemic therapy, family psychoeducation, family conferencing, and wraparound services. This is also a premise in most family-based interventions.

The sense of connectedness is most often a positive motivating feeling. However, connectedness is also a feeling that creates vulnerability because people must consider others during decision making. If people are motivated by self-advancement, they often ignore social connections so individualistic strivings can be maximized (van Kleef et al., 2008; Zurbriggen & Sturman, 2002). Consequently, we must consider the motivating feeling clusters and insert issues of social connection in a manner consistent with client strivings.

Developing Affective Tension

The second affective element associated with client motivation involves developing cognitive tension between the current situation and a client's desired outcomes. Motivation for change requires some self-evaluation where clients identify an alternative vision for their life

(Dijkstra & Dijker, 2005; Marshall et al., 2009). When practitioners explore the vision for change, clients notice a difference between the change vision and their life situation (Aarts, Custers, & Marien, 2009; Principe, Marci, Glick, & Ablon, 2006). As the discrepancy between the alternative visions for living is explored, motivation to change emerges (Riediger & Freund, 2008).

The two visions of their life situations are somewhat explicit for clients who enter service having already evaluated their situation and compared it to how they want to live. Other clients enter service with less clarity, which requires the practitioner to help them develop an alternative vision of how their life might be lived. This exploratory process provides detail to client wishes for themselves. As the vision becomes clear, clients can assess how closely their patterns of living approximate their "change" vision. At this point clients are often considered at a contemplative stage of change.

Dual Visions and Change Energy

Developing tension between a status quo and change vision is a common theme among intervention models. Michael White (1986) and practitioners associated with narrative approaches speak of exploring the differences to promote change. Cognitive practitioners use the term "cognitive dissonance." Regardless of the theoretical underpinnings, findings indicate that when people's values and desires are inconsistent with their behaviors, they first experience tension and then attempt to resolve the difference (Festinger, 1957).

The key for using two visions to generate change motivation is to focus on client values and motivating affect (Hart et al., 2009). When these elements diverge from client actions, the disconnection creates motivation to diminish the differences (Vinski & Tryon, 2009). The inherent power in the two visions is that divergence promotes emotional energy, which in turn generates a desire to reduce the discrepancy. Through exploring the differences between the two visions, we help clients generate motivation to change.

Motivating Cognitive Change

When faced with discrepancies between values and actions, many people begin by altering beliefs. When we find that our espoused beliefs diverge from our actions, it is easier to question the beliefs because our actions are more concrete and undeniable. For this reason, altering beliefs becomes the path of lesser resistance. We tend to distort or alter the beliefs slightly to increase the congruence between what we believe and how we act (Rasmussen, 2003). The attitudinal adjustment associated with dissonance reduction can result in long-term tension reduction (Séneméaud & Somat, 2009).

When we want to challenge beliefs and thinking, we use dissonance to highlight client discrepancies. Typically doing this involves first highlighting client beliefs or values. We then juxtapose a description of their incongruent behavior to generate the dissonance. The goal is to place both elements in contrast to each other so clients experience a dilemma and desire to resolve the differences. We explore the dilemma to help clients rethink their beliefs and alter them in a manner congruent with their behavior.

We must be subtle when highlighting the discrepancies between client behaviors and beliefs because this is a form of confrontation that can engender defensiveness. Many people will distort or deny their beliefs or alter perceptions to create the illusion of congruence (Rasmussen, 2003; Williams, Nesselroade, & Nam, 2007). This is especially true if the person's beliefs are rigidly maintained (Williams et al., 2007). If we are descriptive when highlighting the behaviors, we can maintain a value-free observation. This may prevent feelings of scrutiny and judgment that might promote defensiveness.

Motivating Behavioral Change

When a person's beliefs are tightly held, dissonance increases rapidly with the awareness of incongruent behavior, and this dissonance inhibits attitudinal adjustment (Starzyk, Fabrigar, Soryal, & Fanning, 2009; Stone & Fernandez, 2008). Consequently, people with strongly held values often alter behavior to become consistent with their beliefs. Changes in behavior also to yield subsequent thinking changes after the behavior change is enacted. Research has found that when people restrain themselves from engaging in a behavior that yielded positive outcomes, the value of the behavior diminishes

(E. Harmon-Jones, C. Harmon-Jones, Fearn, Sigelman, & Johnson, 2008; Veling, Holland, & van Knippenberg, 2008).

When we seek to motivate behavioral change, first we must determine the strength of the motivating affect and beliefs. When clients have a long history or identity investment in their values, often we can rely on the values and affect to motivate change. We promote the dissonance using the same juxtaposition of values and behavior to highlight the discrepancy for clients. However, when working with strong values, we must ensure that we validate the values in clients as we put them on the table. Doing this affirms the clients prior to presenting the challenge. The affirmation allies us with clients values as we describe the discrepant behaviors.

Managing Ambivalence

Many models of intervention operate on the assumption that clients enter service with high levels of voluntariness and motivation. However, when we discussed the pathways into service, it was clear that some clients do not want to come into service. Clients with little choice often are displeased about having professionals enter their life. Although these clients feel forced to enter service, there will be diversity in their readiness for change. Some may be precontemplative and unable to identify problems, yet many will be contemplative or even ready to take action.

We cannot rely on uniform motivation among our clients. Even clients who elect to enter service without coercion may have mixed feelings because the change process is uncomfortable. In contrast, even a dismal situation is comfortable in its predictability. At best change is unsettling, and at worst it may seem terrifying for clients. Consequently, ambivalence is a normal response when a client enters the helping relationship.

To ensure that clients are committed to change, we explore their feelings of ambivalence (Binder, Holgersen, & Nielsen, 2008b). Such exploration is a central tenet to new evidence-based approaches to intervention such as motivational interviewing (Miller & Rollnick, 2002). Motivational interviewing recognizes that ambivalence is natural. For that reason, exploring the ambivalence is considered an important element in treatment. Two critical elements are involved in exploring the ambivalence: assessing costs/benefits and promoting autonomy.

Costs Versus Benefits

To respond to ambivalence, we explore the costs and benefits of change. Doing this requires us to understand the two visions that underlie clients' cognitive dissonance. Earlier we explored the current situation (status quo vision) and contrasted that to client hopes and desires associated with services (change vision). The differences between these two visions provide dissonance and affective energy to promote change. These same differences promote ambivalence.

Ambivalence emerges as clients consider the package of costs and benefits associated with each vision (McEvoy & Nathan, 2007). Clients already know how to survive the status quo condition. Although they may dislike the status quo costs, they have developed habits for managing those costs. To overcome this comfort level, outcomes in the change vision must be desirable enough to justify the disruption involved in changing (Alessandri, Dacheville, & Zentall, 2008). Concurrently, clients must accept the costs involved in change.

Figure 11.2 depicts the costs and benefits associated with change. When reviewing the figure, notice on the left that there are clear costs involved in changing. Some changes are affective, some cognitive, and others focus on the client actions. Along with the costs, clients will simultaneously derive benefits from changing. By assessing the balance of costs and benefits, clients are put in a position where they can make an informed decision about engaging in change.

As we help clients manage their ambivalence, it is very important to avoid overselling the change condition. Research suggests that people have a tendency to overvalue their positions when beginning a negotiation process (Bendersky & Curhan, 2009). If we overvalue the potential changes and use them to convince clients to accept the change vision, client autonomy is undermined (Miller & Rollnick, 2004).

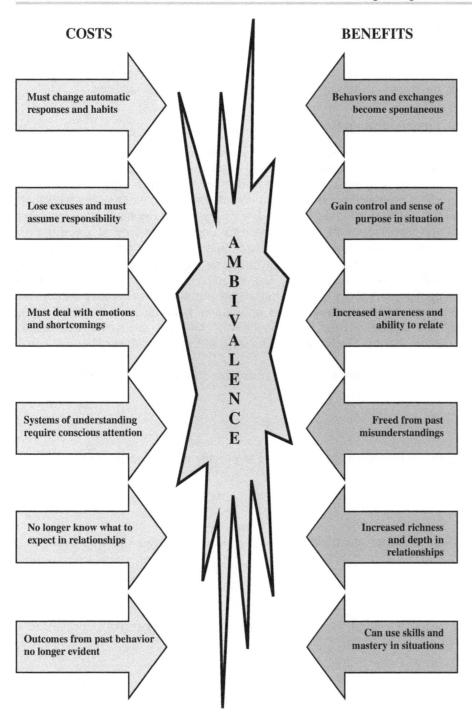

Figure 11.2

Ambivalence about Change

COSTS

- Must change automatic responses and habits
- Lose excuses and must assume responsibility
- Must deal with emotions and shortcomings
- Systems of understanding require conscious attention
- No longer know what to expect in relationships
- Outcomes from past behavior no longer evident

AMBIVALENCE

BENEFITS

- Behaviors and exchanges become spontaneous
- Gain control and sense of purpose in situation
- Increased awareness and ability to relate
- Freed from past misunderstandings
- Increased richness and depth in relationships
- Can use skills and mastery in situations

Promoting Autonomy

For ambivalence to resolve itself, clients must feel that they have choices. This sense of options decreases feelings of being pressured to change. While they may still have people outside the helping relationship who demand changes, in the working alliance it is important to avoid siding with people who have a selfish investment in promoting change. In our relationship with the client, we promote a sense of freedom tempered with an understanding of costs and responsibilities. This allows the client to explore and consider multiple options.

Promoting autonomy is often challenging for the client who may want us to take charge of the changes and tell them what to do. Autonomy can be frightening for clients because the choices they make have consequences. Knowing that they alone are responsible for the consequences often feels daunting for clients. This is especially true for heavily externalized clients who hinge most decisions on their relationships with others.

As we support clients with the autonomy struggles, we must often redirect the client to consider their desires as they continually reflect on how others might respond to decisions. This is sometimes difficult as clients may shift attention away from themselves. Such shifts are most likely to occur when making important decisions. In response we affirm the importance of their relationships and then support an autonomous decision.

Exercise 11.1: Communicating Motivation

You are employed by a mental health agency and are meeting with a woman diagnosed with schizophrenia. When not on her medication, she hears voices talking to her and becomes paranoid. She has been working in a sheltered workshop and living in a group home for the past five years. This woman has not missed a day of work since entering the workshop. However, she has a pattern of doing well for a while, going off her medication, and then regressing. When workshop staff provide feedback on how the lack of medication is influencing her job performance, she is able to reorient herself to take her medication. The woman wants to live in her own apartment and get married. Her boyfriend from the workshop entered competitive employment last year. The two are becoming serious about their relationship. They talk about marriage but cannot afford to marry because she does not make much money in the workshop. The only thing standing in her way of living independently and getting married is her inability to take her medication consistently and obtain a competitive job. She has been doing well, and you want to keep her motivated.

1. Using the stages of change model, what stage has this woman achieved?

2. What elements in this woman's life seem to provide motivation for her?

3. Given these elements, identify feelings that appear to motivate this woman.

4. Review the list of feelings, and identify the associated feeling clusters (connectedness, mastery, fear, etc.).

5. Using the motivating feelings identified earlier, how might these be used to help the woman achieve her goals?

6. What two visions (status quo and change visions) can you use to help motivate this woman to begin working toward competitive employment?

Enhancing Motivation through the Working Alliance

Our ability to access clients' motivating feelings and use two visions to generate motivation provides a foundation for helping clients change. However, it is our ability to respond to clients in interaction that provides the context for change. We cannot simply develop the visions and highlight motivating feelings and believe our work is done. Rather, we remain engaged in back-and-forth discussions of situations. It is our responses during these discussions that support clients in their efforts to change.

Inherent in the working alliance, we must ensure that clients remain in control of their goals and direction. If clients experience self-direction and autonomy in the alliance, they are better able to maximize their situations and achieve well-being (Sheldon, Ryan, Deci, & Kasser, 2004). Doing this requires us to avoid pressuring and arguing for clients to change (Miller & Rollnick, 2004). Rather, our responses must tap into their motivating feelings to keep their desire for and visions of change present during our interactions. The combination of autonomy and support promotes mastery rather than indenturing clients to follow our direction.

Three core skill sets build on client motivation while establishing a working alliance. Some of the skill sets promote an egalitarian relationship focused on achieving goals. Others maintain focus and direction in the relationship. All of the skill sets use the skills outlined in the early chapters of this book. The individual skills described throughout the text are now combined to achieve specific effects in the working alliance. The three critical skill sets are:

1. *Deepening the alliance.* As we work toward client goals, we must attend to the working alliance. Doing this builds on our tuning in and empathy skills as we observe and adjust how we work to mediate the impact on clients.

2. *Seeding change.* Helping clients change while respecting their autonomy requires us to avoid telling them what to do; rather we work with their motivations and perceptions to plant the seeds of change so they can take root.

3. *Providing focus.* To ensure a professional relationship, practitioners must retain client goals and desires for change as a focus in professional exchanges. There are times when we must redirect the focus of discussions to ensure that our interactions are promoting client goals.

Deepening the Alliance

Once established, the working alliance must be nurtured to retain its positive focus and goal direction. Because it is based on goals as well as a relationship, the alliance tends to shift and change over the course of service (Allen et al., 1990; Crits-Christoph et al., 1990). Shifts in the alliance demands the active attentiveness of the practitioner to monitor and adjust the working relationship throughout the delivery of service.

Workers use two basic responses to deepen the working alliance: offering support/feedback and using self-disclosures. If used well, each of these response types can advance both the relationship and the work toward client goals. When nurturing the relationship, the practitioner must be careful to ensure that the alliance also maintains the goal focus.

Strategies for nurturing the alliance require high levels of self-awareness and control by the worker. Most of our communication skills develop in our personal relationships, where we freely share personal information. Such sharing deepens the relationships. With the working alliance, we must resist the impulse to rely on such well-developed methods and instead must filter relationship-nurturing interactions through the professional purpose of the relationship. This means that practitioners will have to limit disclosures and discussions based on the purpose and goals of the working relationship.

Sharing Feedback and Support

When attending to the working alliance, it is helpful to maintain a positive relationship with clients (Chang, 1994; Patterson & Forgatch, 1985). Positive relationship elements include providing support while empowering clients. As clients begin to work toward their goals, support increases feelings of confidence and mastery, which maintains their motivation to work (Nakamura & Tagami, 2008). As we actively support, encourage, and clarify client situations, a collaborative working relationship develops; teaching and confronting, however, decrease collaboration (Allen et al., 1996; Bischoff & Tracey, 1996; W. R. Miller et al., 1993; Najavits & Strupp, 1994; Patterson & Forgatch, 1985).

Another helpful element in maintaining a positive alliance is sharing perceptions of the relationship, client strengths, and quality of work being done (Chang, 1994; Henry, Schacht, & Strupp, 1990). In the sharing of perceptions, it is important to be genuine. The client must be able to recognize him- or herself in the feedback to strengthen the working alliance (Omer, 1997). If practitioner feedback is inconsistent with client self-perceptions, the practitioner will be viewed as deceitful or manipulative.

We must be prepared to support negative and positive client responses, including possible negative feelings about our own performance. Practitioners must hear and validate such feelings and expressions (Safran, Crocker, McMain, & Murray, 1990). Doing this often is difficult because negative feelings create defensive reactions. High levels of self-awareness and control are needed to support clients during these moments of service.

When providing feedback to clients, we go through a four-step process to ensure feedback is accurate and targeted on client goals. Most of the four steps occur internally as we reflectively think about the feedback and predict the potential impact of sharing with clients. The four steps include:

1. *Maintaining a nonjudgmental stance.* The first task is to ensure that the feedback is not a judgment of clients. Even positive judgments, such as praise, are judgments that can disempower clients (Allen et al., 1996). Consequently, we need to avoid evaluative words, such as "good," that communicate practitioner judgment. Enthusiasm should replace such expressions.

2. *Using observations.* When sharing feedback, it is important to base our comments on observations rather than conclusions. Consequently, practitioners must be able to identify specific actions or responses that illustrate some strength or competency that can promote goal achievement.

3. *Describing the observations.* When workers describe their observations, it is easier for clients to see themselves in the feedback and visualize the situations.

4. *Reflecting the progressive meaning of the observation.* The final element of feedback is a reflection to highlight the meaning and link to the motivating feeling or client goals. Doing this allows clients to identify the potential strength in the observed responses.

Case Example

A woman came in to see a practitioner in a family drop-in center. The woman had been struggling with asserting herself with a new boyfriend. When describing events of the past week, the client reported, "I finally let him have it. He was sulking and expecting me to give in again so I said, 'Grow up. . . . You are a man now and need to deal with disappointment.' I then walked out and weeded the garden. He came out and apologized later." The practitioner replied, "When I hear you describe your stand, it gives me goose bumps. I hear power in your voice when you talk. When you said 'grow up,' there was no hesitation. It made me stand at attention. Such assertion is new in that relationship."

In this example, notice the enthusiasm of the practitioner as she responded to the client. When workers feel enthusiastic, they are at high risk for using words such as "good." However, the practitioner used descriptive language to describe her reaction and observations. After the observation, the reflection remains positive for the client and focused on client goals.

Using Self-Disclosure
A second type of communication used to focus and maintain the helping relationship is practitioner self-disclosure. Workers are half of the helping relationship. To develop

mutuality, this half of the relationship must invest. With careful sharing of self-information, practitioners can enhance the working alliance (Hendrick, 1988; Tryon & Kane, 1990; Walborn, 1996). Such sharing, however, must be done very carefully to serve client goals and ensure a clear sense of purpose.

Self-disclosure is a complicated communication that draws heavily on our self-awareness and self-control. It is easy to disclose information that moves the focus away from professional work and into a friendship exchange. We must be wary of this temptation at all times. The risk of moving toward a friendship relationship is associated with common patterns of relating. In friendships, shared information yields reciprocation by the other person. This model often makes the professional relationship awkward because disclosure is one-sided. Any disclosure by the practitioner must have a clear association with client goals.

In using self-disclosure, practitioners follow five critical elements. The first three critical elements employ self-awareness and self-control skills. There is also a need for critical thinking to mentally work through the first three elements of self-disclosing. The final two elements make use of tuning in, engagement, and reflection skills.

1. *Awareness.* Practitioners become aware of an internal impulse to disclose some aspect of their own life to the client (usually a story). For example, the client is upset about work and we are reminded of our past work challenges.

2. *Purpose.* Practitioners reflect on the purpose and goals of the helping relationship. If the disclosure does not clearly promote some service goal, we abandon thoughts of self-disclosure. For example, we consider the client goals of overcoming depression and identify the purpose of the story as instilling hope.

3. *Critical thinking.* Practitioners mentally reflect on potential relationship risks and direction shifts that may evolve from the disclosure. If no risks emerge, we proceed to the next step. If there is some risk, we abandon the urge to disclose. For example, practitioners consider whether the story might be experienced as minimizing the pain or taking focus away from the client.

4. *Limited disclosure.* Practitioners communicate their stories. In this communication, practitioners:
   ○ Introduce the goal or aspect of the client work that triggered the urge to disclose.
   ○ Describe the event or personal story that relates to the client situation.
   ○ Stop the story without further embellishment or personal disclosures.

5. *Transitional reflection.* Practitioners direct the discussion back to the client situation and client goals using a response that will encourage clients to engage further.

Case Example

A recreational worker at a community center noticed that a young man was distraught. The practitioner asked the youth about his situation. The youth replied, "My girlfriend dumped me . . . she traded me in for a new model." The practitioner responded, "It can be so hard when a girlfriend breaks up with you. When you are in the middle of it, you think the pain never ends. As I hear you talk about your pain, I remember feeling that way when my college girlfriend dumped me for another guy. I thought I would never be able to even think about smiling again. How are you managing your feelings?"

Seeding Change

Given that autonomy is vital to client well-being (Miller & Rollnick, 2004; Ryan & Deci, 2008; Sheldon et al., 2004), practitioners must avoid any semblance of overpowering our clients. Doing this requires us to promote client decision making and self-direction toward their goals. At the same time, we are paid to provide direction and support toward goals. To achieve a balance between these two requirements, we select forms of influence that are subtle and empowering. We plant the seeds of change by providing slight nudges and challenges that allow clients to reflect on their life direction.

As we plant seeds and nudge our clients toward change, we rely heavily on transitional responding because it provides incremental influence. Doing this allows us to insert small challenges, observations, thoughts, and direction into discussions planting seeds that can grow rather than telling our clients what they should do. Seeding change allows clients to retain their autonomy and self-motivation during change-focused exchanges (Aarts et al., 2009). Seeding change requires us to work within clients' inherent motivation while helping them to maintain the tension between their two visions.

Highlighting Motivating Feelings

When we know clients' motivating feelings, it is easy to identify the presence of these feelings during interaction. We are also able to identify how feelings promote the problems in clients' lives. When we listen to clients, we develop radar for identifying the presence of motivating feelings. If the feelings on the table reflect a problem direction, we often want to probe for motivating feelings. If motivating feelings are on the table, we often want to highlight and reinforce them to enhance the motivation.

As we work with motivating feelings, it is important to monitor for the positive and negative poles. Negative affect tends to be self-centered so will likely result in selfish motivations (Loroz, 2007). Consequently, as we pick up on feelings to enhance motivation, we often want to highlight the positive poles and feelings that promote connectedness and mastery. To seed change, we do not simply remind clients of their positive or motivating affect; rather we explore the current situation, listening carefully for the existence of neutral/positive affect and feelings that we know underlie client desires for change. When we identify such feelings on the table, we pick up on the feelings so they become part of our conversation.

When working with feelings, we often want either to turn down or to amplify the feelings. This can be accomplished by focusing our discussion on the clients thinking and cognitive processes that influence their feelings (Miron, Parkinson, & Brehm, 2007). If we want to deemphasize problematic feelings, we will insert content that interferes with the feelings. Similarly, when we want to emphasize a feeling, we begin exploring the thinking and values that promote the client motivation. Attenuation and amplification involves a four-step process.

1. *Identify the presence of affect.* As we listen to clients, we notice when feelings that can motivate or promote problems emerge on the table. As we identify these feelings, we experience an impulse to address them.
2. *Identify affect related thinking.* Based on our relationship and the content on the table, we are aware of the thinking associated with client feelings. If we want to deemphasize the feelings, we draw on thinking that can interfere with that feeling state. If we want to amplify a positive feeling, we select thinking that can reinforce that feeling state.
3. *Highlight affect-related thoughts when setting up the response.* As we set up our response, we pick up on client affect and attach thinking that can moderate the feeling.
4. *Deliver a response that will promote client elaboration.* When delivering the response, we engage clients in a way that will elaborate on the attached thinking.

Case Example

A nursing home practitioner was working with a severely depressed elderly man recently placed in the residence. The practitioner's role was to help the client adjust to placement. The client stopped the practitioner and said, "I hate this place. There is nobody here that cares about me." The practitioner noticed themes of connection and responded, "What kinds of things did you do with the people who cared about you?" The client responded, "We used to walk at the mall and stuff." The practitioner explored the activities and found that the client was part of a mall-walking club. As the exploration continued, the practitioner asked, "If opportunities were available for walking at the mall, would you like me to tell you about them?" The client indicated a desire to know. Later the practitioner approached the client, informing him of a group going to the mall and stating, "You mentioned that you would rather be at the mall than hanging out here. Let me introduce you to Tom. He is going to the mall with some others and can show you around if you would like. Are you interested in hearing more?"

Priming Outcomes

Along with working at the affective level, we continue to work with client change visions and goals. As client motivations ebb and flow in the working alliance, we sometimes notice that they are ignoring goals and at other times they appear highly motivated. There will even be times when they appear to believe that they have totally mastered their situation. Depending on the client exchanges, we sometimes want to highlight one of the visions (status quo or change vision) to keep client focus and motivation active.

Priming outcomes requires us to extend elements of the current discussion into the future so clients can reflect on the possible outcomes. Consequently, we pick up on themes in client statements to find content that lends itself well to priming goals. If clients appear to be losing their sense of balance between the two change visions (e.g., overconfident or overly pessimistic), we may pick up on content that allows us to insert a more balanced vision. For example, client with a mental illness was becoming cavalier about medication. When the client stated that medication is no big deal, the practitioner responded, "You certainly have done well. When you first came here, you never took your medication and ended up on the street. Now look at you, you pretty much never miss a day. How have you become so responsible?"

When we want to highlight the potential changes and outcomes, we must be careful to avoid taking over the conversation. To be most effective, we need to change direction in subtle increments (Aarts et al., 2009). These increments involve building on client statements to help them identify possible outcomes and areas of change. Although this skill builds on transitional responding, the skill set emerges as a four-step process when seeding outcomes. These four steps include:

1. *Identify goal-related material.* In the ongoing interaction, there are moments when we tune in to material that is directly related to client goals and visions of change. When we identify this material, we experience an impulse to use it to reinforce potential outcomes.

2. *Pick up on potential direction.* When we identify fertile material for promoting goals, we select the elements in the client statement that best reflect the change direction. In our selection we try to keep the material subtle so we do not launch into long explanations or otherwise disrupt the interactive rhythm.

3. *Include elements of the visions in the setup.* As we prepare our response, we include either the change or status quo vision in our setup. We use the vision to provide an element for contrast and tension generation.

4. *Reinforce the change direction when delivering the response.* After focusing the response, we add a question or reflection to promote a client focus on change-related content. We use questions and prompts if we want to promote an interactive response. Reflections can be used to encourage client thinking.

Providing Focus

The professional working alliance requires focus and purpose. When the focus of the relationship begins to stray away from the main purpose of service, we refocus the relationship to proceed toward the goals. There are times when opportunities naturally arise to reinforce the focus. For example, at the beginning of a meeting, we can affirm the focus prior to engaging in discussion. Likewise, at the end of a meeting, we often summarize the goal-related discussions. At other times we need to shift the focus during interaction with clients, nudging them back toward a goal focus.

Sessional Focusing

At the beginning of each client meeting, we have an opportunity to focus discussion toward achieving client goals. Rather than wasting this opportunity with questions like "How was your week?" we can set a focused tone with questions such as "What did you find yourself using from our last meeting?" Such sessional openers help clients transition from the out-of-service aspects of their lives to the goals of service. Similarly, we can end meetings with a summary of goal-related content. There are three very common strategies of sessional focusing: task follow-up, reflective questions, and integrative focusing.

1. *Task follow-up*. Task-centered focusing ends a session by summarizing the content and negotiating tasks for the week. The next meeting then begins by following up on tasks negotiated during the previous meeting. Workers who use homework assignments or tasks often use a reporting system in which clients describe what they have done between meetings.

2. *Reflective focusing*. Reflective focusing is less structured than tasks. Practitioners often use reflective focusing to end a session by summarizing work and inviting clients to consider how they will use the discussions. The next session begins with a similar question. For example: "What have you found yourself doing differently since our last meeting?"

3. *Integrative focusing*. Integrative focusing is the least structured strategy. Integrative focusing uses a period of catching up on events between meetings. During the catch-up period, clients share information about their week. The practitioner must listen intently to relate content to goal-directed work. Based on client descriptions of events, the practitioner reflects on elements of client stories that build on work from the last meeting.

Practitioners choose their level of structure based on two aspects of the work. First, we want to consider the client and the client needs. When a client is hard to focus, a structured approach may be desirable. However, highly structured strategies limit client ability to table new concerns requiring us to consciously provide opportunities to express emergent needs. A second consideration is agency requirements. With managed care and decreased service availability, some agencies expect highly focused approaches to service. This is consistent with many of the evidence-based practices that prescribe opening and closing sequences. In such situations, reflective focusing and task-centered approaches are more useful.

Focusing Discussions

Refocusing is also used when client work slips off focus. Sometimes client behavior between meetings lacks focus. At other times, the interaction with practitioners tends to shift away from the goal-directed work. During off-focus periods, we begin to notice that focus is slipping, and we become concerned that the alliance has shifted away from the goal-oriented purpose. As we notice slippage occurring, we seek ways to place the slippage on the table for discussion and resolution.

When the focus becomes lost, we end up stopping exchanges to openly address the loss of focus. In a refocusing discussion, we identify the loss of focus and then remind clients of their reasons for meeting. The motivating feelings become critical as we use client desires and visions for change to remind them of the goals of service. There are two common methods for refocusing: redirection and redressing responsibility.

1. *Redirecting focus*. As we develop a working relationship with clients, it is easy for them to share multiple areas of their lives. As broader sharing occurs, the focus of interaction becomes harder to manage because the relationship deepens. When the focus of interaction slips away from the goals and purpose of intervention, we interrupt the flow of discussion and describe our observations to begin correcting the focus of interaction.

2. *Redressing responsibility*. Sometimes we become more invested in the work than our clients. Often this indicates a critical misunderstanding in the alliance that allows clients to become more active in the supportive exchanges and less active in independent goal achievement. When this occurs, we must shift the balance so clients are equally active in goal-related tasks. To accomplish this, we increase the expectations on clients while ensuring that we are not undermining client autonomy by performing tasks on their behalf.

Redirecting focus and redressing responsibility both involve interrupting the flow of discussion, identifying the slippage, and then working collaboratively with clients to refocus the alliance. Both of these methods for bringing focus involve a five-step process that employs the skills from earlier chapters.

1. *Identify the slippage.* We begin by observing past discussions, feelings, thoughts, and actions that indicate that slippage has occurred. As we identify the shift in focus, we interrupt the ongoing process to share the observations.
2. *Describe our observations.* Using descriptive skills, we share our observations with clients. This sharing should be descriptive to avoid any semblance of judging or chastising clients.
3. *Contrast with the motivated past.* We follow our observations with contrasting the current situation with the past motivated alliance.
4. *Ally with the motivating feelings.* Based on past observations of motivation and focused work, we contrast how the current focus inconsistent with the purpose.
5. *Invite clients to engage in discussion.* After contrasting the current situation with the motivated history, we engage clients to help shift the direction of the working alliance.

Case Example

A sheltered workshop practitioner was preparing a client diagnosed with a developmental disability for a work placement. The practitioner wanted to motivate him to acquire important skills but noticed that the client had been talking about reasons to avoid work placement. (*Identification of slippage.*) The practitioner began with this statement: "Frank, I notice you have been focused on reasons not to go to the work placement. (*Describing observations.*) When we first talked about getting a work placement, you talked about what you would do with the money. You had some plans about getting into independent living and being able to go out with Betty. You seemed pretty determined to make it into the workplace. Do you remember? (*Contrasting with motivated past.*) I thought you were working hard in a direction that you wanted to go. You really looked like you had a plan for yourself. (*Ally with the motivating feelings.*) I know that this is a big change; how do you feel about working? (*Invitation.*)

Dealing with the Tension

When we focus the relationship, it is often during times of ambivalence. When we attempt to reassert a focus on goals, ambivalence is accentuated, which can increase tension in the working relationship (Shulman, 1999). Consequently, we must be skilled in managing tension (Edwards & Bess, 1998). This skill requires us to carefully balance support with the demands for work (Miller & Rollnick, 2002). Support helps manage tension in the relationship.

The tension and ambivalence associated with change is natural and should not be approached as a threat to the alliance. Most people notice that tension is present during times of learning and personal growth. Most important relationships have periods of tension. Four types of tension may emerge as we begin to increase the focus on change.

1. *Tension associated with the costs of change.* When the practitioner helps clients identify a need to make changes, tension will increase as clients identify the costs associated with change. At times tension will emerge in the relationship as clients feel helpless in relation to the costs but unable to trust the future benefits.
2. *Tension associated with client responsibility.* (Baenninger-Huber & Widmer, 1999). Part of supporting clients is allowing them to make decisions and do their own work. However, when assuming responsibility for making changes, tension is created. At times, clients want us to take over their problems rather than making their own changes. Although this is tempting, we promote mastery by coaching clients to develop their own skills.
3. *Tension associated with uncertainty.* People do not necessarily know what to expect when they are making changes. Even when a situation is difficult, it is familiar. Change,

however, is unknown. We help clients deal with the anxiety associated with the unknown. As clients begin to trust their new skills in the situation, their ambivalence about change decreases.

4. *Tension associated with perceived criticism*. Even when people know they must change, there are feelings of criticism or inadequacy when others promote the change. Such feelings can promote frustration when clients have difficulty mastering the change or would rather not change. These potential reactions require very active support, exploration of ambivalence, and the ability to reflect on small successes.

Exercise 11.2: Making Demands for Work

You are working with homeless families in a program helping people to get their own homes. You have been working with a single mother and her two young children referred by a domestic violence shelter. She had been in the domestic violence shelter for two months before coming into the homeless shelter associated with your program. She stated that she wanted to provide a stable environment for her children. She connected well with the other residents in the program and is well liked. You are finding that she does not follow through on the homework assignments. She was supposed to search for possible apartments in the paper and arrange to view them on several occasions but took no action. This is a change from when she first came into the program. You want to place some demands on her to assume responsibility for the work.

1. What earlier client statement can be used to rekindle her motivation?

2. What two visions can you construct (status quo versus change) to create motivational energy to change?

3. Using the change vision from question 2, construct a statement that can prime the outcomes for this client.

4. What might be some of the costs and benefits for the woman in this situation?
   Costs:
   Benefits:

5. As the ambivalence is resolved, construct a statement that can increase the demand for work using the steps outlined in this chapter.

Motivation in Larger Client Systems

Most of the discussion in this chapter has focused on individual motivation. A strong understanding of individual-level motivation provides a foundation for understanding larger system motivation and goal-directed action. This is important when working with families, groups, teams, organizations, and communities. Within these larger systems we find shared motivation and goal-directed activity toward mutual goals. For a larger group to achieve motivation, there must be a shared investment and a balance between individual autonomy and collective identity.

Shared Investment

An important element in achieving a collective identity is a mutual investment in shared, rather than individualistic, goals (Beech & Hamilton-Giachritsis, 2005). Part of the shared investment among members involves a shared understanding of the systemic purpose. When the purpose and goals are clear, there is a greater commitment to actively pursuing the collective purpose (van Andel et al., 2003). Individual system members forsake personal agendas to ensure that the group and other members are successful. When shared motivation fails, it is often because some individuals are subverting energy into personal pursuits and goals at the expense of the shared purpose.

As a larger system develops shared values and purpose, these values become normative and influence actions of individual members. Dissonance emerges when an individual's values and actions diverge with the group's normative values and expectations. When significant differences with strongly held values emerge, the members of the system respond in a way that causes violating members to curtail their discrepant activity (Glasford, Pratto, & Dovidio, 2008; McKimmie, Terry, & Hogg, 2009).

When a larger system fails to achieve its stated objectives, it is often because individual strivings interfere with the achievement of a shared vision. This lack of collective direction allows individuals to play out their personal agendas at the expense of the system. It may be that the truly shared values of the members diverge from officially stated values. When we work with larger systems, we carefully observe shared feelings, behaviors, and motivations to determine whether the shared values coincide with publicly stated positions.

Autonomy–Cohesion Balance

In optimally functioning larger systems, there is a synergy between individuals and the larger system. The synergy involves individual autonomy in balance with a shared identity and investment in the system. Systems that support member competence and mastery are able to achieve higher levels of shared commitment because members become more motivated to contribute to the system (Deci et al., 2001; Ryan, Kuhl, & Deci, 1997). As individuals provide meaningful feedback and input to the system, investment in shared outcomes increases, promoting a balanced synergy (Bauer & Mulder, 2006).

As larger systems achieve member commitment to shared goals, a sense of "we-ness," or cohesion, emerges among the members. Cohesion is considered by many to be one of the most important larger system dynamics associated with the accomplishment of group goals (Allen, Sargent, & Bradley, 2003; Chang & Bordia, 2001). This finding is consistent in both work groups (Pollack, 1998) and treatment groups (Beech & Hamilton-Giachritsis, 2005; Marziali, Munroe-Blum, & McCleary, 1997). In the larger system, cohesion provides a foundation for the working alliance among the members. As members commit to mutual goals through the alliance, energy is directed to ensure positive outcomes (Piper, Ogrodniczuk, LaMarche, Hilscher, & Joyce, 2005).

Cultural Considerations

The discussions about motivation have been presented with little reference to cultural influences. Although mastery appears to be a motivating factor across diverse groups (McInerney, 2008), other motivating factors vary according to gender, culture, race, and religion. Diversity emerges from people's orientation toward outcomes and how they organize their efforts toward achieving outcomes. It is very important to consider cultural influences as we work with clients because cultural, racial, religious, and gender-based experiences shape client motivation and orientation toward their goals.

Individualism versus Collectivism

A first cultural influence emerges because some cultures are very individualistic and "self" focused while others are more collectivist and "other" focused (Chen & Carey, 2009). These cultural differences influence how autonomy and relatedness strivings result in motivation. In collectivist cultures, there is a greater likelihood that people will respond to relatedness feelings. More individualistic cultures will respond more strongly to mastery strivings. For example, in the individualistic North American dominant culture, competition and individual gains are highly motivating. However, more collectivist cultures are less competitive and more prone to being motivated by themes of responsibility and prevention (Uskul, Sherman, & Fitzgibbon, 2009). There are similar differences between males and females with males maintaining a stronger individualistic orientation even within the dominant North American culture (Mortazavi, Pedhiwala, Shafiro, & Hammer, 2009).

Given the cultural differences in self versus other orientation, it is important to weigh carefully clients' cultural background when seeking to promote motivation. Although internal motivation often is viewed as preferable (Deci et al., 2001), cultural differences may result in increased externalization with clients from a collectivist culture. This can be observed in an increased need for social support and input from others when setting goals and taking goal-directed action (Gore, Cross, & Kanagawa, 2009). In highly collectivist cultures, it may be necessary to include support people in the meetings to ensure that adequate collective input is garnered and support implemented when pursuing goals (Howard, Ferrari, Nota, Solberg, & Soresi, 2009; Mortenson, Liu, Burleson, & Liu, 2006; Nakamura & Tagami, 2008).

Motivational Differences

The area of greatest motivational diversity is in the area of motivating feelings. Motivating feelings change across racial, cultural, and gender groups. Most of us are aware that males in our society are more highly motivated by achievement and outcomes than female counterparts (Pattnaik & Mishra, 2008). Achievement orientations also vary across cultural, racial, and religious groups. All motivating feelings are filtered through a cultural lens that shapes the motivation and demands different levels of group loyalty in how motivations are expressed. Consequently, as we attempt to access a person's motivating feelings, we must carefully consider diverse backgrounds and experiences.

Experiences as a minority group member can further alter culturally based motivations. For example, members of a minority culture may be achievement motivated to counteract discrimination experiences (Alfaro Umaña-Taylor, Gonzales-Backen, Bámaca, & Zeiders, 2009). Similarly, fear may be more motivating with minority group members where acts of terrorism and death are prevalent (Landau, Greenberg, & Rothschild, 2009). In poor countries, the cultural experiences elevate the importance of survival motivations, leaving achievement motivations less strongly valued (Van de Vliert, 2007).

Identifying Culturally Mismatched Goals

A final cultural consideration is the appropriateness of goals. Motivation will diminish if the goals of service are a poor fit with a client's cultural values. When services attempt to engage people in actions that do not fit with their cultural norms, we may promote the illusion of compliance. However, clients may employ strategies to reduce the discrepancy between our expectations and their cultural norms. Any of the next behaviors may indicate that there is a cultural mismatch interfering with client motivation (Maertz, Hassan, & Magnusson, 2009).

- People attempt to alter their own value base to make the new behavior consistent with values.
- People start to change their attributions or interpretations of the situation to decrease the discrepancy between the behavior and their values.
- People assert their positive attributes in an attempt to convince you that they are indeed good people. Such assertions balance the anxiety associated with engaging in actions that feel culturally wrong.
- People begin to rationalize and justify the fact that they are engaging in a behavior that is inconsistent with their cultural background.

- People confess to you that the behavior feels wrong, taking responsibility for acting in a manner that is inconsistent with their cultural values.

- People reject you and your expectations that they act in a manner that is culturally repugnant. They withdraw and refuse to engage in the behavior.

When these types of reactions are observed with clients, it is important to revisit the goals to ensure that a cultural fit is achieved. If the goals cannot be adjusted (e.g., with court-mandated clients), it may be possible to explore to find culturally relevant values and behaviors that can promote motivation. Although the outcomes may change slightly, the ability to engender motivational energy may make it possible to rekindle a working alliance.

Critical Chapter Themes

1. After clients have engaged, the practitioner must diligently attend to the working alliance to keep work focused on accomplishing client goals. This is accomplished by using combinations of the core skills discussed in previous chapters.

2. Motivational enhancement must occur within a framework of client mastery and autonomy so their efforts to change are meaningful and self-guided.

3. Attending to the working alliance requires motivating, nurturing, and focusing the helping relationship to ensure a positive and focused effort toward achieving client goals.

4. Two polarized dimensions of client motivation can help understand client motivation: internal versus external motivation and emotional versus logical orientations.

5. To help clients remain motivated toward achieving their goals, practitioners tap into clients' innate motivating feelings while helping them to find dissonance between their current and desired situations.

6. Practitioners use combinations of skills to provide feedback, focus, and support as clients seek to achieve their goals. These skills are used differentially based on client readiness to change.

7. Motivations are strongly influenced by ethnicity, culture, and gender. Practitioners must consider these elements as they support client efforts to achieve their goals.

Online Resources

Motivational Interviewing Organization: http://www.motivationalinterview.org/

Stages of Change: http://www.addictioninfo.org/articles/11/1/Stages-of-Change-Model/Page1.html

Center on Alcohol Substance Abuse and Addictions: http://casaa.unm.edu/mi.html

Recommended Reading

Carver, C.S., & Harmon-Jones, E. (2009). Anger is an approach-related affect: Evidence and implications. *Psychological Bulletin*, *135*, 183–204.

Miller, W.R., & Rollnick, S. (2004). Talking oneself into change: Motivational interviewing, stages of change, and therapeutic process. *Journal of Cognitive Psychotherapy: An International Quarterly*, *18*, 299–308.

Patrick, H., Knee, C.R., Canevello, A., & Lonsbary, C. (2007). The role of need fulfillment in relationship functioning and well-being: A self-determination theory perspective. *Journal of Personality and Social Psychology*, *92*, 434–457.

Russell, J.A. (2003). Core affect and the psychological construction of emotion. *Psychological Review*, *110*, 145–172.

Ryan, R.M., & Deci, E.L. (2008). A self-determination theory approach to psychotherapy: The motivational basis for effective change. *Canadian Psychology*, *49*, 186–193.

Chapter 12
Building Multisystemic Working Alliances

Past chapters focused on working with clients from a single-agency perspective. We have learned how to engage clients within an agency context. Although we explored larger client systems, such as families, groups, and organizations, the focus was largely confined to a single agency setting. Some client situations, however, require the working alliance to be extended across multiple systems. This is very common in children's services, mental health, developmental disabilities, and substance abuse fields of practice. Many of the evidence-based practices in these fields are multisystemic, requiring us to be able to work collaboratively in a network of professionals.

Research suggests that coordinated and targeted use of the multiple community resources serving clients improves the outcomes of client services (Anderson, Wright, Kelley, & Kooreman, 2008; Manteuffel et al., 2008). Client reports reinforce these findings; client perceptions of interprofessional collaboration is one of the strongest predictors of client confidence in the services they receive (Reich, Bickman, & Heflinger, 2004). Consequently, many service systems have adopted coordinated and collaborative approaches to serving clients. This is most evident when working with client populations with multiple challenges.

Collaborative Models, Evidence-Based Practice, and Community Partners

The move toward collaborative and coordinated services has been well researched in recent years. Increasingly service providers are encouraged to adopt evidence-based collaborative models. Multisystemic treatment has demonstrated that a coordinated and intensive intervention employing education, mental health, juvenile justice, and other community programs can decrease antisocial behaviors in severely delinquent adolescents (Cunningham & Henggeler, 1999; Swenson, Henggeler, Taylor, & Addison, 2005). Similarly effective evidence-based models of multi-agency intervention include wraparound services (Winters & Metz, 2009) and family group decision making (Pennell & Burford, 2000; Sheets et al., 2009).

These evidence-based practices are often referred to as systems of care. The term "system of care" differentiates a coordinated intervention system from professionals and agencies working in isolation. Seven elements in a system of care that contribute to its effectiveness:

1. Commitment to including client input and cultural needs into service decisions and intervention choice (Cook & Kilmer, 2004).

2. Organizational changes and commitments that maximize the coordinated provision of services (Hernandez & Hodges, 2003).

3. Interprofessional consistency in values, interpretations, and responses among service providers (Young, Daleiden, Chorpita, Schiffman, & Mueller, 2007).

4. Broadly endorsed assessment systems used by service providers as a base for treatment decisions and intervention planning across agencies (Firth, Spanswick, & Rutherford, 2009).

5. Targeted service provision from multiple systems based on the client's identified needs (Foster, Stephens, Krivelyova, & Gamfi, 2007; Stambaugh et al., 2007).

6. Ongoing coordination and planning among the agencies and professionals providing the services (Bunning & Horton, 2007; Rush & Koegl, 2008; Shivram et al., 2009).

7. Organizational commitments to follow through on the commitments and interventions negotiated early in the coordinated intervention (Young et al., 2007).

Given these requirements, a system of care approach requires agencies to commit resources and change the systemic values to a collaborative model (Carstens, Panzano, Massatti, Roth, & Sweeney, 2009). In a system of care, about 40% of a practitioner's time is spent on collaborative activities, such as collegial meetings and phone calls (Ødegård, 2007).

Systems of Care Breakdowns and Solutions

As systems of care are implemented, findings indicate that there are significant differences in effectiveness across communities (Foster et al., 2007). Differences emerge based on the nature of service options and professionals participating in the system. One of the challenges in a coordinated system of care is ensuring that all of the professionals perform their functions. Often service elements get dropped between the early and later phases of intervention (Young et al., 2007). System of care problems sometimes occur when an organization's funding support diminishes, resulting in a subsequent reduction in resource commitment to maintaining the intervention system (Santangelo, 2009).

Three common collaboration problems emerge on the professional level.

1. Problems emerge when professional groups compete with each other to define each other's roles or areas of competence (Lymbery, 2006; Norris & Melby, 2006).
2. Problems emerge when professionals feel they do not have autonomy and are told how to intervene by others (Amir & Auslander, 2003).
3. Problems emerge when individual biases and emotional reactions influence practitioner decisions more than objective assessments of client needs (Farmer, Mustillo, Burns, & Holden, 2008; Mueser & Taub, 2008).

At both the practitioner and organizational levels, collaboration breakdowns tend to emerge from an inability to achieve multiple alliances. At the organizational level, funding considerations cause a rupture in the alliance. At the practitioner level, professional esteem and individual reactivity erode the alliance. The tendency to retreat into individualistic responding occurs when collaborative priorities are less important than self-preservation or self-advancement motivations.

Toward Collaborative Practice

Given the importance of collaboration when working with multiple agencies, it is critical that practitioners develop skill sets that can achieve multiple alliances. Two levels of alliance are necessary to ensure adequate community-level interventions.

1. There must be collaborative alliances between agencies and programs. This requires practitioners to understand and apply policies and interagency agreements to practice situations.
2. Concurrently, practitioners must be able to facilitate alliances among the multiple practitioners working with clients.

These two levels of demand can be challenging at the practice level. The challenge often arises because many times individual practitioners have divergent visions of collaboration. It is important to understand the nature of collaborative interventions. Hodges, Hernandez, and Nesman (2003) developed a five-stage model spanning individualized practice to truly collaborative practice. When you review these stages, notice how the alliance becomes increasingly more complex as the level of collaboration increases.

1. *Individual action.* Professionals work by themselves with little consideration of other professionals and services.
2. *One-on-one collaboration.* Professionals make contact and collaborate with specific other professionals working with the client.

3. *New service development*. Agencies begin to share resources to develop new service delivery programs and strategies.

4. *Professional collaboration*. Collaboration is expected and integrated at the agency, program, and professional levels of participating agencies. There are regular meetings to ensure cross-agency effectiveness.

5. *True collaboration*. Professional collaboration is expanded to include the meaningful participation of clients and family members in service planning and delivery.

Building Multiple Alliances

Extending the alliance across multiple agencies and informal helpers has an enormous impact on how we work with clients. Now the alliance extends to other systems, each with its own interpretations of the situation, service structures, and approaches. Although we continue to use our basic skills, we now use them with colleagues and administrators as well as clients. Doing this requires a cautious use of interpersonal skills because our role with colleagues and administrators is very different from our role with clients. This chapter explores methods of understanding and responding to multisystemic expansions of the working alliance.

As we proceed toward expanding the working alliance, two levels of thinking will influence how we approach potential partners in the alliance.

1. We must understand agency and programs as partners. Doing this requires us to understand policies, agency mandates, and how these contextual realities influence the practice situation. With informal supports, these additional elements can be less clear because there is no formal structure.

2. As we work from an understanding of these organizations and systems, at the same time we must be able to work with a group of colleagues toward achieving client goals. This level of practice occurs at the peer or collegial level.

Alliances and Helping Systems

As the working alliance expands from an individual system to working with multiple organizations, we are exposed to two types of helping systems: formal and informal systems. The term "formal systems" refers to the situations where people are paid to provide assistance to clients. Formal supports include nurses, psychologists, counselors, social workers, occupational therapists, priests, and teachers. We refer to systems as informal when the support people are unpaid. These supports include such people as friends, relatives, coaches, and club leaders.

In each local community, there are networks of formal and informal support systems available to clients. Informal systems include family networks, friends, recreation systems, clubs, and community arts options. Formal networks include agencies, institutions, professionals, and community service groups. Although some communities have significant gaps in their networks' ability to respond to client needs, most communities have some resources that can be engaged to help clients. When we engage these different types of support, we must understand how each type of network is structured and able to support clients.

Multisystemic Alliances and Informal Supports

Most clients live in a network of informal supports that can help them master their situations. Such supports include family, friends, clubs, teams, self-help organizations, and cultural organizations that exist in the community. Informal supports have a different impact from formal services because they are better aligned to client interests and normal network of relationships. Involvement with informal support systems is often cheaper than formal services because there is no professional being paid to spend time with clients. Even when fees are associated with an informal support (e.g., joining a swim team), community organizations often waive fees for people experiencing financial distress.

Informal Support Networks

Informal supports vary in form: Some systems build on common interests while others focus on problems or commonalities among members. Most informal systems are run by people who are not helping professionals. Rather, informal systems involve many peers and volunteers. These systems can provide an excellent source of support with little formality or professional knowledge.

The diversity among informal support systems preempts a unified system of engagement. The support systems involve caring and dedicated people with specific areas of passion. The lack of structure and professional knowledge presents challenges when we use informal systems as part of a collaborative plan of care because we cannot easily monitor or make demands. However, informal supports can be invaluable when we want to enhance clients' current support systems. In the multiple informal supports available, there are different types of support, including social group supports, interest groups, and kinship supports.

Social Group Supports

Most communities have organizations associated with culture, gender, or other demographics. These organizations are often very visible and engage in frequent outreach to members of their community. This type of organization can be a valuable support for clients with appropriate demographic profiles. These types of support are important when clients need people in their life who can understand their cultural background, interests, or particular circumstances.

When we work with clients to engage social group supports, we ensure that the type of support is appropriate for them. There may be times when clients want supports that respond to their unique situations; at other times, clients want to keep their personal situations away from members of their demographic group. When we discuss group-specific supports, we must respect client wishes and sensitivities about engaging focused support systems. Three commonly available social group support systems include:

1. *Cultural-based supports.* Ethnic and cultural groups often have clubs or specific organizations that exist for the sole purpose of supporting members of the social group. These organizations can provide social outlets for clients and multiple types of support.

2. *Spiritual-based supports.* Every community has multiple churches and spiritually based organizations. These systems often have social clubs as well as organized religious activities. Such organizations can be used for structured and unstructured sources of support for clients.

3. *Self-help supports.* When the social group is associated with a problem (e.g., substance abuse or gambling), self-help groups often emerge to support members with common challenges. The groups tend to organize meetings around the problem and use the membership to support each other to overcome the problem.

Interest Group Supports

Many communities have multiple activities and groups organized around people's skills and interests. Such organizations include clubs, teams, musical groups, art guilds, and voluntary pursuits. These groups are very useful when working with clients who feel isolated or who lack social supports. Such activities also can be used to expand a client's range of activity or sense of self-esteem.

Interest group supports can be very useful supplements to formal services because clients can build on their strengths and interests. This activity can be invaluable when clients lack confidence or esteem because the supports can match their strengths. This type of support also views members as peers rather than as people with problems. Two common groups are associated with this type of support. Both types can be useful when we help clients identify social options that can increase their connectedness in the community.

1. *Talent-based supports.* Groups such as teams and musical and artistic groups some- times require members to have a skill or talent prior to entering the group. Other organizations have more of a developmental focus and take members at all levels of talent.
2. *Interest-based supports.* Most communities have clubs and other organizations, similar to talent-based supports that cater to people's interests. Clubs focused on gardening, car restoration, and other interests can provide clients with social supports.

Kinship Group Supports

The last type of informal support involves kinship relationships. These are people who have an invested relationship with clients and are likely to take action to promote clients' successful goal achievement. Because these people have an investment in the clients, they are in a position to better understand and respond to client needs. Often practitioners will attempt to involve some of these supports people in service to ensure that changes begin to occur in clients' life situations.

We must be careful when including kinship supports in clients' service. Clients have a preexisting relationship with kinship supports. Consequently, the reliability and effective- ness of including a person will be influenced by his or her motivation and relationship history. We want to ensure that the relationships are truly supportive or at least malleable to avoid disappointments for clients or the sabotaging of goals. Two types of support are common to kinship group supports:.

1. *Relative supports.* Relative supports are people who are related to clients, including both immediate family and distant relatives with a family connection. The network of relatives can be complex based on marriage and divorce patterns in the family.
2. *Fictive-kin supports.* Fictive kin are people who are not blood-related to clients but operate as if they are family. These people include family friends, neighbors, and people with a long history of involvement with clients.

Using Informal Supports

When we include informal support people in an intervention plan, we engage people from clients' lives who can help them achieve their goals. Engaging people already in the client's life helps support the changes in multiple areas making the intervention broader. Evidence- based interventions, such as multisystemic therapy and wraparound services, routinely include informal support people as part of the intervention.

When we work with clients and seek to employ informal supports as part of our intervention plan, we must have a clear purpose for inclusion. There are four common reasons to include informal supports as part of treatment:

1. *Capacity enhancement.* Informal supports can provide opportunities for clients to explore and expand their interests and skills. As they develop these skills, they are engaged with others of similar interests.
2. *Focused support.* Informal support people can be engaged to perform specific types of support, such as providing information, emotional support, and other tasks needed to promote client success.
3. *Motivational enhancement.* Given that connectedness motivates people to make change, engaging important people can help motivate and promote change.
4. *Situational monitoring.* Informal support people can keep track of the client situation and help practitioners understand client progress in their in vivo relationships.

Engaging Informal Supports

Depending on the reason for inclusion and the role that the informal support people are expected to fill, our strategies for engagement change. If we are hoping to engage clients with new supports, such as relatives, clubs, or support organizations, we often suggest that clients approach the support person and explore possible roles. In this approach we rely on the strength of client interests or relationships to motivate them to follow up on the suggestion. Our role is to discuss the importance of the person or group and help overcome potential obstacles to engagement.

When we have more specific roles for support people, we become more active in facilitating engagement. Doing this often requires us to make contact with potential support people and explore their willingness to participate in the working alliance. As we expand the working alliance to include specific roles, we must ethically ensure that people are making informed decisions about the nature and frequency of their participation. This requires us to talk to each support person about their role, communication expectations, and the amount of involvement. Clients also must be comfortable with the inclusion of others and the roles that each person will play in the intervention.

Multisystemic Alliances With Formal Supports

Expanding the working alliance to include other formal systems is more complex than working with informal supports. Formal systems of support have structures, policies, and procedures that influence how we approach and engage other professionals. This is why these supports are referred to as formal. Formal supports typically operate within funded agencies or organizations that employ practitioners. Given the complexity of formal support systems, clients often have a difficult time accessing services. For that reason, we no longer merely suggest that they contact the support; rather, we become active helping clients connect to services.

Working With Formal Service Networks

With formal services, we must understand the structure of the organization as we engage services on behalf of clients. Formal services typically are funded through an agency or institution of some sort. Typically these organizations provide multiple types of service to members of the community. When we want to engage formal services for clients, we must work closely with them to ensure that the services will meet their needs. Doing this requires exploring the requirements and parameters of the service. These service-related elements are then discussed in light of our assessment of client needs and existing service plans.

When client needs are met through several organizations, the working alliance is complex. Complexity emerges because each organization fulfills unique functions. Organizations orient themselves to specific problems, such as family violence, managing disability, and substance abuse. These orientations influence how problems are defined and how services are structured. The organizational structure of service sets a tone for clients' relationships to service providers and the interrelationships among the providers.

Organizational Structure of Service
A typical organizational structure is illustrated in Figure 12.1. Notice that a funding body generally is as the top of the organization. This body is separate from the organization but provides money to ensure that specific services are provided. Most organizations have a board of directors who oversee the use of the money and develop policies to ensure that the organization abides by its agreements. The board hires an executive director, sometimes called a chief executive officer (CEO), who oversees the daily operations of the agency.

Below the executive director we usually find managers. In Figure 12.1, there is one management level referred to as program directors. In large agencies, there can be several levels of management using different labels. Managers are responsible for ensuring that the agency is providing accountable services. At the lowest managerial level, the main function of the manager is to supervise the practitioners. The practitioners are on the lowest level of the organizational structure. They provide the funded services to clients. The different levels within the organization exist to ensure that the money provided by the funders is being used to provide effective service to clients.

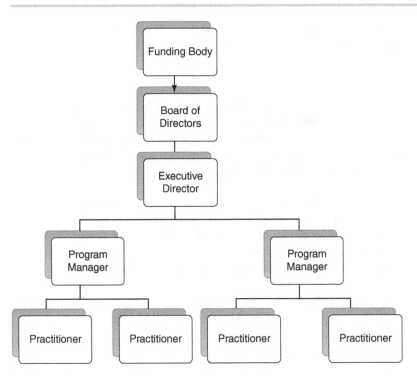

Figure 12.1

Common Organizational Structure

Organizational Impact on the Alliance

As we extend the working alliance across multiple organizations, a web of merging alliances develops. Clients must establish an alliance with every service provider. Each service provider has a preexisting alliance with his or her agency. At the same time, each service provider must achieve an alliance with the other professionals. The resulting web is a very complex network of alliances, each with different levels of relational investment, organizational impact, and professional understandings of the client situation.

Figure 12.2 shows the complex alliances and influences that emerge in multisystemic work. When we explore the figure, we see that the original alliance is nested in a network of

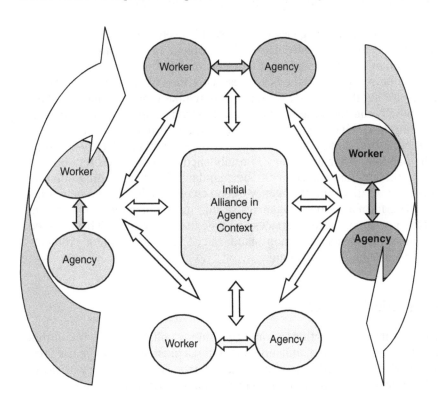

Figure 12.2

Complex Alliances in Multisystemic Work

agencies. Notice that the original alliance between a worker and client is influenced by each worker and agency pairing. These pairings also influence each other, resulting in a very complex array of influences. Managing these influences takes great focus and energy.

Agency Mandates

When working with formal services, it is important to understand the agency mandate and its influence on the working alliance. Mandates are the societal expectations of the agency that accompany funding. These expectations govern the types of service expected and the client populations that can access the agency. Although the nature of mandates changes slightly from state to state, most mandates will include the next elements.

- *Legislation, policies, and funding.* Usually an external social body or institution endorses the existence of the agency. The larger social body (e.g., government, religious group) provides expectations in the form of a funding agreement. Inherent in the agreement is the fact that the agency is contracted to provide services in accordance with the social expectations. The larger body, in turn, agrees to help fund the services.

- *Agency mission.* The agency establishes a mission statement outlining what it hopes to achieve. This mission is consistent with the expectations established in the funding agreements and policy expectations.

- *Programmatic focus.* In the funding agreement and mission statement, agencies limit the program's focus to specific types of problems or populations. For example, children's mental health agencies focus on children with emotional problems. The problem focus sets the context for agency services.

- *Catchment area.* Agency mandates also outline parameters for who can expect services from the agency. Sometimes these parameters are geographic (e.g., any citizen of the county), but they may also include additional parameters, such as religious or ethnic group membership.

- *Accountability structures.* In a formal mandate, the agency outlines a structure of accountability. Accountability is typically maintained through a hierarchy including a board of directors, directors, supervisors, and direct practitioners. Each level has responsibilities associated with providing the mandated services.

To fully understand the nature of agency mandates, it is useful to know how agencies evolve. Initially agencies emerge to address a social problem in the community. This typically begins as concerned citizens meet together to document a problem. As this group continues to meet, members explore methods for resolving the community problem and develop proposals for funding the solution. Although it may take years to achieve a stable agency structure, eventually the concerned citizens develop bylaws and submit legal forms that will allow the group to receive funds, form an agency, and provide services.

As agencies become formalized, they may expand their functions slightly but often remain true to their mandate. After an agency is established, funders often rely on it to respond to any new problems associated with the mandate. Thus, new programs and services emerge over time. At this point the agency often is well established and networked into the community. The formalization of agencies results in organizational policies and procedures that dictate how clients access services and how these services will be provided. Inherent in this progression, agencies develop standardized ways of defining problems, identifying clients, and fulfilling their mandate.

Skills of Multisystemic Alliances

Most of our interactions with other practitioners and community collaborators will continue to use questioning, reflecting, describing, and directing, but we must alter how we use these skills because we are working with colleagues rather than clients. When working with peers, we are more apt to become involved in conflicts, as professional differences inevitably arise.

Conflict risks can be compounded when the practitioners have diverse professional backgrounds. Differences make it difficult to achieve a unified direction for clients. When organizational and professional differences emerge, alliance building requires us first to overcome differences, then find commonalities.

Socialization Challenges to Multiple Alliances

The most challenging element of expanding the working alliance is managing multiple relationships. Most of the socialization challenges discussed in this textbook have focused on how we manage individual interactions based on parental socialization. Although parental problem solving influences our approach to peer situations, our past peer-related experiences also influence how we manage our peer group relationships (Stuart, Fondacaro, Miller, Brown, & Brank, 2008; Tallman, Gray, Kullberg, & Henderson, 1999).

Our skill foundation for peer interaction tends to be developed during our middle school years. This is the developmental period when parents and teachers are less intrusive, allowing peer relations to become a central influence. As we transition toward peer influence, our core skills developed in our families tend to set a tone for peer interactions. Students from highly troubled and stressed families tend to form peer groups identified with a deviance (Harachi et al., 2006) while children from achievement-oriented families cluster with similarly oriented peers (Chen, Chang, & He, 2003; Kindermann, 2007).

Peer Groups and Social Development
Although family influences a general orientation, as we enter middle school, we tend to experiment and often occupy a position in more than one group (England & Petro, 1998). For example, it is possible to be both an athlete and a nerd. These group memberships start to form our identity as we compare ourselves to others (Lubbers, Kuyper, & van der Werf, 2009).

Within the peer group there are pressures to conform with others to avoid feeling isolated (Ohtake, 2007). When disagreement occurs, people susceptible to this pressure withdraw from the argument to avoid taking an unpopular stand. The power of peer group rejection has a significant impact on subsequent self-esteem and social functioning, especially if rejection occurs often (London, Downey, Bonica, & Paltin, 2007; SunWolf & Leets, 2004).

Managing Difference
Our peer group experiences help us learn to cooperate and compete with others as we balance our individual desires with collective pressures (Roseth, Johnson, & Johnson, 2008). Many of us learn to adjust our individual differences to accommodate the group by forming basic collaboration skills that allow us to work toward shared priorities. Some children fail to develop collaborative capacities and remain self-oriented and competitive (Kiefer & Ryan, 2008; Roseth et al., 2008). Such children tend to use social groups to bully others into achieving their personal goals.

Given these peer group dynamics, issues of disagreement and difference are hard to manage. There are four tendencies that emerge as children cope with the group pressures to conform.

1. Children avoid rejection by remaining quiet or acting in agreement even though they disagree with the group position (Burns, Maycock, Cross, & Brown, 2008; Ohtake, 2007).
2. Sometimes children maintain a clearly divergent position vis-à-vis the peer group. This pattern tends to be most pronounced when there is no clear group position (Nathan, Eilam, & Kim, 2007).
3. Inherent in middle school peer conflicts, children secretly talk about others to establish allies and form collusions against other children. This tends to occur when there is no unified set of values and expectations in the group allowing people to vie for power in the group.
4. Some children deal with peer pressure by finding their own source of power. Two common sources of power are coercive threats (e.g., bullying) and discrediting others.

Typically these strategies involve targeting one or two individuals that are perceived as threats.

Socialized Habits and Professional Roles

As adults, we retain these socialized patterns of resolving differences in groups. If we feel impending rejection, we tend to withdraw and remain silent. This behavior can be a problem when we are representing a client's interests among a group of other professionals. When our role is to represent the client's best interests, we must be able to voice concerns rather than withdrawing. from uncomfortable conversations.

The second socialized tendency, to restate positions rather than adjust our thinking, can be equally problematic. It is common for groups of professionals to have divergent positions, which often result in repetitive arguments. When we observe such patterns, it is important to describe our observations so professional problem solving can replace socialized habits. It is also helpful to promote a unified vision so the group pressure toward conformity can mitigate individual agendas.

A third socialized danger is a tendency to triangulate. As we develop a professional peer group, we still compare ourselves to peers who mirror our values while contrasting ourselves to professionals who differ from our approach. If these middle school patterns emerge, we can permanently damage our professional relationships. We must be prepared to engage with all colleagues with the client's best interests in mind.

Finally, when we experience professionals who are competitive, dominating, and aggressive, we will feel the same impulse to withdraw and accommodate that we experienced on the middle school playground. It is important to manage our anxieties so we can act in the best interests of our clients. Doing this often involves confronting other professionals, an act that may diverge from our middle school training.

Challenges for Digital Communicators

If we rely on technology as our main method of peer communication, there are additional challenges to negotiating multiple relationships. Texting, instant messaging, and Facebook wall postings promote a pragmatic approach to communication. These approaches are very direct and succinct. When we communicate using digital means, there is often a flurry of communication until our desired outcomes have been reached.

Although pragmatic communication efficiently takes care of business, challenges emerge when tension emerges. A common approach to online tension management is to break off communication by not responding. This avoidance strategy is not useful when working as part of a collaborative group. Difficulties must be resolved, often through face-to-face communication.

A second habit to avoid is expressing emotion and expecting others to understand and respond. We have all read highly emotional postings on a social networking page. Emotionally expressive posts result in supportive responses, but they also evoke diverse emotional reactions. Emotional expressiveness is not helpful when negotiating collaborative professional relationships.

Skill Adaptations for Multiple Alliances

As we approach multiple professional alliances, we replace our peer group habits by adjusting our interactive skills to the collective context. We still use questioning, reflecting, describing, and directing, but we adapt these skills to forge a collaborative alliance with colleagues and clients. Consequently we use these skills in a network of people all working to achieve client-centered outcomes. We must make four adaptations when applying our skills to multiple alliances:

1. Engaging multiple alliances
2. Achieving collective action
3. Managing conflict
4. Emotional deescalation

Engaging Multiple Alliances

In earlier chapters we learned how to build an alliance with a single client system. In collaborative approaches to intervention, we help the client expand the working alliance forged with us to include other practitioners. Doing this requires us to also ally with other practitioners so that all partners are mutually invested in the outcomes. Even when developing advocacy teams or community groups to address service gaps, we must engage others and establish a focused alliance.

When engaging others in the alliance, we use the same skills outlined in Chapter 5. We must tune in to others to understand and respond. We also go through a diminished type of contracting as we identify goals and discuss each person's role in goal achievement. As we broaden the alliance, we attend to these concerns during the engagement process:

- *Establishing a client-collaborator connection.* As we bring new professionals into the alliance with the client we consider the client's level of autonomy. With informal supports we can often rely on client interests and relationships to facilitate the engagement process. When clients have disabilities or other limitations we must be very active helping them connect with collaborators. We may also need to attend initial meetings and help clients make the initial connection.
- *Establishing interpractitioner connections.* Beyond helping clients connect with other collaborators, we must forge an alliance among the collaborators. Doing this involves meeting with collaborators to discuss our work with clients and listening and negotiating roles that can promote client goals.
- *Maintaining the collaborative alliance.* After the initial connections have been made, it is important to ensure that contact among the collaborators is maintained and focused. Doing this requires ongoing communication and checking in as events occur in the client situation.

Achieving Collective Action

Perhaps the most difficult skill adaptation is helping multiple people to initiate and sustain goal-directed activity. With heavy workloads and demands, it is tempting for collaborators to diminish active involvement when others are visibly serving clients. Each partner must feel that his or her contribution is unique and valued in the collaborative effort. This situation requires us to publicly acknowledge and validate the contribution of every collaborator. We also provide opportunities for all collaborators to shape the service direction. Four sets of interaction help promote collective action:

1. *Clarifying responsibilities.* As collaborators discuss client situations, they are often free with opinions and recommendations. As such contributions are made, we clarify necessary actions. Clarification identifies each person's responsibility in the collective action as suggestions are explored.
2. *Checking in.* When working as part of a collaborative team, it is very important to continue communicating with the other team members. As we check in, we remind collaborators that they important team members. We also reinforce the awareness of mutual goals.
3. *Promoting input.* As events occur in our work with clients, it is important to provide opportunities for other members of the collaborative team to have input into service decisions. When people provide meaningful input, they become more invested in the collaborative goals.
4. *Validating contributions.* All collaborators require feedback and validation. As people fulfill their roles, it is important to acknowledge their contribution to the outcomes. Doing this helps them feel valued in the collaborative relationship.

Managing Conflict

When working as part of a collaborative team, differences in opinion are inevitable. As differences emerge, we openly explore each person's opinion and discuss differences rather than allowing them to remain below the surface. Doing this requires us to identify potential conflicts quickly and immediately get them on the table for discussion.

As we engage the potential conflicts, we describe our observations and use neutral language to avoid reactions among the collaborators. If others believe that we are judging them or taking sides, conflict will escalate rather than resolve. It is important to ensure that all members of a conflict are engaged together in the discussion. Talking behind people's backs elevates the risk of triangulation.

Emotional Deescalation

When conflict emerges, people's feelings become aroused. This arousal can erode collaborative alliances because people are often less logical and more impulsive when emotionally upset (Dutton & Browning, 1988; Sanchez-Navarro, Martinez-Selva, & Román, 2006). When members of a collaborative team become upset, it is often necessary to deescalate their emotions so the difficulties can be resolved in a rational and goal-directed manner.

Deescalation involves exploring the situation in a way that shifts the emotional energy from volatile to benign. This transition sets the stage for rational problem solving by decreasing the emotional energy and providing opportunities for activating cognitive processes. Four common steps are involved in deescalation:

1. *Explore.* The first element of deescalation involves exploring the situation with the emotionally aroused person. Frequently, an angry person's discussion of the situation is externalized (e.g., talking about what others are doing). During the exploration, we shift the focus from action to processing systems so the person begins to talk more about his or her interpretation and feelings and less about other people's actions. Doing this avoids a focus that might escalate the person's emotional reactivity and produces content that remains focused on the aroused person.

2. *Validate.* As the focus shifts to interpretations and feelings, we validate the person's internal experiences and emotions. Validation affirms the person's experience and helps diminish the arousal. When validating the emotional experience, it is helpful to focus on the primary feeling (e.g., powerlessness, hopelessness, inadequacy) rather than secondary emotions such as anger. If we focus on secondary emotions, emotional agitation is likely to persist because secondary emotions often are externalized.

3. *Shift.* As feelings are validated, arousal often diminishes. When the affective power decreases, we can shift our discussion to the interpretations and thinking. We then use interpretative frameworks and meanings to access the underlying beliefs that promote the emotional reactions. As the beliefs are explored, they become available for change.

4. *Challenge interpretations.* As thinking becomes available for change, we promote minor changes in how the situation has been interpreted. We work with the aroused person to help him or her consider alternative interpretations and options in the situation. If we can get the person to consider the alternative interpretations, the level of arousal can diminish further, allowing logical discussions to ensue.

Case Example

A practitioner was meeting with a grandmother living with two teenage daughters and one of their children. Child Protective Services (CPS) was involved with the family and had just threatened to remove the grandchild because of fights between the grandmother and the child's mother. The grandmother was irate and entered the meeting complaining vehemently about the CPS worker. The emotion in the story was fortified with swear words, gestures, and other nonverbal indications of anger. The practitioner listened to the grandmother and validated, "It sucks when people with power don't understand what is happening and start threatening you." The practitioner then continued exploring the grandmother's primary feelings, finding that the grandmother felt powerless in the situation. Eventually the practitioner reflected, "It seems that you are working as hard as you can and desperately need someone on your side . . . but don't know how to get people to understand." The grandmother nodded and asked, "How can I get her [CPS practitioner] to see my side?" The practitioner then started exploring how the grandmother was trying to engage supports and some new options that may be more effective.

Organizational Challenges in Multisystemic Alliances

Although a collaborative approach to intervention is effective, maintaining collaboration across community agencies sometimes can be difficult. Multisystemic interventions place a high demand on agency resources to ensure adequate coordination. Practitioners must be trained, supported, and supervised to ensure that a collaborative alliance is maintained across agencies and between each practitioner and the client. The resource demands and complexity of such interventions make collaborative interventions difficult to maintain.

Challenges emerge in agency practice as administrators must make difficult decisions in response to economic fluctuations and shifts in community priorities. Such decisions often result in compromises that can impact multisystemic working alliances. When insufficient attention is paid to coordinating the multiple services, problems emerge that threaten the expanded working alliance. Three common problems emerge in a community's system of care:

1. Multisystemic overload
2. Service gaps
3. Unresponsive service providers

Multisystemic Overload

Clients with multiple needs tend to be involved with several services and supports (Altshuler, 2003; Hinshaw & DeLeon, 1995). Although each service is involved to respond to specific areas of need, when several services are involved, clients easily can become overwhelmed and experience higher, rather than lower, levels of stress (Ziemba, 2001). Clients must prioritize time and energy to participate in services while respond at the same time to other pressing issues, such as monetary shortages and multiple life demands (J. M. Smith, 2000).

When clients start to feel overloaded, they often miss appointments (Altman, 1993; Rothery & Cameron, 1990). In response, service providers apply pressure to increase the level of commitment. Such pressure can elevate stress levels and threaten the working alliance. Several elements of service contribute stress escalation:

- *Time/resource conflicts.* Clients often are expected to participate with services on a regular basis, resulting in multiple monthly appointments. Each appointment requires clients to adjust their lives (e.g., take time off work, arrange child care), arrange transportation, and then invest time to attend the appointment.
- *Conflicting definitions.* Each agency's mandate and programs apply unique definitions of the client, the problem, and the focus of intervention. When clients attend several services, client and problem definitions vary across settings. Such shifts can become confusing.
- *Conflicting directions.* Intervention is shaped by an agency's mandates and subsequent programs. When clients are faced with divergent advice and interventions, they can become very confused.

To illustrate the confusion of multiple definitions and services, read the next case example. As you read the client story, notice how multiple agencies, each mandated to help, define the client situation differently. Consider how the definitions and programmatic beliefs can create confusion for clients when multiple definitions and approaches are employed simultaneously.

Notice how quickly the involvement of formal services expands during times of crises or when events emerge. Although these services are viewed as potential solutions to perceived problems, the array of services can become quickly overwhelming as the mother and others must balance meetings and attempt to integrate input from the different service providers. Review Table 12.1 to identify how each service differentially defines the problems and the client, creating potential confusion for clients.

Case Example

A woman with her two children entered a battered women's shelter to escape an abusive spouse. Prior to entering the shelter, the spouse had been charged with child abuse because he was also abusive to the children. CPS was monitoring the situation. CPS supported the mother's decision to leave the spouse and facilitated the move to the shelter. The CPS worker also recommended parent skills training because the children tended to be aggressive. The eldest child, 9 years old, also had a severe learning disability and attention deficit disorder/hyperactivity disorder. The school was providing a tutor and had this child in special education programming. The second child was 3 years old and small for his age. He was tested in the past for failure to thrive and was currently being tested for cystic fibrosis. A public health nurse was assigned to help with his development.

The shelter helped the mother access child counseling through the community mental health and also referred the older child to Big Brothers/Big Sisters. To help with the mother's adjustment, the shelter worker also referred her to adult mental health because she seemed very depressed. She was withdrawn in the shelter and often was observed crying. The woman also attended Al-Anon on a weekly basis because her husband had a substance abuse problem.

The woman recently began seeing her husband again. He started substance abuse programming and has entered a violence abatement program. With the potential for reconciliation, the CPS practitioner became more actively involved. The shelter staff strongly encouraged the woman to continue in its support groups and placed the eldest child on a waiting list for their next children's group. At this point, the family is receiving these services:

1. Women's shelter support group
2. Children of Violence Group
3. Children's Protective Services
4. Al Anon
5. Substance abuse services
6. Children's mental health
7. Adult mental health
8. School
9. Tutoring program
10. Big Brothers/Big Sisters
11. Public health nurse
12. Parenting program
13. Probation officer
14. Violence abatement program
15. Lawyer
16. Court

Table 12.1 Multiple Services, Mandates, and Approaches

Service	Mandate	Theory Base and Core Beliefs	Definition of Client	Typical Interventions
Women's shelter	Protect women from domestic violence	Feminist theory—violence is a method of oppression	The *mother* is the victim	Provide safe haven and educate about domestic violence
Children's mental health	Promote optimal mental health in children	Child development—need to correct developmental milestones	The *child* has psychological problems	Child therapy and parent-child therapy
Child Protective Services	Protect children from abuse/neglect	Family systems—parents need to provide a better environment for the child	The *child* is a victim of abusive parents	Hold parents responsible for keeping the child safe

Substance abuse services	Help people stop addictive behavior	Addiction is a disease that controls the addict	The *father* has an illness that causes the problems	Detoxify and support sobriety
Adult mental health	Help people with mental illness manage their illness	Mental illness is caused by biological processes	The *mother* has a mental illness that is influencing the family's life	Prescribe medications and provide supportive counseling
Tutoring program	Help children improve their grades	Children need a solid learning foundation to be successful	The *child* needs help learning important material	Meet with the child to provide lessons and help learning
Probation and parole	Deter repeat criminal activity	Criminals must be monitored and held accountable	The *father* must remain responsible	Meet with the father to monitor for problems
Big Brothers/Big Sisters	Mentor children who are in bad family situations	Children need guidance and support from a reliable adult	The *child* needs support	Take the child on outings to provide a fun, supportive relationship
Violence abatement program	Stop domestic violence	Feminist theory— men need to stop oppressing their partners	The *father* must understand his tactics of power and control	Meet with other men to confront the use of violence and learn alternative behavior
Parent skills training program	Help parents improve their parenting skills	Parents do not adequately understand their children	The *mother* must learn more effective parenting techniques	Meet with other parents to learn about children and appropriate parenting
Al-Anon	Help family members better cope with a family member's addiction	People feed into and support addictive behavior and need to disengage	The *mother* must stop enabling the father and hold him responsible	Meet with others to discuss the addict's behaviors and how to cope
Child Witness Group Program	Help children understand and cope with interparental violence	Violence is an adult problem and children need to understand	The *child* is an unintended victim of the spousal violence	Meet with other children to learn about domestic violence

Responding to Client Overload

When clients are overloaded by the demands and conflicting advice from caregivers, confusion can cause them to withdraw from the working alliance. Consequently, when we notice that clients are overloaded by the systems that are intended to help, we must intervene to salvage the working alliance. Given the nature of the multisystemic alliance, we must simultaneously support overwhelmed clients and the other practitioners to ensure that the integrity of the service plan is maintained. We fulfill four common functions when working with overwhelmed clients:

1. *Support the client.* When clients feel overwhelmed, it is important to listen to them so their pressures are understood. If clients express concerns about elements in the services, guide and support them in finding resolutions with the other practitioners. In this role we support client efforts to resolve problems rather than becoming triangulated by attempting to rescue clients from other providers.

2. *Streamline service delivery.* When multiple services are a result of well-intended but poorly integrated referrals, we discuss client needs with other service providers to identify how to meet needs efficiently, in a streamlined manner.

3. *Establish common understandings.* To correct mandate-related thinking, we meet and discuss the client situation with other service providers to achieve a mutual understanding and definition of family needs.

4. *Mediate misunderstandings.* When clients appear to be distancing themselves from specific practitioners, we work with the practitioners and clients to correct conflicts and misunderstandings.

Service Gaps

In contrast to clients with too many services, we often work in situations where clients have needs that are not adequately met by community services. Clients must then go outside their community, accept inappropriate services, or receive no service. Client needs that the community cannot adequately meet are referred to as service gaps. Service gaps can indicate that the community systems of care have a problem.

Not all service gaps can be resolved in a community. Service gaps are common when clients present with unique needs. For example, a 42-year-old male living in a small rural town approached a practitioner wanting services for men who were sexually abused as children. The practitioner spoke with others in the community and found that no one else had ever requested such services. When the occurrence rate for a problem is low or the community is small, often it is difficult to find services for specific needs.

From Needs to Gaps

When several clients in a community have unmet needs, the service gap indicates a potential community problem. Identifying resolvable service gaps is often a slow process. Initially, we find a pattern of clients with similar unmet needs. As we share the observed patterns with others in the community, common themes emerge. If we find that other practitioners are making similar observations, it is usually a sign that an important service gap exists.

When we identify a service gap, it is important to highlight the gap, allowing others to share their perspectives on the unmet needs. If a service gap remains hidden, it will not be filled. Consequently, we seek others concerned about the impact of the gap on clients. Discussions then become opportunities for multiple practitioners to organize their thinking and plan actions to address the unmet need. As we generate discussions about unmet needs, three elements help us elevate the importance of client needs:

1. *Broader validation.* As we explore service gaps, we expand the discussions from collegial exchanges among practitioners to more formal presentations to administrators. If people with the power to make decisions are not invested in resolving the gap, resources will never be directed toward solving the problem. Consequently, we attempt to have multiple practitioners raise concerns in supervision and staff meetings so the unmet need can become a broader concern.

2. *Client centrality.* As we discuss unmet needs, it is common to speculate about possible solutions. When we shift focus to solutions, we can erode support if others have not participated in defining the needs. Support can erode further if people believe that we are promoting a program without understanding client needs. Consequently, we must be diligent to keep client needs central in our discussions.

3. *Ethics and rights.* As we promote discussions of client needs, it is useful to broaden the discussion to identify client rights. If there is a moral, ethical, or legal right implicit in the unmet needs, it is easier to motivate administrators to respond to the service gap because the system has an inherent obligation to resolve the gap.

Formalizing Discussions

As discussions identify a service gap, administrators and community leaders become involved, which changes the nature of subsequent discussions. Formal action often results in a task force or ad hoc committee to evaluate the service gap and develop recommendations. This transition is important because it legitimizes the discussions and gives the group a mandate to explore possible solutions.

When discussions become formalized, we need an appropriate blend of people on the committee. To ensure that input is gathered from multiple perspectives, it is important for consumer, practitioner, administrative, and community members to participate in the discussions (see Figure 12.3). This blend brings sufficient expertise to assess the adequacy of the current mandates and develop a response that is appropriate to client needs.

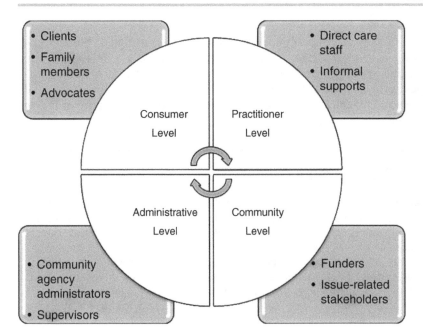

Figure 12.3

Elements Necessary for Formalized Action

- Clients
- Family members
- Advocates

Consumer Level

- Direct care staff
- Informal supports

Practitioner Level

Administrative Level

Community Level

- Community agency administrators
- Supervisors

- Funders
- Issue-related stakeholders

Working with Mandates

As formalized discussions are elevated to include community decision makers and administrators, it is helpful to understand the mandates of the community agencies associated with the client need. It is possible that there are agencies in the community already mandated to respond to the client need. When assessing the agency mandates, consider how well the existing mandates respond to community needs.

When the service gap emerges because the community has no agencies that are mandated to respond to a client need, it may be necessary to convince an agency to expand its mandate to include the unmet client needs. Alternatively, a new service provider may become necessary. In such situations, it is important to have community members and administrators involved because adding services and expanding mandates has implications for organizational bylaws and community funding plans.

Unresponsive Service Providers

The third common organizational challenge is unresponsive service providers. This challenge may involve practitioners who violate a client's right to appropriate services. At other times the lack of responsiveness may occur at the organizational or system level. This type of problem is unique because the actions underlying provider nonresponse emerge from professional decisions rather than the structure of service. Responding to unresponsive collaborators requires us to advocate on behalf of clients.

From Collaboration to Advocacy

In a collaborative system, people share input and negotiate decisions based on others' suggestions. When a practitioner takes a firm stand that is harmful to clients, collaboration breaks down. When the practitioner cannot be persuaded to change his or her position, we must ethically assert ourselves to defend client rights. As we move from collaboration to advocacy, tension will rise in our relationships with the other professionals.

Because advocacy elevates tension, it is important to ensure that the clients are central in all discussions. If we advocate with a focus on a practitioner or agency, our actions can be interpreted as a personal vendetta. Misinterpretation is possible when client concerns become invisible in our discussions. Consequently, it is very important to maintain client centrality by keeping the focus on client rights.

Levels of Advocacy

There are two common levels of advocacy: case-specific and cause-related. Case-specific advocacy is focused on a specific client. In such advocacy efforts, we attempt to alter decisions and actions that are interfering with a specific client's rights. With case-specific advocacy, we often use grievance or appeal procedures to trigger the scrutiny from higher levels within an organization. Almost every agency or service that receives state or federal funding will have an appeals procedure.

Case Example

A practitioner was working with a three-generational family involving a 45-year-old woman, Bianca, her teenage daughter, Fiona, and Fiona's 2-year old child. The family had a significant problem with physical fighting between Bianca and Fiona. As a result, Fiona (aged 15) and her child had been placed in foster care. When they were released from care, Fiona and her child had no food stamps or medical insurance because the social service agency had redirected checks to the foster care agency because the child was in care. The practitioner helped Fiona call her assistance worker to ask for benefits to be reinstated. She was informed that it would be at least three months before changes could be made. The family practitioner worked with Fiona to draft a letter to the supervisor at the family assistance agency. The letter explained that the infant had never been out of the mother's care and appealed the decision asking for special dispensation to restore benefits.

Cause-related advocacy is used when decisions are impinging on the rights of several clients or a population. Typically this type of advocacy seeks to change policies and procedures that interfere with client rights. The policies can be agency-level or larger system-level policies that dictate the parameters of service. Typically cause-related advocacy requires a more complex process involving clients, practitioners, community members, and other advocates working in concert to challenge policies and procedures.

Three Elements of Advocacy

When we transition from collaboration to advocacy, the nature of our discussions changes dramatically. The energy in the discussions is more divisive as we must adopt an argument that is contrary to that of another person. Concurrently, our focus shifts from client needs to client rights. As we assert client rights, we integrate three elements to promote change in the situation (see Figure 12.4). These three elements combine to present an argument for change.

1. *Client rights.* The base for an advocacy discussion is the rights that have been violated. These rights are identified early in the discussion to provide a foundation for our presentation.
2. *Actions.* The second critical element in an advocacy discussion is the action or inaction that contributed to the rights violation. As the discussion unfolds, these actions are contrasted with the rights to establish a cause-and-effect relationship.

Figure 12.4

Three Elements of Advocacy

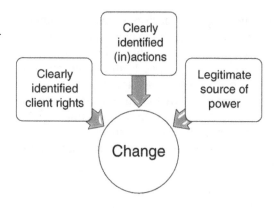

3. *Legitimate power*. The final element used to promote change is a legitimate source of power. To prompt a response, we require a source of power that is meaningful to the other person.

Multiple sources of power can be used for advocacy. Each possible power source is potentially useful, depending on the client situation. Some sources of power are subtle and private while others will cause broader recognition of the situation. It is important to discuss these options with clients before considering action. When the source of power results in client identification, they should be in control of the decisions to avoid ethical breaches and loss of confidentiality. These power sources are commonly used during advocacy:

- *Persuasion*. Often we appeal to a person's logical capacities by presenting a reasonable argument designed to convince the other person to change.
- *Hierarchy*. When there are grievance or appeal procedures, we often help clients use bureaucratic systems to trigger renewed consideration. Typically doing this involves using the hierarchy in organizations, approaching each level to reconsider decisions made at a lower level.
- *Ethics/Values*. When problems arise with professionals, we can help clients register complaints with professional or licensing bodies.
- *Legislation*. When actions violate legal statutes, we can help clients engage lawyers or legal assistance organizations (e.g., American Civil Liberties Union, Juvenile Rights Advocates, Lamda) that can take legal action to force change.
- *Public scrutiny*. Sometimes we use media or other resources to highlight violations in a public forum to bring broad social scrutiny to the situation.

When we engage others in cause advocacy, we often develop an advocacy team. Strong advocacy teams will involve clients and other practitioners. If the advocacy efforts extend beyond the community, administrators and community leaders strengthen the effort. Each type of team member provides unique strengths. For example, clients can advocate using techniques unavailable to professionals. Similarly, administrators and community leaders operate in networks unavailable to practitioners. As we engage others in the advocacy effort, we select invested people who can expand the sources of scrutiny.

Exercise 12.1: Working Across Organizations

You are employed in a child and family therapy agency and are working with a three-generational family involving Kenyata (mother/grandmother), Magena (15-year-old daughter), and Danielle (Magena's 2-year-old daughter). The family referred itself due to frequent arguments that have escalated into physical confrontations between Magena and her mother. Child Protective Services is involved and has been threatening to take the toddler out of the home because of the fighting. The family moved to town about three years ago after Magena's father died of cancer. Reportedly, she was alone in the room with him at the time of his death.

Magena is a very artistic child. She likes cartooning using anime and has developed several comic books with her friend Anthony who lives in her mother's neighborhood. She hopes eventually to do cartooning for a living. She is also very musical. She used to sing in the church choir until her father died. More recently she has started singing with other adolescents who are hoping to form a band. The boys in the band tend to dress goth, which has been the subject of many fights with her mother.

The family lives in subsidized housing because there is currently no work in Kenyata's field. Consequently she is receiving assistance. Last December Magena's older sister also died of cancer. When Kenyata phoned to refer the family for treatment, it was after a severe verbal fight during which Magena had yelled, "Well, I may as well kill myself then." When the intake worker heard of this threat, the family was immediately booked for a crisis session. During the crisis session, it was reported that Magena was not eating well. Based on the lack of eating and potential for suicide, the intake worker arranged for her to be brought into the psychiatric unit for observation. While in the unit Magena was angry and reportedly attacked a social worker when she informed Magena that she would need to go to an out-of-town hospital for the eating disorder assessment.

1. Think about the informal support systems (e.g., clubs, groups, self-help, etc.) in your community that may be helpful for this family.

2. What formal interventions might be appropriate for this family?

    Kenyata (mother/grandmother) and Magena (teen mother) are upset with Jodee (CPS worker). They just informed you that Jodee is unresponsive to their needs. Reportedly, Jodee forced Magena and her daughter into foster care by threatening to take them to court and have Danielle (2-year-old) removed. Magena and Danielle were placed in a private foster home out of the county. Magena is upset because she cannot see her mother or her friends. She also stated that the foster home has been listening in on her phone conversations, looking through her belongings, and refusing to provide Danielle with low-fat milk even though she cannot drink homogenized (whole) milk.. She stated that she had told Jodee about these problems but nothing has been done. When Kenyata phoned Jodee, she was told that the foster home was a good home and if they continued to slander the foster parents she would probably have to place Magena and Danielle in different homes. Kenyata is asking for your advice on how to get Jodee to respond.

3. Identify the client rights that are being violated by the foster parents.

4. Identify the rights being violated by Jodee.

5. Given the rights that are being violated, identify people (roles) inside the CPS system that Kenyata could approach about the violations.

6. Identify people (roles) in the foster care system that could help Kenyata resolve her complaints.

7. Knowing the systems in your area, what external bodies are available for monitoring such problems and ensuring the system is accountable?

8. How would you help Kenyata and Magena advocate against the system? Begin with helping them to frame the problem (rights) and then outline a strategy that can empower them in the situation.

Professional Ethics and Multisystemic Work

Multisystemic alliances give rise to several ethical cautions as the working alliance extends across multiple supports and systems. Collaborative relationships are challenging because we must act ethically with multiple people, each fulfilling a diverse service role. The range of personnel also raises potential problems as we share information and intervention plans. Ethical considerations cover a broad range of practice. Two ethical domains are affected immediately as we broaden the working alliance: collegial relations and informed consent.

The code of ethics insists that we work collaboratively with colleagues and other professionals to maximize client well-being. Two ethical imperatives should guide our responses: We must ensure that our personal feelings toward our peers never impact the client services; and we must behave professionally when talking to, and about, other professionals. Even if we do not like another professional, we must act according to our professional ethics. These three new habits can help to redirect our negative reactions to our peers.

1. *Socialization awareness.* Our socialized habits are automatic responses to collective situations. You may have noticed that these reactions still emerge when engaged in group projects with other students. It is very important that you are aware of your reactions when groups of student or professional peers begin deliberating or planning action. When you notice that you are reacting to others, scan the themes to identify whether this is an automatic response.

2. *Professional reorienting.* When reacting to members of a peer group, it is important to remember professional roles. Not every professional in the group is mandated to achieve the same outcomes. Everyone's job is different, which changes people's approaches to the situation. Consequently, assess each person's thoughts and actions based on his or her professional role in the group. Doing this makes it easier to achieve an alliance because we understand the limits of each position.

3. *Client centeredness.* Whenever working with a group of professional peers, keep client needs and goals in mind when discussing options. All professionals have an obligation to promote the client's best interests. As a result, there is an inherent common outcome that all team members must pursue. . When others take a stand, measure their position based on client outcomes. Even professionals you do not like can provide good service.

When multiple practitioners are involved, informed consent becomes an important consideration. Informed consent begins with clients signing release of information forms allowing information to flow between each professional to all of the others. Often multiple forms are required, identifying each practitioner and his or her setting and specific information to be shared. Practitioners must limit their sharing to the specific content areas that the client has identified in the forms.

Professional Ethics and Informal Supports

Issues of consent are particularly precarious when working with informal supports. Coaches, choirmasters, relatives, and other informal support people are not obligated to follow a code of ethics. Therefore, they have no guidelines for acting on information about clients. Consequently we must be very careful about sharing information or even acknowledging that we know a client.

If it is important that we share information with an informal support person, we first discuss the situation with our client. Doing this requires us to outline reasons for sharing information and the nature of the information that we want to share. The client must then sign a release documenting agreement before any information is shared. Using consent forms can be challenging because the informal support people often know that we are working with the client and are eager to help. In the next excerpt from a telephone call, notice how the practitioner stays within ethical boundaries while still encouraging an informal relationship between her client and the relative.

AUNT: *Hello. My name is Magreet Frances. I know you are working with Nakieta Jones and I wanted to talk to you. I am her aunt.*

PRACTITIONER: *Hi, Mrs. Frances. I have to inform you that I can't even tell you a client's name, regardless of your relationship.*

AUNT: *But I know you are working with her. The family talks about you.*

PRACTITIONER: *It is okay for a family to share information, but I can't even confirm that I know a Nakieta Jones.*

AUNT: *Okay. I understand . . . but can I ask you a question?*

PRACTITIONER: *I can talk with you as a member of the community but really can't share any information about people I know professionally.*

AUNT: *Okay . . . my question is about being a good aunt.*

PRACTITIONER: *What would you like to know about being a good aunt?*

AUNT: *Well . . . I know it is rough for Nakieta at home. She has told me about problems when she is over here (at my house). I really enjoy spending time with her. We bake cookies and go shopping. Her mom doesn't seem too supportive, but I enjoy it when she comes over.*

PRACTITIONER: *It sounds like a really good relationship . . . what is the question for you?*

AUNT: *I wanted to make sure that it is okay to spend time with her.*

PRACTITIONER: *I can't talk about her . . . but I have read a lot of research that suggests that spending time in a positive relationship with relatives is good for any child.*

AUNT: *So it is okay?*

PRACTITIONER: *I am just telling you what is in the research. How does that fit with what you wanted to know?*

AUNT: *Yes . . . it helps a lot.*

PRACTITIONER: *Thank you for calling. You sound like a great aunt that any niece or nephew would enjoy spending time with.*

Exercise 12.2: Supporting Multiple Alliances

You are continuing your work with Magena and her mother (from Exercise 12.1). You are the family's in-home support worker provided through the children's mental health system. You enter the family home for your fifth appointment and find they are very angry because Jodee (the CPS worker) had threatened to take the baby away because Magena was not following the plan to attend school. The family swore at Jodee, who stormed out, telling them that they must follow the plan. When you first sit down, the family is very loud and angry. Kenyata states, "She has no right to try to take Daniele. She is such a bitch. I can't believe she has the nerve to even try. We sure told her, though."

1. You need to deescalate the family and move them toward problem solving. Begin with a statement that will start the exploration.

Your question yielded this information:

KENYATA: *She just wants to get her own way. That's what she wants.*

THERAPIST: *So it feels like she is trying to control you.*

KENYATA: *Damn right. You don't pull a kid just because the mother isn't going to school.*

THERAPIST: *She told you that is why she was thinking of taking Danielle.*

MAGENA: *I haven't been feeling well and I am so far behind now because they stuck me in the hospital.*

KENYATA: *She said that we weren't following the plan so she can't attest to Danielle's safety.*

THERAPIST: *So is she planning to take you to court?*

KENYATA: *She said she was going to.*

THERAPIST: *What did the judge say when you went to court last time?*

KENYATA: *He said she didn't have enough to take Danielle.*

THERAPIST: *What would need to be present for her to have enough to take Danielle?*

KENYATA: *There would have to be violence.*

MAGENA: *We haven't been fighting at all lately. There is no violence.*

THERAPIST: *So what do you think Jodee might say?*

KENYATA: *She could lie about us and say there was violence.*

THERAPIST: *So you feel pretty powerless and vulnerable when it comes to her.*

KENYATA: *Damn right. She is a witch.*

2. You notice that the family is always on the edge of escalating their anger, so you want to validate some aspects of their perspective. Make a statement to the family that can validate the primary feelings of Kenyata.

3. Now identify some alternative understandings of the situation that can build on the validation but shift the emotion.

4. To protect the multiple alliances, devise a plan that can help Jodee restore her working alliance with the family.

Critical Chapter Themes

1. When we work with clients faced with multiple challenges, often several services and professionals are involved with the client system.

2. When multiple services are involved, new challenges emerge as we must maintain an alliance with both the client and the other professionals.

3. Many evidence-based practices adopt a collaborative system of care model where practitioners work closely with other professionals to achieve a well-coordinated array of services.

4. Collaboration places demands on practitioner time and energy because we can no longer work in isolation. Consequently, we are in constant communication with others.

5. There are times when we must advocate on behalf of clients to ensure available and responsive service systems. Advocacy requires an understanding of client rights, policies, and organizational systems. Based on this understanding, we must adjust our use of interpersonal skills.

6. The expanded range of intervention requires us to adapt our skills so we can respond to the needs of the collaborative team and the client.

7. Including the client and managing our professional communication have both clinical and ethical implications. We must be diligent to manage our ethical obligations when collaborating with others.

Online Resources

Center for Effective Collaboration and Practice: http://cecp.air.org/CECP_research_byname.asp

National Resource Center for Community-Based Child Abuse Prevention: www.friendsnrc.org/index.htm

National Resource Center for Family Centered Practice: www.uiowa.edu/~nrcfcp/

Social Care Institute for Excellence: httpwww.scie.org.uk/index.asp

Recommended Reading

Hernandez, M., & Hodges, S. (2003). Building upon the theory of change for systems of care. *Journal of Emotional and Behavioral Disorders. 11*, 17–24.

Hodges, S., Hernandez, M., & Nesman, T. (2003). A developmental framework for collaboration in child-serving agencies. *Journal of Child and Family Services, 12*, 291–305.

Ødegård, A. (2007). Time used on interprofessional collaboration in child mental health care. *Journal of Interprofessional Care, 21*, 45–54.

Santangelo, T. (2009). Collaborative problem solving effectively implemented, but not sustained: A case for aligning the sun, the moon, and the stars. *Exceptional Children, 75*, 185–209.

Winters, N. C., & Metz, W. P. (2009). The wraparound approach in systems of care. *Psychiatric Clinics of North America, 32*, 135–151.

Chapter 13
Managing Threats to the Working Alliance

Throughout this text we explored the need for a positive working alliance between practitioner and client. Service effectiveness and client retention require the development and maintenance of a positive working alliance (Hilsenroth & Cromer, 2007; Spinhoven, Giesen-Bloo, van Dyck, Kooiman, & Arntz, 2007). Although we have learned how to establish a positive alliance, it is important to understand that there will be periodic threats to the working relationship. Some threats emerge in client responses to the worker; some emerge in collegial collaboration; still others emerge through practitioner responses to others (Elkind, 1992).

From Resistance to Alliance Considerations

Client-originated threats to the working alliance historically were referred to as resistance. The term "resistance" located the problem within the client system. Originally, resistance was viewed as a blockage in progress that must be overcome before client goals could be met. In recent years practitioners and theorists shifted the understanding of resistance from a pathological position to ambivalence (Engle & Arkowitz, 2008). Although this shift altered the pathological focus, the locus of resistance remained internal to the client system.

As the concept of resistance was further studied and developed, the location of problems shifted from client personality traits to the nature of the helping relationship (Cullin, 2008; Worrell, 1997). Findings suggest that when clients adopt a subordinate position in the relationship, resistance reactions are common (Whelton, Paulson, & Marusiak, 2007). Research further indicates that resistance can be diminished through three practitioner actions (Jungbluth & Shirk, 2009):

1. Tuning in and attending to client experience as they enter service
2. A relaxed rather than highly structured working atmosphere
3. Exploration of client motivation as they enter service

Inherent in the new understanding of resistance, we seek to understand the client experience as a member of the working alliance (Wong, Beutler, & Zane, 2007). As we monitor client experiences, we watch for alliance ruptures. An alliance rupture occurs when tension, misunderstandings, or collaboration breakdowns emerge (Safran & Muran, 2002). Given that alliance ruptures occur in the relationship rather than in clients, resolution must occur at the interface between practitioner and client.

Alliance Ruptures

To understand alliance ruptures, it is useful first to understand the working alliance. In a working alliance, the practitioner, client, and other collaborators focus their actions and efforts to achieve the goals of intervention. Figure 13.1 illustrates the alliance by an arrow extending toward the goals. The actions of practitioner and client wrap around the arrow. Although their efforts do not mirror each other, they both extend in the general direction of the goals.

When there is a rupture, one member of the alliance directs energy away from the goals. In Figure 13.2, this rupture is depicted by the arrow that is directed downward and away from the goals. Although this arrow is moving from left to right, it does not move upward. This is consistent with an alliance rupture. Even though the client (or other collaborator) remains in the relationship, his or her energy and actions shift direction. This may be due to feelings or a change of mind or because the goals are too difficult.

Figure 13.1

Nature of the Working Alliance

GOALS

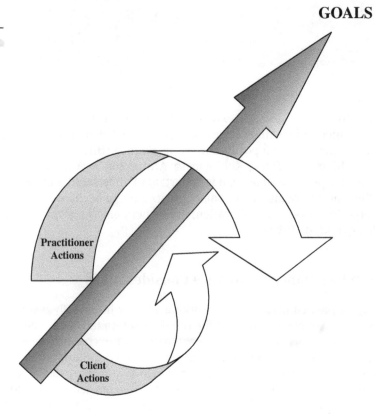

Figure 13.2

Alliance Rupture

GOALS

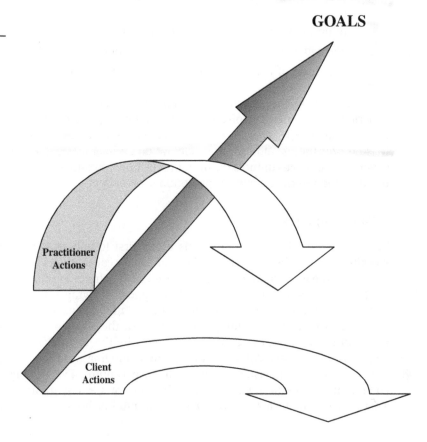

Evidence-Based Practice Implications

Alliance-based research often is identified as different from evidence-based models, but the alliance is an important element in many empirically supported interventions (Borntrager, Chorpita, Higa-McMillan, & Weisz, 2009). Initially, evidence-based practitioners considered the alliance important primarily for retention and compliance (Hayes, McCahon, Panahi, Hamre, & Pohlman, 2008). This concern has expanded to consider issues of active participation and motivation. Increasingly, a working alliance is considered an important element in evidence-based interventions (Garland, Hawley, Brookman-Frazee, & Hurlburt, 2008; Hogue & Liddle, 2009; Kukla & Bond, 2009).

As researchers find that a working alliance is important in evidence-based practice, monitoring for the alliance has begun to emerge in fidelity protocols (Hogue et al., 2008). Practitioners must establish the positive connection and motivate clients toward change. If this alliance wanes, clients will begin to withhold commitment to the change processes, resulting in diminished outcomes (Arbuthnott & Sharpe, 2009).

Sources of Alliance Rupture

Threats to the alliance can emerge from multiple sources. The most common sources involve practitioner actions (Safran et al., 2001), but threats to the alliance also emerge from client responses (Keenan, Tsang, Bobo, & George, 2005; Schröder & Davis, 2004) and the actions of others involved in the client's life (Garber, 2004). When disruptive events occur, a threat to the working alliance emerges.

During intervention, ruptures in the alliance are inevitable (Muran et al., 2009; Safran, Muran, Samstag, & Stevens, 2001). Some are minor and resolve themselves with little effort. Others can be very serious and exert a significant impact on the working alliance (Apsland, Llewelyn, Hardy, Barkham, & Stiles, 2008). If the rupture creates significant discomfort, the working alliance and intervention outcomes can suffer (Muran et al., 2009).

A second important consideration is rupture resolution. When a rupture occurs, the practitioner must tune in to, and appropriately respond to, the client's experience. If the practitioner is responsive and flexible about interventions, it is possible to resolve the rupture and retain a positive working alliance (Kivlighan et al., 1992; Muran et al., 2009). If the practitioner fails to respond, threats to the alliance can interfere with successful intervention.

Responding to Alliance Ruptures

The onus for developing and maintaining a positive working alliance resides with the practitioner (Trepka, Rees, Shapiro, Hardy, & Barkham, 2004). As soon as we identify a possible rupture in the alliance, it is important to mentally assess the intensity and significance of the threat (Apsland et al., 2008). From this initial assessment we decide on a method for getting the threat onto the table so it can be explored and resolved.

This responsibility requires us to scan the relationship to ensure that everyone is invested in achieving client goals. When we identify a possible threat to the alliance, we explore the situation to identify the potential problems. Through this examination we can discover how to resolve the impasse, allowing energy to be redirected toward outcomes (Beutler, Castonguay, & Follette, 2006).

Socialization Challenges

Alliance-related skills, like most professional skills, require some adjustment to our interactional habits. The critical areas of adjustment occur in how we have learned to manage tension and confrontation. We were all guided by our parents and teachers to manage emotional expressiveness (Koesten, Schrodt, & Ford, 2009; Pickens, 2009). In particular, we learned that some emotions are identified as okay to express while others escalate interpersonal tension (Zhang, Chen, & Zhang, 2008).

Depending on our early family experiences, socialization often promotes an impulse to manage interpersonal tension (Shelton & Harolds, 2008). Inherent in our management system, we tend to avoid memories and interpersonal themes associated with past tension (Nelson, Bein, Huemer, Ryst, & Steiner, 2009). Although such socialization influences diminish with age, we tend unconsciously to monitor and respond to tension (Charles, Piazza, Luong, & Almeida, 2009). There are four common socialized systems for managing interpersonal tension:

1. Tension avoidance
2. Defensive reactivity
3. Judgmental confrontation
4. Apologizing

Tension Avoidance

A common socialized habit is tension avoidance. If given a choice, most people elect not to engage others in tension-filled discussions. Even helping professionals have a tendency to avoid difficult discussions (Sportsman & Hamilton, 2007). These inherent tendencies can keep us from putting material on the table that might elevate tension or make others angry. If the material we leave off the table is related to an alliance threat, our tension-avoidant habits can amplify the threat to the working alliance (Afifi, McManus, Steuber, & Coho, 2009).

Threat amplification emerges with avoidance because situations are not explored adequately. Rather, we respond to situations based on untested assumptions (Koesten, Schrodt, & Ford, 2009). With alliance ruptures, it is very important to discuss situations openly rather than basing responses on our assumptions (Beutler et al., 2006; Watson & Greenberg, 2000).

Defensive Reactivity

A second socialization challenge is a tendency to become defensive when criticized. When confronted with negative feedback, we often feel we are being chastised or accused of some inadequacy (Banja, 2008; Polcin, 2006). For that reason, we often experience confrontation as an attack on our self-esteem (Schröder-Abé, Rudolph, & Wiesner, 2007; Sherman & Cohen, 2002). This is particularly acute if our socialization experiences interfered with stable self-esteem development (Kernis, Lakey, & Heppner, 2008).

When clients inform us that we are not being helpful or challenge our approach, we are at risk of an emotional reaction. Emotional reactivity can escalate alliance threats if we respond to our esteem needs rather than to the alliance threat. When working with threats to the alliance, we must use self-awareness and control skills to promote openness to feedback. Such openness allows us to explore the client's experience.

Judgmental Confrontation

An outgrowth of our tension avoidance is a tendency to share judgments, rather than observations, when confronting other people. Inherent in sharing judgments, we often begin with "you" statements. Statements beginning with "you" tend to evoke anger in other people because we assume an expert position, telling them what they are thinking and doing (Kubany, Richard, Bauer, & Miles, 1992).

To temper judgmental confrontations, we use "I" statements. "I" statements tend to be more assertive and report only on our internal experience (Kubany et al., 1992). They are more likely to evoke understanding and engage others rather than creating distance. One of the critical skills involved in making the transition to "I" statements is to describe our observations rather than sharing our conclusions. A descriptive approach makes it easier to avoid "you" focused conclusions.

Apologizing

When our actions create tension or transgressions, we are socialized to respond with an apology. Our parents often insisted on an apology whenever we transgressed as children. Consequently, apologizing is an automatic response. The difficulty with apologizing that many apologies are artificial. Given that many of us have been forced into apologies during our life, we know that many apologies are often rote rather than meaningful.

Apologies serve many functions in our daily communications. One of the main functions of an apology is to achieve forgiveness so the relationship can be restored to its original state (Waldron, Kelley, & Harvey, 2008). When we apologize, it signals that we did not mean to transgress. Consequently, the other person must curtail his or her angry reactions (Krieglmeyer, Wittstadt, & Strack, 2009). As the apology is accepted, the other person relinquishes the right to continue the discussion or maintain anger (Waldron et al., 2008).

Apologizing can be problematic when working with threats to the working alliance because it inhibits exploration. Consequently, discussions may be terminated prematurely before clients can express their feelings fully. Engaging clients fully in an exploration of their experience during an alliance rupture requires us to forgo our impulse to automatically say "I'm sorry." Rather, we must take responsibility for transgressions and explore the impact on clients.

Challenges for Digital Communicators

Some unique challenges exist for people who are more comfortable with digital rather than face-to-face communication. Challenges emerge because resolving threats to the alliance requires us to explore the details of another person's emotional experience. There are three specific challenges associated with digital communication.

1. In digital communication, emotional discussions are simplified through identifying the presence or absence of an emotion (Slatcher, Vazire, & Pennebaker, 2008). The range of emotions tends to be small, and the discussion of emotional events tends to focus more on the context rather than exploring emotional experiences.

2. Digital communication is often more abrupt and direct than face-to-face communication (Gao, Noh, & Koehler, 2009; Zimmerman & Milligan, 2008). Abruptness can escalate alliance threats. When we explore difficult material, it is often important to set up our statements so they are not interpreted negatively. Doing this requires careful crafting of statements to soften how we place material on the table.

3. A final digital communication challenge is managing self-disclosure. Some self-disclosure promotes the working alliance (Watson & Greenberg, 2000), but digital communicators often broadly share information about activities and emotional states as a matter of updating others (Valkenburg & Peter, 2009). These disclosures maintain social relationships. When working with clients, we must be more judicious about our sharing.

Cultural and Social Considerations

Culture, ethnicity, and socioeconomic background all influence the working alliance and how we respond to alliance ruptures. Communication norms are culturally influenced, especially as they pertain to direct feedback and confrontation. Given that alliance-rupture resolution requires us to describe and explore potential threats, we must be very careful to avoid cross-cultural offenses.

Cross-Cultural Timing

The first concern is establishing an integral working alliance. As we begin working with people from diverse cultural groups, we discover that it takes longer to establish a trusting relationship because differences and perceived biases must be resolved before an alliance can emerge (Habib, 2008). Consequently we pace ourselves carefully in cross-cultural work. It is best to avoid early sharing perceptions and confrontation lest we elevate vulnerabilities.

As we meet with people from a different racial group or culture, it is helpful to acknowledge diversity, provided we avoid amplifying the importance of the differences. A helpful approach is to inquire about reference groups that clients draw on for input and advice (Chang & Berk, 2009). Such explorations allow us to learn about people and organizations that inform clients' spiritual, cultural, and situational decisions. Doing this allows us to identify areas of cultural strength and how clients attribute meaning to elements in their situation (Day-Vines et al., 2007).

Cultural Responses to Feedback

Cross-racial and cross-cultural vulnerabilities are amplified when we provide feedback or challenge clients (Hornsey, Frederiks, Smith, & Ford, 2007). Vulnerabilities emerge because members of different cultural groups possess unique self-esteem needs. Emotional reactivity to perceived criticism is an area that requires higher levels of sensitivity because face-saving reactions vary greatly across cultural groups (Kam & Bond, 2008).

Although some cultures react with face-saving strategies when confronted (Kam & Bond, 2008), others prefer to be very open and forthright when dealing with differences (Arcidiancono & Pontecorvo, 2009). We constantly must remain aware of the cultural and racial norms associated with direct communication so we can control our reactivity. If we enter into face-saving responses, alliance ruptures are also possible.

Identifying Threats to the Alliance

The first element in maintaining a positive working alliance is to identify moments that threaten the working alliance. This skill builds on self-awareness and tuning-in skills. Such skills allow us to identify shifts in the relationship that might indicate potential problems. When we identify shifts, we reflect on the situation to determine whether there is a threat to the alliance.

Alliance Ruptures

If problems emerge in the helping relationship, we notice changes in the relationship that help us identify potential problems. Some indicators are logical while others are counter-intuitive. When we know possible indicators, we strengthen our ability to tune in to possible ruptures in the working alliance. Most often problem indicators emerge in how people respond to each other. Some indicators emerge through the processing systems (emotions and thinking) while others involve action systems (behavior and relating).

Processing System Indicators

Many threats to the alliance emerge when feelings are evoked. Although feelings are not directly observable, the content of people's statements and their nonverbal communication often indicates the emergence of an alliance rupture. Typically we notice a change in how the other person responds to our communication. As we tune in to the situation, we start to identify indicators that a problem might be emerging. Some of the common indicators include:

- *Negative sentiments* (Safran, Crocker, McMain, & Murray, 1990). When a person expresses negative sentiments about service or people involved in service, there is a clear indication that the working relationship is in jeopardy.
- *Emotional shifts.* When we notice sudden shifts in emotion, it may indicate a reaction that can threaten the alliance. This is particularly true if the shift occurs immediately after we have provided feedback or described an observation.
- *Face-saving* statements (Safran et al., 1990). When people feel judged, they make statements to protect their self-esteem. Such statements often indicate a possible alliance threat.

Action System Indicators

Sometimes the indicators of risk emerge through interactions and behaviors. Interactional indicators require us to tune into themes and patterns of responding. Action indicators require us to monitor how people's behaviors change during service provision. As we monitor these response systems, we focus on ourselves, our clients, and others involved in the situation. Common action system indicators include:

- *Disagreements about intervention* (Safran et al., 1990). When collaborators argue, disagree, or pressure each other about the direction of service, the working alliance is in trouble.

- *Unquestioning compliance* (Safran et al., 1990). Although many consider compliance a good sign, compliance to avoid angering others or risking rejection indicates threats to the working alliance.
- *Avoidance/nonresponse* (Safran et al., 1990). When people miss meetings and/or fail to complete tasks, there may be a problem in the alliance.
- *Content shifts*. People often change the subject when they feel vulnerable. Sudden shifts in the flow of discussion may indicate an emotional reaction.

Assessing the Rupture

After we identify potential ruptures, it is important to reflect on the situation to decide a course of action. Some ruptures are minor and may correct themselves. In such situations, we continue to monitor to ensure that resolution occurs. Other ruptures will require us to stop the ongoing flow of interaction to explore the potential threat. As we weigh our options, we consider the intensity and type of rupture so we can plan our response.

Rupture Intensity

The phrase "intensity of the rupture" refers to the level of emotional impact evoked in the client. The emotional impact is most often expressed through nonverbal communication because alliance threats diminish trust. Consequently, clients are likely to avoid verbally sharing their emotional response because it will increase vulnerability. Given the lack of verbal expression, we use our observation and describing skills to identify indicators of a possible rupture.

Sometimes reactions are immediate. These are the easiest ruptures to identify and resolve. Other ruptures take time to emerge and are indicated by minor changes in clients over two or three sessions. These ruptures are harder to assess because the rupture emerges as clients reflect on the alliance between meetings. It is harder to resolve these threats to the alliance because we must identify sequence of changes rather than an event-based reaction.

Types of Alliance Rupture

When we assess the potential threats to the alliance, it is useful to consider the nature of the rupture. Although the solution to all ruptures is to explore the situation with our collaborators, the type of rupture influences how sensitive we must be when identifying and exploring the threat. Three types of threats to the working alliance include:

1. *Practitioner-related threats*. Many problems emerge from practitioner statements or actions
2. *"Other-related" threats*. Client and other collaborator traits and actions can disrupt the alliance.
3. *Relationship-related threats*. Some problems emerge from problems in the initial relationship negotiations.

Practitioner-Related Alliance Threats

We all enter our profession to help others, but our attempts to help are the most common source of alliance ruptures. Consequently, it is critical to understand how our behaviors and actions unintentionally disrupt the working alliance. Four common alliance threats include:

1. *Subjugation*. When practitioners tell others what to do or impose their views on clients, the alliance is threatened (Azar & Makin-Byrd, 2007; Bischoff & Tracey, 1995).
2. *Confrontational responding*. When practitioners are confrontational with others, threats to the alliance are likely to emerge (Sommerfeld, Orbach, Zim, and Mikulinger, 2008).
3. *Mistakes*. When practitioners retreat into their thoughts, anxiety is evoked, threatening the working alliance (Ackerman & Hilsenroth, 2001; Sommerfeld et al., 2008). When

practitioners make mistakes but fail to address them, the working alliance can be undermined (Thomas & Millar, 2008).

Subjugation-Based Ruptures

Subjugation-based ruptures occur when we operate from our beliefs and mental constructions rather than working collaboratively to define situations and plan responses. Often subjugation risks emerge when we feel a pressure to solve the client situation and look inward rather than collaborating to find a solution. There are two common forms of subjugation: imposing plans and undermining competencies.

1. *Imposing plans.* Often subjugation-based ruptures involve unilaterally constructing a plan with minimal input from others. This situation may occur if we believe that we understand the situation better than other people. If we find ourselves having to convince others to follow our plan, problems may be evolving.

2. *Undermining competencies.* When we act as if we know more than our collaborators, threats to the alliance emerge (Allen et al., 1996; Elkind, 1992). If we find ourselves constantly explaining, correcting, and educating others, we elevate our status in the collaborative team by implying that others have inferior knowledge or understanding (Patterson & Forgatch, 1985; Vallis, Shaw, & McCabe, 1988).

Managing Subjugation Threats

When we find that others are withdrawing or we have to convince others, we have uncovered an alliance threat. In response, we halt our current activity to reengage others into the working alliance. Doing this involves three elements.

1. *Highlight the rupture.* Subjugation ruptures emerge when we are out of pace with our collaborators. To correct this, we identify how we are out of pace and invite others to share their observations. Doing this allows our collaborators to restart meaningful participation immediately.

2. *Invite commentary.* After people have identified how the collaborative pacing has been disrupted, we invite them to comment on the necessary changes. Doing this allows others to identify alternative directions that might achieve the same outcomes.

3. *Negotiate a new direction.* After collaborators have identified options, we engage them in selecting a mutually agreeable direction.

Confrontational Threats

As practitioners, we often address issues that are ignored or unwelcome. As we identify concerns and attempt to place them on the table, others may feel vulnerable or judged (Schröder-Abé, Rudolph, & Wiesner, 2007; Sherman & Cohen, 2002). Negative reactions are particularly acute when people take feedback personally (Kernis, Lakey, & Heppner, 2008). Two problems emerge during confrontation:

1. *Implicit judgments.* Confrontation often causes people to feel negatively judged (Polcin, 2006). This can result in face-saving arguments and power struggles (Soo-Hoo, 2005). During confrontation, we contrast two conditions: (1) a perceived problem in the current situation, and (2) a preferred direction. Because the two conditions are differentially valued (e.g., one good and one bad), people often feel that their current functioning is negatively judged (Dahmen & Westerman, 2007; Quiamzade & Mugny, 2009).

2. *Empathy erosion.* If confrontation causes us to lose our empathic connection, the working alliance is threatened (Elkind, 1992; Patalano, 1997). Empathy sometimes erodes when confrontation maintains a negative focus (Miller, Benefield, & Tonigan, 1993; Patterson & Forgatch, 1985). To retain a positive working alliance, we need to express genuine concern and support while sharing our observations (Karno, 2007; Moyers et al., 2007).

Managing Confrontations

When placing sensitive material on the table, we can diminish the threat to the alliance by ensuring that our statements do not undermine people's sense of competence (Quiamzade & Mugny, 2009). Feedback should create a sense of concern and support to minimize defensive reactivity (Lizzio, Wilson, & Que, 2009; Polcin, 2006). Doing this requires that we strike a balance between supporting people's self-esteem and sharing information important for goal achievement. These actions can help when we need to confront others.

- *Establish a context of concern.* It is important to introduce the provision of information within a context of concern. We need to set this context in a way that is experienced as genuine and supportive (Lizzio et al., 2009; Polcin, 2006).

- *Affirm the client.* Another critical element is to affirm the client and integrate the information into a positive image. Doing this requires us to affirm people's self-worth prior to providing feedback (Hornsey et al., 2008; Sherman & Cohen, 2002). If we can genuinely integrate the difficult feedback with neutral or positive traits, defensiveness can be reduced (Lakey, Kernis, Heppner, & Lance, 2008; Sherman et al., 2009). An affirmation that taps into the person's motivating feelings can help transition toward a goal focus.

- *Remain descriptive.* We can avoid being judgmental by remaining descriptive. Doing this requires us to clearly and objectively describe our observations as we place the current condition on the table. We describe the actions, or lack of action, that give rise to the concern.

- *Provide a goal-related contrast.* To create emotional energy we contrast the problem behavior with desired outcomes. To achieve this we follow our description with highlighting the goals. The two conditions combined provide a contrast for assessing the desirability of the first condition.

- *Invite collaboration.* After the contrast is developed, invite clients to explore options for resolving the distance between the two conditions. Make sure you avoid leading and allow others to identify what they recommend to reconcile the differences.

Disengagement Threats

The maintenance of an ongoing empathic connection is an important element of a positive working alliance (Ackerman & Hilsenroth, 2003; Constantino et al., 2008). In particular, practitioners need to attend to client communication in a warm and friendly manner (Hersoug, Høglend, Monsen, & Havik, 2001; Samstag, Batchelder, Muran, Safran, & Winston, 1998). Doing this requires practitioners to listen and respond rather than retreating into their thoughts (Littauer, Sexton, & Wynn, 2005). Repeated disengagement creates conditions for the working alliance to break down (Garrison, 2006). Consistent outcomes of disengagement include:

- *Client anxiety.* When we disengage from clients to attend to our thinking, a gap in the interaction develops. Clients become aware that we are no longer listening, which generates client anxiety and speculation about our judgments (Shirk et al., 2008; Sommerfeld et al., 2008).

- *Client confusion.* In addition to generating anxiety, frequent disengagement promotes confusion. We do not develop an accurate understanding of clients if we are constantly retreating into our thinking (Omer, 1997; Patalano, 1997).

- *Worker mistakes.* When we operate from our thinking rather than from client communication, we often make errors. If we do not acknowledge mistakes and assume responsibility for the impact on others, the alliance can suffer (Thomas & Millar, 2008).

Managing Mistakes

When we find that we have created discomfort or made a mistake, the initial response is often remorse (Crigger & Meek, 2007). The initial shock and horror that we have made a mistake can make it difficult to assume responsibility. People often experience an impulse to dismiss the situation or explain the reasons for the mistake (Hollands, 2004; P. H. Kim et al., 2006). Although we may want to deflect responsibility, it is very important to identify the mistake and assume responsibility for its impact on others (Gutheil, 2006; P. H. Kim et al., 2006). These principles can help manage such situations:

- *Avoid apologizing.* Earlier discussions explored our socialization and the use of apologies. In that discussion we learned that apologies function to achieve forgiveness (Waldron, Kelley, & Harvey, 2008) and forestall continued angry reactions (Krieglmeyer et al., 2009). Thus, an apology sweeps the mistake off the table rather than exploring the mistake and its impact on clients (Waldron et al., 2008).

- *Identify that the mistake has been made.* We must identify any mistakes that impact clients and place them on the table for exploration (Thomas & Millar, 2008). If we avoid discussing the mistake, clients are more likely to retain anger about the mistake. Unresolved anger will undermine the alliance.

- *Assume responsibility.* If the potential rupture is caused by our actions (or lack of response), it is important to assume full responsibility for our contribution and the impact on clients (Apsland et al., 2008; P. H. Kim et al., 2006). As we assume responsibility, it is very important to be genuine. If the other person perceives our reaction as contrived, the risk to the relationship will increase (Zechmeister, Garcia, Romero, & Vas, 2004).

- *Work toward resolution.* After exploring the impact on clients and assuming full responsibility, it is important to integrate the experience back into the helping relationship. Doing this involves some renegotiation of the working relationship so clients can have input into how such events can be handled and avoided in the future.

Case Example

A practitioner was working with a family in which a stepmother was very upset with one of her husband's children. The practitioner wanted to help the family resolve the conflict and suggested a family meeting. In the meeting, the stepmother began verbally attacking the child. The attack was vicious, and it took several attempts by the practitioner to curb the barrage. Eventually, the practitioner said, "Betty . . . stop." The stepmother became upset and left the office. The practitioner explored the reactions of other family members and vowed to contact the stepmother the following day. This excerpt is taken from the ensuing phone call.

PRACTITIONER: *Betty, I am sorry you became so upset during our meeting yesterday. I got you to open up about your feelings and then shut you down. I didn't want things to get out of hand and did not know what to do. It was not fair to shut you down like that. You must be very angry with me.* (Notice the beginning of an apology, but the worker shifts to assuming responsibility.)

BETTY: *Damn right I am angry.*

PRACTITIONER: *I know . . . I didn't mean to make you angry. When I saw how upset you were with Nancy [stepchild], I was worried you might say things you would regret later. I set up the meeting to make things better. I should have spent time understanding the power of your feelings before doing that.* (Takes responsibility for setting up ill-fated meeting.)

BETTY: *You shouldn't have told me to stop after getting me started.*

PRACTITIONER: *You're right. I shouldn't have even gotten you started unless I knew you and everyone else would be all right.* (Reinforces responsibility.) *It was my mistake. I am just really glad that you are willing to talk with me still.* (Begins to explore impact on relationship.)

BETTY: *Well . . . I wasn't going to. I was going to just stop everything and not bother trying to make things better.*

PRACTITIONER: *That would be very sad if you gave up on making things better because of my mistake.* (Continued exploration on impact.)

BETTY: *It certainly would.*

PRACTITIONER: *You know, I was trying to get you and Nancy to clear the air so the fighting would stop. I almost set it up so you would continue to fight. I think I missed how upset you were. How can I tell when you are that upset?* (Reinforces impact and begins negotiating.)

BETTY: *I don't like to talk until I get really mad.*

PRACTITIONER: *Is there some way I can ask you, or try to get a feel for things, before making another mistake?* (Continued negotiation.)

BETTY: *Well, you could ask me.*

PRACTITIONER: *How would you respond?*

BETTY: *I would say that everything is okay.*

PRACTITIONER: *And would it be okay?*

BETTY: *Not really.*

PRACTITIONER: *So should I ask you if it is really okay or are you trying to avoid talking?* (Continued negotiation.)

BETTY: *That might work.*

PRACTITIONER: *I would like to do something different from what I did this time.* (Reinforces responsibility.)

BETTY: *Me, too. (Laughs.)*

PRACTITIONER: *Can I make a promise to always check things out rather than moving too fast?* (Finalizing negotiation.)

BETTY: *You better.*

PRACTITIONER: *I promise I will check things out. I think that would be different than most authority figures from your life.*

BETTY: *What do you mean?*

PRACTITIONER: *Well, it seems that authority figures have consistently failed to respond to your needs. It is almost as if I was treating you like your parents . . . I mean, they always seemed to take your sister's side. Did this feel familiar?* (Beginning to integrate the rupture into the goals of service.)

BETTY: *It did, sort of . . . only I got to walk out on you.*

PRACTITIONER: *That is a new response?*

In this example, notice how the practitioner began by voicing responsibility. If the practitioner started making excuses, the discussion would have become counterproductive immediately. After the impact had been established, the practitioner was able to reengage the woman in the relationship. This point of transition can be seen by the rhythm of the exchanges with the practitioner talking less and the client talking more.

Exercise 13.1: Dealing With Worker-Related Problems

A practitioner in a long-term residential facility for older adults helps new residents adjust after being placed in the residence. A new client (placed about one month ago) continually stated he was going home. The practitioner continually reminded him that he is permanently placed, yet the man could not remember due to past strokes. The man's wife visited once in a while, but visits ended with the man getting angry and swearing at her for not taking him home. The wife consequently refused to visit, creating feelings of abandonment in the man. The man became depressed and upset that his wife had abandoned him.

The practitioner met with the wife and found her to be negative about her husband. She spoke of many years of having to live with him but not loving him. There was a suggestion that the man had ruined her life. As she described their life, the practitioner began to feel badly for the male client. At one point the woman said, "You don't know what it was like living with him. It was horrible. I put up with him and his dementia for four years, and it seems that he is still putting stress on me." The practitioner responded to the woman by stating, "You don't know what it's like being abandoned in a place like this. Your husband is hurting, and I don't see you caring one bit about his feelings."

1. What type of mistake was made by this worker?

2. What seems to be the motivating feelings leading to the mistake?

3. Write exactly what you would say to this woman if you had made this mistake.

4. If you were going to try to reengage this woman to help the man adjust, what feelings can you identify that might motivate her to reengage with you?

5. Write exactly what you would say to try to negotiate with her so the two of you could work together.

Collaborator Threats

Most alliance ruptures emerge as a result of practitioner actions, but the working alliance also can be threatened by others involved in the service situation. "Others" includes people such as the client, colleagues, and informal supports. Collaborator threats emerge when people other than the practitioner experience emotions or engage in actions that undermine their commitment to achieving service outcomes.

Working With Collaborator Threats

Collaborator threats emerge in client systems of all sizes. When we work with individuals, the client is the person at highest risk; however, others in the client's life can influence his or her level of commitment (Graff et al., 2009). When working with larger client systems, networks of people influence the alliance on a daily basis because we must deal with alliances among all collaborators.

Identifying Third-Party Ruptures

When a collaborator has difficulty with the working alliance, it most often emerges in how he or she relates to the practitioner. If the collaborator feels vulnerable, alliance problems often emerge behaviorally, which requires us to use observation skills. The most common indicators of collaboration threats include withdrawal, illusions of work, and challenging direction.

- *Withdrawal.* A common response to alliance ruptures is for people to curtail their active involvement toward accomplishing goals. At its worst, this response can involve refusing to participate in service. When people withdraw collaboration, it is often because they feel vulnerable or dismissed in the alliance (Frankel & Levitt, 2009).
- *Illusion of work.* More subtly, collaborators often create an illusion of participation. They attend meetings but have no investment in achieving outcomes (Arbuthnott & Sharpe, 2009). Often tasks are incomplete, and people contribute only minimal effort toward the goals.
- *Challenging direction.* An interactive indicator of other-related problems emerges when collaborators begin to challenge or criticize the practitioner (Watson & McMullen, 2005).

We sometimes notice other-related threats by our reactions to clients. When challenges become negative, we may become upset and emotionally preoccupied (de Oliveira & Vandenberghe, 2009). We may also begin to pathologize our collaborators or feel a need to pressure them to comply. Such responses can undermine the alliance further (Aspland et al., 2008; Safran et al., 2001).

Understanding Other-Related Ruptures

Other-related ruptures often emerge when our collaborators discover that their motivation to participate has changed. When this change is unrelated to our actions, it is often a sign of goal-related problems in the alliance. These problems may relate back to the initial engagement and contracting. Problems also may reflect changes in the client situation. Three common problems underlie other-related threats to the alliance:

1. *Mismatched or unclear goals.* When clients enter service in crisis or in a confused state, they may not be clear about their goals. Consequently, the initial exploration and assessment may lead to mismatched (between client and worker) or unclear goals. As clients becomes clearer about what they want from service, it may not be the same as the worker's understanding, which produces different levels of commitment to the goals.

2. *Changes in goal parameters.* There are times when client motivation early in service is artificially high due to pain or crisis. This motivation level may cause the practitioner to overestimate a collaborator's motivation. When the initial motivating pressures diminish, clients may settle for goal achievement different from the stated goals. The worker, however, not knowing the shift in goals, may continue working toward the initial ones.

3. *Hidden agendas.* There are times when clients come into service with unarticulated expectations. This is common when clients have the secondary felt problem and the person with the primary felt problem is not part of service. In such situations, the practitioner observes clients engaging in activities counter to the agreed goals or failing to engage in activities reflecting work toward goals.

Responding to Collaboration Ruptures

When other-related problems emerge, many practitioners fail to address the alliance, resulting in a seriously compromised working relationship (Bennett, Parry, & Ryle, 2006). When clients or other collaborators begin to distance themselves from service or challenge the direction, it is important to halt intervention activities to explore the rupture. Doing this allows us to correct the relationship by redefining goals, roles, and expectations. When ruptures are openly identified and explored, the relationship can be realigned in a positive direction (Sommerfeld et al., 2008).

When working with professional collaborators, exploring ruptures can be difficult because collegial roles do not permit the same level of exploration. Regardless, it is important to identify ruptures that can interfere with client outcomes (Moore, 2007; Nelson et al., 2008). Doing this can prevent collaboration breakdowns and intervention errors (Baldwin & Daugherty, 2008; Jenkins, Elliott, & Harris, 2006). There are four critical elements when exploring an alliance rupture:

1. Introducing the alliance discussion
2. Setting the emotional tone
3. Describing the observations
4. Inviting and integrating

Introducing the Alliance Discussion

Initiating rupture-related conversations requires us first to introduce the fact that we have made an observation that warrants discussion. Doing this involves interrupting the ongoing interaction to shift focus. As we introduce the change of focus, it is useful to identify that we have made observations that we consider important. The term "observation" is broad and does not single out an individual person. This type of introduction also sets us up to use our describing skills, which can prevent us from using judgments or conclusions.

Setting the Emotional Tone

As we establish a focus on the working alliance, it is important to set a supportive emotional tone. Doing this requires some level of affirmation or validation that acknowledges the other as people of strength and value. If others identify us as concerned and caring, emotional reactivity can be tempered. Stronger cognitive engagement in the ensuing discussion can arise. Some sources of affirmation include:

- *Strengths*. When we put a person's strengths on the table, it provides a visible resource we can use later to master any challenges. For example: "As you speak, I can tell that you have a very incisive mind. You have been able to see through many complex situations."
- *Motivation*. When we want to focus on goals and outcomes, it is useful to tap into the person's motivating feelings. For example: "From what you have told me, I know you really want to get that new job."
- *Current realities*. If internal conflicts or life situations seem pertinent to the discussion, it is helpful to include them in the validation. For example: "From your story, I understand that life has become very hectic and filled with pressure."

The affirmations set an emotional tone through validating a strength or experience. When such elements are highlighted, people feel understood, and a supportive connection is established. In such instances, people can remain comfortable as they engage in the alliance-focused discussion.

Describing the Observations

As we proceed with describing the indicators of a possible rupture, we avoid shifting into conclusions or judgments about others. Doing this requires us to remain very descriptive. To understand the optimal level of description, read the next statements. As you read each statement, pay close attention to the wording.

- "I noticed that you didn't schedule any job interviews."
- "In the last meeting you agreed to schedule some job interviews, but today you reported that you did not attend any interviews."

In the first statement notice how the word "you" is accompanied by a conclusion. This shortens the statement. Such a word choice can result in defensive reactions because it states a judgement about the other person who may feel like we are assigning responsibility. In the second statement, notice how the client is cited ("you reported" and "you agreed"). This phrasing is more descriptive and can help avoid feelings of being judged.

Invitating and Integrating

To engage others in exploration and renegotiation of the relationship, it is important to build on the described observations by inviting active participation. Doing so typically requires us to end our statement with a question so others will feel obligated to respond. As they respond, we can begin an exploration that can reset the working alliance. Three common invitations follow another-related alliance rupture:

1. *Negotiate the relationship*. If the alliance rupture seems to be associated with a relationship problem, the observations lead toward a relationship-focused question. The goal of such questions is to invite clients to express any concerns and renegotiate roles that might feel more comfortable. For example: "I can't help but wonder if we are out of sync on what we are trying to achieve. What are your observations?"
2. *Refocus the work*. When the alliance rupture is caused by a lack of direction or a failure to work toward goal outcomes, describing observations leads to questions about how to refocus energy or assess the feasibility of the goals. For example: "With all the current pressures, are you find yourself rethinking the goals we talked about?"
3. *Explore patterns of reaction*. Often practitioners use alliance ruptures as an opportunity to explore clients' patterns of reacting. When a rupture emerges in the alliance, people often employ their problem-related interpretation systems and emotional responses to

the practitioner's actions (Sommerfeld et al., 2008). In clinical work, practitioners consequently identify the patterns of reaction and explore them in light of the clinical goals. For example: "From what you have told me, this is not the first time you felt someone was trying to interfere in your life. How common is this type of reaction?"

Highlighting Concerns versus Confrontation

As we describe our observations and focus on the alliance rupture, two general approaches can be used: expressing concerns and confrontation. Although both approaches effectively get material on the table, there are subtle differences between expressing a concern and confrontation. With confrontation, we tend to contrast current actions to desired actions. When highlighting concerns, we also include a focus on the other person's internal experience.

Table 13.1 illustrates the differences between confrontation and expressing concerns. Both approaches are explained and illustrated in the table. The last column identifies the critical difference between the two approaches, allowing you to understand each in a step-by-step manner.

Table 13.1 Highlighting Concerns Compared to Confrontation

	Highlighting Concerns	Confrontation	Critical Difference
Introduction/ Setup	The practitioner states that s/he has observed something that seems important to achieving the goals: "I have been noticing something that I think we need to discuss. I feel it is important for achieving our goals."	The practitioner states that s/he has observed something that seems to be out of sync with the goals: "I have noticed something doesn't seem to fit with our goals."	Confrontation introduces two conditions to be contrasted: the current situation and the desired condition (goals).
Setting the Emotional Tone	The practitioner affirms the internal processing of the person (thinking or feeling), focusing concern on well-being: "I know you have a lot on your plate right now, and I want to make sure that we are not overwhelming you."	The practitioner affirms or validates the client in the context of the client's motivation to achieve goals: "I know that you really wanted to get a new job, and I am worried that this might interfere."	Confrontation integrates the affirmation into the contrast between two conditions. Concern is generated in relation to outcomes rather than internal processes.
Describing the Observations	The practitioner describes the observation that promotes the concern: "For the past two meetings together, the tasks that we agreed on were not completed."	The practitioner describes the observation that promotes concern but includes a contrast to goals: "For the past two meetings the tasks we agreed on were not completed. This isn't bringing us closer to getting you that job."	In confrontation, the goals are used as a standard to contrast the current set of actions. In highlighting concerns, the concern stands alone.
Integrating the Alliance	The practitioner puts the helping relationship on the table, extending concern to the other's emotional well-being already on the table (in row 2). "I am worried that we might be pressing too hard and this is overwhelming you."	The practitioner remains focused on the action systems, allowing tension to remain in the unresolved contrast between the two conditions (goals versus incomplete tasks). Presents a dilemma based on the contrast. "I am not sure how we should proceed at this point."	Confrontation puts two conditions on the table, one aligned with goals and one interfering with goals. These two visions present a dilemma about goal achievement. Highlighting concerns remains focused on the relationship and attends to the client's feelings.
Inviting Collaboration	As the practitioner invites the other person to respond, the focus integrates emotional well-being and the helping relationship. "How can we adjust our expectations so they are manageable?"	The practitioner invites the other person to respond, maintaining a focus on proceeding toward the goals: "What are your thoughts about these goals and how we are proceeding toward them?"	Confrontation remains focused on adjusting people's actions using tension between goals and performance. Highlighting concerns remains focused on emotional states underlying the actions.

(continued)

Table 13.1 (*Continued*)

	Highlighting Concerns	Confrontation	Critical Difference
Resolving the Rupture	As the exploration continues, the issues are integrated with the goals of the helping relationship: "You have mentioned other times when things got overwhelming and you kind of shut down. How can we make this different?"	As exploration continues, the goals and methods are renegotiated so direction can be restored. "How can we adjust our expectations so we can help you get that job you want?"	Highlighting concerns generalizes the concern into the client's life while confrontation remains narrowly focused.

When we choose a strategy for describing our observations, it is helpful to consider the desired impact on the other person. Highlighting concerns will couple the identification of potential alliance threats with an experience of being understood and supported. This is likely to lead to a discussion of the relationship. Confrontation tends to focus on how the other person has acted in contrast to the goals. The ensuing discussion is more likely to focus on strategies to ensure goal achievement.

Case Example

When working with a batterer, DiAnthony, to stop his violence (verbal and physical), a practitioner noted a discrepancy between agreements in session and follow-through. Meetings explored stressful situations and how to resolve them without escalating tension. However, DiAnthony never used the alternative solutions. The practitioner had met with the supervisor and decided to confront the batterer with the situation. The next exchange is an excerpt from the meeting.

> **PRACTITIONER:** *I need to talk to you about a concern I have. I am really concerned that our meetings are not helping you as much as we had hoped. We have been meeting for several months. In that time, we have come up with several plans. You decided to use time-out procedures, you developed a cuing system, you were going to use a stress-monitoring system and extra meetings to assure things were cool. I can think of about four other plans that we developed together. Do you remember each of those plans?* (Introduces a concern, describes the observations, then validates the observations.)
>
> **DiANTHONY:** *Yes.*
>
> **PRACTITIONER:** *You know . . . every time we arrive at a plan, we feel pretty hopeful. I see you get motivated and when you leave you seem like the plan might help. Yet none of the plans has been used when you are with your partner. I am concerned that even though we said we were going to change the violence at home, things are not changing.* (Describes the behaviors and discrepancy with the goals.)
>
> **DiANTHONY:** *(Looking angry.) CHANGE . . . are you saying I am not good enough!*
>
> **PRACTITIONER:** *I am not saying you are not good enough, I am saying we are not being true to our goals. The reason we keep meeting is to make these changes, right?* (Maintains the focus on the discrepancy and avoids the bait to engage in defensive justification of the confrontation.)
>
> **DiANTHONY:** *No—I meet with you so you can make me feel better. That's your job, you are my counselor.*
>
> **PRACTITIONER:** *I do want you to be happy, but I don't believe that is what we agreed on when we started meeting. My understanding is we want you to start being happier at home, not just in this office. To be happier at home, we need to get your violence under control. I cannot do that for you; it can only happen through the changes that you make.* (Maintains position and focus on the discrepancy and tries not to invalidate the client.)
>
> **DiANTHONY:** *(Becomes teary.) Everyone tells me that I am not good enough and I have to change.*
>
> **PRACTITIONER:** *I did not make this agreement on my own. Remember when we first met, you were the one who said you wanted to stop beating your partner. Has that changed?* (Still avoiding sidetrack attempts and maintains focus on the discrepancy.)
>
> **DiANTHONY:** *I just want her to treat me better so I can be happy.*
>
> **PRACTITIONER:** *It seems like you would prefer other people to change to make you happy, but we can't control what others do. We can only control what you do. I am concerned we are not making good use of the opportunities we have had to make that change.* (Reflects the thinking themes in the discrepancy.)
>
> **DiANTHONY:** *So you're taking her side?*
>
> **PRACTITIONER:** *No, I am taking your side. If you stop for a minute and look deep inside you, you know what you need to do. You knew the day we first met and I think you still know it. Just stop for a minute and check in with yourself.*

> *(Pause) Do you truly believe that everyone else has to change and not you?* (Tries an expression of support to reach for motivation.)
>
> DiANTHONY: *No . . . .*
>
> PRACTITIONER: *I didn't think so. You are far too bright for that.* (Still supportive.)
>
> DiANTHONY: *(Mumbles something.)*
>
> PRACTITIONER: *Making changes in yourself can be a little uncomfortable, can't it?* (Note that this is a leading question—don't do it.)
>
> DiANTHONY: *Yeah.*
>
> PRACTITIONER: *To meet your goals, you will need to do some things that are uncomfortable and new. Are you still wanting to try to make the changes that we agreed on when you first came in?* (Opens up the possibility for recontracting the goals, still focuses on the discrepancy.)
>
> DiANTHONY: *Well . . . I'll try.*

In the example, the practitioner elected to use confrontation because the client's actions were inconsistent with the goals. There was a clear threat to the alliance because DiAnthony was attending service but was not actively working toward goals. This inactivity creates the illusion of work rather than producing real effort to change. There was a history of support and caring between the two, so shifting the focus to action was appropriate.

Exercise 13.2: Navigating Client Challenges to the Alliance

You are working in a job-readiness program for people diagnosed with a mental illness. You are meeting with a woman diagnosed with bipolar disorder. She has very strong social skills, is punctual, and has attended every meeting. You have worked with her on job interview skills, writing resumes, and developing cover letters. Each week she was assigned a task to complete but never brought back any indication that the task had been accomplished. You feel you need to address the situation.

1. What observed behaviors would you use to focus the discussion?

2. Write exactly what you would say to introduce the discussion.

3. What would you say to set the emotional tone for the discussion?

4. Write exactly what you would say in your descriptive statement to highlight the discrepancy between goals and behavior.

5. Write the question you would use to open up the situation for discussion.

6. Where would you try to guide the discussion so the helping relationship might be renegotiated?

Larger Client System Alliances

Larger client systems, such as families, groups, organizations, and communities, have very complex working alliances because each member must ally with the practitioner and with each other. Inherent in this complex alliance, members must forsake self-focused interests in favor of collective goals (Green, Hill, Friday, & Friday, 2005). The shared alliance is contingent on open communication and goal-consensus (Marvin, 2002).

Alliance Threats in Larger Systems

The complexity of larger systems increases the risk of alliance problems. Success is contingent on focused collective energy. In contrast, failure can hinge on the actions of one or two people within the system. Larger client systems experience two major threats to the working alliance: goal erosion and individualistic divisiveness.

Goal Erosion

Larger system performance directly affects the alliance among the system members. If the system is able to achieve goals, members remain enthusiastic and committed. However, when goal achievement is elusive, members of the system experience feelings of futility, which erodes commitment to the goals (Barlas & Yasarcan, 2006).

Underlying the erosion, system members tend to feel powerless as successive attempts toward goal achievement fail. Eventually, members elect to direct their energy into other pursuits. When the shared commitment to collective goals is low, system members also become tolerant of individual agendas and divergences from the stated collective vision (Fritsche, Kessler, Mummendey, & Neumann, 2009).

Sometimes systemic organization can undermine progress toward goals and subsequent goal erosion. Consequently, we often assess how the system interprets information and responds to the environment. Doing this allows us to understand system-related threats to the working alliance. Two elements seem to influence goal attainment and subsequent alliances:

- *Information processing.* Systems that collect goal-specific information and share it among the members tend to have stronger alliances and commitment toward goals. In contrast, systems that collect larger amounts of unfocused information or limit access often have weaker alliances to goals (Perez-Freije & Enkel, 2007).

- *Member input.* When members receive appropriate information and are allowed to provide input, they maintain a higher commitment toward goals (Perez-Freije & Enkel, 2007). Such systems tend to respond to environmental situations more efficiently and yield better outcomes.

Individual Divisiveness

Collective functioning is best when individual competitiveness is minimized and collective interests are endorsed (Tjosvold & Yu, 2004). When collective interests prevail, people tend to go outside their individual roles and contribute to shared outcomes. In contrast, when individuals fail to collaborate, collective goals are not achieved (Barlas & Yasarcan, 2006; Medina, Munduate, & Guerra, 2008).

There is a natural tension in larger systems between self-interest and the collective interest (Goldstone, Roberts, & Gureckis, 2008). Collective outcomes are contingent on members forsaking individual strivings for the good of the collective. In contrast, self-enhancement increases negativity and decreases the interconnectedness among system members (van den Bos & Stapel, 2008). If inter-member cohesion continues to erode, it can destroy collective action as well as undermine system goals.

Responding to Larger System Threats

Given the value of communication and information in larger systems, it is important to immediately begin open discussions when system members lose their commitment to collective goals (DeCremer, van Knippenberg, van Duk, & van Leeuwen, 2008; Letendre, Gaillard, & Spath, 2008). When committed system members share their commitment, individuals who are wavering can become reengaged in the working alliance (Fristche et al., 2009). There are two common methods for encouraging reengagement: changing the system to enhance inclusion and working with individuals to promote reengagement.

1. *Systemic inclusion*. When collective goals erode, it is important to engage members of the system in an exploration of the dynamics that are interfering with goal achievement. Open discussion among members enhances collaboration and innovation (Müller, Herbig, & Petrovic, 2010). Even digital communication can help to increase group commitment toward outcomes (Lira, Ripoll, Peiró, & González, 2007).

2. *Individual reengagement*. When we help members make progress toward common goals, motivation and commitment to the shared goal increases among the team members (Loersch, Aarts, Payne, & Jefferis, 2008). Often members who are not identified as formal leaders in the system can be instrumental in providing informal leadership and refocusing the system on goal achievement (Rudden, Twemlow, & Ackerman, 2008).

Critical Chapter Themes

1. Resistance is relational and must be interpreted as an indication that practitioner and client are no longer in pace with each other.

2. Threats to the working alliance can be client, worker, or relationship based; each requires a different method of getting potential problems on the table for resolution.

3. Whenever the working alliance is threatened, it is important to get threats onto the table so potential problems can be explored and resolved.

4. When a client-related threat to the alliance is evident, we must:
   ○ Balance support with demands so clients never feel judged or attacked.
   ○ Be descriptive when putting the issue on the table so clients feel supported.
   ○ Explore the situation so the clients' position can be validated and the goals of service can be pursued.

5. When a practitioner-related threat to the alliance is present, one must:
   ○ Acknowledge and validate the impact on clients rather than avoid exploring problems.
   ○ Take full responsibility for the problem rather than minimize or dismiss the situation.
   ○ Move toward resolution of the problem in a way that maintains the service alliance.

6. When a relationship-related threat to service is evident, one must:
   ○ Identify a clearly describable pattern that indicates a loss of pacing.
   ○ Be descriptive when putting the potential problem on the table.
   ○ Explore the situation so that the alliance can be renegotiated.

Online Resources

Management-Related team-building resources: http://managementhelp.org/grp_skll/teams/teams.htm

Positive confrontation skills Web site: www.constructiveconfrontation.com/whitepaper/index.php

Psychotherapy.net article on the working alliance: http://www.psychotherapy.net/article/Therapeutic_Alliance

Tension management and relationships Web site: http://www.tensionmanagementinstitute.org/

Recommended Reading

Apsland, H., Llewelyn, S., Hardy, G. E., Barkham, M., & Stiles, W. (2008). Alliance ruptures and rupture resolution in cognitive-behavior therapy: A preliminary task analysis. *Psychotherapy Research, 18,* 699–710.

de Oliveira, J. A., & Vandenberghe, L. (2009). Upsetting experiences for the therapist in-session: How they can be dealt with and what they are good for. *Journal of Psychotherapy Integration, 19,* 231–245.

Muran, J. C., Safran, J. D., Gorman, B. S., Samstag, L. W., Eubanks-Carter, C., & Winston, A. (2009). The relationship of early alliance ruptures and their resolution to process and outcome in three time-limited psychotherapies for personality disorders. *Psychotherapy: Theory, Research, Practice, Training, 46,* 233–248.

Watson, J. C., & Greenberg, L. S. (2000). Alliance ruptures and repairs in experiential therapy. *Journal of Clinical Psychology, 56,* 175–186.

Chapter 14
Ending the Working Alliance

The helping relationship is by its very nature temporary. When clients achieve their goals, the relationship ends. The experience of ending a relationship is troubling and powerful for many people (Leigh, 1998; Perilloux & Buss, 2008). The working alliance involves a close and personal relationship. As a close relationship impending endings can evoke emotional responses in both the practitioner and the client. This chapter explores the challenges and helpful responses that can make ending the alliance a healthy, rather than a disruptive, experience for clients.

Socialization Challenges to Endings

Throughout our lives we are exposed to various types of ending in our families, friendships, and life situations. Depending on the nature of these endings, we store affective memories that influence how we manage endings. Reactions are most deeply felt when we are invested in the relationship (Hynan, 1990; Tyron & Kane, 1993). The prevalence of the multiple endings in our lives often results in awkwardness when it is time to say good-bye.

Learned Patterns of Ending

Our approach to managing separations emerges through our experiences of ending and the modeling of people in our life. We watch parents respond to losses and follow their guidance as they nurture us through our own endings. We all have endings embedded in our lives. Consider shifting friendships, graduations, past lovers, and kinship losses. These are all natural ending moments. If we have multiple separations our patterns of responding are likely well established. Some of us have also had traumatic endings such as parental losses, untimely deaths, and endings imposed by authority figures (such as entering foster care, incarceration).

Our history of endings provides a template for how we manage impending separations. We may find that memories of these endings emerge as we approach professional endings. This is because our brains tend to retrieve associated memories when we experience emotion. This retrieval system elevates the risk that we will respond to client endings as we would respond to our personal endings. As a professional we should manage our client endings with the same sense of purpose and control that we use in all aspects of the working alliance. To help to gain this level of control, we must often adjust two areas of socialization; emotion management and loss management.

Emotion Management
The first socialization element is how we respond to emotional arousal. Inevitably relationship endings evoke an emotional response and a sense of loss. Even happy endings, such as graduations, can produce mixed feelings when we discover that we will be moving away from friends. Our patterns of managing the emerging feelings are a result of parental modeling and socialization (Yahya, 1999).

The emotional socialization involves two elements: parental modeling and parental guidance.

1. We watch our parents and how they manage their emotions (Yahya, 1999). Such modeling establishes family norms that we follow as we develop.

2. We also learn how to manage emotions based on how our parents responded to our emotional expression. If parents invalidated our emotional experiences, later emotional responses tend to be tainted by anxiety and depression (Krause, Mendelson, & Lynch, 2003).

Past emotional experiences are stored in our memory. As we participate in future experiences that parallel those in our past, the emotion-related memories are retrieved. These memories tend to influence our emotional experiences, often amplifying the intensity of the emotion (Daselaar et al., 2008). Given this pattern, our past experiences of ending will influence our level of emotional arousal and subsequent responses.

Loss Management

The second socialized element emerges through our past experience with relationship endings. Of these experiences, the most powerful involves the loss of family and romantic relationships. When we learn that a relationship is ending, feelings of loss, confusion, and decreased self-esteem are common (Perilloux & Buss, 2008). In response to these feelings, we learn various strategies to manage or minimize the emotional impact of ending. Most strategies seek to increase the sense of controllability. When we feel in control of an ending, we can mediate the negative emotional reactions (Frazier & Cook, 1993). Common strategies include:

- *Withdrawal/avoidance* (Battaglia et al., 1998). A common strategy for managing termination-related feelings is to withdraw from the relationship and decrease active attempts to communicate with the other person.
- *Denial of ending.* Many people refuse to accept the ending. Such refusal often is accompanied by attempts to fix the relationship (Battaglia, Richard, Datteri, & Lord, 1998). Frequently, this includes acts that attempt to replicate early relationship dynamics.
- *Deny relationship investment.* As people approach the end of a relationship, they sometimes deny the importance or emotional investment associated with the relationship (Bettner, 2007). Doing this eases feelings of loss associated with the ending.
- *Argue or fight.* A common strategy for ending relationships is to begin arguing and fighting with the other person (Battaglia et al., 1998). The generation of anger and contention distracts from more vulnerable feelings, such as loss or rejection.
- *Transfer relationships.* Many people enter an alternative relationship prior to ending the current relationship (Battaglia et al., 1998). This strategy allows the person to focus on the new relationship, which distracts from the pain of ending.

Experience of Ending

Inherent in the experience of ending, we often become unsettled and overwhelmed. Our minds shift from memories of the shared past, to painful emotions, to anxiety about a relationship void in the future. These mental shifts are common for most people experiencing a meaningful ending. Some of the disorientation occurs as a result of our habitual life organization and how we manage our time.

Time Orientation and Life Organization

We often live life with very little conscious attention to how we relate to time. Throughout this book you have learned about interactive habits that govern how we interact. We also have organizational habits that allow us to prioritize our mental energy and organize our efforts. One of the organizing principles is our approach to time. Much of our mental energy organizes around a focus on the past, present, or future.

Three Time Orientations

As we organize our lives, we orient discretely to the past, present, and future, depending on environmental demands and personal interests. We seldom focus on more than one time domain; rather we maintain a singular focus on the past, present, or future. This organization allows us to retain focus when performing tasks and engaging in social discourse.

A future orientation is important for visualizing possibilities. In contrast, an absence of future orientation is associated with nihilistic behaviors, such as pathological gambling and substance abuse (Petry, 2001). The future orientation is often associated with goal-directed behavior, such as pursuing an education (Horstmanshof & Zimitat, 2007; Phan, 2009). When we are focused on the future, we tend to think more and are less accepting of our current situation (Öner-Özkan, 2004). Any student who has experienced "senioritis" knows how a future orientation makes it difficult to return to a present orientation.

The present orientation is more strongly associated with acceptance (Öner-Özkan, 2004). When we remain focused on the present, we achieve satisfaction because events in the past and possibilities in the future have no urgency (Sobol-Kwapinska, 2009). A present orientation is also associated with active concentration and mindfulness (Roemer & Orsillo, 2003). We can all remember working on a project, losing track of time, and then reorienting in astonishment to learn how much time had passed. This situation is common when we remain focused on the present.

When we focus on the past, there is a tendency to be more emotional and indecisive (Díaz-Morales, Ferrari, & Cohen, 2008). Rumination about problems is associated with a past focus, whereas worry tends to focus on the future (Watkins, Moulds, & Mackintosh, 2005). Some research has found that people with a negative-focused past orientation are more prone to aggression (Anderson, 2006). However, a positive past orientation is associated with compromise and flexible expectations (Recchia & Howe, 2009).

Time Orientation Flexibility

Although many people have a tendency to orient more strongly toward a single time orientation, our day-to-day orientation shifts. Time orientation also changes with age with people in their 40s more future oriented than those older and people with established careers more present focused (Higata & Okamoto, 2008). On a day-to-day basis, our orientation to time shifts regularly depending on social events, priorities, and demands (Jonas & Huguet, 2008).

Even though time orientation shifts depending on our life circumstances, we have a tendency to focus on a single dimension at any given time. This allows us to immerse ourselves in the mental or emotional experience. When we focus on the past, we tend to bask in an emotional experience, which is qualitatively different from intense planning about the future or focused attention in the present.

Habitual Time Orientation

Inherent in our approach to time is the fact that we tend to ignore two domains and organize our focus on a single time. Notice in Figure 14.1 how the past, present, and future have very little overlap. This is how we typically organize our time. Although the past,

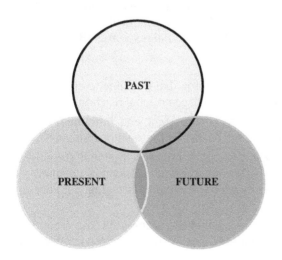

Figure 14.1

Typical Orientation to Time Dimensions

Figure 14.2

Overlapping Times during Termination

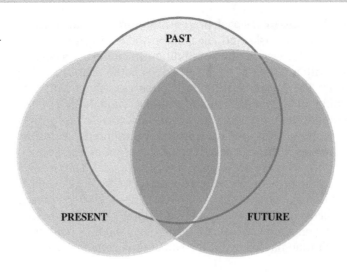

present, and future exist in every moment of life, often it is easier to focus on one time to the exclusion of others. When events demand that we shift priorities, we select a new focus and ignore the other elements of time. These time management habits become central to how we live our lives.

Endings and Time Disorientation

When we deal with an ending, the pattern of focusing on a single time dimension breaks down because all three times have equal urgency. We cannot ignore any of the times because of feelings associated with each. In Figure 14.2 we can see that as the three times converge, there is a greater overlap between the dimensions of time. When this occurs, our method for organizing mental focus breaks down.

When our habitual pattern of singular focus on a time dimension erodes, we become disoriented. During an ending, our mind shifts from feelings of loss (present) to memories of the relationship (past) and then immediately to considering a future without the relationship. As our mind continually shifts focus, we feel disoriented, which amplifies the emotional experience, increasing our desire to avoid endings.

Impact of Ending the Working Alliance

When the helping relationship draws to a close, clients often experience emotional reactions (Younggren & Gottlieb, 2008). Their emotional responses are influenced by the depth of the helping alliance and the practitioner's management of the termination stage. Four sets of conditions tend to modulate clients' emotional responses (Baum, 2005, 2007; Younggren & Gottlieb, 2008):

1. *Source of the termination decision.* The person deciding that it is time to end services has increased control. This sense of control mitigates the emotional reactions to ending.
2. *Working alliance.* When the working alliance is important and influential to the participants, they experience increased feelings of loss as the relationship ends.
3. *Termination process.* Abrupt endings result in more intense emotional responses. Ending requires opportunities to explore the positive and vulnerable elements of termination. Consequently, we must carefully pace and explore the ending relationship during the final meetings.
4. *Intervention outcomes.* When goals have been achieved successfully, the emotional impact of ending is positive. With goal failures, the reasons for nonachievement influence the emotional response.

Ending-Related Disorientation

The experience of ending can become quite disorienting because our singular mental focus on the past, present, and the future experiences breaks down. In an ending we struggle because thinking often shifts from one time orientation to the others. This disrupts our traditional organization which compounds the emotional experience of ending. It is important to consider all three times; the past, present and future as we approach ending the working alliance.

Loss, the Past, and the Working Alliance

The most powerful emotional response for clients is a feeling of loss as the relationship draws to a close (Baum, 2005; Roe, Dekel, Harel, Fennig, & Fennig, 2006). As clients begin to experience the loss-related feelings, internal processes activate loss-related memories (Amini et al., 1996; Daselaar et al., 2008). Memories modify loss because emotional-laden memories tend to amplify the affective experience (Kensinger, 2007; Phelps & Sharot, 2008). Given these dynamics, clients with a history of painful endings are particularly vulnerable as they respond to the termination-related feelings (Zilberstein, 2008).

As feelings and memories of loss are evoked, a past orientation tends to emerge. At times clients will focus on the loss of the helping relationship but occasionally feelings and memories of personal endings emerge. This is a difficult combination, given that many clients have negative history with endings. Consequently the pain of loss can be distracting, leading to rumination and defensive responses.

Present-Focused Feelings

Feelings of loss are not the only ones associated with ending. Negative feelings are balanced by progress and changes that occur during intervention (Roe et al., 2006). Although the negative feelings tend to emerge as an immediate reaction, it is possible to help the clients shift their focus to their successes and growth. Doing this can provide a more balanced emotional experience of ending.

The acknowledgment of progress is a present-focused feeling. Clients typically are aware that they have made progress toward their goals and can understand the logic of ending. When success-focused thoughts emerge, some of the pain associated with loss can diminish. However, if the success is attributed to the practitioner, such feelings can be short-lived.

Anxieties and the Future

When thoughts of the future emerge for clients, anxiety may emerge. It is common for clients to worry about maintaining their changes without continued support. Clients need high levels of confidence and efficacy to launch from the working alliance. If such feelings are not present, the anxieties about a future without practitioner support may cause clients to resist ending.

With a future orientation comes thinking and the potential for worries (Watkins et al., 2005). Thinking and visualizing the future can intrude on clients' experiences, distracting their sense of accomplishment and compounding feelings of loss with anxieties. At times the blend of feelings may become disorienting for clients.

Emotional Cycling

With the equal urgency of the three times (past, present, and future), client attention tends to shift from past, to present, to future in random succession. Each of the times, and its associated feelings, intrudes into client awareness for brief moments, only to be replaced by a different time orientation and a new feeling. If feelings of anxiety or loss are stronger than feelings of success, the ending can be difficult to manage.

Clients with difficult loss histories and/or lower levels of confidence can feel threatened by these affective shifts. Emotional upheaval puts clients in a vulnerable position because the emotional intrusions can interfere with their thinking as they begin to plan how to retain their gains after intervention. If clients struggle with the flow of ending-related feelings, often we must slow down their experience so the ending can become helpful and growth producing.

Managing the Ending Process

With the level of emotionality and disorientation inherent in endings, practitioners have an ethical responsibility to help clients transition from service to a successful future (Rappleyea, Harris, White, & Simon, 2009; Younggren & Gottlieb, 2008). Doing this requires us to reorient clients to the purpose and goals that guide the working alliance. The ending process must be a component of the helping alliance rather than an abrupt abandonment punctuating the end of service.

As we orient clients into the termination phase of intervention, we are concerned with how to get issues of ending gently onto the table and then how to proceed toward ending the alliance in a health-producing manner. Ultimately we want to solidify client gains evidenced throughout intervention and help them to transfer changes into the future. Doing this requires a very careful introduction of termination and responsive pacing throughout the ending process.

Timing the Introduction

Our first ending-related challenge is timing the introduction of ending. If we introduce ending too soon, we may increase client anxiety, causing a rupture in the alliance. If we introduce the ending too late, we will not have enough time to explore and resolve clients' termination-related feelings.

Termination ideally occurs when it is obvious that clients no longer require intervention and their goals have been met (Younggren & Gottlieb, 2008). Client symptoms should be reduced to a level that allows clients to have confidence in their ability to cope in situations similar to those that prompted intervention (Goldfried, 2002).

Managing Avoidance

As ending becomes inevitable, we often must focus on managing avoidance tendencies. Practitioners have a tendency to forestall discussions about the inevitable ending (Mirabito, 2006). Given that clients often are similarly motivated, it is easy to find ways to prolong the relationship beyond the achievement of client goals (Zilberstein, 2008). Some of the common avoidance strategies include:

- *Prolonging the ending.* Practitioners may avoid the ending by extending service through spacing appointments at longer intervals. This method effectively retains the relationship while allowing the alliance to decrease. When the meetings are spaced at longer intervals, the nature of discussions focuses on updating and follow-up. Follow-up is a useful method of supporting gains; however when it is used to avoid discussing the end of active intervention, it reflects practitioner collusion with the client to avoid ending.
- *Illusions of ending.* Some practitioners create the illusion of ending by making the final session qualitatively different from past alliance-based meetings. For example, many group practitioners have a pizza party on the last day of group but fail to discuss the ending prior to the party. This method precludes a meeting to explore and resolve termination-related feelings.
- *Promoting drift.* As clients begin to achieve their goals, they often cancel appointments because they have increased their mastery. As meetings are canceled, it is easy to become unresponsive and allow clients simply to drift away. This method leaves the relationship open and also avoids the termination discussion.
- *Shifting focus..* Many practitioners find new reasons to continue with clients as client goals are achieved. This method extends the relationship by introducing new goals or areas for work. Given that everyone has areas for work, it is perpetually possible to find new areas of focus, allowing the practitioner and client to avoid termination for extended periods.
- *Shifting relationship.* Some practitioners find ways to continue seeing clients after active treatment ends. Relationships shift toward friendships as the practitioner sees

clients in social settings. Although practitioners may consider this follow-up, unless it is part of a formal follow-up plan, it may serve the practitioner's need to retain the relationship more than client needs.

It takes clear thinking and self-awareness to identify that clients are nearing goal achievement and proceed with a balanced ending that avoids abandonment but promotes client autonomy. Strategies of balancing healthy endings differ based on our professional roles. For example, practitioners working with youths in care need to retain a loose relationship into the future because the youths require stability and continuity. Consequently, youth workers may have follow-up systems that extend elements of the working alliance far into the future. This system may be inappropriate for an outpatient clinical practitioner.

Predicting the Client Response

The timing and length of the termination phase emerges from our understanding of clients and their experiences with loss (Zilberstein, 2008). As we move into the ending, it is helpful to extend the maximum level of control to clients. Doing this extends the collaborative alliance into the negotiation of how to end service (Greenberg, 2002).

As we prepare to introduce the inevitable ending, it is important first to reflect on clients' backgrounds and investment in the alliance in order to predict likely responses to ending. Some clients will experience difficult emotional reactions to ending; others may welcome the transition. It is helpful to identify which type of response is likely before initiating a discussion about ending.

Preparation identifies likely reactions to ending and helps us to plan our approach to final discussions of the working alliance. If clients are unlikely to react, we may want to remain goal focused until it is obvious that the ending is due. At this point we can explore goal accomplishments and proceed toward ending as a logical outcome. With clients who may react, we want to allow for time to explore and resolve difficult feelings. To accomplish resolution, we need time.

Anticipating client responses also allows us to find strategies for softening the impact of ending. We may want to introduce the ending in stages, such as first identifying the goals and accomplishments and then exploring how well the accomplishments are generalizing into clients' lives. These accomplishments can then be used as a platform to introduce ending. This platform can be used to balance out negative emotional reactions. There are three considerations as we consider the potential response of clients:

1. *Client history.* Clients have a history with endings that can be expected to influence their experience as we introduce a new ending. If they have had very bad endings (e.g., deaths, multiple placements, parental divorce, abandonments, etc.), we can expect some difficulty. Sometimes difficulty results in emotional expressiveness, but at other times it involves repression of emotion. If there have been difficult endings, it is wise to allow for enough time to explore and resolve the feelings but ensure that the discussion does not occur too early, lest anxiety and avoidance result in an early client departure.

2. *Goal achievements.* When clients have achieved their goals, it is easier to identify that ending is necessary. Goal achievement also provides feelings of success that can moderate the experience of loss so working through termination-related feelings may require less time. When timing the introduction of ending, you may want to allow more time if some of the goals are tenuous.

3. *Alliance investment.* When clients have been heavily invested in the helping relationship and rely on practitioner input for making important decisions, the announcement of termination will likely generate anxiety. It may take extra time to help clients identify goal achievements and the strengths that will ensure success without ongoing intervention. If the alliance is focused and goal directed, ending is naturally assumed with goal achievement. Such organization requires less time between announcement and the eventual termination.

Introducing Termination

As we reflect on possible reactions to ending, an introduction plan emerges. We have a sense of possible reactions, and our knowledge of clients allows us to gently engage them in a discussion of when and how to end the helping alliance. It is useful to build this discussion on a platform of success. The next elements can provide a platform for discussing the impending end of intervention.

- *Describe observations of progress*. When introducing termination, first it is helpful to identify the progress made throughout intervention. When we describe our observations, clients can reflect on their progress. This provides a platform for ending-related discussions.

- *Explore generalization*. Our observations of change often are based on interactions in our client meetings and their verbal reports of social events. We cannot rely totally on such observations so it is helpful to explore how clients have been able to extend their changes into the life situation. As clients describe how their new skills have generalized, we can better plan the ending process.

- *Introduce independent functioning*. At some point in our discussions we need to get independent functioning on the table. Doing this sets a focus on how clients are able to make decisions and perform skills without ongoing practitioner input and assistance. When clients identify how they are able to function independent of the alliance, it is easier for them to consider ending.

- *Introduce the inevitability of ending*. Given the platform that develops with the three elements listed above, it becomes easy to suggest that clients are almost ready to end intervention. This suggestion should be tentative so clients can negotiate the details of ending. If they are anxious, we can adjust the pacing so feelings can be resolved. If they are eager to end, we can test the eagerness to make sure that this is not avoidance and then pace the ending appropriately.

Pacing the Ending Process

The pace of ending is a critical consideration. If we take too long, we prolong intervention, which can undermine client competence. However, if we speed through the ending process, we run the risk of unresolved feelings and cause clients to feel abandoned (Younggren & Gottlieb, 2008). Concurrently, we must ensure that the endings integrate client progress to provide a platform for success. The pace of ending must be sufficient to achieve two critical outcomes:

1. *Resolution of feelings*. The first outcome of the termination phase of intervention is to explore and resolve clients' termination-related feelings (Shapiro & Ginzberg, 2002). The ending of the helping relationship provides a new model of ending that can carry forward into future relationships.

2. *Integration of gains*. As clients end the working alliance, they transition into independent mastery of their life situations. This move provides clients with an opportunity to experience themselves as competent (Roe et al., 2006). With careful planning and facilitation, an experience of success and mastery provides a foundation for considering a successful future without professional supports.

Given the differential emotional impact of the three time elements (past, present and future), it is useful to organize the ending activities around the three times. When moving from time to time, a progression from past, to present, to future provides a facilitative flow because it mimics the progression of time. This flow also addresses the emotions in a logical order allowing clients to separate past related affect from the current ending. This progression is illustrated in Figure 14.3. Notice how the progression manages the distinct emotional experiences as we move through the three time elements.

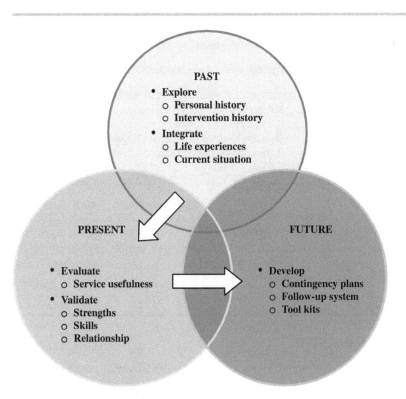

Figure 14.3

**Time-Related
Termination Pacing**

PAST

• **Explore**
  o **Personal history**
  o **Intervention history**
• **Integrate**
  o **Life experiences**
  o **Current situation**

PRESENT

• **Evaluate**
  o **Service usefulness**
• **Validate**
  o **Strengths**
  o **Skills**
  o **Relationship**

FUTURE

• **Develop**
  o **Contingency plans**
  o **Follow-up system**
  o **Tool kits**

Managing Relational Histories

As we proceed toward ending, we have an opportunity to help clients resolve loss-based conflicts (Greenberg, 2002; Many, 2009). Most of these conflicts are based on past ending experiences. Such conflicts are particularly acute with clients who have a history of difficult losses (Zilberstein, 2008). When working with these types of clients, we address clients' personal histories with endings as part of ending the helping relationship (Anthony & Pagano, 1998).

Past to Present Endings

We have learned that ending-related feelings involve a blend of past and current ending experiences. Given that historical endings generate emotional memories, our first task of ending is to help clients discriminate alliance-ending feelings from past endings. If the feelings can be disentwined, affective intensity can be diminished as clients distinguish their history from the current situation.

From Personal to Professional
To access memory-related affect, it is helpful to begin with an exploration of old personal endings. This brief exploration can distinguish past endings from the current termination process. As feelings about past endings are identified, we can help clients make the current ending qualitatively different from past experiences. As we explore past endings, we identify the nature of difficult endings, the associated feelings, and the resulting adaptations.

After exploring personal endings, we can shift our focus to the current ending. As we transition from past personal endings to the ending of the working alliance, the history of the alliance provides an opportunity to explore and validate the shared history. This exploration builds an awareness of the client progress and the value of the collaborative alliance (Garland, Jones, & Kolodny, 1976; Murphy & Dillon, 1998).

Exploring the Alliance History
The exploration of personal endings helps disentangle past ending reactions from the current ending. Exploration of the personal endings seeks to identify painful endings and how these

Table 14.1 Areas of Past-Focused Exploration

Personal History of Endings	History of the Helping Relationship
Past difficult endings	Concerns and functioning when starting service
Emotional impact of past endings	Milestones and important events
Adaptations to avoid repeated pain	Memories of the helping relationship
Past good endings	Changes noticed throughout intervention
Differences between good and bad	Differences between then and now
Unmet needs in past endings	

have affected the client. This allows us to differentiate the past painful endings from the current termination. When we shift focus to the professional ending we begin to track the history of the working alliance and changes noted through intervention. These different areas of exploration are provided in Table 14.1. Notice how each column develops very different material.

Case Example

As part of an internship, a student ran a social skills group for men with developmental disabilities who were preparing for independent living. The group had become cohesive, and the men had arranged to continue the group with another staff member after the student left. The group had also explored ways to raise money to fund social events. There were five men in the group. All were in their mid-20s and operating in the mild range of mental retardation. They worked in a sheltered workshop with periodic placements in competitive employment settings. The men lived with parents, in foster homes, or in group home settings. All of the men also had been placed in institutions as children. The men included Raulf, Roberto, Anthony, Cleveland, and Dennis.

Raulf was a 25-year-old Egyptian male. He was not a highly active member of the group; he followed the lead of the more dominant members, such as Roberto, Anthony, and Dennis. He was bright and functioned well in his placements. He had a physical problem that resulted in a severe limp. He did not talk much. Raulf was placed in an institution at the age of 6. His parents visit him at Christmas but have little contact beyond special occasions.

Roberto was a 27-year-old Hispanic male. He was very high functioning and often served as the group spokesperson due to his advanced verbal skills. Roberto was active in the community and lived in specialized foster care. He disliked having people tell him what to do. He was placed in an institution at the age of 4 and has not seen his parents since his placement. Roberto was first on the list for a supported independent-living apartment.

Anthony was a 25-year-old African American male. He lived in an institution from the age of 3 until 22. He cannot remember his parents. He currently lives in a specialized foster home and is slated for a supported independent-living apartment.

Cleveland was a 26-year-old African American male. He was one of the lower-functioning group members. He was placed in the institution at the age of 5 and remained there until 12, when his parents returned him to their home, where he still lives. He was scheduled for competitive employment and was being considered for a supported independent-living placement.

Dennis was a 24-year-old Caucasian male living in a group home. He was placed in an institution at birth, and his parents never attempted to keep in contact. He was moved to a community placement at 12, when it was discovered that he was misdiagnosed. Apparently, most of his difficulty was a hearing impairment. He is fairly high functioning mentally and can now hear with hearing aids.

In the last official group meeting, the group leader had tuned into the past good-byes and wanted to be sure that the power in the ending did not create problems for the men. The practitioner was aware that frequent staff changes in the setting had jaded the men somewhat about how professionals would come and go. The practitioner consequently began the discussion of ending with the rotten good-byes technique.

> PRACTITIONER: *I hate good-byes. Most of them are not very good. Have you guys had any crappy good-byes?* (Introduce the issue of ending.)
>
> ROBERTO: *Yeah . . . I had crappy good-byes. I never see my parents. They didn't want me because I had a disability.*
>
> DENNIS: *Me, too . . . I see my parents sometimes but when I was a kid, I was stuck at the state school.*
>
> CLEVELAND: *Me, too.*
>
> ANTHONY (ALMOST SIMULTANEOUSLY WITH CLEVELAND): *Me, too.*
>
> PRACTITIONER: *Raulf, these guys have had difficult good-byes, especially around the institution; what have your good-byes been like?* (Making sure all are engaged.)

RAULF: *Not good.*

PRACTITIONER: *What do you think makes good-byes so crappy?* (Trying to engage in exploration.)

RAULF: *They hurt inside.*

ROBERT:*o Yeah . . . and people leave because they don't want to be with you.*

OTHERS (MUMBLING): *Uh-huh.*

PRACTITIONER: *So it seems that most good-byes are painful, and it seems like people are dumping you.* (Reflecting meaning.)

ALL: *Uh-huh.*

PRACTITIONER: *Have there been any good endings that you can think of?* (Trying to elicit exceptions.)

ROBERTO: *There aren't any . . . people just leave and you stay. You never see them again.*

PRACTITIONER: *That is difficult because the group is ending. That is a difficult good-bye. I feel like I am leaving you guys in the middle of something—like the middle of a stream.* (Introduce the group ending, reflecting emotion.)

ROBERTO: *You are abandoning us in the middle of the stream. You are like one of them [staff] leaving us. We should get him.*

DENNIS: *Like how?*

ROBERTO: *Well . . . he is Canadian. We can have him deported back to Canada.*

CLEVELAND: *That will show him.*

DENNIS: *Yeah . . . let's plant some pot in his briefcase and call the cops.*

ROBERTO: *And immigration.*

ANTHONY: *Yeah . . . call them both on him.*

ROBERTO: *That will fix him for leaving us.*

PRACTITIONER: *Sounds like you are angry with me for making you go through another good-bye.* (Reflecting meaning.)

ALL: *We sure are.*

PRACTITIONER: *I bet, we have done a lot together. You guys don't even seem like the same guys who started this group five months ago.* (Begin the review.)

DENNIS: *What do you mean?*

PRACTITIONER: *Well, what do you remember from when we first got together?* (Using questioning to continue the review.)

ROBERTO: *I remember you were supposed to teach us cooking or something like that.*

ANTHONY: *Yeah, we got pretty good at cooking.*

CLEVELAND: *. . . and now we got a club.*

ROBERTO: *. . . and the club will keep going because it is ours.*

DENNIS: *As long as you don't start wearing diapers again.*

ALL: (Laughing)

PRACTITIONER: *So Roberto has made some changes you like.* (Reflecting meaning.) *What other changes have you noticed?* (Using questioning to continue the review.)

In the group exchange, notice how difficult the good-byes were for these men. The history still evoked emotion as they spoke about past good-byes and about ending the alliance. With permission, the men were able to express feelings about the group ending. They were also able to use fantasy to try to feel they had some control over the ending. Notice how the practitioner's activity levels were much higher earlier as he tried to get the men engaged about the ending. Practitioner activity again increased when he tried to transition the group into reviewing the shared history.

Exercise 14.1: Responding to the Past

Based on the preceding example, think about the ending issues evident with this group.

1. Identify historical events and themes that might make the ending difficult for the group members.
   a. Raulf:

   b. Roberto:

c. Cleveland:

d. Anthony:

e. Dennis:

2. Based on the histories of the group members, what do you think are the important shared themes to explore in this ending?

3. What was the practitioner statement that actually engaged the group in the exploration of past issues? Why do you think this worked?

4. When Roberto made his statement about the practitioner abandoning the group and wanted to "get him," what reflective statement would you use to capture Roberto's processing?

5. When Raulf said that good-byes hurt, others agreed with him. Write a question that you might use to explore the group experiences with painful good-byes.

Processing Present Endings

After we explore clients' past-related feelings, the review of the helping relationship progresses to a present focus. During the review of the helping alliance, we can identify service milestones and events. This reminiscence helps us transition from a past to a present orientation. As we orient to the present, the review of the alliance allows us to also reflect on client progress.

Validating Progress

In our shift to the present, it is important to affirm and recap client progress (Walsh & Harrigan, 2003). The shift from exploring painful feelings of loss to observations of progress changes the emotional experience from one of loss to one of pride (Zilberstein, 2008). Feelings of pride and accomplishment tend to lighten the discussion as clients begin to identify their success.

When clients are supported to identify their accomplishments and progress, they can integrate and understand incremental changes that occur through intervention. We share observations about client change noticed throughout the alliance and help clients identify how they have extended their changes into life situations. Doing this helps clients form an emotional foundation for launching into a service-free future (Greenberg, 2002).

Exploring the Ending

As a positive foundation is established, we can begin to explore the present ending. Although this change of focus may create a melancholy emotion, building the exploration of termination onto a discussion of accomplishments allows us to make ending the working alliance qualitatively different from other good-byes. The difference emerges as we explore and process the ending with clients. As we share our experiences and invite clients to share, a new model for ending emerges. The next elements can help to create vital difference in the good-bye experience:

- *Extending control.* We can collaborate with clients to make the current ending different from past endings. Doing this helps clients gain mastery over the ending so they can shape their experience.
- *Updating impressions.* As we share our observations of growth, we are able to contrast clients at the beginning and end of the working alliance. By sharing our impressions, clients can integrate positive messages.
- *Identifying mutual impact.* Concurrent with updating progress, the exploration of the alliance allows us to share how clients have influenced our professional development. When we share client contributions, clients learn that the alliance has a mutual impact.
- *Evaluation.* As clients leave service, it is helpful to have them evaluate their experience (Murphy & Dillon, 1998). Doing this involves soliciting feedback about (1) what was helpful, (2) what was not helpful, and (3) changes they would recommend in any upcoming services. Evaluation allows clients to express feelings about service in a structured manner while introducing the inevitability of the future without service.

Case Example

In the group described earlier, the practitioner wanted to get members to discuss current feelings. Although the group was going to continue with a new leader, there was still an ending of the group as it existed. (In a situation in which a group continues but the leader leaves, it is easy for members to avoid present feelings because only one person is leaving.) The practitioner felt it was important to attend to the ending, given the turnover of people in the lives of the group members. The practitioner especially wanted to help the members explore abandonment feelings, given their histories. The next excerpt demonstrates how the group struggled with the present issues.

> PRACTITIONER: *You know, you guys have all had such icky good-byes in the past. How can we make this good-bye better?* (Try to focus on present and making it different.)
>
> ROBERTO: *This isn't really a good-bye for us; we are just getting rid of you.*
>
> ALL: (Laughing)
>
> PRACTITIONER: *How will getting rid of me change the group?* (Trying to engage rather than avoid)
>
> DENNIS: *Well, Carmine is prettier than you.*
>
> ALL: (Laughing)
>
> PRACTITIONER: *She is prettier . . . how will it change the way you guys act?* (Still working on engagement.)
>
> CLEVELAND: *We'll act better.*
>
> ROBERTO: *Yeah, we won't be able to make fun of her like we do with you.*
>
> ANTHONY: *No.*
>
> RAULF: *No way.*
>
> PRACTITIONER: *So really, the way you guys are acting will change plus the group will look better. Sounds like the group as you know it today will never be the same.* (Reflecting on meaning and pushing engagement in dealing with the ending.)
>
> ROBERTO: *Yeah, I guess so.*
>
> PRACTITIONER: *I know it sure will for me because I won't be there. You guys will be working with someone else. You know, I sometimes try not to even think about that because it is hard to think of this group without me as part of it. I am really going to miss you guys.* (Reflecting on themes of loss.)

(continued)

(Continued)

RAULF: *Me, too.*

DENNIS: *You are not going anywhere, Raulf.*

PRACTITIONER: *I think Raulf is saying that when the group changes, that will be a bit of a loss . . . is that right?* (Reflecting the meaning.)

RAULF: (Nodding)

DENNIS: *I don't like thinking about the change, either. I like the group the way it is.*

ROBERTO: *Yeah, I didn't always like it when you guys made me do things, but I kind of like the way things are now.*

CLEVELAND: *I am going to miss things.*

PRACTITIONER: *What about you, Anthony—what will you miss?*

ANTHONY: *I will miss the way we joke around with you.*

ROBERTO: *Yeah, most staff get mad when you tease them.*

ALL: *Uh-huh.*

PRACTITIONER: *So you guys will have to learn new ways of getting along when Carmine comes into the group. Will it be hard to let go of the teasing and things that we do together?* (Reflecting on meaning then exploring with questions.)

DENNIS: *Yeah, that is half the fun of the group.*

ROBERTO: *Yeah, we should tell Carmine that that is one of the rules.*

ALL: *Uh-huh.*

PRACTITIONER: *It does sound like it is ending—so you guys have been avoiding my question. How can we make this good-bye different?* (Redirecting back to the issue.)

ROBERTO: *You could come back! Not like those other staff.*

DENNIS: *Yeah, for the car wash.*

PRACTITIONER: *I could help with the car wash.* (Negotiating how to be different.)

DENNIS: *. . . and the coffee house, too.*

PRACTITIONER: *I am willing to help out, but if you keep bringing me back, we won't have an ending, will we?* (Still negotiating and reflecting on the avoidance.)

DENNIS: *No.*

PRACTITIONER: *. . . and I will be graduating and having to move on to a new job. So we will have to make this ending a good one. I can do my part to help out on those things, but what will you do differently this time?* (Still stressing the meaning of the ending for all system members—pushing for the difference.)

ROBERTO: *I usually swear at people when they are going, it is a fight.*

PRACTITIONER: *Can we do this one without fighting?* (Negotiating the difference.)

ROBERTO: *I'll try, but I get mad when people leave—I feel like they are leaving me.*

RAULF: *Yeah.*

PRACTITIONER: *When people have those sad feelings, is it easier to fight?* (Reflecting the feeling.)

ALL: *Uh-huh.*

PRACTITIONER: *When we fight, what feelings are we trying to avoid?* (Exploring the feelings.)

CLEVELAND: *Sad.*

ANTHONY: *Yeah, sad ones.*

DENNIS: *I hate good-byes.*

EVERYONE: *Me, too.*

PRACTITIONER: *I find it really hard because I am the one to leave and I am being replaced. Carmine will get to have the fun with you guys now.* (Reflecting the ending and orienting to the future.)

DENNIS: *She better have fun and joke around, like you.*

PRACTITIONER: *That is one of the things you would like to keep, is it? Are there any other things about the group or how I was working in the group that you would recommend doing again in other groups?* (Moving to evaluation.)

ROBERTO: *I liked the cooking. I have a recipe book now.*

DENNIS: *I just liked the way that we got to decide on what to do . . . not like a staff or a teacher.*

ANTHONY: *I like that and the joking.*

PRACTITIONER: *What would you recommend never doing again?* (Continued evaluation.)

CLEVELAND: *Leaving.*

ALL: *Yeah.*

PRACTITIONER: *What else?*

ROBERTO: *I like the group. I wouldn't change anything.*

PRACTITIONER: *There is usually something. I wouldn't want to inflict others with the same mistakes I made here.* (Continued evaluation.)

DENNIS: *I think we could have a better room for the weeks that we are not cooking.*

ROBERTO: *That would be good.*

PRACTITIONER: *Okay.*

In this example, notice how active the practitioner is directing the flow of discussion toward the present issues. We can also see how members try to deny or minimize the endings to avoid their feelings. However, when the feelings surface, the practitioner picks up on them so they can be safely explored among the group members.

Exercise 14.2: Present-Oriented Responding

Based on the preceding example, think through the next questions and issues related to present-oriented responding.

1. What was the issue that seemed toughest to the practitioner and made him want to avoid discussing the ending?

2. What do you think might have been toughest for you if you were ending with this group?

3. Using your interactive tuning-in skills, what seemed to be the most critical issue for each of the members?

   a. Raulf:

   b. Roberto:

   c. Dennis:

   d. Anthony:

   e. Cleveland:

4. Identify three ways that group members tried to avoid talking about their feelings associated with the ending.

5. What was the statement that finally got the group members engaged in talking about their feelings associated with the ending?

6. When Dennis was negotiating with the practitioner about what to do differently, there seemed to be a feeling underneath his statements. Write a reflective statement that you would use in response to this theme.

7. Anthony and Cleveland seemed tuned in to feelings when the practitioner asked them about what feelings were under the fighting. Write a question that you could use in response to help them explore their feelings.

Developing the Future Orientation

As clients shift their focus to the future, we begin to explore how to sustain progress as they transition out of service (Baum, 2005). Discussions of future success project the goal achievements back into the client's life situations. Inherent in this new focus is the demise of the working alliance. Even if the client and practitioner meet each other in the community, the working alliance ends forever, changing the nature of their interactions (Murphy & Dillon, 1998).

Future-Oriented Tasks

There are two critical tasks in this phase of ending: helping clients visualize a postservice future and solidifying gains. Although the two tasks are related, there are qualitative differences. Visualizing the future seeks to diminish client anxieties about ending. The goal is to help them become confident in their progress and ability to succeed without support (Epston & White, 1995). The second consideration is to ensure that clients maintain and generalize their gains from service (Okun, 1997; Perri, 1998; Rzepnicki, 1991).

Visualizing the Future

The first critical element in visualizing the future is to help clients face the future without undue anxiety. Strategies for managing client anxiety sometimes focus on extending access into the future. Other strategies seek to help clients feel secure about their ability to manage future challenges in the absence of the working alliance. Three common strategies include:

1. *Providing pathways back to service.* Although the ending of the helping relationship may be permanent, it is helpful to leave the door open for clients to return in the future (Frank, 2009; Greenberg, 2002; Lebow, 1995). Pathways include identifying risk indicators and a reconnection plan (e.g., coupons for free follow-up meetings). Even if clients do not reconnect, they will feel that there is a safety net. Feelings of security associated with the ability to reconnect diminish the emotional impact associated with a "final" ending to intervention (Zilberstein, 2008).

2. *Progress affirmations.* Practitioners often promote closure of the relationship by reflecting on the learning they will take with them as a result of this helping relationship. The practitioner can then ask the clients to describe what learning they will take with them to use in their lives. This strategy provides feedback about the helping relationship while promoting future postulations (Epston & White, 1995).

3. *Providing transitional objects.* Many practitioners provide clients with keepsakes and reminders of service. Such mementos can be useful tools so client take a reminder of the positive outcomes and work into the future (Zilberstein, 2008). Common objects include certificates, symbolic gifts, and other tokens that will remind clients of their service experiences and progress.

Solidifying Gains

As we orient clients to the future, we help them see and organize their gains. Strategies for solidifying gains tend to focus more on clients and how they will function into the future. Some strategies tend to predict future challenges and help clients anticipate how they can use their new skills and understandings. Other strategies focus on extending elements of the helping relationship into the future. Common strategies include:

- *Relapse prevention plans.* As clients leave the helping relationship, it can be useful to predict future challenges and explore how they might use their service experiences to interpret and respond in a more empowered manner (Greenberg, 2002). When discussing challenges, we can suggest that clients will recall discussions from service. The suggestion that clients will hear the practitioner's voice helping to solve a problem has been effective in helping clients move into the future with success (Rosen, 1982).

- *Follow-up plans.* As clients end active intervention, it is possible to negotiate a follow-up system to help them integrate changes into their life situations. Follow-up involves planning meetings at specific intervals after intervention has ended so the practitioner and clients can review how clients are applying their learning and maintaining changes (Clifford, 2004). Doing this often involves a schedule (diminishing over time) of meetings so the practitioner can monitor and support changes. In developing a follow-up plan, practitioners still must address the ending because the current helping relationship will end.

- *Visualizing success.* When clients have mastered important changes, it is useful to have them visualize challenging situations in which they successfully use their new skills (Epston & White, 1995). Doing this helps them visualize success in the future and outside of the helping relationship. This exploration also reinforces progress by mentally extending accomplishments to external situations.

Case Example

When ending with the group discussed in the previous two sections, the practitioner wanted to shift the focus to the future. The practitioner felt this was important, given that there was to be a new person helping the group members. The next excerpt captures some of the exchange that occurred during the future-oriented discussions.

PRACTITIONER: *You mentioned that you want to have fun when Carmine begins helping you with the group; what other things do you hope might happen?*

RAULF: *Eating.*

PRACTITIONER: *You want to keep the cooking part of the group?*

RAULF: *Yes.*

PRACTITIONER: *. . . and what else?*

ROBERTO: *Well, we want to keep on raising money so we can put on fun things for everyone.*

DENNIS: *Yeah, that is why we are together, and we want to keep control of our own money.*

PRACTITIONER: *What will you say to her to convince her that these things are important to you?*

ANTHONY: *We'll just tell her that this is what we want.*

PRACTITIONER: *What room will you be meeting in?* (Moving to visualize success.)

ANTHONY: *This one.*

PRACTITIONER: *Where will she sit?*

CLEVELAND: *She can sit where you are.*

PRACTITIONER: *Okay, now picture her sitting here. What exactly will you say?* (Continuing the visualization.)

ROBERTO: *I can speak for the group. I will say, "Carmine, the group wants you to know the kinds of things we do. We get together and cook, but while we eat we plan things that we can do for fun."*

PRACTITIONER: *You sound impressive to me.* (Reflecting success.) *Do you think she will go along with you?*

ROBERTO: *She better . . . or we will find someone else to help us.*

In this exchange, notice how the group was able to orient to the future and begin to picture a successful discussion with the new staff member. The group was working cooperatively and was able to visualize themselves with the new person rather than with the leader who was leaving.

Exercise 14.3: Future-Oriented Responding

1. In tuning in to the themes among the members in the previous excerpt, what seems to be the critical issue for the members as they add the new practitioner?

2. What do you think will need to happen in order for the group to stay together and succeed in the future?

3. What do you base this conclusion on?

4. What would you say to the group members to engage them in an exploration of what they need to do to make that happen?

5. Write a reflective statement that indicates how important this is to the group's beliefs about success in the future.

6. What did you observe in the content themes of each member that identifies what is important to him?
   a. Roberto:

   b. Raulf:

   c. Cleveland:

d. Anthony:

e. Dennis:

Critical Considerations

The discussions in this chapter presented an ideal vision of endings with no consideration that some helping relationships will end before goals are achieved. Although the discussions help to identify core issues of and techniques for facilitating an ending, it is important to understand the variations and contextual elements that can influence endings sometimes resulting in premature termination of services.

This final section of the chapter focuses on important considerations that can vary the experience and process of ending. This exploration begins with considerations of early termination, because a premature ending unfolds differently from what has been explored earlier in the chapter. This discussion is followed by an exploration of population and service contexts that can influence the ending of service.

Premature Termination

The ideal ending involves the successful completion of goal-directed intervention; many service endings, however, occur before goals are achieved successfully. Along with alliance ruptures, there are many situations and events that can lead to premature endings (Gelman, Fernandez, Hausman, Miller, & Weiner, 2007; Watchel, 2002; Younggren & Gottlieb, 2008). Some reasons for premature termination include:

- *Client resources.* Often clients leave intervention when social and financial pressures require them to prioritize life events over service continuation (Self, Oates, Pinnock-Hamilton, & Leach, 2005).
- *Alliance problems.* If there are irreconcilable alliance problems and either the practitioner or client is unable to keep intervention working toward client goals, services often are terminated. When clients are ambivalent and withdraw, there is little opportunity to refer them elsewhere. If the alliance problem is a result of practitioner responses, clients should be helped to engage with another practitioner.
- *Safety issues.* When safety for either client or practitioner is threatened by events in the helping relationship, services may be terminated.
  - *Practitioner safety.* When clients exhibit a threat to the practitioner's well-being, services with that practitioner often are terminated and clients are helped (most often by the supervisor) to engage with another practitioner.
  - *Client safety.* If clients are being harmed by the intervention or their problem situation interferes with forming an alliance with the practitioner (for example, a male practitioner who reminds a victim of her rapist), the client may change to a different practitioner. Often such changes involve initiating the change through a supervisor who assists clients to engage with an alternative practitioner.
- *Forced termination.* If service conditions change causing a forced termination (e.g., end of employment, reimbursement limitations, student placement), clients are informed of the options and helped to engage with a service or other practitioner who can meet their needs.
- *Ethical problems.* If there are boundary violations or ethical breaches on the part of the practitioner, the supervisor should meet with clients to explain the problem and then facilitate engagement with another practitioner.

Managing Premature Termination

When premature termination occurs, it is very difficult for us to facilitate a healthy ending to the alliance. Many practitioners struggle with premature endings, especially if clients initiate the ending (Tyron & Kane, 1993). Such endings can diminish our self-esteem, which inhibits motivation to facilitate a healthy ending experience for clients (Baum, 2007).

With client-initiated early termination, client absence sometimes further undermines our ability to promote a healthy ending. Although an early exit inhibits our ability to provide feedback and create a positive ending experience, it is possible to provide feedback through a feedback letter that outlines how to reengage in services in the future (Rappleyea et al., 2009).

Cultural and Social Considerations

Diversity considerations influence clients' experience of ending. Social diversity often results in premature endings because clients' life situations overwhelm their ability to fully engage in the working alliance. Cultural diversity may cause clients to be sensitive to specific feelings or experiences during the ending process.

Socioeconomic Diversity

Research finds that clients who are socioeconomically disadvantaged are more likely to end service before their goals have been achieved (Self et al., 2005). With socioeconomic disadvantage comes stresses and environmental demands that inhibit client ability to participate fully in some types of service. Participation inhibitions cause priorities to shift, resulting in early termination.

Many premature endings with economically stressed clients occur in office-based services that expect regular attendance and maintain a focus on "curing" client problems. The inherent assumptions of such programs often set expectations that are unrealistic for clients who must balance multiple stresses. It is important to reach out and affirm such clients to promote a positive ending and potential pathways back to service.

Cultural Diversity

Some ethnic and cultural groups have experiences, beliefs, and orientations that can influence their experience of ending. We constantly must be sensitive and aware that cultural influences may emerge. Doing this is particularly important with cultural groups that have a history of traumatic separations and social exclusion (Glasgow & Gouse-Sheese, 1995; Kiang, Blumenthal, Carlson, Lawson, & Shell, 2009; Rousseau, Mekki-Berrada, & Moreau, 2001). Such cultural histories can stimulate difficult reactions to the ending.

A second consideration emerges when working with cultural groups whose orientation to time diverges from our cultural orientation (Brislin & Kim, 2003; Sharma & Kerl, 2002). Some cultural groups have unique orientations to time and how time-linked events are understood (Briley, 2009). We need to be aware that some clients will more naturally orient to one time dimension, making it difficult to transition to different perspectives. When we attempt to shift from past, to present, to future, some clients may find transitions awkward.

In cross-cultural services, when we notice a client hesitate it is important to explore the hesitation for cultural elements. Concurrently, we should consider culturally relevant ending rituals or culturally relevant tokens that can be used (Zilberstein, 2008). When using rituals and gifts as part of termination, the practitioner can explore the meaning with each person to capture the unique cultural experiences and meaning (Shapiro & Ginzberg, 2002).

Endings and Evidence-Based Practice

Our approach to intervention also can influence the ending phase of service. Some intervention programs are structured so that termination occurs in a predetermined fashion rather than emerging through goal achievement. This change in termination criteria influences how we approach both intervention and managing endings.

Many short-term and evidence-based interventions are time limited, which structures termination from the very beginning of service. For this reason, issues of ending are discussed during the contracting phase of intervention and implicit in the working alliance (Goldfried, 2002). Some structured interventions are program dependent and end with little consideration of clients' goal achievement. The evaluation at the end of service tends to focus more on the program outcomes than individual client goals.

Many researchers and professionals have raised concerns about the ethical need to determine adequate termination procedures in evidence-based practice (Rappleyea et al., 2009). The current ethical standard is that practitioners must competently manage engagement, assessment, intervention, and termination (Rappleyea et al., 2009; Younggren & Gottlieb, 2008). Doing this requires practitioners to allow clients to express and explore their reactions to ending so they can be resolved (Kato, 2003).

Increasingly there is an expectation that all intervention systems attend to the client experience when ending intervention. Although the termination phase of treatment has not been studied extensively in evidence-based practice, it has been included in some models of intervention. Motivational interviewing has begun exploring relapse prevention as an element of the evidence-based intervention (Tan, 2010), as have some cognitive-behavioral interventions (Paykel et al., 2005). This trend is likely to gather momentum and provide strong recommendations in the near future.

Critical Chapter Themes

1. It is very common for people, including practitioners, to avoid the difficult feelings associated with endings. Practitioners must take control of their own feelings to help explore their reactions to ending service.

2. The power associated with endings comes from the convergence of past, present, and future in the act of ending. Practitioners must attend to all three times when helping clients with the ending.

3. Issues of the past include feelings associated with past difficult endings along with the ending of the service relationship. It is important to focus on both personal past endings as well as the current ending.

4. Issues of the present include helping clients explore their feelings about ending along with evaluating their experience of service.

5. Future-oriented issues include helping clients to move out of service without undue anxiety and helping them maintain their gains into the future.

6. Different cultural and ethnic groups have diverse orientations to the dynamics of ending. Practitioners must be responsive to these unique experiences.

Online Resources

A Guide to Psychology Web site: www.guidetopsychology.com/termin.htm

PsychCentral Web site: http://psychcentral.com/blog/archives/2009/05/27/termination-10-tips-when-ending-psychotherapy/

Zur Institute Web site: www.zurinstitute.com/ethicsoftermination.html

Recommended Reading

Baum, N. (2007). Therapists' responses to treatment termination: An inquiry into the variables that contribute to therapists' experiences. *Clinical Social Work Journal, 35,* 97–106.

Gelman, C. R., Fernandez, P., Hausman, N., Miller, S., & Weiner, M. (2007). Challenging endings: First year MSW interns' experiences with forced termination and discussion points for supervisory guidance. *Clinical Social Work Journal, 35,* 79–90.

Many, M. M. (2009). Termination as a therapeutic intervention when treating children who have experienced multiple losses. *Infant Mental Health Journal, 30,* 23–39.

Younggren, J. N., & Gottlieb, M. C. (2008). Termination and abandonment: History, risk, and risk management. *Professional Psychology: Research and Practice, 39,* 498–504.

Zilberstein, K. (2008). Au revoir: An attachment and loss perspective on termination. *Clinical Social Work Journal, 36,* 301–311.

References

Aarts, H., Custers, R., & Marien, H. (2009). Priming an authorship ascription: When nonconscious goals turn into conscious experiences of self agency. *Journal of Personality and Social Psychology, 96*, 967–979.

Abbott, G., & Rosinski, P. (2007). Global coaching and evidence based coaching: Multiple perspectives operating in a process of pragmatic humanism. *International Journal of Evidence Based Coaching and Mentoring, 5*, 58–77.

Arbuthnott, A., & Sharpe, D. (2009). The effect of physician-patient collaboration on patient adherence in non-psychiatric medicine. *Patient Education and Counseling, 77*, 60–67.

Ackerman, S. J., & Hilsenroth, M. J. (2003). A review of therapist characteristics and techniques positively impacting the therapeutic alliance. *Clinical Psychology Review, 23*, 1–33.

Adams, J. F. (1997). Questions as interventions in therapeutic conversation. *Journal of Family Psychotherapy, 8*, 17–35.

Adie, J. W., Duda, J. L., & Ntoumanis, N. (2008). Autonomy support, basic need satisfaction and the optimal functioning of adult male and female sport participants: A test of basic needs theory. *Motivation and Emotion, 32*, 189–199.

Adúriz, M. E., Bluthgen, C., & Knopfler, C. (2009). Helping child flood victims using group EMDR intervention in Argentina: Treatment outcome and gender differences. *International Journal of Stress Management, 16*, 138–153.

Afifi, T. D., McManus, T., Steuber, K., & Coho, A. (2009). Verbal avoidance and dissatisfaction in intimate conflict situations. *Human Communication Research, 35*, 357–383.

Alesandri, J., Darcheville, J-C., & Zentall, T. R. (2008). Cognitive dissonance in children: Justification of effort or contrast? *Psychonomic Bulletin & Review, 15*, 673–677.

Alfaro, E. C., Umaña-Taylor, A. J., Gonzales-Backen, M. A., Bámaca, M. Y., & Zeiders, K. H. (2009). Latino adolescents' academic success: The role of discrimination, academic motivation, and gender. *Journal of Adolescence, 32*, 941–962.

Alissi, A. (1980). *Perspectives in group work practice.* New York, NY: Research Press.

Allcorn, S. (1995). Understanding organizational culture as the quality of workplace subjectivity. *Human Relations, 48*, 73–96.

Allcorn, S., & Diamond, M. A. (1997). *Managing people during stressful times: The psychologically defensive workplace.* Westport, CT: Quorum Books.

Allen, B. C., Sargent, L. D., & Bradley, L. M. (2003). Differential effects of task and reward interdependence on perceived helping behavior, effort, and group performance. *Small Group Research, 34*, 716–740.

Allen, J. G., Coyne, L., Colson, D. B., Horwitz, L., Gabbard, G. O., Frieswyk, S. J., & Newson, G. (1996). Pattern of therapist interventions associated with patient collaboration, *Psychotherapy, 33*, 254–261.

Allen, J. G., Gabbard, G. O., Newsom, G. E., & Coyne, L. (1990). Detecting patterns of change in patients' collaboration within individual psychotherapy sessions. *Psychotherapy, 27*, 522–530.

Altman, N. (1993). Psychoanalysis and the urban poor. *Psychoanalytic Dialogues, 3*, 29–49.

Altshuler, S. J. (2003). From barriers to successful collaboration: Public schools and child welfare working together. *Social Work, 48*, 52–63.

Amini, F., Lewis, T., Lannon, R., Louie, A., Baumbacher, G., McGuinness, T., & Schiff, E. Z. (1996). Affect, attachment, memory: Contributions toward psychobiologic integration. *Psychiatry, 59*(3), 213–239.

Amir, V., & Auslander, G. K. (2003). Inter-organizational collaboration among social workers: The case of community mental health centers and local social service departments in Israel. *British Journal of Social Work, 33*, 557–566.

Anderson, J. (1997). *Social work with groups.* New York, NY: Longman Publishing.

Anderson, J. A., Wright, E. R., Kelley, K., & Kooreman, H. (2008). Patterns of clinical functioning over time for young people served in a system of care. *Journal of Emotional and Behavioral Disorders, 16*, 90–104.

Anderson, J. W. (2006). Past focus, present danger: An investigation of aggression and past time orientation. *Dissertation Abstracts International Section B: The Sciences and Engineering, 67*(2B), 1139.

Anderson, N. B., & Armstead, C. A. (1995). Toward understanding the association of socioeconomic status and health: A new challenge for the biopsychosocial approach. *Psychosomatic Medicine, 57*, 213–225.

Angell, B. G. (1996). Neurolinguistic programming theory and social work treatment. In F. J. Turner (Ed.), *Social work treatment: Interlocking theoretical approaches* (4th ed., pp. 480–502). New York, NY: Free Press.

Angus, L., & Kagan, F. (2007). Empathic relational bonds and personal agency in psychotherapy: Implications for psychotherapy supervision, practice, and research. *Psychotherapy: Theory, Research, Practice, Training, 44*, 371–377.

Annesi, J. J. (2006). Sex differences in correlations between personal incentives, and self-motivation, and occurrence of perceived positive feeling states after exercise. *Psychological Reports, 98*, 95–98.

Anthony, E. K., Austin, M. H., & Cormier, D. R. (2010). Early detection of prenatal substance exposure and the role of child welfare. *Children and Youth Services Review, 32*, 6–12.

Anthony, S., & Pagano, G. (1998). The therapeutic potential for growth during the termination process. *Clinical Social Work Journal, 26*, 281–296.

Apsland, H., Llewelyn, S., Hardy, G. E., Barkham, M., & Stiles, W. (2008). Alliance ruptures and rupture resolution in cognitive-behavior therapy: A preliminary task analysis. *Psychotherapy Research*, *18*, 699–710.

Arcidiacono, F., & Pontecorvo, C. (2009). Cultural practices in Italian family conversations: Verbal conflict between parents and preadolescents. *European Journal of Psychology of Education*, *24*, 97–117.

Arndt, J., Cox, C. R., Goldenberg, J. L., Vess, M., Routledge, C., Cooper, D. P., & Cohen, F. (2009). Blowing in the (social) wind: Implications of extrinsic esteem contingencies for terror management and health. *Journal of Personality and Social Psychology*, *96*, 1191–1205.

Aron, A., Fisher, H., Mashek, D. J., Strong, G., Haifang, L., & Brown, L. L. (2005). Reward, motivation, and emotion systems associated with early-stage intense romantic love. *Journal of Neurophysiology*, *94*, 327–337.

Arthur, N. (1998). Counsellor education for diversity: Where do we go from here? *Canadian Journal of Counselling*, *32*, 88–103.

Ashwin, C., Baron-Cohen, S., Wheelwright, S., O'Riordan, M., & Bullmore, E. T. (2007). Differential activation of the amydala and the "social brain" during fearful face-processing in Asperger syndrome. *Neuropsychologia*, *45*(1), 2–14.

Aspland, H., Llewelyn, S., Hardy, G. E., Barkham, M., & Stiles, W. (2008). Alliance ruptures and rupture resolution in cognitive-behavior therapy: A preliminary task analysis. *Psychotherapy Research*, *18*, 699–710.

Azar, S. T., & Makin-Byrd, K. N. (2007). When family values clash with therapist's goals and treatment delivery. In T. A. Cavell & K. T. Malcolm (Eds.), *Anger, aggression and interventions for interpersonal violence* (pp. 349–392). Mahwah, NJ: Lawrence Erlbaum.

Bach, D. R., Herdener, M., Grandjean, D., Sander, D., Seifritz, E., & Strik, W. K. (2009). Altered lateralization of emotional prosody processing in schizophrenia. *Schizophrenia Research*, *110*, 180–187.

Bachelor, A. (1995). Clients' perception of the therapeutic alliance: A qualitative analysis. *Journal of Counseling Psychology*, *42*, 323–337.

Bachelor, A., Laverdière, O., Gamache, D., & Bordeleau, V. (2007). Perceptions and relationships with client psychological functioning, interpersonal relations, and motivation. *Psychotherapy: Theory, Research, Practice, Training*, *44*, 175–192.

Badger, D. (1985). Learning for transfer: A further contribution. *Issues in Social Work Education*, *5*, 63–66.

Bados, A., Balaguer, G., & Saldaña, C. (2007). The efficacy of cognitive-behavioral therapy and the problem of dropout. *Journal of Clinical Psychology*, *63*, 585–592.

Baenninger-Huber, E., & Widmer, C. (1999). Affective relationship patterns and psychotherapeutic change. *Psychotherapy Research*, *9*, 74–87.

Bagarozzi, D. A., & Anderson, S. A. (1989). *Personal, marital, and family myths—theoretical formulations and clinical strategies*. New York, NY: W. W. Norton.

Bailey, C. T., & Butcher, D. J. (1983). Interpersonal skills training: I. The nature of skill acquisition and its implications for training design and management. *Management Education and Development*, *14*, 48–54.

Balconi, M., Falbo, L., & Brambilla, E. (2009). BIS/BAS responses to emotional cues: Self report, autonomic measure and alpha band modulation. *Personality and Individual Differences*, *47*, 858–863.

Baldwin, D. C. Jr., & Daugherty, S. R. (2008). Interprofessional conflict and medical errors: Results of a national multispecialty survey of hospital residents in the US. *Journal of Interprofessional Care*, *22*, 573–586.

Baltes, P. B., Reese, H., & Lipsett, L. (1980). Lifespan developmental psychology, *Annual Review of Psychology*, *31*, 65–110.

Bandler, R., & Grinder, J. (1975). *The structure of magic*. Palo Alto, CA: Science and Behavior Books.

Bandura, A., Caprara, G. V., Barbaranelli, C., Pastorelli, C., & Regalia, C. (2001). Sociocognitive self-regulatory mechanisms governing transgressive behavior. *Journal of Personality and Social Psychology*, *80*, 125–135.

Banja, J. D. (2008). Toward a more empathic relationship in pain medicine. *Pain Medicine*, *9*, 1125–1129.

Banks, S. (1998). Professional ethics in social work—what future? *British Journal of Social Work*, *28*, 213–231.

Banks, S. J., Kamryn, T. E., Angstadt, M., Pradeep, J. N., & Phan, K. L. (2007). Amygdala-frontal connectivity during emotion regulation. *Scan*, *2*, 303–312.

Barber, J. P., Gallop, R., Crits-Christoph, P., Frank, A., Thase, M. E., Weiss, R. D., & Gibbons, M. B.C. (2006). The role of therapist adherence, therapist competence, and alliance in predicting outcome of individual drug counseling: Results from the National Institute Drug Abuse Collaborative Cocaine Treatment Study. *Psychotherapy Research*, *16*, 229–240.

Barlas, Y., & Yasarcan, H. (2006). Goal setting, evaluation, learning and revision: A dynamic modeling approach. *Evaluation and Program Planning*, *29*, 79–87.

Barnett, M.A. (2008). Economic disadvantage in complex family systems: Expansion of family stress models. *Clinical Child and Family Psychology Review*, *11*, 145–161.

Baron, J. (1994). *Thinking and deciding* (2nd ed.). Cambridge, UK: Cambridge University Press.

Barratt, M. S., Roach, M. A., Morgan, K. M., & Colbert, K. K. (1996). Adjustment to motherhood by single adolescents. *Family Relations*, *45*, 209–215.

Battaglia, D. M., Richard, F. D., Datteri, D. L., & Lord, C. G. (1998). Breaking up is (relatively) easy to do: A script for the dissolution of close relationships. *Journal of Social and Personal Relationships*, *15*, 829–845.

Bauer, J., & Mulder, R. H. (2006). Upward feedback and its contribution to employees' feeling of self-determination. *Journal of Workplace Learning*, *18*, 508–521.

Baum, N. (2005). Correlates of clients' emotional and behavioral responses to treatment termination. *Clinical Social Work Journal*, *33*, 309–326.

Baum, N. (2007). Therapists' responses to treatment termination: An inquiry into the variables that contribute to therapists' experiences. *Clinical Social Work Journal*, *35*, 97–106.

Bauman, C. W., & Skitka, L. J. (2009). Moral disagreement and procedural justice: Moral mandates as constraints to voice effects. *Australian Journal of Psychology*, *61*, 40–49.

Bauman, S. (2009). Group work in the economic downturn. *Journal for Specialists in Group Work*, *34*, 97–100.

Bavelas, J. B., Coates, L., & Johnson, T. (2002). Listener responses as a collaborative process: The role of gaze. *Journal of Communication, 52,* 566–580.

Bayazit, M., & Mannix, E. A. (2003). Should I stay or should I go? Predicting team members' intent to remain in the team. *Small Group Research, 34,* 290–321.

Bechara, A., & Bar-On, R. (2006). Neurological substrates of emotional and social intelligence: Evidence from patients with focal brain lesions. In J. T. Cacioppo, P. S. Visser, & C. L. Pickett (Eds.), *Social neuroscience: People thinking about thinking people* (pp. 13–40). Cambridge, MA: MIT Press.

Beck, J. G., Coffey, S. F., Foy, D. W., Keane, T. M., & Blanchard, E. B. (2009). Group cognitive behavior therapy for chronic posttraumatic stress disorder: An initial randomized pilot study. *Behavior Therapy, 40,* 82–92.

Beck, M., Friedlander, M. L., & Escudero, V. (2006). Three perspectives on clients' experiences of the therapeutic alliance: A discovery-oriented investigation. *Journal of Marital and Family Therapy, 32,* 355–368.

Beech, A. R., & Hamilton-Giachritsis, C. E. (2005). Relationship between therapeutic climate and treatment outcome in group-based sexual offender treatment programs. *Sexual Abuse: Journal of Research and Treatment, 17,* 127–140.

Bendersky, C., & Curhan, J. R. (2009). Cognitive dissonance in negotiation: Free choice or justification. *Social Cognition, 27,* 455–474.

Bennett, D., Parry, G., & Ryle, A. (2006). Resolving threats to the therapeutic alliance in cognitive analytic therapy of borderline personality disorder: A task analysis. *Psychology and Psychotherapy: Theory, Research and Practice, 79,* 395–418.

Berg, A. L., Sandahl, C., & Clinton, D. (2008). The relationship of treatment preferences and experiences to outcome in generalized anxiety disorder (GAD). *Psychology and Psychotherapy: Theory, Research and Practice, 81,* 247–259.

Berlin, S. B., & Marsh, J. C. (1993). *Informing practice decisions.* New York, NY: Macmillan.

Berliner, L. (2005). The results of randomized clinical trials move the field forward. *Child Abuse and Neglect, 29,* 103–105.

Bernstein, S. (1976). Conflict and group work. In S. Bernstein (Ed.), *Explorations in group work* (pp. 72–106). Boston, MA: Charles River Books.

Berry, G. W., & Sipps, G. J. (1991). Interactive effects of counselor—client similarity and client self-esteem on termination type and number of sessions. *Journal of Counseling Psychology, 38,* 120–125.

Betancourt, H., & Lopez, S. R. (1995). The study of culture, ethnicity, and race in American psychology. In N. R. Goldberger & J. B. Veroff (Eds.), *The culture and psychology reader* (pp. 87–107). New York, NY: New York University Press.

Bettner, B. L. (2007). Recreating sibling relationships in marriage. *Journal of Individual Psychology,* 339–344.

Beutler, L. E., & Clarkin, J. F. (1990). *Systematic treatment selection: Toward targeted therapeutic interventions.* San Francisco, CA: Brunner/Mazel.

Beutler, L. E., Catonguay, L. G., & Follette, W. C. (2006). Therapeutic factors in dysphoric disorders. *Journal of Clinical Psychology, 62,* 639–647.

Bianchi-Demicheli, F., Grafton, S. T., & Ortigue, S. (2006). The power of love on the human brain. *Social Neuroscience, 1*(2), 90–103.

Binder, J.L. & Strupp, H.H. (1997). Supervision of psychodynamic psychotherapies. In C.E. Watkin Jr. (ed). *Handbook of psychotherapy supervision* (pp. 44–62). New York, NY: John Wiley & Sons.

Binder, P.-E., Holgersen, H., & Nielsen, G. H. (2008a). Establishing a bond that works: A qualitative study of how psychotherapists make contact with adolescent patients. *European Journal of Psychotherapy and Counselling, 10,* 55–69.

Binder, P.-E., Holgersen, H., & Nielsen, G. H. (2008b). Reestablishing contact: A qualitative exploration of how therapists work with alliance ruptures in adolescent psychotherapy. *Counselling and Psychotherapy Research, 8,* 239–245.

Biringen, Z. (1990). Direct observation of maternal sensitivity and dyadic interactions in the home: Relations to maternal thinking. *Developmental Psychology, 26,* 278–284.

Bischoff, M. M., & Tracey, T. J. G. (1995). Client resistance as predicted by therapist behavior: A study of sequential dependence. *Journal of Counseling Psychology, 42,* 487–495.

Block-Lerner, J., Adair, C., Plumb, J. C., Rhatigan, D. L., & Orsillo, S. M. (2007). The case for mindfulness-based approaches in the cultivation of empathy: Does nonjudgmental, present-moment awareness increase capacity for perspective-taking and empathic concern? *Journal of Marital and Family Therapy, 33,* 501–516.

Bloom, J.S., & Hynd, G.W. (2005). The role of the corpus callosum in interhemispheric transfer of information: Excitation or inhibition? *Neuropsychology Review, 15,* 59–71.

Bloom, M., Fischer, J., & Orme, J. G. (1995). *Evaluating practice: Guidelines for the accountable professional* (2nd ed.). Boston, MA: Allyn & Bacon.

Boardman, T., Delwyn, C., Grobe, J. E., Little, T. D., & Ahluwalia, J. S. (2006). Using motivational interviewing with smokers: Do therapist behaviors relate to engagement and therapeutic alliance? *Journal of Substance Abuse Treatment, 31,* 329–339.

Bond, M. H., & Ng, I. W.-C. (2004). The depth of a group's personality resources: Impacts on group process and group performance. *Asian Journal of Social Psychology, 7,* 285–300.

Borge, S. (2007). Unwarranted questions and conversation. *Journal of Pragmatics, 39,* 1689–1701.

Bornhofen, C., & McDonald, S. (2008). Comparing strategies for treating emotion perception deficits in traumatic brain injury. *Journal of Head Trauma Rehabilitation, 23,* 103–115.

Borntrager, C. F., Chorpita, B. F., Higa-McMillan, C., & Weisz, J. R. (2009). Provider attitudes toward evidence-based practices: Are the concerns with the evidence or with the manuals? *Psychiatric Services, 60,* 677–681.

Borrell-Carrio, F., & Epstein, R. M. (2004). Preventing errors in clinical practice: A call for self-awareness. *Annals of Family Medicine, 2,* 310–316.

Boverie, P. E. (1991). Human systems consultant: Using family therapy in organizations. *Family Therapy, 18,* 61–71.

Bowen, M. (1974). Toward the differentiation of self in one's family of origin. In E. Andres & J. Lorio (Eds.), *Georgetown Family Symposium, Vol. 1*. Washington, DC: Department of Psychiatry, Georgetown University Medical Center.

Bowen, M. (1978). *Family therapy in clinical practice*. New York, NY: Jason Aronson.

Boyd, G. E. (2003). Pastoral conversation: Relational listening and open-ended questions. *Pastoral Psychology, 51*, 345–359.

Boyer, S. P., & Hoffman, M. A. (1993). Counselor affective reactions to termination: Impact of counselor loss history and perceived client sensitivity to loss. *Journal of Counseling Psychology, 40*, 271–277.

Bozarth, J. D. (1997). Empathy from the framework of client-centered theory and the Rogerian hypothesis. In A. C. Bohart & L. S. Greenberg (Eds.), *Empathy reconsidered: New directions in psychotherapy* (pp. 81–102). Washington, DC: American Psychological Association.

Brabender, V. (2007). The ethical group psychotherapist: A coda. *International Journal of Group Psychotherapy, 57*, 41–47.

Brehm, J. W., Miron, A. M., & Miller, K. (2009). Affect as a motivational state. *Cognition and Emotion, 23*, 1069–1089.

Brewin, C. R., Wheatley, J., Patel, T., Fearon, P., Hackmann, A., Wells, A. . . . Myers, S. (2009). Imagery rescripting as a brief stand-alone treatment for depressed patients with intrusive memories. *Behaviour Research and Therapy, 47*, 569–576.

Briley, D.A. (2009). Looking forward, looking back: Cultural differences and similarities in time orientation. In R.S. Wyer, C. Chiu, & Hong, Y. (Eds.) *Understanding culture: Theory, research, and application* (pp. 311–325). New York, NY: Psychology Press.

Brislin, R.W., & Kim, E.S. (2003). Cultural diversity in people's understanding and uses of time. *Applied Psychology: An International Review, 52*, 363–382.

Bromley, E., & Braslow, J. T. (2008). Teaching critical thinking in psychiatric training: A role for the social sciences. *American Journal of Psychiatry, 165*, 1396–1401.

Brookfield, S. D. (1987). *Developing critical thinkers: Challenging adults to explore alternate ways of thinking and acting*. San Francisco, CA: Jossey-Bass.

Brooks, R. C. (2007). Microsimulations: Bridging theory and practice in the composition practicum. *Simulation & Gaming, 38*, 352–361.

Broome, B. J. (1991). Building shared meaning: Implications of a relational approach to empathy for teaching intercultural communication. *Communication Education, 40*, 235–249.

Bross, A. (1982). *Family Therapy. A Recursive Model of Strategic Practice*. Toronto, ONT: Methuen Press.

Brown, J. E. (1997a). Circular questioning: An introductory guide. *Australian & New Zealand Journal of Family Therapy, 18*, 109–114.

Brown, J. E. (1997b). The question cube: A model for developing question repertoire in training couple and family therapists. *Journal of Marital and Family Therapy, 23*, 27–40.

Brown, J. R., & Dunn, J. (1996). Continuities in emotion understanding from 3–6 yrs. *Child Development, 67*, 789–802.

Browne, N. M., & Hausmann, R. G. (1998). The friendly sound of critical thinking. *Korean Journal of Thinking and Problem Solving, 8*, 47–53.

Browne, N. M., & Keeley, S. M. (1994). *Asking the right questions: A guide to critical thinking* (4th ed.). Englewood Cliffs, NJ: Prentice-Hall.

Brownell, K. D., Marlatt, G. A., Lichtenstein, E., & Wilson, G. T. (1986). Understanding and preventing relapse. *American Psychologist, 41*, 765–782.

Brubacher, M. R., Fondacaro, M. R., Brank, E. M., Brown, V. E., & Miller, S. A. (2009). Procedural justice in resolving family disputes: Implications for childhood bullying. *Psychology, Public Policy, and Law, 15*, 149–167.

Buchanan, T. W. (2007). Retrieval of emotional memories. *Psychological Bulletin, 133*(5), 761–779.

Buchbinder, E. (2007). Being a social worker as an existential commitment: from vulnerability to meaningful purpose. *Humanistic Psychologist, 35*, 161–174.

Bueno, J., Weinberg, R. S., Fernández-Castro, J., & Capdevila, L. (2008). Emotional and motivational mechanisms mediating the influence of goal setting on endurance athletes' performance. *Psychology of Sport and Exercise, 9*, 786–799.

Bugg, A., Graham, T., Mason, S., & Scholes, C. (2009). A randomized controlled trial of the effectiveness of writing as a self-help intervention for traumatic injury patients at risk of developing post-traumatic stress disorder. *Behaviour Research and Therapy, 47*, 6–12.

Bunning, K., & Horton, S. (2007). "Border crossing" as a rout to inclusion: A shared cause with people with a learning disability? *Aphasiology, 21*, 9–22.

Burchard, J. D., Burchard, S. N., Sewell, R., & VanDenBerg, J. (1993). *One kid at a time: Evaluative case studies and descriptions of the Alaska Youth Initiative Demonstration Project*. Washington, DC: SAMHSA Center for Mental Health Services.

Burke, S. M., Carron, A. V., Patterson, M. M., Estabrooks, P. A., Hill, J. L., Loughead, T. M. . . . Spink, K. S. (2005). Cohesion as shared beliefs in exercise classes. *Small Group Research, 36*, 267–288.

Burns, S., Maycock, B., Cross, D., & Brown, G. (2008). The power of peers: Why some students bully others to conform. *Qualitative Health Research, 18*, 1704–1716.

Burton, M., & Kagan, C. (2007). Psychologists and torture: More than a question of interrogation. *Psychologist, 20*, 484–487.

Butler, M. H., & Gardner, B. C. (2003). Adapting enactments to couple reactivity: Five developmental stages. *Journal of Marital and Family Therapy, 29*, 311–327.

Buttner, A.K. (2007). Questions versus statements: Challenging an assumption about semantic illusions. *The Quarterly Journal of Experimental Psychology, 60*, 779–789.

Buttny, R. (1996). Clients' and therapist's joint construction of the clients' problems. *Research on Language and Social Interaction, 29*, 125–153.

Byng-Hall, J. (1988). Scripts and legends in families and family therapy. *Family Process, 27*, 167–179.

Cameron, G., & Wren, A. M. (1999). Reconstructing organizational culture: A process using multiple perspectives. *Public Health Nursing, 16*, 96–101.

Carbaugh, D. (1999). "Just listen": "Listening" and landscape among the Blackfeet. *Western Journal of Communication, 63,* 250–270.

Carnegie, E., & Kiger, A. (2009). Being and doing politics: An outdated model or 21st century reality? *Journal of Advanced Nursing, 65,* 1976–1984.

Carpenter, J., & Treacher, A. (1989). *Problems and solutions in marital and family therapy.* Oxford, UK: Basil Blackwell.

Carstens, C. A., Panzano, P. C., Massatti, R., Roth, D., & Sweeney, H. A. (2009). A naturalistic study of MST dissemination in 13 Ohio communities. *Journal of Behavioral Health Services & Research, 36,* 344–360.

Cartwright, D., & Zander.A. (1968). *Group dynamics* (3rd ed.). New York, NY: Harper & Row.

Carver, C. S., & Harmon-Jones, E. (2009). Anger is an approach-related affect: Evidence and implications. *Psychological Bulletin, 135,* 183–204.

Castonguay, L.G., Goldfried, M.R., Wiser, S., Raue, P.J., & Hayes, A.M. (1996). Predicting the effect of cognitive therapy for depression: A study of unique and common factors. *Journal of Consulting and Clinical Psychology, 64,* 497–504.

Chang, A., & Bordia, P. (2001). A multidimensional approach to the group cohesion-group performance relationship. *Small Group Research, 32,* 379–405.

Chang, D. F., & Berk, A. (2009). Making cross-racial therapy work: A phenomenological study of clients' experiences of cross-racial therapy. *Journal of Counseling Psychology, 56,* 521–536.

Chang, P. (1994). Effects of interviewer question and response type on compliance: An analogue study. *Journal of Counseling Psychology, 41,* 74–82.

Charles, S. T., Piazza, J. R., Luong, G., & Almeida, D. M. (2009). Now you see it, now you don't: Age differences in affective reactivity to social tensions. *Psychology and Aging, 24,* 645–653.

Chen, E. Y., Matthews, L., Charese, A., Kuo, J. R., & Linehan, M. M. (2008). Dialectical behavior therapy for clients with binge-eating disorder or bulimia nervosa and borderline personality disorder. *International Journal of Eating Disorders, 41,* 505–512.

Chen, S. X., & Carey, T. P. (2009). Assessing citizenship behavior in educational contexts: The role of personality, motivation, and culture. *Journal of Psychoeducational Assessment, 27,* 125–137.

Chen, X., Chang, L., & He, Y. (2003). The peer group as a context: Mediating and moderating effects on relations between academic achievement and social functioning in Chinese children. *Child Development, 74,* 710–727.

Clark, C. (1998). Self-determination and paternalism in community care: Practice and prospects. *British Journal of Social Work, 28,* 387–402.

Clarke, J., Rees, A., & Hardy, G. E. (2004). The big idea: Clients' perspectives of change processes in cognitive therapy. *Psychology and Psychotherapy: Theory, Research and Practice, 77,* 67–89.

Clifford, M. T. (2004). Termination and two-year follow-up to prevent relapse. In J. S. Gottman (Ed.), *The Marriage Clinic Casebook* (pp. 213–227). New York, NY: W. W. Norton.

Cohen, J. A., Mannarino, A. P., & Knudsen, K. (2005). Treating sexually abused children: 1 year follow-up of a randomized controlled trial. *Child Abuse & Neglect, 29,* 135–145.

Collins, D. (1995). Death of a gainsharing plan: Power politics and participatory management. *Organizational Dynamics, 24,* 23–38.

Conger, J. A. (1998). The dark side of leadership. In G. R. Hickman (Ed.), *Leading organizations: Perspectives for a new era* (pp. 250–260). Thousand Oaks, CA: Sage.

Cook, J. R., & Kilmer, R. P. (2004). Evaluating systems of care: Missing links in children's mental health research. *Journal of Community Psychology, 32,* 655–674.

Conroy, D. E., Elliot, A. J., & Pincus, A. L. (2009). The expression of achievement motives in interpersonal problems. *Journal of Personality, 77,* 495–526.

Constantino, M. J., Marnell, M. E., Haile, A. J., Kanther-Sista, S. N., Wolman, K., Zappert, L., & Arnow, B. A. (2008). Integrative cognitive therapy for depression: A randomized pilot comparison. *Psychotherapy Theory, Research, Practice, Training, 45,* 122–134.

Conway, L. G., III, Thoemmes, F., Allison, A. M., Towgood, K. H., Wagner, M. J., Davey, K. . . . Conway, K. R. (2008). Two ways to be complex and why they matter: Implications for attitude strength and lying. *Journal of Personality and Social Psychology, 95,* 1029–1044.

Corcoran, K. (1998). Clients without a cause: Is there a legal right to effective treatment? *Research on Social Work Practice, 8,* 589–596.

Corey, G., & Corey, M. S. (1998). *Issues and ethics in the helping professions* (5th ed.). Pacific Grove, CA: Brooks/Cole.

Corey, G., Corey, M. S., & Callanan, P. (1998). *Issues and ethics in the helping professions.* Pacific Grove, CA: Brooks/ Cole.

Corey, G., & Herlihy, B. (1996). Client rights and informed consent. In B. Herlihy & G. Corey (Eds.), *ACA ethical standards casebook* (5th ed., pp. 181–191). Alexandria, VA: American Counseling Association.

Cormier, S., & Cormier, B (1998). *Interviewing strategies for helpers: Fundamental skills and cognitive behavioral interventions* (4th ed.). Pacific Grove, CA: Brooks/Cole.

Courtright, J. A., Millar, F. E., Rogers, L. E., & Bagarozzi, D. (1990). Interaction dynamics of relational negotiation: Reconciliation versus termination of distressed relationships. *Western Journal of Speech Communication, 54,* 429–453.

Creed, T. A., & Kendall, P. C. (2005). Therapist alliance-building behavior within a cognitive-behavioral treatment for anxiety in youth. *Journal of Consulting and Clinical Psychology, 73,* 498–505.

Crigger, N. J., & Meek, V. L. (2007). Toward a theory of self-reconciliation following mistakes in nursing practice. *Journal of Nursing Scholarship, 39,* 177–183.

Creswell, J.D., Welch, W.T., Taylor, S.E., Sherman, D.K., Gruenewald, T.L., & Mann, T. (2005). Affirmation of personal values buffers neuroendocrine and psychological stress responses. *Psychological Science, 16,* 846–851.

Crits-Christoph, P., Demorest, A., & Connolly, M. B. (1990). Quantitative assessment of interpersonal themes over the course of psychotherapy, *Psychotherapy, 27,* 513–521.

Croxton, T. A., Churchill, S. R., & Fellin, P. (1988). Counseling minors without parental consent. *Child Welfare, 67,* 3–14.

Cueva, M. (2006). Moving beyond edutainment to engagement. *Journal of Cancer Education, 21,* 141.

Cullin, J. (2008). Levels of sameness: Understanding "resistance" at the level of the therapeutic system. *Psychodynamic Practice: Individuals, Groups and Organisations, 14,* 295–311.

Cunningham, J. N., Kliewer, W., & Garner, P. W. (2009). Emotion socialization, child emotion understanding and regulation, and adjustment in urban African American families: Differential associations across child gender. *Development and Psychopathology, 21,* 261–283.

Cunningham, P. B., & Henggeler, S. W. (1999). Engaging multiproblem families in treatment: Lessons learned throughout the development of multisystemic therapy. *Family Process, 38,* 265–286.

Dahmen, B. A., & Westerman, M. A. (2007). Expectations about the long-term consequences of recurring defensive interpersonal behavior. *Journal of Research in Personality, 41,* 1073–1090.

Dalenberg, C. J. (2004). Maintaining the safe and effective therapeutic relationship in the context of distrust and anger: Countertransference and complex trauma. *Psychotherapy: Theory, Research, Practice, Training, 41,* 438–447.

Daley, J. M., Wong, P., & Applewhite, S. (1992). Serving on the boards of mental health agencies: The experiences of Mexican American community leaders. *Administration and Policy in Mental Health, 19,* 353–365.

Daniel, J. H., Roysircar, G., Abeles, N., & Boyd, C. (2004). Individual and cultural-diversity competency: Focus on the therapist. *Journal of Clinical Psychology, 60,* 755–770.

Daselaar, S. M., Rice, H. J., Greenberg, D. L., Cabeza, R., LaBar, K. S., & Rubin, D. C. (2008). The spatiotemporal dynamics of autobiographical memory: Neural correlates of recall, emotional intensity, and reliving. *Cerebral Cortex, 18,* 217–229.

Davis, S. D., & Butler, M. H. (2004). Enacting relationships in marriage and family therapy: A conceptual and operational definition of an enactment. *Journal of Marital and Family Therapy, 30,* 319–333.

Davitt, J. K., & Kaye, L. W. (1996). Supporting patient autonomy: Decision making in home health care. *Social Work, 41,* 41–50.

Dawes, R. M. (1988). *Rational choice in an uncertain world.* San Diego, CA: Harcourt Brace.

Day-Vines, N. L., Wood, S. M., Grothaus, T., Craigen, L., Holman, A., Dotson-Blake, K., & Douglass, M. J. (2007). Broaching the subjects of race, ethnicity, and culture during the counseling process. *Journal of Counseling & Development, 85,* 401–409.

Dean, H. E. (1998). The primacy of the ethical aim in clinical social work: Its relationship to social justice and mental health. *Smith College Studies in Social Work, 69,* 9–24.

Deci, E. L., Ryan, R. M., Gagné, M., Leone, D. R., Usunov, J., & Kornazheva, B. P. (2001). Need satisfaction, motivation, and well-being in the work organizations of a former Eastern bloc country: A cross-cultural study of self-determination. *Personality and Social Psychology Bulletin, 27,* 930–942.

De Cremer, D., van Knippenberg, D., van Duk, E., & van Leeuwen, E. (2008). Cooperating if one's goals are collective-based: Social identification effects in social dilemmas as a function of goal transformation. *Journal of Applied Social Psychology, 38,* 1562–1579.

Dehaene, S., & Naccache, L. (2001). Towards a cognitive neuroscience of consciousness: Basic evidence and a workspace framework. *Cognition, 79,* 1–37.

DeJong, P., & Berg, I. K. (1998). *Interviewing for solutions.* Pacific Grove, CA: Brooks/Cole.

DeJong, P., & Miller, S. D. (1995). How to interview for client strengths. *Social Work, 40,* 729–736.

de Luynes, M. (1995). Neuro linguistic programming. *Educational and Child Psychology, 12,* 34–47.

Demaree, H. A., Everhart, D. E., Youngstrom, E. A., & Harrison, D. W. (2005). Brain lateralization of emotional processing: Historical roots and a future incorporating "dominance." *Behavioral and Cognitive Neuroscience Review, 4,* 3–29.

Denby, R., & Alford, K. (1996). Understanding African American discipline styles: Suggestions for effective social work intervention. *Journal of Multicultural Social Work, 4,* 81–98.

de Oliveira, J. A., & Vandenberghe, L. (2009). Upsetting experiences for the therapist in-session: How they can be dealt with and what they are good for. *Journal of Psychotherapy Integration, 19,* 231–245.

Dettlaff, A. J., Moore, L. S., & Dietz, T. J. (2006). Personality type preferences of social work students: Enhancing education through understanding personality variables. *The Journal of Baccalaureate Social Work, 11,* 88–101.

Devaux, F. (1995). Intergenerational transmission of cultural family patterns. *Family Therapy, 22,* 17–23.

de Vignemont, F., & Singer, T. (2006). The empathic brain: How, when and why? *Trends in Cognitive Sciences, 10* (10), 435–441.

DeWall, C. N., Baumeister, R. F., & Masicampo, E. J. (2008). Evidence that logical reasoning depends on conscious processing. *Consciousness and Cognition, 17,* 628–645.

Diamond, G. M., Diamond, G. S., & Hogue, A. (2007). Attachment-based family therapy: Adherence and differentiation. *Journal of Marital & Family Therapy, 33,* 177–191.

Diaz-Morales, J. F., Ferrari, J. R., & Cohen, J. R. (2008). Indecision and avoidant procrastination: The role of morningness-evingness and time perspective in chronic delay lifestyles. *Journal of General Psychology, 135,* 228–240.

Dickson, D. T. (1998). *Confidentiality and privacy in social work: A guide to the law for practitioners and students.* New York, NY: Free Press.

Dietrich, S., Hertrich, I., Alter, K., Ischebeck, A., & Ackermann, H. (2007). Semiotic aspects of human nonverbal vocalizations: A functional imaging study. *Neuroreport, 18,* 1891–1894.

Dijkstra, A., & Dijker, L. D. (2005). Physical threat and self-evaluative emotions in smoking cessation. *Journal of Applied Social Psychology, 35,* 1859–1878.

Dilallo, J. J., & Weiss, G., (2009). Motivational interviewing and adolescent psychopharmacology. *Journal of the American Academy of Child & Adolescent Psychiatry, 48,* 108–113.

Docherty, N.M., St-Hilaire, A., Aakre, J.M., & Seghers, J. P. (2009). Life events and high-trait reactivity together predict psychotic symptom increases in schizophrenia. *Schizophrenia Bulletin, 35*, 638–645.

Dolgoff, R., & Skolnik, L. (1996). Ethical decision making in social work with groups: An empirical study. *Social Work with Groups, 19*, 49–65.

Dong-Min, K., Wampold, B. E., & Bolt, D. M. (2006). Therapist effects in psychotherapy: A random-effects modeling of the National Institute of Mental Health treatment of depression collaborative research program data. *Psychotherapy Research, 16*, 161–172.

Dougal, S., Phelps, E. A., & Davachi, L. (2007). The role of medial temporal lobe in item recognition and source recollection of emotional stimuli. *Cognitive, Affective & Behavioral Neuroscience, 7*(3), 233–242.

Dowd, E. T., & Sanders, D. (1994). Resistance, reactance, and the difficult client. *Canadian Journal of Counselling, 28*, 13–24.

Downie, M., Mageau, G. A., & Koestner, R. (2008). What makes for a pleasant social interaction? Motivational dynamics of interpersonal relations. *Journal of Social Psychology, 148*, 523–534.

Dozier, R. M., Micks, M. W., Cornille, T. A., & Peterson, G. W. (1998). The effect of Tomm's Therapeutic questioning styles on therapeutic alliance: A clinical analog study. *Family Process, 37*, 189–200.

Draine, J., & Herman, D. B. (2007). Critical time intervention for reentry from prison for persons with mental illness. *Psychiatric Services, 58*, 1577–1581.

Dumas, J. E., Nissley-Tsiopinis, J., & Moreland, A. D. (2006). From intent to enrollment, attendance, and participation in preventive parenting groups. *Journal of Child and Family Studies, 16*, 1–26.

Dunbar, R. I.M. (2009). Darwin and the ghost of Phineas Gage: Neuro-evolution and the social brain. *Cortex, 45*, 119–125.

Duncan, S. (1072). Some signals and rules for taking speaking turns in conversation. *Journal of Personality and Social Psychology, 23*, 283–292.

Dunn, W. N., & Ginsberg, A. (1986). A sociocognitive network approach to organizational analysis. *Human Relations, 39*, 955–975.

Durana, C. (1998). The use of touch in psychotherapy: Ethical and clinical guidelines. *Psychotherapy, 35*, 269–280.

Dutton, D. G., & Browning, J. J. (1988). Concern for power, fear of intimacy and aversive stimuli for wife abuse. In G. T. Hotaling, D. Finkelhor, J. T. Kilpatric, & M. Straus (Eds.), *New Directions in Family Violence Research* (pp. 163–175). Newbury Park, CA: Sage.

Edwards, J. K., & Bess, J. M. (1998). Developing effectiveness in the therapeutic use of self. *Clinical Social Work Journal, 26*, 89–105.

Egan, G. (2010). *The Skilled Helper* (9th ed.). Belmont, CA: Cengage (Brooks/Cole).

Egan, S. J., Piek, J. P., Dyck, M. J., & Rees, C. S. (2007). The role of dichotomous thinking and rigidity in perfectionism. *Behaviour Research and Therapy, 45*, 1813–1822.

Eippert, F., Veit, R., Weiskopf, N., Erb, M., Birbaumer, N., & Anders, S. (2007). Regulation of emotional responses elicited by threat-related stimuli. *Human Brain Mapping, 28*(5), 409–423.

Eisenberger, N. I., & Lieberman, M. D. (2004). Why rejection hurts: A common neural alarm system for physical and social pain. *Trends in Cognitive Sciences, 8*, 294–300.

Elkind, S. N. (1992). *Resolving impasses in therapeutic relationships.* New York, NY: Guilford Press.

Ellis, A. (1996). Thinking processes involved in irrational beliefs and their disturbed consequences. *Journal of Cognitive Psychotherapy, 9*, 105–116.

Enfield, N. J. (2009). Relationship thinking and human pragmatics. *Journal of Pragmatics, 41*, 60–78.

Engel, G. L. (1977). The need for a new medical model: A challenge for biomedicine. *Science, 196*, 129–136.

England, E. M., & Petro, K. D. (1998). Middle school students' perceptions of peer groups: Relative judgments about group characteristics. *Journal of Early Adolescence, 18*, 349–373.

Engle, D., & Arkowitz, H. (2008). Viewing resistance as ambivalence: Integrative strategies for working with resistant ambivalence. *Journal of Humanistic Psychology, 48*, 389–412.

Englebrecht, C., Peterson, D., Scherer, A., & Naccarato, T. (2008). "It's not my fault": Acceptance of responsibility as a component of engagement in juvenile residential treatment. *Children and Youth Services Review, 30*, 466–484.

Engström, A., & Söerberg, S. (2007). Receiving power through confirmation: The meaning of close relatives for people who have been critically ill. *Journal of Advanced Nursing, 53*, 569–576.

Epston, D., & White, M. (1995). Termination as a rite of passage: Questioning strategies for a therapy of inclusion. In R. A. Neimeyer & M. J. Manoney (Eds.) *Constructivism in psychotherapy* (pp. 339–354). Washington, DC: American Psychological Association.

Ericsson, K. A., Krampe, R. T., & Tesch-Romer, C. (1993). The role of deliberate practice in the acquisition of expert performance. *Psychological Review, 100*(3), 363–406.

Estrada, A. U., & Holmes, J. M. (1999). Couples' perceptions of effective and ineffective ingredients of marital therapy. *Journal of Sex and Marital Therapy, 25*, 151–162.

Etkin, A., & Wager, T. D. (2007). Functional neuroimaging of anxiety: A meta-analysis of emotional processing in PTSD, social anxiety disorder, and specific phobia. *American Journal of Psychiatry, 164*, 1476–1488.

Evans, D. R., Hearn, M. T., Uhlemann, M. R., & Ivey, A. E. (1998). *Essential interviewing: A programmed approach to effective communication* (5th ed.). Pacific Grove, CA: Brooks/Cole.

Evans, K. M., & Federmeier, K. D. (2009). Left and right memory revisited: Electrophysiological investigations of hemispheric asymmetries at retrieval. *Neuropsychologia, 47*, 303–313.

Everts, R., Lidzba, K., Wilke, M., Kiefer, C., Mordasini, M., Schroth, G. . . . & Seinlin, M. (2009). Strengthening of laterality of verbal and visuospatial functions during childhood and adolescence. *Human Brain Mapping, 30*, 473–483.

Fabiano, G. A., Chacko, A., Pelham, W. E. Jr., Robb, J., Walker, K. S., Wymbs, F., Sastry, A. L., Flammer, L., Keenan, J. K., Visweswaraiah, J., Shulman, S., Herbst, L., & Pirvics, L. (2009). A comparison of behavioral parent training programs for fathers of children with attention-deficit/hyperactivity disorder. *Behavior Therapy, 40*, 190–204.

Fahrenwald, N. L., Bassett, S. D., Tschetter, L., Carson, P. P., White, L., & Winterboer, V. J. (2005). Teaching core nursing values. *Journal of Professional Nursing, 21*, 46–51.

Falicov, C. J. (1998). *Latino families in therapy: A guide to multicultural practice.* New York, NY: Guilford Press.

Farmer, E. M. Z., Mustillo, S., Burns, B. J., & Holden, E. W. (2008). Use and predictors of out-of-home placements within systems of care. *Journal of Emotional and Behavioral Disorders, 16,* 5–14.

Felthous, A. R. (2006). Warning a potential victim of a person's dangerousness: Clinician's duty or victim's right? *Journal of the American Academy of Psychiatry and the Law, 34,* 338–348.

Festinger, L. (1957). *A theory of cognitive dissonance.* Palo Alto, CA: Stanford University Press.

Finn, R. (2008). The language of teamwork: Reproducing professional divisions in the operating theatre. *Human Relations, 61,* 103–130.

Fiorentine, R., & Hillhouse, M. P., (1999). Drug treatment effectiveness and client-counselor empathy: Exploring the effects of gender and ethnic congruency. *Journal of Drug Issues, 229,* 59–74.

Firth, H., Spanswick, M., & Rutherford, L. (2009). Managing multiple risks: Use of a concise risk assessment format. *Child and Adolescent Mental Health, 14,* 48–52.

Fischer, L., & Sorenson, G. P. (1996). *School law for counselors, psychologists, and social workers* (3rd ed.). New York, NY: Longman.

Fisher, C. B. (2004). Challenges in constructing a cross-national ethics code for psychologists. *European Psychologist, 9,* 273–277.

Fiske, S. T. (1995). Controlling other people: The impact of power on stereotyping. In N. R. Goldberger & J. B. Veroff (Eds.), *The culture and psychology reader* (pp. 438–456). New York, NY: New York Univesity Press.

Flaskas, C. (2004). Thinking about the therapeutic relationship: Emerging themes in family therapy. *Australian and New Zealand Journal of Family Therapy, 25,* 13–20.

Flaskerud, J. H. (2007). Cultural competence column: Can we achieve it? *Issues in Mental Health Nursing, 28,* 309–311.

Flemke, K., & Allen, K. R. (2008). Women's experience of rage: A critical feminist analysis. *Journal of Marital and Family Therapy, 34,* 58–74.

Floyd, K., Whelan, J. P., & Meyers, A. W. (2006). Use of warning messages to modify gambling beliers and behavior in a laboratory investigation. *Psychology of Addictive Behaviors, 20,* 69–74.

Fluckiger, C., & Holtforth, M.G. (2008). Focusing the therapist's attention on the patient's strengths: A preliminary study to foster a mechanism of change in outpatient psychotherapy. *Journal of Clinical Psychology, 64,* 876–890.

Ford, F. R. (1983). Rules: The invisible family. *Family Process, 22,* 135–145.

Forgatch, M. S. (1989). Patterns and outcome in family problem solving: The disrupting effect of negative emotion. *Journal of Marriage and the Family, 51,* 115–124.

Fosha, D. (2004). "Nothing that feels bad is ever the last step": The role of positive emotions in experiential work with difficult emotional experiences. *Clinical Psychology and Psychotherapy, 11,* 30–43.

Foster, E. M., Stephens, R., Krivelyova, A., & Gamfi, P. (2007). Can system integration improve mental health outcomes for children and youth? *Children and Youth Services Review, 29,* 1301–1319.

Fox, M. P. (2009). A systematic review of the literature reporting on studies that examined the impact of interactive, computer-based patient education programs. *Patient Education & Counseling, 77,* 6–13.

Frank, K. A. (2009). Ending with options. *Psychoanalytic Inquiry, 29,* 136–156.

Frankel, Z., & Levitt, H. M. (2009). Clients' experiences of disengaged moments in psychotherapy: A grounded theory analysis. *Journal of Contemporary Psychotherapy, 39,* 171–186.

Frazier, P. A., & Cook, S. W. (1993). Correlates of distress following heterosexual relationship dissolution. *Journal of Social and Personal Relationships, 10,* 55–67.

Freedman, J., & Combs, G. (1993). Invitations to new stories: Using questions to explore alternative possibilities. In S. G. Gilligan & R. Price (Eds.), *Therapeutic Conversations* (pp. 291–308). New York, NY: W. W. Norton.

Freeman, J. B. (1993). *Thinking logically* (2nd ed.). Englewood Cliffs, NJ: Prentice-Hall.

French, R., Reardon, M., & Smith, P. (2003). Engaging with a mental health service: Perspectives of at-risk youth. *Child & Adolescent Social Work Journal, 20,* 529–548.

Fritsche, I., Kessler, T., Mummendey, A., & Neumann, J. (2009). Minimal and maximal goal orientation and reactions to norm violations. *European Journal of Social Psychology, 39,* 3–21.

Frueh, B. C., Grubaugh, A. L., Cusack, K. J., Kimble, M. O., Elhai, J. D., & Knapp, R. G. (2009). Exposure-based cognitive-behavioral treatment of PTSD in adults with schizophrenia or schizoaffective disorder. A pilot study. *Journal of Anxiety Disorders, 23,* 665–675.

Gacitua, R., Sawyer, P., & Rayson, P. (2008). A flexible framework to experiment with ontology learning techniques. *Knowledge-Based Systems, 21,* 192–199.

Gagné, F. (2007). Ten commandments for academic talent development. *Gifted Child Quarterly, 51,* 93–118.

Gainotti, G. (2007). Face familiarity feeling, the right temporal lobe and the possible underlying neural mechanisms. *Brain Research Reviews, 56,* 214–235.

Gambrill, E. (1990). *Critical thinking in clinical practice: Improving the accuracy of judgments and decisions about clients.* San Francisco, CA: Jossey-Bass.

Gambrill, E. (1994). What critical thinking offers to clinicians. *Behavior Therapist, 17,* 141–147.

Gambrill, E. (1997). *Social work practice: A critical thinker's guide.* New York, NY: Oxford University Press.

Gao, F., Noh, J. J., & Koehler, M. J. (2009). Comparing role-playing activities in Second Life and face-to-face environments. *Journal of Interactive Learning Research, 20,* 423–443.

Garber, B. D. (2004). Therapist alienation: Foreseeing and forestalling third-party dynamics undermining psychotherapy with children of conflicted caregivers. *Professional Psychology: Research and Practice, 35,* 357–363.

Garland, A. F., Hawley, K. M., Brookman-Frazee, L., & Hurlburt, M. S. (2008). Identifying common elements of evidence-based psychosocial treatment for children's disruptive behavior problems. *Journal of the American Academy of Child & Adolescent Psychiatry, 47,* 505–514.

Garland, J. A., Jones, H. E., & Kolodny, R. L. (1976). A model for stages of development in social work groups. In S. Bernstein (Ed.), *Explorations in group work* (pp. 17–71). Boston, MA: Charles River Books.

Garrett, J., & Landau, J. (2007). Family motivation to change: A major factor in engaging alcoholics in treatment. *Alcoholism Treatment Quarterly, 25*, 65–83.

Garrison, M. (2006). Misalliance movements in psychotherapy. *Journal of Individual Psychology, 62*, 168–179.

Gaston, L. (1990). The concept of the alliance and its role in psychotherapy: Theoretical and empirical considerations. *Psychotherapy, 27*, 143–153.

Gaston, L., Marmar, C. R., Thompson, L. W., & Gallagher, D. (1988). Relation of patient pretreatment characteristics to the therapeutic alliance in diverse psychotherapies. *Journal of Consulting and Clinical Psychology, 56*, 483–489.

Gelman, C. R., Fernandez, P., Hausman, N., Miller, S., & Weiner, M. (2007). Challenging endings: First year MSW interns' experiences with forced termination and discussion points for supervisory guidance. *Clinical Social Work Journal, 35*, 79–90.

Gelso, C. J., & Hayes, J. A. (1998). *The psychotherapy relationship: Theory, research, and practice.* New York, NY: John Wiley.

Giampaolo, S., Conti, L., Fiore, D., Carcione, A., Dimaggio, G., & Semerari, A. (2006). Disorganized narratives: Problems in treatment and therapist intervention hierarchy. *Journal of Constructivist Psychology, 19*, 191–207.

Gibbs, L. E. (1991). *Scientific reasoning for social workers.* New York, NY: Macmillan.

Gibbs, L. E. (1994). Teaching clinical reasoning. *Behavior Therapist, 17*, 1–6.

Gibbs, L. E., & Gambrill, E. (1999). *Critical thinking for social workers—Exercises for the helping profession.* Thousand Oaks, CA: Pine Forge Press.

Gladwin, T. E., Hart, B. M., & de Jong, R. (2008). Dissociations between motor-related EEG measures in a cued movement sequence task. *Cortex, 44*, 521–536.

Glasford, D. E., Pratto, F., & Dovidio, J. F. (2008). Intragroup dissonance: Responses to ingroup violation of personal values. *Journal of Experimental Social Psychology, 44*, 1057–1064.

Glasgow, G. F., & Gouse-Sheese, J. (1995). Theme of rejection and abandonment in group work with Caribbean adolescents. *Social Work with Groups, 17*, 3–27.

Glassner, A., & Schwarz, B. B. (2007). What stands and develops between creative and critical thinking? Argumentation? *Thinking Skills and Creativity, 2*, 10–18.

Godwin, D. D., & Scanzoni, J. (1989). Couple consensus during marital joint decision-making: A context, process, outcome model. *Journal of Marriage and the Family, 51*, 943–956.

Goldfried, M. R. (2002). A cognitive-behavioral perspective on termination. *Journal of Psychotherapy Integration, 12*, 364–372.

Goldin, E., & Doyle, R. E. (1991). Counselor predicate usage and communication proficiency on ratings of counselor empathic understanding. *Counselor Education and Supervision, 30*, 212–224.

Goldsmith, H. H., & Davidson, R. J. (2004). Disambiguating the components of emotion regulation. *Child Development, 75*, 361–365.

Goldstone, R. L., Roberts, M. E., & Gureckis, T. M. (2008). Emergent processes in group behavior. *Current Directions in Psychological Science, 17*, 10–15.

Goodson, B. D., Layzer, J. I., St. Pierre, R. G., Bernstein, L. S., & Lopez, M. (2000). Effectiveness of a comprehensive, five-year family support program for low-income children and their families: Findings from the comprehensive child development program. *Early Childhood Research Quarterly, 15*, 5–39.

Goodyear, R. K., & Sinnett, E. R. (1984). Current and emerging ethical issues for counseling psychology. *Counseling Psychologist, 12*, 87–98.

Gore, J. S., Cross, S. E., & Kanagawa, C. (2009). Acting in our interests: Relational self-construal and goal motivation across cultures. *Motivation and Emotion, 33*, 75–87.

Graff, F. S., Morgan, T. J., Epstein, E. E., McCrady, B. S., Cook, S. M., Jensen, N. K., & Kelly, S. (2009). Engagement and retention in outpatient alcoholism treatment for women. *American Journal on Addictions, 18*, 277–288.

Green, A. L., Hill, A. Y., Friday, E., & Friday, S. S. (2005). The use of multiple intelligences to enhance team productivity. *Management Decision, 43*, 349–359.

Greenberg, L. S. (2002). Termination of experiential therapy. *Journal of Psychotherapy Integration, 12*, 358–363.

Greenberg, L. S. (2004). Emotion-focused therapy. *Clinical Psychology & Psychotherapy, 11*, 3–16.

Greenberg, L. S., Warwar, S. H., & Malcolm, W. M. (2008). Differential effects of emotion-focused therapy and psychoeducation in facilitating forgiveness and letting go of emotional injuries. *Journal of Counseling Psychology, 55*, 185–196.

Greenblatt, M. (1986). "End runs" and "reverse end runs": A note on organizational dynamics. *American Journal of Social Psychiatry, 6*, 114–119.

Greene, G. J., Lee, M., Mentzer, R. A., Pinnell, S. R., & Niles, D. (1998). Miracles, dreams, and empowerment: A brief therapy practice note. *Families in Society, 79*, 395–399.

Greene, J. O. (2003). Models of adult communication skill acquisition: Practice and the course of performance improvement. In J. O. Greene & B. R. Burleson (Eds.) *Handbook of Communication and Social Interaction Skills* (pp. 51–91). Mahwah, NJ: Lawrence Erlbaum.

Gregory, J., & Embrey, D. G. (2009). Companion recovery model to reduce the effects of profound catastrophic trauma for former child soldiers in Ganta, Liberia. *Traumatology, 15*, 40–51.

Grizenko, N. & Pawliuk, N. (1994). Risk and protective factors for disruptive behavior disorders in children. *American Journal of Orthopsychiatry, 64*, 534–544.

Grover, S. (2004). Advocating for children's rights as an aspect of professionalism: The role of frontline workers and Children's Rights Commissions. *Child & Youth Care Forum, 33*, 405–423.

Groves, K., Vance, C., & Paik, Y. (2008). Linking linear/nonlinear thinking style balance and managerial ethical decision-making. *Journal of Business Ethics, 80*, 305–325.

Guilfoyle, M. (2003). Dialogue and power: A critical analysis of power in dialogical therapy. *Family Process, 42*, 331–343.

Gummer, B. (1994). Managing diversity in the work force. *Administration in Social Work, 18*, 123–140.

Gunner, A. L.C. (2006). Feedback loops in clinical practice: An integrative framework. *Australian and New Zealand Journal of Family Therapy, 27*, 143–152.

Gutheil, T. G. (2006). Commentary: Systems, sensitivity, and "sorry." *Journal of the American Academy of Psychiatry and the Law, 34*, 101–102.

Habib, R. (2008). Humor and disagreement: Identity construction and cross-cultural enrichment. *Journal of Pragmatics, 40*, 1117–1145.

Haen, C. (2005). Rebuilding security: Group therapy with children affected by September 11. *International Journal of Group Psychotherapy, 55*, 391–414.

Haen, C., & Brannon, K. H. (2002). Superheroes, monsters, and babies: Roles of strength, destruction and vulnerability for emotionally disturbed boys. *Arts in Psychotherapy, 29*, 31–40.

Haga, S. M., Kraft, P., & Corby, E.-K. (2009). Emotion regulation: Antecedents and well-being outcomes of cognitive reappraisal and expressive suppression in cross-cultural samples. *Journal of Happiness Studies, 10*, 271–291.

Hakman, M., Chaffin, M., Funderburk, B., & Silovsky, J. F. (2009). Change trajectories for parent-child interaction sequences during parent-child interaction therapy for child physical abuse. *Child Abuse & Neglect, 33*, 461–470.

Hall, A. S., & Jugovic, H. J. (1997). Adolescents' self-determination: Assuming competency until otherwise proven. *Journal of Mental Health Counseling, 19*, 256–267.

Hall, J. C. (2008). A practitioner's application and deconstruction of evidence-based practice. *Families in Society: Journal of Contemporary Social Services, 89*, 385–393.

Halonen, M., & Sorjonen, M-L. (2008). Using niin-interrogative to treat the prior speaker's action as an exaggeration. *Discourse Studies, 10*, 37–53.

Halvorsen, K., Forde, R., & Nortvedt, P. (2009). The principle of justice in patient priorities in the intensive care unit: The role of significant others. *Journal of Medical Ethics, 35*, 483–487.

Hammond, R. T., & Nichols, M. P. (2008). How collaborative is structural family therapy? *Family Journal, 16*, 118–124.

Hancock, T. U. (2007). Come the revolution: Human rights, the far right, and new direction for social work education. *Journal of Baccalaureate Social Work, 12*, 1–12.

Hänze, M., & Berger, R. (2007). Cooperative learning, motivational effects, and student characteristics: An experimental study comparing cooperative learning and direct instruction in 12th grade physics classes. *Learning and Instruction, 17*, 29–41.

Harachi, T. W., Fleming, C. B., White, H. R., Ensminger, M. E., Abbott, R. D., Catalano, R. F., & Haggerty, K. P. (2006). Aggressive behavior among girls and boys during middle childhood: Predictors and sequelae of trajectory group membership. *Aggressive Behavior, 32*, 279–293.

Hare, A. P. (1982). *Creativity in small groups.* Beverly Hills, CA: Sage.

Harmon-Jones, E., Harmon-Jones, C., Fearn, M., Sigelman, J. D., & Johnson, P. (2008). Left frontal cortical activation and spreading of alternatives: Tests of the action-based model of dissonance. *Journal of Personality and Social Psychology, 94*, 1–15.

Harrell, S. P., & Bond, M. A. (2006). Listening to diversity stories: Principles for practice in community research and action. *American Journal of Community Psychology, 37*, 365–376.

Harris, G. A. (1996). Dealing with difficult clients. In F. Flash (Ed.), *The Hatherleigh Guide to Psychotherapy.* (pp. 47–61). New York, NY: Hatherleigh Press.

Hart, W., Albarracín, D., Eagly, A. H., Brechan, I., Lindberg, M. J., Merrill, L. (2009). Feeling validated versus being correct: A meta-analysis of selective exposure to information. *Psychological Bulletin, 135*, 555–588.

Hartman, A. (1978). Diagramatic assessment of family relationships. *Social Casework, 59*, 465–476.

Harvey, J. B. (1988). The Abilene Paradox: The management of agreement. *Organizational Dynamics, 17*, 17–34.

Hay, C. E. & Kinnier, R. T. (1998). Homework in counseling. *Journal of Mental Health Counseling, 20*, 122–132.

Hayes, E., McCahon, C., Panahi, M. R., Hamre, T., & Pohlman, K. (2008). Alliance not compliance: Coaching strategies to improve type 2 diabetes outcomes. *Journal of the American Academy of Nurse Practitioners, 20*, 155–162.

Heard, W. G. (1996). Feelings from a dialogical perspective: Ontology and clinical application. *Humanistic Psychologist, 24*, 95–115.

Hedges, L. E. (1992). *Interpreting the countertransference.* Northvale, NJ: Jason Aronson.

Heineman, T. (2008). Questions of accountability: Yes no interrogatives that are unanswerable. *Discourse Studies, 10*, 55–71.

Helms, J. E. (1995). Why is there no study of cultural equivalence in standardized cognitive ability testing? In N. R. Goldberger & J. B. Veroff (Eds.), *The culture and psychology reader* (pp. 674–719). New York, NY: New York University Press.

Hendrick, S. S. (1988). Counselor self-disclosure. *Journal of Counseling and Development, 66*, 419–424.

Henggeler, S., & Borduin, C. (1990). Family therapy and beyond: A multisystemic approach to treating the behavior problems of children and adolescents. Pacific Grove, CA: Brooks/Cole.

Henry, W. P., Schacht, T. E., & Strupp, H. H. (1990). Patient and therapist introject, interpersonal process, and differential psychotherapy outcome. *Journal of Consulting and Clinical Psychology, 58*, 768–774.

Herlihy, B., & Remley, T. P. (1995). Unified ethical standards: A challenge for professionalism. *Journal of Counseling and Development, 74*, 130–133.

Hernandez, M., & Hodges, S. (2003). Building upon the theory of change for systems of care. *Journal of Emotional and Behavioral Disorders, 11*, 17–24.

Hersoug, A. G., Høglend, P., Monsen, J. T., & Havik, O. E. (2001). Quality of working alliance in psychotherapy—therapist variables and patient/therapist similarity as predictors. *Journal of Psychotherapy Practice and Research, 10*, 205–216.

Hess, P. M., & Hess, H. J. (1998). Values and ethics in social work practice with lesbian and gay persons. In G. P. Mallon (Ed.), *Foundations of social work practice with lesbian and gay persons* (pp. 31–46). New York, NY: Harrington Park Press.

Higata, A., & Okamoto, Y. (2008). The relationship between time perspective and mental health in middle age. *Japanese Journal of Developmental Psychology, 19*, 144–156.

Hillyer, D. (1996). Solution-oriented questions: An analysis of a key intervention in solution-focused therapy. *Journal of the American Psychiatric Nurses Association, 2*, 3–10.

Hilsenroth, M. J., & Cromer, T. D. (2007). Clinician interventions related to alliance during the initial interview and psychological assessment. *Psychotherapy: Theory, Research, Practice, Training, 44*, 205–218.

Hilsenroth, M. J., Peters, E. J., & Ackerman, S. J. (2004). The development of therapeutic alliance during psychological assessment: Patient and therapist perspectives across treatment. *Journal of Personality Assessment, 83*, 332–344

Hinshaw, A. W., & DeLeon, P. H. (1995). Toward achieving multidisciplinary professional collaboration. *Professional Psychology: Research & Practice, 26*, 115–116.

Hobbs, L. J., & Yan, Z., (2008). Cracking the walnut: Using a computer game to impact cognition, emotion, and behavior of highly aggressive fifth grade students. *Computers in Human Behavior, 24*, 421–438.

Hodges, S., Hernadez, M., & Nesman, T. (2003). A developmental framework for collaboration in child-serving agencies. *Journal of Child and Family Services, 12*, 291–305.

Hoeksma, J. B., Oosterlaan, J. & Schipper, E. M. (2004). Emotion regulation and the dynamics of feelings: A conceptual and methodological framework. *Child Development, 75*, 354–360.

Hoenderdos, H. T. W., & van Romunde, L. K. J. (1995). Information exchange between client and the outside world from the NLP perspective. *Communication and Cognition, 28*, 343–350.

Hogan, B. E., & Linden, W. (2004). Anger response styles and blood pressure: At least don't ruminate about it! *Annals of Behavioral Medicine, 27*, 38–49.

Hogue, A., Dauber, S., Chinchilla, P., Fried, A., Henderson, C., Inclan, J., Reiner, R. H., & Liddle, H. A. (2008). Assessing fidelity in individual and family therapy for adolescent substance abuse. *Journal of Substance Abuse Treatment, 35*, 137–147.

Hogue, A., & Liddle, H. A. (2009). Family-based treatment for adolescent substance abuse: controlled trials and new horizons in services research. *Journal of Family Therapy, 31*, 126–154.

Hollands, D. (2004). Reflections on client-counsellor communications. *Psychodynamic Practice: Individuals, Groups and organizations, 10*, 490–499.

Hornickel, J., Skoe, E., & Kraus, N. (2009). Subcortical laterality of speech encoding. *Audiology & Neurotology, 14*, 198–207.

Hornsey, M. J., Frederiks, E., Smith, J. R., & Ford, L. (2007). Strategic defensiveness: Public and private responses to group criticism. *British Journal of Social Psychology, 46*, 697–716.

Hornsey, M. J., Robson, E., Smith, J., Esposo, S., & Sutton, R. M. (2008). Sugaring the pill: Assessing rhetorical strategies designed to minimize defensive reactions to group criticism. *Human Communication Research, 34*, 70–98.

Horton, J. (1998). Further research on the patient's experience of touch in psychotherapy. In E. W. L. Smith & P. R. Clance (Eds.), *Touch in psychotherapy: Theory, research, and practice* (pp. 127–141). New York, NY: Guilford Press.

Horstmanshof, L., & Zimitat, C. (2007). Future time orientation predicts academic engagement among first-year university students. *British Journal of Educational Psychology, 77*, 703–718.

House, S. (1994). Blending NLP representational systems with the RT counseling environment. *Journal of Reality Therapy, 14*, 61–65.

Howard, K. A. S., Ferrari, L., Nota, L., Solberg, V. S. H., & Soresi, S. (2009). The relation of cultural context and social relationships to career development in middle school. *Journal of Vocational Behavior, 75*, 100–108.

Huber, C. H. (1994). *Ethical, legal, and professional issues in the practice of marriage and family therapy* (2nd ed.). Columbus, OH: Merrill.

Huber, D., Henrich, G., & Brandl, T. (2005). Working relationship in a psychotherapeutic consultation. *Psychotherapy Research, 15*, 129–139.

Hugdahl, K., & Westerhausen, R. (2009). What is left is right—How speech asymmetry shaped the brain. *European Psychologist, 14*, 78–89.

Huppert, J. D., Barlow, D. H., Gorman, J. M., Shear, M. K., & Woods, S. W. (2006). The interaction of motivation and adherence predicts outcome in cognitive behavioral therapy for panic disorder: Preliminary findings. *Cognitive and Behavioral Practice, 13*, 198–204.

Hurvitz, S., & Schlesinger, I. M. (2009). Studying implicit messages: A different approach. *Journal of Pragmatics, 41*, 738–752.

Hynan, D. J. (1990). Client reasons and experiences in treatment that influence termination of psychotherapy. *Journal of Clinical Psychology, 46*, 891–895.

Insel, T. R., & Fernald, R. D. (2004). How the brain processes social information: Searching for the social brain. *Annual Review of Neuroscience, 27*, 697–722.

Isaacs, M. L., & Stone, C. (1999). School counselors and confidentiality: Factors affecting professional choices. *Professional School Counseling, 2*, 258–266.

Iwakabe, S. (2008). Psychotherapy integration in Japan. *Psychotherapy Integration, 18*, 103–125.

Ivey, A. E., & Ivey, M. B. (1998). Reframing DSM-IV: Positive strategies from developmental counseling and therapy. *Journal of Counseling and Development, 76*, 334–350.

Izard, C., Stark, K., Trentacosta, C., & Schultz, D. (2008). Beyond emotion regulation: Emotion utilization and adaptive functioning. *Child Development Perspectives, 2*, 156–163.

Jackson, Y. (1998). Applying APA ethical guidelines to individual play therapy with children. *International Journal of Play Therapy, 7*, 1–15.

Jahoda, A., Selkirk, M., Trower, P., Pert, C., Kroese, B. S., Dagnan, D., & Burford, B. (2009). The balance of power in therapeutic interactions with individuals who have intellectual disabilities. *British Journal of Clinical Psychology, 48*, 63–77.

James, W. (1894). Discussion: The physical basis of emotion. *Psychological Review, 1*, 516–529.

Jenkins, C. L., Elliott, A. R., & Harris, J. R. (2006). Identifying ethical issues of the Department of the Army Civilian and Army Nurse Corps certified registered nurse anesthetists. *Military Medicine, 171*, 762–769.

Jennings, L., D'Rozario, V., Goh, M., Sovereign, A., Brogger, M., & Skovholt, T. (2008). Psychotherapy expertise in Singapore: A qualitative investigation. *Psychotherapy Research, 18*, 508–522.

Jennings, L., & Skovholt, T. M. (1999). The cognitive, emotional, and relational characteristics of master therapists. *Journal of Counseling Psychology, 46*, 3–11.

Johansson, H., & Eklund, M. (2006). Helping alliance and early dropout from psychiatric out-patient care: The influence of patient factors. *Social Psychiatry and Psychiatric Epidemiology, 41,* 140–147.

Johnson, A. (2003). Procedural memory and skill acquisition. In A. F. Healy & R. W. Proctor (Eds.), *Handbook of Psychology: Experimental Psychology, Vol. 4* (pp. 499–523). New York, NY: John Wiley.

Johnson, D. W. (1997). *Reading out: Interpersonal effectiveness and self-actualization.* Boston, MA: Allyn & Bacon.

Johnson, S. M. (1996). *The practice of emotionally focused marital therapy: Creating connection.* New York, NY: Brunner/Mazel.

Jonas, K. J., & Huguet, P. (2008). What day is today? A social psychological investigation into the process of time orientation. *Personality and Social Psychology Bulletin, 34,* 353–365.

Jones, S. H., Sellwood, W., McGovern, J. (2005). Psychological therapies for bipolar disorder: The role of model-driven approaches to therapy integration. *Bipolar Disorders, 7,* 22–32.

Joseph, J. E., Liu, X., Jiang, Y., Lynam, D., & Kelly, T. H., (2009). Neural correlates of emotional reactivity in sensation seeking. *Psychological Science, 20,* 215–223.

Jungbluth, N. J., & Shirk, S. R. (2009). Therapist strategies for building involvement in cognitive-behavioral therapy for adolescent depression. *Journal of Consulting and Clinical Psychology, 77,* 1179–1184.

Kahane, H. (1992). *Logic and contemporary rhetoric: The use of reason in everyday life* (6th ed.). Belmont, CA: Wadsworth.

Kakkad, D. (2005). A new ethical praxis: Psychologists' emerging responsibilities in issues of social justice. *Ethics & Behavior, 15,* 293–308.

Kalmuss, D. (1984). The intergenerational transmission of marital aggression. *Journal of Marriage and the Family, 46,* 11–19.

Kam, C. C.-S., & Bond, M. H. (2008). Role of emotions and behavioural responses in mediating the impact of face loss on relationship deterioration: Are Chinese more face-sensitive than Americans? *Asian Journal of Social Psychology, 11,* 175–184.

Karno, M. P. (2007). A case study of mediators of treatment effectiveness. *Alcoholism: Clinical and Experimental Research, 31,* 33s–95s.

Karp, J., & Dugas, M. J. (2003). Stuck behind a wall of fear: How cognitive-behavior therapy helped one woman with social phobia. *Cognitive Therapy, 2,* 171–187.

Karver, M., Shirk, S., Handelsman, J. B., Fields, S., Crisp, H., Gudmundsen, G., & McMakin, D. (2008). Relationship processes in youth psychotherapy: Measuring alliance, alliance-building behaviors, and client involvement. *Journal of Emotional and Behavioral Disorders, 16,* 15–28.

Kasper, G., & Ross, S.J. (2007). Multiple questions in oral proficiency interviews. *Journal of Pragmatics, 39,* 2045–2070.

Kasper, L. B., Hill, C. E., & Kivlighan, D. M., Jr. (2008). Therapist immediacy in brief psychotherapy: Case study I, *Psychotherapy Theory, Research, Practice, Training, 45,* 281–297.

Kassierer, J. P., & Kopelman, R. I. (1991). *Learning clinical reasoning.* Baltimore, MD: Williams & Wilkins.

Kato, S. (2003). A study of the psychological mechanism and counselor's actions in the unexpected termination of

counseling. *Japanese Journal of Counseling Science, 36,* 156–164.

Kearns, J., Forbes, A., & Gardiner, M. (2007). A cognitive behavioural coaching intervention for the treatment of perfectionism and self-handicapping in a nonclinical population. *Behaviour Change, 24,* 157–172.

Keenan, E. K., Tsang, A. K. T., Bogo, M., & George, U. (2005). Micro ruptures and repairs in the beginning phase of cross-cultural psychotherapy. *Clinical Social Work Journal, 33,* 271–289.

Keijsers, G. P.J., Schaap, C. P.D. R., & Hoogduin, C. A. L. (2000). The impact of interpersonal patient and therapist behavior on outcome in cognitive-behavior therapy. *Behavior Modification, 24,* 264–297.

Kennedy, S. S., Mercer, J., Mohr, W., & Huffine, C. W. (2002). Snake oil, ethics, and the first amendment: What's a profession to do? *American Journal of Orthopsychiatry, 72,* 5–15.

Kensinger, E. A. (2007). Negative emotion enhances memory accuracy behavioral and neuroimaging evidence. *Current Directions in Psychological Science, 16*(4), 213–218.

Kernis, M. H., Lakey, C. E., & Heppner, W. L. (2008). Secure versus fragile high self-esteem as a predictor of verbal defensiveness: Converging findings across three different markers. *Journal of Personality, 76,* 477–512.

Kerr, P. L., Muehlenkamp, J., Larsen, M. A. (2009). Implementation of DBT-informed therapy at a rural university training clinic: A case study. *Cognitive and Behavioral Practice, 16,* 92–100.

Kessel, L., Todres, M., & Av-Ron, S. (2001). Leaving the "professional home": Women in mental health professions. *Journal of Feminist Family Therapy, 13,* 47–56.

Kiang, L., Blumenthal, T. D., Carlson, E. N., Lawson, Y. N., & Shell, J. C. (2009). Physiologic responses to racial rejection images among young adults from African-American backgrounds. *Journal of Youth and Adolescence, 38,* 164–174.

Kiefer, S. M., & Ryan, A. M. (2008). Striving for social dominance over peers: The implications for academic adjustment during early adolescence. *Journal of Educational Psychology, 100,* 417–428.

Kim, P. H., Dirks, K. T., Cooper, C. D., & Ferrin, D. L. (2006). When more blame is better than less: The implications of internal vs. external attributions for the repair of trust after a competence vs. integrity-based trust violation. *Organizational Behavior and Human Decision Processes, 99,* 49–65.

Kim, S., Kverno, K., Lee, E. M., Jeong, H. P., Lee, J. J., & Kim, H. L. (2006). Intervention for the primary prevention of adjustment difficulties in Korean adolescent girls. *Journal of Child and Adolescent Psychiatric Nursing, 19,* 103–111.

Kindermann, T. A. (2007). Effects of naturally existing peer groups on changes in academic engagement in a cohort of sixth graders. *Child Development, 78,* 1186–1203.

Kita, S. (2009). Cross-cultural variation of speech-accompanying gesture: A review. *Language and Cognitive Processes, 24,* 145–167.

Kivlighan, D.M. Jr., Mullison, D.D., Flohr, D.F., Proudman, S., Francis, A.M.R. (1992). The interpersonal structure of "good" versus "bad" group counseling sessions: A multiple-case study. *Psychotherapy: Theory, Research, Practice, Training, 29,* 500–508.

Klann, J., Kastrau, F., Semeny, S., & Huber, W. (2002). Perception of signs of written words: An fMRI study. *Cortex*, *38*, 874–877.

Koesten, J., Schrodt, P., & Ford, D. J. (2009). Cognitive flexibility as a mediator of family communication environments and young adults' well-being. *Health Communication*, *24*, 82–94.

Kong, K. C. C. (2003). "Are you my friend?": Negotiating friendship in conversations between network marketers and their prospects. *Language in Society*, *32*, 487–522.

Kopp, R. R. (1995). *Metaphor therapy: Using client-generated metaphors in psychotherapy*. New York, NY: Brunner/ Mazel.

Krause, E. D., Mendelson, T., & Lynch, T. R. (2003). Childhood emotional invalidation and adult psychological distress: The mediating role of emotional inhibition. *Child Abuse and Neglect*, *27*, 199–213.

Krieglmeyer, R., Wittstadt, D., & Strack, F. (2009). How attribution influences aggression: Answers to an old question by using an implicit measure of anger. *Journal of Experimental Social Psychology*, *45*, 379–385.

Kubany, E. S., Richard, D. C., Bauer, G. B., & Miles, Y. M. (1992). Verbalized anger and accusatory "you" messages as cues for anger and antagonism among adolescents. *Adolescence*, *27*, 505–516.

Kukla, M., & Bond, G. R. (2009). The working alliance and employment outcomes for people with severe mental illness enrolled in vocational programs. *Rehabilitation Psychology*, *54*, 157–163.

Lacharite, C., Ethier, L. & Couture, G. (1995). The influence of partner on parental stress of neglectful mothers. *Child Abuse Review*, *5*, 18–33.

Lachman, P., & Bernard, C. (2006). Moving from blame to quality: How to respond to failures in child protective services. *Child Abuse & Neglect*, *30*, 963–968.

Lafave, L., Desportes, L., & McBride, C. (2009). Treatment outcomes and perceived benefits: A qualitative and quantitative assessment of a women's substance abuse treatment program. *Women & Therapy*, *32*, 51–68.

Lafferty, P., Beutler, L. E., & Crago, M. (1989). Differences between more and less effective psychotherapists: A study of select therapist variables. *Journal of Consulting and Clinical Psychology*, *57*, 76–80.

Lahmann, C., Nickel, M., Schuster, T., Sauer, N., Ronel, J., Noll-Jussong, M., Tritt, K., Nowak, D., Röhricht, F., & Loew, T. (2009). Functional relaxation and guided imagery as complementary therapy in asthma: A randomized controlled clinical trial. *Psychotherapy and Psychosomatics*, *78*, 233–239.

Lakey, C. E., Kernis, M. H., Heppner, W. L., & Lance, C. E. (2008). Individual differences in authenticity and mindfulness as predictors of verbal defensiveness. *Journal of Research in Personality*, *42*, 230–238.

Landau, M. H., Greenberg, J., & Rothschild, Z. K. (2009). Motivated cultural worldview adherence and culturally loaded test performance. *Personality and Social Psychology Bulletin*, *35*, 442–453.

Lane, S. M., Mathews, R. C., Sallas, B., Prattini, R., & Sun, R. (2008). Facilitative interactions of model-and experience-based processes. Implications for type and flexibility of representation. *Memory & Cognition*, *36*, 157–169.

Lansberg, I. (1988). Social categorization, entitlement, and justice in organizations: Contextual determinants and cognitive underpinnings. *Human Relations*, *41*, 871–899.

LeBaron, M., & Carstarphen, N. (1997). Negotiating intractable conflict: The common ground dialogue process and abortion. *Negotiation Journal*, *13*, 341–361.

Lebow, J. L. (1995). Open-ended therapy: Termination in marital and family therapy. In R. H. Mikesell & D. Lusterman (Eds.), *Integrating family therapy: Handbook of family psychology and systems theory* (pp. 73–86). Washington, DC: American Psychological Association.

Le Foll, D., Rascle, O., & Higgins, N. C. (2008). Attributional feedback-induced changes in functional and dysfunctional attributions, expectations of success, hopefulness, and short-term persistence in a novel sport. *Psychology of Sport and Exercise*, *9*, 77–91.

Leigh, A. (1998). *Referral and termination issues for counsellors*. London, UK: Academy of Hebrew Language.

Leis, J. A., Mendelson, T., Tandon, S. D., & Perry, D. F. (2009). A systematic review of home-based interventions to prevent and treat postpartum depression. *Archives of Women's Mental Health*, *12*, 3–13.

Leszcz, M., & Yalom, I. D. (2005). *The Theory and Practice of Group Psychotherapy*, 5th ed. New York, NY: Basic Books.

Letendre, J., Gaillard, B. V., & Spath, R. (2008). Getting the job done: Use of a work group for agency change. *Groupwork*, *18*, 52–68.

Levitt, D. H. (2001). Active listening and counselor self-efficacy: Emphasis on one microskill in beginning counselor training. *Clinical Supervisor*, *20*, 101–115.

Lewis, M. D., & Todd, R. M. (2007). The self-regulating brain: Cortical-subcortical feedback and the development of intelligent action. *Cognitive Development*, *22*, 406–430.

Libri, V., & Kemp, T. (2006). Assessing the efficacy of a cognitive behavioural executive coaching program. *International Coaching Psychology Review*, *1*, 9–18.

Linder-Pelz, S., & Hall, L. M. (2007). The theoretical roots of NLP-based coaching. *Coaching Psychologist*, *3*, 12–17.

Linder-Pelz, S., & Hall, L. M. (2008). Meta-coaching: A methodology grounded in psychological theory. *International Journal of Evidence Based Coaching and Mentoring*, *6*, 43–56.

Link, B. G., & Phelan, J. (1995). Social conditions as fundamental causes of disease. *Journal of Health and Social Behavior* (Extra Issue), 80–94.

Lira, E. M., Ripoll, P., Peiró, J. M., & González, P. (2007). The roles of group potency and information and communication technologies in the relationship between task conflict and team effectiveness: A longitudinal study. *Computers in Human Behavior*, *23*, 2888–2903.

Littauer, J., Sexton, H., & Wynn, R. (2005). Qualities clients wish for in their therapists. *Scandinavian Journal of Caring Sciences*, *19*, 28–31.

Lizzio, A., Wilson, K., & Que, J. (2009). Relationship dimensions in the professional supervision of psychology graduates: Supervisee perceptions of processes and outcome. *Studies in Continuing Education*, *31*, 127–140.

Loersch, C., Aarts, H., Payne, B. K., & Jefferis, V. E. (2008). The influence of social groups on goal contagion. *Journal of Experimental Social Psychology*, *44*, 1555–1558.

London, B., Downey, G., Bonica, C., & Paltin, I. (2007). Social causes and consequences of rejection sensitivity. *Journal of Research on Adolescence, 17,* 481–506.

Lopez, V. (2008). Understanding adolescent property crime using a delinquent events perspective. *Deviant Behavior, 29,* 581–610.

Loroz, P. S. (2007). The interaction of message frames and reference points in prosocial persuasive appeals. *Psychology and Marketing, 24,* 1001–1023.

Lowy, L. (1976). Decision-making and group work. In S. Bernstein (Ed.), *Explorations in group work* (pp. 107–136). Boston, MA: Charles River Books.

Lubbers, M. J., Kuyper, H., & van der Werf, M. P. C. (2009). Social comparison with friends versus non-friends. *European Journal of Social Psychology, 39,* 52–68.

Lucey, C. F., & Staton, A. R. (2003). Constructing a solutions timeline: Creating possibilities in counseling. *Family Journal: Counseling and Therapy for Couples and Families, 11,* 409–412.

Lum, D. (1992). *Social work and people of color: A process-stage approach.* Pacific Grove, CA: Brooks/Cole.

Lupu, V., & Iftene, F. (2009). The impact of rational emotive behavior education on anxiety in teenagers. *Journal of Cognitive and Behavioral Psychotherapies, 9,* 95–105.

Lutcke, H., & Frahm, J. (2008). Lateralized anterior cingulated function during error processing and conflict monitoring as revealed by high-resolution fMRI. *Cerebral Cortex, 18,* 508–515.

Lutz, W., Leon, S. C., Martinovich, Z., Lyons, J. S., & Stiles, W. B. (2007). Therapist effects in outpatient psychotherapy: A three-level growth curve approach. *Journal of Counseling Psychology, 54,* 32–39.

Lymbery, M. (2006). United we stand? Partnership working in health and social care and the role of social work in services for older people. *British Journal of Social Work, 36,* 1119–1137.

Macpherson, R., Hovey, N., Ranganath, K., Uppal, A., & Thompson, A. (2007). An audit of clinical practice in an ACT team against NICE guidelines in schizophrenia. *Journal of Psychiatric Intensive Care, 3,* 113–117.

Maertz, C. P., Jr., Hassan, A., & Magnusson, P. (2009). When learning is not enough: A process model of expatriate adjustment as cultural cognitive dissonance reduction. *Organizational Behavior and Human Decision Processes, 108,* 66–78.

Mallinckrodt, B. (1993). Session impact, working alliance, and treatment outcome in brief counseling. *Journal of Counseling Psychology, 40,* 25–32.

Manteuffel, B., Stephens, R. L., Sondheimer, D. L., & Fisher, S. K. (2008). Characteristics, service experiences, and outcomes of transition-aged youth in systems of care: Programmatic and policy implications. *Journal of Behavioral Health Services & Research, 35,* 469–487.

Manthei, R. J. (1997). The response-shift bias in a counsellor education program. *British Journal of Guidance and Counselling, 25,* 229–237.

Many, M. M. (2009). Termination as a therapeutic intervention when treating children who have experienced multiple losses. *Infant Mental Health Journal, 30,* 23–39.

Marchewka, A., Brechmann, A., Nowicka, A., Jednorog, K., Scheich, H., & Grabowska, A., (2008). False recognition of emotional stimuli is lateralized in the brain: An fMRI study. *Neurobiology of Learning and Memory, 90,* 280–284.

Marlin, E. (1989). *Genograms: The new tool for exploring the personality, career, and love patterns you inherit.* Chicago, IL: Contemporary Books.

Marshall, E. C., Vujanovic, A. A., Kutz, A., Gibson, L., Leyro, T., & Zvolensky, M. J. (2009). Reasons for quitting smoking prior to a self-quit attempt among smokers with and without posttraumatic stress disorder or other anxiety/mood psychopathology. *American Journal of Addictions, 18,* 309–315.

Marshall, R.J. (2003). Use of the group therapist's personality via the countertransferences. *Group, 27,* 107–120.

Marshall, W. L., Ward, T., Mann, R. E., Moulden, H., Fernadez, Y. M., Serran, G., & Marshall, L. E. (2005). Working positively with sexual offenders—maximizing the effectiveness of treatment. *Journal of Interpersonal Violence, 20,* 1096–1114.

Martin, R. C., & Dahlen, E. R. (2004). Irrational beliefs and the experience and expression of anger. *Journal of Rational-Emotive & Cognitive Behavior Therapy, 22,* 3–20.

Martin, S. N., Milne, C., & Scantlebury, K. (2006). Eye-rollers, risk-takers, and turn sharks: Target students in a professional science education program. *Journal of Research in Science Teaching, 43,* 819–851.

Marvin, F. (2002). Consensus is primary to group facilitation. *Group Facilitation, 4,* 56–58.

Marziali, E., Munroe-Blum, H., & McCleary, L. (1997). The contribution of group cohesion and group alliance to the outcome of group psychotherapy. *International Journal of Group Psychotherapy, 47,* 475–497.

Matsunaga, M., Isowa, T., Kimura, K., Miyakoshi, M., Kanayama, N., Murakami, H. . . . Ohira, H. (2008). Associations among central nervous, endocrine, and immune activities when positive emotions are elicited by looking at a favorite person. *Brain, Behavior, and Immunity, 22,* 408–417.

McAuliffe, G., & Lovell, C. (2006). The influence of counselor epistemology on the helping interview: A qualitative study. *Journal of Counseling and Development, 84,* 308–317.

McCollum, V. J. C. (1997). Evolution of the African American family personality: Considerations for family therapy. *Journal of Multicultural Counseling and Development, 25,* 219–229.

McCord, J. (1988). Parental behavior in the cycle of aggression. *Psychiatry, 51,* 14–23.

McEvoy, P. M., & Nathan, P. (2007). Perceived costs and benefits of behavior change: Reconsidering the value of ambivalence for psychotherapy outcomes. *Journal of Clinical Psychology, 63,* 1217–1229.

McGoldrick, M., Gerson, R., & Shellenberger, S. (1999). *Genograms: Assessment and Intervention.* New York, NY: W. W. Norton.

McGovern, M. P., Newman, F. L., & Kopta, S. M. (1986). Metatheoretical assumptions and psychotherapy orientation. *Journal of Consulting and Clinical Psychology, 54,* 476–481.

McInerney, D. M. (2008). Personal investment, culture and learning: Insights into school achievement across Anglo,

Aboriginal, Asian and Lebanese students in Australia. *International Journal of Psychology, 43,* 870–879.

McKay, M. M., Nudelman, R., McCadam, K., & Bonzales, J. (1996). Evaluating a social work engagement approach to involving inner-city children and their families in mental health care. *Research on Social Work Practice, 6,* 462–472.

McKay, N., & Lashutka, S. (1983). The basics of organization change: An eclectic model. *Training and Development Journal, 37,* 64–69.

McKelley, R. A. (2007). Men's resistance to seeking help: Using individual psychology to understand counseling-reluctant men. *Journal of Individual Psychology, 63,* 48–58.

McKelley, R. A., & Rochlen, A. B. (2007). The practice of coaching: Exploring alternative to therapy for counseling-resistant men. *Psychology of Men & Masculinity, 8,* 53–65.

McKimmie, B. M., Terry, D. J., & Hogg, M. A. (2009). Dissonance reduction in the context of group membership: The role of metaconsistency. *Group Dynamics: Theory, Research, and Practice, 13,* 103–119.

McLennan, J., Culkin, K., & Courtney, P. (1994). Telephone counsellors' conceptualizing abilities and counselling skills. *British Journal of Guidance and Counselling, 22,* 183–195.

McNeese, C. A., & Thyer, B. A. (2004). Evidence-based practice and social work. *Journal of Evidence-Based Social Work, 1,* 7–25.

McNulty, J.K., O'Mara, E.M., & Karney, B.R. (2008). Benevolent cognitions as a strategy of relationship maintenance: "Don't sweat the small stuff" . . . but it is not all small stuff. *Journal of Personality and Social Psychology, 94,* 631–646.

McPherson, J. M., Popeilarz, P. A., & Drobnic, S. (1992). *American Sociological Review, 57,* 153–170.

Medina, F. J., Munduate, L., & Guerra, J. M. (2008). Power and conflict in cooperative and competitive contexts. *European Journal of Work and Organizational Psychology, 17,* 349–362.

Meichenbaum, D. (1997). The evolution of a cognitive-behavior therapist. In J. K. Zeig (Ed.), *The evolution of psychotherapy* (pp. 95–104). New York, NY: Brunner/Mazel.

Mertens, D. M., & Ginsberg, P. E. (2008). Deep in ethical waters: Transformative perspectives for qualitative social work research. *Qualitative Social Work, 7,* 484–503.

Miller, L. A., Taber, K. H., Gabbard, G. O., & Hurley, R. A. (2008). *Neural underpinnings of fear and its modulation: Implications for anxiety disorders.* Arlington, VA: American Psychiatric Publishing.

Miller, R. (1999). The first session with a new client: Five stages. In R. Bor & M. Watts (Eds.), *The trainee handbook: A guide for counselling and psychotherapy* (pp. 146–167). Thousand Oaks, CA: Sage.

Miller, S. D. (1994). Some questions (not answers) for the brief treatment of people with drug and alcohol problems. In M. F. Hoyt (Ed.), *Constructive therapies* (pp. 92–110). New York, NY: Guilford Press.

Miller, W. R., Benefield, R. G., & Tonigan, J. S. (1993). Enhancing motivation for change in problem drinking: A controlled comparison of two therapist styles. *Journal of Consulting and Clinical Psychology, 61,* 455–461.

Miller, W. R., & Rollnick, S. (2002). *Motivational interviewing: Preparing people for change.* New York, NY: Guilford Press.

Miller, W. R., & Rollnick, S. (2004). Talking oneself into change: Motivational interviewing, stages of change, and therapeutic process. *Journal of Cognitive Psychotherapy: An International Quarterly, 18,* 299–308.

Minuchin, S. (1974). *Families and family therapy.* London, UK: Tavistock.

Miron, A. M., Parkinson, S. K., & Brehm, J. W. (2007). Does happiness function like a motivational state? *Cognition and Emotion, 21,* 248–267.

Mirabito, D. M. (2006). Revisiting unplanned termination: Clinicians' perceptions of termination from adolescent mental health treatment. *Families in Society, 87,* 171–180.

Mishel, M. H., Germino, B. B., Belyea, M., Stewart, J. L., Bailey, D. E., Jr., Mohler, J., & Robertson, C. (2003). Moderators of an uncertainty management intervention for men with localized prostate cancer. *Nursing Research, 52,* 89–97.

Mishra, R. C., & Singh, D. V. (2008). Psychological differentiation in relation to some socialisation variables: a study with rural children. *Psychology & Developing Societies, 20,* 241–256.

Mitrany, E. (2009). Is psychoanalytic psychotherapy still an option in Anorexia Nervosa? *International Journal of Child and Adolescent Health, 2,* 197–204.

Miville, M. L., Carlozzi, A. F., Gushue, G. V., Schara, S. L., & Ueda, M. (2006). Mental health counselor qualities for a diverse clientele: Linking empathy, universal-diverse orientation, and emotional intelligence. *Journal of Mental Health Counseling, 28,* 151–165.

Mohr, C., Landis, T., & Brugger, P. (2006). Lateralized semantic priming: Modulation by levodopa, semantic distance, and participants' magical beliefs. *Neuropsychiatric Disease & Treatment, 2,* 71–84.

Moller, A. C., Elliot, A. J., & Friedman, R. (2008). When competence and love are at stake: Achievement goals and perceived closeness to parents in an achievement context. *Journal of Research in Personality, 42,* 1386–1391.

Montague, J. (1996). Counseling families from diverse cultures: A non-deficit approach. *Journal of Multicultural Counseling and Development, 24,* 37–41.

Monzoni, C.M. (2008). Introducing direct complaints through questions: The interactional achievement of 'presequences'? *Discourse Studies, 10,* 73–87.

Moore, L. J. (2007). Ethical and organizational tensions for work-based learners. *Journal of Workplace Learning, 19,* 161–172.

Moosbruker, J. (1983). OD with a community mental health center: A case of building structures patiently. *Group and Organization Studies, 8,* 45–59.

Morgan, M.L., & Wampler, K.S. (2003). Fostering client creativity in family therapy: A process research study. *Contemporary Family Therapy, 25,* 207–228.

Morsette, A., Swaney, G., Stolle, D., Schuldberg, D., van den Pol, R., & Young, R. (2009). Cognitive behavioral intervention for trauma in schools (CBITS): School-based treatment on a rural American Indian reservation. *Journal of Behavior Therapy and Experimental Psychiatry, 40,* 169–178.

Mortazavi, S., Pedhiwala, N., Shafiro, M., & Hammer, L. (2009). Work-family conflict related to culture and gender. *Community, Work & Family, 12,* 251–273.

Mortenson, S., Liu, M., Burleson, B. R., & Liu, Y. (2006). A fluency of feeling—Exploring cultural and individual differences (and similarities) related to skilled emotional support. *Journal of Cross-Cultural Psychology, 37,* 366–385.

Mouratidis, A., Vanseenkiste, M., Lens, W., Vanden Auweele, Y. (2009). Beyond positive and negative affect: Achievement goals and discrete emotions in the elementary physical education classroom. *Psychology of Sport and Exercise,* 10, 336–343.

Moyers, T. B., & Martin, T. (2006). Therapist influence on client language during motivational interviewing sessions. *Journal of Substance Abuse Treatment, 30,* 245–251.

Moyers, T. B., Martin, T., Christopher, P. J., Houck, J. M., Tonigan, J. S., & Amrhein, P. C. (2007). Client language as a mediator of motivational interviewing efficacy: Where is the evidence? *Alcoholism: Clinical and Experimental Research, 31,* 40S–47S.

Mueser, K. T., & Bellack, A. S. (2007). Social skills training: Alive and well? *Journal of Mental Health, 16,* 549–552.

Mueser, K. T., Glynn, S. M., Cather, C., Zarate, R., Fox, L., Feldman, J., Wolfe, R., & Clark, R. E. (2009). Family intervention for co-occurring substance use and severe psychiatric disorders: Participant characteristics and correlates of initial engagement and more extended exposure in a randomized controlled trial. *Addictive Behaviors, 34,* 867–877.

Mueser, K. T., & Taub, J. (2008). Trauma and PTSD among adolescents with severe emotional disorders involved in multiple service systems. *Psychiatric Services, 59,* 627–634.

Müller, A., Herbig, B., & Petrovic, K. (2010). The explication of implicit team knowledge and its supporting effect on team processes and technical innovations—An action regulation perspective on team reflexivity. *Small Group Research, 40,* 28–51.

Muran, J. C., Safran, J. D., Gorman, B. S., Samstag, L. W., Eubanks-Carter, C., & Winston, A. (2009). The relationship of early alliance ruptures and their resolution to process and outcome in three time-limited psychotherapies for personality disorders. *Psychotherapy: Theory, Research, Practice, Training, 46,* 233–248.

Muraven, M., Rosman, H., & Gagné, M. (2007). Lack of autonomy and self-control: Performance contingent rewards lead to greater depletion. *Motivation and Emotion, 31,* 322–330.

Murphy, B. C., & Dillon, C. (1998). *Interviewing in action process and practice.* Pacific Grove, CA: Brooks/Cole.

Myyry, L., & Helkama, K. (2007). Socio-cognitive conflict, emotions and complexity of thought in real-life morality. *Scandinavian Journal of Psychology, 48,* 247–259.

Nabi, R. L. (2002). Anger, fear, uncertainty, and attitudes: A test of the cognitive-functional model. *Communication Monographs, 69,* 204–216.

Najavits, L. M., & Strupp, H. H. (1994). Differences in the effectiveness of psychodynamic therapists: A process-outcome study. *Psychotherapy, 31,* 114–123.

Nakamura, K., & Tagami, F. (2008). Relationship between fulfillment feeling in guidance room and returning to classrooms for junior high school students. *Japanese Journal of Counseling Science, 41,* 254–265.

Nathan, M. J., Eilam, B., & Kim, S. (2007). To disagree, we must also agree: How intersubjectivity structures and perpetuates discourse in a mathematics classroom. *Journal of Learning Sciences, 16,* 523–563.

Nebbitt, V. E., Lombe, M., & Lindsey, M. A. (2007). Perceived parental behavior and peer affiliations among urban African American Adolescents. *Social Work Research, 31,* 163–169.

Neimeyer, G. J., Macnair, R., Metzler, A. E., & Courchaine, K. (1991). Changing personal beliefs: Effects of forewarning, argument quality, prior bias, and personal exploration. *Journal of Social and Clinical Psychology, 10,* 1–20.

Nelson, K. L., Bein, E., Huemer, J., Ryst, E., & Steiner, H. (2009). Listening for avoidance: Narrative form and defensiveness in adolescent memories. *Child Psychiatry and Human Development, 40,* 561–573.

Nelson, M. L., Barnes, K. L., Evans, A. L., & Triggiano, P. J. (2008). Working with conflict in clinical supervision: Wise supervisors' perspectives. *Journal of Counseling Psychology, 55,* 172–184.

Nelson, M. L., & Neufeldt, A. (1996). Building on an empirical foundation: Strategies to enhance good practice. *Journal of Counseling and Development, 74,* 609–615.

Neuner, F., Catani, C., Ruf, M., Schauer, E., Schauer, M., & Llbert, T. (2008). Narrative exposure therapy for the treatment of traumatized children and adolescents (KidNET): From neurocognitive theory to field intervention. *Child and Adolescent Psychiatric Clinics of North America, 17,* 641–664.

Newman, M. G., & Stiles, W. B. (2006). Therapeutic factors in treating anxiety disorders. *Journal of Clinical Psychology, 62,* 649–659.

Newnham-Kanas, C., Irwin, J. D., & Morrow, D. (2008). Co-active life coaching as a treatment for adults with obesity. *International Journal of Evidence Based Coaching and Mentoring, 6,* 1–12.

Niemiec, C. P., Ryan, R. M., & Deci, E. L. (2009). The path taken: Consequences of attaining intrinsic and extrinsic aspirations in post-college life. *Journal of Research in Personality, 43,* 291–306.

Nishii, L. H., & Mayer, D. M. (2009). Do inclusive leaders help to reduce turnover in diverse groups? The moderating role of leader-member exchange in the diversity to turnover relationship. *Journal of Applied Sociology, 94,* 1412–1426.

Nixon, R., & Spearmon, M. (1991). Building a pluralistic workplace. In R. L. Edwards & J. Yankey (Eds.), *Skills for effective human services management* (pp. 155–170). Silver Spring, MD: NASW Press.

Nolan, P., & Bradley, E. (2008). Evidence-based practice: Implications and concerns. *Journal of Nursing Management, 16,* 388–393.

Nordbø, R. H. S., Gulliksen, K. S., Espeset, E. M. S., Skårderud, F., Geller, J., & Holte, A. (2008). Expanding the concepts of motivation to change: The content of patients' wish to recover from anorexia nervosa. *International Journal of Eating Disorders, 41,* 635–642.

Norris, T., & Melby, V. (2006). The acute care nurse practitioner: Challenging existing boundaries of emergency nurses in the United Kingdom. *Journal of Clinical Nursing, 15*, 253–263.

Northen, H. (1998). Ethical dilemmas in social work with groups. *Social Work with Groups, 21*, 5–18.

Obleser, J., Eisner, F., & Kotz, S. A. (2008). Bilateral speech comprehension reflects differential sensitivity to spectral and temporal features. *Journal of Neuroscience, 28*, 8116–8124.

Ødegård, A. (2007). Time used on interprofessional collaboration in child mental health care. *Journal of Interprofessional Care, 21*, 45–54.

Ohtake, S. (2007). The influence of social isolation avoidance norms on interpersonal relationships among middle school girls. *Japanese Journal of Counseling Science, 40*, 267–277.

Okada, R. (2007). Motivational analysis of academic help-seeking: Self-determination in adolescents' friendship. *Psychological Reports, 100*, 1000–1012.

Okun, B. F. (1997). *Effective helping: Interviewing and counseling techniques.* Pacific Grove, CA: Brooks/Cole.

Olson, I. R., Plotzker, A., & Ezzyat, Y. (2007). The enigmatic temporal pole: A review of findings on social and emotional processing. *Brain, 130*, 1718–1731.

Omer, H. (1997). Narrative empathy. *Psychotherapy, 34*, 19–27.

Öner-Özkan, B. (2004). Future time orientation in romantic relationships and the minding theory of relating. *Social Behavior and Personality, 32*, 797–804.

Osborn, C. J., West, J. D., Kindsvatter, A., & Paez, S. B. (2008). Treatment planning as collaborative care map construction: reframing clinical practice to promote client involvement. *Journal of Contemporary Psychotherapy, 38*, 169–176.

Pachankis, J.E., & Goldfried, M.R. (2007). An integrative, principle-based approach to psychotherapy. In S.G. Hofmann & J. Weinberger (Eds.) *The art and science of psychotherapy* (pp. 49–68). New York, NY: Routledge/Taylor & Francis.

Pack-Brown, S. P., Thomas, T. L., & Seymour, J. M. (2008). Infusing professional ethics into counselor education programs: a multicultural/social justice perspective. *Journal of Counseling and Development, 86*, 296–302.

Palazzoli-Selvini, M., Boscolo, L., Cecchin, G., & Prata, G. (1980). Hypothesizing-circularity-neutrality: Three guidelines for the conductor of the session. *Family Process, 19*, 3–12.

Palmero, G. B. (2009). Psychologists and offenders: Rights versus duties. *International Journal of Offender Therapy and Comparative Criminology, 53*, 123–125.

Palut, B. (2008). The relationship between thinking styles and level of externality: A study of Turkish female preschool student teachers. *Social Behavior and Personality, 36*, 519–528.

Panagua, F. (1995). *Assessing culturally diverse clients.* Thousand Oaks, CA: Sage.

Paradise, R., & Rogoff, B. (2009). Side by side: Learning by observing and pitching in. *Ethos, 37*, 102–138.

Park, S.-Y., & Cheah, C. S.L. (2005). Korean mothers' proactive socialization beliefs regarding preschoolers' social skills. *International Journal of Behavioral Development, 29*, 24–34.

Patalano, F. (1997). Developing the working alliance in marital therapy: A psychodynamic perspective. *Contemporary Family Therapy: An International Journal, 19*, 497–505.

Paterson, B. L., Duggett-Leger, L., & Cruttenden, K. (2009). Contextual factors influencing the evolution of nurses' roles in a primary health care clinic. *Public Health Nursing, 26*, 421–429.

Patrick, H., Knee, C. R., Canevello, A., & Lonsbary, C. (2007). The role of need fulfillment in relationship functioning and well-being: A self-determination theory perspective. *Journal of Personality and Social Psychology, 92*, 434–457.

Patterson, G. R., & Forgatch, M. S. (1985). Therapist behavior as a determinant for client noncompliance: A paradox for the behavior modifier. *Journal of Consulting and Clinical Psychology, 63*, 846–851.

Pattnaik, N., & Mishra, S. (2008). Work culture, gender and occupational stress. *Social Science International, 24*, 3–13.

Patton, M. Q. (1980). *Qualitative evaluation methods.* Beverly Hills, CA: Sage.

Paulson, R., Herinckx, H., Demmler, J., Clarke, G., Culter, D., & Birecree, E. (1999). Comparing practice patterns of consumer and non-consumer mental health service providers. *Community Mental Health Journal, 35*, 251–269.

Paykel, E.S., Scott, J., Cornwall, P.L., Abbott, R., Crane, C., Pope, M., & Johnson, A.L. (2005). Duration of relapse prevention after cognitive therapy in residual depression: Follow-up of controlled trial. *Psychological Medicine: A Journal of Research in Psychiatry and the Allied Sciences, 35*, 59–68.

Payne, J. W., Samper, A., Bettman, J. R., & Luce, M. F. (2008). Boundary conditions on unconscious thought in complex decision making. *Psychological Science, 19*, 1118–1123.

Peile, C. (1998). Emotional and embodied knowledge: Implications for critical practice. *Journal of Sociology and Social Welfare, 25*, 39–59.

Penn, P. (1982). Circular questioning. *Family Process, 21*, 267–280.

Pennell, J., & Burford, G. (2000). Family group decision making: Protecting children and women. *Child Welfare Journal, 79*, 131–158.

Perez, A., Peers, P. V., Valdes-Sosa, M., Galan, L., Garcia, L., & Martinez-Montes, E. (2009). Hemispheric modulations of alpha-band power reflect the rightward shift in attention induced by enhanced attentional load. *Neuropsychologia, 47*, 41–49.

Perez-Freije, J., & Enkel, E. (2007). Creative tension in the innovation process: How to support the right capabilities. *European Management Journal, 25*, 11–24.

Perilloux, C., & Buss, D. M. (2008). Breaking up romantic relationships: Costs experienced and coping strategies employed. *Evolutionary Psychology, 6*, 164–181.

Perri, M. G. (1998). The maintenance of treatment effects in the long-term management of obesity. *Clinical Psychology: Science and Practice, 5*, 526–543.

Perry, R. P., Stupnisky, R. H., Daniels, L. M., & Haynes, T. L. (2008). Attributional (explanatory) thinking about failure in new achievement settings. *European Journal of Psychology of Education, 23*, 459–475.

Pettifor, J. L. (2004). Professional ethics across national boundaries. *European Psychologist, 9*, 264–272.

Petry, N.M. (2001). Pathological gamblers, with and without substance abuse disorders, discount delayed rewards at high rates. *Journal of Abnormal Psychology, 110*, 482–487.

Phan, H.P. (2009). Amalgamation of future time orientation, epistemological beliefs, achievement goals and study strategies: Empirical evidence established. *British Journal of Educational Psychology, 79,* 155–173.

Phan, M. B. (2008). We're all in this together: Context, contacts, and social trust in Canada. *Analyses of Social Issues and Public Policy, 8,* 23–51.

Phelps, E. A. (2004). Human emotion and memory: Interactions of the amygdala and hippocampal complex. *Current Opinion in Neurobiology, 14,* 198–202.

Phelps, E. A., & Sharot, T. (2008). How (and why) emotion enhances the subjective sense of recollection. *Current Directions in Psychological Science, 17*(2), 147–152.

Pickens, J. (2009). Socio-emotional programme promotes positive behavior in preschoolers. *Child Care in Practice, 15,* 261–278.

Piers, J. C. & Ragg, D. M. Confronting Family Socialization: A Critical Element When Developing Family Practice Skills. Presented at the CSWE-APM, Philadelphia, November 2008.

Pietrofesa, J. J., Pietrofesa, C. J., Pietrofesa, J. D. (1990). The mental health counsellor and duty to warn. *Journal of Mental Health Counselling, 12*(2), 129–137.

Pincus, D., Fox, K. M., Perez, K. A., Turner, J. S., & McGeehan, A. R. (2008). Nonlinear dynamics of individual and interpersonal conflict in an experimental group. *Small Group Research, 39,* 150–178.

Pingree, R. J. (2007). How messages affect their senders: A more general model of message effects and implication for deliberation. *Communication Theory, 17,* 439–461.

Piper, W. E., Ogrodniczuk, J. S., LaMarche, C., Hilscher, T., & Joyce, A. S. (2005). Level of alliance, pattern of alliance, and outcome in short-term group therapy. *International Journal of Group Psychotherapy, 55,* 527–550.

Polcin, D. L. (2006). Reexamining confrontation and motivational interviewing. *Addictive Disorders and Their Treatment, 5,* 201–209.

Pollack, B. N. (1998). The impact of the sociophysical environment on interpersonal communication and feelings of belonging in work groups. In J. Sanford & B. R. Connell (Eds.), *People, places and public policy* (pp. 71–78). Edmond, OK: Environmental Design Research Association.

Poynor, C., & Haws, K.L. (2009). Lines in the sand: The role of motivated categorization in the pursuit of self-control goals. *Journal of Consumer Research, 35,* 772–787.

Pratt, M. W., Hunsberger, B., Pancer, S. M., & Alisat, S. (2003). A longitudinal analysis of personal values socialization: Correlates of a moral self-ideal in late adolescence. *Social Development, 12,* 563–585.

Price, P. B., & Jones, E. E. (1998). Examining the alliance using the Psychotherapy Process Q-Set. *Psychotherapy: Theory, Research, Practice, Training, 35,* 392–404.

Principe, J. M., Marci, C. D., Glick, D. M., & Ablon, J. S. (2006). The relationship among patient contemplation, early alliance, and continuation in psychotherapy. *Psychotherapy: Theory, Research, Practice, Training, 43,* 238–243.

Pritchard, C., Cotton, A., Bowen, D., & Williams, R. (1998). A consumer study of young people's views on their educational social worker: Engagement as a measure of an effective relationship. *British Journal of Social Work, 28,* 915–938.

Prochaska, J. O., DiClemente, C. C., & Norcross, J. C. (1992). In search of how people change: Applications to addictive behavior. *American Psychologist, 47,* 1102–1114.

Proudfoot, J. G., Corr, P. J., Guest, D. E., & Dunn, G. (2009). Cognitive-behavioural training to change attributional style improves employee well-being, job satisfaction, productivity, and turnover. *Personality and Individual Differences, 46,* 147–153.

Prout, S. M., DeMartino, R. A., & Prout, H. T. (1999). Ethical and legal issues in psychological interventions with children and adolescents. In H. T. Prout & D. T. Brown (Eds.), *Counseling and psychotherapy with children and adolescents: Theory and practice for school and clinical settings,* 3rd ed. (pp. 26–48). New York, NY: John Wiley.

Quiamzade, A., & Mugny, G. (2009). Social influence and threat in confrontations between competent peers. *Journal of Personality and Social Psychology, 97,* 652–666.

Quintana, S. M., & Holahan, W. (1992). Termination in short-term counseling: Comparison of successful and unsuccessful cases. *Journal of Counseling Psychology, 39,* 299–305.

Ragg, D. M. (2001). *Building effective helping skills.* Boston, MA: Allyn & Bacon.

Ragg, D. M. (2006). *Building family practice skills.* Pacific Grove, CA: Cengage.

Raikes, H.A., & Thompson, R.A. (2005). Links between risk and attachment security: Models of influence. *Journal of Applied Developmental Psychology, 26,* 440–455.

Ramirez, J. M., Santisteban, C., Fujihara, T. & Van Goozen, S. (2002). Differences between experiences of anger and readiness to angry action: A study of Japanese and Spanish students. *Aggressive Behavior, 28,* 429–438.

Rappleyea, D. L., Harris, S. M., White, M., & Simon, K. (2009). Termination: Legal and ethical considerations for marriage and family therapists. *American Journal of Family Therapy, 37,* 12–27.

Rasmussen, P. R. (2003). Emotional reorientation: A clinical strategy. *Journal of Individual Psychology, 59,* 345–359.

Ray, R. D., Upson, J. D., & Henderson, B. J. (1977). A systems approach to behavior: III. Organismic pace and complexity in time-space fields. *Psychological Record, 27,* 649–682.

Raw, S. D. (1998). Who is to define effective treatment for social work clients? *Social Work, 43,* 81–86.

Raz, A. E., & Atar, M. (2003). Nondirectiveness and its lay interpretations: The effect of counseling style, ethnicity and culture on attitudes towards genetic counseling among Jewish and Bedouin respondents in Israel. *Journal of Genetic Counseling, 12,* 313–332.

Reamer, R. G. (1998). Clients' right to competent and ethical treatment. *Research on Social Work Practice, 8,* 597–603.

Reandeau, S. G., & Wampold, B. E. (1991). Relationship of power and involvement to working alliance: A multiple-case sequential analysis of brief therapy. *Journal of Counseling Psychology, 38,* 107–114.

Recchia, H. E., & Howe, N. (2009). Sibling relationship quality moderates the associations between parental interventions and siblings' independent conflict strategies and outcomes. *Journal of Family Psychology, 23,* 551–561.

Reibeiro, K.L., & Cook, J.V. (1999). Opportunity, not prescription: An exploratory study of the experience of occupational engagement. *Canadian Journal of Occupational Therapy, 66,* 176–187.

Reich, S., Bickman, L., & Heflinger, C. A. (2004). Covariates of self-efficacy: Caregiver characteristics related to mental health services self-efficacy. *Journal of Emotional and Behavioral Disorders, 12,* 99–108.

Rennie, D. L. (1994). Clients' accounts of resistance in counselling: A qualitative analysis. *Canadian Journal of Counselling, 28,* 43–57.

Reynolds, J. R., & Burge, S. W. (2008). Educational expectations and the rise of women's post-secondary attainments. *Social Science Research, 37,* 485–499.

Richards, P. S., & Bergin, A. E. (2005). Spiritual interventions used by contemporary psychotherapists. In P. S. Richards & A. E. Bergin (eds.), *A Spiritual Strategy for Counseling and Psychotherapy* (2nd ed., pp. 281–309). Washington, DC: American Psychological Association.

Ridgway, I. R., & Sharpley, C. F. (1990). Multiple measures for the prediction of counsellor trainee effectiveness. *Canadian Journal of Counselling, 24,* 165–177.

Riediger, M., & Freund, A. M. (2008). Me against myself: Motivational conflicts and emotional development in adulthood. *Psychology and Aging, 23,* 479–494.

Ringwalt, C., Pankratz, M. M., Hansen, W. B., Dusenbury, L., Jackson-Newsom, J., Giles, S. M., & Brodish, P. H. (2009). The potential of coaching as a strategy to improve the effectiveness of school-based substance use prevention curricula. *Health Education & Behavior, 36,* 696–710.

Robbins, S. P. (1993). *Organizational behavior: Concepts, controversies, and applications* (6th ed.). Englewood Cliffs, NJ: Prentice-Hall.

Rober, P. (1999). The therapist's inner conversation in family therapy practice: Some ideas about the self of the therapist, therapeutic impasse, and the process of reflection. *Family Process, 38,* 209–228.

Robinson, J. L., & Demaree, H. A. (2009). Experiencing and regulating sadness: Physiological and cognitive effects. *Brain and Cognition, 70,* 13–20.

Roe, D., Dekel, R., Harel, G., Fennig, S., & Fennig, S. (2006). Clients' feelings during termination of psychodynamically oriented psychotherapy. *Bulletin of the Menninger Clinic, 70,* 68–81.

Roemer, L., & Orsillo, S. M. (2003). Mindfulness: A promising intervention strategy in need of further study. *Clinical Psychology: Science and Practice, 10,* 10–18.

Rollnick, S., & Morgan, M. (1996). Motivational interviewing: Increasing readiness for change. In A. M. Washton (Ed.), *Psychotherapy and substance abuse: A practitioner's handbook* (pp. 179–191). New York, NY: Guilford Press.

Rosen, S. (1982). *My voice will go with you: The teaching tales of Milton Erickson.* San Francisco, CA: Brunner/Mazel.

Roseth, C. J., Johnson, D. W., & Johnson, R. T. (2008). Promoting early adolescents' achievement and peer relationships: The effects of cooperative and individualistic goal structures. *Psychological Bulletin, 134,* 223–246.

Ross, E. (2008). The intersection of cultural practices and ethics in a rights-based society: Implications for South African social workers. *International Social Work, 51,* 384–395.

Rothery, M., & Cameron, G. (1990). *Child maltreatment: Expanding our concept of helping.* Hillsdale, NJ: Lawrence Erlbaum.

Rothman, J. C. (1999). *Self-awareness workbook for social workers.* Boston, MA: Allyn & Bacon.

Rousseau, C., Mekki-Berrada, A., & Moreau, S. (2001). Trauma and extended separation from family among Latin American and African refugees in Montreal. *Psychiatry: Interpersonal and Biological Processes, 64,* 40–59.

Rowe, C. E., Jr., & MacIsaac, D. S. (1989). *Empathic attunement: The "technique" of psychoanalytic self psychology.* Northvale, NJ: Jason Aronson.

Rudden, M. G., Twemlow, S., & Ackerman, S. (2008). Leadership and regressive group processes: A pilot study. *International Journal of Psychoanalysis, 89,* 993–1010.

Ruge, J., & Naumann, E. (2006). Brain-electrical correlates of negative location priming under sustained and transient attentional context conditions. *Journal of Psychophysiology, 20,* 160–169.

Rusbult, C. E., Johnson, D. J., & Morrow, G. D. (1986). Impact of couple patterns of problem solving on distress and nondistress in dating relationships. *Journal of Personality and Social Psychology, 50,* 744–753.

Rush, B., & Koegl, C. J. (2008). Prevalence and profile of people with co-occurring mental and substance use disorders within a comprehensive mental health system. *Canadian Journal of Psychiatry, 53,* 810–821.

Russell, J. A. (2003). Core affect and the psychological construction of emotion. *Psychological Review, 110,* 145–172.

Russell, J. A., & Barrett, L. F. (1999). Core affect, prototypical emotional episodes, and other things called emotion: Dissecting the elephant. *Journal of Personality and Social Psychology, 76,* 805–819.

Ruzickova, E. (2007). Strong and mild requestive hints and positive-face redress in Cuban Spanish. *Journal of Pragmatics, 39,* 1170–1202.

Ryan, R. M., & Deci, E. L. (2000). Self-determination theory and the facilitation of intrinsic motivation, social development, and well-being. *American Psychologist, 55,* 749–761.

Ryan, R. M., & Deci, E. L. (2006). Self-regulation and the problem of human autonomy: Does psychology need choice, self-determination, and will? *Journal of Personality, 74,* 1557–1585.

Ryan, R. M., & Deci, E. L. (2008). A self-determination theory approach to psychotherapy: The motivational basis for effective change. *Canadian Psychology, 49,* 186–193.

Ryan, R. M., Kuhl, J., & Deci, E. L. (1997). Nature and autonomy: An organizational view of social and neurobiological aspects of self-regulation in behavior and development. *Development and Psychopathology, 9,* 701–728.

Rzepnicki, T. L. (1991). Enhancing the durability of intervention gains: A challenge for the 1990s. *Social Service Review, 65,* 92–109.

Sabourin, S. (1990). Problem-solving, self-appraisal and coping efforts in distressed and nondistressed couples. *Journal of Marital and Family Therapy, 16,* 89–97.

Sacco, W. P., Malone, J. I., Morrison, A. D., Friedman, A., & Wells, K. (2009). Effect of a brief, regular telephone intervention by paraprofessionals for type 2 diabetes. *Journal of Behavioral Medicine, 32,* 349–359.

Sachs-Ericsson, N., Cromer, K., Hernandez, A., & Kendall-Tackett, K. (2009). A review of childhood abuse, health, and pain-related problems: The role of psychiatric disorders and current life stress. *Journal of Trauma & Dissociation, 10,* 170–188.

Safran, J. D., Crocker, P., McMain, S., & Murray, P. (1990). Therapeutic alliance rupture as a therapy event for empirical investigation. *Psychotherapy, 27,* 154–165.

Safran, J. D., & Muran, J. C. (2002). Intervention strategies: Impasses and transformations. *NYS Psychologist*, *14*, 2–4.

Safran, J.D., Muran, J.C., Samstag, L.W., & Stevens, C. Repairing alliance ruptures. *Psychotherapy: Theory, Research, Practice, Training*, *38*, 406–412.

Saleebey, D. (1997). The strengths approach to practice. In D. Saleebey (Ed.), *The strengths perspective in social work practice* (2nd ed., pp. 49–57). New York, NY: Longman.

Saleebey, D. (2009). *The strengths perspective in social work practice* (5th ed.). Boston, MA: Allyn & Bacon.

Samstag, L. W., Batchelder, S. T., Muran, J. C., Safran, J. D., & Winston, A. (1998). Early identification of treatment failures in short-term psychotherapy: An assessment of therapeutic alliance and interpersonal behavior. *Journal of Psychotherapy Practice and Research*, *7*, 126–143.

Sanchez-Navarro, J. P., Martinez-Selva, J. M., & Román, F. (2006). Uncovering the relationship between defense and orienting in emotion: Cardiac reactivity to unpleasant pictures. *International Journal of Psychophysiology*, *61*, 34–46.

Sani, F. (2005). When subgroups secede: Extending and refining the social psychological model of schism in groups. *Personality and Social Psychology Bulletin*, *31*, 1074–1086.

Santangelo, T. (2009). Collaborative problem solving effectively implemented, but not sustained: A case for aligning the sun, the moon, and the stars. *Exceptional Children*, *75*, 185–209.

Santa Rita, E. Jr. (1998). What do you do after asking the miracle question in solution-focused therapy? *Family Therapy*, *25*, 189–195.

Sarkisian, C. A., Prohaska, T. R., Davis, C., & Weiner, B. (2007). Pilot test of an attribution retraining intervention to raise walking levels in sedentary older adults. *Journal of the American Geriatrics Society*, *55*, 1842–1846.

Satterfield, W. A., & Lyddon, W. J. (1998). Client attachment and the working alliance. *Counselling Psychology Quarterly*, *11*, 407–415.

Saunders, C. (2008). Double-edged swords? Collective identity and solidarity in the environment movement. *British Journal of Sociology*, *59*, 227–253.

Saunders, S. M. (1999). Clients' assessment of the affective environment of the psychotherapy session: Relationship to session quality and treatment effectiveness. *Journal of Clinical Psychology*, *55*, 597–605.

Savicki, B., & Kelley, M. (2000). Computer mediated communication: Gender and group composition. *CyberPsychology & Behavior*, *3*, 817–826.

Scannapieco, M., & Jackson, S. (1996). Kinship care: The African American response to family preservation. *Social Work*, *41*, 190–196.

Schaap, C., Bennun, I., Schindler, L., & Hoogduin, K. (1993). *The therapeutic relationship in behavioural psychotherapy*. Chichester, UK: John Wiley.

Scheel, M.J., Hanson, W. E., & Razzhavaikina, T. I. (2004). The process of recommending homework in psychotherapy: A review of therapist delivery methods, client acceptability, and factors that affect compliance. *Psychotherapy: Theory, Research, Practice, Training*, *41*, 38–55.

Scheel.M. J., Seaman, S., Roach, K., Mulling, T. & Mahoney, K. B. (1999). Families' implementation of therapist recommendations predicted by families' perception of fit,

difficulty of implementation, and therapist influence. *Journal of Counseling Psychology*, *46*, 308–316.

Scheyett, A., Kim, M., Swanson, J., Swartz, M., Elbogen, E., Van Dorn, R., & Ferron, J. (2009). Autonomy and the use of directive intervention in the treatment of individuals with serious mental illnesses: A survey of social work practitioners. *Social Work in Mental Health*, *7*, 283–306.

Schlesinger, I. M., & Hurvitz, S. (2008). The structure of misunderstandings. *Pragmatics & Cognition*, *16*, 568–585.

Schmidt, G. L., & Seger, C. A. (2009). Neural correlates of metaphor processing: The roles of figurativeness, familiarity and difficulty. *Brain and Cognition*, *71*, 375–386.

Schmidt, J. J. (1987). Parental objections to counseling services: An analysis. *School Counselor*, *34*, 387–391.

Schröder, T. A., & Davis, J. D. (2004). Therapists' experience of difficulty in practice. *Psychotherapy Research*, *14*, 328–345.

Schröder-Abé, M., Rudolph, A., & Wiesner, A. (2007). Self-esteem discrepancies and defensive reactions to social feedback. *International Journal of Psychology*, *42*, 174–183.

Schwebel, M., & Coster, J. (1998). Well-functioning in professional psychologists: As program heads see it. *Professional Psychology: Research and Practice*, *29*, 284–292.

Seedall, R. B., & Butler, M. H. (2006). The effect of proxy voice intervention on couple softening in the context of enactments. *Journal of Marital and Family Therapy*, *32*, 421–437.

Self, R., Oates, Pl, Pinnock-Hamilton, T., & Leach, C. (2005). The relationship between social deprivation and unilateral termination (attrition) from psychotherapy at various stages of the health care pathway. *Psychology and Psychotherapy: Theory, Research and Practice*, *78*, 95–111.

Sells, J. N., & Hays, K. A. (1997). A comparison of time-limited and brief time-limited group therapy at termination. *Journal of College Student Development*, *38*, 136–142.

Séneméaud, C., & Somat, A. (2009). Dissonance arousal and persistence in attitude change. *Swiss Journal of Psychology*, *68*, 25–31.

Sexton, H., Littauer, H., Sexton, A., & Tømmerås, E. (2005). Building an alliance: Early therapy process and the client therapist connection. *Psychotherapy Research*, *15*, 103–116.

Shapiro, E. L., & Ginzberg, R. (2002). Parting gifts: Termination rituals in group therapy. *International Journal of Group Psychotherapy*, *52*, 319–336.

Sharma, P., & Kerl, S.B. (2002). Suggestions for psychologists working with Mexican American individuals and families in health care settings. *Rehabilitation Psychology*, *47*, 230–239.

Shaw, H. K., & Degazon, C. (2008). Integrating the core professional values of nursing: A profession, not just a career. *Journal of Cultural Diversity*, *15*, 44–50.

Shaw, M. E. (1971). *Group dynamics*. New York, NY: McGraw-Hill.

Shebilske, W. L., Goettl, B. P., Corrington, K., & Day, E. A. (1999). Interlesson spacing and task-related processing during complex skill acquisition. *Journal of Experimental Psychology: Applied*, *5*, 413–437.

Shechtman, Z. (2004). Client behavior and therapist helping skills in individual and group treatment of aggressive boys. *Journal of Counseling Psychology*, *51*, 463–472.

Sheets, J., Wittenstrom, K., Fong, R., James, J., Tecci, M., Baumann, D. J., & Rodriquez, C. (2009). Evidence-based practice in family group decision-making for Anglo, African American, and Hispanic families. *Children and Youth Services Review, 31,* 1187–1191.

Sheldon, K. M., Ryan, R. M., Deci, E. L., & Kasser, T. (2004). The independent effects of goal contents and motives on well-being: It's both what you pursue and why you pursue it. *Personality and Social Psychology Bulletin, 30,* 475–486.

Shelton, K. H., & Harold, G. T. (2008). Pathways between interparental conflict and adolescent psychological adjustment: Bridging links through children's cognitive appraisals and coping strategies. *Journal of Early Adolescence, 28,* 555–582.

Sherman, D. K., & Cohen, G. L. (2002). Accepting threatening information: Self-affirmation and the reduction of defensive biases. *Current Directions in Psychological Science, 11,* 119–123.

Sherman, D. K., Cohen, G. L., Nelson, L. D., Nussbaum, A. D., Bunyan, D. P., & Garcia, J. (2009). Affirmed yet unaware: Exploring the role of awareness in the process of self-affirmation. *Journal of Personality and Social Psychology, 97,* 745–764.

Shilts, L., & Gordon, A. B. (1996). What to do after the miracle occurs. *Journal of Family Psychotherapy, 7,* 15–22.

Shin, E., Fabiani, M., & Gratton, G. (2006). Multiple levels of stimulus representation in visual working memory. *Journal of Cognitive Neuroscience, 18,* 844–858.

Shirk, S. R., Gudmundsen, G., Kaplinski, H. C., & McMakin, D. L. (2008). Alliance and outcome in cognitive-behavioral therapy for adolescent depression. *Journal of Clinical Child and Adolescent Psychology, 37,* 631–639.

Shivram, R., Bankart, J., Meltzer, H., Ford, T., Vostanis, P., & Goodman, R. (2009). Service utilization by children with conduct disorders: Findings from the 2004 Great Britain child mental health survey. *European Child and Adolescent Psychiatry, 18,* 555–563.

Shmelvov, A. G., & Naumenko, A. S. (2009). Developing culture-specific assessments. In E. L. Grigorenko (Ed.) *Multicultural psychoeducational assessment* (pp. 335–349). New York, NY: Springer Publishing.

Shulman, L. (1985/6). The dynamics of mutual aid. *Social Work with Groups, 8,* 51–60.

Shulman, L. (1999). *The skills of helping individuals, families, groups and communities* (4th ed.). Itasca, IL: Peacock.

Skowron, E.A., Stanley, K.L., & Shapiro, M.D. (2009). A longitudinal perspective on differentiation of self, interpersonal and psychological well-being in young adulthood. *Contemporary Family Therapy: An International Journal, 31,* 3–18.

Skultans, V. (2006). Psychiatry through the ethnographic lens. *International Journal of Social Psychiatry, 52,* 73–93.

Slatcher, R. B., Vazire, S., & Pennebaker, J. W. (2008). Am "I" more important than "we"? Couples' word use in instant messages. *Personal Relationships, 15,* 407–424.

Slonim-Nevo, V. (1996). Clinical practice: Treating the nonvoluntary client. *International Social Work, 39,* 117–129.

Smith, D., & Fitzpatrick, M. (1995). Patient-therapist boundary issues: An integrative review of theory and research. *Professional Psychology: Research and Practice, 26,* 499–506.

Smith, J. M. (2000). Psychotherapy with people stressed by poverty. In A. Sabo & L Havens (Eds.), *The Real World Guide to Psychotherapy Practice* (pp. 71–92). Cambridge, MA: Harvard University Press.

Smith, K. J., Subich, L. M., & Kalodner, C. (1995). The transtheoretical model's stages and processes of change and the relation to premature termination. *Journal of Counseling Psychology, 42,* 34–39.

Smith, K. K., Kamistein, D. S., & Makadok, R. J. (1995). The health of the corporate body: Illness and organizational dynamics. *Journal of Applied Behavioral Science, 31,* 328–351.

Smith, P. K., Dijksterhuis, A., & Wigboldus, D. H. J. (2008). Powerful people make good decisions even when they consciously think. *Psychological Science, 19,* 1258–1259.

Smokowski, P. R., Rose, S., & Bacallao, M. L. (2001). Damaging experiences in therapeutic groups—how vulnerable consumers become group casualties. *Small Group Research, 32,* 223–251.

Snow, N., & Austin, W. J. (2009). Community treatment orders: The ethical balancing act in community mental health. *Journal of Psychiatric and Mental Health Nursing, 16,* 177–186.

Sobol-Kwapinska, M. (2009). Forms of present time orientation and satisfaction with life in the context of attitudes toward the past and future. *Social Behavior and Personality, 37,* 433–440.

Sommerfeld, E., Orbach, I., Zim, S., & Mikulinger, M. (2008). An in-session exploration of ruptures in working alliance and their associations with clients' core conflictual relationship themes, alliance-related discourse, and clients' postsession evaluations. *Psychotherapy Research, 18,* 377–388.

Sommers-Flanagan, J., & Sommers-Flanagan, R. (1997). *Tough kids, cool counseling: User-friendly approaches with challenging youth.* Alexandria, VA: American Counseling Association.

Somov, P. G. (2008). A psychodrama group for substance use relapse prevention training. *Arts in Psychotherapy, 35,* 151–161.

Sonkin, D.J. (1986). Clairvoyance vs. common sense: Therapist's duty to warn and protect. *Violence and Victims, 1,* 7–22.

Soo-Hoo, T. (2005). Transforming power struggles through shifts in perception in marital therapy. *Journal of Family Psychotherapy, 16,* 19–38.

Spence, S. A., & Frith, C. D. (1999). Towards a functional anatomy of volition. *Journal of Consciousness Studies, 6,* 11–29.

Spinhoven, P., Giesen-Bloo, J., van Dyck, R., Kooiman, K., & Arntz, A. (2007). The therapeutic alliance in schema-focused therapy and transference-focused psychotherapy for borderline personality disorder. *Journal of Consulting and Clinical Psychology, 75,* 104–115.

Spironelli, C., Tagliabue, M., & Umilta, C. (2009). Response selection and attention orienting—a computational model of Simon effect asymmetries. *Experimental Psychology, 56,* 274–282.

Sportsman, S., & Hamilton, P. (2007). Conflict management styles in the health professions. *Journal of Professional Nursing, 23,* 157–166.

Springer, C., & Reddy, L. (2004). Measuring adherence in behavior therapy: Opportunities for practice and research. *The Behavior Therapist, 27,* 99–101.

Spoth, R., Redmond, C., Hockaday, C., & Chung, C. Y. (1996). Barriers to participation in family skills preventive interventions and their evaluations: A replication and extension. *Family Relations, 45,* 247–254.

Spurling, L., & Dryden, W. (1989). The self and the therapeutic domain. In W. Dryden & L. Spurling (Eds.), *On becoming a psychotherapist* (pp. 191–214). London, UK: Tavistock/Routledge.

Stalker, C. A., Mandell, D., Frensch, K. M., Harvey, C., & Wright, M. (2007). Child welfare workers who are exhausted yet satisfied with their jobs: How do they do it? *Child and Family Social Work, 12,* 182–191.

Staller, K. M., & Kirk, S. A. (1998). Knowledge utilization in social work and legal practice. *Journal of Sociology and Social Welfare, 25,* 91–113.

Stambaugh, L. F., Mustillo, S. A.Burns, B. J., Stephens, R. L., Baxter, B., Edwards, D., & DeKraai, M. (2007). Outcomes from Wraparound and Multisystemic Therapy in a center for mental health services system-of-care demonstration site. *Journal of Emotional and Behavioral Disorders, 15,* 143–155.

Stancombe, J., & White, S. (2005). Cause and responsibility: Towards an interactional understanding of blaming and "neutrality" in family therapy. *Journal of Family Therapy, 27,* 330–351.

Starzyk, K. B., Fabrigar, L. R., Soryal, A. S., & Fanning, J. J. (2009). A painful reminder: The role of level and salience of attitude importance in cognitive dissonance. *Personality and Social Psychology, 35,* 126–137.

Steensig, J. & Larsen, T. (2008). Affiliative and disaffiliative uses of you say x questions. *Discourse Studies, 10,* 113–132.

Stein, R. (1995). The role of affects in the process of change in psychotherapy. *Israel Journal of Psychiatry and Related Sciences, 32,* 167–173.

Stein, R. H. (1990). *Ethical issues in counseling.* Buffalo, NY: Prometheus Books.

Stephens, C., Porter, J., Nettleton, C., & Willis, R. (2006). Disappearing, displaced, and undervalued: A call to action for indigenous health worldwide. *Lancet, 367,* 2019–2028.

Stephens, J., & Beattie, G. (1986). On judging the ends of speaker turns in conversation. *Journal of Language and Social Psychology, 5,* 119–134.

Sternberg, R. J., Grigorenko, E. L., & Zhang, L.-F. (2008). Styles of learning and thinking matter in instruction and assessment. *Perspectives on Psychological Science, 3,* 486–506.

Stone, J., & Fernandez, N. C. (2008). To practice what we preach: The use of hypocrisy and cognitive dissonance to motivate behavior change. *Social and Personality Psychology Compass, 2,* 1024–1051.

Stuart, J., Fondacaro, M., Miller, S. A., Brown, V., & Brank, E. M. (2008). Procedural justice in family conflict resolution and deviant peer group involvement among adolescents: The mediating influence of peer conflict. *Journal of Youth and Adolescence, 37,* 674–684.

Sue, D. W., Ivey, A. R., & Pedersen, P. B. (1996). *A theory of multicultural counseling and therapy.* Pacific Grove, CA: Brooks/Cole.

Sue, D. W., & Sue, D. (1990). *Counseling the culturally different* (2nd ed.). New York, NY: John Wiley.

Suedfeld, P., & Coren, S. (1992). Cognitive correlates of conceptual complexity. *Personality and Individual Differences, 13,* 1193–1199.

Sunwolf, & Leets, L. (2004). Being left out: Rejecting outsiders and communicating group boundaries in childhood and adolescent peer groups. *Journal of Applied Communication Research, 32,* 195–223.

Sutherland, O. (2007). Therapist positioning and power in discursive therapies: a comparative analysis. *Contemporary Family Therapy, 29,* 193–209.

Sutherland, O., & Couture, S. (2007). The discursive performance of the alliance in family therapy: A conversation analytic perspective. *Australian and New Zealand Journal of Family Therapy, 28,* 210–217.

Suyemoto, K. L., Liem, J. H., Kuhn, J. C., Mongillow, E. A., & Tauriac, J. J. (2007). Training therapists to be culturally sensitive with Asian American women clients. *Women & Therapy, 30,* 209–227.

Sween, E. (2003). Accessing the rest-of-the-story in couples therapy. *Family Journal, 11*(1), 61–67.

Swenson, C. C., Henggeler, S. W., Taylor, I. S., & Addison, O. W. (2005). *Multisystemic Therapy and neighborhood partnerships: Reducing adolescent violence and substance abuse.* New York, NY: Guilford Press.

Szentagotai, A., David, D., Lupu, V., & Cosman, D. (2008). Rational emotive behavior therapy versus cognitive therapy versus pharmacotherapy in the treatment of major depressive disorder: Mechanisms of change analysis. *Psychotherapy theory, Research, Practice, Training, 45,* 523–538.

Tafrate, R. C., & Kassinove, H. (1998). Anger control in men: Barb exposure with rational, irrational, and irrelevant self-statements. *Journal of Cognitive Psychotherapy,* 187–211.

Takimoto, M. (2007). The effects of input-based tasks on the development of learners' pragmatic proficiency. *Applied Linguistics, 30,* 1–25.

Talley, P. F., Strupp, H. H., & Morey, L. C. (1990). Matchmaking in psychotherapy: Patient-therapist dimensions and their impact on outcome. *Journal of Consulting and Clinical Psychology, 58,* 182–188.

Tallman, I., Gray, L. N., Kullberg, V., & Henderson, D. (1999). The intergenerational transmission of marital conflict: Testing a process model. *Social Psychology Quarterly, 62,* 219–239.

Tan, V. (2010). Alcohol dependence treated by a psychiatry resident. In C.B. Taylor (Ed.) *How to practice evidence-based psychiatry: Basic principles and case studies* (pp. 337–348). Arlington, VA: American Psychiatric Publishing.

Tansey, M. J., & Burke, W. F. (1989). *Understanding countertransference: From projective identification to empathy.* Hillsdale, NJ: Analytic Press.

Thielscher, A., & Pessoa, L. (2007). Neural correlates of perceptual choice and decision making during fear-disgust discrimination. *Journal of Neuroscience, 27*(11), 2908–2917.

Thøgersen-Ntoumani, C., & Fox, K. R. (2007). Exploring the role of autonomy for exercise and its relationship with mental well-being: A study with non-academic university employees. *International Journal of Sport and Exercise Psychology, 5,* 227–239.

Thomas, J. A., & Barron, K. E. (2006). A test of multiple achievement goal benefits in physical education activities. *Journal of Applied Sport Psychology, 18,* 114–135.

Thomas, R. L., & Millar, M. G. (2008). The impact of failing to give an apology and the need-for-cognition on anger. *Current Psychology, 27,* 126–134.

Thompson, R. A., Lewis, M. D., & Calkins, S. D. (2008). Reassessing emotion regulation. *Child Development Perspectives, 2*, 124–131.

Thyer, B. A. (2007). Social work education and clinical learning: Towards evidence-based practice? *Clinical Social Work Journal, 35*, 25–32.

Thyer, B. A., & Myers, L. L. (1998). Supporting the client's right to effective treatment: Touching a raw nerve? *Social Work, 43*, 87–91.

Tice, D. M., Bratslavsky, E. & Baumeister, R. F. (2001). Emotional distress regulation takes precedence over impulse control: If you feel bad, do it! *Journal of Personality & Social Psychology, 80*, 53–67.

Timler, G. R., Olswang, L. B., & Coggins, T. E. (2005). "Do I know what I need to do?" A social communication intervention for children with complex clinical profiles. *Language, Speech, and Hearing Services in Schools, 36*, 73–85.

Tjosvold, D., Andrews, I. R., & Struthers, J. T. (1991). Power and interdependence in work groups: Views of managers and employees. *Group and Organizational Studies, 16*, 285–299.

Tjosvold, D., & Yu, Z.-Y. (2004). Goal interdependence and applying abilities for team in-role and extra-role performance in China. *Group Dynamics: Theory, Research, and Practice, 8*, 98–111.

Tokar, D. M., Hardin, S. I., Adams, E. M., & Brandel, I. W. (1996). Clients' expectations about counseling and perceptions of the working alliance. *Journal of College Student Psychotherapy, 11*, 9–26.

Tomarken, A. J., & Zald, D. H. (2009). Conceptual, methodological, and empirical ambiguities in the linkage between anger and approach: comment on Carver and Harmon-Jones. *Psychological Bulletin, 135*, 209–214.

Tomasello, M. (1999). *The cultural origins of human cognition.* Cambridge, MA: Harvard University Press.

Tomm, K. (1987). Interventive interviewing: Part II. Reflexive questioning as a means to enable self-healing. *Family Process, 26*, 167–184.

Tomm, K. (1988). Interventive interviewing: III. Intending to ask lineal, circular, strategic, or reflexive questions? *Family Process, 27*, 1–15.

Trepka, C., Rees, A., Shapiro, D. A., Hardy, G. E., & Barkham, M. (2004). Therapist competence and outcome of cognitive therapy for depression. *Cognitive Therapy and Research, 28*, 143–157.

Triandis, H. C. (1995). The self and social behavior in differing cultural contexts. In N. R. Goldberger & J. B. Veroff (Eds.), *The culture and psychology reader* (pp. 326–365). New York, NY: New York University Press.

Trosper, S. E., Buzzella, B. A., Bennett, S. M., & Ehrenrich, J. T. (2009). Emotion regulation in youth with emotional disorders: Implications for a unified treatment approach. *Clinical Child and Family Psychology Review, 12*, 234–254.

Tryon, G. S., & Kane, A. S. (1990). The helping alliance and premature termination. *Counselling Psychology Quarterly, 3*, 233–238.

Tufnell, G., (2005). Eye movement desensitization of reprocessing in the treatment of pre-adolescent children with post-traumatic symptoms. *Clinical Child Psychology and Psychiatry, 10*, 587–600.

Türan, B., & Stemberger, R. M.T. (2000). The effectiveness of matching language to enhance perceived empathy. *Communication and Cognition, 33*, 287–300.

Türküm, A. S. (2007). Differential effects between group counseling and group guidance in conducting a "Coping with Stress Training Program" for Turkish university students. *International Journal for the Advancement of Counselling, 29*, 69–81.

Tyron, G. S., & Kane, A. S. (1993). Relationship of working alliance to mutual and unilateral termination. *Journal of Counseling Psychology, 40*, 33–36.

Uhlemann, M. R., Lee, D. Y., & Martin, J. (1994). Client cognitive responses as a function of quality of counselor verbal responses. *Journal of Counseling and Development, 73*, 198–203.

Umberson, D., Williams, K. & Anderson, K. (2002). Violent behavior: A measure of emotional upset? *Journal of Health & Social Behavior, 43*, 189–206.

Uskul, A. K., Sherman, D. K., & Fitzgibbon, J. (2009). The cultural congruency effect: Culture, regulatory focus, and the effectiveness of gain- vs.-loss-framed health messages. *Journal of Experimental Social Psychology, 45*, 535–541.

Valkenburg, P. M., & Peter, J. (2009). The effects of instant messaging on the quality of adolescents' existing friendships: A longitudinal study. *Journal of Communication, 59*, 79–94.

Vallis, T. M., Shaw, B. F., & McCabe, S. B. (1988). The relationship between therapist competency in cognitive therapy and general therapy skill. *Journal of Cognitive Psychotherapy, 2*, 237–249.

van Andel, P., Erdman, R. A. M., Karsdorp, P. A., Appels, A., & Trijsburg, R. W. (2003). Group cohesion and working alliance: Prediction of treatment outcome in cardiac patients receiving cognitive behavioral group psychotherapy. *Psychotherapy and Psychosomatics, 72*, 141–149.

Vance, C. M., Groves, K. S., Paik, Y., & Kindler, H. (2007). Understanding and measuring linear-nonlinear thinking style for enhanced management education and professional practice. *Academy of Management Learning & Education, 6*, 167–185.

van den Bos, A., & Stapel, D. A. (2008). The impact of comprehension versus self-enhancement goals on group perception. *Social Psychology, 39*, 222–230.

Van de Vliert, E. (2007). Climates create cultures. *Social and Personality Psychology Compass, 1*, 53–67.

van Kleef, G. A., Oveis, C. van der Löwe, I., Luokogan, A., Goetz, J., & Keltner, D. (2008). Power, distress, and compassion: Turning a blind eye to the suffering of others. *Psychological Science, 19*, 1315–1322.

van Stegeren, A. H. (2009). Imaging stress effects on memory: A review of neuroimaging studies. *Canadian Journal of Psychiatry, 54*, 16–27.

Velicer, W. F., Norman, G. J., Fava, J. L., & Prochaska, J. O. (1999). Testing 40 predictions from the transtheoretical model. *Addictive Behaviors, 24*, 455–469.

Veling, H., Holland, R. W., & van Knippenberg, A. (2008). When approach motivation and behavioral inhibition collide: Behavior regulation through stimulus devaluation. *Journal of Experimental Social Psychology, 44*, 1013–1019.

Venning, A., Kettler, L., Eliott, J., & Wilson, A. (2009). The effectiveness of cognitive-behavioural therapy with hopeful elements to prevent the development of depression in young people: A systematic review. *International Journal of Evidence-Based Healthcare, 7*, 15–33.

Verbeke, W. J., Belschak, F. D., Bakker, A. B., & Dietz, B. (2008). When intelligence is (dys)functional for achieving sales performance. *Journal of Marketing, 72*, 44–57.

Verbrugge, R., & Mol, L. (2008). Learning to apply theory of mind. *Journal of Logic, Language and Information, 17*, 489–511.

Vincent, D., LaForest, M., & Bergeron, A. (2009). Lies, rebukes and social norms: On the unspeakable in interactions with health-care professionals. *Discourse Studies, 9*, 226–245.

Vinski, E. J., & Tryon, G. S. (2009). Study of a cognitive dissonance intervention to address high school students' cheating attitudes and behaviors. *Ethics & Behavior, 19*, 218–226.

Vivino, B. L., Thompson, B. J., Jill, C. E., & Ladany, N. (2009). Compassion in psychotherapy: The perspective of therapists nominated as compassionate. *Psychotherapy Research, 19*, 157–171.

Vogel, J. J., Bowers, C. A., & Vogel, D. S. (2003). Cerebral lateralization of spatial abilities: A meta analysis. *Brain and Cognition, 52*, 197–204.

Voth, J., & Sirois, F. M. (2009). The role of self-blame and responsibility in adjustment to inflammatory bowel disease. *Rehabilitation Psychology, 54*, 99–108.

Wachtel, P. L. (2002). Termination of therapy: An effort at integration. *Journal of Psychotherapy Integration, 12*, 373–383.

Walborn, F. S. (1996). *Process variables: Four common elements of counseling and psychotherapy.* Pacific Grove, CA: Brooks/Cole.

Walcott, D. M., Cerundolo, P., Beck, J. C. (2001). Current analysis of the Tarasoff Duty: An evolution toward the limitation of the duty to protect. *Behavioral Sciences and the Law, 19*, 325–343.

Waldman, J. D. (2007). Thinking systems need systems thinking. *Systems Research & Behavioral Science, 24*, 271–284.

Waldron, H. B., Turner, C. W., Barton, C., Alexander, J. F., & Cline, V. B. (1997). Therapist defensiveness and marital therapy process and outcome. *American Journal of Family Therapy, 25*, 233–243.

Waldron, V. R., Kelley, D. L., & Harvey, J. (2008). Forgiving communication and relational consequences. In M. T. Motley (ed.) *Studies in Applied Interpersonal Communication* (pp. 165–183). Thousand Oaks, CA: Sage.

Walitzer, K. S., Dermen, K. H., & Barrick, C. (2009). Facilitating involvement in Alcoholics Anonymous during outpatient treatment: A randomized clinical trial. *Addiction, 104*, 391–401.

Walsh, J., & Harrigan, M. (2003). The termination phase in structural family intervention. *Family Therapy, 30*, 13–26.

Walter, A., Bundy, C., & Dornan, T. (2005). How should trainees be taught to open a clinical interview? *Medical Education, 39*, 492–496.

Walton, D. (2006). Examination dialogue: An argumentation framework for critically questioning an expert opinion. *Journal of Pragmatics, 38*, 745–777.

Wang, J. (2006). Questions and the exercise of power. *Discourse & Society, 17*, 529–548.

Ward, T., Gannon, T., & Vess, J. (2009). Human rights, ethical principles, and standards in forensic psychology. *International Journal of Offender Therapy and Comparative Criminology, 53*, 126–144.

Wareneken, F., & Tomasello, M. (2008). Extrinsic rewards undermine altruistic tendencies in 20-month-olds. *Developmental Psychology, 44*, 1785–1788.

Warwar, S.H., Links, P.S., Greeberg, L., & Bergmans, Y. (2008). Emotion-focused principles for working with borderline personality disorder. *Journal of Psychiatric Practice, 14*, 94–104.

Watkins, E., Moulds, M., & Mackintosh, B. (2005). Comparisons between rumination and worry in a non-clinical population. *Behaviour Research and Therapy, 43*, 1577–1585.

Watson, D. (2009). Locating anger in the hierarchical structure of affect: Comment of Carver and Harmon-Jones (2009). *Psychological Bulletin, 135*, 205–208.

Watson, J. C., & Greenberg, L. S. (2000). Alliance ruptures and repairs in experiential therapy. *Journal of Clinical Psychology, 56*, 175–186.

Watson, J. C., & McMullen, E. J. (2005). An examination of therapist and client behavior in high- and low-alliance sessions in cognitive-behavioral therapy and process experiential therapy. *Psychotherapy: Theory, Research, Practice, Training, 42*, 297–310.

Watt, J. W., & Kallmann, G. L. (1998). Managing professional obligations under managed care: A social work perspective. *Family and Community Health, 21*, 40–49.

Watzlawick, P., Beavin, J. H., & Jackson, D. D. (1967). *Pragmatics of human communication: A study of interactional patterns, pathologies, and paradoxes.* New York, NY: W. W. Norton.

Watzlawick, P., Weakland, J., & Fisch, R. (1974). *Change: Principles of problem formation and problem resolution.* New York: Norton.

Weaver, H. N., & White, B. J. (1997). The Native American family circle: Roots of resiliency. *Journal of Family Social Work, 2*, 67–79.

Webb, A., & Wheeler, S., II (1998). A social dilemma perspective on cooperative behavior in organizations: The effects of scarcity, communication, and unequal access on the use of a shared resource. *Group and Organizational Management, 23*, 509–524.

Weigesberg, M. J., Lane, C. J., Winners, O., Wright, T., Nguyen-Rodriguez, S., Goran, M. I., & Spruijt-Metz, D. (2009). Acute effects of stress-reduction interactive guided imagery on salivary cortisol in overweight Latino adolescents. *Journal of Alternative and Complementary Medicine, 15*, 297–303.

Weisbuch, M., & Ambady, N. (2008). Non-conscious routes to building culture: Nonverbal communication components of socialization. *Journal of Consciousness Studies, 15*, 159–183.

Welch, M. R., Rivera, R. E. N., Conway, B. P., Yonkoski, J., Lupton, P. M., & Giancola, R. (2005). Determinants and consequences of social trust. *Sociological Inquiry, 75*, 453–473.

Wells, B., & Local, J. (2009). Prosody as an interactional resource: A clinical linguistic perspective.

International Journal of Speech-Language Pathology, 11, 321–325.

Wesley, C. A. (1996). Social work and end-of-life decisions: Self-determination and the common good. *Health and Social Work, 21,* 115–121.

Whelton, W. J. (2004). Emotional processes in psychotherapy: Evidence across therapeutic modalities. *Clinical Psychology & Psychotherapy, 11,* 58–71.

Whelton, W. J., Paulson, B., & Marusiak, C. W. (2007). Self-criticism and the therapeutic relationship. *Counselling Psychology Quarterly, 20,* 135–148.

Wheelan, S. A., McKeage, R. L., Verdi, A. F., Abraham, M., Krasick, C., & Johnston, F. (1994). Communication and developmental patterns in a system of interacting groups. In L. R. Frey (Ed.), *Group communication in context: Studies of natural groups* (pp. 153–178). Hillsdale, NJ: Lawrence Erlbaum.

White, M. (1984). Pseudo-encopresis: From avalanche to victory, from vicious cycles to virtuous cycles. *Family Systems Medicine, 2,* 150–160.

White, M. (1986). Negative explanation, restraint, and double description: A template for family therapy. *Family Process, 25,* 169–184.

White, M. (1988). The process of questioning: A therapy of literary merit? *Dulwich Centre Newsletter.* Dulwich Centre, NZ.

White, S. (1989). Backchannels across cultures: a study of Americans and Japanese. *Language in Society, 18,* 59–76.

Wiggins, M. I. (2009). Therapist self-awareness of spirituality. In J. D. Atken & M. M. Leach (Eds.) *Spirituality and the Therapeutic Process: A Comprehensive Resource from Intake to Termination* (pp. 53–74). Washington, DC: American Psychological Association.

Wildgruber, D., Hertrich, I., Riecker, A., Erb, M., Anders, S., Grodd, W., & Ackermann, H. (2004). Distinct frontal regions subserve evaluation of linguistic and emotional aspects of speech intonation. *Cerebral Cortex, 14,* 1384–1389.

Willemen, A.M., Schuengel, C., & Koot, H.M. (2009). Physiological regulation of stress in referred adolescents: The role of the parent-adolescent relationship. *Journal of Child Psychology and Psychiatry, 50,* 482–490.

Williams, E. N. (2008). A psychotherapy researcher's perspective on therapist self-awareness and self-focused attention after a decade of research. *Psychotherapy Research, 18,* 139–146.

Williams, J. K., Nesselroade, K. P., Jr., & Nam, R. K. (2007). When dissonance intervenes: Effects of perceived moral weight and issue of opinion on self-enhancement of opinion objectivity. *Journal of Psychology and Christianity, 26,* 227–235.

Windrass, G., & Nunes, T. (2003). Montserratian mothers' and English teachers' perceptions of teaching and learning. *Cognitive Development, 18,* 555–577.

Winstok, Z., Eisikovits, Z., & Gelles, R. (2002). Structure and dynamics of escalation from the batterer's perspective. *Families in Society, 83,* 129–141.

Winters, N. C., & Metz, W. P. (2009). The wraparound approach in systems of care. *Psychiatric Clinics of North America, 32,* 135–151.

Wiseman, H., & Rice, L. N. (1989). Sequential analyses of therapist-client interaction during change events: A task-focused approach. *Journal of Consulting and Clinical Psychology, 57,* 281–286.

Wolynski, B., Schott, B. H., Kanowski, M., & Hoffmann, M. B. (2009). Visuo-motor integration in humans: Cortical patterns of response lateralization and functional connectivity. *Neuropsychologia, 47,* 1313–1322.

Wong, D. F. K., Chau, P., Kwok, A., & Kwan, J. (2007). Cognitive-behavioral treatment groups for people with chronic physical illness in Hong Kong: Reflections on a culturally attuned model. *International Journal of Group Psychotherapy, 57,* 367–385.

Wong, E. C., Beutler, L. E., & Zane, N. W. (2007). Using mediators and moderators to test assumptions underlying culturally sensitive therapies: An exploratory example. *Cultural Diversity and Ethnic Minority Psychology, 13,* 169–177.

Wong, K. F. E., Kwong, J. Y. L., Ng, C. K. (2008). When thinking rationally increases biases: The role of rational thinking style in escalation of commitment. *Applied Psychology: An International Review, 57,* 246–271.

Wood, J. V., Heimpel, S. A., Manwell, L. A., & Whittington, E. J. (2009). This mood is familiar and I don't deserve to feel better anyway: Mechanisms underlying self-esteem differences in motivation to repair sad moods. *Journal of Personality and Social Psychology, 96,* 363–380.

Woody, E. Z., Lewis, V., Snider, L., Grant, H., Kamath, M., & Szechtman, H. (2005). Induction of compulsive-like washing by blocking the feelings of knowing: An experimental test of the security-motivation hypothesis of obsessive-compulsive disorder. *Behavioral and Brain Functions, 1.*

Worrell, M. (1997). An existential-phenomenological perspective on the concept of "resistance" in counselling and psychotherapy. *Counselling Psychology Quarterly, 10,* 5–15.

Wubbolding, R. E. (1996). Professional issues: The use of questions in reality therapy. *Journal of Reality Therapy, 16,* 122–127.

Wynn, R., & Wynn, M. (2006). Empathy as an interactionally achieved phenomenon in psychotherapy—characteristics of some conversational resources. *Journal of Pragmatics, 38,* 1385–1397.

Yahya, K. (1999). Relationship of coping strategies of 7th, 8th and 9th grade students to parental socialization practices and emotional state, gender and great. *Dirasat: Educational Sciences, 26,* 514–528.

Yalom, I. D. (1995). *The theory and practice of group psychotherapy* (4th ed.). New York, NY: Basic Books.

Yamaguchi, R., & Maehr, M. L. (2004). Children's emergent leadership—the relationships with group characteristics and outcomes. *Small Group Research, 35,* 388–406.

Yan, M. C. (2005). How cultural awareness works: An empirical examination of the interaction between social workers and their clients. *Canadian Social Work Review, 22,* 5–29.

Young, J., Daleiden, E. L., Chorpita, B. F., Schiffman, J., & Mueller, C. W. (2007). Assessing stability between treatment planning documents in a system of care. *Administration and Policy in Mental Health and Mental Health Services Research, 34,* 530–539.

Young, P. (2004). *Understanding NLP Principles and Practice.* Norwalk, CT: Crown House.

Younggren, J. N., & Gottlieb, M. C. (2008). Termination and abandonment: History, risk, and risk management. *Professional Psychology: Research and Practice, 39*, 498–504.

Yu, M.-C., (2003). On the universality of face: Evidence from Chinese compliment response behavior. *Journal of Pragmatics, 35*, 1679–1710.

Zechmeister, J. S., Garcia, S., Romero, C., & Vas, S. N. (2004). Don't apologize unless you mean it: A laboratory investigation of forgiveness and retaliation. *Journal of Social and Clinical Psychology, 23*, 532–564.

Zhang, L.-F. (2002). Thinking styles: Their relationships with modes of thinking and academic performance. *Educational Psychology, 22*, 331–348.

Zhang, L.-F. (2003). Are parents' and children's thinking styles related? *Psychological Reports, 93*, 617–630.

Zhang, L.-F. (2006). Thinking styles and the big five personality traits revisited. *Personality and Individual Differences, 40*, 1177–1187.

Zhang, X., Chen, H-C., & Zhang, G-F. (2008). Children's relationships with mothers and teachers: Linkages to problem behavior in their first preschool years. *Acta Psychologica Sinica, 40*, 418–426.

Zhang, L.-F., & Sternberg, R. J. (2005). A threefold model of intellectual styles. *Educational Psychology Review, 17*, 1–53.

Ziemba, S. J. (2001). Therapy with families in poverty: Application of feminist family therapy principles. *Journal of Feminist Family Therapy, 12*, 205–237.

Zilberstein, K. (2008). Au revoir: An attachment and loss perspective on termination. *Clinical Social Work Journal, 36*, 301–311.

Zimmerman, L., & Milligan, A. T. (2008). Perspectives on communicating with the next generation. *Innovate: Journal of Online Education, 4*. http://www.innovateonline.info/index.php?view=article&id=338

Zurbriggen, E. L., & Sturman, T. S. (2002). Linking motives and emotions: A test of McClelland's hypothesis. *Personality and Social Psychology Bulletin, 28*, 521–535.

Author Index

Subject Index

Abuse, 42–43, 47
Accessibility:
  of motivating emotions, 259–266
  of parents, 10–11
Action systems:
  alliance rupture indicators in, 308–309
  defined, 7–8
  reflective responding with, 157
  response system as, 7–8, 125, 157, 236–237, 239, 308–309
  transitional responding and, 236–237, 239
  tuning in to, 125
Activity-based interventions:
  affective processing influenced in, 204–209
  challenging thinking patterns in, 203–204
  coaching in, 219–222
  contextual issues with, 202–203, 210–211
  direction in, 201–211, 214–217, 219–222
  facilitation activities in, 214–217
  feedback in, 204, 209, 219–220, 221–222
  information provided in, 201–202
  instructions in, 215–216
  with larger client systems, 210, 219, 221
  problem context altered in, 210–211
  setting up, 214–215, 221
  sharing/applying concepts in, 202
  skills and behavior influenced in, 209–210
Advice giving, 8, 124, 128, 142, 174–175
Advocacy, 34, 295–297
Affective issues. See Emotions
Agencies:
  client concerns about, 112, 115, 118
  formal support through, 284–286
  mandates for, 286, 295
  multisystemic working alliances among, 279–301, 314–320
Alliances. See Working alliances
Alternatives:

developing alternative thinking, 204
engaging alternative practitioner, 341–342
nonlinear thinking generating, 68
Ambivalence, 251–252, 264–265, 273, 303
American Association of Pastoral Counselors, 29
American Counseling Association, 30
American Nursing Association, 30
American Occupational Therapy Association, 30
American Psychiatric Association *Diagnostic and Statistical Manual,* 77, 89–90
American Psychological Association, 30–31, 41
Apologies, 306–307, 312
Applied thinking, 64–69
Arbitration, 124
Art-based activities, 209
Assessment:
  assessment reports, 95–97
  case examples of, 79, 89
  cultural and social influences on, 86, 91–92, 97
  data collection in, 80–86
  data weighing in, 87–92
  ethical issues in, 76, 77
  exercises on, 94–95
  formulating dynamic assessment, 92–93
  process of, 79–97
  professional affiliation influencing, 75–79
  service direction identified through, 95–97
  theoretical approaches to, 78–79, 88–89
Assumptions:
  challenging, 68
  of competence, 42
  of informed consent, 42
  of least intrusive intervention, 42
  legal, 41–42 (See also Legal duties)
Autonomy, clients', 252–253, 262, 265–266, 267, 269–270, 275. See also Self-determination, clients'

Behavior patterns:
  action systems reflecting, 7–8, 125, 157, 236–237, 239, 308–309
  activity-based interventions influencing, 209–210
  cognitive-emotional processes associated with, 206–207
  identifying, 65
  professional (See Professional code of behavior)
  socialization influencing, 7–8, 21
  working alliance influencing, 231
Beliefs. See also Ideologies; Spirituality/religion; Thinking; Values
  identifying irrational, 203
  socialization providing, 9, 22–23
Biopsychosocial theoretical models, 54–55, 57, 78
Brain function:
  description and, 190, 192
  emotional processing and, 205, 207
  observation and, 180–181, 183

Capacity issues. See also Competency issues
  in activity-based interventions, 202–203, 210, 214
  capacity enhancement through informal support, 283
  diversity of ability-related influences, 45
  goal development based on capacity, 100–101
Case examples. See also Exercises
  of assessment issues, 79, 89
  of change promotion, 255, 256, 261, 268, 269, 270, 273
  of client concern responses, 118, 119, 121, 122
  of description, 196
  of ending working alliances, 332–333, 335–337, 339–340
  of ethical prioritization, 47
  of goal development, 99, 101
  of maintaining interactive engagement, 133
  of motivation orientation, 255, 256, 261, 268, 269, 270, 273

About the DVD

Introduction

This appendix provides you with information on the contents of the DVD that accompanies this book. For the latest information, please refer to the ReadMe file located at the root of the DVD.

System Requirements

- A computer with a processor running at 120 Mhz or faster
- At least 32 MB of total RAM installed on your computer; for best performance, we recommend at least 64 MB
- A DVD-ROM drive

NOTE: Many popular word processing programs are capable of reading Microsoft Word files. However, users should be aware that a slight amount of formatting might be lost when using a program other than Microsoft Word.

Using the DVD with Windows

To install the items from the DVD to your hard drive, follow these steps:

1. Insert the DVD into your computer's DVD-ROM drive.
2. The DVD interface will appear. The interface provides a simple point-and-click way to explore the contents of the DVD.

If the opening screen of the DVD does not appear automatically, follow these steps to access the DVD:

1. Click the Start button on the left end of the taskbar and then choose Run from the menu that pops up.
2. In the dialog box that appears, type *d* :\start.exe. (If your DVD-ROM drive is not drive d, fill in the appropriate letter in place of *d*.) This brings up the DVD Interface described in the preceding set of steps.

Using the DVD with Macintosh

To install the items from the DVD to your hard drive, follow these steps:

1. Insert the DVD into your computer's DVD-ROM drive.
2. The DVD icon will appear on your desktop; double-click to open.
3. Double-click the Start button.
4. Read the license agreement and click the Accept button to use the DVD.
5. The DVD interface will appear. Here you can install the programs and run the demos.

What's on the DVD

The following sections provide a summary of the software and other materials you'll find on the DVD.

Content

Organized by chapter to correspond directly to topics in the book, the companion DVD contains both video and text supplementary materials designed to reinforce and expand upon competencies introduced in the book. These exercises provide instructors with additional resources to enhance the classroom experience as well as engage students and strengthen their helping skills, knowledge, and values. Students will also find these supplementary materials useful in practicing the skills presented throughout the book.

Applications

The following applications are on the DVD:

Adobe Reader
Adobe Reader is a freeware application for viewing files in the Adobe Portable Document format.

Word Viewer
Microsoft Word Viewer is a freeware viewer that allows you to view, but not edit, most Microsoft Word files. Certain features of Microsoft Word documents may not display as expected from within Word Viewer.

PowerPoint Viewer
Microsoft PowerPoint Viewer is a freeware viewer that allows you to view, but not edit, Microsoft PowerPoint files. Certain features of Microsoft PowerPoint presentations may not work as expected from within PowerPoint Viewer.

OpenOffice.org
OpenOffice.org is a free multi-platform office productivity suite. It is similar to Microsoft Office or Lotus SmartSuite, but OpenOffice.org is absolutely free. It includes word processing, spreadsheet, presentation, and drawing applications that enable you to create professional documents, newsletters, reports, and presentations. It supports most file formats of other office software. You should be able to edit and view any files created with other office solutions.

Shareware programs are fully functional, trial versions of copyrighted programs. If you like particular programs, register with their authors for a nominal fee and receive licenses, enhanced versions, and technical support.

Freeware programs are copyrighted games, applications, and utilities that are free for personal use. Unlike shareware, these programs do not require a fee or provide technical support.

GNU software is governed by its own license, which is included inside the folder of the GNU product. See the GNU license for more details.

Trial, demo, or evaluation versions are usually limited either by time or functionality (such as being unable to save projects). Some trial versions are very sensitive to system date changes. If you alter your computer's date, the programs will "time out" and no longer be functional.

Customer Care

If you have trouble with the DVD, please call the Wiley Product Technical Support phone number at (800) 762-2974. Outside the United States, call 1(317) 572-3994. You can also contact Wiley Product Technical Support at http://support.wiley.com. John Wiley & Sons will provide technical support only for installation and other general quality control items. For technical support on the applications themselves, consult the program's vendor or author.

To place additional orders or to request information about other Wiley products, please call (80077) 762-2974.